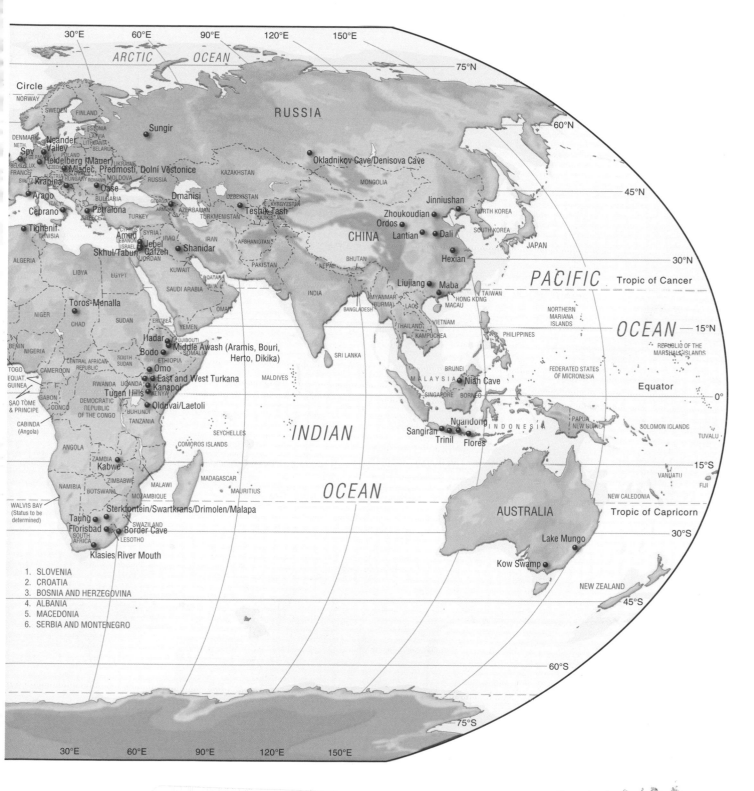

1. SLOVENIA
2. CROATIA
3. BOSNIA AND HERZEGOVINA
4. ALBANIA
5. MACEDONIA
6. SERBIA AND MONTENEGRO

Physical Anthropology

THE ESSENTIALS

NINTH EDITION

Robert Jurmain

Professor Emeritus, San Jose State University

Lynn Kilgore

University of Colorado, Boulder

Wenda Trevathan

Professor Emerita, New Mexico State University

WADSWORTH
CENGAGE Learning™

Australia • Brazil • Japan • Korea • Mexico • Singapore • Spain • United Kingdom • United States

WADSWORTH
CENGAGE Learning™

Physical Anthropology: The Essentials
Ninth Edition, International Edition
Robert Jurmain, Lynn Kilgore,
and Wenda Trevathan

Acquiring Sponsoring Editor: Erin Mitchell

Developmental Editor: Lin Gaylord

Assistant Editor: Mallory Ortberg

Media Editor: John Chell

Marketing Program Manager: Janay Pryor

Content Project Manager: Cheri Palmer

Art Director: Caryl Gorska

Manufacturing Planner: Judy Inouye

Rights Acquisitions Specialist: Dean Dauphinais

Design, Production Services, and Composition:
Hespenheide Design

Photo Researcher: Patti Zeman

Text Researcher: Ashley Liening

Copy Editor: Cheryl Smith

Illustrator: Hespenheide Design

Cover Image: toonman

International Edition:

ISBN-13: 978-1-111-83815-7

ISBN-10: 1-111-83815-1

Cengage Learning International Offices

Asia
www.cengageasia.com
tel: (65) 6410 1200

Australia/New Zealand
www.cengage.com.au
tel: (61) 3 9685 4111

Brazil
www.cengage.com.br
tel: (55) 11 3665 9900

India
www.cengage.co.in
tel: (91) 11 4364 1111

Latin America
www.cengage.com.mx
tel: (52) 55 1500 6000

UK/Europe/Middle East/Africa
www.cengage.co.uk
tel: (44) 0 1264 332 424

Represented in Canada by
Nelson Education, Ltd.
www.nelson.com
tel: (416) 752 9100 / (800) 668 0671

Cengage Learning is a leading provider of customized learning solutions with office locations around the globe, including Singapore, the United Kingdom, Australia, Mexico, Brazil, and Japan. Locate your local office at: **www.cengage.com/global**

For product information and free companion resources:
www.cengage.com/international

Visit your local office: **www.cengage.com/global**

Visit our corporate website: **www.cengage.com**

Printed in Canada
1 2 3 4 5 6 7 16 15 14 13 12

Brief Contents

Contents

NASA

Peter Jones

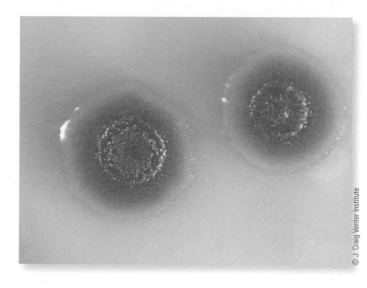

© J. Craig Venter Institute

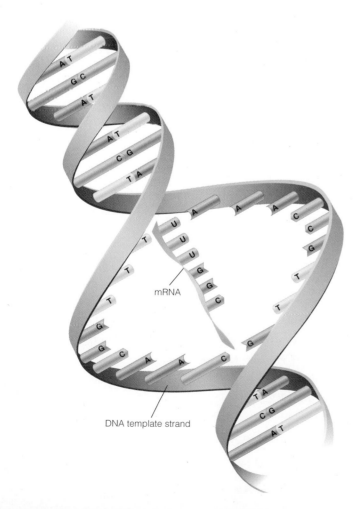

mRNA

DNA template strand

© Nelson Ting

CHAPTER 7
Survey of the Living Primates   152

CHAPTER 8
Primate Behavior   186

© 2010 Photo E. Daynes – Reconstruction Atelier Daynes Paris

Lynn Kilgore

CHAPTER 13

The Anthropological Perspective on the Human Life Course   342

CHAPTER 14

Legacies of Human Evolutionary History: Effects on the Individual   366

APPENDIX A

Atlas of Primate Skeletal Anatomy   378

APPENDIX B

Summary of Early Hominin Fossil Finds from Africa   386

APPENDIX C

Population Genetics   391

APPENDIX D

Sexing and Aging the Skeleton   394

© iStockphoto.com / Joseph Luoman

Preface

This book is about human evolution and how our species is biologically connected to all life on earth. At its foundation, our topic is a part of human biology and, more generally, directly linked to all the biological sciences.

Biology is a field that is changing dramatically as new methods are developed and major discoveries are made almost daily. Much of the most crucial, and certainly the most exciting breakthroughs, come from molecular studies of DNA.

The academic discipline that studies human evolution specifically is called physical (or biological) anthropology. In this field, too, there have been major advances within the last few years. Perhaps most significantly, this very new knowledge has revealed how complicated are the genetic mechanisms that build and regulate all organisms on earth, including humans. What's more, as new fossils relating to the evolution of the human lineage are found, the picture of our evolutionary history becomes all the more complicated.

These exciting developments pose a challenge for students, instructors, and textbook authors alike, but they also provide the opportunity for a deeper understanding of our subject. Each of the authors of this textbook has taught the introductory physical anthropology course for many years. From this long experience, we realize that many of the students taking this course have had limited biological or anthropological instruction in high school and may find much of the material in this book entirely new. To help students more easily grasp this new subject area, we provide clear explanations and examples enhanced by many visual aids.

Within these pages, there are many opportunities for students to seek help in learning about topics, ideas, and developments encountered for the first time. To provide even greater assistance than in previous editions, much of the artwork has been completely redrawn, and we have also added many new photos. All these changes reflect our long-term commitment to make our textbook an effective teaching and learning instrument.

Because genetic mechanisms lie at the heart of understanding evolution, we address the basic aspects of life, cells, and DNA, in the early chapters of this text (Chapters 2 through 4). We next turn to the nature of modern human variation (including the meaning of "race") and patterns of adaptation in recent human populations (Chapter 5) before looking at the ways species change (Chapter 6). In Chapters 7 and 8 we explore our evolutionary cousins, the nonhuman primates, and how they relate to us both physically and behaviorally. In Chapters 9 through 12, we briefly discuss the evolutionary history of early primates and then turn to a more detailed exploration of our specific human evolutionary history over the past 6 million years. This evolutionary journey takes us back to our small-brained ancestors in Africa and follows the development of their descendants through time and over their expanding ranges into Asia and Europe and much later into Australia and the Americas.

In the last section of this book (Chapter 13), we trace the ongoing evolution of our species and the developmental changes experienced by humans through the life course. In our mostly new concluding chapter, "Legacies of Human Evolutionary History: Effects on the Individual," we discuss how humans now adapt to and alter the planet and compare these recent developments with our species' long evolutionary past, when humans were not so numerous or so dependent on nonrenewable resources. These dramatic alterations to our world will pose enormous challenges to people throughout the twenty-first century and beyond. We hope that this book will better prepare all of you for what lies ahead.

What's New in the Ninth Edition

First of all, we have incorporated the unifying concept of our 'connection' to all life as the framework for presenting the material throughout the text. To further reinforce this central focus, each chapter now opens with a pedagogical aid that clearly shows students the biological connections as they are organized within and between chapters.

In addition, we have updated much of the book, reflecting recent advances in virtually every aspect of physical anthropology. There is no area of biological research today that advances more rapidly than the study of genetics. Because genetics underlies evolution and thus every topic in this book, we strive to keep our coverage as up to date as possible. At the same time, it's important to make this complicated topic understandable and (we hope) enjoyable to college students, whose lives are impacted by genetic research every day.

As genetic technology continues to grow at an unprecedented pace, it is our task to present the most relevant new discoveries in as simple a manner as possible. In addition to discussing the newly developed synthetic bacterial cell in Chapter 3, we've added to Chapter 4 a new discussion of how DNA deletions and duplications impact the evolutionary process. As an example, we used changes in the skulls of bull terriers over a 35-year period to show how duplications of DNA segments in developmental genes can cause dramatic and rapid anatomical changes in species if there is strong selection pressure acting on them (in this case, breeding by humans). We have added more nonhuman examples of genetic phenomena because we want to underscore the theme of biological connections—that humans are part of a biological spectrum and that we are related to all life on earth. We have also added some new artwork and revised a number of figures in Chapters 3 and 4 to help clarify difficult concepts.

Our focus next turns to modern human biology. Understanding human variation (discussed in Chapter 5) has been completely transformed by more complete DNA data, published in just the last two years. We have updated and modified our main perspective in this chapter to reflect the remarkable new findings contributed by molecular biology. For example, in Chapter 12, there's a new discussion of recent research demonstrating a population-wide genetic mutation in Tibetan highlanders that increases their ability to adapt to living at high altitude.

Primatologists are regularly reporting on new discoveries about our closest relatives, the nonhuman primates, revealing our continuity with them. Since many of our primate cousins are unfamiliar to our readers, we've added several new photos in the two primate chapters and replaced many others. Today, many nonhuman primates are endangered, and we hope to raise awareness of them among students who read this book. In Chapter 8, we've updated the discussion of intergroup aggression, including new findings concerning male aggression in chimpanzees. We've also broadened our discussion of nonaggressive behaviors, providing new evidence for empathy in nonhuman primates.

Remarkable new discoveries of fossil hominins are discussed in Chapters 9 through 12. Chapter 9 covers the earliest hominins and presents controversial new interpretations of *Ardipithecus*, especially relating to the partial skeleton known as "Ardi." Exciting discoveries from South Africa of a brand-new species called *Australopithecus sediba* provide us with new insights from remarkably preserved fossils dating to 2 million years ago.

Chapter 10 has updates relating to how childhood development occurred in *Homo erectus* as well as key new dating for fossil sites in Africa and Europe. Chapters 11 and 12 have been extensively reorganized and refocused to reflect the startling new evidence obtained from the analysis of Neandertal DNA. These molecular discoveries show that Neandertals interbred with modern human populations, and their genes can still be found in many contemporary human populations! What's more, evaluation of very incomplete hominin remains from Siberia show that one is a Neandertal and the other may be a new species altogether. Lastly, newly found archaeological finds from Europe indicate that Neandertals may have made use of novel materials for personal adornment, suggesting more advanced symbolic thought than previously assumed.

Chapter 12 builds on this emerging new story about the origins of modern people, and the main focus of the chapter has been modified to reflect a lot of new evidence. What's more, physical anthropologists are learning more all the time about the little hominins from Indonesia (popularly called "hobbits"), and the most recent findings (including some new archaeological discoveries) suggest that these highly unusual hominins perhaps diverged from other hominins far earlier than previously thought.

One theme that we emphasize throughout the book is that we are the result of not only biological but also cultural evolutionary factors. In other words, we are a *biocultural* species. In Chapter 13, "The Anthropological Perspective on the Human Life Course," we focus on ways in which biology and culture act on the human life course from conception, through reproduction, to the end of life. There are a number of ways in which our biology, resulting from millions of years of evolution, seems to be mismatched with the lives we lead today, leading in some cases to compromised health. For example, the biology of women may not be well suited to the highly frequent menstrual cycling that results from the use of modern forms of birth control. Some health disorders that we are dealing with today may stem from the dramatic differences between the diets of our ancestors and the foods we eat today. We also discuss how the rapidly growing field of *epigenetics* helps to resolve the age-old nature-nurture debate by showing how environmental factors can influence gene expression.

Finally, in Chapter 14, we focus on another theme that runs through the book—*why it matters* that we know and understand human evolutionary history, its impact on the world today, and how we have distanced ourselves from other living species with which we share so many connections. We humans and the consequences of our activities are probably the most important influences on evolution today, causing the extinction or near-extinction of thousands of other life-forms and threatening the very planet on which we live. Our disconnection from other life forms and from our own evolutionary past poses the biggest challenges our species has ever faced. Only by understanding how we got to this point can we begin to respond to the challenges that are in our future and the futures of our children and grandchildren.

In-Chapter Learning Aids

Connections graphic at beginning of each chapter shows the biological relationships emphasized in the chapter in context of topics in other chapters.

A running glossary in the margins provides definitions of terms immediately adjacent to the text where the term is first introduced. A full glossary is provided at the back of the book.

At a Glance boxes found throughout the book briefly summarize complex or controversial material in a visually simple fashion.

Why it Matters sections at the end of chapters (except for Chapter 14 which is all about "why it matters") make the case for the importance of studying the material presented in the chapters by relating that material to students' lives.

What's Important tables that summarize the most significant fossil discoveries discussed are included at the end of relevant chapters to help students as they review the chapter material.

Figures, including numerous photographs, line drawings, and maps, most in full color, are carefully selected to clarify text materials and directly support the discussion in the text. Much of the art, especially anatomical drawings, have been redrawn for this edition.

Critical Thinking Questions at the end of each chapter reinforce key concepts and encourage students to think critically about what they have read.

Full bibliographical citations throughout the book provide sources from which the materials are drawn. This type of documentation guides students to published, peer-reviewed source materials and illustrates for students the proper use of references. All cited sources are listed in the comprehensive bibliography at the back of the book.

Photo Essays periodically fall between chapters and visually show students how physical anthropologists work in the field. Topics include forensic anthropology, Paleoanthropology, and Paleopathology.

Acknowledgments

Over the years, many friends and colleagues have assisted us with our books. For this edition we are especially grateful to the reviewers who so carefully commented on the manuscript and made such helpful suggestions: Anna Belissari, Wright University; Chi-Hua Chiu, Kent State; William Doonan, Sacramento City College; Renee Garcia, Saddleback College; Ellen Ingmanson, Bridgewater College; Elizabeth Lamble, Oakland Community College; Tony Tessandori, Bellevue College; Patricia Vinyard, University of Akron.

We wish to thank the team at Cengage Learning: Erin Mitchell, Lin Marshall Gaylord, Mallory Ortberg, John Chell, Caryl Gorska, and Cheri Palmer. Moreover, for their unflagging expertise and patience, we are grateful to our copy editor, Cheryl Smith, our production coordinator,

Gary Hespenheide, and his skilled staff at Hespenheide Design: Patti Zeman, Bridget Neumayr, and Randy Miyake.

To the many friends and colleagues who have generously provided photographs we are greatly appreciative: Zeresenay Alemseged, Art Aufderheide, Lee Berger, C. K. Brain, Günter Bräuer, Peter Brown, Chip Clark, Desmond Clark, Ron Clarke, Raymond Dart, Henri de Lumley, Emanuelle de Merode, Jean DeRousseau, Michael S. Donnenberg, Denis Etler, Diane France, Robert Franciscus, David Frayer, Kathleen Galvin, David Haring, John Hodgkiss, Almut Hoffman, Ellen Ingmanson, Fred Jacobs, Don Johanson, Peter Jones, John Kappelman, Richard Kay, William Kimbel, Arlene Kruse, Richard Leakey, Linda Levitch, Barry Lewis, Carol Lofton,

David Lordkipanidze, Giorgio Manzi, Tetsuo Matsuzawa, Russell Mittermeier, Lorna Moore, Gerald Newlands, John Oates, Bonnie Pedersen, David Pilbeam, William Pratt, Judith Regensteiner, Charlotte Roberts, Sastrohamijoyo Sartono, Eugenie Scott, Rose Sevick, Elwyn Simons, Meredith Small, Fred Smith, Thierry Smith, Masanaru Takai, Heather Thew, Nelson Ting, Li Tianyuan, Phillip Tobias, Erik Trinkaus, Alan Walker, Carol Ward, Dietrich Wegner, James Westgate, Randy White, Milford Wolpoff, and Xinzhi Wu and João Zilhão.

Robert Jurmain
Lynn Kilgore
Wenda Trevathan

January 2012

Supplements

Physical Anthropology: The Essentials Ninth Edition, comes with an outstanding supplement program to help instructors create an effective learning environment so that students can more easily master the latest discoveries and interpretations in the field of physical anthropology.

Supplements for Teachers

Online Instructor's Manual with Test Bank for *Physical Anthropology: The Essentials Ninth Edition*

This online resource includes a sample syllabus showing how to integrate CourseMate with the text, as well as chapter outlines, key terms and concepts, lecture suggestions, enrichment topics, and 40–60 test questions per chapter.

PowerLecture™ with Exam View® (Windows/Macintosh) for *Physical Anthropology: The Essentials Ninth Edition*

This easy-to-use, one-stop digital library and presentation tool includes the following book-specific resources as well as direct links to many of Wadsworth's highly valued electronic resources for anthropology:

- Ready-to-use Microsoft® PowerPoint® lecture slides with photos and graphics from the text, making it easy for the instructor to assemble, edit, publish, and present customized lectures.
- ExamView® testing software, which provides all the test items from the text's *test bank* in elec-

tronic format, enabling the instructor to create customized tests of up to 250 items that can be delivered in print or online.

- The text's *Instructor's Resource Manual and Test Bank* in electronic format.

Anthropology CourseMate

This website for *Physical Anthropology: The Essentials Ninth Edition* brings chapter topics to life with interactive learning, study, and exam preparation tools, including quizzes and flash cards for each chapter's key terms and concepts. The website also provides an eBook version of the text with highlighting and note-taking capabilities. For instructors, this text's CourseMate also includes Engagement Tracker, a first-of-its-kind tool that monitors student engagement in the course. WebTutor™ for Blackboard® and WebCT®

Instructors can jump-start their course with customizable, rich, text-specific content within your Course Management System.

- **Jump-start**—Simply load a WebTutor cartridge into your Course Management System.
- **Customize**—Easily blend, add, edit, reorganize, or delete content. The rich, text-specific content includes media assets, quizzes, web links, discussion topics, interactive games and exercises, and more.

The Wadsworth Anthropology Video Library Vol. 1–3

The Wadsworth Anthropology Video Library drives home the relevance of

course topics through short, provocative clips of current and historical events. Perfect for enriching lectures and engaging students in discussion, many of the segments on this volume have been gathered from BBC Motion Gallery. Ask your Cengage Learning representative for a list of contents.

Supplements for Students

Anthropology CourseMate

This website for *Physical Anthropology: The Essentials Ninth Edition* brings chapter topics to life with interactive learning, study, and exam preparation tools, including quizzes, flash cards, videos, animations, and more! The site also provides an eBook version of the text with highlighting and note-taking capabilities. Students can access this new learning tool and all other online resources through www.cengagebrain.com.

Classic and Contemporary Readings in Physical Anthropology

Edited by Mary K. Sandford and Eileen Jackson. This accessible reader presents primary articles with introductions and questions for discussion, helping students to better understand the nature of scientific inquiry. Students will read highly accessible classic and contemporary articles on key topics, including the science of physical anthropology, evolution and heredity, primates, human evolution, and modern human variation.

International Edition of Lab Manual and Workbook for Physical Anthropology, Seventh Edition

Written by Diane L. France, this edition of the workbook and lab manual includes a new "Introduction to Science and Critical Thinking" that precedes the first chapter. Using hands-on exercises, this richly illustrated full-color lab manual balances the study of genetics, human osteology, anthropometry, and forensic anthropology with the study of primates and human evolution. In addition to providing hands-on lab assignments that apply the field's perspectives and techniques to real situations, this edition provides more explanatory information and sample exercises throughout the text to help make the concepts of physical anthropology easier to understand. Contact your Cengage sales representative to package this with the text.

Virtual Laboratories for Physical Anthropology, CD-ROM, Fourth Edition, by John Kappelman

Through the use of video segments, interactive exercises, quizzes, 3-D animations, and sound and digital images, students can actively participate in 12 labs on their own terms—at home, in the library—at any time! Recent fossil discoveries are included, as well as exercises in behavior and archaeology and critical thinking and problem-solving activities. *Virtual Laboratories* includes web links, outstanding fossil images, exercises, and a post-lab self-quiz.

Basic Genetics in Anthropology CD-ROM: Principles and Applications, Version 2.0, by Jurmain/ Kilgore/Trevathan

This student CD-ROM expands on basic biological concepts covered in the book, focusing on biological inheritance (such as genes and DNA sequencing) and its applications to modern human populations. Interactive animations and simulations bring these important concepts to life so that students can fully understand the essential biological principles underlying human evolution. Also available are quizzes and interactive flash cards for further study.

Hominid Fossils CD-ROM: An Interactive Atlas, by James Ahern

This CD-based interactive atlas includes over 75 key fossils that are important for a clear understanding of human evolution. The Quick-Time® Virtual Reality (QTVR) "object" movie format for each fossil will enable students to have a near-authentic experience working with these important finds by allowing them to rotate the fossil 360°. Unlike some VR media, QTVR objects are made using actual photographs of the real objects and thus better preserve details of color and texture. The fossils used are high-quality research casts and real fossils.

The organization of the atlas is nonlinear, with three levels and multiple paths, enabling students to start with a particular fossil and work their way "up" to see how the fossil fits into the map of human evolution in terms of geography, time, and evolution. The CD-ROM offers students an inviting, authentic learning environment, one that also contains a dynamic quizzing feature that will allow students to test their knowledge of fossil and species identification as well as provide more detailed information about the fossil record.

Wadsworth Anthropology's Module Series

This series includes:

Evolution of the Brain Module: Neuroanatomy, Development, and Paleontology

The human species is the only species that has ever created a symphony, written a poem, developed a mathematical equation, or studied its own origins. The biological structure that has enabled humans to perform these feats of intelligence is the human brain. This module, created by Daniel D. White, of the University of Albany, SUNY, explores the basics of neuroanatomy, brain development, lateralization, and sexual dimorphism and provides the fossil evidence for hominin brain evolution. This module in chapter-like format can be packaged for free with the text.

Human Environment Interactions: New Directions in Human Ecology

This module by Kathy Galvin, of Colorado State University, begins with a brief discussion of the history and core concepts of the field of human ecology, the study of how humans interact with the natural environment, before looking in depth at how the environment influences cultural practices (environmental determinism) as well as how aspects of culture, in turn, affect the environment. Human behavioral ecology is presented within the context of natural selection and how ecological factors influence the development of cultural and behavioral traits and how people subsist in different environments. The module concludes with a discussion of resilience and global change as a result of human-environment interactions. This module in chapter-like format can be packaged for free with the text.

Forensic Anthropology Module

The forensic application of physical anthropology is exploding in popularity. Written by Diane L. France, this module explores the myths and realities of the search for human remains in crime scenes, what can be expected from a forensic anthropology expert in the courtroom, some of the special challenges in responding to mass fatalities, and the issues a student should consider if pursuing a career in forensic anthropology. This module in chapter-like format can be packaged for free with the text.

Molecular Anthropology Module

This module explores how molecular genetic methods are used to understand the organization and expression of genetic information in humans and nonhuman primates. Students will learn about the common laboratory methods used to study variation and evolution in molecular anthropology. Examples are drawn from up-to-date research on human evolutionary origins and comparative primate genomics to demonstrate that scientific research is an ongoing process, with theories frequently being questioned and reevaluated.

These resources are available to qualified adopters, and ordering options for student supplements are flexible. Please consult your local Cengage sales consultant for more information or to evaluate examination copies of any of these resources or to receive product demonstrations.

Connections

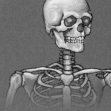

Physical anthropology investigates how humans have evolved.

Evolutionary theory, particularly natural selection, explains how life forms have changed over time.

1

Introduction to Physical Anthropology

Introduction

One day, perhaps during the rainy season some 3.7 million years ago, two or three animals walked across a grassland **savanna** (see next page for definitions of terms on this page) in what is now northern Tanzania, in East Africa. These individuals were early **hominins**, members of the evolutionary lineage that also includes our own **species**, *Homo sapiens*. Fortunately for us, a record of their passage on that long-forgotten day remains in the form of fossilized footprints, preserved in hardened volcanic deposits. As chance would have it, shortly after heels and toes were pressed into the damp soil, a nearby volcano erupted. The ensuing ash fall blanketed everything on the ground. In time, the ash layer hardened into a deposit that remarkably preserved the tracks of numerous animals, including those early hominins, for nearly 4 million years (**Fig. 1-1**).

These now famous prints indicate that two individuals, one smaller than the other and perhaps walking side by side, left parallel sets of tracks. But because the larger individual's prints are obscured, possibly by those of a third, it's unclear how many actually made that journey so long ago. What is clear is that the prints were made by an animal that habitually walked **bipedally** (on two feet), and that fact tells us that those ancient travelers were hominins.

In addition to the footprints, scientists working at this site (called Laetoli) and at other locations have discovered many fossilized parts of skeletons of an animal we call *Australopithecus afarensis*. Because the remains have been extensively studied, we know that these hominins were anatomically similar to ourselves, although their brains were only about one-third the size of ours. They may have used stones and sticks as simple tools, but there is no evidence that they actually made stone tools. In fact, they were very much at the mercy of nature's whims. They certainly could not outrun most predators, and their canine teeth were fairly small, so compared to many other animals, they were pretty much defenseless.

◄This illustration emphasizes the fact that all life-forms on earth, including humans, are ultimately connected by DNA.

▶ **Figure 1-1**
Early hominin footprints at Laetoli, Tanzania. The tracks to the left were made by one individual, while those to the right appear to have been made by two individuals, the second stepping in the tracks of the first.

Peter Jones

savanna (also spelled savannah) A large flat grassland with scattered trees and shrubs. Savannas are found in many regions of the world with dry and warm-to-hot climates.

hominins Colloquial term for members of the evolutionary group that includes modern humans and now-extinct bipedal relatives.

species A group of organisms that can interbreed to produce fertile offspring. Members of one species are reproductively isolated from members of all other species (i.e., they cannot mate with them to produce fertile offspring).

bipedally On two feet; walking habitually on two legs.

We've asked hundreds of questions about the Laetoli hominins, but we will never be able to answer them all. They walked down a path into what became their future, and their immediate journey has long since ended. So it remains for us to learn as much as we can about them, and as we continue to do this, their greater journey continues.

On July 20, 1969, a television audience numbering in the hundreds of millions watched as two human beings stepped out of a spacecraft onto the surface of the moon. People born after that date have always lived in an age of space exploration; therefore, many

may now take that first moon landing for granted. But the significance of that first moonwalk actually can't be overstated, because it represents humankind's presumed mastery over the natural forces that govern our presence on earth. For the first time ever, people actually walked upon the surface of a celestial body that, as far as we know, has never given birth to biological life.

As the astronauts gathered geological specimens and frolicked in near weightlessness, they left traces of their fleeting presence in the form of footprints in the lunar dust (**Fig. 1-2**). On the surface of the moon, where no rain falls and no wind blows, the footprints remain undisturbed to this day. They survive as silent testimony to a brief visit by a medium-sized, big-brained creature that presumed to challenge the very forces that created it.

You may wonder why anyone would care about early hominin footprints and how they can possibly be relevant to your life. You may also wonder why a physical **anthropology** textbook would begin by discussing two such seemingly unrelated events as ancient hominins walking across an African savanna and a moonwalk. But the fact is, these two events are very closely connected.

Physical, or biological, anthropology is a scientific discipline concerned with the biological and behavioral characteristics of human beings, as well as our closest relatives, the non-human **primates** (apes, monkeys, tarsiers, lemurs, and lorises), and their ancestors. This kind of research helps us explain what it means to be human and how we came to be the way we are. This is an ambitious goal, and it probably isn't fully attainable, but it's certainly worth pursuing. We're the only species to ponder our own existence and question how we fit into the spectrum of life on earth. Most people view humanity as quite separate from the rest of the animal kingdom. But at the same time, many are curious about the similarities we share with other species. Maybe, as a child, you looked at your dog and tried to figure out how her front legs might correspond to your arms. Or perhaps during a visit to the zoo, you recognized the similarities between a chimpanzee's hands or facial expressions and your own. Maybe you wondered if he also shared your thoughts and feelings. If you've ever had thoughts and questions like these, then you've indeed been curious about humankind's place in nature.

We humans, who can barely comprehend a century, can't begin to grasp the enormity of nearly 4 million years. But we still want to know more about those creatures who walked across the savanna that day. We want to know how an insignificant but clever bipedal primate such as *Australopithecus afarensis*, or perhaps a close relative, gave rise to a species that would eventually walk on the surface of the moon, some 230,000 miles from earth.

How did *Homo sapiens*, a result of the same evolutionary forces that produced all other forms of life on this planet, gain the power to control the flow of rivers and even alter the climate on a global scale? As tropical animals, how were we able to leave the tropics and eventually occupy most of the earth's land surfaces? How did we adjust to different environmental conditions as we dispersed? How could our species, which numbered fewer than 1 billion until the mid-nineteenth century, come to number more than 7 billion worldwide today and, as we now do, add another billion people every 11 years?

These are some of the many questions that physical anthropologists try to answer through the study of human **evolution**, variation, and **adaptation**. These issues, and many others, are covered in this textbook, because physical anthropology is, in large part, human biology seen from an evolutionary perspective. On hearing the term *evolution*, most people think of the appearance of new species. Certainly, new species are one important consequence of evolution; but it isn't the only one, because evolution is an ongoing biological process with more than one outcome. Simply stated, evolution is a change in the **genetic** makeup of a population from one generation to the next, and it can be defined and studied at two levels. Over time, some genetic changes in populations do result in the appearance of a new species (or *speciation*), especially when those populations are isolated from one another. Change at this level is called *macroevolution*. At the other level, there are genetic alterations *within* populations; and though this type of change may not lead to speciation, it does cause populations of a species to differ from one another in the frequency of certain traits. Evolution at this level is referred to as *microevolution*. Evolution at both these levels will be discussed in this book.

▲ **Figure 1-2**
Human footprints left on the lunar surface during the *Apollo* mission.

anthropology The field of inquiry that studies human culture and evolutionary aspects of human biology; includes cultural anthropology, archaeology, linguistics, and physical, or biological, anthropology.

primates Members of the mammalian order Primates (pronounced "pry-may´-tees"), which includes lemurs, lorises, tarsiers, monkeys, apes, and humans.

evolution A change in the genetic structure of a population. The term is also frequently used to refer to the appearance of a new species.

adaptation An anatomical, physiological, or behavioral response of organisms or populations to the environment. Adaptations result from evolutionary change (specifically, as a result of natural selection).

genetic Having to do with the study of gene structure and action and the patterns of inheritance of traits from parent to offspring. Genetic mechanisms are the foundation for evolutionary change.

The Human Connection

The unifying theme of this textbook is how human beings are linked to all other life on earth. We can see how we are connected to other organisms in countless ways, as you will learn throughout this book. For example, most of our DNA is structurally identical to that of every living thing. Indeed, we share genes that are involved in the most fundamental life processes with even the simplest of animals, such as sponges. These genes have changed very little over the course of several hundred million years of evolution. Our cells have the same structure and work the same way as in all life-forms, with few exceptions. Anatomically, we have the same muscles and bones as many other animals. What's more, many aspects of our **behavior** have direct connections to nonhuman species, especially other primates.

The countless connections we share with other organisms show that humans are a product of the same evolutionary forces that produced all living things. But, clearly we aren't identical to any other species. In fact, all species are unique in some ways. We humans are one contemporary component of a vast biological **continuum** at a particular point in time; and in this regard, we aren't really all that special. Stating that humans are part of a continuum doesn't imply that we're at the peak of development on that continuum. Depending on the criteria used, humans can be seen to exist at one end of the spectrum or the other, or somewhere in between, but we don't necessarily occupy a position of inherent superiority over other species (**Fig. 1-4** on page 8).

However, human beings are truly unique in one significant dimension, and that is intellect. After all, humans are the only species, born of earth, to stir the lunar dust. We're the only species to develop language and complex culture as a means of buffering nature's challenges; and by doing so we have gained the power to shape the planet's very destiny.

Biocultural Evolution

Biological anthropologists don't just study physiological and biological systems. When these topics are considered within the broader context of human evolution, another factor must be considered, and that factor is **culture**. Culture is an extremely important concept, not only as it relates to modern humans but also because of its critical role in human evolution. Quite simply, and in a very broad sense, culture can be defined as the strategy by which humans adapt to the natural environment. In fact, culture has so altered and dominated our world that it's become the environment in which we live. Culture includes technologies ranging from stone tools to computers; subsistence patterns, from hunting and gathering to global agribusiness; housing types, from thatched huts to skyscrapers; and clothing, from animal skins to high-tech synthetic fibers (**Fig. 1-3**). Technology, religion, values, social organization, language, kinship, marriage rules, gender roles, dietary practices, inheritance of property, and so on, are all aspects of culture. Each culture shapes people's perceptions of the external environment, or **worldview**, in particular ways that distinguish that society from all others.

One important point to remember is that culture isn't genetically passed from one generation to the next. We aren't born with innate knowledge that leads us to behave in ways appropriate to our own culture. Culture is *learned*, and the process of learning one's culture begins, quite literally, at birth. All people are products of the culture they're raised in, and since most human behavior is learned, it follows that most human behaviors, perceptions, values, and reactions are shaped by culture.

behavior Anything organisms do that involves action in response to internal or external stimuli; the response of an individual, group, or species to its environment. Such responses may or may not be deliberate, and they aren't necessarily the result of conscious decision making (which is absent in single-celled organisms, insects, and many other species).

continuum A set of relationships in which all components fall along a single integrated spectrum (for example, color). All life reflects a single biological continuum.

culture Behavioral aspects of human adaptation, including technology, traditions, language, religion, marriage patterns, and social roles. Culture is a set of learned behaviors transmitted from one generation to the next by nonbiological (i.e., nongenetic) means.

worldview General cultural orientation or perspective shared by members of a society.

▶ **Figure 1-3**

Traditional and recent technologies. **(a)** An early stone tool from East Africa. This artifact represents one of the oldest types of stone tools found anywhere. **(b)** The Hubble Space telescope, a late twentieth-century tool, orbits the earth every 96 minutes at an altitude of 360 miles. Because it is above the earth's atmosphere, it provides distortion-free images of objects in deep space. **(c)** A cuneiform tablet. Cuneiform, the earliest form of writing, involved pressing symbols into clay tablets. It originated in southern Iraq some 5,000 years ago. **(d)** Text messaging, a fairly recent innovation in satellite communication, has generated a new language of sorts. Today, more than 500 million text messages are sent every day worldwide. **(e)** A Samburu woman in East Africa building a traditional but complicated dwelling of stems, small branches, and mud. **(f)** These Hong Kong skyscrapers are typical of cities in industrialized countries today.

Connections

Figure 1-4
Humans are biologically connected to all life. This central theme will be addressed in every chapter of the text, as shown in this figure.

CHAPTER 1

Physical anthropology is a biological science that investigates how humans have evolved and continue to do so.

CHAPTER 2

Evolutionary theory, particularly natural selection, explains how life forms have changed over time and how new species are produced.

CHAPTER 14

Humans have recently become disconnected from other life and are rapidly altering the planet.

CHAPTER 13

Human development and adaptation is best understood from an evolutionary perspective.

CHAPTER 9

Hominins began to disperse out of Africa around 2 million years ago, and during the next 1 million years inhabited much of Eurasia.

CHAPTER 12

Modern human variation is best understood by looking at patterns of DNA in different populations.

CHAPTER 10

The immediate predecessors of modern humans, including the Neandertals, were much like us, but had some anatomical and behavioral differences.

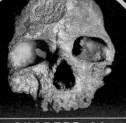

CHAPTER 11

Modern humans first evolved in Africa and later spread to other areas of the world, where they occasionally interbred with Neandertals and other pre-modern humans.

CHAPTER 3

DNA molecule is the basis of all life.

CHAPTER 3

All forms of life are made up of cells.

CHAPTER 4

Heredity is based on the transmission of DNA from one generation to the next.

CHAPTER 8

The first more human-like animals (hominins) appeared in Africa more than 6 million years ago and evolved into a variety of different species.

CHAPTER 4

Evolution occurs when DNA changes, and genetic variation is further influenced by natural selection and other factors.

CHAPTER 7

Partly because of common evolution-ary history, many human behaviors are also seen in other primates.

CHAPTER 6

Humans are primates and share many biological characteristics with other primates.

CHAPTER 5

Humans are both vertebrates and mammals, and their evolutionary history over many millions of years explains our early roots.

At the same time, however, it's important to emphasize that even though culture isn't genetically determined, the human predisposition to assimilate culture and function within it is very much influenced by biological factors. Most nonhuman animals, including birds and especially primates, rely to varying degrees on learned behavior. This is especially true of the great apes (gorillas, chimpanzees, bonobos, and orangutans), which exhibit several aspects of culture.

The predisposition for culture is perhaps the most critical component of human evolutionary history, and it was inherited from our early hominin or even prehominin ancestors. In fact, the common ancestor we share with chimpanzees may have had this predisposition. But during the course of human evolution, the role of culture became increasingly important. Over time, culture influenced many aspects of our biological makeup; and in turn, aspects of biology influenced cultural practices. For this reason, humans are the result of long-term interactions between biology and culture, and we call these interactions **biocultural evolution**; in this respect, humans are unique.

Biocultural interactions have resulted in many anatomical, biological, and behavioral changes during the course of human evolution: the shape of the pelvis, increased brain size, reorganization of neurological structures, smaller teeth, and the development of language, to name a few. Today, biocultural interactions are as important as ever, especially with regard to health and disease. Air pollution and exposure to dangerous chemicals have increased the prevalence of respiratory disease and cancer. While air travel makes it possible for people to travel thousands of miles in just a few hours, we aren't the only species that can do this. Millions of disease-causing organisms travel on airplanes with their human hosts, making it possible for infectious diseases to spread, literally within hours, across the globe.

Many human activities have changed the patterns of such infectious diseases as tuberculosis, influenza, and malaria. After the domestication of nonhuman animals, close contact with chickens, pigs, and cattle greatly increased human exposure to some of the diseases these animals carry. Through this contact we've also changed the genetic makeup of disease-causing microorganisms. For example, the H1N1 "swine flu" virus that caused the 2009 pandemic actually contains genetic material derived from bacteria that infect three different species: humans, birds, and pigs. As it turned out, that pandemic wasn't as serious as had originally been feared, but the next one could be. Because we've overused antibiotics, we've made many bacteria resistant to treatment and even deadly. Likewise, although we're making progress in treating malaria, the microorganism that causes it has developed resistance to some treatments and preventive medications. We've also increased the geographical distribution of malaria-carrying mosquitoes through agricultural practices and global climate change. But while it's clear that we humans have influenced the development and spread of infectious disease, we still don't know the many ways that changes in infectious disease patterns are affecting human biology and behavior. Anthropological research in this one topic alone is extremely relevant, and there are many other critical topics that biological anthropologists explore.

What Is Anthropology?

Many anthropology students contemplate this question when their parents or friends ask, "What are you studying?" The answer is often followed by a blank stare or a comment

biocultural evolution The mutual, interactive evolution of human biology and culture; the concept that biology makes culture possible and that developing culture further influences the direction of biological evolution; a basic concept in understanding the unique components of human evolution.

about dinosaurs. So, what *is* anthropology, and how is it different from several related disciplines?

In the United States, anthropology is divided into four main subfields: cultural, or social, anthropology; archaeology; linguistic anthropology; and physical, or biological, anthropology. Each of these, in turn, is divided into several specialized areas of interest. This four-field approach concerns all aspects of humanity across space and time. Each subdiscipline emphasizes different aspects of the human experience, but together, they offer a means of explaining variation in human biological and behavioral adaptations. In addition, each of these subfields has practical applications, and many anthropologists pursue careers outside the university environment. This kind of anthropology is called **applied anthropology**, and it's extremely important today.

Cultural Anthropology

Cultural, or social, anthropology is the study of patterns of belief and behavior found in modern and historical cultures. The origins of cultural anthropology can be traced to the nineteenth century, when travel and exploration brought Europeans in contact (and sometimes conflict) with various cultures in Africa, Asia, and the New World.

This interest in so-called "traditional" societies led many early anthropologists to study and record lifestyles that are now mostly extinct. These studies produced many descriptive **ethnographies** that covered a range of topics such as religion, ritual, myth, use of symbols, diet, technology, gender roles, and child-rearing practices. Ethnographic accounts, in turn, formed the basis for comparative studies of numerous cultures. By examining the similarities and differences among cultures, cultural anthropologists have been able to formulate many

hypotheses regarding fundamental aspects of human behavior.

The focus of cultural anthropology shifted over the course of the twentieth century. Cultural anthropologists still work in remote areas, but increasingly they've turned their gaze toward their own cultures and the people around them. Increasingly, ethnographic techniques have been applied to the study of diverse subcultures and their interactions with one another in contemporary metropolitan areas (urban anthropology). For example, many contemporary cultural anthropologists are concerned with the welfare of refugees and study their resettlement and cultural integration (or lack thereof) in countries such as the United States.

Archaeology

Archaeology is the study of earlier cultures by anthropologists who specialize in the scientific recovery, analysis, and interpretation of the material remains of past societies. Archaeologists obtain information from **artifacts** and structures left behind by earlier cultures. The remains of earlier societies, in the form of tools, structures, art, eating implements, fragments of writing, and so on, provide a great deal of information about many important aspects of a society, such as religion and social structure.

Unlike in the past (or in movies such as *Tomb Raider* or *Indiana Jones*), sites aren't excavated simply for the artifacts or "treasures" they may contain. Rather, they're excavated to gain information about human behavior. For example, patterns of behavior are reflected in the dispersal of human settlements across a landscape and in the distribution of cultural remains within them. Archaeological research may focus on specific localities or peoples and attempt to identify, for example, various aspects of social organization, subsistence techniques, or factors that led to the collapse of a civilization.

applied anthropology The practical application of anthropological and archaeological theories and techniques. For example, many biological anthropologists work in the public health sector.

ethnographies Detailed descriptive studies of human societies. In cultural anthropology, an ethnography is traditionally the study of a non-Western society.

artifacts Objects or materials made or modified for use by hominins. The earliest artifacts are usually tools made of stone or, occasionally, bone.

Alternatively, inquiry may reflect an interest in broader issues relating to human culture in general, such as the development of agriculture or the rise of cities.

Linguistic Anthropology

Linguistic anthropology is the study of human speech and language, including the origins of language in general as well as specific languages. By examining similarities between contemporary languages, linguists have been able to trace historical ties between particular languages and groups of languages, thus facilitating the identification of language families and perhaps past relationships between human populations.

Because the spontaneous acquisition and use of language is a uniquely human characteristic, it's an important topic for linguistic anthropologists, who, along with specialists in other fields, study the process of language acquisition in infants. Because insights into the process may well have implications for the development of language in human evolution, as well as in growing children, it's also an important subject to physical anthropologists.

Physical Anthropology

As we've already said, *physical anthropology* is the study of human biology within the framework of evolution with an emphasis on the interaction between biology and culture. This subdiscipline is also referred to as *biological anthropology*, and you'll find the terms used interchangeably. *Physical anthropology* is the original term, and it reflects the initial interests anthropologists had in describing human physical variation. The American Association of Physical Anthro-

pologists, its journal, many college courses, and numerous publications retain this term. The designation *biological anthropology* reflects the shift in emphasis to more biologically oriented topics, such as genetics, evolutionary biology, nutrition, physiological adaptation, and growth and development. This shift occurred largely because of advances in the field of genetics and molecular biology since the late 1950s. Although we've continued to use the traditional term in the title of this textbook, you'll find that all of the major topics we discuss pertain to biological issues.

The origins of physical anthropology can be traced to two principal areas of interest among nineteenth-century European and American scholars (at that time called *naturalists* or *natural historians*): the origins of modern species and human variation. Although most of these naturalists held religious convictions, they were beginning to doubt the literal interpretation of the biblical account of creation and to support explanations that emphasized natural processes rather than supernatural phenomena. Eventually, the sparks of interest in biological change over time were fueled into flames by the publication of Charles Darwin's *On the Origin of Species* in 1859.

Today, **paleoanthropology**, the study of anatomical and behavioral human evolution as revealed in the fossil record, is a major subfield of physical anthropology (**Fig. 1-5**). Thousands of fossilized remains of early primates, including human ancestors, are now kept in research collections. Taken together, these fossils span at least 7 million years of human prehistory. Although most of these fossils are incomplete, they provide us with a significant wealth of knowledge that increases each year. It's the ultimate goal of paleoanthropological research to identify the various early human and humanlike species, establish a chronological sequence of relationships among them, and gain insights into their adaptation and behavior. Only

paleoanthropology The interdisciplinary approach to the study of earlier hominins—their chronology, physical structure, archaeological remains, habitats, and so on.

a

© HO/Reuters / Corbis

b

© Russell L. Ciochon

▲ **Figure 1-5**

(a) Paleoanthropologists excavating at the Drimolen site, South Africa. **(b)** Primate paleontologist Russell L. Ciochon (left) and Le Trang Kha (right), a vertebrate paleontologist, examine the fossil remains of *Gigantopithecus* from a 450,000-year-old site in Vietnam. *Gigantopithecus* is the name given to the largest apes that ever lived. In the background is a reconstruction of this enormous animal.

then will we have a clear picture of how and when modern humans came into being.

Human variation was the other major area of interest for early physical anthropologists. Enormous effort was spent in measuring, describing, and explaining visible differences among various human populations, with particular attention being focused on skin color, body proportions, and shape of the head and face. Although some approaches were misguided and even racist, they gave birth to many body measurements that are sometimes still used. They've been used to design everything from wheelchairs to office furniture. Undoubtedly, they've also been used to determine the absolute

minimum amount of leg room a person needs in order to remain sane during a 3-hour flight on a commercial airliner. They're also very important to the study of skeletal remains from archaeological sites (**Fig. 1-6**).

Today, physical anthropologists are concerned with human variation because of its possible *adaptive significance* and because they want to identify the factors that have produced not only visible physical variation but genetic variation as well. In other words, many traits that typify certain populations evolved as biological adaptations, or adjustments, to local environmental conditions such as sunlight, altitude, or infectious disease. Other

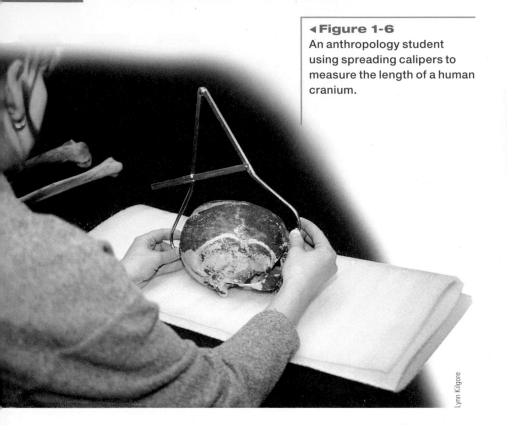

◄**Figure 1-6**
An anthropology student using spreading calipers to measure the length of a human cranium.

Lynn Kilgore

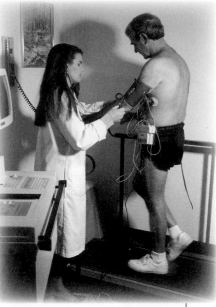

© Tom McCarthy / Photo Edit

▲**Figure 1-7**
This researcher is using a treadmill test to assess a subject's heart rate, blood pressure, and oxygen consumption.

characteristics may be the result of geographical isolation or the descent of populations from small founding groups. Examining biological variation between populations of any species provides valuable information as to the mechanisms of genetic change in groups over time, and this is really what the evolutionary process is all about.

Modern population studies also examine other important aspects of human variation, including how different groups respond physiologically to different kinds of environmentally induced stress (**Fig. 1-7**). Such stresses may include high altitude, cold, or heat. *Nutritional anthropologists* study the relationships between various dietary components, cultural practices, physiology, and certain aspects of health and disease (**Fig. 1-8**). Investigations of human fertility, growth, and development also are closely related to the topic of nutrition. These fields of inquiry, which are fundamental to studies of adaptation in modern human populations, can provide insights into hominin evolution, too.

It would be impossible to study evolutionary processes without some knowledge of how traits are inherited. For this reason and others, genetics is a crucial field for physical anthropologists. Modern physical anthropology wouldn't exist as an evolutionary science if it weren't for advances in the understanding of genetic mechanisms.

Molecular anthropologists use cutting-edge technologies to investigate evolutionary relationships between human populations as well as between humans and nonhuman primates. To do this, they examine similarities and differences in **DNA** sequences between individuals, populations, and species. What's more, by extracting DNA from certain fossils, these researchers have contributed to our understanding of evolutionary relationships between extinct and living species. As genetic technologies continue to be developed, molecular anthropologists will play a key role in explaining human evolution, adaptation, and our biological relationships with other species (**Fig. 1-9**).

DNA (deoxyribonucleic acid) The double-stranded molecule that contains the genetic code. DNA is a main component of chromosomes.

◄ Figure 1-8

Dr. Kathleen Galvin measures upper arm circumference in a young Maasai boy in Tanzania. Data derived from various body measurements, including height and weight, were used in a health and nutrition study of groups of Maasai cattle herders.

▲ Figure 1-9

(a) Cloning and sequencing methods are frequently used to identify genes in humans and nonhuman primates. This graduate student is working with genetically modified bacterial clones.

(b) Molecular anthropologist Nelson Ting collecting red colobus fecal samples for a study of genetic variation in small groups of monkeys isolated from one another by agricultural clearing.

However, before genetic and molecular techniques became widespread, **osteology**, the study of the skeleton, was the only way that anthropologists could study our immediate ancestors. In fact, a thorough knowledge of skeletal structure and function is still critical to the interpretation of fossil material today. For this reason, osteology has long been viewed as central to physical anthropology. In fact, it's so important that when many people think of biological anthropology, the first thing that comes to mind is bones!

Bone biology and physiology are of major importance to many other aspects of physical anthropology besides human evolution. Many oste-ologists specialize in the measurement of skeletal elements, essential for identifying stature and growth patterns in archaeological populations. In the last 30 years or so, the study of human skeletal remains from archaeological sites has sometimes been called **bioarchaeology**.

Paleopathology, the study of disease and trauma in ancient skeletal populations, is a major component of bioarchaeology. Paleopathologists investigate the prevalence of trauma, certain infectious diseases (such as syphilis and tuberculosis), nutritional deficiencies, and numerous other conditions that may leave evidence in bone (**Fig. 1-10**). This research can tell us a

▼**Figure 1-10**

Two examples of pathological conditions in human skeletal remains from the Nubian site of Kulubnarti in Sudan. These remains are approximately 1,000 years old. **(a)** A partially healed fracture of a child's left femur (thigh bone). This child died around the age of 6, probably of an infection that resulted from this injury. **(b)** Very severe congenital scoliosis in an adult male. The curves are due to developmental defects in individual vertebrae. (This is not the most common form of scoliosis.)

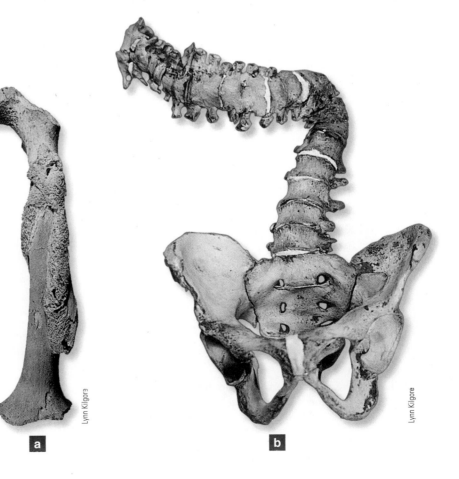

a

b

Lynn Kilgore

Lynn Kilgore

osteology The study of skeletal material. Human osteology focuses on the interpretation of the skeletal remains from archaeological sites, skeletal anatomy, bone physiology, and growth and development. Some of the same techniques are used in paleoanthropology to study early hominins.

bioarchaeology The study of skeletal remains from archaeological sites.

paleopathology The branch of osteology that studies the evidence of disease and injury in human skeletal (or, occasionally, mummified) remains from archaeological sites.

© Reuters / Corbis

U.S. Army Corps of Engineers, and the Regime Crime Liaison Office

◀**Figure 1-11**
(a) Forensic anthropologists Vuzumusi Madasco (from Zimbabwe) and Patricia Bernardi (from Argentina) excavating the skeletal remains and clothing of one of many victims of a civil war massacre in El Salvador. The goal is to identify as many of the victims as possible. **(b)** These forensic anthropologists, working in a lab near Baghdad, are examining the skeletal remains of Khurdish victims of genocide. They cataloged the injuries of 114 individuals buried in a mass grave, and some of their evidence was used against Saddam Hussein during his trial in 2006.

great deal about the lives of individuals and populations in the past. Paleopathology also yields information regarding the history of certain disease processes, and for this reason it's of interest to scientists in biomedical fields.

Forensic anthropology, is directly related to osteology and paleopathology, and has become of increasing interest to the public because of forensic TV shows like *Bones* (based on a character created by a practicing forensic anthropologist) and *Crime Scene Investigation*. Technically, this approach is the application of anthropological (usually osteological and sometimes archaeological) techniques to legal issues. Forensic anthropologists help identify skeletal remains in mass disasters or other situations in which a human body has been found. They've been involved in numerous cases having important legal, historical, and human consequences (**Fig. 1-11**). They were instrumental in identifying the skeletons of most of the Russian imperial family, executed in 1918; and many participated in the overwhelming task of trying to identify the remains of victims

forensic anthropology An applied anthropological approach dealing with legal matters. Forensic anthropologists work with coroners and others in identifying and analyzing human remains.

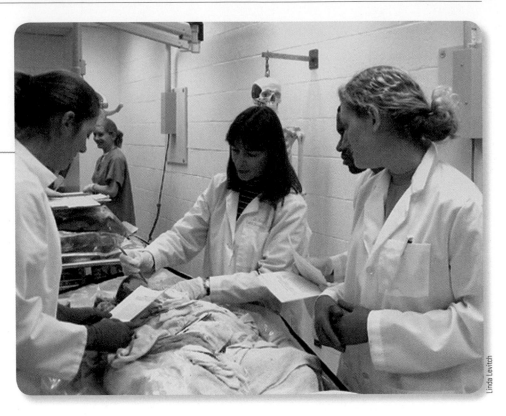

▶ **Figure 1-12**
Dr. Linda Levitch teaching a human anatomy class at the University of North Carolina School of Medicine.

Linda Levitch

of the September 11, 2001, terrorist attacks in the United States.

Anatomy is yet another important area of interest for physical anthropologists. In living organisms, bones and teeth are intimately linked to the soft tissues that surround and act on them. Consequently, a thorough knowledge of soft tissue anatomy is essential to understanding the biomechanical relationships involved in movement. Such relationships are important in assessing the structure and function of limbs and other components of fossilized remains. For these reasons and others, many physical anthropologists specialize in anatomical studies. In fact, several physical anthropologists are professors in anatomy departments at universities and medical schools (**Fig. 1-12**).

But humans aren't the only species studied by biological anthropologists. Given our evolutionary focus and the fact that we ourselves are primates, it's natural that **primatology**, the study of the living nonhuman primates, has become increasingly important since the late 1950s (**Fig. 1-13**). Today, doz-

ens of nonhuman primate species have been, and are being, studied. Because nonhuman primates are our closest living relatives, identifying the underlying factors related to their social behavior, communication, infant care, reproductive behavior, and so on, helps us develop a better understanding of the natural forces that have shaped so many aspects of modern human behavior. Nonhuman primates are also important to study in their own right. This is particularly true today because the majority of primate species are threatened or seriously endangered. Only through study will scientists be able to recommend policies that can better ensure the survival of many nonhuman primates as well as thousands of other species.

Applied Anthropology

There are many applied approaches in anthropology in general and biological anthropology in particular. Though *applied anthropology* is the practical use of anthropological theories and methods outside the academic setting,

primatology The study of the biology and behavior of nonhuman primates (lemurs, lorises, tarsiers, monkeys, and apes).

▲ Figure 1-13
(a) Primatologist Emmanuelle Grundmann using ropes and a harness to observe an orangutan in Borneo.
(b) Primatologist Jill Pruetz follows a chimpanzee in Senegal, in West Africa.

applied and academic anthropology aren't mutually exclusive approaches. In fact, applied anthropology relies on the research and theories of academic anthropologists and at the same time has much to contribute to theory and techniques.

Within biological anthropology, forensic anthropology is a good example of the applied approach. But the practical application of the techniques of physical anthropology isn't new. During World War II, for example, physical anthropologists were extensively involved in designing gun turrets and airplane cockpits. Since then, many physical anthropologists have pursued careers in genetic and biomedical research, public health, evolu-tionary medicine, medical anthropology, and conservation of nonhuman primates, and many hold positions in museums and zoos. In fact, a background in physical anthropology is excellent preparation for almost any career in the medical and biological fields (**Fig. 1-14**).

▶ **Figure 1-14**
Nanette Barkey, a medical anthropologist involved in a repatriation project in Angola, photographed this little girl being vaccinated at a refugee transit camp. Vaccinations were being administered to Angolan refugees returning home in 2004 from the Democratic Republic of Congo, where they had fled to escape warfare in their own country.

© Nanette Barkey

science A body of knowledge gained through observation and experimentation; from the Latin *scientia*, meaning "knowledge."

hypotheses (*sing.*, hypothesis) A provisional explanation of a phenomenon. Hypotheses require verification or falsification through testing.

empirical Relying on experiment or observation; from the Latin *empiricus*, meaning "experienced."

scientific method An approach to research whereby a problem is identified, a hypothesis (provisional explanation) is stated, and that hypothesis is tested by collecting and analyzing data.

data (*sing.*, datum) Facts from which conclusions can be drawn; scientific information.

quantitatively Pertaining to measurements of quantity and including such properties as size, number, and capacity. When data are quantified, they're expressed numerically and can be tested statistically.

theory A broad statement of scientific relationships or underlying principles that has been substantially verified through the testing of hypotheses.

Physical Anthropology and the Scientific Method

Science is a method of gaining information to explain natural phenomena. It involves observation; developing **hypotheses** to explain what has been observed; and developing a research design or series of experiments to test the hypotheses. This is an **empirical** approach to gaining information. Because biological anthropologists are engaged in scientific pursuits, they adhere to the principles of the **scientific method** by identifying a research problem and then gathering information to solve it.

Once a question has been asked, the first step usually is to explore the existing literature (books and journals) to determine what other people have done to resolve the issue. Based on this preliminary research and other observations, one or even several tentative explanations (hypotheses) are then proposed. The next step is to develop a research design or methodology to test the hypothesis. These methods involve collecting information, or **data**, that

can then be studied and analyzed. Data can be analyzed in many ways, most of them involving various statistical tests. During the data collection and analysis phase, it's important for scientists to use a rigorously controlled approach so they can precisely describe their techniques and results. This precision is critical because it enables others to repeat the experiments and allows scientists to make comparisons between their study and the work of others.

For example, when scientists collect data on tooth size in hominin fossils, they must specify which teeth are measured, how they're measured, and the results of the measurements (expressed numerically, or **quantitatively**). Then, by analyzing the data, the investigators try to draw conclusions about the meaning and significance of their measurements. This body of information then becomes the basis of future studies, perhaps by other researchers, who can compare their own results with those already obtained.

Hypothesis testing is the very core of the scientific method, and although it may seem contradictory at first, it's based on the potential to *falsify* the hypothesis. Falsification doesn't mean that the entire hypothesis is untrue, but it does indicate that the hypothesis may need to be refined and subjected to further testing.

Eventually, if a hypothesis stands up to repeated testing, it may become part of a **theory** or perhaps a theory itself. There's a popular misconception that a theory is nothing more than conjecture, or a "hunch." But in science, theories are proposed explanations of relationships between natural phenomena. Theories usually concern broader, more universal views than hypotheses, which have a narrower focus and deal with more specific relationships between phenomena. But like hypotheses, theories aren't facts. *They are tested explanations of facts.* For example, it's a fact that when you drop an object, it falls to the ground. The explanation for this fact is the theory of gravity. But, like hypotheses, theories can be altered over time with further experimentation and by using newly developed technologies in testing. The theory of gravity has been tested many times and qualified by experiments showing how the mass of objects affects how they're attracted to one another. So far, the theory has held up.

Scientific testing of hypotheses may take several years (or longer) and may involve researchers who weren't involved with the original work. What's more, new methods may permit different kinds of testing that weren't previously possible, and this is a strength, not a weakness, of scientific research. For example, since the 1970s, primatologists have reported that male nonhuman primates (as well as males of many other species) sometimes kill infants. One hypothesis has been that infanticidal males only killed the offspring of other males. But many scientists have objected to this hypothesis and have proposed several alternatives. For one thing, there was no way to know for certain that the males weren't killing their own offspring; and if they were, this would argue against the hypothesis. However, in a fairly recent study, scientists collected DNA samples from dead infants and the males who killed them. The evidence showed that most of the time, the males weren't related to their victims. This result doesn't prove that the original hypothesis is accurate, but it does strengthen it. This study is described in more detail in Chapter 8, but we mention it here to emphasize that science is an ongoing process that builds on previous work and benefits from newly developed techniques (in this case, DNA testing) in ways that constantly expand our knowledge.

There's one more extremely important fact about hypotheses and theories: *Any proposition that is stated as absolute or does not allow the possibility of falsification is not a scientific hypothesis and should never be considered as such.* For a statement to be considered a scientific hypothesis, there must be a way to evaluate its validity. Statements such as "Heaven exists" may well be true but there is no rational, empirical means (based on experience or experiment) of testing them. Therefore, acceptance of such a view is based on faith rather than on scientific verification. The purpose of scientific research is not to establish absolute truths; rather, it's to generate ever more accurate and consistent explanations of phenomena in our universe based on observation and testing. At its very heart, scientific methodology is an exercise in rational thought and critical thinking.

The development of critical thinking skills is an important and lasting benefit of a college education. Such skills enable people to evaluate, compare, analyze, critique, and synthesize information so they won't accept everything they hear at face value. Critical thinking skills are perhaps most needed when it comes to advertising and politics. People spend billions of dollars every year on "natural" dietary supplements based on marketing claims that may not have been tested. So when a salesperson tells you that, for example, echinacea helps prevent colds, you should ask if that statement has been scientifically tested, how it was tested, when, by whom, and where the results were published. Similarly, when politicians make claims in 30-second sound bites, check those claims before you accept them as truth. Be skeptical, and if you do check the validity of advertising and political statements, you'll find that frequently they're either misleading or just plain wrong.

The Anthropological Perspective

Perhaps the most important benefit you'll receive from this textbook, and this course, is a wider appreciation of the human experience. To understand human beings and how our species came to be, we must broaden our viewpoint through both time and space. All branches of anthropology

scientific testing The precise repetition of an experiment or expansion of observed data to provide verification; the procedure by which hypotheses and theories are verified, modified, or discarded.

fundamentally seek to do this in what we call the *anthropological perspective*.

Physical anthropologists, for example, are interested in how humans both differ from and are similar to other animals, especially nonhuman primates. For example, we've defined *hominins* as bipedal primates, but what are the major anatomical components of bipedal locomotion, and how do they differ from, say, those in a **quadrupedal** ape? To answer these questions, we would need to study the anatomical structures involved in human locomotion (muscles, hips, legs, and feet) and compare them with the same structures in various nonhuman primates.

Through a perspective that is broad in space and time, we can begin to grasp the diversity of the human experience within the context of biological and behavioral connections with other species. In this way, we may better understand the limits and potentials of humankind. And by extending our knowledge to include cultures other than our own, we may hope to avoid the **ethnocentric** pitfalls inherent in a more limited view of humanity.

This **relativistic** view of culture is perhaps more important now than ever before, because in our increasingly interdependent global community, it allows us to understand other people's concerns and to view our own culture from a broader perspective. Likewise, by examining our species as part of a wide spectrum of life, we realize that we can't judge other species using human criteria. Each species is unique, with needs and a behavioral repertoire not exactly like that of any other. By recognizing that we share many similarities (both biological and behavioral) with other animals, perhaps we may come to recognize that they have a place in nature just as surely as we ourselves do.

We hope that after reading the following pages, you'll have an increased understanding not only of the similarities we share with other biological organisms, but also of the processes that have shaped the traits that make us unique. We live in what may well be our planet's most crucial period in the past 65 million years. We are members of the one species that, through the very agency of culture, has wrought such devastating changes in ecological systems that we must now alter our technologies or face potentially unspeakable consequences. In such a time, it's vital that we attempt to gain the best possible understanding of what it means to be human. We believe that the study of physical anthropology is one endeavor that aids in this attempt, and that is indeed the goal of this textbook.

quadrupedal Using all four limbs to support the body during locomotion; the basic mammalian (and primate) form of locomotion.

ethnocentric Viewing other cultures from the inherently biased perspective of one's own culture. Ethnocentrism often results in other cultures being seen as inferior to one's own.

relativistic Viewing entities as they relate to something else. Cultural relativism is the view that cultures have merits within their own historical and environmental contexts.

Why It Matters

Today, the trend in advanced education is toward greater and greater specialization, with the result that very few people or professions have the broad overview necessary to implement policy and make effective changes that could lead to improved standards of living, a safer geopolitical world, and better planetary health. This is acutely felt in medicine, where specialists focusing on one part of the body sometimes ignore other parts, often to the detriment of overall health (especially mental and emotional) of the patient. Anthropology is one of the few disciplines that encourages a broad view of the human condition.

An example is seen in AIDS prevention research. The wealth of knowledge that biologists and medical researchers have provided on the characteristics and behavior of HIV (the virus that causes AIDS) is useless for preventing its transmission unless we also have an understanding of human behavior at both the individual and the sociocultural levels. Behavioral scientists, including anthropologists, are prepared to examine the range of social, religious, economic, political, and historical contexts surrounding sexuality to devise AIDS prevention strategies that will vary from population to population and even from subculture to subculture. Whether or not you choose a career in anthropology, the perspectives that you gain from studying this discipline will enable you to participate in research and policy decisions on future challenges to human and planetary well-being.

Summary of Main Topics

- The major subfields of anthropology are cultural anthropology, linguistic anthropology, archaeology, and physical anthropology.
- Physical anthropology is a discipline that seeks to explain how and when human beings evolved. This requires a detailed examination of the primate, and particularly hominin, fossil record (primate paleontology). Another major topic of physical anthropology is human biological variation, its genetic basis, and its adaptive significance. In addition, physical anthropologists study the behavior and biology of nonhuman primates, partly as a method of understanding humans, but also because nonhuman primates are important in their own right.

- Because physical anthropology is a scientific approach to the investigation of all aspects of human evolution, variation, and adaptation, research in this field is based on the scientific method. The scientific method is a system of inquiry that involves the development of hypotheses to explain some phenomenon. To determine the validity of hypotheses, scientists develop research designs aimed at collecting information (data) and testing the data to see if they support the hypothesis. If the hypothesis is not supported by the data, then it may be rejected or modified and retested. If it is supported, it may also be modified or refined over time and further tested. Further tests frequently use new technologies that have been developed since the original hypothesis was proposed. If a hypothesis stands up to continued testing, then it may eventually be accepted as a theory or part of a theory.

Critical Thinking Questions

1. Given that you've only just been introduced to the field of physical anthropology, why do you think subjects such as anatomy, genetics, nonhuman primate behavior, and human evolution are integrated into a discussion of what it means to be human?

2. Is it important to you, personally, to know about human evolution? Why or why not?

3. Do you see a connection between hominin footprints that are almost 4 million years old and human footprints left on the moon in 1969? If so, do you think this relationship is important? What does the fact that there are human footprints on the moon say about human adaptation? (Consider both biological and cultural adaptation.)

Making a Difference:
Forensic Anthropologists in the Contemporary World

Due to wide media coverage, especially several popular television shows, forensic anthropology has captured the imagination of many people. In addition to their well-known participation in assisting law enforcement officials investigating crime scenes, forensic anthropologists also work in a variety of other interesting situations. They are often called to join recovery teams at scenes of mass disasters such as the World Trade Center, plane crashes, or in areas devastated by an earthquake or tsunami. Additionally, they're involved in excavating mass graves where victims of political atrocities have been secretly buried. Sadly, these sites of such enormous human tragedy are found in many parts of the world, from Iraq to Bosnia, to Argentina, to Rwanda. Forensic anthropologists also help search for and identify soldiers missing in action from prior wars. In all these difficult circumstances, wherever possible, the goal is to determine the identity of missing people and to return their remains to family members.

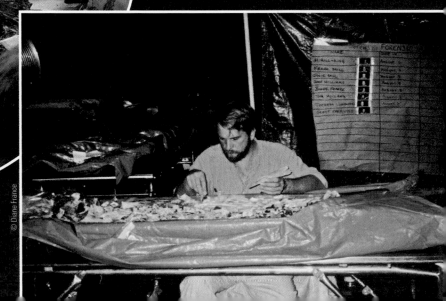

◀ Scene of a Korean Airlines crash in 1996 in the U.S. territory of Guam, that killed 228 people. The U.S. government immediately sent numerous DMORT (Disaster Mortuary Operation Response) teams, each of which usually has at least one forensic anthropologist.

▼ All human remains were evaluated in the field laboratory where Tom Holland (Director of the Central Identification Laboratory in Hawaii) is shown identifying fragmentary skeletal elements, many of which were extensively burned (as were many of the bodies). Nevertheless, all the passengers and crew were accounted for.

© Diane France

© Diane France

U.S. Army Corps of Engineers, and the Regime Crime Liaison Office

▲ Forensic anthropologists, including both physical anthropologists and archaeologists, recovered 114 Kurdish victims of genocide from this site in southern Iraq.

U.S. Army Corps of Engineers, and the Regime Crime Liaison Office

Forensic anthropology has captured the imagination of many people.

▲ Forensic anthropologists working in a lab near Baghdad catalogued the injuries suffered by every individual from the mass grave shown above. Some of this evidence was used in the trial of Saddam Hussein and helped lead to his conviction. After the trial, the human remains were turned over to Kurdish officials for reburial

▶ Lower Right: Heather Thew, who was trained as an anthropologist, is shown working at the Armed Forces DNA Laboratory where remains of missing soldiers are identified.

Craig King, Armed Forces DNA Identification Laboratory

25

Connections

Physical anthropology investigates how humans have evolved.

Evolutionary theory, particularly natural selection, explains how life forms have changed over time.

DNA molecule is the basis of all life.

2

The Development of Evolutionary Theory

Has anyone ever asked you, "If humans evolved from monkeys, then why do we still have monkeys?" Or maybe, "If evolution happens, then why don't we ever see new species?" These are the kinds of questions people sometimes ask if they don't understand evolutionary processes or they don't believe evolution occurs. Evolution is one of the most fundamental of all biological processes, and yet it's one of the most misunderstood. The explanation for the misunderstanding is simple: Evolution is not taught in most primary and secondary schools. In fact, it's frequently avoided. Even in colleges and universities, evolution is barely touched on, sometimes even in biology classes. In general, it receives the most detailed treatment in biological anthropology. If you're not an anthropology or biology major and you're taking a class in biological anthropology mainly to fulfill a science requirement, you'll probably never study evolution again.

By the end of this course, you'll know the answers to the questions in the preceding paragraph. Briefly, no one who studies evolution would ever say that humans evolved from monkeys, because we didn't. We didn't evolve from chimpanzees either. The earliest human ancestors evolved from a species that lived some 6 to 8 million years ago (mya). That ancestral species was the *last common ancestor* we share with chimpanzees. In turn, the lineage that eventually gave rise to the apes and humans separated from a monkey-like ancestor some 20 mya, and monkeys are still around because as early primate lineages diverged from one another, each went its separate way. Over millions of years, some of these groups became extinct while others evolved into the species we see today. Thus, all living species are the current results of processes that go back millions of years. Because the evolution of new species takes time, and lots of it, we rarely witness the appearance of new species except in microorganisms. But we do see *microevolutionary* changes in many species, including humans.

The subject of evolution is controversial, especially in the United States, because some religious views hold that evolutionary statements run counter to biblical teachings. In fact, as you're probably aware, there is strong opposition in the United States to the teaching of evolution in public schools. Opponents of

◄ Common Cactus Finch on Santa Cruz Island, Galapagos Islands.

evolution often say, "It's just a theory," meaning that evolution is just an idea, a hunch. As we pointed out in Chapter 1, scientific theories aren't just ideas, although that's how the word *theory* is commonly used in everyday conversation. But, when dealing with scientific issues, referring to a concept as "theory" supports it. Theories have been tested and subjected to verification through accumulated evidence, and they haven't been disproved, sometimes after decades of experimentation. It's absolutely true that evolution is a theory, one that's supported by a mounting body of genetic evidence that, quite literally, grows daily. It's a theory that explains how biological change occurs in species over time, and it's stood the test of time. Today, evolutionary theory stands as the most fundamental unifying force in biological science, and evolutionary biologists can explain many evolutionary processes in ways that were impossible even 10 years ago.

Because physical anthropology is concerned with all aspects of how humans came to be and how we adapt physiologically to the external environment, the details of the evolutionary process are crucial to the field. Given the central importance of evolution to biological anthropology, it's helpful to know how the mechanics of the process came to be discovered. Also, if we want to understand and make critical assessments of the controversy that surrounds the issue today, we need to explore the social and political events that influenced the discovery of evolutionary principles.

A Brief History of Evolutionary Thought

The discovery of evolutionary principles first took place in western Europe and was made possible by advances in scientific thinking that

date back to the sixteenth century. Having said this, we must recognize that Western science borrowed many of its ideas from other cultures, especially the Arabs, Indians, and Chinese. In fact, intellectuals in these cultures and in ancient Greece had developed notions of biological evolution centuries before Charles Darwin (Teresi, 2002), but they never formulated them into a cohesive theory.

Charles Darwin was the first person to explain the basic mechanics of the evolutionary process. But while he was developing his theory of **natural selection**, a Scottish naturalist named Alfred Russel Wallace independently reached the same conclusion. That natural selection, the single most important force of evolutionary change, was proposed at more or less the same time by two British men in the mid-nineteenth century may seem like a strange coincidence. But actually, if Darwin and Wallace hadn't made their simultaneous discoveries, someone else soon would have, and that someone would probably have been British or French. That's because the groundwork had already been laid in Britain and France, and many scientists there were prepared to accept explanations of biological change that would have been unacceptable even 25 years before.

Like other human endeavors, scientific knowledge is usually gained through a series of small steps rather than giant leaps. And just as technological change is based on past achievements, scientific knowledge builds on previously developed theories. Therefore, it's informative to examine the development of ideas that led Darwin and Wallace to independently arrive at the theory of evolution by natural selection.

Throughout the Middle Ages, one predominant feature of the European worldview was that all aspects of nature, including all forms of life and their relationships to one another, never changed. This view was partly shaped by a feudal society that was itself a rigid class system that hadn't

natural selection The most critical mechanism of evolutionary change, first described by Charles Darwin; refers to genetic change or changes in the frequencies of certain traits in populations due to differential reproductive success between individuals.

Italian School (16th century)/Museo di San Marco dell'Angelico, Florence, Italy/Alinari/The Bridgeman Art Library

◄ **Figure 2-1**
Portion of a Renaissance painting that depicts the execution of Father Girolamo Savonarola in 1498 in Florence, Italy (artist unknown). Savonarola wasn't promoting scientific arguments, but he did run afoul of church leaders. His execution by burning was the typical punishment of those, including many scientists and philosophers, who promoted scientific explanations of natural phenomena.

changed much for centuries. But the most important influence was an extremely powerful religious system in which the teachings of Christianity were held to be the only "truth." Consequently, it was generally accepted that all life on earth had been created by God exactly as it existed in the present, and this belief that life-forms couldn't and didn't change came to be known as **fixity of species**. Anyone who questioned the assumptions of fixity, especially in the fifteenth and sixteenth centuries, could be accused of challenging God's perfection, and that was heresy. Generally, it was a good idea to avoid accusations of heresy because it was a crime that could be punished by a nasty and often fiery death (**Fig. 2-1**).

The plan of the entire universe was viewed as God's design. In what's called the "argument from design," anatomical structures were engineered to meet the purpose for which they were required. Limbs, internal organs, and eyes all fit the functions they performed; and they, along with the rest

of nature, were a deliberate plan of the Grand Designer. Also, the Grand Designer was thought to have completed his works as recently as 4004 B.C. The prevailing notion of the earth's brief existence, together with fixity of species, was a huge obstacle to the development of evolutionary theory. The idea of immense geological time, which today we take for granted, simply didn't exist. In fact, until the concepts of fixity and time were fundamentally altered, it was impossible to conceive of evolution by means of natural selection.

The Scientific Revolution

So, what transformed centuries-old beliefs in a rigid, static universe to a view of worlds in continuous motion? How did the earth's brief history become an immense expanse of incomprehensible time? How did the scientific method as we know it today develop? These are important questions, but we could also ask why it took so long for Europe to break away from traditional

fixity of species The notion that species, once created, can never change; an idea diametrically opposed to theories of biological evolution.

▶ **Figure 2-2**
This beautifully illustrated seventeenth-century map shows the earth at the center of the solar system. Around it are seven concentric circles depicting the orbits of the moon, sun, and the five planets that were known at the time. (Note also the signs of the zodiac.)

beliefs. After all, scholars in India and the Arab world had developed concepts of planetary motion, for example, centuries earlier.

For Europeans, the discovery of the New World and circumnavigation of the globe in the fifteenth century overturned some very basic ideas about the planet. For one thing, the earth could no longer be thought of as flat. Also, as Europeans began to explore the New World, their awareness of biological diversity was expanded as they encountered plants and animals they'd never seen before.

There were other attacks on traditional beliefs. In 1514, a Polish mathematician named Copernicus challenged a notion proposed more than 1,500 years earlier by the fourth-century B.C. Greek philosopher Aristotle. Aristotle had taught that the sun and planets existed in a series of concentric spheres that revolved around the earth (**Fig. 2-2**). This system of planetary spheres was, in turn, surrounded by the stars. This meant, of course, that the earth was the center of the solar system. In fact, scholars in India

had figured out that the earth orbited the sun long before Copernicus did; but Copernicus is generally credited with removing the earth as the center of all things.

Copernicus' theory was discussed in intellectual circles, but it didn't attract much attention from the Catholic Church. (Catholicism was the only form of Christianity until the 1520s.) Nevertheless, the theory did contradict a major premise of church doctrine, which at that time wholeheartedly embraced the teachings of Aristotle. By the 1300s, the church had accepted these teachings as dogma because they reinforced the notion that the earth, and the humans on it, were the central focus of God's creation and must therefore have a central position in the solar system.

However, in the early 1600s, an Italian mathematician named Galileo Galilei restated Copernicus' views, using logic and mathematics to support his claim. To his misfortune, Galileo was eventually confronted by the highest-ranking officials of the Catholic Church (including his former friend, the pope), and he spent the last nine years of his life under house arrest. Nevertheless, in intellectual circles, the solar system had changed; the sun was now at its center, and the earth and other planets revolved around it as the entire system journeyed through space.

Throughout the sixteenth and seventeenth centuries, European scientists developed other methods and theories that revolutionized scientific thought. The seventeenth century, in particular, saw the discovery of the principles of physics (such as motion and gravity), and the invention of numerous scientific instruments, including the microscope. These advances permitted the investigation of many previously misunderstood natural phenomena. But even with these advances, the idea that living forms could change over time simply didn't occur to people.

Precursors to the Theory of Evolution

Before early naturalists could begin to understand the many forms of organic life, they needed to list and describe them. And as research progressed, scholars were increasingly impressed with the amount of biological diversity they saw.

The concept of species, as we think of them today, wasn't proposed until the seventeenth century, when John Ray, a minister educated at the University of Cambridge, developed it. He recognized that groups of plants and animals could be differentiated from other groups by their ability to mate with one another and produce fertile offspring. He placed such groups of **reproductively isolated** organisms into categories, which he called species (*sing.*, species). Thus, by the late 1600s, the biological criterion of reproduction was used to define species, much as it is today (Young, 1992). Ray also recognized that species frequently share similarities with other species, and he grouped these together in a sec-

ond level of classification he called the genus (*pl.*, genera). He was the first to use the labels *genus* and *species* in this way, and they're the terms we still use.

Carolus Linnaeus (1707–1778) was a Swedish naturalist who developed a method of classifying plants and animals. In his famous work, *Systema Naturae* (Systems of Nature), first published in 1735, he standardized Ray's use of genus and species terminology and established the system of **binomial nomenclature**. He also added two more categories: class and order. Linnaeus' four-level system became the basis for **taxonomy**, the system of classification we continue to use.

Linnaeus also included humans in his classification of animals, placing them in the genus *Homo* and species *sapiens*. (Genus and species names are always italicized.) Including humans in this scheme was controversial because it defied contemporary thought that humans, made in God's image, should be considered unique and separate from the rest of the animal kingdom.

For all his progressive tendencies, Linnaeus still believed in fixity of species, although in later years, faced with mounting evidence to the contrary, he came to question it. Indeed, fixity was being challenged on many fronts, especially in France, where voices were being raised in favor of a universe based on change and, more to the point, in favor of a biological relationship between similar species based on descent from a common ancestor.

A French naturalist, Georges-Louis Leclerc de Buffon (1707–1788), recognized the dynamic relationship between the external environment and living forms. In his *Natural History*, first published in 1749, he recognized that different regions have unique plants and animals. He also stressed that animals had come from a "center of origin," but he never discussed the diversification of life over time. Even so, Buffon recognized that alterations of the external environment, including the climate, were agents of change in species. For this reason, the late

reproductively isolated Pertaining to groups of organisms that, mainly because of genetic differences, are prevented from mating and producing offspring with members of other such groups. For example, dogs cannot mate and produce offspring with cats.

binomial nomenclature (*binomial*, meaning "two names") In taxonomy, the convention established by Carolus Linnaeus whereby genus and species names are used to refer to species. For example, *Homo sapiens* refers to human beings.

taxonomy The branch of science concerned with the rules of classifying organisms on the basis of evolutionary relationships.

▲ Figure 2-3
Portrait of Jean-Baptiste Lamarck. Lamarck believed that species change was influenced by environmental change. He is best known for his theory of the inheritance of acquired characteristics.

Oil on canvas, Thevenin, Charles (1764–1838) / Private Collection / The Bridgeman Art Library International

catastrophism The view that the earth's geological landscape is the result of violent cataclysmic events. Cuvier promoted this view, especially in opposition to Lamarck.

evolutionary biologist Ernst Mayr said of him: "He was not an evolutionist, yet he was the father of evolutionism" (Mayr, 1981, p. 330).

Today, Erasmus Darwin (1731–1802) is best known as Charles Darwin's grandfather. But he was also a physician, a poet, and a leading member of an important intellectual community in England. In fact, Darwin counted among his friends some of the leading figures of the industrial revolution, a time of rapid technological and social change. In his most famous poem, Darwin expressed the view that life had originated in the seas and that all species had descended from a common ancestor. Thus, he introduced many of the ideas that his grandson would propose 56 years later. These concepts include vast expanses of time for life to evolve, competition for resources, and the importance of the environment in evolutionary processes. From letters and other sources, we know that Charles Darwin read his grandfather's writings, but we don't know how much he was influenced by them.

Neither Buffon nor Erasmus Darwin attempted to *explain* the evolutionary process, but a French naturalist named Jean-Baptiste Lamarck (1744–1829) did. Lamarck (**Fig. 2-3**) suggested a dynamic relationship between species and the environment such that if the external environment changed, an animal's activity patterns would also change to accommodate the new circumstances. This would result in the increased or decreased use of certain body parts; consequently, those body parts would be modified. According to Lamarck, the parts that weren't used would disappear over time. However, the parts that continued to be used, perhaps in different ways, would change. Such physical changes would occur in response to bodily "needs," so that if a particular part of the body felt a certain need, "fluids and forces" would be directed to that point, and the structure would be modified. Because the alteration would make the animal better suited to its habitat, the new

trait would be passed on to offspring. This theory is known as the *inheritance of acquired characteristics*, or the *use-disuse* theory.

One of the most frequently given hypothetical examples of Lamarck's theory is the giraffe, which, having stripped all the leaves from the lower branches of a tree (environmental change), tries to reach leaves on upper branches. As "vital forces" move to tissues of the neck, it becomes slightly longer, and the giraffe can reach higher. The longer neck is then transmitted to offspring, with the eventual result that all giraffes have longer necks than their predecessors had (**Fig. 2-4**). So, according to this theory, *a trait acquired by an animal during its lifetime can be passed on to offspring*. Today we know that this explanation is wrong because only those traits that are influenced by genetic information contained within sex cells (eggs and sperm) can be inherited (see Chapter 3).

Because Lamarck's explanation of species change isn't genetically correct, he is frequently scorned even today. But in fact, Lamarck deserves a great deal of credit because he emphasized the importance of interactions between organisms and the external environment in the evolutionary process. He also coined the term *biology* to refer to the study of living organisms, and a central feature of this new discipline was the idea of species change.

Lamarck's most vehement opponent was a French vertebrate paleontologist named Georges Cuvier (1769–1832). Cuvier introduced the concept of extinction to explain the disappearance of animals represented by fossils. Cuvier was a brilliant anatomist, but he never grasped the dynamic concept of nature and continued to insist on the fixity of species. So, rather than assuming that similarities between fossil forms and living species indicate evolutionary relationships, Cuvier proposed a variation of a doctrine known as **catastrophism**.

Catastrophism was the belief that the earth's geological features are the

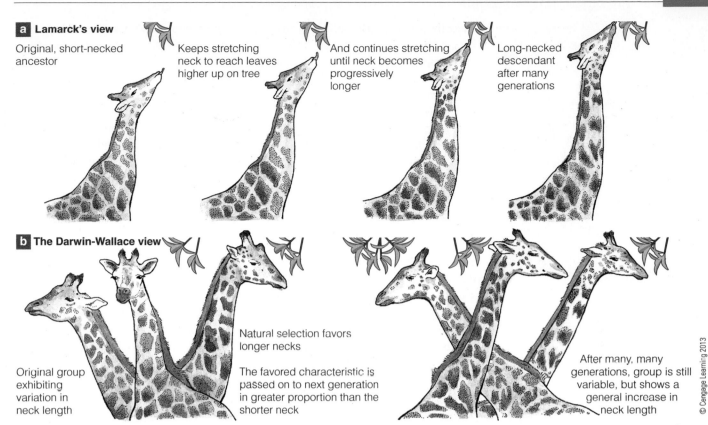

a **Lamarck's view**

Original, short-necked ancestor

Keeps stretching neck to reach leaves higher up on tree

And continues stretching until neck becomes progressively longer

Long-necked descendant after many generations

b **The Darwin-Wallace view**

Original group exhibiting variation in neck length

Natural selection favors longer necks

The favored characteristic is passed on to next generation in greater proportion than the shorter neck

After many, many generations, group is still variable, but shows a general increase in neck length

© Cengage Learning 2013

▲ **Figure 2-4**

Contrasting ideas about the mechanism of evolution. (a) Lamarck's theory held that acquired characteristics can be passed to offspring. Short-necked giraffes stretched to reach higher into trees for food, and their necks grew longer. According to Lamarck, this acquired trait was passed on to offspring, who were born with longer necks.
(b) The Darwin-Wallace theory of natural selection states that among giraffes there is variation in neck length. If having a longer neck provides an advantage for feeding, the trait will be passed on to a greater number of offspring, leading to an overall increase in the length of giraffe necks over many generations.

results of sudden, worldwide cataclysmic events. Cuvier's version of catastrophism suggested that a series of regional disasters had destroyed most or all of the local plant and animal life in many places. These areas were then restocked with new, similar forms that migrated in from unaffected regions. Because he needed to be consistent with emerging fossil evidence, which indicated that organisms had become more complex over time, Cuvier proposed that after each disaster, the incoming migrants were more similar to living species because they had been produced by more recent creation events. In this way, Cuvier's explanation of increased complexity over time avoided any notion of evolution, but it still managed to account for the evidence of change so well preserved in the fossil record.

In 1798, an English economist named Thomas Malthus (1766–1834) wrote *An Essay on the Principle of Population*. This important essay inspired both Charles Darwin and Alfred Russel Wallace in their separate discoveries of natural selection. Considering the enormous influence that Malthus had on these two men, it's noteworthy that he wasn't interested in species change at all. Instead, he was arguing for limits to human population growth. He pointed out that in nature, there is a tendency for animal populations to increase in size, but the amount of resources (food and water) remains relatively the same. Therefore, population size is held in

© Hulton-Deutsch Collection / Corbis

▲ **Figure 2-5**
Portrait of Charles Lyell.

check by resource availability. Even though humans can reduce constraints on population size by producing more food, Malthus argued that the lack of resources would always be a constant source of "misery" and famine for humankind if our numbers continued to increase. (Unfortunately, we're already testing Malthus' hypothesis as the number of humans on earth reached 7 billion in 2011!)

Both Darwin and Wallace extended Malthus' principles to all organisms, not just humans. Moreover, they recognized the important fact that when population size is limited by resource availability, there must be constant competition for food and water. This is a crucial point because competition between individuals is the ultimate key to understanding natural selection.

Charles Lyell (1797–1875) is considered the founder of modern geology (**Fig. 2-5**). He was a lawyer, a geologist, and, for many years, Charles Darwin's friend and mentor. Before meeting Darwin in 1836, Lyell had earned acceptance in Europe's most prestigious scientific circles, thanks to his highly praised *Principles of Geology*, first published during the years 1830–1833.

In this extremely important work, Lyell argued that the geological processes we see today are the same as those in the past. This theory, called geological **uniformitarianism**, didn't originate entirely with Lyell, having been proposed by James Hutton in the late 1700s. Even so, it was Lyell who demonstrated that forces such as wind, water erosion, local flooding, frost, decomposition of vegetable matter, volcanoes, earthquakes, and glacial movements had all contributed in the past to produce the geological landscape that we see today. What's more, these processes were ongoing, indicating that geological change was still happening and that the forces driving such change were consistent, or *uniform*, over time. In other words, various aspects of the earth's surface (for example, climate, plants, animals, and land surfaces)

vary through time, but the *underlying processes* that influence them are constant.

Lyell also emphasized the obvious: namely, that for such slow-acting forces to produce momentous change, the earth must be far older than anyone had previously suspected. By providing an immense time scale and thereby changing perceptions of the earth's history from a few thousand to many millions of years, Lyell changed the framework within which scientists viewed the geological past. Thus, the concept of "deep time" (Gould, 1987) remains one of Lyell's most significant contributions to the discovery of evolutionary principles, because the immensity of geological time permitted the necessary time depth for the inherently slow process of evolutionary change (**Fig. 2-6**).

As you can see, the roots of evolutionary theory are deeply embedded in the late eighteenth and early nineteenth centuries. During that time, many lesser-known but very important people also contributed to this intellectual movement. We have discussed only a very few, but it should be noted that these few were influenced by many others.

The Discovery of Natural Selection

Having already been introduced to Erasmus Darwin, you shouldn't be surprised to learn that his grandson Charles grew up in an educated family with ties to intellectual circles. Charles Darwin (1809–1882) was one of six children of Dr. Robert and Susanna Darwin (**Fig. 2-7**). Being the grandson not only of Erasmus Darwin but also of the wealthy Josiah Wedgwood (of Wedgwood china fame), Charles grew up enjoying the comfortable lifestyle of the landed gentry in rural England.

As a boy, Darwin had a keen interest in nature and spent his days fishing and collecting shells, birds' eggs, and rocks. However, this interest in natural history didn't dispel the generally held

uniformitarianism The theory that the earth's features are the result of long-term processes that continue to operate in the present just as they did in the past. Elaborated on by Lyell, this theory opposed catastrophism and contributed strongly to the concept of immense geological time.

◄ Figure 2-6
(a) These limestone cliffs in southern France were formed around 300 million years ago from shells and the skeletal remains of countless sea creatures. **(b)** Part of a block of stone cut from the same limestone containing fossilized shells.

Lynn Kilgore

Lynn Kilgore

view among family and friends that he was in no way remarkable. In fact, his performance at school was no more than ordinary.

After his mother's death when he was 8 years old, Darwin was raised by his father and older sisters. Because he showed little interest in anything except hunting, shooting, and perhaps science, his father sent him to Edinburgh University to study medicine. It was there that Darwin first became acquainted with the evolutionary theories of Lamarck and others.

During that time (the 1820s), notions of evolution were becoming feared in England and elsewhere. Anything identified with postrevolutionary France was viewed with suspicion by the established order in England, and Lamarck, partly because he was French, was especially vilified by British scientists.

It was also a time of growing political unrest in Britain. The Reform Movement, which sought to undo the many inequalities of the traditional class sys-

tem, was under way, and like most social movements, it had a radical faction. Because many of the radicals were atheists and socialists who also supported Lamarck's ideas, many

◄ Figure 2-7
Charles Darwin, photographed five years before the publication of *On the Origin of Species*.

© Bettmann / Corbis

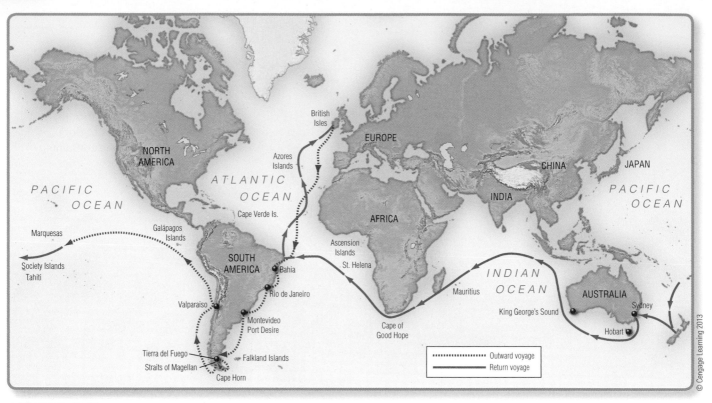

▲ **Figure 2-8**
The route of HMS *Beagle*.

people came to associate evolution with atheism and political subversion. The growing fear of evolutionary ideas led many to believe that if these ideas were generally accepted, "the Church would crash, the moral fabric of society would be torn apart, and civilized man would return to savagery" (Desmond and Moore, 1991, p. 34). It's unfortunate that some of the most outspoken early proponents of species change were so vehemently anti-Christian, because their rhetoric helped establish the entrenched suspicion and misunderstanding of evolutionary theory that persists today.

While at Edinburgh, Darwin studied with professors who were outspoken supporters of Lamarck. So, even though he hated medicine and left Edinburgh after two years, his experience there was a formative period in his intellectual development.

Although Darwin was fairly indifferent to religion, he next went to Cambridge to study theology. It was during his Cambridge years that he cultivated interests in natural science, immersing himself in botany and geol-

ogy. Following his graduation in 1831 he was invited to join a scientific expedition that would circle the globe. And so it was that Darwin set sail aboard HMS *Beagle* on December 17, 1831 (**Fig. 2-8**). The famous voyage of the *Beagle* would take almost five years and would forever change not only the course of Darwin's life but also the history of biological science (**Fig. 2-9**).

Darwin went aboard the *Beagle* believing in fixity of species. But during the voyage, he privately began to have doubts. For one thing, he came across fossils of ancient giant animals that, except for size, looked very much like species that still lived in the same vicinity. The similarities he saw caused him to speculate that the fossils represented ancestors of those living forms.

During the now famous stopover at the Galápagos Islands, off the coast of Ecuador, Darwin noticed that the vegetation and animals (especially birds) shared many similarities with those on the South American mainland. But they weren't identical to them. What's more, the birds varied from island to island. Darwin collected 13 varieties

◄ **Figure 2-9**
A painting by John Chancellor of the HMS *Beagle* sailing through the Galápagos Islands in 1835.

of Galápagos finches, and it was clear that they represented a closely related group; but some of their physical traits were different, particularly the shape and size of their beaks (**Fig. 2-10**). Darwin also collected finches from the mainland, and these appeared to represent only one group, or species.

The insight that Darwin gained from the finches is legendary. But, contrary to popular misconception, it wasn't until *after* he returned to England that he recognized the significance of the variation in beak structure. In fact, dur-

ing the voyage, he had paid little attention to the finches. It was only later that he considered the factors that could lead to the modification of one species into many (Gould, 1985; Desmond and Moore, 1991). He realized that the various Galapagos finches had all descended from a common mainland ancestor and had been modified over time in response to different island habitats and dietary preferences.

Darwin returned to England in October 1836, and was immediately accepted into the most prestigious

▼ **Figure 2-10**
Beak variation in Darwin's Galápagos finches.

Ground finch	Tree finch	Tree finch (called wood-pecker finch)	Ground finch (known as warbler finch)
Main Food: seeds	Main food: leaves, buds, blossoms, fruits	Main food: insects	Main food: insects
Beak: heavy	Beak: thick, short	Beak: stout, straight	Beak: slender

▶ **Figure 2-11**
Down House, as seen from the rear. *On the Origin of Species* and numerous other publications were written here.

Robert Jurmain

scientific circles. He married his cousin, Emma Wedgwood, and moved to the village of Down, near London, where he spent the rest of his life writing on topics ranging from fossils to orchids (**Fig. 2-11**). But the question of species change was his overriding passion.

At Down, Darwin began to develop his views on what he called *natural selection*. This concept was borrowed from animal breeders, who choose, or "select," as breeding stock those animals that possess certain traits they want to emphasize in offspring. Animals with undesirable traits are "selected against," or prevented from breeding. A dramatic example of the effects of selective breeding can be seen in the various domestic dog breeds shown in **Figure 2-12**. Darwin applied his knowledge of domesticated species to naturally occurring ones, and he recognized that in undomesticated organisms, the selective agent was nature, not humans.

By the late 1830s, Darwin had realized that biological variation within a species (that is, differences among individuals) was crucial. Furthermore, he realized that sexual reproduction increased variation, although he didn't know why. Then, in 1838, he read Malthus' essay; and there he found the

answer to the question of how new species came to be. He accepted Malthus' idea that populations increase at a faster rate than resources do, and he recognized that in nonhuman animals, population size is always limited by the amount of available food and water. He also recognized that these two facts lead to a constant "struggle for existence." The idea that in each generation more offspring are born than survive to adulthood, coupled with the notions of competition for resources and biological diversity, was all Darwin needed to develop his theory of natural selection. He wrote: "It at once struck me that under these circumstances favourable variations would tend to be preserved, and unfavourable ones to be destroyed. The result of this would be the formation of a new species" (F. Darwin, 1950, pp. 53–54). Basically, this quotation summarizes the entire theory of natural selection.

By 1844, Darwin had written a short summary of his natural selection hypothesis, but he didn't think he had enough data to support it, so he continued his research without publishing. He also had other reasons for not publishing what he knew would be a highly controversial work. He was deeply troubled that his wife, Emma,

saw his ideas as running counter to her strong religious convictions (Keynes, 2002). Also, as a member of the established order, he knew that many of his friends and associates were concerned with threats to the status quo, and evolutionary theory was viewed as a very serious threat indeed.

In Darwin's Shadow

Unlike Darwin, Alfred Russel Wallace (1823–1913) was born into a family of modest means (**Fig. 2-13**). He went to work at the age of 14 and, with little formal education, he moved from one job to the next. Eventually, he became interested in collecting plants and animals and joined expeditions to the Amazon and Southeast Asia, where he acquired firsthand knowledge of many natural phenomena.

In 1855, Wallace published an article suggesting that current species were descended from other species and that the appearance of new ones was influenced by environmental factors (Trinkaus and Shipman, 1992). This article caused Lyell and others to urge Darwin to publish, but he continued to hesitate.

Then, in 1858, Wallace sent Darwin another paper, "On the Tendency of Varieties to Depart Indefinitely from the Original Type." In it, Wallace described evolution as a process driven by competition and natural selection. When he received Wallace's paper,

▲ **Figure 2-12**
All domestic dog breeds share a common ancestor, the wolf. The extreme variation exhibited by dog breeds today has been achieved in a relatively short time through artificial selection. In this situation, humans allow only certain dogs to breed to emphasize specific characteristics. (We should note that not all traits desired by human breeders are advantageous to the dogs themselves.)

▲ Figure 2-13
Alfred Russel Wallace independently identified natural selection as the key to the evolutionary process.

Oil on canvas by Evstafieff (19th century) Down House, Downe, Kent, UK/ © English Heritage Photo Library / The Bridgeman Art Library

▲ Figure 2-14
Charles Darwin's *Origin of Species*, the book that revolutionized biological science.

fitness Pertaining to natural selection, a measure of the relative reproductive success of individuals. Fitness can be measured by an individual's genetic contribution to the next generation compared with that of other individuals. The terms genetic fitness, reproductive fitness, and *differential reproductive success* are also used.

Darwin realized he could wait no longer or Wallace might get credit for a theory (natural selection) that he himself had developed. He quickly wrote a paper presenting his ideas, and both papers were read before the Linnean Society of London. Neither author was present. Wallace was out of the country, and Darwin was mourning the recent death of his young son.

The papers received little notice at the time. But in December 1859, when Darwin completed and published his greatest work, *On the Origin of Species*,* the storm broke, and it still hasn't abated (**Fig. 2-14**). Although public opinion was negative, there was much scholarly praise for the book, and scientific opinion gradually came to Darwin's support. The question of species was now explained: Species could change, they weren't fixed, and they evolved from other species through the mechanism of natural selection.

---
* The full title is *On the Origin of Species by Means of Natural Selection, or the Preservation of Favoured Races in the Struggle for Life.*

Natural Selection

Early in his research, Darwin had realized that natural selection was the key to evolution. With the help of Malthus' ideas, he saw *how* selection in nature could be explained. In the struggle for existence, those *individuals* with favorable variations would survive and reproduce, but those with unfavorable variations would not. For Darwin, the explanation of evolution was simple. The basic processes, as he understood them, are as follows:

1. All species are capable of producing offspring at a faster rate than food supplies increase.
2. There is biological variation within all species.
3. In each generation more offspring are produced than survive, and because of limited resources, there is competition among individuals. (*Note:* This statement doesn't mean that there is constant fierce fighting.)
4. Individuals who possess favorable variations or traits (for example, speed, resistance to disease, protective coloration) have an advantage over those who don't have them. In other words, they have greater **fitness** because favorable traits increase the likelihood that they will survive to adulthood and reproduce.
5. The environmental context determines whether or not a trait is beneficial. What is favorable in one setting may be a liability in another. Consequently, the traits that become most advantageous are the results of a natural process.
6. Traits are inherited and passed on to the next generation. Because individuals who possess favorable traits contribute more offspring to the next generation than do others, over time those favorable traits become more common in the pop-

ulation. Less favorable characteristics aren't passed as frequently, so they become less common over time and are "weeded out." Individuals who produce more offspring in comparison to others are said to have greater **reproductive success** or fitness.

7. Over long periods of time, successful variations accumulate in a population, so that later generations may be distinct from ancestral ones. Thus, in time, a new species may appear.

8. Geographical isolation also contributes to the formation of new species. As populations of a species become geographically isolated from one another, for whatever reasons (for example, distance or natural barriers such as oceans), they begin to adapt to different environments. Over time, as populations continue to respond to different **selective pressures** (that is, different ecological circumstances), they may become distinct species. The 13 species of Galápagos finches are presumably all descended from a common ancestor on the South American mainland, and they provide an example of the role of geographical isolation.

Before Darwin, individual members of species weren't considered important, so they weren't studied. But as we've seen, Darwin recognized the uniqueness of individuals and realized that variation among them could explain how selection occurs. Favorable variations are selected, or chosen, for survival by nature; unfavorable ones are eliminated. *Natural selection operates on individuals*, either favorably or unfavorably, but *it's the population that evolves*. It's important to emphasize that the unit of natural selection is the individual; the unit of evolution is the population. This is because individuals don't change genetically, but over time, populations do.

▲ **Figure 2-15**
Variation in the peppered moth.
(a) The dark form is more visible on the light, lichen-covered tree.
(b) On trees darkened by pollution, the lighter form is more visible.

Natural Selection in Action

One of the most frequently cited examples of natural selection relates to changes in the coloration of a species of moth. In recent years, the moth story has come under some criticism; but the premise remains valid, so we use it to illustrate how natural selection works.

Before the nineteenth century, the most common variety of the peppered moth in England was a mottled gray color. During the day, as the moths rested on lichen-covered tree trunks, their coloration provided camouflage (**Fig. 2-15**). There was also a dark gray variety of the same species, but because

reproductive success The number of offspring an individual produces and rears to reproductive age; an individual's genetic contribution to the next generation.

selective pressures Forces in the environment that influence reproductive success in individuals.

the dark moths were not as well camouflaged, they were more frequently eaten by birds and so they were less common. (In this example, the birds are the *selective agent*, and they apply *selective pressures* on the moths.) Yet, by the end of the nineteenth century, the darker form had almost completely replaced the common gray one.

The cause of this change was the changing environment of industrialized nineteenth-century England. Coal dust from factories and fireplaces settled on the trees, turning them dark gray and killing the lichen. The moths continued to rest on the trees, but the light gray ones became more conspicuous as the trees became darker, and they were increasingly targeted by birds. Fewer of the light gray moths were living long enough to reproduce, so they contributed fewer genes to the next generation than the darker moths did, and the proportion of lighter moths decreased while the dark moths became more common. A similar color shift also occurred in North America. But with the advent of clean air acts in both Britain and the United States reducing the amount of air pollution (at least from coal), the predominant color of the peppered moth once again became the light mottled gray. This kind of evolutionary shift in response to environmental change is called *adaptation*.

The medium ground finch of the Galápagos Islands provides another example of natural selection. In 1977, drought killed many of the plants that produced the smaller, softer seeds favored by these birds. This forced a population of finches on one of the islands to feed on larger, harder seeds. Even before 1977, some birds had smaller, less robust beaks than others (that is, there was variation). During the drought, because they were less able to process the larger seeds, more smaller-beaked birds died than larger-beaked birds. So, although overall population size declined, average beak thickness in the survivors and their offspring increased, simply because

thicker-beaked individuals were surviving in greater numbers and producing more offspring. In other words, they had greater reproductive success. But during heavy rains in 1982–1983, smaller seeds became more plentiful again and the pattern in beak size reversed itself, demonstrating again how reproductive success is related to environmental conditions (Grant, 1986; Ridley, 1993).

The best illustration of natural selection, however—and certainly one with potentially grave consequences for humans—is the recent increase in resistant strains of disease-causing microorganisms. When antibiotics were first introduced in the 1940s, they were seen as the cure for bacterial disease. But that optimistic view didn't take into account that bacteria, like other organisms, possess genetic variability. Consequently, though an antibiotic will kill most bacteria in an infected person, any bacterium with an inherited resistance to that particular therapy will survive. In turn, the survivors reproduce and pass their drug resistance to future generations, so that eventually, the population is mostly made up of bacteria that don't respond to treatment. What's more, because bacteria produce new generations every few hours, antibiotic-resistant strains are continuously appearing. As a result, many types of infection no longer respond to treatment. For example, tuberculosis was once thought to be well controlled, but there's been a resurgence of TB in recent years because some strains of the bacterium that causes it are resistant to most of the antibiotics used to treat it.

These examples (moths, finches, and bacteria) provide the following insights into the fundamentals of evolutionary change produced by natural selection:

1. *A trait must be inherited if natural selection is to act on it.* A characteristic that isn't hereditary (such as a temporary change in hair color produced by the hairdresser)

Quick Review

The Mechanism of Natural Selection

Individuals in a population vary in most inherited characteristics (i.e., they don't all express these traits in the same way)

Environment (selective agents)

Some individuals have higher reproductive success than others because they possess advantageous expressions of certain traits

Increase in the proportion of individuals with the advantageous expression of the trait; decrease in the proportion having a less beneficial expression

© Cengage Learning 2013

won't be passed on to offspring. In finches, for example, beak size is a hereditary trait.

2. *Natural selection cannot occur without population variation in inherited characteristics.* If, for example, all the peppered moths had initially been light gray and the trees had become darker, the survival and reproduction of the moths could have been so low that the population might have become extinct. *Selection can work only with variation that already exists.*

3. *Fitness is a relative measure that changes as the environment changes.* Fitness is simply differential net reproductive success. In the initial stage, the lighter moths were more fit because they produced more offspring. But as the environment changed, the dark gray moths became more fit. Later, a further change reversed the pattern again. Likewise, the majority of Galápagos finches will have larger or smaller beaks, depending on external conditions. So it should be obvious that statements regarding the "most fit" don't mean anything without reference to specific environments.

4. *Natural selection can act only on traits that affect reproduction.* If a characteristic isn't expressed until later in life, after organisms have reproduced, then natural selection can't influence it. This is because the trait's inherited components have already been passed on to offspring. Many forms of cancer and cardiovascular disease are influenced by hereditary factors, but because these diseases usually affect people after they've had children, natural selection can't act against them. By the same token, if a condition usually kills or compromises the individual before he or she reproduces, natural selection is able to act against it because the trait won't be passed on.

So far, our examples have shown how different death rates influence natural selection (for example, moths or finches that die early leave fewer offspring). But mortality is only part of the picture. Another important aspect of natural selection is **fertility**, because an animal that gives birth to more young contributes more genes to the next generation than an animal that produces fewer offspring. But fertility isn't the entire story either, because the crucial element is the number of young raised successfully to the point where they themselves reproduce. We call this *differential net reproductive success*. The way this mechanism works can be demonstrated through another example.

In swifts (small birds that resemble swallows), data show that producing more offspring doesn't necessarily guarantee that more young will be successfully raised. The number of eggs hatched in a breeding season is a measure of fertility. The number of birds that mature and are eventually able to leave the nest is a measure of net reproductive success, or successfully raised offspring. The following table shows the correlation between the number of eggs hatched (fertility) and the number of young that leave the nest (reproductive success), averaged over four breeding seasons (Lack, 1966):

Number of eggs hatched (fertility)	2 eggs	3 eggs	4 eggs
Average number of young raised (reproductive success)	1.92	2.54	1.76
Sample size (number of nests)	72	20	16

As you can see, the most efficient number of eggs is three, because that number yields the highest reproductive success. Raising two offspring is less beneficial to the parents, because the end result isn't as successful as with three eggs. Trying to raise more than three is actually detrimental, as the parents may not be able to provide enough nourishment for any of the offspring. Offspring that die before

reaching reproductive age are, in evolutionary terms, equivalent to never being born. Moreover, an offspring that dies can be a minus to the parents, because before it dies, it drains parental resources. It may even inhibit their ability to raise other offspring, thus reducing their reproductive success even further. Selection favors those genetic traits that yield the maximum net reproductive success. If the number of eggs laid is a genetic trait in birds (and it seems to be), natural selection in swifts should act to favor laying three eggs as opposed to two or four.

Constraints on Nineteenth-Century Evolutionary Theory

Darwin argued for the concept of evolution in general and the role of natural selection in particular. But he didn't understand the exact mechanisms of evolutionary change.

As we've already seen, natural selection acts on *variation* within species, but what Darwin didn't understand was where the variation came from. In the nineteenth century, this remained an unanswered question, plus no one understood how offspring inherited traits from their parents. Almost without exception, nineteenth-century scientists believed inheritance to be a *blending* process in which parental characteristics are mixed together to produce intermediate expressions in offspring. Given this notion, we can see why the true nature of genes was unimaginable; and, with no alternative explanation, Darwin accepted the blending theory of inheritance. As it turns out, a contemporary of Darwin's had actually worked out the rules of heredity. However, the work of this Augustinian monk named Gregor Mendel (whom you'll meet in Chapter 4) wasn't recognized until the beginning of the twentieth century.

fertility The ability to conceive and produce healthy offspring.

The first three decades of the twentieth century saw the merger of natural selection theory and Mendel's discoveries. This was a crucial development because until then, scientists thought these concepts were unrelated. Then, in 1953, the structure of DNA was discovered. This landmark achievement has been followed by even more amazing advances in the field of genetics. The human **genome** was sequenced in 2003, followed by the chimpanzee genome in 2005. The genomes of many other species have also now been sequenced. By comparing the genomes of different species (a field called comparative genomics), scientists can examine how genetically similar (or different) they are. This can explain many aspects of how these species evolved. Also, since the early 1990s, several scientists have merged the fields of evolutionary and developmental biology into a new field called "evo-devo." This approach, which compares the actions of different developmental genes and the factors that regulate them, is making it possible to explain evolution in ways that were impossible even 15 years ago. Scientists are truly on the threshold of revealing many secrets of the evolutionary process. If only Darwin could know!

Opposition to Evolution Today

One hundred and fifty years after the publication of *Origin of Species*, the debate over evolution is far from over, especially in the United States and, increasingly, in several Muslim countries. For most biologists, evolution is indisputable. The genetic evidence for it is solid and accumulating daily. Anyone who appreciates and understands genetic mechanisms can't avoid the conclusion that populations and species evolve. What's more, the majority of Christians don't believe that biblical depictions should be taken literally. But at the same time, some surveys show that about half of all Americans don't believe that evolution occurs. There are a number of reasons for this.

The mechanisms of evolution are complex and do not lend themselves to simple explanations. Understanding them requires some familiarity with genetics and biology, a familiarity that most people don't have unless they took related courses in school. What is more, many people want definitive, clear-cut answers to complex questions. But as you learned in Chapter 1, science doesn't always provide definitive answers to questions; it doesn't establish absolute truths; and it doesn't *prove* facts. Another thing to consider is that regardless of their culture, most people are raised in belief systems that don't emphasize **biological continuity** between species or offer scientific explanations for natural phenomena.

The relationship between science and religion has never been easy (remember Galileo), even though both serve, in their own ways, to explain natural phenomena. As you read in Chapter 1, scientific explanations are based in data analysis, hypothesis testing, and interpretation. Religion, meanwhile, is a system of faith-based beliefs. A major difference between science and religion is that religious beliefs and explanations aren't amenable to scientific testing. Religion and science concern different aspects of the human experience, but they aren't inherently mutually exclusive approaches. That is, belief in God doesn't exclude the possibility of biological evolution; and acknowledgment of evolutionary processes doesn't preclude the existence of God. What's more, evolutionary theories aren't rejected by all religions or by most forms of Christianity.

Some years ago, the Vatican hosted an international conference on human evolution; in 1996, Pope John Paul II issued a statement that "fresh knowledge leads to recognition of the theory of evolution as more than just a hypothesis." Today, the official position

genome The entire genetic makeup of an individual or species.

biological continuity A biological continuum. When expressions of a phenomenon continuously grade into one another so that there are no discrete categories, they exist on a continuum. Color is one such phenomenon, and life-forms are another.

of the Catholic Church is that evolutionary processes do occur, but that the human soul is of divine creation and not subject to evolutionary processes. Likewise, mainstream Protestants don't generally see a conflict. Unfortunately, those who believe in an absolutely literal interpretation of the Bible (called *fundamentalists*) accept no compromise.

A Brief History of Opposition to Evolution in the United States

There are historical reasons for the opposition to teaching of evolution in the United States. Reacting to rapid cultural change after World War I, conservative Christians in the United States sought a revival of what they considered "traditional values." In their view, one way to achieve this was to prevent any mention of Darwinism in public schools. One result of this effort was a state law passed in Tennessee in 1925 that banned the teaching of any theory (particularly evolution) that did not support the biblical version of the creation of humankind. To test the validity of this law, the American Civil Liberties Union persuaded a high school teacher named John Scopes to submit to being arrested and tried for teaching evolution (**Fig. 2-16**). The subsequent trial, called the "Scopes Monkey Trial." was a 1920s equivalent of current celebrity trials. In the end, Scopes was convicted and fined $100, though the conviction was later overturned. Although most states didn't actually forbid the teaching of evolution, Arkansas, Tennessee, and a few others continued to prohibit any mention of it until 1968, when the U.S. Supreme Court struck down the ban against teaching evolution in public schools. (One coauthor of this textbook remembers when her junior high school science teacher was fired for mentioning evolution in Little Rock, Arkansas.)

As coverage of evolution in textbooks increased by the mid-1960s, **Christian fundamentalists** renewed their campaign to eliminate evolution from public school curricula or to introduce antievolutionary material into public school classes. Out of this

▶ **Figure 2-16**
Photo taken at the "Scopes Monkey Trial." The well-known defense attorney Clarence Darrow is sitting on the edge of the table. John Scopes, wearing a white shirt, is sitting with his arms folded behind Darrow.

© Bettmann / Corbis

Christian fundamentalists
Adherents to a movement in American Protestantism that began in the early twentieth century. This group holds that the teachings of the Bible are infallible and that the scriptures are to be taken literally.

effort, the *creation science* movement was born.

Proponents of creation science are called "creationists" because they explain the existence of the universe as the result of a sudden creation event that occurred over the course of six 24-hour days as described in the book of Genesis. The premise of creation science is that the biblical account of the earth's origins and the Noah flood can be supported by scientific evidence.

Creationists have insisted that what they used to call "creation science" and now call "intelligent design" (ID) is a valid scientific explanation of the earth's origins. They've argued that in the interest of fairness, a balanced view should be offered in public schools: If evolution is taught as science, then cre-

ationism should also be taught as science. Sounds fair, doesn't it? But ID isn't science at all, for the simple reason that creationists insist that their view is absolute and infallible. Therefore, creationism isn't a hypothesis that can be tested, nor is it amenable to falsification. And because hypothesis testing is the basis of all science, creationism, by its very nature, cannot be considered science.

Since the 1970s, creationists have become increasingly active in local school boards and state legislatures, promoting laws that mandate the teaching of creationism in public schools. However, state and federal courts have consistently overruled these laws because they violate the "establishment clause" of the First Amendment of the U.S. Constitution,

Why It Matters

As you've just seen, one of the greatest controversies regarding education in the United States and some other parts of the world is the teaching of evolution. Although some political leaders advocate equal time for "intelligent design," they also express concern over the continuous threat that current strains of new influenza virus will change (that is, evolve) into more deadly forms. But many of these leaders don't recognize the link between developing vaccines or other medical tools to fight an emerging disease and the teaching of evolution in the public schools. (Though creationists accept that microorganisms change, they don't believe that these changes constitute evolution.)

Actually, there are several ways an evolutionary view can contribute to understanding contemporary health challenges. One of these is the recognition that the inevitable outcome of our more aggressive methods of fighting disease-causing

microorganisms such as bacteria and viruses will lead to modified organisms that have evolved to resist therapies such as antibiotics. This is because the antibiotics used to treat bacterial infections actually weed out the vulnerable bacteria microbes and leave the less vulnerable ones to reproduce. Unfortunately, the latter can sometimes cause even more serious forms of disease than the organisms that were eliminated.

For example, we've seen the appearance of resistant and even deadly strains of *Staphylococcus* bacteria, tuberculosis, and *E. coli*. Moreover, many disease-causing microorganisms such as HIV (the virus that causes AIDS) mutate so quickly that all attempts to develop a vaccine against them have failed so far. For the most part, the antibiotic–bacteria arms race has led to the development of increasingly lethal strains of bacteria. However, the evolutionary process doesn't have to go in that direction. In fact, one suggestion for defeating disease-causing organisms such as HIV is to turn the evolutionary process around so that it pro-

duces less virulent strains. Ewald (1994, 1999) has called this procedure "domesticating" disease-causing organisms and cites the bacterium that causes diphtheria as an example that has apparently evolved into milder strains because of vaccination. The primary argument is that treatments that can respond to the emergence and evolution of disease organisms are much more likely to be successful in the long run than those that target specific disease variants and their manifestations.

Consider, for example, the influenza viruses that appear every autumn. Medical researchers try to predict which of several strains will pose the most serious threat. Then they try to develop a vaccine that targets that specific strain. If their prediction is wrong, an influenza epidemic may emerge. If future physicians and biomedical researchers don't understand evolutionary processes, there is little hope that they can do anything to forestall the potential medical crises that lie ahead as the pace of change in pathogens exceeds that of the treatments designed to defeat them.

which states that "Congress shall make no law respecting an establishment of religion, or prohibiting the free exercise thereof." This statement guarantees the separation of church and state, and it means that the government can neither promote nor inhibit the practice of any religion. Therefore, the use of public institutions (including schools) paid for by taxes to promote any particular religion is unconstitutional. Of course, this doesn't mean that individuals can't have private religious discussions or pray in publicly funded institutions; but it does mean that such places can't be used for organized religious events. This hasn't stopped creationists, who encourage teachers to claim "academic freedom" to teach creationism. To avoid objections based on the guarantee of separation of church and state, proponents of ID claim that they don't emphasize any particular reli-gion. But this argument doesn't address the essential point that teaching *any* religious views in a way that promotes them in publicly funded schools is a violation of the U.S. Constitution.

It is curious that the biological process that has led to the appearance of millions of plants and animals on our planet should generate such controversy. Our current understanding of evolution is directly traceable to developments in intellectual thought over the past 400 years. Many people contributed to this shift in perspective, and we've named only a few to provide a short historical view. It is quite likely that in the next 20 years, scientists will identify many of the secrets of our evolutionary past through advances in genetic technologies and the continued discovery of fossil material. For evolutionary science, the early twenty-first century is indeed an exciting time.

Summary of Main Topics

- Our current understanding of evolutionary processes is directly traceable to developments in intellectual thought in western Europe and the East over the past 400 years. Darwin and Wallace were able to discover the process of natural selection and evolution because of the discoveries of numerous scientists who had laid the groundwork for them. Among others, Galileo, Lyell, Lamarck, Linnaeus, and Malthus all contributed to a dramatic shift in how people viewed the planet and themselves as part of a system governed by natural processes.

- Charles Darwin and Alfred Russel Wallace recognized that there was variation among individuals in any population (human or non-human). By understanding how animal breeders selected for certain traits in cattle, pigeons, and other species, Darwin formulated the theory of natural selection. Stated in the simplest terms, natural selection is a process whereby individuals who possess favorable traits (characteristics that permit them to survive and reproduce in a specific environment) will produce more offspring than individuals who have less favorable traits. Over time, the beneficial characteristics will become more frequent in the population, and the makeup of the population (or even a species) will have changed.

- As populations of a species become reproductively isolated from one another (perhaps due to distance or geographical barriers), they become increasingly different as each population adapts, by means of natural selection, to its own environment. Eventually, the populations may become distinct enough that they can no longer interbreed; at this point, they are considered separate species.

- In the United States, and increasingly in some Muslim countries, evolutionary processes are denounced because they are seen as contradictory to religious teaching. In recent years, Christian fundamentalists in the United States have argued in favor of teaching "creation science" or "intelligent design" in public schools. So far, courts have ruled against various attempts to promote "creation science" because of separation of church and state as provided for in the U.S. Constitution.

Critical Thinking Questions

1. After having read this chapter, how would you respond to the question, "If humans evolved from monkeys, why do we still have monkeys?"

2. Given what you've read about the scientific method in Chapter 1 how would you explain the differences between science and religion as methods of explaining natural phenomena? Do you personally see a conflict between evolutionary and religious explanations of how species came to be?

3. Can you think of some examples of artificial and natural selection that weren't discussed in this chapter? For your examples, what traits have been selected for? In the case of natural selection, what was the selective agent?

Connections

Evolutionary theory, particularly natural selection, explains how life forms have changed over time.

DNA molecule is the basis of all life.

All forms of life are made up of cells.

Heredity is based on the transmission of DNA from one generation to the next.

3

The Biological Basis of Life

You've just gotten home after a rotten day, and you're watching the news on TV. The first story, after about 20 minutes of commercials, is about genetically modified foods, a newly cloned species, synthetic DNA, or the controversy over stem cell research. What do you do? Change the channel? Press the mute button? Go to sleep? Or do you follow the story? If you watch it, do you understand it, and do you think it's important or relevant to you personally? Actually, all of these stories are important to you because you live in an age when genetic discoveries and genetically based technologies are advancing daily, and one way or another, they're going to profoundly affect your life.

At some point in your life, you or someone you love will probably need lifesaving medical treatment, perhaps for cancer, and this treatment will almost certainly be based on genetic research. Like it or not, you already eat genetically modified foods, and you may eventually take advantage of developing reproductive technologies. Sadly, you may also see the development of biological weapons based on genetically altered bacteria and viruses. But fortunately, you'll also live to see many of the secrets of evolution revealed through genetic research. So even if you haven't been particularly interested in genetic issues, you should be aware that they affect your life every day.

As you already know, this book is about human evolution, variation, and adaptation, all of which are intimately linked to life processes that involve cells, the duplication and decoding of genetic information, and the transmission of this information between generations. So before we go any further, we need to examine the basic principles of genetics. Genetics is the study of how genes work and how traits are passed from one generation to the next. Although most physical anthropologists don't specialize in this field, they're very familiar with it because genetics unifies the various subdisciplines of biological anthropology.

◄ Lily cells in various stages of division.

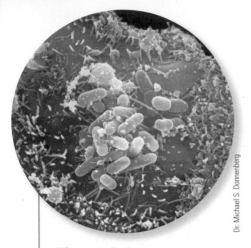

▲ Figure 3-1
Each one of these pink sausage-shaped structures is a single-celled bacterium.

Cells

To discuss genetic and evolutionary principles, it's necessary to understand the basic functions of cells. Cells are the fundamental units of life in all organisms. In some life-forms, such as bacteria, the entire organism consists of a single cell (**Fig. 3-1**). However, more complex *multicellular* forms, such as plants, insects, and animals, are composed of billions of cells. In fact, an adult human body may be composed of as many as 1 trillion (1,000,000,000,000) cells, all functioning in complex ways that ultimately promote the survival of the individual.

Life on earth began at least 3.7 billion years ago in the form of single-celled organisms, represented today by bacteria and blue-green algae. Structurally more complex cells, called *eukaryotic* cells, appeared approximately 1.2 billion years ago, and because they're the kind of cell found in multicellular organisms, they will be the focus of this chapter. Despite the numerous differences among various life-forms, it's important to understand that the cells of all living organisms share many similarities as a result of their common evolutionary past.

In general, a eukaryotic cell is a three-dimensional structure composed of carbohydrates, lipids (fats), nucleic acids, and **proteins**. It also contains several kinds of substructures called *organelles,* one of which is the **nucleus** (*pl.,* nuclei), a discrete unit surrounded by a thin membrane, the *nuclear membrane* (**Fig. 3-2**). Inside the nucleus are two kinds of **molecules**, which contain the genetic information that controls the cell's functions. These two molecules are **DNA (deoxyribonucleic acid)** and **RNA (ribonucleic acid).**

The nucleus is surrounded by a gel-like substance called **cytoplasm**, which contains many other types of organelles involved in activities related to the function of the cell and organism. These activities include converting nutrients into other substances, storing and releasing energy, elimi-

proteins Three-dimensional molecules that serve a wide variety of functions through their ability to bind to other molecules.

nucleus A structure (organelle) found in all eukaryotic cells. The nucleus contains DNA that, during cell division, is organized into chromosomes.

molecules Structures made up of two or more atoms. Molecules can combine with other molecules to form more complex structures.

DNA (deoxyribonucleic acid) The double-stranded molecule that contains the genetic code. DNA is a main component of chromosomes.

RNA (ribonucleic acid) A single-stranded molecule similar in structure to DNA. Three forms of RNA are essential to protein synthesis: messenger RNA (mRNA), transfer RNA (tRNA), and ribosomal RNA (rRNA).

cytoplasm The semifluid substance contained within the cell membrane. The nucleus and numerous other kinds of structures involved with cell function are found within the cytoplasm.

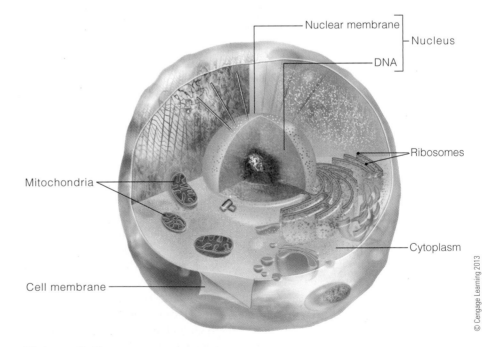

▲ Figure 3-2
Structure of a generalized eukaryotic cell, illustrating its three-dimensional nature. Various organelles are shown, but for simplicity, only those we discuss are labeled.

nating waste, and manufacturing proteins through a process called **protein synthesis**.

Two of these organelles, **ribosomes** and **mitochondria** (*sing.,* mitochondrion), require further mention. Ribosomes are roughly spherical and partly composed of RNA. They're important because they're essential to protein synthesis. Mitochondria (**Fig. 3-3**) produce energy and can loosely be thought of as the cell's engines. Mitochondria are oval structures enclosed within a folded membrane, and they contain their own distinct DNA, called **mitochondrial DNA (mtDNA)**, which directs mitochondrial activities. Mitochondrial DNA has the same molecular structure and function as the DNA found in the nucleus, but it's organized somewhat differently. In recent years, mtDNA has attracted a lot of attention because of the traits it influences and because it can be used to study certain evolutionary processes. For these reasons, we'll discuss mitochondrial inheritance in more detail later.

There are basically two types of cells: **somatic cells** and **gametes**. Somatic cells make up body tissues, such as muscles, bones, organs, skin, and the brain. Gametes, or sex cells, are specifically involved in reproduction and aren't important as structural components of the body. There are two types of gametes: egg cells, produced in female ovaries, and sperm cells, which develop in male testes. The sole function of a sex cell is to unite with a gamete from another individual to form a **zygote**, which has the potential of developing into a new individual. In this way, gametes transmit genetic information from parents to offspring.

DNA Structure

DNA is the very basis of life because it directs all cellular activities. The exact physical and chemical properties of DNA were unknown until 1953, when, at the University of Cambridge in England, an American researcher named James Watson and three British scientists, Francis Crick, Maurice Wilkins, and Rosalind Franklin, developed a structural model of DNA (Watson and Crick, 1953a, 1953b). It's impossible to overstate the importance of this achievement because it completely revolutionized the fields of biology and medicine and forever altered our understanding of biological and evolutionary mechanisms.

The DNA molecule is composed of two chains of even smaller units called **nucleotides**. A nucleotide, in turn, is made up of three components: a sugar molecule (deoxyribose), a phosphate group (a molecule composed of phosphorus and oxygen), and one of four nitrogenous *bases* (**Fig. 3-4**). In DNA, nucleotides are stacked on top of one another to form a chain that is bonded by its bases to another nucleotide chain. Together the two chains twist to form a spiral, or helical, shape. Thus, the DNA molecule is double-stranded and is described as forming a *double helix* that resembles a twisted ladder. If we follow the twisted ladder analogy, the sugars and phosphates represent the two sides, whereas the bases and the bonds that join them form the rungs.

The four bases are the key to how DNA works. The bases are *adenine, guanine, thymine,* and *cytosine,* usually referred to by their initial letters: A, G, T, and C. When the double helix is formed, one type of base can pair or bond with only one other type: A can only pair with T, and G can only pair with C (Fig. 3-5). This specificity is absolutely essential to the DNA molecule's ability to **replicate**, or make an exact copy of itself.

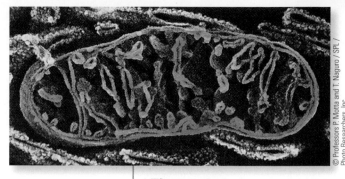

▲**Figure 3-3**
Scanning electron micrograph of a mitochondrion.

protein synthesis The manufacture of proteins; the assembly of chains of amino acids into functional protein molecules. Protein synthesis is directed by DNA.

ribosomes Structures composed of a form of RNA called ribosomal RNA (rRNA) and protein. Ribosomes are found in a cell's cytoplasm and are essential to the manufacture of proteins.

mitochondria (*sing.,* mitochondrion) Structures contained within the cytoplasm of eukaryotic cells that convert energy, derived from nutrients, to a form that can be used by the cell.

mitochondrial DNA (mtDNA) DNA found in the mitochondria. Mitochondrial DNA is inherited only from the mother.

somatic cells Basically, all the cells in the body except those involved with reproduction.

gametes Reproductive cells (eggs and sperm in animals) developed from precursor cells in ovaries and testes.

zygote A cell formed by the union of an egg cell and a sperm cell. It contains the full complement of chromosomes (in humans, 46) and has the potential to develop into an entire organism.

nucleotides Basic units of the DNA molecule, composed of a sugar, a phosphate, and one of four DNA bases.

replicate To duplicate. The DNA molecule is able to make copies of itself.

▶ **Figure 3-4**
Part of a DNA molecule. The illustration shows the two DNA strands with the sugar (gray) and phosphate (purple) backbone and the bases (labeled T, A, G, and C) extending toward the center.

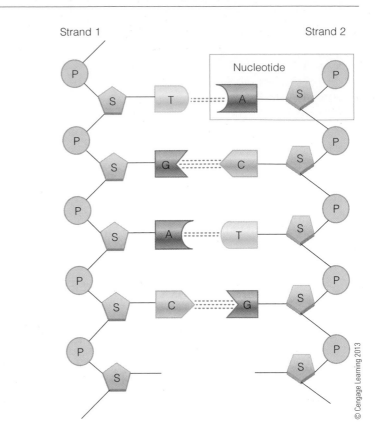

DNA Replication

Cells multiply by dividing, making exact copies of themselves. This, in turn, enables organisms to grow and injured tissues to heal. There are two kinds of cell division. In the simpler form, a cell divides one time to produce two "daughter" cells, each of which receives a full set of genetic material. This is important, because a cell can't function properly without the right amount of DNA. But before a cell can divide, its DNA must replicate.

Replication begins when **enzymes** break the bonds between bases throughout the DNA molecule, separating the two previously joined strands of nucleotides and leaving their bases exposed (**Fig. 3-5**). These bases then attract unattached DNA nucleotides that have been made by DNA elsewhere in the cell nucleus. Because each base can pair with only one other, the attraction between bases occurs in a **complementary** way. This means that the two previously joined parental nucleotide chains serve as models,

or templates, for forming new strands of nucleotides. As each new strand is formed, its bases are joined to the bases of an original strand. When the process is complete, there are two double-stranded DNA molecules exactly like the original one, and each newly formed molecule consists of one original nucleotide chain joined to a newly formed chain (Fig. 3-5).

Protein Synthesis

One of the most important activities of DNA is to direct the assembly of proteins (protein synthesis) within cells. Proteins are complex, three-dimensional molecules that function through their ability to bind to other molecules. For example, the protein **hemoglobin (Fig. 3-6)**, found in red blood cells, is able to bind to oxygen, which it carries to cells throughout the body.

Proteins function in countless ways. Some, such as collagen, are structural components of tissues. Collagen is the

enzymes Specialized proteins that initiate and direct chemical reactions in the body.

complementary In genetics, referring to the fact that DNA bases form pairs (called base pairs) in a precise manner. For example, adenine can bond only to thymine. These two bases are said to be complementary because one requires the other to form a complete DNA base pair.

hemoglobin A protein molecule that occurs in red blood cells and binds to oxygen molecules.

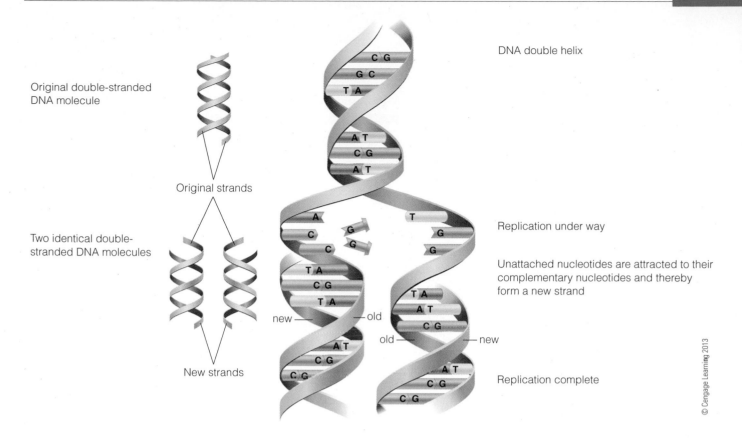

Original double-stranded DNA molecule

Original strands

Two identical double-stranded DNA molecules

New strands

new — old

old — new

DNA double helix

Replication under way

Unattached nucleotides are attracted to their complementary nucleotides and thereby form a new strand

Replication complete

© Cengage Learning 2013

most common protein in the body and is a major component of all connective tissues. Enzymes are also proteins, and they regulate chemical reactions. For example, a digestive enzyme called *lactase* breaks down *lactose,* or milk sugar, into two simpler sugars. Another class of proteins includes many types of **hormones**. Hormones are produced by specialized cells and then released into the bloodstream to circulate to other parts of the body, where they produce specific effects in tissues and organs. Insulin is a hormone produced by cells in the pancreas, and it causes cells in the liver to absorb energy-producing glucose (sugar) from the blood. Lastly, many kinds of proteins can attach directly to DNA. This is very important because when these proteins bind to DNA, they can regulate its activity and change how a cell functions. From this brief description, you can see that proteins make us what we are. So protein synthesis must occur accurately, because if it doesn't, physiological development and cellular activities can be disrupted or even prevented.

Proteins are made up of chains of smaller molecules called **amino acids**. In all, there are 20 amino acids, 8 of which must be obtained from foods (see Chapter 5). The remaining 12 are produced in cells. These 20 amino acids are combined in different amounts and sequences to produce at least 90,000 different proteins. What makes proteins different from one another is the number and sequence of their amino acids.

▲ **Figure 3-5**
DNA replication. During DNA replication, the two strands of the DNA molecule (purple) are separated, and each strand serves as a template for the formation of a new strand (brown). When replication is complete, there are two DNA molecules, each consisting of one new strand and one original strand.

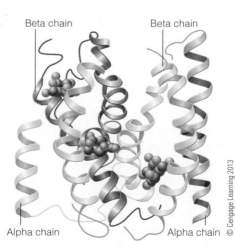

Beta chain   Beta chain

Alpha chain   Alpha chain

© Cengage Learning 2013

◄ **Figure 3-6**
Diagrammatic representation of a hemoglobin molecule. Hemoglobin molecules are composed of four chains of amino acids (two alpha chains and two beta chains).

hormones Substances (usually proteins) that are produced by specialized cells and that travel to other parts of the body, where they influence chemical reactions and regulate various cellular functions.

amino acids Small molecules that are the components of proteins.

TABLE

3.1 The Genetic Code

Amino Acid Symbol	Amino Acid	mRNA Codon	DNA Triplet
Ala	Alanine	GCU, GCC, GCA, GCG	CGA, CGG, CGT, CGC
Arg	Arginine	CGU, CGC, CGA, CGG, AGA, AGG	GCA, GCG, GCT, GCC, TCT, TCC
Asn	Asparagine	AAU, AAC	TTA, TTG
Asp	Aspartic acid	GAU, GAC	CTA, CTG
Cys	Cysteine	UGU, UGC	ACA, ACG
Gln	Glutamine	CAA, CAG	GTT, GTC
Glu	Glutamic acid	GAA, GAG	CTT, CTC
Gly	Glycine	GGU, GGC, GGA, GGG	CCA, CCG, CCT, CCC
His	Histidine	CAU, CAC	GTA, GTG
Ile	Isoleucine	AUU, AUC, AUA	TAA, TAG, TAT
Leu	Leucine	UUA, UUG, CUU, CUC, CUA, CUG	AAT, AAC, GAA, GAG, GAT, GAC
Lys	Lysine	AAA, AAG	TTT, TTC
Met	Methionine	AUG	TAC
Phe	Phenylalanine	UUU, UUC	AAA, AAG
Pro	Proline	CCU, CCC, CCA, CCG	GGA, GGG, GGT, GGC
Ser	Serine	UCU, UCC, UCA, UCG, AGU, AGC	AGA, AGG, AGT, AGC, TCA, TCG
Thr	Threonine	ACU, ACC, ACA, ACG	TGA, TGG, TGT, TGC
Trp	Tryptophan	UGG	ACC
Tyr	Tyrosine	UAU, UAC	ATA, ATG
Val	Valine	GUU, GUC, GUA, GUG	CAA, CAG, CAT, CAC
Terminating triplets		UAA, UAG, UGA	ATT, ATC, ACT

In part, DNA is a recipe for making a protein, because it's the sequence of DNA bases that ultimately determines the order of amino acids in a protein. In the DNA instructions, a *triplet,* or group of three bases, specifies a particular amino acid. For example, if a triplet consists of the base sequence cytosine, guanine, and adenine (CGA), it specifies the amino acid arginine (**Table 3-1**). Therefore, a small portion of a DNA recipe might look like this (except there would be no spaces between the triplets): AGA CGA ACA ACC TAC TTT TTC CTT AAG GTC.

Protein synthesis actually takes place outside the cell nucleus, in the cytoplasm at one of the previously mentioned organelles, the ribosomes. But the DNA molecule can't leave the cell's nucleus. Therefore, the first step in protein synthesis is to copy the DNA message into a form of RNA called **messenger RNA (mRNA)**, which can pass through the nuclear membrane into the cytoplasm. RNA is similar to DNA, but different in some important ways:

1. It is single-stranded. (This is true for the forms we discuss here, but not for all forms of RNA.)
2. It contains a different type of sugar.

messenger RNA (mRNA) A form of RNA that's assembled on a sequence of DNA bases. It carries the DNA code to the ribosome during protein synthesis.

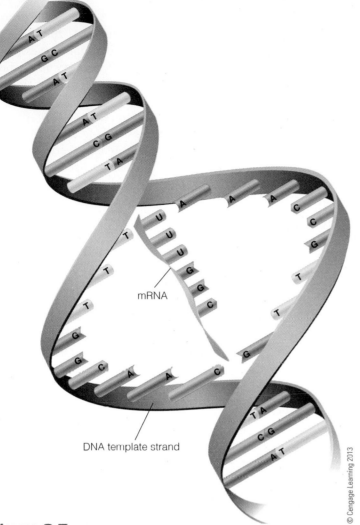

▲**Figure 3-7**

Transcription. In this illustration, the two DNA strands have partly separated. Messenger RNA (mRNA) nucleotides have been drawn to the template strand, and a strand of mRNA is being made. Note that the mRNA strand will exactly complement the DNA template strand, except that uracil (U) replaces thymine (T).

a As the ribosome binds to the mRNA, tRNA brings a particular amino acid, specified by the mRNA codon, to the ribosome.

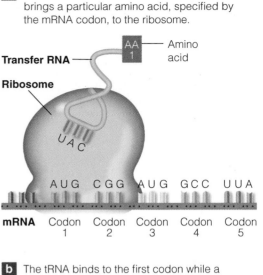

b The tRNA binds to the first codon while a second tRNA–amino acid complex arrives at the ribosome.

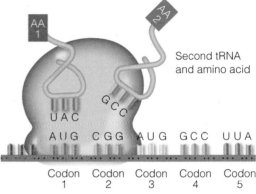

c The ribosome moves down the mRNA, allowing a third amino acid to be brought into position by another tRNA molecule. Note that the first two amino acids are now joined together.

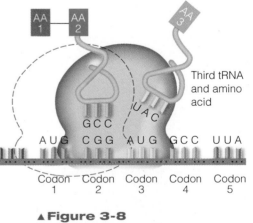

▲**Figure 3-8**
Assembly of an amino acid chain in protein synthesis.

3. It contains the base uracil (U) as a substitute for the DNA base thymine. (Uracil binds to adenine in the same way thymine does.)

The mRNA molecule forms on the DNA template in pretty much the same way that new DNA molecules do. As in DNA replication, the two DNA strands separate, but only partially, and one of these strands attracts free-floating RNA nucleotides (also produced in the cell), which are joined together on the DNA template. The formation of mRNA is called *transcription* because, in fact, the DNA code is being copied, or transcribed (**Fig. 3-7**). Once the appropriate segment has been copied, or transcribed, the mRNA strand peels away from the DNA model, and a portion of it travels through the nuclear membrane to the ribosome. Meanwhile, the bonds between the DNA bases are reestablished, and the DNA molecule is once more intact.

As the mRNA strand arrives at the ribosome, its message is translated, or decoded (**Fig. 3-8**). Just as each DNA triplet specifies one amino acid, so do mRNA triplets, which are called **codons**. Therefore, the mRNA strand is "read" in codons, or groups of three mRNA bases at a time (see Table 3-1). Subsequently, another form of RNA, called **transfer RNA (tRNA)**, brings each amino acid to the ribosome. The ribosome then joins that amino acid to another amino acid in the order dictated by the sequence of mRNA codons (or, ultimately, DNA triplets). In this way, amino acids are linked together to form a molecule that will eventually be a protein or part of a protein. But it's important to mention that if a DNA base or sequence of bases is changed through **mutation**, some proteins may not be made or they may be defective. In this case, cells won't function properly, if at all.

What Is a Gene?

The answer to this question is complicated, and the definition of the term **gene** is currently the subject of some debate. In the past, textbooks compared genes to a string of beads, with each bead representing one gene on a chromosome. For 50 years or so, biologists considered a gene to be an uninterrupted sequence of DNA bases responsible for the manufacture of a protein or part of a protein. Or, put another way, a gene could be defined as *a segment of DNA that specifies the sequence of amino acids in a particular protein*. This definition, based on the concept of a one gene–one protein relationship, was a core principle in biology for decades, but it's been substantially modified, partly in recognition of the fact that DNA codes not only for proteins, but also for RNA and other DNA nucleotides. Moreover, when the human **genome** was sequenced in 2001 (International

Human Genome Sequencing Consortium, 2001; Venter et al., 2001), scientists learned that humans have only about 25,000 genes; pretty much the same number as most other mammals. Yet, we produce as many as 90,000 proteins! Therefore, the one gene–one protein hypothesis has fallen by the wayside. This shift in perspective is a good example of what we discussed in Chapter 1, that hypotheses and theories can, and do, change over time as we continue to acquire new knowledge.

Geneticists have also learned that only some parts of genes, called **exons**, are actually transcribed into mRNA and thus code for specific amino acids. In fact, most of the nucleotide sequences in genes aren't expressed during protein synthesis. (By *expressed* we mean that the DNA sequence is actually making a product.) Some **noncoding DNA** sequences, called **introns**, are initially transcribed into mRNA and then clipped out (**Fig. 3-9**). Therefore, introns aren't translated into amino acid sequences. Moreover, the introns that are snipped out of a gene aren't always the same ones, and this means that the exons can be combined in dif-

▼**Figure 3-9**
Diagram of a DNA sequence being transcribed. The introns are deleted from pre-mRNA before it leaves the cell's nucleus. The remaining mature RNA contains only exons, which will code for a protein or part of a protein.

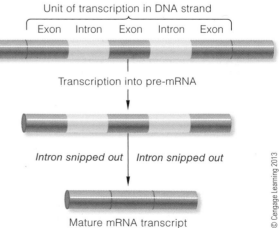

Unit of transcription in DNA strand

Exon   Intron   Exon   Intron   Exon

Transcription into pre-mRNA

Intron snipped out | *Intron snipped out*

Mature mRNA transcript

© Cengage Learning 2013

---

codons Triplets of messenger RNA bases that code for specific amino acids during protein synthesis.

transfer RNA (tRNA) The form of RNA that binds to specific amino acids and transports them to the ribosome during protein synthesis.

mutation A change in DNA. The term can refer to changes in DNA bases (specifically called point mutations) as well as to changes in chromosome number and/or structure.

gene A sequence of DNA bases that specifies the order of amino acids in an entire protein, a portion of a protein, or any functional product (for example., RNA). A gene may be made up of hundreds or thousands of DNA bases organized into coding and noncoding segments.

genome The entire genetic makeup of an individual or species.

exons Segments of genes that are transcribed and are involved in protein synthesis. (The prefix *ex* denotes that these segments are expressed.)

noncoding DNA DNA that does not direct the production of proteins. However, such DNA segments may produce other important molecules, so the term *noncoding* DNA is not really accurate.

introns Segments of genes that are initially transcribed and then deleted. Because they aren't expressed, they aren't involved in protein synthesis. However, a DNA sequence that is deleted during the manufacture of one protein may not be deleted in another. Therefore, the terms "introns" and "noncoding DNA" aren't synonymous.

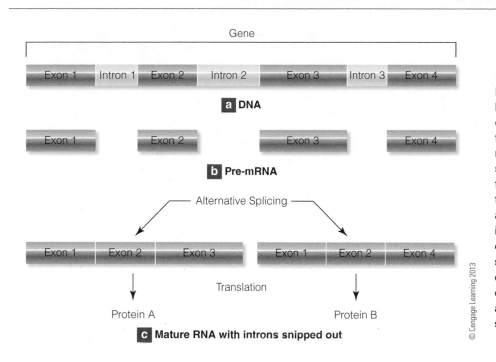

Gene

a DNA

| Exon 1 | Intron 1 | Exon 2 | Intron 2 | Exon 3 | Intron 3 | Exon 4 |

b Pre-mRNA

| Exon 1 | Exon 2 | Exon 3 | Exon 4 |

Alternative Splicing

| Exon 1 | Exon 2 | Exon 3 | | Exon 1 | Exon 2 | Exon 4 |

Translation

Protein A   Protein B

c Mature RNA with introns snipped out

© Cengage Learning 2013

◄ **Figure 3-10**
Diagrammatic representation of how our views of gene function have changed. (a) According to the traditional view, genes are discrete segments of DNA, each coding for a specific protein, and only one of the two DNA strands is involved in protein synthesis. (b) We now know that as different introns are deleted during translation, the remaining exons can form several overlapping coding sequences, each of which can be considered a gene. That is, a portion of one gene can also be part of another gene. Also, both DNA strands are functional.

ferent ways to make segments that code for more than one protein. Genes can also overlap one another, and there can be genes within genes (**Fig. 3-10**). Clearly, the answer to the question "What is a gene?" is complicated, and a completely accurate definition may be a long time coming. However, a proposed and more inclusive definition simply states that a gene is "a complete chromosomal segment responsible for making a functional product" (Snyder and Gerstein, 2003).

In spite of all the recently obtained information that has changed some of our views and expanded our knowledge of DNA, there is one fact that doesn't change. The genetic code is *universal*, and at least on earth, DNA is the molecule that governs the expression, inheritance, and evolution of biological traits in all forms of life. The DNA of all organisms, from bacteria to oak trees to fruit flies to human beings, is composed of the same molecules using the same kinds of instructions. The DNA triplet CGA, for example, specifies the amino acid alanine, regardless of species. These similarities imply biological relationships between all forms of life—and a common ancestry as well. What makes fruit flies distinct from humans isn't differences in the DNA

material itself, but differences in how that material is arranged and regulated.

Regulatory Genes

Some genes act solely to control the expression of other genes. Basically, these **regulatory genes** make molecules that switch other genes on or off. Thus, their functions are critical for individual organisms, and they also play a fundamental and critical role in evolution. In fact, the study of regulatory genes will enable us to answer many of the remaining questions we have about the evolution of species.

Homeobox genes are a critically important type of regulatory genes, and there are several different kinds. Perhaps the best known are the *Hox* genes that direct early segmentation of embryonic tissues, including those that give rise to the spine and thoracic muscles. They also interact with other genes to determine the characteristics of developing body segments and structures, but not their actual development. For example, *Hox* genes determine where, in a developing embryo, limb buds will appear. They also establish the number and overall pattern of the different types of vertebrae,

regulatory genes Genes that influence the activity of other genes. Regulatory genes direct embryonic development and are involved in physiological processes throughout life. They are extremely important to the evolutionary process.

homeobox genes An evolutionarily ancient group of regulatory genes. One type (called *Hox* genes) directs segmentation of the body during embryonic development.

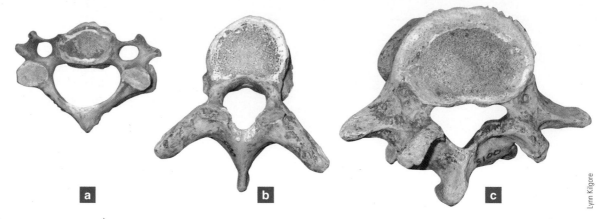

a   b   c

Lynn Kilgore

▲**Figure 3-11**
The differences in these three vertebrae, from different regions of
the spine, are caused by the action
of Hox genes during embryonic
development. **(a)** The cervical
(neck) vertebrae have characteristics that differentiate them from
(b) thoracic vertebrae, which are
attached to the ribs, and also from
(c) lumbar vertebrae of the lower
back. Hox genes determine the
overall pattern not only of each
type of vertebra but also of each
individual vertebra.

the bones that make up the spine
(**Fig. 3-11**).

All homeobox genes are highly conserved, meaning they've been maintained throughout evolutionary history. They're present in all invertebrates
(such as worms and insects) and vertebrates, and they don't vary greatly from
species to species. This type of conservation means not only that these
genes are vitally important, but also
that they evolved from genes that were
present in some of the earliest forms of
life. Moreover, changes in the behavior
of homeobox genes are responsible for
various physical differences between
closely related species or different
breeds of domesticated animals.

There are many other types of
highly conserved genes as well. For
example, recent sequencing of the sea
sponge genome has shown that humans
share many genes with sea sponges
(Srivastava et al., 2010). This doesn't
mean that sponges were ancestral to
humans, but it does mean that we have

Quick Review

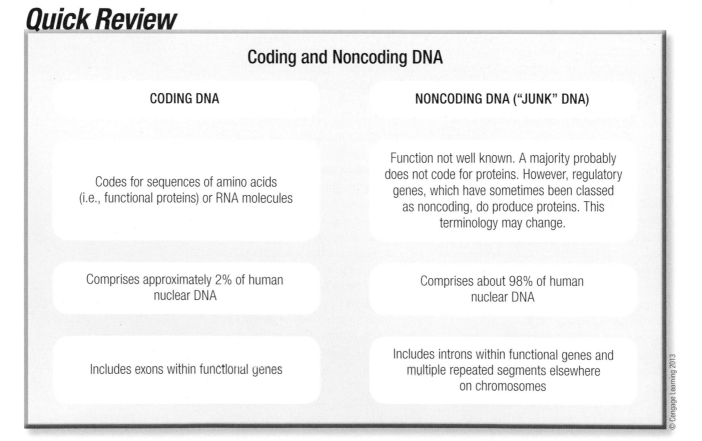

Coding and Noncoding DNA

CODING DNA	NONCODING DNA ("JUNK" DNA)
Codes for sequences of amino acids (i.e., functional proteins) or RNA molecules	Function not well known. A majority probably does not code for proteins. However, regulatory genes, which have sometimes been classed as noncoding, do produce proteins. This terminology may change.
Comprises approximately 2% of human nuclear DNA	Comprises about 98% of human nuclear DNA
Includes exons within functional genes	Includes introns within functional genes and multiple repeated segments elsewhere on chromosomes

© Cengage Learning 2013

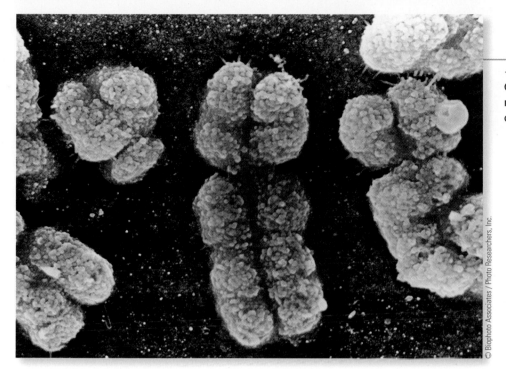

◄ Figure 3-12
Colorized scanning electron micrograph of human chromosomes.

genes that were already in existence some 600 mya. These genes ultimately laid the foundation for the evolution of complex animals, and they're crucial to many of the basic cellular processes that are fundamental to life today. These processes include cell growth; the ability to recognize foreign cells (immunity), the development of specific cell types; and signaling between cells during growth and development.

We cannot overstate the importance of regulatory genes in evolution. And the fact that these genes, with little modification, are present in all complex (and some not so complex) organisms, including humans, is the basis of biological continuity or connections between species.

Cell Division

Throughout much of a cell's life, its DNA (all 6 feet of it!) directs cellular functions and exists as an uncoiled, granular substance. However, at various times in the life of most types of cells, normal activities stop and the cell divides. Cell division produces new cells, and at the beginning of this process, the DNA becomes tightly coiled and is visible under a microscope as a set of discrete structures called **chromosomes** (**Fig. 3-12**).

Every species has a specific number of chromosomes in somatic cells (**Table 3-2**). Humans have 46, while chimpanzees and gorillas have 48. This doesn't mean that humans have less DNA than chimpanzees and gorillas, it just means that the DNA is packaged differently.

Chromosomes

Chromosomes are composed of a DNA molecule and proteins (**Fig. 3-13**). During normal cell function, if the DNA were organized into chromosomes, they would look like single-stranded structures. However, during the early stages of cell division when chromosomes become visible, they're made up of two strands, or two DNA molecules, joined together at a constricted area called the *centromere*. The reason there are two strands is simple: The DNA molecules have *replicated*, and one strand is an exact copy of the other.

There are two basic types of chromosomes: **autosomes** and **sex chromosomes**. Autosomes carry genetic

chromosomes Discrete structures composed of DNA and proteins found only in the nucleus of cells. Chromosomes are visible under magnification only during certain phases of cell division.

autosomes All chromosomes except the sex chromosomes.

sex chromosomes In mammals, the X and Y chromosomes.

TABLE 3.2	Standard Chromosomal Complement in Various Organisms	
Organism	**Chromosome Number in Somatic Cells**	**Chromosome Number in Gametes**
Human (*Homo sapiens*)	46	23
Chimpanzee (*Pan troglodytes*)	48	24
Gorilla (*Gorilla gorilla*)	48	24
Dog (*Canis familiaris*)	78	39
Chicken (*Gallus domesticus*)	78	39
Frog (*Rana pipiens*)	26	13
Housefly (*Musca domestica*)	12	6
Onion (*Allium cepa*)	16	8
Corn (*Zea mays*)	20	10
Tobacco (*Nicotiana tabacum*)	48	24

Source: Cummings, 2000, p. 16.

© Cengage Learning 2013

information that governs all physical characteristics except primary sex determination. In mammals, the two sex chromosomes are the X and Y chromosomes, and the Y chromosome is directly involved in determining maleness. Although the X chromosome is called a "sex chromosome," it actually functions more like an autosome because it's not involved in primary sex determination, and it influences many other traits. Among mammals, all genetically normal females have two X chromosomes (XX), and they're female only because they don't have a Y chromosome. (Female is the default setting.) All genetically normal males have one X and one Y chromosome (XY). In other classes of animals, such as birds or insects, primary sex determination is governed by various other chromosomal mechanisms and factors.

Chromosomes occur in pairs, so all normal human somatic cells have 22 pairs of autosomes and one pair of sex chromosomes (23 pairs in all). Abnormal numbers of autosomes, with few exceptions, are fatal—usually soon after conception. Although abnormal numbers of sex chromosomes aren't usually fatal, they may result in sterility and frequently have other consequences as well. So, to function normally, it's essential for a human cell to possess both members of each chromosomal pair, or a total of 46 chromosomes.

Offspring inherit one member of each chromosomal pair from the father and one member from the mother. Members of chromosomal pairs are alike in size and position of the centromere, and they carry genetic information governing the same traits. But this doesn't mean that partner chromosomes are genetically identical; it just means they influence the same traits.

Mitosis

As we mentioned earlier, normal cellular function is periodically interrupted so the cell can divide. Cell division in somatic cells is called **mitosis**, and it's the way somatic cells reproduce. It occurs during growth and development; repairs injured tissues; and

mitosis Simple cell division; the process by which somatic cells divide to produce two identical daughter cells.

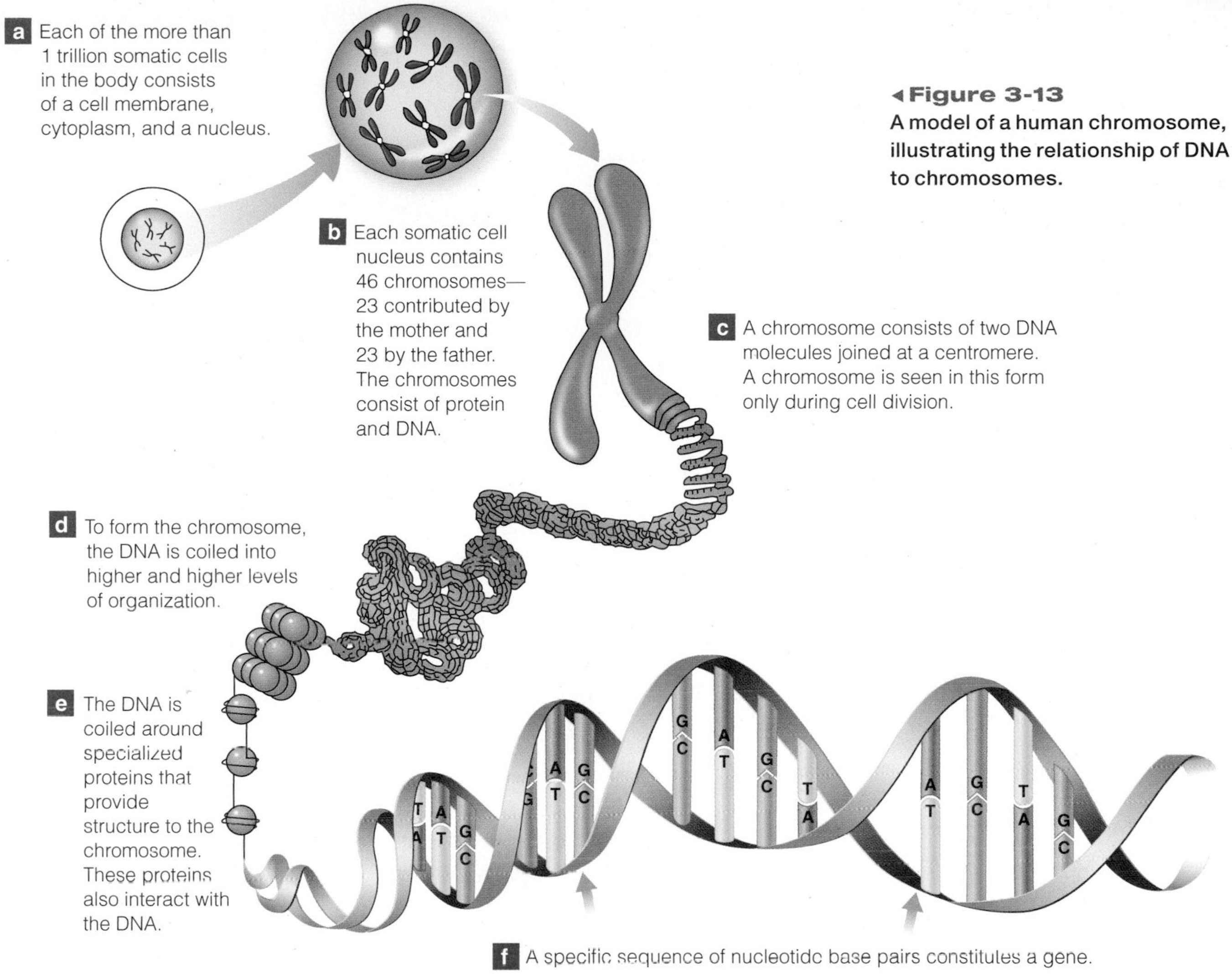

a Each of the more than 1 trillion somatic cells in the body consists of a cell membrane, cytoplasm, and a nucleus.

◀**Figure 3-13**
A model of a human chromosome, illustrating the relationship of DNA to chromosomes.

b Each somatic cell nucleus contains 46 chromosomes—23 contributed by the mother and 23 by the father. The chromosomes consist of protein and DNA.

c A chromosome consists of two DNA molecules joined at a centromere. A chromosome is seen in this form only during cell division.

d To form the chromosome, the DNA is coiled into higher and higher levels of organization.

e The DNA is coiled around specialized proteins that provide structure to the chromosome. These proteins also interact with the DNA.

f A specific sequence of nucleotide base pairs constitutes a gene.

© Cengage Learning 2013

replaces older cells with newer ones. In the early stages of mitosis, a human somatic cell has 46 double-stranded chromosomes, and as the cell begins to divide, these chromosomes line up along its center and split apart so that the two strands separate (**Fig. 3-14**). Once the two strands are apart, they pull away from each other and move to opposite ends of the dividing cell. At this point, each strand is a distinct chromosome, *composed of one DNA molecule*. Following the separation of chromosome strands, the cell membrane pinches in and seals, so that there are two new cells, each with a full complement of DNA, or 46 chromosomes.

Mitosis is referred to as "simple cell division" because a somatic cell divides one time to produce two daughter cells that are genetically identical to each other and to the original cell. In mitosis, the original cell possesses 46 chromosomes, and each new daughter cell inherits an exact copy of all 46. This precision is made possible by the DNA molecule's ability to replicate. Therefore, DNA replication is what ensures that the amount of genetic material remains constant from one generation of cells to the next.

Meiosis

While mitosis produces new cells, **meiosis** can lead to the development of an entire new organism because it produces reproductive cells (gametes). Meiosis is similar to mitosis, but a little

meiosis Cell division in specialized cells in ovaries and testes. Meiosis involves two divisions and results in four daughter cells, each containing only half the original number of chromosomes. These cells can develop into gametes.

▶ **Figure 3-14**
Diagrammatic representation of mitosis. The blue images next to some of these illustrations are photomicrographs of actual chromosomes in a dividing cell.

a The cell is involved in metabolic activities. DNA replication occurs, but chromosomes are not visible.

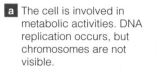

b The nuclear membrane disappears, and double-stranded chromosomes are visible.

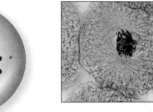

c The chromosomes align themselves at the center of the cell.

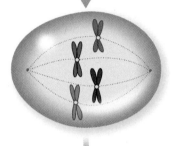
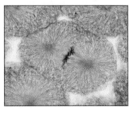

d The chromosomes split at the centromere, and the strands separate and move to opposite ends of the dividing cell.

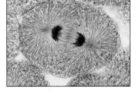

e The cell membrane pinches in as the cell continues to divide. The chromosomes begin to uncoil (not shown here).

f After mitosis is complete, there are two identical daughter cells. The nuclear membrane is present, and chromosomes are no longer visible.

more complicated. In meiosis, there are two divisions instead of one. Also, meiosis produces four daughter cells, not two, and each of these four cells contains only half the original number of chromosomes.

During meiosis, specialized cells in male testes and female ovaries divide and eventually develop into sperm and egg cells. Initially, these cells contain the full complement of chromosomes (46 in humans), but after the first division (called *reduction division*), the number of chromosomes in the two daughter cells is 23, or half the original number (**Fig. 3-15**). This reduction of chromosome number is important because the resulting gamete, with its 23 chromosomes, may eventually unite with another gamete that also has 23 chromosomes. The product of this union is a *zygote,* or fertilized egg, in which the original number of chromosomes (46) has been restored. In other words, a zygote inherits the exact amount of DNA it needs (half from each parent) to develop and function normally. If it weren't for reduction division in meiosis, it wouldn't be possible to maintain the correct number of chromosomes from one generation to the next.

During the first division, partner chromosomes come together to form pairs of double-stranded chromosomes that line up along the cell's center. Pairing of partner chromosomes is essential, because while they're together, members of pairs exchange genetic information in a process called **recombination**. Pairing is also important because it ensures that each new daughter cell receives only one member of each pair.

As the cell begins to divide, the chromosomes themselves remain intact (that is, double-stranded), but *members of pairs* pull apart and move to opposite ends of the cell. After the first division, there are two new daughter cells, but they aren't identical to each other or to the parental cell. They're different because each cell contains only one member of each chromosome pair (that is, only 23 chromosomes), each of which still has two strands. Also, because of recombination, each chromosome now contains some combinations of genes it didn't have before.

The second meiotic division is similar to division in mitosis. (For a comparison of mitosis and meiosis, see **Fig. 3-16**.) In the two newly formed cells, the 23 double-stranded chromosomes line up at the cell's center and, as in mitosis, the strands of each chromosome separate from each other and move apart. Once this second division is completed, there are four daughter cells, each with 23 single-stranded chromosomes, or 23 DNA molecules.

The Evolutionary Significance of Meiosis Meiosis occurs in all sexually reproducing organisms, and it's an extremely important evolutionary innovation because it increases genetic variation in populations. As you have already learned, genetic variation is essential if species are to adapt to changing selective pressures. Because they receive genetic contributions from two parents, members of sexually reproducing species aren't genetically identical **clones** of one another.

Problems with Meiosis For fetal development to occur normally, the process of meiosis needs to be exact. If chromosomes or chromosome strands don't separate during either of the two divisions, serious problems can develop. This failure to separate is called *nondisjunction*, and when it happens one of the daughter cells receives two copies of the affected chromosome, while the other daughter cell receives none. If such an affected gamete unites with a normal gamete containing 23 chromosomes, the resulting zygote will have either 45 or 47 chromosomes. If there are 47, then there will be three copies of one chromosome instead of two, a situation called *trisomy.*

You can appreciate the potential effects of an abnormal number of chromosomes if you remember that the

recombination The exchange of genetic material between paired chromosomes during meiosis; also called *crossing over.*

clones Organisms that are genetically identical to another organism.

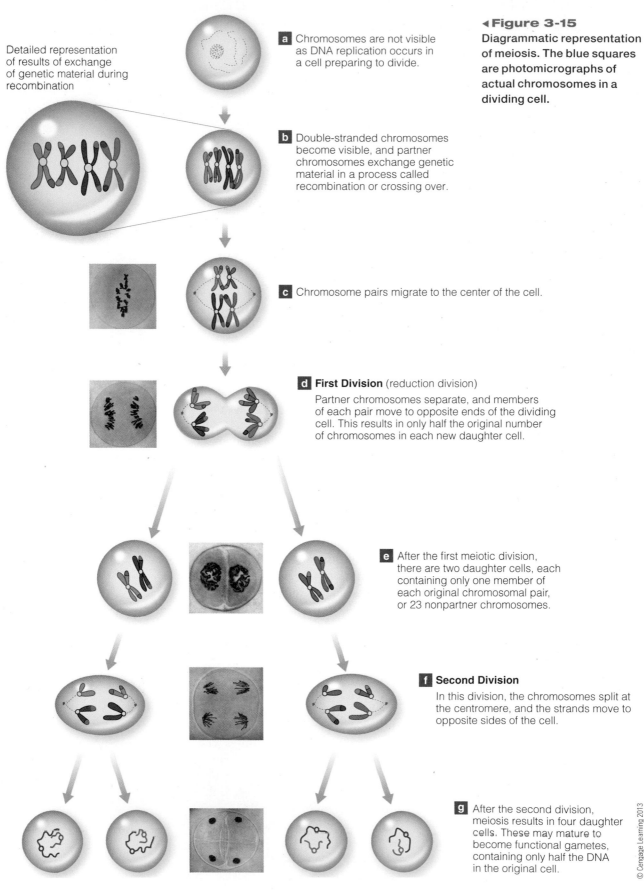

Detailed representation of results of exchange of genetic material during recombination

a Chromosomes are not visible as DNA replication occurs in a cell preparing to divide.

◀**Figure 3-15**
Diagrammatic representation of meiosis. The blue squares are photomicrographs of actual chromosomes in a dividing cell.

b Double-stranded chromosomes become visible, and partner chromosomes exchange genetic material in a process called recombination or crossing over.

c Chromosome pairs migrate to the center of the cell.

d **First Division** (reduction division)
Partner chromosomes separate, and members of each pair move to opposite ends of the dividing cell. This results in only half the original number of chromosomes in each new daughter cell.

e After the first meiotic division, there are two daughter cells, each containing only one member of each original chromosomal pair, or 23 nonpartner chromosomes.

f **Second Division**
In this division, the chromosomes split at the centromere, and the strands move to opposite sides of the cell.

g After the second division, meiosis results in four daughter cells. These may mature to become functional gametes, containing only half the DNA in the original cell.

© Cengage Learning 2013

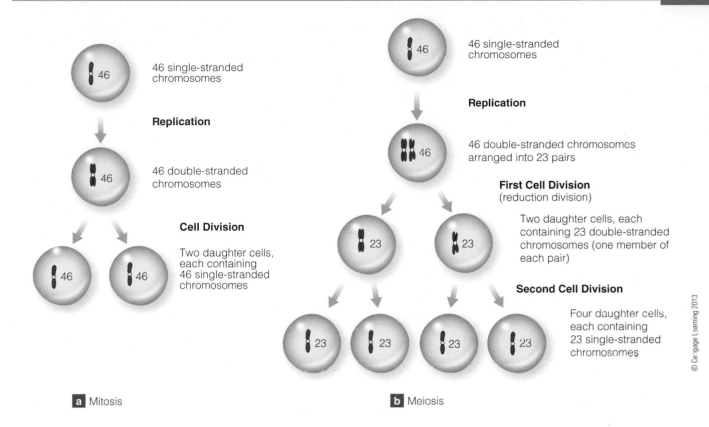

46 single-stranded chromosomes

Replication

46 double-stranded chromosomes

Cell Division

Two daughter cells, each containing 46 single-stranded chromosomes

46 single-stranded chromosomes

Replication

46 double-stranded chromosomes arranged into 23 pairs

First Cell Division (reduction division)

Two daughter cells, each containing 23 double-stranded chromosomes (one member of each pair)

Second Cell Division

Four daughter cells, each containing 23 single-stranded chromosomes

a Mitosis

b Meiosis

© Cengage Learning 2013

zygote, by means of mitosis, ultimately gives rise to all the cells in the developing body. Consequently, every one of these cells will inherit the abnormal chromosome number. And because most abnormal numbers of autosomes are lethal, the embryo is usually spontaneously aborted, frequently before the pregnancy is even recognized.

Trisomy 21 (formerly called Down syndrome) is the only example of an abnormal number of autosomes that's compatible with life beyond the first few years after birth. Trisomy 21 is caused by the presence of three copies of chromosome 21. It occurs in approximately 1 out of every 1,000 live births and is associated with various developmental and health problems. These problems include congenital heart defects (seen in about 40 percent of affected newborns), increased susceptibility to respiratory infections, and leukemia. However, the most widely recognized effect is mental impairment, which is variably expressed and ranges from mild to severe.

Nondisjunction also occurs in sex chromosomes. For example, a man may have two X chromosomes and one Y chromosome, or one X chromosome and two Y chromosomes. Likewise, a woman may have only one X chromosome, or she may have more than two. Although abnormal numbers of sex chromosomes don't always result in spontaneous abortion or death, they can cause sterility, some mental impairment, and other problems. And though it's possible to live without a Y chromosome (roughly half of all people do), it's impossible for an embryo to survive without an X chromosome. (Remember, X chromosomes carry genes that influence many traits.) Clearly, normal development depends on having the correct number of chromosomes.

New Frontiers

Since the discovery of DNA structure and function in the 1950s, the field of genetics has revolutionized biological science and reshaped our understanding of inheritance, genetic

▲ **Figure 3-16**
Mitosis and meiosis compared. In mitosis, one division produces two daughter cells, each of which contains 46 chromosomes. In meiosis there are two divisions. After the first, there are two cells, each containing only 23 chromosomes (one member of each original chromosome pair). Each daughter cell divides again, so that the final result is four cells, each with only half the original number of chromosomes.

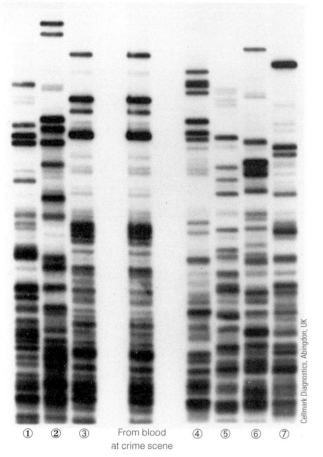

① ② ③ From blood at crime scene ④ ⑤ ⑥ ⑦

Cellmark Diagnostics, Abingdon, UK

▲ **Figure 3-17**
Eight DNA fingerprints, one of which is from a blood sample left at an actual crime scene. The other seven are from suspects. By comparing the banding patterns, it's easy to identify the guilty person.

polymerase chain reaction (PCR) A method of producing thousands of copies of a DNA sample.

Human Genome Project An international effort aimed at sequencing and mapping the entire human genome, completed in 2003.

disease, and evolutionary processes. For example, a technique developed in 1986, called **polymerase chain reaction (PCR)**, enables scientists to make thousands of copies of small samples of DNA, which can then be analyzed. In the past, DNA samples from crime scenes or fossils were usually too small to be studied. But PCR makes it possible to examine DNA sequences in, for example, Neandertal fossils and Egyptian mummies; and it has limitless potential for many disciplines, including forensic science, medicine, and paleoanthropology.

Another application of PCR allows scientists to identify *DNA fingerprints,* so-called because they appear as patterns of repeated DNA sequences that are unique to each individual (**Fig. 3-17**). For example, one person might have a segment of 6 bases such as ATTCTA repeated 3 times, while another person might have 20 copies of the same sequence. DNA fingerprinting is perhaps the most powerful tool available for human identification. Scientists have used it to identify scores of unidentified remains, including members of the Russian royal family murdered in 1918 and victims of the September 11, 2001, terrorist attacks in the United States. Just as importantly, the technique has been used to exonerate many innocent people wrongly convicted of crimes, in some cases decades after they were imprisoned.

Over the last two decades, scientists have used the techniques of *recombinant DNA technology* to transfer genes from the cells of one spe-

cies into those of another. One common method has been to insert human genes that direct the production of various proteins into bacterial cells in laboratories. The altered bacteria can then produce human gene products such as insulin. Until the early 1980s, people with diabetes relied on insulin derived from nonhuman animals. However, this insulin wasn't plentiful, and some patients developed allergies to it. But since 1982, abundant supplies of human insulin, produced by bacteria, have been available; and bacteria-derived insulin doesn't cause allergic reactions.

Cloning has been one of the more controversial new genetic technologies. But cloning isn't as new as you might think. Anyone who has ever taken a cutting from a plant and rooted it to grow a new one has produced a clone. Many species have now been cloned, and geneticists recently produced clones of dead mice that were frozen for as long as 16 years. This gives rise to hopes that eventually it may be possible to clone extinct animals, such as mammoths, from the frozen bodies of animals that died several thousand years ago (Wakayama et al., 2008). But don't count on visiting a *Jurassic Park* type zoo anytime soon. No one knows how successful cloning will become. Long-term studies have yet to show whether cloned animals live out their normal life span, but some evidence from mice suggests that they don't. Also, Dolly, a sheep clone born in 1997, developed health problems and was euthanized at the relatively young age of 6 years (Giles and Knight, 2003).

As exciting as these innovations are, probably the single most important advance in genetics has been the progress made by the **Human Genome Project** (International Human Genome Sequencing Consortium, 2001; Venter et al., 2001). The goal of this international effort, begun in 1990, was to sequence the entire human genome, which consists of some 3 billion bases making up approximately 25,000 protein-coding genes. This extremely important project was completed in 2003. The potential for anthropological applications is enormous.

While scientists were sequencing human genes, the genomes of other organisms were also being studied. As of now, the genomes of hundreds of species have been sequenced, including mice (Waterston et al., 2002), chimpanzees (Chimpanzee Sequencing and Analysis Consortium, 2005), and rhesus macaques (Rhesus Macaque Genome Sequencing and Analysis Consortium, 2007).

In May 2010, researchers finished sequencing the Neandertal genome (Green et al., 2006; 2010). To date, the most exciting announcement stemming from this research is that modern Europeans and Asians, but not Africans, inherited 1 to 4 percent of their genes from ancient Neandertal ancestors. This finding sheds light on debates concerning whether or not early modern humans interbred with Neandertals. These debates have been ongoing in physical anthropology for more than 50 years, and while this new genetic evidence does not conclusively end the discussion, it strongly supports the argument that some interbreeding did occur and that many of us carry a few Neandertal genes.

Eventually, comparative genome analysis should provide a thorough assessment of genetic similarities and differences, and thus the evolutionary relationships, between humans and other primates. What's more, we can already look at human variation in an entirely different light than we could even 10 years ago (see Chapter 5). Among other things, genetic comparisons between human groups can inform us about population movements in the past and what selective pressures may have been exerted on different populations to produce some of the variability we see.

Completion of the Neandertal genome sequence wasn't the only groundbreaking achievement in 2010. After 10 years of effort, scientists cre-

ated a functional, synthetic bacterial genome (Gibson et al., 2010). This synthetic genome is the first life-form ever made by humans, and it has major implications for biotechnology. (Understandably, it has also raised many ethical concerns.) Basically, geneticists sequenced the 1 million bases in a bacterial chromosome. (Bacterial DNA is organized into a single ring-shaped chromosome.) They then produced an artificial chromosome by assembling DNA segments and splicing them together, interspersed with "noncoding" sequences they had invented. These noncoding sequences allowed them to distinguish the genome they had created from the natural one. The new synthetic DNA was then inserted into a bacterial cell of a different species. The original DNA of the recipient cell had been removed, and the cell began to follow the instructions of the new DNA. That is, it produced proteins characteristic of a different bacterial species! Moreover, the recipient cell replicated, and now there are laboratory colonies of the "new" bacterium (**Fig. 3-18**).

It's important to emphasize that this project did not create a completely new synthetic life-form because the

▼ **Figure 3-18**
Self-replicating synthetic bacteria. Researchers inserted a gene into the synthetic bacteria that makes this colony appear blue. This was so they could distinguish these cells from the original bacteria (which aren't blue) and therefore determine if the new cells were indeed replicating.

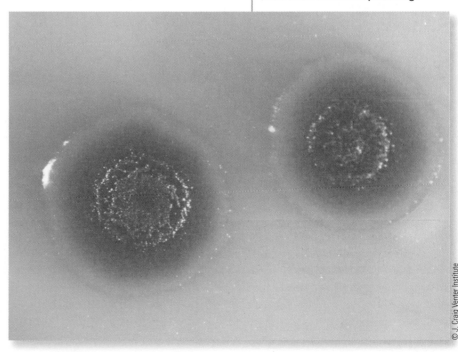

genome had been transferred into an already existing cell. Nevertheless, the door has been opened for the development of artificial organisms. Though it may never be possible to create new species as complex as birds and mammals, we can almost certainly expect to see the production of artificial, single-celled organisms, many of which will have medical applications. But the potential for abuse,

especially in the development of biological weapons, will obviously be of grave concern. Still, the human development of a self-replicating bacterium with altered DNA from another species is an extraordinary milestone in biology. It is not an exaggeration to say that this is the most exciting time in the history of evolutionary biology since Darwin published *On the Origin of Species*.

Why It Matters

You may be wondering why it's important to compare human genes with those of other species. Actually, there are countless reasons for this kind of research. The latest developments in assessing the complete genetic sequences of chimpanzees and humans have confirmed the many similarities in genes that code for proteins, but they also show many previously unanticipated differences in sequences that *don't* code for proteins. Also, research has shown how tiny differences in protein-

coding sequences may explain why humans are susceptible to diseases such as cholera, malaria, and influenza whereas chimpanzees apparently are not. For example, the human form of a molecule called sialic acid differs from the chimpanzee molecule by a single oxygen atom (Varki, 2000). The chimpanzee version of the sialic acid gene is the one found in other mammals, so it's been suggested that the human sialic acid gene probably evolved after the chimpanzee and human lines split (see Chapter 9).

Sialic acid serves as a binding site for microorganisms that cause diseases

such as cholera, malaria, and some forms of influenza (Muchmore, Diaz, and Varki, 1998), and the discovery of this genetic difference may lead to treatments for these diseases. It's also an important reminder that even one genetic difference between humans and chimpanzees can have an extensive and as yet unforeseen impact. Without full knowledge of the gene sequences of humans, chimpanzees, and other animals, we wouldn't be aware of these tiny differences that may have huge impacts on individual health, growth, and development.

Summary of Main Topics

- Cells are the fundamental units of life, and in multicellular organisms, there are basically two types. Somatic cells make up body tissues, and gametes (eggs and sperm) are reproductive cells that transmit genetic information from parents to offspring.
- Genetic information is contained in the DNA molecule, found in the nucleus of cells and in mitochondria. The DNA molecule is capable of replication, or making copies of itself. Replication makes it possible

for daughter cells to receive a full complement of DNA (contained in chromosomes). DNA also controls protein synthesis by directing the cell to arrange amino acids in the proper sequence for each protein. Also involved in the process of protein synthesis is another, similar molecule called RNA.
- There are many genes that regulate the function of other genes. One class of regulatory genes, the homeobox genes, direct the development of the body plan. Other

regulatory genes turn genes on and off.
- Most of our DNA doesn't actually code for protein production, and much of its function is unknown. Some of these noncoding sequences, called introns, are contained within genes. Introns are initially transcribed into mRNA but are then deleted before the mRNA leaves the cell nucleus. The function of most noncoding DNA is unknown, but some is involved in gene regulation.

- Cells multiply by dividing, and during cell division, DNA is visible under a microscope in the form of chromosomes. In humans, there are 46 chromosomes (23 pairs). If the full complement isn't precisely distributed to succeeding generations of cells, there may be serious consequences.

- Somatic cells divide during growth or tissue repair or to replace old, worn-out cells. Somatic cell division is called mitosis. A cell divides one time to produce two daughter cells, each possessing a full and identical set of chromosomes. Sex cells are produced when specialized cells in the ovaries and testes divide during meiosis. Unlike mitosis, meiosis is characterized by two divisions that produce four nonidentical daughter cells, each containing only half the amount of DNA (23 chromosomes).

Critical Thinking Questions

1. Before reading this chapter, were you aware that the DNA in your body is structurally the same as in all other organisms? Do you see this fact as having potential to clarify some of the many questions we still have regarding biological evolution? Why?

2. Do you think proteins are exactly the same in all species? If not, how do you think they would differ in terms of their composition, and why might these differences be important to physical anthropologists?

3. Do you approve of cloning? If so, would you restrict cloning to certain species? Would you have a pet cloned? Why or why not?

4. Do you approve of the recent development of a "synthetic" bacterial genome? Why or why not? How do you think this technology might be used in the future?

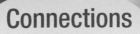

Connections

All forms of life are made up of cells.

Heredity is based on the transmission of DNA from one generation to the next.

Evolution results from DNA changes and the action of other evolutionary factors.

Humans are both vertebrates and mammals and we've shared evolutionary history for millions of years.

4

Heredity and Evolution

Have you ever had a cat with five, six, or even seven toes? Even if you haven't, you may have seen one, because extra toes are fairly common in cats. Or, maybe you've known someone with an extra finger or toe, because some people have them, too. Anne Boleyn, mother of England's Queen Elizabeth I and the first of Henry VIII's wives to lose her head, apparently had at least part of an extra little finger. (Of course, this had nothing to do with her early demise; that's another story.)

Having extra digits (fingers and toes) is called *polydactyly*, and it's pretty certain that one of Anne Boleyn's parents was also polydactylous (**Fig. 4-1**). It's also likely that any polydactylous cat has a parent with extra toes. But how do we know this? Actually, it's fairly simple. We know it because polydactyly is a Mendelian trait inherited in a predictable way, and its pattern of inheritance is one of those discovered almost 150 years ago by a monk named Gregor Mendel (**Fig. 4-2**).

For at least 10,000 years, people have raised domesticated plants and animals. However, it wasn't until the twentieth century that scientists understood how **selective breeding** (see definition on next page) could increase the frequency of desirable characteristics. From the time ancient Greek philosophers considered the question of how traits were inherited until well into the nineteenth century, the most common belief was that the traits seen in offspring resulted from the blending of parental traits. There were different explanations of how this happened, but numerous scholars, including Charles Darwin, accepted some aspects of the theory.

◀ Embryonic stem cells.

▶ **Figure 4-1**
(a) Hand of a person with polydactyly. **(b)** Front foot of a polydactylous cat.

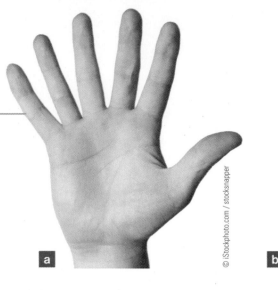

The Genetic Principles Discovered by Mendel

▶ **Figure 4-2**
Portrait of Gregor Mendel.

It may seem strange that after discussing recent discoveries about DNA we now turn our attention back to the middle of the nineteenth century, but that's when the science of genetics was born. By examining how the basic principles of inheritance were discovered, we can more easily understand them. It wasn't until Gregor Mendel (1822–1884) considered the question of heredity that it began to be resolved. Mendel was living in an abbey in what is now the Czech Republic. At the time he began his research, he'd already studied botany, physics, and mathematics at the University of Vienna. He had also performed various experiments in the monastery gardens, and this background led him to investigate how physical traits, such as color or height, could be expressed in plant **hybrids**.

Mendel worked with garden peas, concentrating on seven different traits, each of which could be expressed two ways (**Fig. 4-3**). You may think it's unusual to discuss peas in an anthropology book, but they provide a simple example of the basic rules of inheritance. The principles Mendel discovered apply to all biological organisms, including humans, another fact that illustrates biological connections among all living things.

Segregation

First, Mendel grew groups of pea plants that were different from one another with regard to at least one trait. For example, in one group all the plants were tall, while in another they were all short. To see how the expression of height would change from one generation to the next, Mendel crossed tall plants with short plants, and he called this first generation of plants the *parental generation*. According to traditional views, all the hybrid offspring, which he called the F_1 *generation*, should have been intermediate in height. But they weren't. Instead, they were all tall (**Fig. 4-4**).

Next, Mendel let the F_1 plants self-fertilize to produce a second generation (the F_2 generation). But this time, only about ¾ of the offspring were tall, and the remaining ¼ were short. One expression (short) of the trait (height) had completely disappeared in the F_1

selective breeding A practice whereby animal or plant breeders choose which individual animals or plants will be allowed to mate based on the traits (such as body size) they hope to produce in the offspring. Animals or plants that don't have the desirable traits aren't allowed to breed.

hybrids Offspring of parents who differ from each other with regard to certain traits or certain aspects of genetic makeup; heterozygotes.

Trait Studied	Dominant Form	Recessive Form

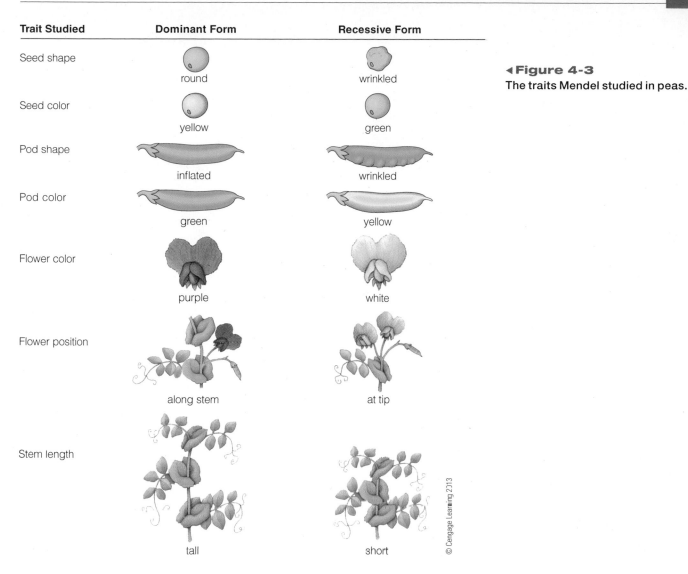

Seed shape	round	wrinkled
Seed color	yellow	green
Pod shape	inflated	wrinkled
Pod color	green	yellow
Flower color	purple	white
Flower position	along stem	at tip
Stem length	tall	short

© Cengage Learning 2013

◄ **Figure 4-3**
The traits Mendel studied in peas.

generation and then reappeared in the F$_2$ generation. Moreover, the expression that was present in all the F$_1$ plants was more common in the F$_2$ plants, occurring in a ratio of approximately 3:1 (three tall plants for every short one).

These results suggested that different expressions of a trait were controlled by discrete *units* (we would call them genes), which occurred in pairs, and that offspring inherited one unit from each parent. Mendel realized that the members of a pair of units that controlled a trait somehow separated into different sex cells and were again united with another member during fertilization of the egg. This is Mendel's *first principle of inheritance*, known as the **principle of segregation**.

Today we know that meiosis explains Mendel's principle of segregation. During meiosis, paired chromosomes, and the genes they carry, separate from each other and end up in different gametes. However, in the zygote, the full complement of chromosomes is restored, and both members of each chromosome pair are present in the offspring.

Dominance and Recessiveness

Mendel also realized that the "unit" for the absent characteristic (shortness) in the F$_1$ plants hadn't actually disappeared. It was still there, but somehow, it wasn't expressed. Mendel

principle of segregation Genes (alleles) occur in pairs because chromosomes occur in pairs. During gamete formation, the members of each pair of alleles separate, so that each gamete contains one member of each pair.

▶ **Figure 4-4**
Results of crosses when only one trait (height) at a time is considered.

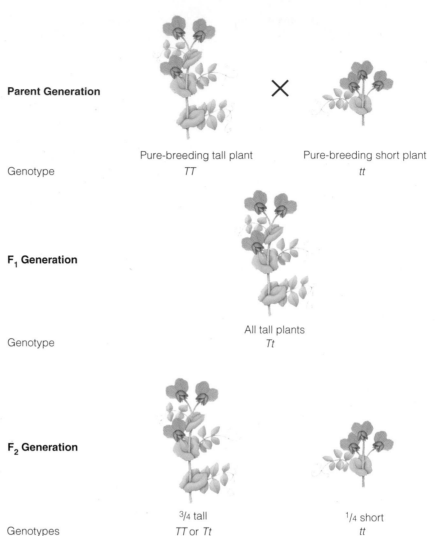

Parent Generation

Pure-breeding tall plant
TT

×

Pure-breeding short plant
tt

Genotype

F₁ Generation

All tall plants
Tt

Genotype

F₂ Generation

³/₄ tall
TT or *Tt*

¹/₄ short
tt

Genotypes

© Cengage Learning 2013

recessive Describing a trait that isn't expressed in heterozygotes; also refers to the allele that governs the trait. For a recessive allele to be expressed, an individual must have two copies of it (that is, the individual must be homozygous).

dominant In genetics, describing a trait governed by an allele that's expressed in the presence of another allele (that is, in heterozygotes). Dominant alleles prevent the expression of recessive alleles in heterozygotes. (This is the definition of *complete* dominance.)

locus (*pl.*, loci) (lo-kus, lo-sigh) The position on a chromosome where a given gene occurs. The term is frequently used interchangeably with *gene*.

alleles Alternate forms of a gene. Alleles occur at the same locus on both members of a pair of chromosomes, and they influence the same trait. But because they're slightly different from one another, their action may result in different expressions of that trait. The term *allele* is sometimes used synonymously with *gene*.

homozygous Having the same allele at the same locus on both members of a pair of chromosomes.

described the expression that seemed to be lost as "**recessive**," and he called the expressed trait "**dominant**." Thus, the principles of *dominance and recessiveness* were developed, and they remain important concepts in genetics today.

You already know that one definition of a gene is *a segment of DNA that directs the production of a specific protein, part of a protein, or any functional product*. Furthermore, the location of a gene on a chromosome is its **locus** (*pl.*, loci). At many genetic loci, however, there is more than one possible form of the gene, and these variations of genes at specific loci are called **alleles** (**Fig. 4-5**). Simply stated, alleles are different versions of a gene, each of which can direct the cell to produce a slightly modified form of the same product

and, perhaps, a different expression of the trait.

As it turns out, height in pea plants is controlled by two different alleles at the same genetic locus. (We'll call it the height locus.) The allele that specifies tall is dominant to the allele for short. (Height is not controlled this way in all plants.) In Mendel's experiments, all the parent plants had two copies of the same allele, either dominant or recessive, depending on whether they were tall or short. When two copies of the same allele are present, the individual is said to be **homozygous**. Thus, all the tall parent plants were homozygous for the dominant allele, and all the short parent plants were homozygous for the recessive allele. This explains why crossing tall plants with tall plants produced only tall offspring. Likewise, crosses between short plants produced only short offspring. All the plants in the parent generation had the same allele (that is, they lacked genetic variation) at the height locus. However, all the F_1 plants (hybrids) inherited one allele from each parent (one tall allele and one short allele). Therefore, they all inherited two different alleles at the height locus. Individuals with two different alleles at a locus are **heterozygous**.

Figure 4-6 illustrates the crosses that Mendel initially performed. By convention, letters that represent alleles or genes are italicized, with uppercase letters referring to dominant alleles (or dominant traits) and lowercase letters referring to recessive alleles (or recessive traits). Therefore,

T = the allele for tallness
t = the allele for shortness

The same symbols are combined to describe an individual's actual genetic makeup, or **genotype**. The term *genotype* can be used to refer to an organism's entire genetic makeup or only to the alleles at a specific genetic locus. Thus, the genotypes of the plants in Mendel's experiments were

TT = homozygous tall plants
Tt = heterozygous tall plants
tt = homozygous short plants

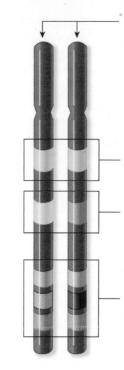

Members of a pair of chromosomes. One chromosome is from a male parent, and its partner is from a female parent.

Gene locus. The location for a specific gene on a chromosome.

Pair of alleles. Although they influence the same characteristic, their DNA varies slightly, so they produce somewhat different expressions of the same trait.

Three pairs of alleles (at three loci on this pair of chomosomes). Note that at two loci the alleles are identical (homozygous), and at one locus they are different (heterozygous).

© Cengage Learning 2013

▲**Figure 4-5**

This illustration depicts alleles residing at the same locus on paired chromosomes. Note that the alleles aren't always identical (indicated here by different shades of the same color.) For the sake of simplicity, the alleles are shown on single-stranded chromosomes.

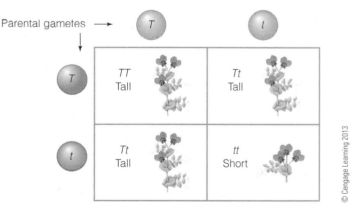

Parental gametes →

© Cengage Learning 2013

▲**Figure 4-6**

Diagram representing possible genotypes and phenotypes and their proportions in the F_2 generation. The circles across the top and at the left of the square represent the gametes of the F_1 parents. Each small square receives one allele from the gamete above it and another from the gamete to the left. Thus, the square at the upper left has two dominant (T) alleles. The upper right square receives a recessive (t) allele from the blue gamete above it and a dominant (T) allele from the orange gamete to its left. In this way, the four squares illustrate that ¼ of the F_2 plants can be expected to be homozygous tall (TT); another ½ of the plants can also be expected to be tall but will be heterozygous (Tt); and the remaining ¼ can be expected to be short because they are homozygous for the recessive "short" allele (tt). Thus, ¾ can be expected to be tall and ¼ to be short.

heterozygous Having different alleles at the same locus on members of a pair of chromosomes.

genotype The genetic makeup of an individual. Genotype can refer to an organism's entire genetic makeup or to the alleles at a particular locus.

Figure 4-6 also shows the different ways alleles can be combined when the F_1 plants are self-fertilized to produce an F_2 generation. Therefore, the figure illustrates all the *genotypes* that are possible in the F_2 generation; and statistically speaking, it shows that we would expect ¼ of the F_2 plants to be homozygous dominant (*TT*), ½ to be heterozygous (*Tt*), and the remaining ¼ to be homozygous recessive (*tt*).

You can also see the proportions of F_2 **phenotypes**, the observed physical manifestations of genes, illustrating why Mendel saw approximately three tall plants for every short plant in the F_2 generation. One quarter of the F_2 plants are tall because they have the *TT* genotype. Furthermore, an additional ½ are also tall because they're heterozygous (*Tt*), and *T* is dominant to *t*. The remaining ¼ are homozygous recessive (*tt*), and they're short because no dominant allele is present. It's important to understand that the *only* way a recessive allele can be expressed is if it occurs with another recessive allele, that is, if the individual is homozygous recessive at the locus in question.

Independent Assortment

Mendel also demonstrated that different characteristics aren't necessarily inherited together by showing that plant height and seed color are independent of each other. That is, any tall pea plant had a 50-50 chance of producing either yellow or green peas. Because of this fact, he developed the **principle of independent assortment**. According to this principle, the units (genes) that code for different traits (in this example, plant height and seed color) sort out independently of each other during gamete formation. Today we know that this happens because the genes that control plant height and seed color are located on different, nonpartner chromosomes, and during meiosis, the chromosomes travel to newly forming cells independently of one another in a process called **random assortment**.

But if Mendel had used just *any* two traits, his results would have been different at least some of the time. This is because genes on the same chromosome aren't independent of each other, and they usually stay together during meiosis. Even though Mendel didn't know about chromosomes, he certainly knew that all characteristics weren't independent of one another. But because he wanted to emphasize independence, he only reported on those traits that illustrated independent assortment.

In 1866, Mendel's results were published, but the methodology and statistical nature of the research were beyond the thinking of the time, and their significance was overlooked and unappreciated. But, by the end of the nineteenth century, several investigators had made important contributions to the field of biology. For example, chromosomes had been discovered and cell division had been explained. In just 34 years new discoveries and further hypothesis testing had revised many scientists' views of inheritance. Thus, Mendel's work was generally accepted by biologists by 1900.

Mendelian Inheritance in Humans

Mendelian traits, also called *discrete traits*, are controlled by alleles at only one genetic locus (or, in some cases, two or more very closely linked loci). The most comprehensive listing of Mendelian traits in humans is available on the Internet as *Online Mendelian Inheritance in Man* (OMIM) at: www.ncbi.nlm.nih.gov/omim/. Currently this listing includes more than 20,000 human characteristics that are inherited according to Mendelian principles.

Although some Mendelian characteristics have readily visible phenotypic expressions (such as polydactyly), most don't. The majority of Mendelian traits are biochemical in nature, and many

phenotypes The observable or detectable physical characteristics of an organism; the detectable expressions of genotypes, frequently influenced by environmental factors.

principle of independent assortment The distribution of one pair of alleles into gametes does not influence the distribution of another pair. The genes controlling different traits are inherited independently of one another.

random assortment The chance distribution of chromosomes to daughter cells during meiosis. Along with recombination, random assortment is an important source of genetic variation (but not new alleles).

Mendelian traits Characteristics that are influenced by alleles at only one genetic locus. Examples include many blood types, such as ABO. Many genetic disorders, including sickle-cell anemia and Tay-Sachs disease, are also Mendelian traits.

TABLE 4.1 Some Mendelian Traits in Humans

Dominant Traits Condition	Manifestations	Recessive Traits Condition	Manifestations
Achondroplasia	Dwarfism due to growth defects involving the long bones of the arms and legs; trunk and head size usually normal.	Cystic fibrosis	Among the most common genetic (Mendelian) disorders among European Americans; abnormal secretions of the exocrine glands, with pronounced involvement of the pancreas; most patients develop obstructive lung disease. Until the recent development of new treatments, only about half of all patients survived to early adulthood.
Brachydactyly	Shortened fingers and toes.		
Familial hyper-cholesterolemia	Elevated cholesterol levels and cholesterol plaque deposition; a leading cause of heart disease, with death frequently occurring by middle age.		
Neurofibromatosis	Symptoms range from the appearance of abnormal skin pigmentation to large tumors resulting in severe deformities; can, in extreme cases, lead to paralysis, blindness, and death.	Tay-Sachs disease	Most common among Ashkenazi Jews; degeneration of the nervous system beginning at about 6 months of age; lethal by age 2 or 3 years.
Marfan syndrome	The eyes and cardiovascular and skeletal systems are affected; symptoms include greater than average height, long arms and legs, eye problems, and enlargement of the aorta; death due to rupture of the aorta is common. Abraham Lincoln may have had Marfan syndrome.	Phenylketonuria (PKU)	Inability to metabolize the amino acid phenylalanine; results in mental impairment if left untreated during childhood; treatment involves strict dietary management and some supplementation.
Huntington disease	Progressive degeneration of the nervous system accompanied by dementia and seizures; age of onset variable but commonly between 30 and 40 years.	Albinism	Inability to produce normal amounts of the pigment melanin; results in very fair, untannable skin, light blond hair, and light eyes; may also be associated with vision problems. (There is more than one form of albinism.)
Camptodactyly	Malformation of the hands whereby the fingers, usually the little finger, is permanently contracted.	Sickle-cell anemia	Abnormal form of hemoglobin (Hb^S) that results in collapsed red blood cells, blockage of capillaries, reduced blood flow to organs, and, without treatment, death.
Hypodontia of upper lateral incisors	Upper lateral incisors are absent or only partially formed (peg-shaped). Pegged incisors are a partial expression of the allele.	Thalassemia	A group of disorders characterized by reduced or absent alpha or beta chains in the hemoglobin molecule; results in severe anemia and, in some forms, death.
Cleft chin	Dimple or depression in the middle of the chin; less prominent in females than in males.		
PTC tasting	The ability to taste the bitter substance phenylthiocarbamide (PTC). Tasting thresholds vary, suggesting that alleles at another locus may also exert an influence.	Absence of permanent dentition	Failure of the permanent dentition to erupt. The primary dentition is not affected.

© Cengage Learning 2013

genetic disorders result from harmful alleles inherited in Mendelian fashion (Table 4-1). So if it seems like textbooks overly emphasize genetic disease in discussions of Mendelian traits, it's because so many Mendelian characteristics are the results of harmful alleles.

A number of genetic disorders are caused by dominant alleles (see Table 4-1). This means that if a person inherits a harmful dominant allele, he or she will have the condition it causes, even if there is a different, recessive allele on the partner chromosome.

Recessive conditions are commonly associated with the lack of a substance, usually an enzyme (see Table 4-1). For a person actually to have a recessive disorder, he or she must have *two* copies of the recessive allele that causes it. People who have only one copy of a harmful recessive allele are unaffected, but they can still pass that allele on to offspring. (Remember, half their gametes will carry the recessive allele.) For this reason they're frequently called *carriers*. If their mate is also a carrier, it's possible for them to have a child who will be homozygous for the allele, and that child will be affected. In fact, in a mating between two carriers, the risk of having an affected child is 25 percent (refer back to Fig. 4-5).

Blood groups, such as the ABO system, provide one of the best examples of Mendelian traits in humans. The ABO system is governed by three alleles, *A*, *B*, and *O*, found at the ABO locus on the ninth chromosome. These alleles determine a person's ABO blood type by coding for the production of molecules called **antigens** on the surface of red blood cells. If only antigen A is present, the blood type (phenotype) is A; if only B is present, the blood type is B; if both are present, the blood type is AB; and when neither is present, the blood type is O (**Table 4-2**).

The *O* allele is recessive to both *A* and *B*; therefore, if a person has type O blood, he or she must have two copies of the *O* allele. However, since both *A* and *B* are dominant to *O*, an individual with blood type A can have one of two genotypes: *AA* or *AO*. The same is true of type B, which results from the genotypes *BB* and *BO* (see Table 4-2). However, type AB presents a slightly different situation called **codominance**, where two different alleles are present and both are expressed. Therefore, when both *A* and *B* alleles are present, both A and B antigens occur on the surface of red blood cells because neither allele is dominant to the other.

Misconceptions about Dominance and Recessiveness

Most people have the impression that dominance and recessiveness are all-or-nothing situations. This misconception especially pertains to recessive alleles, and the general view is that when these alleles occur in carriers (heterozygotes), they have no effect on the phenotype; that is, they are completely inactivated by the presence of another (dominant) allele. Certainly, this is how it appeared to Gregor Mendel.

However, various biochemical techniques available today show that many

antigens Large molecules found on the surface of cells. Several different loci govern various antigens on red and white blood cells. (Foreign antigens provoke an immune response.)

codominance The expression of two alleles in heterozygotes. In this situation, neither allele is dominant or recessive, so they both influence the phenotype.

TABLE 4.2	ABO Genotypes and Associated Phenotypes	
Genotypes	**Antigens on Red Blood Cells**	**ABO Blood Type (Phenotype)**
AA, AO	A	A
BB, BO	B	B
AB	A and B	AB
OO	None	O

© Cengage Learning 2013

recessive alleles actually do have some effect on the phenotype, although these effects aren't usually detectable through simple observation. It turns out that in heterozygotes, the products of many recessive alleles are reduced but not completely eliminated. Therefore, our perception of recessive alleles greatly depends on whether we examine them at the directly observable phenotypic level or the biochemical level.

There are also a number of misconceptions about dominant alleles. Many people think of dominant alleles as somehow "stronger" or "better," and there is always the mistaken idea that dominant alleles are more common in populations because natural selection favors them. These misconceptions undoubtedly stem from the label "dominant" and the connotations of that term. But in genetic usage, this view is misleading. Just think about it. If dominant alleles were always more common, then a majority of people would have conditions such as achondroplasia and Marfan syndrome (see Table 4-1). But obviously, that's not true.

Previously held views of dominance and recessiveness were influenced by available technologies, and as genetic technologies continue to change, new theories will emerge, and our perceptions will be further altered. (This is another example of how new techniques and continued hypothesis testing can lead to a revision of hypotheses and theories.) In fact, although dominance and recessiveness will remain important factors in genetics, it's clear that the ways in which these concepts will be taught will be adapted to accommodate new discoveries.

Polygenic Inheritance

Mendelian traits are described as *discrete*, or *discontinuous*, because their phenotypic expressions don't overlap; instead, they fall into clearly defined categories (**Fig. 4-7a**). For example, in the ABO system, the four phenotypes are completely distinct from one another; that is, there is no intermediate form between type A and type B. In other words, Mendelian characteristics don't show *continuous* variation.

However, many characteristics do have a wide range of phenotypic expressions that form a graded series. These are called **polygenic**, or *continuous*, traits (**Fig. 4-7b and c**). While Mendelian traits are governed by only one genetic locus, polygenic characteristics are governed by alleles at two or more loci, and each locus has some influence on the phenotype. Throughout the history of physical anthropology, the most frequently discussed examples of polygenic inheritance in humans have been skin, hair, and eye color (**Fig. 4-8**).

Coloration is determined by melanin, a **pigment** produced by specialized cells called melanocytes (see Chapter 5); and the amount of melanin that is produced determines how dark or light a person's skin will be. Melanin production is influenced by interactions between several different loci. Interestingly, a study by Lamason and colleagues (2005) showed that one single, highly *conserved* gene (called *MC1R*) with two alleles makes a greater contribution to melanin production than some other melanin-producing genes do.* Moreover, geneticists know of at least four other pigmentation genes. This is very important because they can now examine the complex interactions between these genes. The story of melanin production is a complicated one, but it's exciting that

---

*Highly conserved genes are genes that are present in most, if not all, animal species and sometimes in plants. Genes that are found in most species are extremely important; they're evidence for shared ancestry and biological continuity. Variations in the *MC1R* gene that cause pigmentation differences occur throughout the animal kingdom in species ranging from zebra fish to dogs to humans. Similar variations have also been identified in preserved DNA of extinct species, including mammoths and Neandertals.

polygenic Referring to traits that are influenced by genes at two or more loci. Examples include stature, skin color, eye color, and hair color. Many (but not all) polygenic traits are influenced by environmental factors such as nutrition and exposure to sunlight.

pigment In this context, a molecule that influences the color of skin, hair, and eyes.

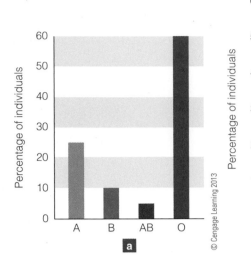

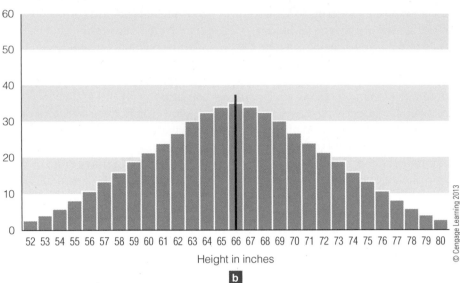

© Cengage Learning 2013

© Cengage Learning 2013

a

Height in inches

b

▲ **Figure 4-7**

(a) This bar graph shows the discontinuous distribution of a Mendelian trait (ABO blood type) in a hypothetical population. Expression of the trait is described in terms of frequencies. **(b)** This histogram represents the continuous expression of a polygenic trait (height) in a large group of people. Notice that the percentage of extremely short or tall individuals is low; most people are closer to the mean, or average height, represented by the vertical line at the center of the distribution. **(c)** A group of male students arranged according to height. The most common height is 70 inches, which is the mean, or average, for this group.

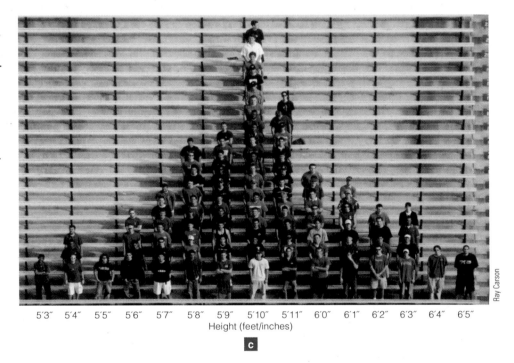

Ray Carson

Height (feet/inches)

c

many long-standing questions about variation in human skin color will be answered in the not too distant future. (See Chapter 5 for further discussion of variation in pigmentation.)

Polygenic traits actually account for most of the readily observable phenotypic variation in humans and other species, and they've traditionally served as a basis for racial classification (see Chapter 5). In addition to skin, hair, and eye color, there are many other polygenic characteristics, including stature, shape of the face, and fingerprint pattern, to name a few. Because they show continuous variation, most polygenic traits can be measured on a scale composed of equal increments. For example, height (stature) is measured in feet and inches (or meters and centimeters). If we were to measure height in a large number of individuals, the distribution of measurements would continue uninterrupted from the shortest extreme to the tallest (see Fig. 4-7b and c). That's what is meant by the term *continuous traits*.

Quick Review

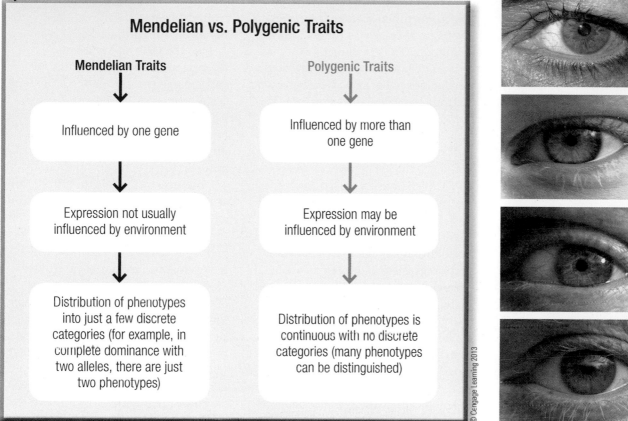

Mendelian vs. Polygenic Traits

Mendelian Traits

↓

Influenced by one gene

↓

Expression not usually influenced by environment

↓

Distribution of phenotypes into just a few discrete categories (for example, in complete dominance with two alleles, there are just two phenotypes)

Polygenic Traits

↓

Influenced by more than one gene

↓

Expression may be influenced by environment

↓

Distribution of phenotypes is continuous with no discrete categories (many phenotypes can be distinguished)

© Cengage Learning 2013

Mendelian traits can't be measured in the same way because they're either present or absent or manifested one way or another. But this doesn't mean that Mendelian characteristics provide less information about genetic processes. Mendelian characteristics can be described in terms of frequency within populations, and this makes it possible to compare groups for differences in prevalence. For example, one population may have a high frequency of blood type A, while in another group, type A may be almost completely absent. Also, Mendelian traits can be analyzed for mode of inheritance (dominant or recessive). Lastly, for many Mendelian traits, the approximate or exact positions of genetic loci are known, and this makes it possible to examine the mechanisms and patterns of inheritance at these loci. This type of study isn't yet possible for polygenic traits because they're influenced by several genes that are only now being traced to specific loci.

Genetic and Environmental Factors

By now you may have the impression that phenotypes are entirely the expressions of genotypes; but that's not true. (Here the terms *genotype* and *phenotype* are used in a broader sense to refer to an individual's *entire* genetic makeup and *all* observable or detectable characteristics.) Genotypes set limits and potentials for development, but they also interact with the environment, so that certain phenotypic expressions are influenced by this genetic–environmental interaction. For example, adult stature is influenced by both genes and the environment. Even though the maximum height a person can achieve is genetically determined, childhood nutrition (an environmental factor) is also important. Other important

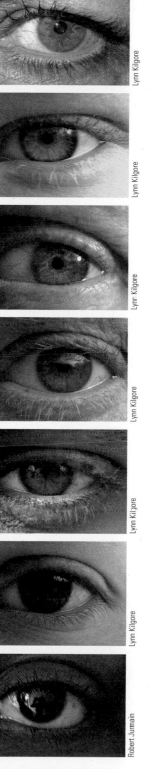

▲ **FIGURE 4-8**
Eye color is a polygenic characteristic and is a good example of continuous variation.

environmental factors include exposure to sunlight, altitude, temperature, and, unfortunately, increasing levels of exposure to toxic waste and airborne pollutants. These and many other factors contribute in complex ways to the continuous phenotypic variation seen in traits governed by several genetic loci. However, for many characteristics, it's not possible to identify the *specific* environmental components that influence the phenotype.

Mendelian traits are less likely to be influenced by environmental factors. For example, ABO blood type is determined at fertilization and remains fixed throughout an individual's lifetime, regardless of diet, exposure to ultraviolet radiation, temperature, and so forth.

Mendelian and polygenic inheritance produce different patterns of phenotypic variation. In the former, variation occurs in discrete categories, while in the latter, it's continuous. However, it's important to understand that even for polygenic characteristics, Mendelian principles still apply at individual loci. In other words, if a trait is influenced by six loci, each one of those loci may have two or more alleles, with some perhaps being dominant to others. It's the combined action of the alleles at all six loci, interacting with the environment that produces the phenotype.

Mitochondrial Inheritance

Another component of inheritance involves the organelles called *mitochondria* (see Chapter 3). All cells contain several hundred of these oval-shaped structures that convert energy (derived from the breakdown of nutrients) to a form that can be used by cells.

Each mitochondrion contains several copies of a ring-shaped DNA molecule, or chromosome. While *mitochondrial DNA (mtDNA)* is distinct from chromosomal DNA, its molecular structure and functions are the same. The entire molecule has been sequenced and is known to contain around 40 genes that direct the conversion of energy within cells.

Like the DNA in a cell's nucleus, mtDNA is subject to mutations, and some of these mutations cause certain genetic disorders that result from impaired energy conversion. Importantly, animals of both sexes inherit all their mtDNA, and thus all mitochondrial traits, from their mothers. Because mtDNA is inherited from only one parent, meiosis and recombination don't occur. This means that all the variation in mtDNA among individuals is caused by mutation, which makes mtDNA extremely useful for studying genetic change over time. So far, geneticists have used mutation rates in mtDNA to investigate evolutionary relationships between species, to trace ancestral relationships within the human lineage, and to study genetic variability among individuals and/or populations. While these techniques are still being refined, it's clear that we have a lot to learn from mtDNA.

Modern Evolutionary Theory

By the beginning of the twentieth century, the foundations for evolutionary theory had already been developed. Darwin and Wallace had described natural selection 40 years earlier, and the rediscovery of Mendelian genetics in 1900 contributed the other major component, namely, a mechanism for inheritance. We might expect that these two basic contributions would have been combined into a consistent theory of evolution, but they weren't. For the first 30 years of the twentieth century, some scientists argued that mutation was the main factor in evolution, while others emphasized natural selection. What they really needed was a merger of the two views; but this didn't happen until the 1930s.

The Modern Synthesis

In the late 1920s and early 1930s, biologists realized that mutation and natural selection weren't opposing processes. Rather, they *both* contributed to biological evolution. The two major foundations of the biological sciences had finally been brought together in what is called the Modern Synthesis. From this perspective, we define evolution as a two-stage process:

1. The production and redistribution of **variation** (inherited differences among organisms);
2. *Natural selection* acting on this variation, whereby inherited differences, or variation, among individuals differentially affect their ability to successfully reproduce.

A Current Definition of Evolution

As we discussed in Chapter 2, Darwin saw evolution as the gradual unfolding of new varieties of life from pre-existing ones. Certainly, this is one result of the evolutionary process. But these long-term effects can come about only through the accumulation of many small genetic changes occurring over many generations. Today, we can demonstrate how evolution works by examining some of the small genetic changes and how they increase or decrease in frequency. From this perspective, we define evolution as *a change in* **allele frequency** *from one generation to the next.*

Allele frequencies are indicators of the genetic makeup of a **population**, the members of which share a common **gene pool**. To show how allele frequencies change, we'll use a simplified example of an inherited trait, again the ABO blood types.

Let's assume that the students in your anthropology class represent a population and that we've determined everyone's ABO blood type. (To be considered a population, individuals must choose mates more often from *within* the group than from outside it. Obviously, your class won't meet this requirement, but we'll overlook this point.) The proportions of the *A*, *B*, and *O* alleles are the allele frequencies for this trait. If 50 percent of all the *ABO* alleles in your class are *A*, 40 percent are *B*, and 10 percent are *O*, then the frequencies of these alleles are *A* = .50, *B* = .40, and *O* = .10.

Since the frequencies of these alleles represent proportions of a total, it's obvious that allele frequencies can refer only to groups of individuals, or populations. Individuals don't have allele frequencies; they have either *A*, *B*, or *O* in any combination of two. Also, from conception onward, a person's genetic composition is fixed. If you start out with blood type A, you'll always have type A. Therefore, only a population can evolve over time; individuals can't.

Assume that 20 years from now, we calculate the frequencies of the *ABO* alleles for the children of our classroom population and find the following: *A* = .30, *B* = .40, and *O* = .30. We can see that the relative proportions have changed: *A* has decreased, *O* has increased, and *B* has remained the same. This wouldn't be a big deal, but in a biological sense, minor changes such as this constitute evolution. Over the short span of just a few generations, changes in the frequencies of inherited traits may be very small; but if they continue to happen, and particularly if they go in one direction as a result of natural selection, they can produce new adaptations and even new species.

Whether we're talking about the short-term effects (as in our classroom population) from one generation to the next, which is sometimes called **microevolution**, or the long-term effects through time, called speciation or **macroevolution**, the basic evolutionary mechanisms are similar. But how do allele frequencies change? Or, to put it another way, what causes evolution? As we've already said, evolution is a two-stage process. Genetic variation must first be produced by mutation, and then it can be acted on by natural selection.

variation In genetics, inherited differences among individuals; the basis of all evolutionary change.

allele frequency In a population, the percentage of all the alleles at a locus accounted for by one specific allele.

population Within a species, a community of individuals where mates are usually found.

gene pool All of the genes shared by the reproductive members of a population.

microevolution Small changes occurring within species, such as changes in allele frequencies.

macroevolution Changes produced only after many generations, such as the appearance of a new species.

Factors That Produce and Redistribute Variation

Mutation

You've already learned that a change in DNA is a type of mutation, and that many genes have two or more forms called alleles (*A*, *B*, or *O*, for example). If one allele changes to another, that is, if the gene itself is altered, a mutation has occurred. In fact, alleles are the results of mutation. Even the substitution of one single DNA base for another, called a *point mutation*, can cause the allele to change. But point mutations have to occur in sex cells if they're going to have evolutionary consequences. This is because, in order for evolutionary change to happen, mutations must be passed from one generation to the next. If a mutation doesn't occur in a gamete, the individual will possess it but won't pass it on to offspring. If, however, a genetic change occurs in the sperm or egg of one of the students in our classroom (*A* mutates to *B*, for instance), the offspring's blood type will be different from that of the parent, causing a minute shift in the allele frequencies of the next generation.

Actually, except in microorganisms, it's rare for evolution to happen solely because of mutations. Mutation rates for any given trait are usually low, so we wouldn't really expect to see a mutation at the *ABO* locus in so small a population as your class. In larger populations, mutations might occur in 1 individual out of 10,000, but by themselves they would have no impact on allele frequencies. However, when mutation is combined with natural selection, evolutionary changes can occur more rapidly.

It's important to remember that mutation is the basic creative force in evolution, since it's the *only* way to produce *new* genes (that is, variation). Its role in the production of variation is key to the first stage of the evolutionary process.

Gene Flow

Gene flow is the exchange of genes between populations. The term *migration* is also sometimes used; but strictly speaking, migration refers to the movement of people. In contrast, gene flow only occurs when the migrants interbreed. Also, even if individuals move temporarily and have offspring in the new population (thus leaving a genetic contribution), they don't necessarily stay there. For example, the children of U.S. soldiers and Vietnamese women represent gene flow. Even though the fathers returned to the United States after the Vietnam War, some of their genes remained behind, although not in sufficient numbers to appreciably change allele frequencies.

In humans, mating patterns are mostly determined by social factors, and cultural anthropologists can work closely with biological anthropologists to isolate and measure this aspect of evolutionary change. Human population movements (particularly in the last 500 years) have reached previously unheard of proportions, and very few breeding isolates remain. But migration on a smaller scale has been a consistent feature of human evolution, and gene flow between populations (even though sometimes limited) helps explain why speciation has been rare during the past million years or so.

One example of how gene flow influences microevolutionary changes in modern human populations is seen in African Americans. African Americans are largely of West African descent, but there has also been considerable genetic admixture with European Americans. By measuring allele frequencies for specific genetic loci, we can estimate the amount of migration of European alleles into the African American gene pool. Data from northern and western U.S. cities (including New York, Detroit, and Oakland) have shown that the proportion of *non*-African genes in the African American gene pool is 20 to 25 percent (Cummings, 2000). However,

gene flow Exchange of genes between populations.

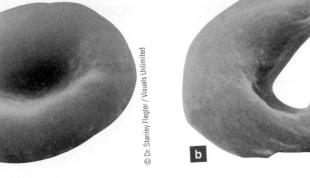

1
lectron micrograph
ly oxygenated red
Scanning electron
a collapsed,
d red blood cell that
oglobin S.

© Dr. Stanley Flegler / Visuals Unlimited

© Dr. Stanley Flegler / Visuals Unlimited

Natural Selection Is Directional and Acts on Variation

The evolutionary factors just discussed (mutation, gene flow, genetic drift, and recombination) interact to produce variation and to distribute genes within and between populations. But there is no long-term *direction* to any of these factors, and for adaptation and evolution to occur, a population's gene pool needs to change in a specific direction. This means that some alleles must consistently become more common, while others become less common, and natural selection is the one factor that can cause directional change in allele frequency *relative to specific environmental factors*. If the environment changes, selection pressures change, and ultimately, allele frequencies also change. Such a shift in allele frequencies is called *adaptation*.

In humans, the best-documented example of natural selection involves hemoglobin S (Hb^S), an abnormal form of hemoglobin that results from a point mutation in the gene that produces part of the hemoglobin molecule. Worldwide, the Hb^S allele is rare. Most people are homozygous for the Hb^A allele (Hb^A/Hb^A), and they produce normal hemoglobin. People who have one copy of each allele (that is, they're heterozygotes with the Hb^A/Hb^S genotype) have a condition called **sickle-cell trait**, and although some of their hemoglobin is abnormal, enough of it

is normal to allow them to function normally under most circumstances. But people who inherit the Hb^S allele from both parents (Hb^S/Hb^S) produce no normal hemoglobin, and they have a very serious condition called **sickle-cell anemia.**

Sickle-cell anemia has numerous manifestations, but basically, the abnormal hemoglobin S reduces the ability of red blood cells to transport oxygen throughout the body. When people with sickle-cell anemia increase their body's demand for oxygen (for example, while exercising or traveling to high altitude), their red blood cells collapse and form a shape similar to a sickle (**Fig. 4-11**). Consequently, these cells can't carry adequate amounts of oxygen. What's more, they also clump together and block small capillaries, restricting blood flow and depriving vital organs of oxygen. Even with treatment, life expectancy in the United States today is less than 45 years for patients with sickle-cell anemia. Worldwide, sickle-cell anemia causes an estimated 100,000 deaths each year, and in the United States, approximately 40,000 to 50,000 individuals, mostly of African descent, suffer from this condition.

The Hb^S mutation occurs occasionally in all human populations. However, in some populations, especially in western and central Africa, it's more common than elsewhere, with frequencies as high as 20 percent. The Hb^S allele is also fairly common in parts of Greece and India (**Fig. 4-12**).

ell trait Heterozygous
h which a person has one Hb^A
ne Hb^S allele. Thus they have
al hemoglobin.

cell anemia A severe inher-
globin disorder in which red
collapse when deprived of
t results from inheriting two
a mutant allele. This allele is
y a single base substitution in

Time

A small population with considerable genetic variability. Note that the dark green and blue alleles are less common than the other alleles.

After just a few generations, the population is approximately the same size but genetic variation has been reduced. Both the dark green and blue alleles have been lost. Also, the red allele is less common and the frequency of the light green allele has increased.

Original population with considerable genetic variation

A small group leaves to colonize a new area, or a bottleneck occurs, so that population size decreases and genetic variation is reduced.

Population size restored but the dark green and purple alleles have been lost. The frequencies of the red and yellow alleles have also changed.

Population size

a

Population size

b

© Cengage Learning 2013

▲ **Figure 4-9**

Small populations are subject to genetic drift, where rare alleles can be lost because, just by chance, they weren't passed to offspring. Also, although more common alleles may not be lost, their frequencies may change for the same reason. **(a)** This diagram represents six alleles (different-colored dots) that occur at one genetic locus in a small population. You can see that in a fairly short period of time (three or four generations), rare alleles can be lost and genetic diversity consequently reduced. **(b)** This diagram illustrates founder effect, a form of genetic drift where diversity is lost

because a large population is drastically reduced in size and consequently passes through a genetic "bottleneck." Founder effect also happens when a small group leaves the larger group and "founds" a new population elsewhere. (In this case, the group of founders is represented by the bottleneck.) Those individuals that survive (or the founders) and the alleles they carry represent only a sample of the variation that was present in the original population. And future generations, all descended from the survivors (founders), will therefore have less variability.

more restricted data from the southern United States (Charleston and rural Georgia) indicated less gene flow than the rest of the country (4 to 11 percent).

Genetic Drift and Founder Effect

Genetic drift is the random factor in evolution, and it's a function of population size. *Drift occurs solely because the population is small.* If an allele is rare in a small population, it may completely disappear because, just by chance, it isn't passed on to offspring (**Fig. 4-9a**).

A particular kind of genetic drift, called **founder effect**, is seen in many

modern human and nonhuman populations. Founder effect can occur when a small band of "founders" leaves its parent group and forms a colony somewhere else. Over time, a new population will be established, and as long as mates are chosen only from within this population, all of its members will be descended from the small original group of founders. Therefore, all the genes in the expanding group will have come from the original colonists. In such a case, an allele that was rare in the parent population but was carried by even one of the founders can eventually become common among the founders' descendants (**Fig. 4-9b**). This

genetic drift Evolutionary changes, or changes in allele frequencies, that are produced by random factors in small populations. Genetic drift is a result of small population size.

founder effect A type of genetic drift in which allele frequencies are altered in small populations that are taken from, or are remnants of, larger populations.

is because a high proportion of people in later generations are all descended from that one individual.

Colonization isn't the only way founder effect can happen. Small founding groups may be the survivors of a larger group that was mostly wiped out by a disaster of some sort. But like the small group of colonists, the survivors possess only a sample of all the alleles that were present in the original population. Therefore, just by chance alone, some alleles may be completely lost from a population's gene pool, while others may become the only allele at a locus that previously had two or more. Whatever the cause, the outcome is a reduction in genetic diversity, and the allele frequencies of succeeding generations may be substantially different from those of the original, larger population. The loss of genetic diversity in this type of situation is called a *genetic bottleneck*, and the effects can be extremely detrimental to a species.

There are many known examples (both human and nonhuman) of species or populations that have passed through genetic bottlenecks. (In fact, right now many species are currently going through genetic bottlenecks.) Genetically, cheetahs (**Fig. 4-10**) are an extremely uniform species, and biologists believe that at some point in the

past, these magnificent cats suffered a catastrophic decline in numbers. For unknown reasons related to the species-wide loss of numerous alleles, male cheetahs produce a high percentage of defective sperm compared to other cat species. Decreased reproductive potential, greatly reduced genetic diversity, and other factors, including human hunting, have combined to jeopardize the continued existence of this species. Other species that have passed through genetic bottlenecks include California elephant seals, sea otters, and condors. Indeed, our own species is much more genetically uniform than chimpanzees, and it appears that all modern human populations are the descendants of a few small groups.

Many examples of founder effect have been documented in small, usually isolated populations (such as island groups or small agricultural villages in New Guinea or South America). Even larger populations that are descended from fairly small groups of founders can show the effects of genetic drift many generations later. For instance, French Canadians in Quebec, who currently number close to 6 million, are all descended from about 8,500 founders who left France during the sixteenth and seventeenth centuries. Because the genes carried by the initial founders represented only a sample of the gene pool from which they were derived, a number of alleles now occur in different frequencies from those of the current population of France. These differences include an increased presence of several harmful alleles, including those that cause some of the diseases listed in Table 4-1, such as cystic fibrosis, a variety of Tay-Sachs, thalassemia, and PKU (Scriver, 2001).

Examples such as this provide insight into the evolutionary factors that acted on our ancestors in the past. Throughout at least the last 4 to 5 million years, homi-

▶ **Figure 4-10**
Cheetahs, like many other species, have passed through a genetic bottleneck. Consequently, as a species they have little genetic variation.

Lynn Kilgore

nins probably lived in small groups, and drift probably had a significant impact. Also, there is good evidence to suggest that in the last 100,000 to 200,000 years, our species experienced a genetic bottleneck that considerably influenced the pattern of genetic variation seen in all human populations today.

As we've seen, both gene flow and genetic drift can produce some evolutionary changes by themselves. However, these changes are usually *microevolutionary* ones; that is, they produce changes within species over the short term. To produce the kind of evolutionary changes that ultimately result in new species (for example, the diversification of the first primates or the appearance of the earliest hominins), natural selection is necessary. But natural selection can't operate independently of the other evolutionary factors: mutation, gene flow, and genetic drift.

Recombination

As we saw in Chapter 3, members of chromosome pairs exchange segments of DNA during meiosis. By itself, recombination doesn't change allele frequencies, or cause evolution. However, when paired chromosomes exchange DNA, genes sometimes find themselves in different genetic environments. (It's like they've moved to a new neighborhood.) This fact can be important because the functions of some genes can be influenced simply by the alleles they're close to. Thus, recombination not only changes the composition of parts of chromosomes but also can affect how some genes act, and slight changes of gene function can become material for natural selection to act on. (The levels of organization in the evolutionary process are summarized in **Table 4-3**.)

▶ **Figure 4-**
(a) Scanning e
of a normal, fu
blood cell. (b)
micrograph o
sickle-shaped
contains hem

TABLE **4.3** Levels of Organization in the Evolutionary Process			
Evolutionary Factor	**Level**	**Evolutionary Process**	**Te of**
Mutation	DNA	Storage of genetic information; ability to replicate; influences phenotype by production of proteins	Bioc
Mutation	Chromosomes	A vehicle for packaging and transmitting genetic material (DNA)	Light
Recombination (sex cells only)	Cell	The basic unit of life that contains the chromosomes and divides for growth and for production of sex cells	Light
Natural selection	Organism	The unit, composed of cells, that reproduces and that we observe for phenotypic traits	Visual s
Drift, gene flow	Population	A group of interbreeding organisms; changes in allele frequencies between generations; it's the population that evolves	Statistica

sickle-c
condition
allele and
some nor

sickle-c
ited hemo
blood ce
oxygen.
copies o
caused
the DNA

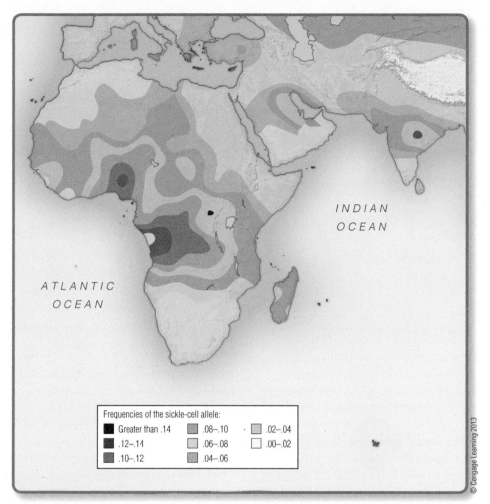

▲**Figure 4-12**
The distribution of the sickle-cell allele in the Old World.

Given the devastating effects of hemoglobin S in homozygotes, you may wonder why it's so common in some populations. It seems like natural selection would eliminate it, but it doesn't. The explanation for this situation can be summed up in one word: malaria.

Malaria is an infectious disease caused by a single-celled parasitic organism (**Fig. 4-13**). The organism is transmitted to humans by mosquitoes, and it kills an estimated 1 to 3 million people worldwide every year. After an infected mosquito bite, these parasites invade red blood cells, where they obtain oxygen, which they need for reproduction. The consequences of this infection include fever, chills, headache, nausea, vomiting, and frequently death. In parts of western and

central Africa, where malaria is always present, as many as 50 to 75 percent of 2- to 9-year-olds are afflicted.

In the mid-twentieth century, the geographical correlation between malaria and the distribution of the sickle-cell allele (Hb^S) was the only evidence of a biological relationship between the two (Figs. 4-12 and **4-14**). But now we know that people with sickle-cell trait have greater resistance to malaria than people with only normal hemoglobin. This is because people with sickle-cell trait have some red blood cells that contain hemoglobin S, and these cells don't provide a suitable environment for the malarial parasite. In other words, having some hemoglobin S is beneficial because it affords some protection from malaria. So, in

▶**Figure 4-13**
The distribution of malaria in the Old World.

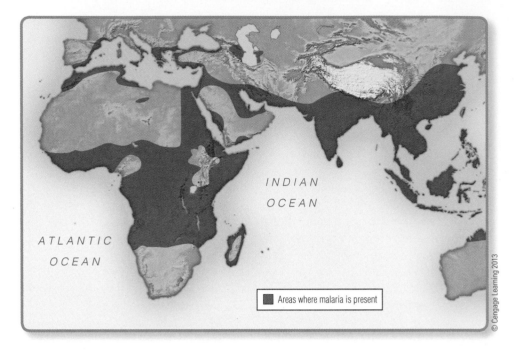

INDIAN OCEAN

ATLANTIC OCEAN

▪ Areas where malaria is present

© Cengage Learning 2013

regions where malaria is present, it acts as a selective agent that favors the heterozygous phenotype, because people with sickle-cell trait produce more offspring than those with only normal hemoglobin, who may die of malaria. But selection for heterozygotes means that the Hb^S allele will be maintained in the population. Thus, there will always be some people with sickle-cell anemia, and they, of course, have the lowest reproductive success, since without treatment, most die before reaching adulthood.

▼**Figure 4-14**
The life cycle of the parasite that causes malaria.

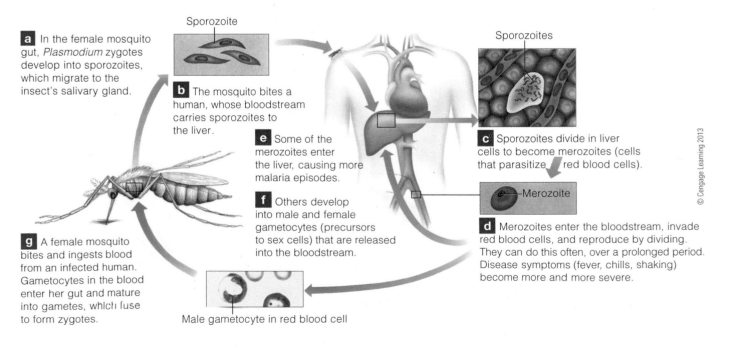

a In the female mosquito gut, *Plasmodium* zygotes develop into sporozoites, which migrate to the insect's salivary gland.

Sporozoite

b The mosquito bites a human, whose bloodstream carries sporozoites to the liver.

e Some of the merozoites enter the liver, causing more malaria episodes.

f Others develop into male and female gametocytes (precursors to sex cells) that are released into the bloodstream.

g A female mosquito bites and ingests blood from an infected human. Gametocytes in the blood enter her gut and mature into gametes, which fuse to form zygotes.

Male gametocyte in red blood cell

Sporozoites

c Sporozoites divide in liver cells to become merozoites (cells that parasitize red blood cells).

Merozoite

d Merozoites enter the bloodstream, invade red blood cells, and reproduce by dividing. They can do this often, over a prolonged period. Disease symptoms (fever, chills, shaking) become more and more severe.

© Cengage Learning 2013

Review of Genetics and Evolutionary Factors

In this chapter, discussion focused on how genetic information is passed from one generation to the next. We also reviewed evolutionary theory, emphasizing the crucial role of natural selection. The various levels (molecular, cellular, individual, and populational) are different components of the evolutionary process, and they're related to each other in ways that can eventually produce evolutionary change. A step-by-step example will make this clear.

Consider a population in which almost everyone has hemoglobin A. Thus, there is almost no variation regarding this trait, and without some source of new variation, evolution isn't possible. However, in every generation, a few people carry a spontaneous mutation that changes just one DNA base in the Hb^A gene. This base substitution, which actually creates a new allele (Hb^S), slightly alters the protein product (the hemoglobin molecule). But for the mutated allele to have any evolutionary potential, it must be transmitted to offspring. And, if a person has the mutation on only one member of a pair of chromosomes, there's a 50-50 chance that the mutation will be passed on to each offspring.

To repeat an earlier definition, evolution is a change in allele frequencies in a population from one generation to the next. The key point here is that we are considering populations, because it's populations that change over time. We can determine if allele frequencies have changed in a population where sickle-cell hemoglobin is found by calculating the percentage of individuals with the Hb^S allele versus those with the normal allele (Hb^A). If the relative proportions of these alleles change with time, the population is evolving at the Hb^A locus. But in addition to knowing that evolution is happening, it's important to know why, and there are several possible explanations. First, the only way the new Hb^S allele could have arisen is by mutation, and we've shown how this can happen in a single individual. But this isn't an evolutionary change, since in a large population, the alteration of one person's genes won't change allele frequencies. Somehow, this new allele must *spread* in the population; and in the case of Hb^S, the allele spread because it was favored by natural selection.

As you learned earlier, genetic drift can also greatly alter the frequencies of alleles in small populations. Just by chance, some alleles may not be passed on, and after a few generations, they're completely lost. Other alleles, meanwhile, may end up being the only allele at a particular locus.

In the course of human evolution, drift has probably played a significant role, and it's important to remember that at this microevolutionary level, drift and/or gene flow can (and will) produce evolutionary change, even in the absence of natural selection. However, such change will be random because natural selection is the only factor that can cause allele frequencies to change in a particular direction. The way this has worked in the past and still operates today (as with sickle-cell hemoglobin) is through differential reproduction. That is, individuals who carry a particular allele or combination of alleles produce more offspring than other individuals with different alleles. Hence, the frequency of a new allele in the population may increase slowly from generation to generation. When this process is compounded over hundreds of generations at numerous loci, the result is significant evolutionary change. The levels of organization in the evolutionary process are summarized in Table 4-3 on page 89.

Why It Matters

As you learned on pages 76 and 77, many human disorders are caused by mutations in genes (alleles) at one locus. This has practical implications for many of us who may eventually have to make important life decisions due to a family history of genetic disease. Obviously, the more we know about Mendelian disorders, the better prepared we are to make such decisions.

Huntington disease is a neurological disorder that affects approximately 1 out of every 100,000 people, and it's caused by a dominant mutation on chromosome 4. Because this disease is caused by a dominant allele, you only have to inherit one copy of the mutant allele to eventually get the disease. Also, a person who has the allele has a 50-50 chance of passing it on to each child he or she has.

In Huntington disease, brain cells are destroyed. Symptoms include erratic behavior, confusion, uncontrollable movement, loss of cognitive abilities, and eventually death. There is no cure, and tragically, the symptoms of most forms of Huntington disease don't appear until a person is between the ages of 35 and 45. By this time, most people who want children have already had them and may have unknowingly passed the mutant allele on to their offspring.

There's a test for Huntington disease, and people who have a parent with symptoms can learn whether or not they themselves have inherited it. Certainly, anyone who has an affected parent should be tested before they, in turn, have children. But just suppose that one of your parents has been diagnosed with Huntington disease. What would you do? Would you be tested?

Because you know about Mendelian traits, you know that you have a 50 percent chance of having the Huntington disease allele. If you have the test, there are only two outcomes: You'll either be extremely relieved by the results or you'll have to cope with the knowledge that you're going to develop a severe neurological disease that ultimately will kill you. It's just this kind of scenario that makes it important for people to be at least minimally informed about how traits are inherited. After all, it's estimated that every one of us has inherited around seven detrimental alleles that have huge impacts on individual health, growth, and development.

Summary of Main Topics

- In the mid-nineteenth century, Gregor Mendel discovered the principles of segregation, independent assortment, and dominance and recessiveness. Although the field of genetics progressed dramatically during the twentieth century, the concepts first put forth by Mendel remain the basis of our current knowledge of how traits are inherited.
- Basic Mendelian principles are applied to the study of the various modes of inheritance we're familiar with today. The most important factor in all the Mendelian modes of inheritance is the role of segregation of chromosomes, and the alleles they carry, during meiosis.
- Building on fundamental nineteenth-century contributions by Charles Darwin and the rediscovery of Mendel's work in 1900, advances in genetics throughout the twentieth century contributed to contemporary evolutionary thought. In particular, the combination of natural selection with Mendel's principles of inheritance and experimental evidence concerning the nature of mutation have all been synthesized into a modern understanding of evolutionary change, appropriately called the Modern Synthesis. In this, the contemporary theory of evolution, evolutionary change is seen as a two-stage process. The first stage is the production and redistribution of variation. The second stage is the process whereby natural selection acts on the accumulated genetic variation.
- Mutation is crucial to all evolutionary change because it's the only source of completely new genetic material (that is, new alleles), which increases variation. In addition, the factors of recombination, genetic drift, and gene

flow redistribute variation within individuals (recombination), within populations (genetic drift), and between populations (gene flow).

- Natural selection is the central determining factor that influences the long-term direction of evolutionary change. How natural selection works can best be explained as differential net reproductive success, or how successful individuals are, compared to others, in producing offspring who, in turn, reproduce. The detailed history of the evolutionary spread of the sickle-cell allele provides the best-documented example of natural selection among recent human populations. It must be remembered that evolution is an integrated process, and this chapter concluded with a discussion of how the various evolutionary factors can be integrated into a single comprehensive view of evolutionary change.

Critical Thinking Questions

1. If two people with blood type A, both with the *AO* genotype, have children, what *proportion* of their children would be expected to have blood type O? Understanding the underlying principles that allow you to answer this question could potentially be relevant to you personally. How?

2. After having read this chapter, do you understand evolutionary processes more completely? What questions do you still have?

3. Sickle-cell anemia is frequently described as affecting only Africans or people of African descent; it's considered a "racial" disease that doesn't affect other populations. How would you explain to someone that this view is wrong?

4. Give some examples of how selection, gene flow, genetic drift, and mutation have acted on populations or species in the past. Try to think of at least one human and one nonhuman example. Why do you think genetic drift might be important today to endangered species?

Connections

Modern humans first evolved in Africa and later spread to other areas of the world.

Modern human variation is best understood by looking at patterns of DNA in different populations.

Human development and adaptation is best understood from an evolutionary perspective.

BROWN

5

Modern Human Biology: Patterns of Variation and Adaptation

Notions about human diversity have played an enormous role in human relations for at least a few thousand years, and they still influence political and social perceptions. Although we'd like to believe that informed views have become universal, the gruesome record of genocidal and ethnic cleansing atrocities in recent years tells us that, worldwide, we have a long way to go before tolerance becomes the norm.

In this chapter, we continue to discuss a topic that directly relates to genetics, namely, human biological diversity and how humans adapt physically to environmental challenges. After discussing historical attempts at explaining variations in human phenotypes and racial classification, we examine current methods of interpreting some aspects of variation. In recent years, techniques have been developed that allow scientists to directly examine the DNA molecule, and this research is revealing differences among people even at the level of single nucleotides. But as discoveries of different levels of diversity emerge, geneticists have also shown that our species is genetically very uniform, particularly when compared with other species.

Historical Views of Human Variation

The first step toward understanding diversity in nature is to organize it into categories that can then be named, discussed, and perhaps studied. Historically, when different groups of people came into contact with one another, they tried to account for the physical differences they saw. Because skin color is so noticeable, it was one of the more frequently explained traits, and most systems of racial classification were based on it.

As early as 1350 B.C., the ancient Egyptians had classified humans based on their skin color: red for Egyptian, yellow for people to the east, white for those to the north, and black for sub-Saharan Africans (Gossett, 1963). In the sixteenth

◄ Research station in Antarctica.

century, after the discovery of the New World, several European countries embarked on a period of intense exploration and colonization in both the New and Old Worlds. One result of this contact was an increased awareness of human diversity.

Throughout the eighteenth and nineteenth centuries, European and American scientists concentrated primarily on describing and classifying the biological variation in humans as well as in nonhuman species. The first scientific attempt to describe variation among human populations was Linnaeus' taxonomic classification (see Chapter 2), which placed humans into four separate categories (Linnaeus, 1758). Linnaeus assigned behavioral and intellectual qualities to each group, with the least complimentary descriptions going to sub-Saharan, dark-skinned Africans. This ranking was typical of the period and reflected the almost universal European ethnocentric view that Europeans were superior to everyone else.

Johann Friedrich Blumenbach (1752–1840), a German anatomist, classified humans into five races, which were often simply described as white, yellow, red, black, and brown. Blumenbach also used criteria other than skin color, and he acknowledged that his system had limitations. For example, he emphasized that categories based on skin color were arbitrary and that many traits, including skin color, weren't discrete phenomena because their expression often overlapped between groups. He also pointed out that classifying all humans using such a system would omit everyone who didn't neatly fall into a specific category. (That means ignoring a lot of people!)

Nevertheless, by the mid-nineteenth century, populations were essentially ranked on a scale based on skin color (along with size and shape of the head), again with sub-Saharan Africans at the bottom. The Europeans themselves were also ranked, with northern, light-skinned populations considered superi-

or to their southern, somewhat darker-skinned neighbors in Italy and Greece.

To many Europeans, the fact that non-Europeans weren't Christian suggested that they were "uncivilized," and implied an even more basic inferiority of character and intellect. This view was rooted in a concept called **biological determinism**, which in part holds that there's an association between physical characteristics and such attributes as intelligence, morals, values, abilities, and even social and economic status. In other words, cultural variations were believed to be *inherited* in the same way that biological differences are. It followed, then, that there are inherent behavioral and cognitive differences between groups and that some groups are by nature superior to others.

After 1850, biological determinism was a constant theme underlying common thinking as well as scientific research in Europe and the United States. Most people, including such notables as Thomas Jefferson, Georges Cuvier, Benjamin Franklin, Charles Lyell, Abraham Lincoln, Charles Darwin, and Supreme Court justice Oliver Wendell Holmes, held deterministic (and what today we'd call racist) views. Commenting on this usually de-emphasized characteristic of such respected historical figures, the late evolutionary biologist Stephen J. Gould (1981, p. 32) remarked that "all American culture heroes embraced racial attitudes that would embarrass public-school mythmakers."

Francis Galton (1822–1911), Charles Darwin's cousin, shared an increasingly common fear among nineteenth-century Europeans that "civilized society" was being weakened by the failure of natural selection to eliminate unfit and inferior members (Greene, 1981, p. 107). Galton wrote and lectured on the necessity of "race improvement" and suggested government regulation of marriage and family size, an approach he called **eugenics**. Although eugenics had its share of critics, its popularity flourished until the 1930s. Nowhere was it more embraced

biological determinism The concept that phenomena, including various aspects of behavior (e.g., intelligence, values, morals) are governed by biological (genetic) factors; the inaccurate association of various behavioral attributes with certain biological traits, such as skin color.

eugenics The philosophy of "race improvement" through the forced sterilization of members of some groups and increased reproduction among others; an overly simplified, often racist view that's now discredited.

than in Germany, where the viewpoint took a horrifying turn. The false idea of pure races was increasingly extolled as a means of reestablishing a strong and prosperous state, and eugenics was seen as scientific justification for purging Germany of its "unfit." Many of Germany's scientists supported the policies of racial purity and eugenics during the Nazi period (Proctor, 1988, p. 143), when these ideologies served as justification for condemning millions of people to death.

But at the same time, many scientists were turning away from racial typologies and classification in favor of a more evolutionary approach. No doubt for some, this shift in direction was motivated by their growing concerns over the goals of the eugenics movement. Probably more important, however, was the synthesis of genetics and Darwin's theories of natural selection during the 1930s. As discussed in Chapter 4, this breakthrough influenced all the biological sciences, and some physical anthropologists soon began applying evolutionary principles to the study of human variation.

The Concept of Race

All contemporary humans are members of the same **polytypic** species, *Homo sapiens*. A polytypic species is composed of local populations that differ in the expression of one or more traits. Still it's crucial to recognize that even *within local populations, there's a great deal of genotypic and phenotypic variation between individuals.*

Nevertheless, in discussions of human variation, most people have traditionally combined various characteristics, such as skin color, face shape, nose shape, hair color, hair form (curly or straight), and eye color. People who have particular combinations of these and other traits have been placed together in categories associated with specific geographical localities. These categories are called *races*.

We all think we know what we mean by the word *race*, but in reality, the term has had various meanings since the 1500s, when it first appeared in the English language. Race has been used synonymously with *species*, as in "the human race." Since the 1600s, race has also referred to various culturally defined groups, and this meaning is still common. For example, you'll hear people say, "the English race" or "the Japanese race," when they actually mean nationality. Another phrase you've probably heard is "the Jewish race," when the speaker is really talking about an ethnic and religious identity.

So even though race is usually a term with biological connotations, it also has enormous social significance. There's also still a widespread perception that certain physical traits (skin color, in particular) are associated with intelligence and numerous cultural attributes (such as occupational preferences, and even morality). As a result, in many cultural contexts, a person's social identity is strongly influenced by the way he or she expresses those physical traits traditionally used to define "racial groups." Characteristics such as skin color are highly visible, and they make it easy to superficially place people into socially defined categories. However, so-called racial traits aren't the only phenotypic expressions that contribute to social identity. Sex and age are also critically important. But aside from these two variables, an individual's biological and/or ethnic background is still inevitably a factor that influences how he or she is initially perceived and judged by others.

References to national origin (for example, African, Asian) as substitutes for racial labels have become more common in recent years, both within and outside anthropology. Within anthropology, the term *ethnicity* was proposed in the early 1950s to avoid the more emotionally charged race. Strictly speaking, ethnicity refers to cultural factors, but the fact that the words ethnicity and race are used interchangeably reflects the social importance of

polytypic Referring to species composed of populations that differ in the expression of one or more traits.

phenotypic expression and demonstrates once again how phenotype is mistakenly associated with culturally defined variables.

In its most common biological usage, the term *race* refers to geographically patterned phenotypic variation within a species. By the seventeenth century, naturalists were beginning to describe races in plants and nonhuman animals. They had recognized that when populations of a species occupied different regions, they sometimes differed from one another in the expression of one or more traits. But even today, there are no established criteria for assessing races of plants and animals, including humans. As a result, biologists now almost never refer to "races" of other species, but more typically talk about *populations* or, for major subdivisions, *subspecies*.

Before World War II, most studies of human variation focused on visible phenotypic variation between large, geographically defined populations, and these studies were largely descriptive. But in the last 60 years or so, the emphasis has shifted to examining the differences in allele frequencies (and, more basically, DNA differences) within and between populations, as well as considering the adaptive significance of phenotypic and genotypic variation. This shift in focus occurred partly because of the Modern Synthesis in biology. But now, armed with genome data sets for populations, biologists have an unprecedented opportunity to study and explain human variation and the role evolutionary factors have played in producing it (Pritchard et al, 2010).

In the twentieth century, the application of evolutionary principles to the study of modern human variation replaced the superficial nineteenth-century view of race *based solely on observed phenotype.* Additionally, the genetic emphasis dispelled previously held misconceptions that races are fixed biological entities that don't change over time and that are composed of individuals who all conform to a particular *type.* Clearly, there are phenotypic differences between humans, and some of these differences roughly correspond to particular geographical locations. But we need to ask if there's any adaptive significance attached to these differences. Is genetic drift a factor? What is the degree of underlying genetic variation that influences phenotypic variation? What influence has culture played in the past? These questions place considerations of human variation within a contemporary evolutionary, biocultural framework.

Although physical anthropology is partly rooted in attempts to explain human diversity, no contemporary anthropologist subscribes to pre–Modern Synthesis concepts of races (human or nonhuman) as fixed biological entities. Anthropologists recognize that such outdated concepts of race are no longer valid, because the amount of genetic variation accounted for by differences *between* groups is vastly exceeded by the variation that exists *within* groups. Many anthropologists also argue that race is an outdated creation of the human mind that attempts to simplify biological complexity by organizing it into categories. Simplistic racial classification may have been an acceptable approach 100 years ago, but given the current state of genetic and evolutionary science, it's absolutely meaningless.

However, many biological anthropologists continue to study differences in such traits as skin or eye color because these characteristics, and the genes that influence them, can yield information about population adaptation, genetic drift, mutation, and gene flow. Forensic anthropologists, in particular, find the phenotypic criteria associated with ancestry (especially as reflected in the skeleton) to have practical applications. Law enforcement agencies frequently call on forensic anthropologists to help identify human remains. Because unidentified human remains are often those of crime victims, identification must be as accurate as possible. The most important variables in such identification are the individual's sex, age, stature, and ancestry ("racial" and ethnic background). Forensic anthropologists use various techniques to determine the ancestry of a person whose remains have been found, and their findings are accurate about 80 percent of the time (Owsley et al., 2009).

Another major limitation of traditional classification schemes derives from their inherently *typological* nature, meaning that categories are distinct and based on stereotypes or ideals that comprise a specific set of traits. So in general, typologies are

inherently misleading because any grouping always includes many individuals who don't conform to all aspects of a particular type. In any so-called racial group, there are individuals who fall into the normal range of variation for another group based on one or several characteristics. For example, two people of different ancestry might differ in skin color, but they could share any number of other traits, including height, shape of head, hair color, eye color, and ABO blood type. In fact, they could easily share more similarities with each other than they do with many members of their own populations (**Fig. 5-1**).

▲ **Figure 5-1**
Some examples of phenotypic variation among Africans.
(a) San (South African)
(b) West African (Bantu)
(c) Ethiopian
(d) Ituri (central African)
(e) North African (Tunisia)

To blur this picture further, the characteristics that have traditionally been used to define races are *polygenic;* that is, they're influenced by more than one gene and therefore exhibit a continuous range of expression. So it's difficult, if not impossible, to draw distinct boundaries between populations with regard to many traits. This limitation becomes clear if you ask yourself, At what point is hair color no longer dark brown but medium brown, or no longer light brown but dark blond? (Look back at Figure 4-8 for an illustration showing variability in eye color.)

The scientific controversy over race will fade as we enhance our understanding of the genetic diversity (and uniformity) of our species. Given the rapid advances in genome studies, dividing the human species into racial categories is not a biologically meaningful way to look at human variation. But among the general public, variations on the theme of race will undoubtedly continue to be the most common view of human variation. Keeping all this in mind, anthropologists and biologists must continue exploring the issue so that, to the best of our abilities, accurate information about human variation is available to anyone who seeks informed explanations of complex phenomena.

Contemporary Interpretations of Human Variation

Because the physical characteristics (such as skin color and hair form) that are used to define race are *polygenic*, precisely measuring the genetic influence on them hasn't been possible. But geneticists are now able to identify many of the genes that influence continuous traits (Gibbons, 2010), so the genetic basis of these characteristics is beginning to be revealed.

Beginning in the 1950s, studies of modern human variation focused on various components of blood as well as other aspects of body chemistry. Some phenotypes, such as the ABO blood types, are the direct products of genotypes. (Recall that protein-coding genes direct cells to make proteins, and the antigens on blood cells and many constituents of blood serum are partly composed of proteins; **Fig.5-2**.) During the twentieth century, the study of many Mendelian traits was very successful, identifying dozens of loci and the frequencies of many specific alleles for many human populations. Even so, in all these cases, it was the phenotype that was observed, and information about the underlying genotype remained largely unobtainable. But by the 1990s, the development of new techniques made genomic studies possible. It's now possible to directly sequence DNA, and we can actually identify entire genes and even larger DNA segments and make comparisons between individuals and populations. A decade ago, only a small portion of the human genome was accessible to physical anthropologists, but now we have the capacity to obtain DNA profiles for virtually every human population on earth. And we can expect that, in the next decade, our understanding and knowledge of human biological variation and adaptation will dramatically increase.

Human Polymorphisms

Traits (or the DNA sequences that code for them) that differ in expression between populations and individuals are called **polymorphisms**, and they're the main focus of human variation studies. A genetic trait is *polymorphic* if the locus that governs it has two or more alleles. A locus can consist of hundreds of nucleotides or just one nucleotide.

Polymorphisms have been essential to the study of evolutionary processes in modern populations. For some time, geneticists have examined polymorphic traits to compare allele frequencies between different popula-

polymorphisms Loci with more than one allele. Polymorphisms can be expressed in the phenotype as the result of gene action (as in ABO), or they can exist solely at the DNA level within noncoding regions.

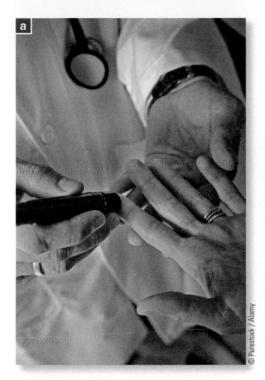

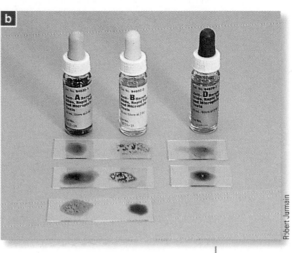

▲Figure 5-2

Blood typing. **(a)** A blood sample is drawn. **(b)** To determine an individual's blood type, a few drops of blood are treated with specific chemicals. The ABO and Rh blood types can be detected by using commercially available chemicals. The glass slides below the blue- and yellow-labeled bottles show reactions for the ABO system: The blood on the top slide is type AB; the middle is type B; and the bottom is type A. The two samples to the right depict Rh-negative blood (top) and Rh-positive blood (bottom).

tions. These comparisons have then been used to reconstruct the evolutionary events that link human populations with one another.

The ABO system is interesting from an anthropological perspective because the frequencies of the *A*, *B*, and *O* alleles vary tremendously among humans. In most groups, *A* and *B* are rarely found in frequencies greater than 50 percent, and usually their frequencies are much lower. Most human groups are still polymorphic for all three alleles, but there are exceptions. For example, the frequency of the *O* allele is virtually 100 percent in indigenous populations of South America. Exceptionally high frequencies of *O* are also found in northern Australia. In these populations, the predominance of the *O* allele is probably due to genetic drift (founder effect),

although the influence of natural selection cannot be entirely ruled out.

Examining single traits can be informative regarding potential influences of natural selection or gene flow. This approach, however, is limited when we try to sort out population relationships, since the study of single traits, by themselves, can lead to confusing interpretations of possible relationships between populations. A more meaningful approach is to study several traits simultaneously.

Polymorphisms at the DNA Level

As a result of the Human Genome Project, we've gained remarkable insights into human variation at the DNA level, and molecular biologists have recently discovered many variations in the human genome. For example, there are thousands of DNA segments called copy number variants (CNVs) where DNA segments are repeated, in some cases just a few times and in other cases hundreds of times. These segments vary tremendously from person to person and, in fact, every person has his or her own unique arrangement that defines their distinctive "DNA fingerprint."

Researchers are expanding their approach to map patterns of variation for individual nucleotides. As you know, point mutations have been recognized for some time. But what's only been recently appreciated is that single-nucleotide changes also frequently occur in *non–protein-coding* portions of DNA. These point mutations, together with those in coding regions of DNA, are all referred to as *single-nucleotide polymorphisms (SNPs)*. From years of detailed analyses, about 15 million SNPs have been recognized. These 15 million SNPs are dispersed throughout the human genome (the majority found in noncoding DNA), and they're extraordinarily variable (Durbin et al., 2010). SNPs are only one of several recent genetic discoveries and indeed, geneticists have gained access to a vast biological "library" that documents the genetic history of our species.

The most recent and most comprehensive population data regarding worldwide patterns of variation come from analysis of extremely large portions of DNA, called "whole-genome" analysis. Three recent studies have evaluated molecular information for the entire genome in more than 1,000 total individuals. The first two studies each identified and traced the patterning of more than 500,000 SNPs in a few dozen populations worldwide (Jakobsson et al., 2008; Li et al., 2008). The most recent study, called the "1000 Genomes Project," is a massive collaboration of more than 400 scientists worldwide, and its preliminary findings reported on close to 15 million SNPs

(as well as other DNA variants such as insertions and deletions). Indeed, with these more detailed sequencing methods, the researchers conclude they already have discovered the molecular basis for 95 percent of all fairly common patterns of human variation (Durbin et al., 2010). They have also identified between 50 and 100 gene variants associated with disease. This study was also able to reconstruct the *entire* genome for 179 individuals (with an ultimate goal of completing whole genome sequences for 2,500 people from all around the world). These more complete data, particularly as they are enhanced, will provide the basis for the next generation of human population genetics studies.

So far, the results of these new studies are significant because they confirm earlier findings from more restricted molecular data and they provide new insights. The higher degree of genetic variation seen in African populations as compared to any other geographical group was once again clearly seen. All human populations outside Africa combined have much less genetic variation than that seen in Africa. These findings further verify the earlier genetic studies (as well as fossil discoveries) that suggest a fairly recent African origin of all modern humans (as discussed in Chapter 12). Moreover, these new data shed light on the genetic relationships between populations worldwide and the nature of human migrations out of Africa. They also provide evidence of the role of genetic drift (founder effect) in recent human evolution, as successively smaller populations split off from larger ones. Finally, preliminary results suggest that the patterning of human variation at the global level may help scientists identify genetic risk factors that influence how susceptible different populations are to various diseases. Specifically, the relative genetic uniformity in non-African populations (for example, European Americans) as compared to those of more recent African descent (such as African

Americans) exposes them to a greater risk of developing disease (Lohmueller et al., 2008). How such information might be put to use, however, is controversial.

Human Biocultural Evolution

We've defined culture as the human strategy of adaptation. Humans live in cultural environments that are continually modified by their own activities; thus, evolutionary processes are understandable only within a *cultural* context. You'll recall that natural selection operates within specific environmental settings, and for humans and many of our hominin ancestors, this means an environment dominated by culture. For example, you learned in Chapter 4 that the altered form of hemoglobin called Hb^S confers resistance to malaria. But the sickle-cell allele hasn't always been an important factor in human populations. Before the development of agriculture, humans rarely, if ever, lived close to mosquito-breeding areas for long periods of time. But with the spread in Africa of **slash-and-burn agriculture**, perhaps in just the last 2,000 years, penetration and clearing of tropical forests occurred. As a result, rainwater was left to stand in open, stagnant pools that provided mosquito-breeding areas close to human settlements. DNA analyses have further confirmed a recent origin and spread of the sickle-cell allele in a population from Senegal, in West Africa. One study estimates that the Hb^s allele appeared (through mutation) in this group sometime at between 2,100 and 1,250 ya (Currat et al., 2002). Thus, it appears that at least in some areas, malaria began to have an impact on human populations only recently. But once it did, it became a powerful selective force.

The increase in the frequency of the sickle-cell allele is a biological adaptation to an environmental change. However, as you learned in Chapter 4, this type of adaptation comes with a huge cost. Heterozygotes (people with sickle-cell trait) have increased resistance to malaria and presumably higher reproductive success, but prior to modern medical treatment, some of their offspring died from sickle-cell anemia. This situation still persists in much of the developing world. So there's a counterbalance between selective forces with an advantage for carriers *only* in malarial environments. The genetic patterns of recessive traits such as sickle-cell anemia are discussed in Chapter 4.

Following World War II, the World Health Organization began spraying mosquito-breeding areas in the tropics with DDT. Sixty years of DDT spraying killed millions of mosquitoes; but at the same time, natural selection acted to produce several strains of DDT-resistant mosquitoes (**Fig. 5-3**). Accordingly, malaria is again on the rise, with up to 500 million new cases reported annually and more than one million people dying each year.

Lactose intolerance, which involves a person's ability to digest milk, is another example of human biocultural evolution. In all human populations, infants and young children are able to digest milk, an obvious necessity for any young mammal. One ingredient of milk is *lactose*, a sugar that is broken down by the enzyme *lactase*, and. in most mammals, including many humans, the gene that codes for lactase production "switches off" in adolescence. Once this happens, if a person drinks fresh milk, the lactose ferments in the large intestine, leading to diarrhea and severe gastrointestinal upset. So, as you might expect, adults stop drinking milk. Among many African and Asian populations, most adults are

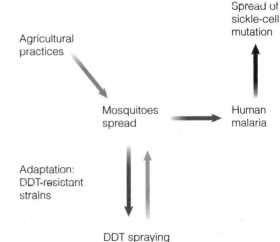

Agricultural practices

Mosquitoes spread

Human malaria

Adaptation: DDT-resistant strains

Spread of sickle-cell mutation

DDT spraying

© Cengage Learning 2013

▲ **Figure 5-3**
Evolutionary interactions affecting the frequency of the sickle-cell allele.

TABLE 5.1 Frequencies of Lactose Intolerance

Population Group	Percent
U.S. whites	2–19
Finnish	18
Swiss	12
Swedish	4
U.S. blacks	70–77
Ibos	99
Bantu	90
Fulani	22
Thais	99
Asian Americans	95–100
Native Americans	85

Source: Lerner, I. M., and W. J. Libby, 1976. Heredity, Evolution, and Society. San Francisco: W. H. Freeman.

lactase persistence In adults, the continued production of lactase, the enzyme that breaks down lactose (milk sugar). This allows adults in some human populations to digest fresh milk products. The discontinued production of lactase in adults leads to lactose intolerance and the inability to digest fresh milk.

lactose-intolerant (**Table 5-1**). But in other populations, including some Africans and Europeans, adults continue to produce lactase and are able to digest fresh milk. This continued production of lactase is called **lactase persistence**.

Throughout most of hominin evolution, milk was unavailable after weaning. Perhaps, in such circumstances, the continued action of an unnecessary enzyme might inhibit digestion of other foods. Therefore, there may be a selective advantage for the gene coding for lactase production to switch off. So why can some adults (the majority in some populations) tolerate milk? The distribution of lactose-tolerant populations may provide an answer to this question, and it suggests a powerful cultural influence on this trait.

Europeans, who are generally lactose-tolerant, are partly descended from Middle Eastern populations. Often economically dependent on pastoralism, these groups raised cows and/or goats and probably drank considerable quantities of milk. In such a cultural environment, strong selection pressures apparently favored lactose tolerance, a trait that has been retained in modern Europeans. Recent genetic evidence from north-central Europe supports this interpretation.

DNA analysis of both cattle and humans suggests that these species have, to some extent, influenced each other genetically. The interaction between humans and cattle resulted in cattle that produce high-quality milk and humans with the ability to digest it (Beja-Pereira et al., 2003). In other words, more than 5,000 ya, populations of north-central Europe were selectively breeding cattle for higher milk yields. Moreover, as these populations were increasing their dependence on fresh milk, they were inadvertently selecting for the gene that produces lactase persistence in themselves.

Most human populations in Africa are lactose-intolerant, but at some point in the past, certain groups became cattle herders and began to consume fresh milk (**Fig. 5-4**). Interestingly, a pattern of coevolution similar to that seen in Europe has recently been identified in humans and cattle in East Africa (Tishkoff et al., 2007). However, the mutations (SNPs) that allow the continued production of lactase in African adults are different from the European version, suggesting that lactase persistence evolved independently in Africa and Europe. In fact, the data show that lactase persistence has evolved several times just in East Africa alone. Clearly, the domestication of cattle, partly to provide milk, was a cultural and dietary shift of sufficient importance to cause allele frequencies to change (and lactase persistence to increase) in at least two distinct areas.

As we've seen, the geographical distribution of lactase persistence is related to a history of cultural dependence on fresh milk products. But some populations rely on dairying yet don't have high rates of lactase persistence (**Fig. 5-5**). It's been suggested that such populations traditionally have consumed their milk in the form of cheese and yogurt, in which the lactose has been broken down by bacterial action.

The interaction of human cultural environments and changes in lactase persistence in human populations is an excellent example of biocultural evolution. In the last few thousand years, cultural factors have initiated specific evolutionary changes in human groups. Such cultural factors have probably influenced the course of human

◀ Figure 5-4
Fulani cattle herder with his cattle.

© Atlantide Phototravel / Corbis

▼ Figure 5-5
Natives of Mongolia rely heavily on milk products from goats and sheep, but mostly consume these foods in the form of cheese and yogurt.

© Michael S. Yamashita / Corbis

evolution for at least 3 million years, and today they are still of paramount importance.

Population Genetics

Physical anthropologists use the approach of **population genetics** to interpret microevolutionary patterns of human variation. Population genetics is the area of research that, among other things, examines allele frequencies in populations and attempts to identify the various factors that cause allele frequencies to change over time. As we defined it in Chapter 4, a *population* is a group of interbreeding individuals that share a common **gene pool**. As a rule, a population is the group within which individuals are most likely to find mates.

In theory, this is a straightforward concept. In every generation, the genes (alleles) in a gene pool are mixed by recombination and then reunited with their counterparts (located on paired chromosomes) through mating. What emerges in the next generation is a direct product of the genes going into

the pool, which in turn is a product of who is mating with whom.

Factors that determine mate choice are geographical, ecological, and social. If people are isolated on a remote island in the middle of the Pacific, there isn't much chance they'll find a mate outside the immediate vicinity. Such **breeding isolates** are fairly easily defined and are a favorite subject of microevolutionary studies. Geography plays a dominant role in producing

population genetics The study of the frequency of alleles, genotypes, and phenotypes in populations from a microevolutionary perspective.

gene pool The total complement of genes shared by the reproductive members of a population.

breeding isolates Populations that are clearly isolated geographically and/ or socially from other breeding groups.

these isolates by strictly determining the range of available mates. But even within these limits, cultural rules can play a deciding role by prescribing who is most appropriate among those who are potentially available.

Most humans today aren't so clearly defined as members of particular populations as they would be if they belonged to breeding isolates. Inhabitants of large cities may appear to be members of a single population, but within the city, socioeconomic, ethnic, and religious boundaries cross-cut in complex ways to form smaller population segments. In addition to being members of these smaller local populations, we're also members of overlapping gradations of larger populations: the immediate geographical region (a metropolitan area or perhaps a state), a section of the country, a nation, and ultimately the entire species.

Once specific human populations have been identified, the next step is to ascertain what evolutionary forces, if any, are operating on them. To determine whether evolution is taking place at a given locus, population geneticists measure allele frequencies for specific traits and compare these observed frequencies with a set predicted by a mathematical model called the **Hardy-Weinberg equilibrium** equation. Just how the equation is used is illustrated in Appendix C. The Hardy-Weinberg formula provides a tool to establish whether allele frequencies in a population are indeed changing. In Chapter 4, we discussed several factors that act to change allele frequencies.

The Adaptive Significance of Human Variation

As you have seen, human variation is the result of several evolutionary factors: genetic drift, founder effect, gene flow, and adaptations to environmental conditions, both past and present. Cultural adaptations have also played a critical role in the evolution of our species, so we must consider the influence of cultural practices on human adaptive responses.

To survive, all organisms must maintain the normal functions of organs, tissues, and cells within the context of an ever-changing environment. Even during the course of a single, seemingly uneventful day, there are numerous fluctuations in temperature, wind, solar radiation, humidity, and so on. Physical activity also places **stress** on physiological mechanisms. The body accommodates these environmental changes by compensating in some manner to maintain internal constancy, or **homeostasis**, and all forms of life have evolved physiological mechanisms that, within limits, achieve this goal.

Physiological responses to environmental change are influenced by genetic factors. We've already defined adaptation as a functional response to environmental conditions in populations and individuals. In a narrower sense, adaptation refers to long-term evolutionary (that is, genetic) changes that characterize all individuals within a population or species.

Examples of long-term adaptations in humans include physiological responses to heat (sweating) and excessive levels of ultraviolet (UV) light (deeply pigmented skin in tropical regions). Such characteristics are the results of evolutionary change in species or populations, and they don't vary because of short-term environmental change. For example, the ability to sweat isn't lost in people who spend their entire lives in predominantly cool areas. Likewise, individuals born with dark skin wouldn't become lighter even if they were never exposed to sunlight.

Acclimatization is another kind of physiological response to environmental conditions, and it can be short-term, long-term, or even permanent. The physiological responses to environmental factors are influenced by genes,

Hardy-Weinberg equilibrium The mathematical relationship expressing—under conditions in which no evolution is occurring—the predicted distribution of alleles in populations; the central theorem of population genetics.

stress In a physiological context, any factor that acts to disrupt homeostasis; more precisely, the body's response to any factor that threatens its ability to maintain homeostasis.

homeostasis A condition of balance, or stability, within a biological system, maintained by the interaction of physiological mechanisms that compensate for changes (both external and internal).

acclimatization Physiological responses to changes in the environment that occur during an individual's lifetime. Such responses may be temporary or permanent, depending on the duration of the environmental change and when in the individual's life it occurs. The capacity for acclimatization may typify an entire population or species, and because it's under genetic influence, it's subject to evolutionary factors such as natural selection and genetic drift.

but also affected by the duration and severity of the exposure, technological buffers (such as shelter or clothing), and individual behavior, weight, and overall body size.

The simplest type of acclimatization is a temporary and rapid adjustment to an environmental change (Hanna, 1999). Tanning, which can occur in everyone (except people with albinism), is one example. Another, which you may have unknowingly experienced, is the very rapid increase in hemoglobin production that occurs when people who live at low elevations travel to higher ones. This increase provides the body with more oxygen in an environment where oxygen is less available. In both of these situations, the physiological change is temporary. Tans fade once exposure to sunlight is reduced, and hemoglobin production drops to original levels following a return to a lower elevation.

On the other hand, *developmental acclimatization* is irreversible and results from exposure to an environmental challenge during growth and development. Lifelong residents of high altitude exhibit certain expressions of developmental acclimatization.

In the following discussion, we present some examples of how humans respond to environmental challenges. Some of these characterize our entire species, whereas others illustrate adaptations seen in only some populations.

Solar Radiation and Skin Color

Skin color is a commonly cited example of adaptation through natural selection in humans. In general, pigmentation in indigenous populations prior to European contact (beginning around 1500) followed a particular geographical distribution, especially in the Old World (**Fig. 5-6**). In general, this pattern is still seen today. Populations with the greatest amount of pigmentation are found in the tropics, and lighter skin color is associated with more northern latitudes, particularly the inhabitants of northwestern Europe.

Skin color is mostly influenced by the pigment *melanin*, a granular

▼ **Figure 5-6**
Geographical distribution of skin color in indigenous human populations.

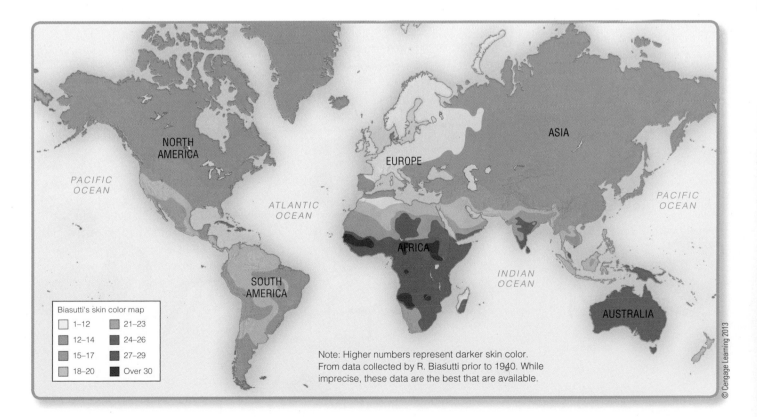

Biasutti's skin color map
1–12	21–23
12–14	24–26
15–17	27–29
18–20	Over 30

Note: Higher numbers represent darker skin color. From data collected by R. Biasutti prior to 1940. While imprecise, these data are the best that are available.

© Cengage Learning 2013

substance produced by cells called *melanocytes*, found in the epidermis (**Fig. 5-7**). All humans have approximately the same number of melanocytes. It's the amount of melanin and the size of the melanin granules that vary. Melanin is important because it acts as a built-in sunscreen by absorbing potentially dangerous ultraviolet (UV) rays present in sunlight. Thus, melanin protects us from overexposure to UV radiation, which can cause genetic mutations in skin cells. These mutations may lead to skin cancer, which, if left untreated, can eventually spread to other organs and result in death.

Exposure to sunlight triggers a protective mechanism in the form of tanning, the result of temporarily increased melanin production. This response is a form of acclimatization and it occurs in all humans except albinos, who have a genetic mutation that prevents their melanocytes from producing melanin (**Fig. 5-8**).

Darker Skin In areas closest to the equator (the tropics), where the sun's rays are most direct and thus exposure to UV light is most intense, natural selection has favored deeply pigmented skin. In considering the negative effects of UV radiation from an evolutionary perspective, three points must be kept in mind:

1. Early hominins lived in the tropics, where solar radiation is more intense than in temperate areas to the north and south.
2. Unlike modern city dwellers, early hominins were outdoors all the time.

▼ Figure 5-7
Ultraviolet rays penetrate the skin and can eventually damage the DNA within skin cells. The three major types of cells that can be affected are squamous cells, basal cells, and melanocytes.

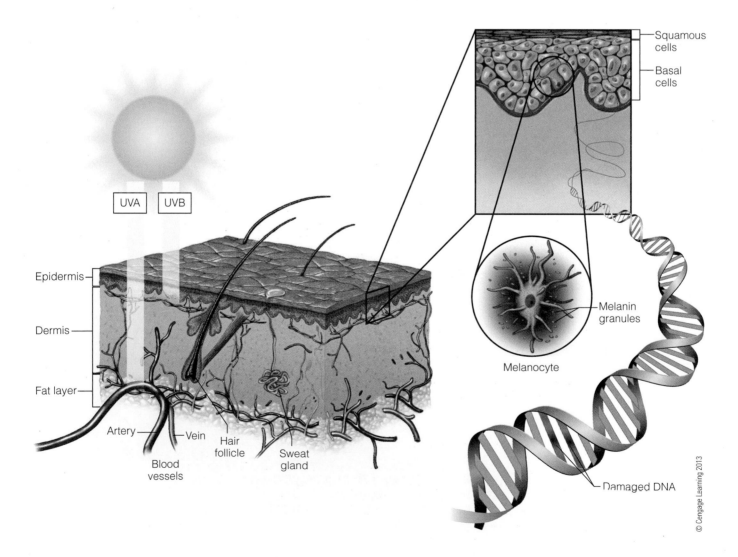

(a) © Reuters / STR / Landov; (b) © Juniors Bildarchiv / Alamy

◄Figure 5-8
(a) A Tanzanian woman with her albino young son. Tragically, since the mid-2000s, there has been a dramatic increase in the trade of albino body parts, which are used in witchcraft, especially in Tanzania. **(b)** This albino horse is unquestionably beautiful but, with virtually no pigmentation, if kept outdoors, it is highly susceptible to sunburn and various forms of skin cancer.

3. Early hominins didn't wear clothing that would have protected them from the sun.

Given these conditions, UV radiation was a powerful agent selecting for high levels of melanin production to provide protection from UV radiation.

Jablonski (1992) and Jablonski and Chaplin (2000, 2010) offer an additional explanation for the distribution of skin color, one that de-emphasizes the role of cancer, and instead, focuses on the degradation of folate (a B vitamin) by UV radiation. Because folate isn't stored in the body, it must be replenished through dietary sources such as leafy green vegetables and certain fruits.

Adequate levels of folate are required for cell division, and this is especially important during embryonic and fetal development, when cell division is rapid and continuous. In pregnant women, insufficient levels of folate are associated with numerous fetal developmental disorders, including **neural tube** defects such as **spina bifida**. The consequences of severe neural tube defects can include pain, infection, paralysis, and even failure of the brain to develop. It goes without saying that neural tube defects can dramatically reduce the reproductive success of affected individuals.

Some studies have shown that UV radiation rapidly depletes folate serum levels in fair-skinned individuals. Therefore, Jablonski and Chaplin suggest that the earliest hominins may have had light skin covered with dark hair, as seen in chimpanzees and gorillas. (Both have darker skin on exposed parts of the body such as faces and hands.) But as loss of body hair occurred in hominins, dark skin evolved rather quickly as a protective response to the damaging effects of UV radiation on folate.

Skin cancer and the maintenance of sufficient levels of folate have no doubt been selective agents favoring dark skin in humans living where UV radiation is most intense. Therefore, we have a

neural tube In early embryonic development, the anatomical structure that develops to form the brain and spinal cord.

spina bifida A condition in which the arch of one or more vertebrae fails to fuse and form a protective barrier around the spinal cord. This can lead to spinal cord damage and paralysis.

good explanation for darker skin in the tropics. But why do populations in higher latitudes, farther from the equator, have lighter skin? There are several closely related hypotheses, and recent studies have added strength to these arguments.

Lighter skin As hominins migrated out of Africa into Asia and Europe, they faced new selective pressures. In particular, those populations that eventually occupied northern Europe encountered cold temperatures and cloudy skies, frequently during summer as well as in winter. Winter also meant fewer hours of daylight, and with the sun well to the south, solar radiation was very indirect. What's more, people in these areas wore animal skins and other types of clothing, which blocked the sun's rays.

It appears that natural selection acted rapidly against darker skin as humans moved to northern latitudes. This change probably occurred because the need for a physiological UV filter was reduced and outweighed by another important biological necessity, the production of vitamin D. The theory concerning the possible role of vitamin D, known as the *vitamin D hypothesis*, offers the following explanation.

Vitamin D is produced in the body partly as a result of the interaction between ultraviolet radiation and a substance similar to cholesterol. It's also available in some foods, including liver, fish oils, egg yolks, butter, and cream. Vitamin D is necessary for normal bone growth and mineralization, and some exposure to ultraviolet radiation is therefore essential. Insufficient amounts of vitamin D during childhood result in *rickets*, a condition that often leads to bowing of the long bones of the legs and deformation of the pelvis (**Fig. 5-9**). Pelvic deformities are of particular concern for women, because they can lead to a narrowing of the birth canal, which, in the absence of surgical intervention, frequently results in the death of both mother and infant during childbirth.

Rickets may have been a significant selective factor that favored lighter skin in regions with less sunlight. Lower levels of UV light and the increased use of clothing could have been detrimental to dark-skinned individuals in more northern latitudes. In these people, melanin would have blocked absorption of the already reduced amounts of available UV radiation required for vitamin D synthesis. Therefore, selection pressures would have shifted to favor lighter skin. There is substantial evidence, both historically and in contemporary populations, to support this theory.

During the latter decades of the nineteenth century in the United States, African American inhabitants of northern cities suffered a higher incidence of rickets than whites. (The solution to this problem was fairly simple: the supplementation of milk with vitamin D.) Another example is seen in Britain, where darker-skinned East Indians and Pakistanis show a higher incidence of rickets than do people with lighter skin (Molnar, 1983).

In addition to its role in bone mineralization, vitamin D is critical to numerous other biological processes. In the body, vitamin D is converted to a different molecule called 1,25D that can attach directly to DNA, after which it can regulate more than 1,000 different genes (Tavera-Mendoza and White, 2007). Some of these genes are involved in cell replication, and because 1,25D acts to regulate this activity, it appears to provide some protection against certain cancers, especially prostate and colon cancer (Lin and White, 2004). (Cancer is caused by uncontrolled cell replication.) Other genes influenced by 1,25D produce proteins that act as natural antibiotics to kill certain bacteria and viruses, including the bacterium that causes tuberculosis. This could well explain why, in the early twentieth century, tuberculosis patients often

▲ Figure 5-9
A child with rickets. Her leg bones have not been properly mineralized due to lack of vitamin D. Thus, they are bowed because they aren't strong enough to support the weight of her upper body.

© Biophoto Associates / Photo Researchers, Inc.

improved after being sent to sanitariums in sunny locations.

Jablonski and Chapin (2000) have also looked at the *potential* for vitamin D synthesis in people with different skin color based on the yearly average of UV radiation at various latitudes (**Fig. 5-10**). Their conclusions support the vitamin D hypothesis to the point of stating that the requirement for vitamin D synthesis in northern latitudes was as important to natural selection as the need for protection from UV radiation in the tropics.

More than 100 genetic loci are thought to be involved in pigmentation in vertebrates, and one of the more important ones is referred to as *MC1R*, which influences coloration in all mammals (yet another example of biological connections among species). The human version of this gene has at least 30 alleles, some of which are associated with red hair combined with fair skin and a tendency to freckle (Lin and Fisher, 2007). Research on Neandertal DNA has shown that some Neandertals possessed an *MC1R* allele

that reduces the amount of pigment in skin and hair. But this allele is not found in modern humans. The fact that less pigmented skin developed in two hominin species, but through different mutations in the same gene, strongly reinforces the hypothesis that there is a significant selective advantage to lighter skin in higher latitudes.

Except for a person's sex, more social importance has been attached to differences in skin color than to any other single human biological trait. But aside from its probable adaptive significance relative to UV radiation, skin color is no more important physiologically than many other characteristics. However, from an evolutionary perspective, skin color provides an outstanding example of how the forces of natural selection have produced geographically patterned variation as the result of two conflicting selective forces: the need for protection from overexposure to UV radiation, on the one hand, and the necessity of adequate UV exposure for vitamin D synthesis on the other.

▼**Figure 5-10**
Populations indigenous to the tropics (brown band) receive enough UV radiation for vitamin D synthesis year-round. The dark orange band shows areas where people with moderately pigmented skin don't receive enough UV light for vitamin D synthesis for one month of the year. The light orange band shows areas where even light-skinned people don't receive enough UV light for vitamin D synthesis during most of the years. (Adapted from Jablonski and Chaplin, 2000, 2002.)

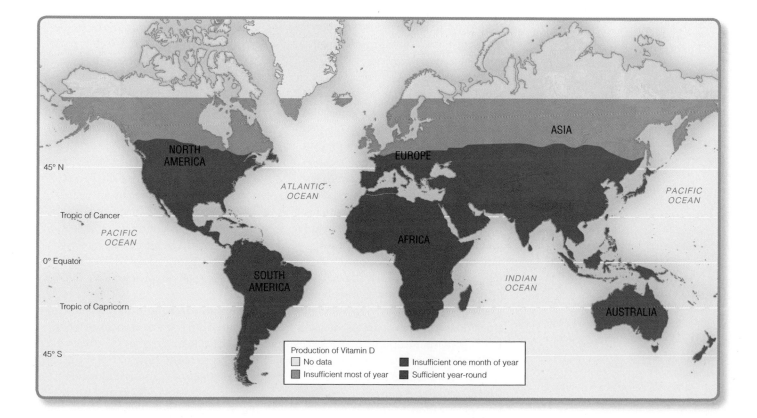

The Thermal Environment

Mammals and birds have evolved complex mechanisms to maintain a constant internal body temperature. Reptiles rely on exposure to external heat sources to raise body temperature and energy levels, but mammals and birds have physiological mechanisms that, within certain limits, increase or reduce the loss of body heat. The optimum internal body temperature for normal cellular functions is species-specific, and for humans it's approximately 98.6°F.

People are found in a wide variety of habitats, with temperatures ranging from over 120°F to lower than –60°F. In these extremes, human life wouldn't be possible without cultural innovations. But even accounting for the artificial environments in which we live, such external conditions place the human body under enormous stress.

Response to Heat All available evidence suggests that the earliest hominins evolved in the warm-to-hot woodlands and savannas of East Africa. The fact that humans cope better with heat than they do with cold is testimony to the long-term adaptations to heat that evolved in our ancestors.

In humans, as well as certain other species, such as horses, sweat glands are distributed throughout the skin. This wide distribution of sweat glands makes it possible to lose heat at the body surface through **evaporative cooling**, a mechanism that has evolved to the greatest degree in humans. The ability to dissipate heat by sweating is seen in all people to an almost equal degree, with the average number of sweat glands per individual (approximately 1.6 million) being fairly constant. However, people who aren't generally exposed to hot conditions do experience a period of acclimatization that initially involves significantly increased perspiration rates (Frisancho, 1993). An additional factor that enhances the cooling effects of sweating is increased exposure of the

skin because of reduced amounts of body hair. We don't know when in our evolutionary history we began to lose body hair, but it represents a species-wide adaptation. (Although, on average, some populations have more body hair than others.)

Although effective, heat reduction through evaporation can be expensive, and indeed dangerous, because of water and sodium loss. For example, a person engaged in heavy work in high heat can lose up to 3 liters of water per hour. To appreciate the importance of this fact, consider that losing 1 liter of water is approximately equivalent to losing 1.5 percent of total body weight, and losing 10 percent of body weight can be life threatening. So water must be continuously replaced during exercise in heat.

Basically, there are two types of heat, arid and humid. Arid environments, such as those of the southwestern United States, the Middle East, and parts of Africa, can have high temperatures, wind, and low water vapor. Humid heat, associated with increased water vapor, occurs in regions with a great deal of vegetation and precipitation, conditions found in the eastern and southern United States, parts of Europe, and much of the tropics. Because the increased water vapor in humid climates inhibits the evaporation of sweat on the skin's surface, humans adjust much more readily to dry heat. In fact, people exercising in dry heat may be unaware that they're sweating because the perspiration evaporates as soon as it reaches the skin's surface. While rapid evaporation increases comfort, it can lead to dehydration. Therefore, especially in dry heat, it's important to keep drinking water, even if you aren't particularly thirsty.

Vasodilation, another mechanism for radiating body heat, occurs when capillaries near the skin's surface widen to increase blood flow to the skin. The visible effect of vasodilation is flushing, or increased redness and warming of the skin, particularly of the face.

evaporative cooling A physiological mechanism that helps prevent the body from overheating. It occurs when perspiration is produced from sweat glands and then evaporates from the surface of the skin.

vasodilation Expansion of blood vessels, permitting increased blood flow to the skin. Vasodilation permits warming of the skin and facilitates radiation of warmth as a means of cooling. Vasodilation is an involuntary response to warm temperatures, various drugs, and even emotional states (blushing).

But the physiological effect is to permit heat, carried by the blood from the interior of the body, to be radiated from the skin's surface to the surrounding air. (Some drugs, including alcohol, also produce vasodilation, which accounts for the increased redness and warmth of the face in some people after they've had a couple of drinks.)

Body size and proportions are also important in regulating body temperature. Indeed, there seems to be a general relationship between climate and body size and shape in birds and mammals. In general, within a species, body size (weight) is greater in populations living farther from the equator. In humans, this relationship holds up fairly well, but there are numerous exceptions.

Two rules that pertain to the relationship between body size, body proportions, and climate are *Bergmann's rule* and *Allen's rule.*

1. *Bergmann's rule concerns the relationship of body mass or volume to surface area.* In mammals, body size tends to be greater in populations that live in colder climates. This is because as mass increases, the relative amount of surface area decreases proportionately. Because heat is lost at the surface, it follows that increased mass allows for greater heat retention.
2. *Allen's rule concerns shape of the body, especially appendages.* In colder climates, shorter appendages, with increased mass-to-surface ratios, are adaptive because they're more effective at preventing heat loss. Conversely, longer appendages, with increased surface area relative to mass, are more adaptive in warmer climates because they promote heat loss.

According to these rules, the most suitable body shape in hot climates is linear with long arms and legs. In a cold climate, a more suitable body type is stocky with shorter limbs. Several studies have shown that human populations conform to these principles to some degree. In colder climates, body mass tends, on average, to be greater and characterized by a larger trunk relative to arms and legs (Roberts, 1973). People living in the Arctic tend to be short and stocky, while many sub-Saharan Africans, especially East African pastoralists, are, on average, tall and linear (**Fig. 5-11**). But there's a great deal of variability regarding human body proportions, and not all populations conform so readily to Bergmann's and Allen's rules.

Response to Cold Human physiological responses to cold combine factors that increase heat production with those that enhance heat retention. Of the two, heat retention is more efficient because it requires less energy. This is an important point because energy is derived from food. Unless food is abundant (and in winter it frequently wasn't for traditional cultures), any factor that conserves energy can have adaptive value. As an analogy, you can think of keeping your house warm either by increasing insulation and saving energy

▲ **Figure 5-11**
(a) These Samburu women (and men in the background) have the linear proportions characteristic of many inhabitants of East Africa. The Samburu are cattle herding people who live in northern Kenya. **(b)** By comparison, these Canadian Inuit women are shorter and stockier. Although the people in these two pictures don't typify everyone in their populations, they do serve as good examples of Bergmann's and Allen's rules.

or by turning up the heat and using more energy.

An increase in metabolic rate and shivering are short-term responses that generate body heat. Increases in metabolic rate (the rate at which cells break up nutrients into their components) release energy in the form of heat. Shivering also generates muscle heat, as does voluntary exercise. But both these methods are costly because they require an increased intake of nutrients to provide needed energy.

Vasoconstriction, the opposite of vasodilation, is another short-term response that restricts heat loss and also conserves energy. Vasoconstriction restricts capillary blood flow to the surface of the skin, thus reducing heat loss at the body surface. Because retaining body heat is more economical than creating it, vasoconstriction is very efficient, provided temperatures don't drop below freezing. However, if temperatures do fall below freezing, continued vasoconstriction can lower skin temperature to the point of frostbite or worse.

In general, people exposed to chronic cold (meaning much or most of the year) maintain higher metabolic rates than those living in warmer climates. The Inuit (Eskimo) people living in the Arctic maintain metabolic rates between 13 and 45 percent higher than observed in non-Inuit control subjects (Frisancho, 1993). Moreover, the highest metabolic rates are seen in inland Inuit, who are exposed to even greater cold stress than coastal populations. Traditionally, the Inuit had the highest animal protein and fat diet of any human population in the world. Their diet was dictated by the available resource base (fish and mammals but little to no vegetable material), and it also made it possible to maintain the high metabolic rates required to live in regions where extreme cold persisted for months at a time.

Long-term responses to cold vary among human groups. For example, in the past, desert-dwelling native Australian populations were exposed to wide temperature fluctuations from day to night. Since they wore no clothing and didn't build shelters, their only protection from temperatures that hovered only a few degrees above freezing was provided by sleeping fires. They also experienced continuous vasoconstriction throughout the night, permitting a degree of skin cooling most people would find extremely uncomfortable. As there was no threat of frostbite, continued vasoconstriction was an efficient adaptation that helped prevent excessive internal heat loss.

By contrast, the Inuit experience intermittent periods of vasoconstriction and vasodilation. This compromise provides periodic warmth to the skin that helps prevent frostbite in subfreezing temperatures. At the same time, because vasodilation is intermittent, energy loss is restricted, to retain more heat at the body's core.

Humans, and some other animals, also have a subcutaneous (beneath the skin) fat layer that provides insulation throughout the body. In many overfed populations today, this fat layer is an annoyance to many and a major health issue for others. But in the not-too-distant past, our hunting and gathering ancestors relied on it not only for some protection against the cold but also as a source of nutrients when food was scarce.

These examples illustrate some of the ways adaptations to cold vary among human populations. Obviously, winter conditions exceed our ability to adapt physiologically in many parts of the world. If our ancestors hadn't developed cultural innovations, they would have remained in the tropics and the history of humanity, and the planet, would have been entirely different.

High Altitude

Studies of high-altitude residents have greatly contributed to our understanding of physiological adaptation. As you would expect, altitude studies have focused on inhabited mountainous

vasoconstriction Narrowing of blood vessels to reduce blood flow to the skin. Vasoconstriction is an involuntary response to cold and reduces heat loss at the skin's surface.

regions, particularly in the Himalayas, Andes, and Rocky Mountains. Of these three areas, permanent human habitation probably has the longest history in the Himalayas (Moore et al., 1998). Today, perhaps as many as 25 million people live at altitudes above 10,000 feet. In Tibet, permanent settlements exist above 15,000 feet, and in the Andes, they can be found as high as 17,000 feet (**Fig. 5-12**).

Because the mechanisms that maintain homeostasis in humans evolved at lower altitudes, we're compromised by conditions at higher elevations. At high altitudes, humans face numerous environmental challenges. These include **hypoxia**, more intense solar radiation, cold, low humidity, wind, a reduced nutritional base, and rough terrain. Of these, hypoxia causes the greatest amount of stress for human physiological systems, especially the heart, lungs, and brain.

Hypoxia results from reduced barometric pressure. It isn't that there is less oxygen in the atmosphere at high altitudes, it's just less concentrated. Therefore, to obtain the same amount of oxygen at 9,000 feet as at sea level, people must make physiological alterations that increase the body's ability to transport and efficiently use the oxygen that's available.

◀ Figure 5-12
(a) Namche Bazaar, Tibet, situated at an elevation of over 12,000 feet above sea level. **(b)** La Paz, Bolivia, at just over 12,000 feet, is home to more than 1 million people.

hypoxia Insufficient levels of oxygen in body tissues; oxygen deficiency.

These challenges with oxygen supply at high altitudes affect reproduction through increased infant mortality rates, miscarriage, low birth weights, and premature birth. In general, the problems related to childbearing are attributed to issues that compromise the vascular supply (and thus oxygen transport) to the fetus. One cause of fetal and maternal death is preeclampsia, a severe elevation of blood pressure in pregnant women. Palmer and colleagues (1999) reported that among pregnant women living at elevations over 10,000 feet in Colorado, the prevalence of preeclampsia was 16 percent, compared to 3 percent at around 4,000 feet.

People born at lower altitudes and high-altitude natives differ somewhat in how they adapt to hypoxia. When people born at low elevations travel to higher ones, the process of acclimatization begins within a day or two. These changes include an increase in respiration rate, heart rate, and production of red blood cells. (Red blood cells contain hemoglobin, the protein responsible for transporting oxygen to organs and tissues.)

Developmental acclimatization occurs in high-altitude natives during growth and development. This type of acclimatization is present only in people who grow up in high-altitude areas, not in those who move there as adults. Lifelong residents of high elevations have greater heart and lung capacity than do people from lower elevations. They are also more efficient than migrants at diffusing oxygen from blood to body tissues, and geneticists are beginning to identify the genes that regulate this ability. Developmental acclimatization to high-altitude hypoxia is an excellent example of physiological flexibility that illustrates how, within the limits set by genetic factors, development can be influenced by environmental factors.

The best evidence for permanent high-altitude adaptation is provided by the indigenous peoples of Tibet. These people have inhabited regions higher than 12,000 feet for at least 7,000 years (Simonson et al., 2010) and perhaps as long as 25,000 years. Altitude doesn't affect reproduction in high altitude Tibetans to the degree it does in other populations. Infants have birth weights as high as those of lowland Tibetan groups and higher than those of recent Chinese immigrants. This disparity in birth weights may be the result of alterations in maternal blood flow to the uterus during pregnancy (Moore et al., 2001; 2006). Another line of evidence concerns how the body processes glucose (blood sugar). Glucose is critical because it's the only source of energy used by the brain, and it's also used, although not exclusively, by the heart. Both highland Tibetans and the Quechua (inhabitants of high-altitude regions of the Peruvian Andes) burn glucose in a way that permits more efficient use of oxygen. This implies the presence of genetic mutations in the mitochondrial DNA because mtDNA directs how cells use glucose.

We now have firm evidence that natural selection has acted strongly and rapidly to increase the frequency of certain alleles that have produced adaptive responses to altitude in Tibetans. Ninety percent of Tibetan highlanders possess a mutation in a gene involved in red blood cell production. In effect, this mutation inhibits the increased red blood cell production normally seen in high-altitude inhabitants. Tibetan highlanders have red cell counts similar to those of populations living at sea level. Interestingly, the Quechua and other high-altitude residents of the Andes do not have this mutation and have higher red cell counts than lowland inhabitants. But if increased red blood cell production is advantageous at high altitude, why would selection favor a mutation that acts against it in Tibetans? The answer is that beyond certain levels, elevated numbers of red cells can actually "thicken" the blood and lead to increased risk of stroke, blood clots, and heart attack. In pregnant women, they can also lead to impaired fetal growth and even fetal death. Thus, although the mechanisms aren't yet understood, Tibetans have acquired a number of genetically influenced adaptations to hypoxic conditions while still producing the same amount of hemoglobin we would expect at sea level. Because the mutation is believed to have appeared only around 4,000 ya, its presence throughout most high-altitude Tibetan populations is the strongest and most rapid example of natural selection documented for humans (Yi et al., 2010).

Infectious Disease

Infectious diseases are pathological conditions caused by microorganisms (viruses, bacteria, and certain other one-celled organisms). Throughout the course of human evolution, they have exerted enormous selective pressures on our species, influencing the frequency of numerous alleles that affect the immune response. In fact, it would be difficult to overstate the importance of infectious disease as an agent of natural selection in human populations.

The effects of infectious disease on humans are mediated culturally as well as biologically. Innumerable cultural factors, such as architectural styles, subsistence techniques, and exposure to domesticated animals affect how infectious disease develops and persists within and between populations.

Until about 15,000 ya, all humans lived in small nomadic hunting and gathering groups. These groups rarely stayed in one location for long, so they had minimal contact with refuse heaps that house disease **vectors**. But with the domestication of plants and animals, people became more sedentary and began living in small villages. Gradually, villages became towns, and towns, in turn, developed into densely crowded, unsanitary cities.

As long as humans lived in small bands, there was little opportunity for infectious disease to affect large numbers of people. Even if an entire local group or band were wiped out, the effect on the overall population in a given area would have been negligible. Moreover, for a disease to become **endemic** in a population, there must be enough people to sustain it. Therefore, small bands of hunter-gatherers weren't faced with continuous exposure to endemic disease.

But with the advent of settled living and close proximity to domesticated animals, opportunities for disease greatly increased. As sedentary life permitted larger group size, it became possible for diseases to become permanently established in some populations. Moreover, exposure to domestic animals, such as cattle and fowl, provided an opportune environment for the spread of several **zoonotic** diseases, such as tuberculosis and influenza. Also, the crowded, unsanitary conditions that characterized parts of all cities until the late nineteenth century and that persist in much of the world today further added to the disease burden borne by human inhabitants.

AIDS (acquired immunodeficiency syndrome) provides an excellent example of the influence of human infectious disease as a selective agent. In the United States, the first cases of AIDS were reported in 1981. Since that time, at least 1.5 million Americans have been infected by HIV (human immunodeficiency virus), the agent that causes AIDS. However, most of the burden of AIDS is borne by developing countries, where 95 percent of all HIV-infected people live. According to World Health Organization estimates, between 33 and 35 million people worldwide were living with HIV infection as of November 2009, and more than 25 million had died (UNAIDS/WHO, 2010).

By the early 1990s, scientists were aware of a number of patients who had been HIV positive for 10 to 15 years but continued to show few if any symptoms. This led researchers to suspect that some people are naturally resistant to HIV infection. This was shown to be true in late 1996 with the publication of

vectors Agents that transmit disease from one carrier to another. Mosquitoes are vectors for malaria, just as fleas are vectors for bubonic plague.

endemic Continuously present in a population.

zoonotic (zoh-oh-no´-tic) Pertaining to a zoonosis (*pl.*, zoonoses), a disease that's transmitted to humans through contact with nonhuman animals.

▲ **Figure 5-13**
This 1974 photo shows a young boy with smallpox. His body is covered with the painful pustules that are typical of the disease. These lesions frequently leave severe scarring on the skin of survivors.

two different studies (Dean et al., 1996; Samson et al., 1996) that demonstrated a mechanism for HIV resistance.

These two reports describe a genetic mutation that involves a receptor site on the surface of certain immune cells. (Receptor sites are protein molecules that enable HIV and other viruses to invade cells.) As a result of the mutation, the receptor site doesn't function properly and HIV can't enter the cell. Current evidence suggests that individuals who are homozygous for the mutant allele may be completely resistant to many types of HIV infection. In heterozygotes, infection may still occur, but the course of HIV disease is slowed.

For unknown reasons, the mutant allele occurs mainly in people of European descent, among whom its frequency is about 10 percent. The mutation was absent in certain Japanese and West African groups that were studied (Samson et al., 1996). Researchers suggested that this polymorphism exists in Europeans as a result of selective pressures favoring an allele that originally occurred as a rare mutation. But the original selective agent was *not* HIV. Instead, it was some other, as yet unidentified, pathogen that requires the same receptor site as HIV, and some scientists have implicated the virus that causes smallpox. Though this conclusion hasn't been proved, it offers a very interesting avenue of research. It may reveal how a mutation that originally was favored by selection because it provides protection against one type of infection (perhaps smallpox) can also increase resistance to another (AIDS).

Smallpox, once a deadly viral disease, is estimated to have accounted for 10 to 15 percent of all deaths in parts of Europe during the eighteenth century. Today, this once devastating killer is the only condition to have been successfully eliminated by modern medical technology. By 1977, through massive vaccination programs, the World Health Organization was able to declare the smallpox virus extinct, except for a few colonies in research labs in the United States and Russia (**Fig. 5-13**).

The best-known epidemic in history was the Black Death (bubonic plague) in the mid-fourteenth century. Bubonic plague is caused by a bacterium and is transmitted from rodents to humans by fleas. In just a few years, this deadly disease had spread from the Caspian Sea throughout the Mediterranean area to northern Europe. During the initial exposure to this disease, as many as one-third of the inhabitants of Europe died.

Although we have no definite evidence of a selective role for bubonic plague or smallpox, this doesn't mean that one doesn't exist. The tremendous mortality that these diseases (and others) can cause certainly would very likely influence human adaptive responses. Understanding how natural selection has altered the frequency of specific genes is a major focus of biomedical research.

The Continuing Impact of Infectious Disease

It's important to understand that humans and pathogens exert selective pressures on each other, creating a dynamic relationship between disease organisms and their human (and nonhuman) hosts. Just as disease exerts selective pressures on host populations to adapt, microorganisms also evolve and adapt to various pressures exerted on them by their hosts.

Evolutionarily speaking, it's to the advantage of any pathogen not to be so deadly as to kill its host too quickly. If the host dies soon after becoming infected, the virus or bacterium may not have time to reproduce and infect other hosts. Thus, selection sometimes acts to produce resistance in host populations and/or to reduce the virulence of disease organisms, to the benefit of both. However, members of populations exposed for the first time to a new disease frequently die in huge numbers. This type of exposure was a major factor in the decimation of indigenous New World populations after contact with Europeans introduced smallpox into Native American groups. Similar lack of resistance also helps explain the current worldwide spread of HIV.

Of the known disease-causing organisms, HIV provides the best-documented example of evolution and adaptation in a pathogen. It's also one of several examples of interspecies transfer of infection. HIV is the most mutable and genetically variable virus known, and the type that's responsible for the AIDS epidemic is HIV-1. Another far less common type is HIV-2, which is present only in populations in West Africa. HIV-2 also exhibits a wide range of genetic diversity, and whereas some strains cause AIDS, others are far less virulent.

Since the late 1980s, researchers have been comparing the DNA sequences of HIV and a closely related virus called *simian immunodeficiency virus (SIV)*. SIV is found in chimpanzees, gorillas, and several African monkey species. Comparisons of HIV

and SIV DNA have demonstrated that HIV-1 almost certainly evolved from the strain of chimpanzee SIV that infects the central African subspecies *Pan troglodytes troglodytes* (Gao et al., 1999).

Unfortunately for both species, chimpanzees are routinely hunted by humans for food in parts of West Africa. Consequently, SIV was probably first transmitted from chimpanzees to humans through the hunting and butchering of chimpanzees (Gao et al., 1999; Weiss and Wrangham, 1999). Thus, HIV/AIDS is a zoonotic disease (**Fig. 5-14**). The DNA evidence further suggests that there were at least three separate human exposures to chimpanzee SIV, and at some point the virus was altered to the form we call HIV. When chimpanzee SIV was first transmitted to humans is unknown, but the oldest evidence of human infection is a blood sample taken from a West African patient in 1959. Therefore, although human exposure to SIV/HIV probably occurred many times in the past, the virus didn't become firmly established in humans until the latter half of the twentieth century.

Influenza, is a zoonotic, contagious respiratory disease caused by various

▲**Figure 5-14**
These women selling butchered chimpanzees in West Africa probably don't realize that by handling this meat they could be exposing themselves to HIV.

© Karl Ammann

► **Figure 5-15**
This woman, selling chickens in a Chinese market, is wearing a scarf over her nose and mouth in an attempt to protect herself from exposure to avian flu.

© Hoang Dinh Nam / AFP / Getty Images

strains of virus. It has probably killed more humans than any other infectious disease. There were two flu pandemics in the twentieth century; the first killed between 20 and 100 million people worldwide in 1918. Moreover, "seasonal flu," which comes around every year, killed an annual average of 36,000 people in the United States during the 1990s (Centers for Disease Control, 2009). Worldwide, seasonal flu accounts for several hundred thousand deaths every year.

The influenza viruses that infect humans are initially acquired through contact with domestic pigs and fowl (**Fig. 5-15**). For this reason, influenza is frequently referred to as swine or avian (bird) flu. In 2009, a new swine flu virus called H1N1 caused great fear of another pandemic. This epidemic proved not to be as severe as originally feared. By mid-November 2009, about 50 million Americans had been infected (Reinberg, 2009), but most cases

were mild. Still, health officials are always on the alert for the possibility of an influenza **pandemic**, partly because of the ever-present danger presented by close contact between humans, pigs, and domestic fowl.

Until the twentieth century, infectious disease was the number one cause of death in all human populations. Even today, in many developing countries, as much as half of all mortality is due to infectious disease, compared to only about 10 percent in the United States. For example, there are an estimated one million deaths due to malaria each year. Ninety percent of these deaths occur in sub-Saharan Africa, where 5 percent of children die of malaria before their fifth birthday (Greenwood and Mutabingwa, 2002; Weiss, 2002).

In the United States and other industrialized nations, with improved living conditions and sanitation, and the widespread use of antibiotics and

pandemic An epidemic that spreads through many populations and may affect people worldwide. Examples include HIV/ AIDS and the "Spanish flu" pandemic of 1918-1919.

pesticides since the 1940s, infectious disease has given way to heart disease and cancer as the leading causes of death. Optimistic predictions held that infectious disease would one day be a thing of the past. However, mortality in the United States due to infectious disease has increased substantially in recent years (Pinner et al., 1996). This increase is partly due to the overuse of antibiotics. It's estimated that half of all antibiotics prescribed in the United States are used to treat viral conditions such as colds and flu. Because antibiotics are completely ineffective against viruses, antibiotic therapy not only is useless, but may actually have dangerous long-term consequences. There's considerable concern in the biomedical community over the indiscriminate use of antibiotics since the 1950s. Antibiotics have exerted selective pressures on bacterial species that have, over time, evolved antibiotic-resistant strains (an excellent example of natural selection). So in the past few years, we've seen the reemergence of many bacterial diseases, including pneumonia, cholera, and tuberculosis (TB), in forms that are less responsive to treatment. To make matters worse, at the present time there are no new antibiotics on the horizon capable of treating the increasing number of resistant strains of bacteria.

Tuberculosis is now listed as the world's leading killer of adults by the World Health Organization (Colwell, 1996). In fact, the number of tuberculosis cases has risen 28 percent worldwide since the mid-1980s, with an estimated 10 million people infected in the United States alone. Although not all infected people develop active disease, in the 1990s an estimated 30 million persons worldwide are believed to have died from TB. One very troubling aspect of the increase in tuber-

Why It Matters

Although humans could be seen as a highly successful species, we are not as "dominant" as we might think. Indeed, we are in an arms race with other species that could attack and kill millions of people. The most dangerous of these biological rivals include microorganisms, specifically bacteria and viruses.

In much of the world over the last 80 years, medical technology has reduced the dangers from bacterial infections such as tuberculosis through use of antibiotics. But, the bacteria don't just disappear, because they have their own ways to fight back biologically. What they do is to *evolve*, and they do it remarkably quickly. Bacteria can reproduce about every 20 minutes, compared to a human generational span of 20 years. What's more, they're far more numerous than any other life form.

One estimate suggests bacteria make up about 98 percent of all cells on earth.

We've mentioned earlier that when bacteria are exposed to antibiotics, some of them (due to earlier random mutations) will probably be resistant. They will be the ones that reproduce, and, in just a few years resistant strains could potentially spread around the world. Of course, this is an excellent example of natural selection. Humans certainly can't fight back simply by waiting for natural selection to make us immune to bacteria. We use technology instead and invent different and stronger antibiotics. The bacteria then evolve further through more natural selection, and the biological arms race continues.

Recently, our technology has seriously begun to lose ground to the microbes. The last ten years have seen the appearance of at least two new mutations that make some bacteria resistant to even our most powerful antibiotics. One of these mutations apparently originated in southern Asia (India or Pakistan), and the other was first indentified in U.S. hospitals. These bacterial strains now have spread to Europe, China, and South America.

With no antibiotics that can predictably combat these resistant strains, some hospital patients have died, despite the best efforts of doctors using the entire arsenal of drugs now available. Pharmaceutical companies could develop yet stronger and more creative antibiotics that would work—at least for now. But . . . such new drugs require up to 10 years to develop, and there are none currently even in early stages of such development (McKenna, 2011).

So, in the absence of new antibiotics there is a real danger of increasing lethal infections caused by resistant bacterial strains. The war with microbes is one we can never completely win, and the next decade will certainly see increased threats to humans due to a lack of effective pharmaceutical weapons.

culosis infection is that new strains of *Mycobacterium tuberculosis*, the bacterium that causes TB, are resistant to many antibiotics.

In addition to threats posed by resistant strains of pathogens, there are other factors that may contribute to the emergence (or reemergence) of infectious disease. Political leaders in some (mostly European) countries and the overwhelming majority of scientists worldwide are becoming increasingly concerned over the potential for global warming to expand the geographical range of numerous tropical disease vectors, such as mosquitoes. And the destruction of natural environments not only contributes to global warming; it also has the potential of causing disease vectors formerly restricted to local areas to spread to new habitats.

Fundamental to all these factors is human population size, which, as it continues to soar, causes more environmental disturbance and, through additional human activity, adds further to global warming. One could scarcely conceive of a better set of circumstances for the appearance and spread of communicable disease, and it remains to be seen if scientific innovation and medical technology are able to meet the challenge.

Summary of Main Topics

- Visible traits, traditionally used in attempts to classify humans into clearly defined "races," have emphasized such features as skin color, hair color, hair form, and shape of the head and face. The concept of race is a simplistic view of human variation that doesn't take into account evolutionary factors and adaptation to environmental conditions. Since the 1990s, the development and rapid application of comparative genomics have drastically expanded genetic data. These powerful new tools allow evaluation of human population variation using thousands (or hundreds of thousands) of precisely defined DNA sequences. Such population studies are aimed at reconstructing the microevolutionary population history of our species and understanding the varied roles of natural selection, genetic drift, gene flow, and mutation.

- For humans, culture also plays a crucial evolutionary role. Interacting with biological influences, these factors define the distinctive biocultural nature of human evolution. Two excellent examples of recent human biocultural evolution relate to resistance to malaria (involving the sickle-cell allele) and lactase persistence.

- Even today, populations living in the tropics have darker skin whereas those living in northern latitudes usually have lighter skin. This patterning is due to natural selection that favored increased melanin production as protection from overexposure to UV radiation in regions where the sun's rays are most direct. Research suggests that this protection served to prevent skin cancer and degradation of folate.

- Fair-skinned populations are limited to northern latitudes, particularly Northern Europe. Natural selection favored less melanin production in areas where exposure to UV radiation is less intense in order to facilitate the production of vitamin D. Vitamin D is critical to bone mineralization and regu-

lates a number of gene functions, one of which is the production of a protein that provides protection from tuberculosis by killing the bacterium that causes it.

- Various forms of acclimatization have evolved in humans to accommodate environmental factors such as heat, cold, and high altitude. Natural selection favoring several genetic mutations has allowed Tibetan highlanders to adapt to extremely high altitudes. There has been especially rapid and strong selection favoring a particular mutation that permits them to retain red blood cell counts that are normal for sea-level residents. This, in turn, avoids life-threatening problems associated with overproduction of red blood cells.

- Cultural innovations and contact with nonhuman animals have increased the spread of infectious diseases. Examples of this are HIV/AIDS, influenza, and malaria.

Critical Thinking Questions

1. Imagine you're with some friends talking about variation and how many races there are. One person says that there are three, and another thinks that there are five. Would you agree with either one? Why or why not?

2. For the same group of friends in question 1 (none of whom have had a course in biological anthropology), how would you explain how scientific knowledge doesn't support their preconceived notions about human races?

3. In the twentieth century, how did the scientific study of human diversity change from the more traditional approach?

4. Why can we say that variations in human skin color are the result of natural selection in different environments? Why can we say that less pigmented skin is a result of conflicting selective factors?

5. Do you think that infectious disease has played an important role in human evolution? Do you think it plays a *current* role in human adaptation?

6. How have human cultural practices influenced the patterns of infectious disease seen today? Provide as many examples as you can, including some not discussed in this chapter.

Paleopathology:
What Bones Can Tell Us About Ancient Diseases and Injury

The branch of physical anthropology that studies injury and disease in earlier populations is called *paleopathology*. Within this subdiscipline, anthropologists, often working with medical specialists, contribute to our knowledge of the history and geographical distribution of human diseases such as tuberculosis and syphilis. In addition, patterns of disease and trauma in specific groups can further illuminate how these peoples were affected by various environmental and cultural factors. In most cases, paleopathologists work exclusively with dry, skeletonized specimens.

Occasionally, however, under unusual circumstances, soft tissues—such as skin, hair, cartilage, or even internal organs—may also be preserved. For example, artificial mummification was practiced in ancient Egypt and Chile, and natural mummification may also occur in extremely dry climates (such as in the American Southwest and parts of North Africa).

◄ Naturally mummified tissue on a cranium from Nubia (part of the modern country of the Sudan; c. A.D. 700–1400).

Lynn Kilgore

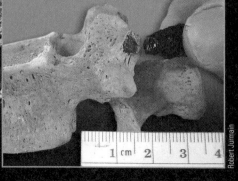

Robert Jurmain

▲ Embedded piece of obsidian projectile point in a lumbar vertebra from a central California male, 25 to 40 years old. The portion being held was found with the burial and may have been retained during life in soft tissue (muscle?). The injury shows some healing.

Lynn Kilgore

▲ Fracture of a right femur (thigh bone) seen from the rear. (The normal left femur is shown for comparison.) Such an injury is extremely severe, even life-threatening, but in this individual the bone healed remarkably well.

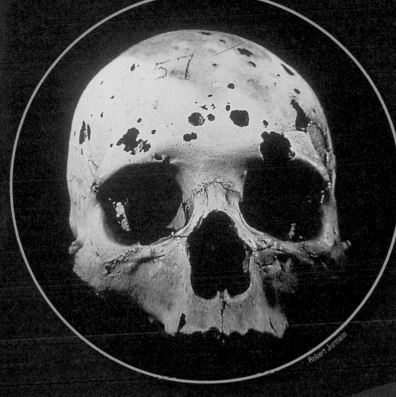

◄ Numerous lesions of the cranium (such erosive lesions were also found in other bones), probably the result of a disseminated (metastasized) cancer, possibly originating from the breast, shown here in an Inuit (Eskimo) female.

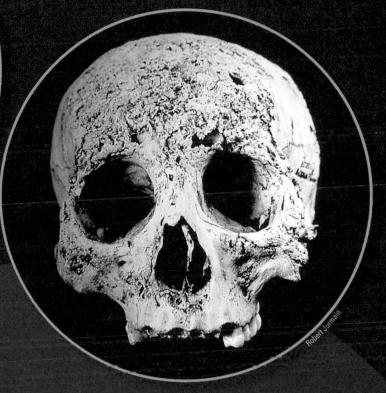

▲ Extreme reaction in a cranium from an Alaskan Eskimo, diagnostic of syphilis (although other possibilities must be considered).

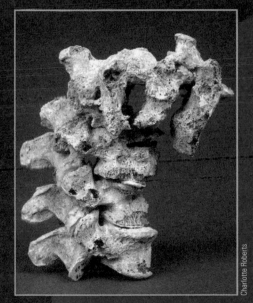

▲ Mid portion of spinal column with severe bone loss, collapse of vertebral bodies and deformity resulting from tuberculosis (from medieval England, male, 17–25 years old, dated to 6th century A.D.).

▶ Dr. Arthur Aufderheide (right) and Dr. Wilmar Salo (left) examine DNA fingerprints obtained by PCR. From this analysis these researchers were the first to obtain such clear molecular evidence of tuberculosis in the pre-Columbian New World.

127

Connections

Evolution results from DNA changes and the action of other evolutionary factors.

Humans are both vertebrates and mammals and we've shared evolutionary history for millions of years.

Humans are primates and share many biological characteristics with other primates.

Macroevolution: Processes of Vertebrate and Mammalian Evolution

Many people think that paleontology is a pretty dreary subject and only interesting to overly serious academics. But have you ever been to a natural history museum—or perhaps to one of the larger, more elaborate toy stores? If so, you may have seen a full-size mock-up of *Tyrannosaurus rex*, one that might even have moved its head and arms and screamed threateningly. These displays are usually encircled by enthralled adults and flocks of noisy, excited children. These same onlookers, however, show almost no interest in the display cases containing fossils of early marine organisms. And yet every trace of early life has a fascinating story to tell.

The study of the history of life on earth is full of mystery and adventure. The bits and pieces of fossils are the remains of once living, breathing animals (some of them extremely large and dangerous). Searching for these fossils in remote corners of the globe, from the Gobi Desert in Mongolia, to the rocky outcrops of Madagascar, to the badlands of South Dakota, is not a task for the faint of heart. Piecing together the tiny clues and ultimately reconstructing what *Tyrannosaurus rex* or a small, 50-million-year-old primate looked like and how it might have behaved is really much like detective work. Sure, it can be serious; but it's also a lot of fun.

In this chapter, we'll look back at the very ancient roots of human evolution. We are a primate, which, in turn, is one type of mammal; what's more, mammals are one of the major groups of vertebrates. It's important to understand these more general aspects of evolutionary history so that we can place our species in its proper biological context. *Homo sapiens* is only one of millions of species that have evolved. More than that, people have been around for just an instant in the vast expanse of time that life has existed, and we want to know where we fit in this long and complex story of life on earth. To discover how humans connect within this incredibly long story of life on earth, we also discuss some contemporary issues relating to evolutionary theory. In particular, in this chapter we emphasize concepts relating to large-scale evolutionary processes—that is, *macroevolution* (in contrast to the microevolutionary focus of Chapter 4). The fundamental

◀ Paleontologists excavating a mammoth skeleton from North America.

perspectives reviewed here concern geological history, principles of classification, and the nature of evolutionary change. These perspectives will serve as a basis for topics covered throughout much of the remainder of this book.

How We Connect: Discovering the Human Place in the Organic World

There are millions of species living today; if we were to include microorganisms, the total would likely exceed tens of millions. If we added in the multitudes of species that are now extinct, the total would be staggering—perhaps *hundreds* of millions! Where do we fit in, and what types of evidence do scientists use to answer this question?

Biologists need to develop methods to deal scientifically with all this diversity. One way to do this is to develop a system of **classification** that organizes diversity into categories and, at the same time, indicates evolutionary relationships.

Multicellular organisms that move about and ingest food are called animals (**Fig. 6-1**). Within the kingdom Animalia, there are more than 20 major groups called *phyla* (*sing.*, phylum). **Chordata** is one of these phyla and it includes all animals with a nerve cord, gill slits (at some stage of development), and a supporting cord along the back. In turn, most (but not all) chordates are **vertebrates**—so-called because they have a vertebral column. Vertebrates also have a developed brain and paired sensory structures for sight, smell, and balance.

The vertebrates themselves are subdivided into five classes: cartilaginous fishes, bony fishes, amphibians, reptiles/birds, and mammals. We'll discuss mammalian classification later in this chapter.

By putting organisms into increasingly narrow groupings, we organize diversity into categories and also make statements about evolutionary and genetic relationships between species and groups of species. Further dividing mammals into orders makes the statement that, for example, all carnivores (Carnivora) are more closely related to each other than they are to any species placed in another order. Consequently, bears, dogs, and cats are more closely related to each other than they are to cattle, pigs, or deer (Artiodactyla). At each succeeding level (suborder, superfamily, family, subfamily, genus, and species), finer distinctions are made between categories until, at the species level, only those animals that can potentially interbreed and produce viable offspring are included.

Principles of Classification

Before we go any further, we need to discuss the basis of animal classification. The field that specializes in establishing the rules of classification is called *taxonomy*. Organisms are classified first, and most traditionally, according to their physical similarities. This was the basis of the first systematic classification devised by Linnaeus in the eighteenth century (see Chapter 2).

Today, basic physical similarities are still considered a good starting point. But for similarities to be useful, they *must* reflect evolutionary descent. For example, the bones of the forelimb of those vertebrates whose ancestors initially adapted to terrestrial (land) environments are so similar in number and form (**Fig. 6-2**) that the obvious explanation for the striking resemblance is that all of these "four-footed" (tetrapod) animals ultimately derived their forelimb structure from a common ancestor.

How could such seemingly major evolutionary modifications in structure occur? They quite likely began with

classification In biology, the ordering of organisms into categories, such as orders, families, and genera, to show evolutionary relationships.

Chordata The phylum of the animal kingdom that includes vertebrates.

vertebrates Animals with segmented, bony spinal columns; includes fishes, amphibians, reptiles (including birds), and mammals.

▼ Figure 6-1

In this classification chart, modified from Linnaeus, all animals are placed in certain categories based on structural similarities. Not all members of categories are shown; for example, there are up to 20 orders of placental mammals (8 are depicted). Chapter 7 presents a more comprehensive classification of the primate order.

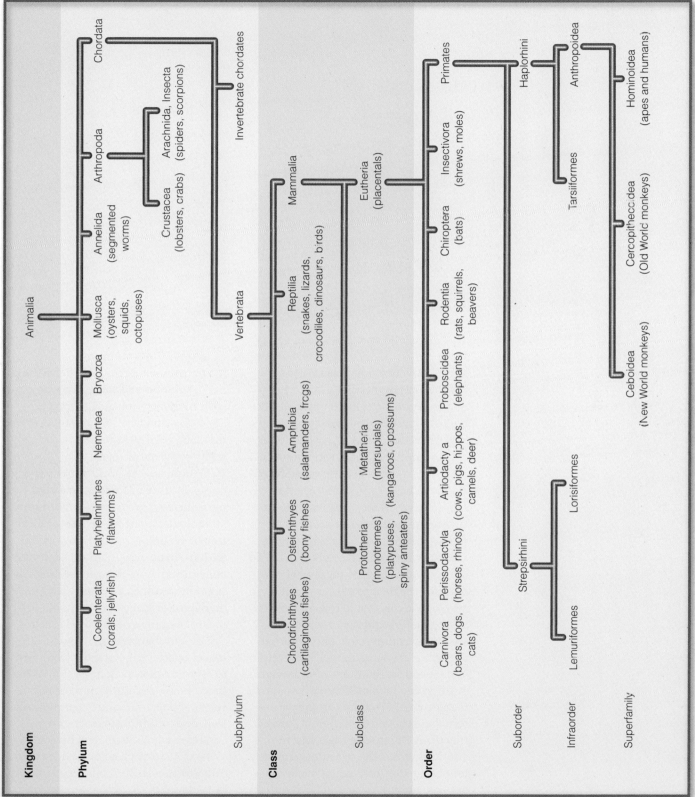

▶ **Figure 6-2**

Homologies. Similarities in the fore-limb bones of these land vertebrates can be most easily explained by descent from a common ancestor.

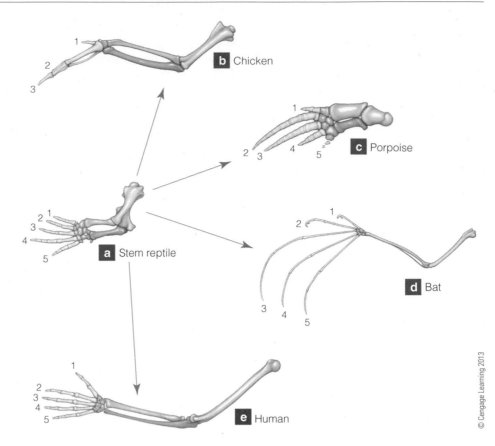

only relatively minor genetic changes. For example, molecular research shows that forelimb development in all vertebrates is directed by just a few regulatory genes (Shubin et al., 1997; Riddle and Tabin, 1999). A few mutations in certain *Hox* genes in early vertebrates led to the basic limb plan seen in all subsequent vertebrates, including us. With additional small mutations in these genes or in the genes they regulate, the varied structures that make up the wing of a chicken, the flipper of a porpoise, or the upper limb of a human developed. You should recognize that *basic* genetic regulatory mechanisms are highly conserved in animals; that is, they've been maintained relatively unchanged for hundreds of millions of years. Like a musical score with a basic theme, small variations on the pattern can produce the different "tunes" that differentiate one organism from another. This is the essential genetic foundation for most macroevolutionary change. Large anatomical modifications, therefore, don't always require

major genetic rearrangements. This is a crucial point and shows how we quite easily connect biologically with other life-forms and how our and their evolutionary histories are part of the same grand story of life on earth.

Structures that are shared by species on the basis of descent from a common ancestor are called **homologies**. Homologies alone are reliable indicators of evolutionary relationship, but we have to be careful not to draw hasty conclusions from superficial similarities. For example, both birds and butterflies have wings, but they shouldn't be grouped together on the basis of this single characteristic; butterflies (as insects) differ dramatically from birds in several other, even more fundamental ways. (For example, birds have an internal skeleton, central nervous system, and four limbs; insects don't.)

Here's what's happened in evolutionary history: From quite distant ancestors, both butterflies and birds have developed wings *independently*. So their (superficial) similarities

homologies Similarities between organisms based on descent from a common ancestor.

are a product of separate evolutionary responses to roughly similar functional demands. Such similarities, based on independent functional adaptation and not on shared evolutionary descent, are called **analogies**. The process that leads to the development of analogies (also called analogous structures) such as wings in birds and butterflies is termed **homoplasy**.

Constructing Classifications and Interpreting Evolutionary Relationships

Evolutionary biologists typically use two major approaches, or "schools," when interpreting evolutionary relationships, with the goal of producing classifications. The first approach, called **evolutionary systematics**, is the more traditional. The second approach, called **cladistics**, has emerged primarily in the last three decades. Although aspects of both approaches are still used by most evolutionary biologists, in recent years cladistic methodologies have predominated among anthropologists. Indeed, one noted primate evolutionist commented that "virtually all current studies of primate phylogeny involve the methods and terminology" of cladistics (Fleagle, 1999, p. 1).

Comparing Evolutionary Systematics with Cladistics

Before we begin drawing distinctions between these two approaches, it's first helpful to note features shared by both evolutionary systematics and cladistics. First, both schools are interested in tracing evolutionary relationships and in constructing classifications that reflect these relationships. Second,

both schools recognize that organisms must be compared using specific features (called *characters*) and that some of these characters are more informative than others. And third (deriving directly from the previous two points), both approaches focus exclusively on homologies.

But these approaches also have some significant differences—in how characters are chosen, which groups are compared, and how the results are interpreted and eventually incorporated into evolutionary schemes and classifications. The primary difference is that cladistics more explicitly and more rigorously defines the kinds of homologies that yield the most useful information. For example, at a very basic level, all life (except for some viruses) shares DNA as the molecule underlying all organic processes. However, beyond inferring that all life most likely derives from a single origin, the mere presence of DNA tells us nothing further regarding more specific relationships among different kinds of life-forms. To draw further conclusions, we need to look at particular characters that certain groups share as the result of more recent ancestry.

This perspective emphasizes an important point: Some homologous characters are much more informative than others. We saw earlier that all terrestrial vertebrates share homologies in the number and basic arrangement of bones in the forelimb. Even though these similarities are broadly useful in showing that these large evolutionary groups (amphibians, reptiles, and mammals) are all related through a distant ancestor, they don't provide information we can use to distinguish one group from another (a reptile from a mammal, for example). These kinds of characters (also called traits) that are shared through such remote ancestry are said to be **ancestral**, or primitive. We prefer the term *ancestral* because it doesn't reflect negatively on the evolutionary value of the character in question. In biological anthropology, the term *primitive* or *ancestral*

analogies Similarities between organisms based strictly on common function, with no assumed common evolutionary descent.

homoplasy (*homo*, meaning "same," and *plasy*, meaning "growth") The separate evolutionary development of similar characteristics in different groups of organisms.

evolutionary systematics A traditional approach to classification (and evolutionary interpretation) in which presumed ancestors and descendants are traced in time by analysis of homologous characters.

cladistics An approach to classification that attempts to make rigorous evolutionary interpretations based solely on analysis of certain types of homologous characters (those considered to be derived characters).

ancestral Referring to characters inherited by a group of organisms from a remote ancestor and thus not diagnostic of groups (lineages) that diverged after the character first appeared; also called primitive.

simply means that a character seen in two organisms is inherited in both of them from a distant ancestor.

In most cases, analyzing ancestral characters doesn't supply enough information to make accurate evolutionary interpretations of relationships between different groups. In fact, misinterpretation of ancestral characters can easily lead to inaccurate evolutionary conclusions. Cladistics focuses on traits that distinguish particular evolutionary lineages; such traits are far more informative than ancestral traits. Lineages that share a common ancestor are called a **clade**, giving the name *cladistics* to the field that seeks to identify and interpret these groups.

When we try to identify a clade, the characters of interest are said to be **derived**, or **modified**. Thus, though the general ancestral bony pattern of the forelimb in land vertebrates doesn't allow us to distinguish among them, the further modification of this pattern in certain groups (as hooves, flippers, or wings, for instance) does.

An Example of Cladistic Analysis: The Evolutionary History of Cars and Trucks

A simplified example might help clarify the basic principles used in cladistic analysis. **Figure 6-3a** shows a hypothetical "lineage" of passenger vehicles. All of the "descendant" vehicles share a common ancestor, the prototype passenger vehicle. The first major division (I) differentiates passenger cars from trucks. The second split (that is, diversification) is between luxury cars and sports cars (you could, of course, imagine many other subcategories). Modified (derived) traits that distinguish trucks from cars might include type of frame, suspension, wheel size, and, in some forms, an open cargo bed. Derived characters that might distinguish sports cars from luxury cars

could include engine size and type, wheel base size, and a decorative racing stripe.

Now let's assume that you're presented with an "unknown" vehicle (meaning one not yet classified). How do you decide what kind of vehicle it is? You might note such features as four wheels, a steering wheel, and a seat for the driver, but these are *ancestral* characters (found in the common ancestor) of all passenger vehicles. If, however, you note that the vehicle lacks a cargo bed and raised suspension (so it's not a truck) but has a racing stripe, you might conclude that it's a car, and more than that, a sports car (because it has a derived feature presumably of *only* that group).

All this seems fairly obvious, and you've probably noticed that this simple type of decision making characterizes much of human mental organization. Still, we frequently deal with complications that aren't so obvious. What if you're presented with a sports utility vehicle (SUV) with a racing stripe (**Fig. 6-3b**)? SUVs are basically trucks; the presence of a racing stripe could be seen as a homoplasy with sports cars. The lesson here is that we need to be careful, look at several traits, decide which are ancestral and which are derived, and finally try to recognize the complexity (and potential confusion) introduced by homoplasy.

Our example of passenger vehicles is useful up to a point. Because it concerns human inventions, the groupings possess characters that humans can add and delete in almost any combination. Naturally occurring organic systems are more limited in this respect. Any species can possess only those characters that have been inherited from its ancestor or that have been subsequently modified (derived) from those shared with the ancestor. So any modification in *any* species is constrained by that species' evolutionary legacy—that is, what the species starts out with.

clade A group of organisms sharing a common ancestor. The group includes the common ancestor and all descendants.

derived (modified) Referring to characters that are modified from the ancestral condition and thus diagnostic of particular evolutionary lineages.

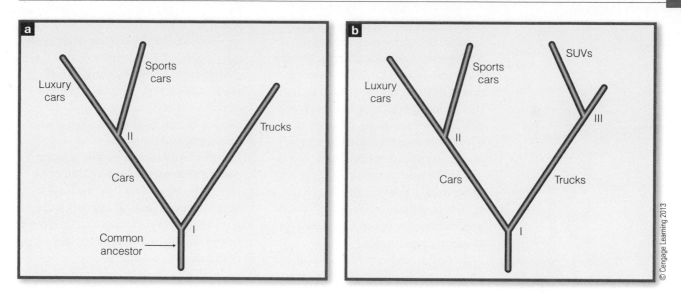

▲ **Figure 6-3**
Evolutionary "trees"
showing development of
passenger vehicles.

Using Cladistics to Interpret Real Organisms

Another example, one drawn from paleontological (fossil) evidence of actual organisms, can help clarify these points. Most people know something about dinosaur evolution, and you may know about the recent controversies surrounding this topic. There are several intriguing issues concerning the evolutionary history of dinosaurs, and recent fossil discoveries have shed considerable light on them. Here we'll consider one of the more fascinating questions: the relationship of dinosaurs to birds.

Traditionally, it was thought that birds were a distinct group from reptiles and not especially closely related to any of them (including extinct forms, such as the dinosaurs; **Fig. 6-4a**). Still, the early origins of birds were clouded in mystery and have been much debated for more than a century. In fact, the first fossil evidence of a very primitive bird (now known to be about 150 million years old) was discovered in 1861, just two years following Darwin's publication of *Origin of Species.* Despite some initial and quite remarkably accurate interpretations linking these early birds to dinosaurs, most experts concluded that there was no close relationship. This view persisted through most of the twentieth

▼ **Figure 6-4**
Evolutionary relationships
of birds and dinosaurs.
(a) Traditional view, showing
no close relationship.
(b) Revised view, showing
common ancestry of birds
and dinosaurs.

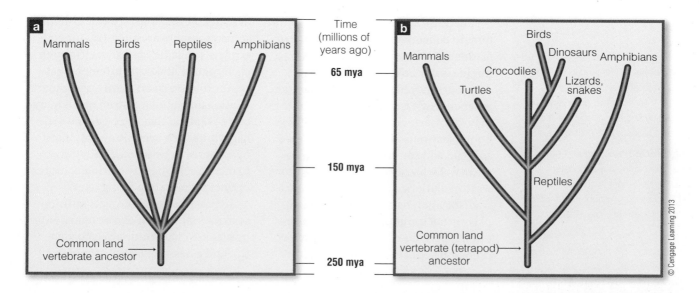

century, but discoveries made in the last two decades have supported the hypothesis that birds *are* closely related to some dinosaurs. Two developments in particular have influenced this change of opinion: some remarkable discoveries in the 1990s from China, Madagascar, and elsewhere and the application of cladistic methods to the interpretation of these and other fossils. (Here is another example of how new discoveries as well as new approaches can become the basis for changing hypotheses.)

Recent finds from Madagascar of chicken-sized, primitive birds dated to 70–65 million years ago (mya) show an elongated second toe (similar, in fact, to that seen in the dinosaur *Velociraptor*, made infamous in the film *Jurassic Park*). Indeed, these primitive birds from Madagascar show many other similarities to *Velociraptor* and its close cousins. Even more extraordinary finds have been unearthed recently in China, where the traces of what were once *feathers* have been found embossed in fossilized sediments! For many researchers, these new finds have finally solved the mystery of bird origins (Fig. 6-4b), leading them to conclude that "birds are not only *descended* from dinosaurs, they *are* dinosaurs (and reptiles)—just as humans are mammals, even though people are as different from other mammals as birds are from other reptiles" (Padian and Chiappe, 1998, p. 43).

There are some doubters who remain concerned that the presence of feathers in dinosaurs (145–125 mya) might simply be a homoplasy (that is, dinosaurs may have developed the trait independently from its appearance in birds). Certainly, the possibility of homoplasy must always be considered, as it can add considerably to the complexity of what seems like a straightforward evolutionary interpretation. Strict cladistic analysis assumes that homoplasy is not a common occurrence; if it were, perhaps no evolutionary interpretation could be very straightforward! When we discuss our own more recent evolutionary lineage (the hominins, beginning in Chapter 9), we'll see that possible homoplasy might well really mess up any simple interpretation. Fortunately, in the case of the proposed relationship between some dinosaurs and birds, the presence of feathers looks like an excellent example of a **shared derived** characteristic, which therefore *does* link the forms. What's more, cladistic analysis emphasizes that several characteristics should be examined, because homoplasy might muddle an interpretation based on just one or two shared traits. In the bird/dinosaur case, several other characteristics further suggest their evolutionary relationship.

One last point needs to be mentioned. Traditional evolutionary systematics illustrates the hypothesized evolutionary relationships using a *phylogeny*, more properly called a **phylogenetic tree**. Strict cladistic analysis, however, shows relationships in a **cladogram** (Fig. 6-5). If you examine the charts in Figures 6-4 and 6-5, you'll see some obvious differences. A phylogenetic tree incorporates the dimension of time, as shown in Figure 6-4 (you can find many other examples in this and upcoming chapters). A cladogram doesn't indicate time; all forms (fossil and modern) are shown along one dimension. Phylogenetic trees usually attempt to make some hypotheses regarding ancestor–descendant relationships (for example, some dinosaurs are ancestral to modern birds). Cladistic analysis (through cladograms) makes no attempt whatsoever to discern ancestor–descendant relationships. In fact, strict cladists are quite skeptical that the evidence really permits such specific evolutionary hypotheses to be scientifically confirmed (because there are many more extinct species than living ones).

In practice, most physical anthropologists (and other evolutionary biologists) use cladistic analysis to identify and assess the utility of traits and

shared derived Relating to specific character traits shared in common between two life-forms and considered the most useful type of characteristic for making evolutionary interpretations.

phylogenetic tree A chart showing evolutionary relationships as determined by evolutionary systematics. It contains a time component and implies ancestor–descendant relationships.

cladogram A chart showing evolutionary relationships as determined by cladistic analysis. It's based solely on interpretation of shared derived characters. It contains no time component and does not imply ancestor-descendant relationships.

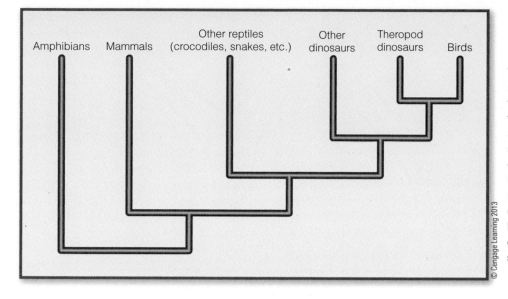

◄**Figure 6-5**
This cladogram shows the relationships of birds, dinosaurs, and other terrestrial vertebrates. Notice that there's no time scale, and both living and fossil forms are shown along the same dimension—that is, ancestor–descendant relationships aren't indicated. The chart is slightly simplified, as there are other branches (not shown) within the reptiles (with birds slightly more closely related to crocodiles than to other reptiles, such as snakes and lizards).

to make testable hypotheses regarding the relationships between groups of organisms. They also frequently extend this basic cladistic methodology to further hypothesize likely ancestor–descendant relationships shown relative to a time scale (that is, in a phylogenetic tree). In this way, aspects of both traditional evolutionary systematics and cladistic analysis are combined to produce a more complete picture of evolutionary history. We'll have lots to say about hominin evolutionary relationships, and we'll use this combined approach to make interpretations.

Definition of Species

Whether biologists are doing a cladistic or more traditional phylogenetic analysis, they're comparing groups of organisms—that is, different species, genera (*sing.,* genus), families, orders, and so forth. Fundamental to all these levels of classification is the most basic, the species. It's appropriate, then, to ask how biologists define species. We addressed this issue briefly in Chapters 1 and 2, where we used the most common definition, one that emphasizes interbreeding and reproductive isolation. While it's not the only definition of species, this view, called the **biologi-**

cal species concept (Mayr, 1970), is the one preferred by most biologists.

To understand what species are, you might consider how they come about in the first place—what Darwin called the "origin of species." This most fundamental of macroevolutionary processes is called **speciation**. According to the biological species concept, the way new species are first produced involves some form of isolation. Picture a single species (baboons, for example) composed of several populations distributed over a wide geographical area. Gene exchange between populations (gene flow) will be limited if a geographical barrier, such as an ocean or a large river, effectively separates these populations. This extremely important form of isolating mechanism is called *geographical isolation.*

If one baboon population (A) is separated from another baboon population (B) by a river that has changed course, individual baboons of population A won't mate with individuals from population B (**Fig. 6-6**). As time passes (perhaps hundreds or thousands of generations), genetic differences will accumulate in both populations. If population size is small, we can assume that genetic drift will also cause allele frequencies to change in both populations. And because drift

biological species concept A depiction of species as groups of individuals capable of fertile interbreeding but reproductively isolated from other such groups.

speciation The process by which a new species evolves from an earlier species. Speciation is the most basic process in macroevolution.

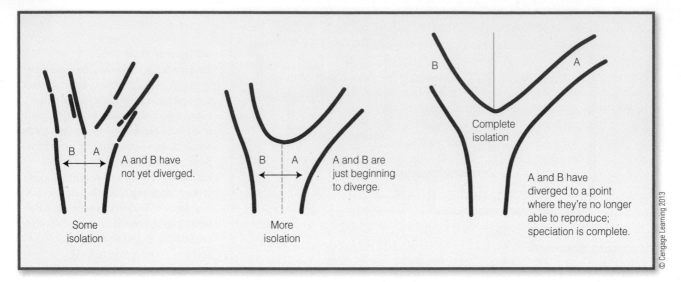

© Cengage Learning 2013

▲ **Figure 6-6**
This speciation model illustrates branching evolution, or cladogenesis, which is caused by increasing reproductive isolation.

is *random*, we wouldn't expect the effects to be the same. Consequently, the two populations will begin to diverge genetically.

As long as gene exchange is limited, the populations can only become more genetically different over time. What's more, further difference can be expected if the baboon groups are occupying slightly different habitats. These additional genetic differences would be incorporated through the process of natural selection. Certain individuals in population A would be more reproductively fit in their own environment, but they would show less reproductive success in the environment occupied by population B. So allele frequencies will shift further, resulting in even greater divergence between the two groups.

With the cumulative effects of genetic drift and natural selection acting over many generations, the result will be two populations that—even if they were to come back into contact—could no longer interbreed. More than just geographical isolation might now apply. There may, for instance, be behavioral differences that interfere with courtship—what we call *behavioral isolation*. Using our *biological* definition of species, we would now recognize two distinct species where initially only one existed.

Interpreting Species and Other Groups in the Fossil Record

Throughout much of this text, we'll be using various taxonomic terms to refer to fossil primates (including fossil hominins). You'll be introduced to such names as *Proconsul*, *Sivapithecus*, *Australopithecus*, and *Homo*. (Of course, *Homo* is still a living primate.) But it's especially difficult to make these types of designations from remains of animals that are long dead (and only partially preserved as skeletal remains). In these contexts, what do such names mean in evolutionary terms?

Our goal when applying species, genus, or other taxonomic labels to groups of organisms is to make meaningful biological statements about the variation that's represented. When looking at populations of living or long-extinct animals, we certainly are going to see variation; this happens in *any* sexually reproducing organism due to recombination (see Chapter 3). As a result of recombination, each individual organism is a unique combination of genetic material, and the uniqueness is often reflected to some extent in the phenotype.

Besides such *individual variation*, we see other kinds of systematic variation in all biological populations. *Age changes* alter overall body size, as well as shape, in many mammals. One pertinent example for fossil human and ape studies is the change in number, size, and shape of teeth from deciduous (also known as baby or milk) teeth (only 20 teeth are present) to permanent dentition (32 are present). It would be an obvious error to distinguish two fossil forms based solely on such age-dependent criteria. If one individual were represented just by milk teeth and another (seemingly very different) individual were represented just by adult teeth, they easily could be different-aged individuals from the *same* population. Researchers dealing with fragmentary remains must be alert to variation of this sort. Otherwise, one could make such a silly mistake as thinking pieces of a two-year-old were from a different species than his/her mother!

Variation due to sex also plays an important role in influencing differences among individuals observed in biological populations. Differences in physical characteristics between males and females of the same species, called **sexual dimorphism**, can result in marked variation in body size and proportions in adults of the same species (we'll discuss this important topic in more detail in Chapter 7).

Recognition of Fossil Species

Keeping in mind all the types of variation present within interbreeding groups of organisms, the minimum biological category we'd like to define in fossil primate samples is the *species*. As already defined (according to the biological species concept), a species is a group of interbreeding or potentially interbreeding organisms that is reproductively isolated from other such groups. In modern organisms, this concept is theoretically testable by observations of reproductive behavior. In animals long extinct, such observations are obviously impossible. Our only way, then, to get a handle on the variation we see in fossil groups is to refer to living animals.

When studying a fossil group, we may observe obvious variation, such as some individuals being larger and with bigger teeth than others. The question then becomes: What's the biological significance of this variation? Two possibilities come to mind. Either the variation is accounted for by individual, age, and sex differences seen *within* every biological species (that is, it is **intraspecific**), or the variation represents differences *between* reproductively isolated groups (that is, it is **interspecific**). To decide which answer is correct, we have to look at contemporary species.

If the amount of variation we observe in fossil samples is comparable to that seen today *within species of closely related forms*, then we shouldn't "split" our sample into more than one species. We must, however, be careful in choosing modern analogues, because rates of evolution vary among different groups of mammals. So, for example, when studying extinct fossil primates, it's necessary to compare them with well-known modern primates. Even so, studies of living groups show that defining exactly where species boundaries begin and end is often difficult. In dealing with extinct species, the uncertainties are even greater. In addition to the overlapping patterns of variation *spatially* (over space), variation also occurs *temporally* (through time). In other words, even more variation will be seen in **paleospecies**, because individuals may be separated by thousands or even millions of years. Applying a strict Linnaean taxonomy to such a situation presents an unavoidable dilemma. Standard Linnaean classification, as used by biologists, is designed to take into account the variation present at any given time; that is, it describes a static situation. But when we deal with paleospecies, the time frame is expanded and the situation can be dynamic (in other words, later forms might be different from earlier forms). In such a

sexual dimorphism Differences in physical characteristics between males and females of the same species. For example, humans are slightly sexually dimorphic for body size, with males being taller, on average, than females of the same population. Sexual dimorphism is very pronounced in many species, such as gorillas.

intraspecific Within species; refers to variation seen within the same species.

interspecific Between species; refers to variation beyond that seen within the same species to include additional aspects seen between two different species.

paleospecies Species defined from fossil evidence, often covering a long time span.

dynamic situation, taxonomic decisions (where to draw species boundaries) will unavoidably be somewhat arbitrary.

Because the task of interpreting paleospecies is so difficult, paleoanthropologists have sought various solutions. Most researchers today define species using clusters of derived traits (identified cladistically). But owing to the ambiguity of how many derived characters are required to identify a fully distinct species (as opposed to a subspecies), the frequent mixing of characters into novel combinations, and the always difficult problem of homoplasy, there continues to be disagreement. A good deal of the dispute is driven by philosophical orientation. Exactly how much diversity should one expect among fossil primates, especially among fossil hominins?

Some researchers, called "splitters," claim that speciation occurred frequently during hominin evolution, and they often identify numerous fossil hominin species in a sample being studied. As the nickname suggests, these scientists are inclined to split groups into many species. Others, called "lumpers," assume that speciation was less common and see much variation as being intraspecific. These scientists lump groups together, so that fewer hominin species are identified, named, and eventually plugged into evolutionary schemes. As you'll see in the following chapters, debates of this sort pervade paleoanthropology, perhaps more than in any other branch of evolutionary biology.

Recognition of Fossil Genera

The next and broader level of taxonomic classification, the **genus** (*pl.*, genera), presents another challenge for biologists. To have more than one genus, we obviously must have at least two species (reproductively isolated groups), and the species of one genus must differ in a basic way from the species of another genus. A genus is there-

fore defined as a group of species composed of members more closely related to each other than they are to species from any other genus.

Grouping species into genera can be quite subjective and is often much debated by biologists. One possible test for contemporary animals is to check for results of hybridization between individuals of different species—rare in nature, but quite common in captivity. If members of two normally separate species interbreed and produce live (though not necessarily fertile) offspring, the two parental species probably are not too different genetically and should therefore be grouped in the same genus. A well-known example of such a cross is horses with donkeys (*Equus caballus* × *Equus asinus*), which normally produces live but sterile offspring (mules).

As previously mentioned, we can't perform breeding experiments with extinct animals, which is why another definition of genus becomes highly relevant. Species that are members of the same genus share the same broad adaptive zone. An adaptive zone represents a general ecological lifestyle more basic than the narrower **ecological niches** characteristic of individual species. This ecological definition of genus can be an immense aid in interpreting fossil primates. Teeth are the most frequently preserved parts, and they often can provide excellent general ecological inferences. Cladistic analysis also helps scientists to make judgments about evolutionary relationships. That is, members of the same genus should all share derived characters not seen in members of other genera.

As a final comment, we should stress that classification by genus is not always a straightforward decision. For instance, in emphasizing the very close genetic similarities between humans (*Homo sapiens*) and chimpanzees (*Pan troglodytes*), some current researchers (Wildman et al., 2003) place both in the same genus (*Homo sapiens, Homo troglodytes*). This philosophy has caused some to support extending basic

genus (*pl.*, genera) A group of closely related species.

ecological niche The position of a species within its physical and biological environments. A species' ecological niche is defined by such components as diet, terrain, vegetation, type of predators, relationships with other species, and activity patterns, and each niche is unique to a given species. Together, ecological niches make up an ecosystem.

fossils Traces or remnants of organisms found in geological beds on the earth's surface.

human rights to great apes (as proposed by members of the Great Ape Project). Such thinking might startle you. Of course, when it gets this close to home, it's often difficult to remain objective!

What Are Fossils and How Do They Form?

Much of what we know about the history of life comes from studying **fossils**. Fossils are traces of ancient organisms and can be formed in many ways. The oldest fossils found thus far date back to more than 3 billion years ago; because they are the remains of microorganisms, they are extremely small and are called *microfossils*.

These very early traces of life are fragile and very rare. Most of our evidence comes from later in time and usually in the form of pieces of shells, bones, or teeth, all of which, even in a living animal, were already partly made of mineral. After the organism died, these "hard" tissues were further impregnated with other minerals, being eventually transformed into a stone-like composition in a process called **mineralization** (**Fig. 6-7**).

There are, however, many other ways in which life-forms have left traces of their existence. Sometimes insects were trapped in tree sap, which

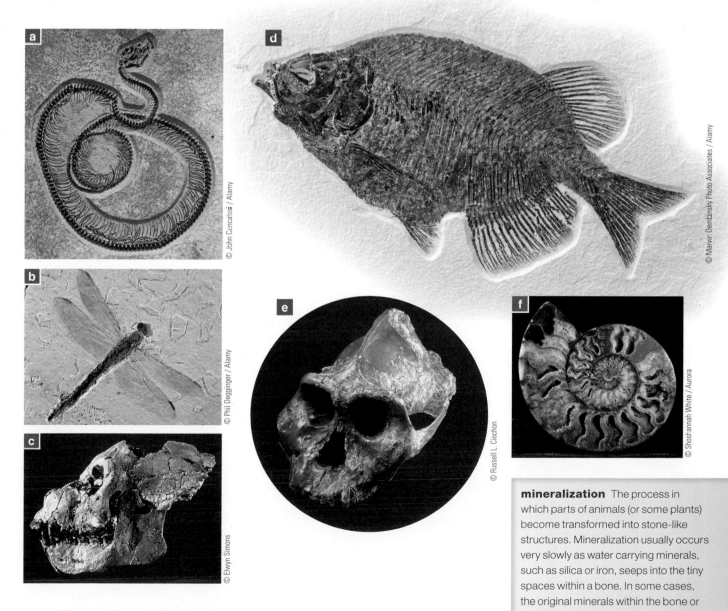

© John Cencalosi / Alamy
© Phil Degginger / Alamy
© Elwyn Simons
© Russell L. Ciochon
© Marvin Dembinsky Photo Associates / Alamy
© Shoshannah White / Aurora

▼ Figure 6-7
Examples of mineralized fossils. **(a)** A mineralized snake caste from geological deposits in Wyoming (dated to about 50 mya). **(b)** A fossil dragonfly from Brazil, dated to more than 100 mya. **(c)** An early primate skull from Egypt, dated to about 30 mya. **(d)** A fossil fish (a relative of the piranha) from the same deposits as the snake above (also dated to approximately 50 mya). **(e)** A fossilized skull of a hominin from East Africa, dated to 2.5 mya. **(f)** A nautilus, a relative of living snails.

mineralization The process in which parts of animals (or some plants) become transformed into stone-like structures. Mineralization usually occurs very slowly as water carrying minerals, such as silica or iron, seeps into the tiny spaces within a bone. In some cases, the original minerals within the bone or tooth can be completely replaced, molecule by molecule, with other minerals.

▶ **Figure 6-8**
A spider fossilized in amber.

© Kazuo Unno / Minden Pictures

later became hardened and chemically altered. Because there was little or no oxygen inside the hardened amber, the insects have remained remarkably well preserved for millions of years, with even soft tissue and DNA still present (**Fig. 6-8**). This fascinating circumstance led author Michael Crichton to conjure the events depicted in the novel (and motion picture) *Jurassic Park*.

Dinosaur footprints as well as much more recent hominin tracks, leaf imprints in hardened mud or similar impressions of small organisms, and even the traces of dinosaur feathers—all of these are fossils. Recently, beautifully preserved dinosaur feathers have been discovered in northeastern China (dated to approximately 125 mya). These remains are so superbly preserved that even microscopic cell structures have been indentified. These tiny structures directly influenced feather color in ancient dinosaurs; what's more, these same structures influence feather color in modern birds. Researchers are now able to deduce that some stripes in the feathers of one dinosaur were chestnut/reddish brown in color (Zhang et al., 2010)!

A spectacular discovery of a 47-million-year-old early primate fossil was widely publicized in 2009. This fossil is remarkable, preserving more than 95 percent of the skeleton as well as outlines of soft tissue and even fossilized remains of digestive tract contents (see Chapter 9) (Franzen et al., 2009). The amazing preservation of this small primate occurred because it died on the edge of a volcanic lake and was quickly covered with sediment. It reminds us that whether a dead animal will become fossilized and how much of it will be preserved depends partly on *how* it dies, but even more on *where* it dies.

Some ancient organisms have left vast amounts of fossil remains. Indeed, limestone deposits can be hundreds of feet thick and are largely made up of fossilized remains of marine shellfish. (see Chapter 2).

Fossils of land animals are not nearly so common. After an animal dies—let's say it's an early hominin from 2 mya—it will probably be eaten and its bones scattered and broken, and eventually they will decompose. After just a few weeks, there will be hardly anything left to fossilize. But suppose, by chance, this recently deceased hominin became quickly covered by sediment, perhaps by sand and mud in a streambed or along a lakeshore or by volcanic ash from a

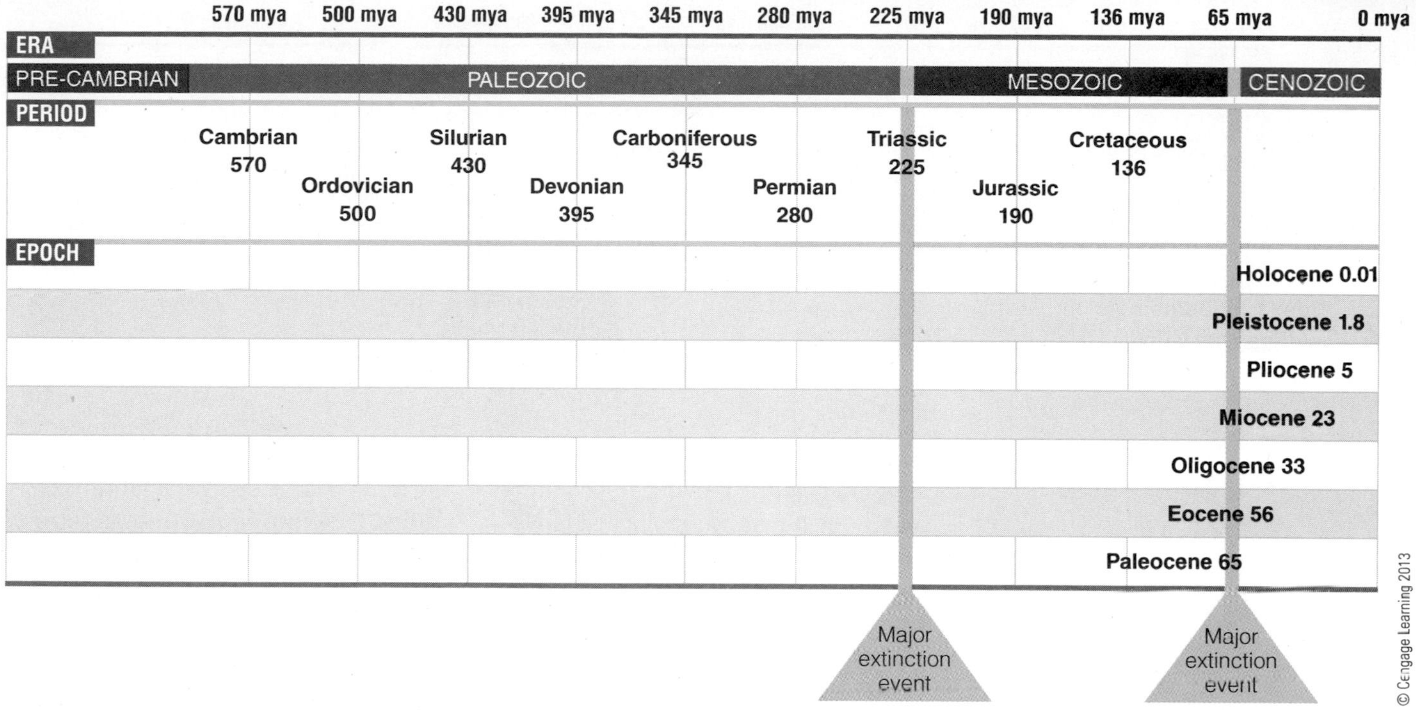

	570 mya	500 mya	430 mya	395 mya	345 mya	280 mya	225 mya	190 mya	136 mya	65 mya	0 mya
ERA											
	PRE-CAMBRIAN		PALEOZOIC					MESOZOIC			CENOZOIC
PERIOD											
		Cambrian 570		Silurian 430		Carboniferous 345	Triassic 225		Cretaceous 136		
			Ordovician 500		Devonian 395		Permian 280	Jurassic 190			
EPOCH											
											Holocene 0.01
											Pleistocene 1.8
											Pliocene 5
											Miocene 23
											Oligocene 33
											Eocene 56
											Paleocene 65

Major extinction event   Major extinction event

© Cengage Learning 2013

▲ **Figure 6-9**
Geological time scale.

nearby volcano. As a result, the long, slow process of mineralization may eventually turn at least some parts of the hominin into a fossil.

The study of how bones and other materials come to be buried in the earth and preserved as fossils is called **taphonomy**. Among the topics that taphonomists try to understand are processes of sedimentation, including the action of streams, preservation properties of bone, and carnivore disturbance factors.

Vertebrate Evolutionary History: A Brief Summary

Biologists must contend with not only the staggering array of living and extinct life-forms, but also with the vast amount of time that life has been evolving on earth. Again, scientists have devised simplified schemes— but in this case to organize *time*, not biological diversity.

Geologists have formulated the **geological time scale** (Fig. 6-9), in which immense time spans are orga-

nized into eras that include one or more periods. Periods, in turn, can be broken down into epochs. For the time span encompassing vertebrate evolution, there are three eras: the Paleozoic, the Mesozoic, and the Cenozoic. The earliest vertebrate fossils date to early in the Paleozoic at 500 mya, and their origins are probably much older. It's the vertebrate capacity to form bone that accounts for their more complete fossil record *after* 500 mya.

During the Paleozoic, several varieties of fishes (including the ancestors of modern sharks and bony fishes), amphibians, and reptiles appeared. At the end of the Paleozoic, close to 250 mya, several varieties of mammal-like reptiles were also diversifying. It's generally thought that some of these forms gave rise to the mammals.

The evolutionary history of vertebrates and other organisms during the Paleozoic and Mesozoic was profoundly influenced by geographical events. We know that the positions of the earth's continents have dramatically shifted during the last several hundred million years. This process, called **continental drift**, is explained by the geological theory of *plate tectonics*,

taphonomy The study of how bones and other materials come to be buried in the earth and preserved as fossils.

geological time scale The organization of earth history into eras, periods, and epochs; commonly used by geologists and paleoanthropologists.

continental drift The movement of continents on sliding plates of the earth's surface. As a result, the positions of large landmasses have shifted drastically during the earth's history.

570 mya	500 mya	430 mya	395 mya	345 mya	
ERA					
				PALEOZOIC	
PERIOD					
Cambrian	**Ordovician**	**Silurian**	**Devonian**	**Carboniferous**	
Trilobites abundant; also brachiopods, jellyfish, worms, and other invertebrates	First fishes; trilobites still abundant; graptolites and corals become plentiful; possible land plants	Jawed fishes appear; first air-breathing animals; definite land plants	Age of Fishes; first amphibians and first forests appear	First reptiles; radiation of amphibians; modern insects diversify	

which states that the earth's crust is a series of gigantic moving and colliding plates. Such massive geological movements can induce volcanic activity (as, for example, all around the Pacific Rim), mountain building (for example, the Himalayas), and earthquakes. Living on the juncture of the Pacific and North American plates, residents of the Pacific coast of the United States are very much aware of some of these consequences, as illustrated by the explosive volcanic eruption of Mt. St. Helens and the frequent earthquakes in Alaska and California.

While reconstructing the earth's physical history, geologists have determined the earlier positions of major continental landmasses. During the late Paleozoic, the continents came together to form a single colossal landmass called *Pangea*. During the early Mesozoic, the southern continents began to split off from Pangea, forming a large southern landmass called *Gondwanaland* (**Fig. 6-10a**). Similarly, the northern continents were consolidated into a northern landmass called *Laurasia*. During the Mesozoic, Gondwanaland and Laurasia continued to drift apart and to break up into smaller segments. By the end of the Mesozoic (about 65 mya), the continents were beginning to assume their current positions (**Fig. 6-10b**).

The evolutionary ramifications of this long-term continental drift were profound. Groups of animals became effectively isolated from each other by oceans, significantly influencing the distribution of mammals and other land vertebrates. These continental movements continued in the Cenozoic and indeed are still happening, although without such dramatic results.

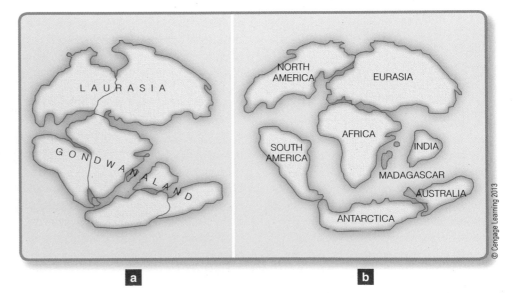

▶ **Figure 6-10**
Continental drift. **(a)** Positions of the continents during the Mesozoic (ca. 125 mya). Pangea is breaking up into a northern landmass (Laurasia) and a southern landmass (Gondwanaland). **(b)** Positions of the continents at the beginning of the Cenozoic (ca. 65 mya).

© Cengage Learning 2013

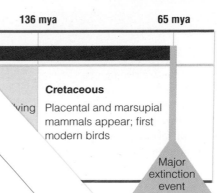

136 mya	65 mya

Cretaceous

Placental and marsupial mammals appear; first modern birds

Major extinction event

© Cengage Learning 2013

Figure 6-11

This time line depicts major events in early vertebrate evolution.

Neocortex

Cerebellum

© Cengage Learning 2013

...was ...birds, ...eptiles as ...g vertebrates. ...nt for the rela- ...ss of the mammals ...e Mesozoic and early ...ic? Several characteristics relat- ...learning and general flexibility ...havior are of prime importance. ...mmals were selected for larger ...ins than those typically found in ...ptiles, making them better equipped ...process information. In particu- ar, the cerebrum became generally enlarged, especially the outer covering, the neocortex, which controls higher brain functions (**Fig. 6-12**). In some mammals, the cerebrum expanded so much that it came to comprise most of the brain volume; the number of surface convolutions also increased, creating more surface area and thus providing space for even more nerve cells (neurons). As we discuss in Chapter 7, this is a trend even further emphasized among the primates.

For such a large and complex organ as the mammalian brain to develop, a longer, more intense period of growth is required. Slower development can occur internally (*in utero*) as well as after birth. Internal fertilization and internal development aren't unique to mammals, but the latter was a major innovation among terrestrial vertebrates. Other forms (most fishes and

epochs Categories of the geological time scale; subdivisions of periods. In the Cenozoic era, epochs include the Paleocene, Eocene, Oligocene, Miocene, and Pliocene (from the Tertiary Period) and the Pleistocene and Holocene (from the Quaternary Period).

▶ Figure 6-12
Lateral view of the brain in fishes, reptiles, and primates. You can see the increased size of the cerebral cortex (neocortex) of the primate brain. The cerebral cortex integrates sensory information and selects responses.

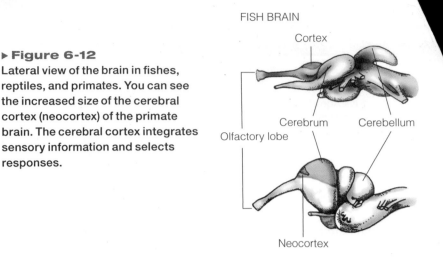

FISH BRAIN

Cortex

Cerebrum   Cerebellum

Olfactory lobe

Cerebrum

Neocortex

REPTILE BRAIN   PRIMATE E

reptiles—including birds) lay eggs, and "prenatal" development occurs externally, outside the mother's body. Mammals, with very few exceptions, give birth to live young. Even among mammals, however, there's considerable variation among the major groups in how mature the young are at birth; and in **placental** mammals, including ourselves, *in utero* development goes farthest.

Another distinctive feature of mammals is the dentition. Although many living reptiles (such as lizards and snakes) consistently have similarly shaped teeth (called a *homodont* dentition), mammals have differently shaped teeth (**Fig. 6-13**). This varied pattern, termed a **heterodont** dentition, is reflected in the ancestral (primitive) mammalian arrangement of teeth,

which includes 3
premolars, and 3 m
ter of the mouth. S
each quarter of the
tral mammalian der
includes a total of 44
erodont arrangemen
mals to process a wid
Incisors are used for c
for grasping and pierc
molars and molars for
grinding.

A final point regardi
to their disproportionat
tion in the fossil record.
est, most durable portion
brate skeleton, teeth have
likelihood of becoming fo
is, mineralized), because t
dominantly composed of n
begin with. As a result, the

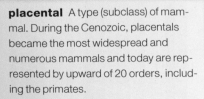

a REPTILIAN (alligator): homodont

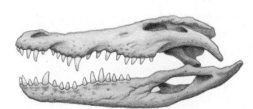

Incisors

Canine

Premolars   Molars

Cheek teeth

b MAMMALIAN: heterodo

▲ Figure 6-13
Reptilian and mammalian teeth.

ity of available fossil data for most vertebrates, including primates, consists of teeth.

Another major adaptive complex that distinguishes contemporary mammals from reptiles (except birds) is the maintenance of a constant internal body temperature. Known colloquially (and incorrectly) as warm-bloodedness, this crucial physiological adaptation is also seen in contemporary birds and may have characterized many dinosaurs as well. Except for birds, reptiles maintain a constant internal body temperature through exposure to the sun; these reptiles are said to be *ectothermic*. In mammals and birds, however, energy is generated *internally* through metabolic activity (by processing food or by muscle action); for this reason, mammals and birds are said to be **endothermic**.

The Emergence of Major Mammalian Groups

There are three major subgroups of living mammals: the egg-laying mammals, or monotremes; the pouched mammals, or marsupials; and the placental mammals. The monotremes, of which the platypus is one example (**Fig. 6-14**), are extremely primitive and are considered more distinct from marsupials or placentals than these two subgroups are from each other. The recent sequencing of the full genome of the platypus (Warren et al., 2008) has confirmed the very ancient origins of the monotremes and their distinctiveness from other mammals.

The most notable difference between marsupials and placental mammals concerns fetal development. In marsupials, the young are born extremely immature and must complete development in an external pouch (**Fig. 6-15**). But placental mammals develop over a longer period of time *in utero*, made possible by the evolutionary develop-

ment of a specialized tissue (the placenta) that provides for fetal nourishment.

With a longer gestation period, the central nervous system develops more completely in the placental fetus. What's more, after birth, the "bond of milk" between mother and young allows more time for complex neural structures to form. We should also emphasize that from a *biosocial* perspective, this dependency period not only allows for adequate physiological development but also provides for a wider range of learning stimuli. That is, a vast amount of information is channeled to the young mammalian brain through observation of the mother's behavior and through play with age mates. It's not enough to have evolved a brain capable of learning. Collateral evolution of mammalian social systems has ensured that young mammal brains are provided with ample learning opportunities and are thus put to good use.

Processes of Macroevolution

As we noted earlier, evolution operates at both microevolutionary and macroevolutionary levels. We discussed evolution primarily from a microevolutionary perspective in Chapter 4; in this chapter, our focus is on macroevolution. Macroevolutionary mechanisms operate more on the whole species than on individuals or populations, and they take much longer than microevolutionary processes to have a noticeable impact.

Adaptive Radiation

As we mentioned in Chapter 2, the potential capacity of a group of organisms to multiply is practically unlimited, but its ability to increase its numbers is regulated largely by the availability of resources (food, water,

▲**Figure 6-14**
A duck-billed platypus (monotreme).

▲**Figure 6-15**
A wallaby with an infant in the pouch (marsupials).

endothermic (*endo*, meaning "within" or "internal") Able to maintain internal body temperature by producing energy through metabolic processes within cells; characteristic of mammals, birds, and perhaps some dinosaurs.

shelter, and space). As population size increases, access to resources decreases, and the environment will ultimately prove inadequate. Depleted resources induce some members of a population to seek an environment in which competition is reduced and the opportunities for survival and reproductive success are increased. This evolutionary tendency to exploit unoccupied habitats may eventually produce an abundance of diverse species.

This story has been played out countless times during the history of life, and some groups have expanded extremely rapidly. This evolutionary process, known as **adaptive radiation**, can also be seen in the divergence of the stem reptiles into the profusion of different forms of the late Paleozoic and especially those of the Mesozoic. It's a process that takes place when a life-form rapidly takes advantage, so to speak, of the many newly available ecological niches.

The principle of evolution illustrated by adaptive radiation is fairly simple, but important. It may be stated this way: A species, or group of species, will diverge into as many variations as two factors allow. These factors are (1) its adaptive potential and (2) the adaptive opportunities of the available niches.

In the case of reptiles, there was little divergence in the very early stages of evolution, when the ancestral form was little more than one among a variety of amphibian water dwellers. Later, a more efficient egg (one that could incubate out of water) developed in reptiles; this new egg, with a hard, watertight shell, had great adaptive potential, but initially there were few zones to invade. When reptiles became fully terrestrial, however, a wide array of ecological niches became accessible to them. Once freed from their attachment to water, reptiles were able to exploit landmasses with no serious competition from any other animal. They moved into the many different ecological niches on land (and to some extent in the air

and sea), and as they adapted to these areas, they diversified into a large number of species. This spectacular radiation burst forth with such evolutionary speed that it may well be termed an adaptive explosion.

Of course, the rapid expansion of placental mammals during the late Mesozoic and throughout the Cenozoic is another excellent example of adaptive radiation. The worldwide major extinction event at the end of the Cenozoic left thousands of econiches vacant as the dinosaurs became extinct. Small-bodied, mostly nocturnal mammals had been around for at least 70 million years, and once they were no longer in competition with the dinosaurs, they were free to move into previously occupied habitats. Thus, over the course of several million years, there was a major adaptive radiation of mammals as they diversified to exploit previously unavailable habitats.

Generalized and Specialized Characteristics

Another aspect of evolution closely related to adaptive radiation involves the transition from *generalized* characteristics to *specialized* characteristics. These two terms refer to the adaptive potential of a particular trait. A trait that's adapted for many functions is said to be generalized, whereas one that's limited to a narrow set of functions is said to be specialized.

For example, a generalized mammalian limb has five fairly flexible digits, adapted for many possible functions (grasping, weight support, and digging). In this respect, human hands are still quite generalized. On the other hand (or foot), there have been many structural modifications in our feet to make them suited for the specialized function of stable weight support in an upright posture.

The terms *generalized* and *specialized* are also sometimes used when speaking of the adaptive potential of

adaptive radiation The relatively rapid expansion and diversification of life-forms into new ecological niches.

whole organisms. Consider, for example, the aye-aye of Madagascar, an unusual primate species. The aye-aye is a highly specialized animal, structurally adapted to a narrow, rodent/woodpecker-like econiche—digging holes with prominent incisors and removing insect larvae with an elongated bony finger (**Fig. 6-16**).

It's important to note that only a generalized ancestor can provide the flexible evolutionary basis for rapid diversification. Only a generalized species with potential for adaptation to varied ecological niches can lead to all the later diversification and specialization of forms into particular ecological niches.

An issue that we've already raised also bears on this discussion: the relationship of ancestral and derived characters. It's not always the case, but ancestral characters *usually* tend to be more generalized. And specialized characteristics are nearly always derived ones as well.

Working Together: Microevolution and Macroevolution

For many years, evolutionary biologists generally agreed that microevolutionary mechanisms could be translated directly into the larger-scale macroevolutionary changes, especially the most central of all macroevolutionary processes, speciation. However, four decades ago, some leading evolutionary biologists challenged this traditional view.

Over the last 40 years evolutionary biologists have debated whether there are fundamental differences between the processes of micro- as compared to macroevolution. This discussion continues, and divergent views, framed as specific hypotheses, are further tested against new evidence. At present, the major difference seems to be one of

▲**Figure 6-16**
An aye-aye, a specialized primate native to Madagascar. Note the elongated middle finger, which is used to probe under bark for insects.

scale. That is, both processes are driven by similar factors; however, macroevolution takes much longer to occur than does microevolution.

For example, several species of very early hominins evolved over more than 4 million years, initially separating from their common ancestor with chimpanzees, and some of these species eventually adapted to more ground-living niches. These changes clearly reflect macroevolutionary processes. Much more recently, some modern human populations adapted in just a couple of thousand years to living at high altitudes, which was made more possible by changes in particular genes. This is a good example of microevolution.

We should note that rates of evolutionary change can speed up at certain times and slow down during other periods. Most crucially, natural selection is influenced by how fast the environment is changing (and how fast genetic changes appear and spread within a species). Both fossil and molecular evidence (Pagel et al., 2006) indicate that both gradual (slow) and rapid (also called "punctuated") changes have occurred in the evolution of both plant and animal species.

In all lineages, the pace assuredly speeds up and slows down due to factors that influence the size and relative isolation of populations. As we've said, environmental changes that influence the pace and direction of natural selection must also be considered. So, in general accordance with the Modern Synthesis and as indicated by molecular evidence, microevolution and macroevolution don't need to be considered separately, as some evolutionary biologists have suggested. Some groups of primates, for instance, simply have slower or faster durations of speciation, which is why Old World monkeys typically speciate more slowly than the great apes.

Why It Matters

Why is it useful to know about the age of the earth and continental drift? A scientific understanding of earth history reveals that life on our planet stretches back hundreds of millions of years. During this time, the continents have dramatically changed in location, and these changes influenced the distribution of life-forms. But what does any of this have to do with us and our world today? In fact, what does it *really* matter if the earth is only a few thousand years old, as some people claim?

Some of us who have lived in California or other *tectonically* active regions are well aware of earthquakes. Anyone who has experienced an earthquake knows that they're more than unsettling; they can be downright dangerous. For example, a 1976 earthquake in China is estimated to have killed 250,000 people, and the 2010 earthquake in Haiti is thought to have killed at least 200,000 people. Even more recently, in 2011, the gigantic earthquake and ensuing tsunami in Japan killed more than 20,000 people. Volcanoes also pose major risks to millions of people. It's the movement of the earth's crust on sliding plates that have led to earthquakes, volcanoes, and ultimately continental drift during the vast spans of earth's geological history. You've heard of the explosive eruption of Mt. Vesuvius in A.D. 79 that destroyed Pompeii and decimated a large region of southern Italy. Today, this brooding and still active volcanic mountain looms over nearby Naples, a city of over 3 million people. We have reason to be concerned about the power of nature, but can we predict future catastrophes and perhaps save thousands of lives? Geologists are currently researching ways to do exactly this, and one major approach is to study geological beds that are millions of years old. From this long geological record it becomes possible to compute the *periodicity* of major earthquakes or volcanic eruptions. This information allows geologists to make general predictions, for example, of when the next major quake in San Francisco or Los Angeles will occur or when Vesuvius will next explode in lethal fury. By the way, insurance companies make regular use of such information to evaluate which properties to insure and how much they will charge.

Summary of Main Topics

- To understand the large-scale evolutionary history of life on earth, two major organizing perspectives prove indispensable: (1) schemes of formal classification to organize organic diversity and (2) the geological time scale to organize geological time.
- There are two differing approaches to classifying and interpreting life-forms: evolutionary systematics and cladistics.

- Because primates are vertebrates and, more specifically, mammals, it's important to understand how these major groups are connected to our own origins.
- Theoretical perspectives relating to contemporary understanding of macroevolutionary processes (especially the concepts of species and speciation) are crucial to any interpretation of long-term aspects of evolutionary history, be it vertebrate, mammalian, or primate.

- Because genus and species designation is the common form of reference for both living and extinct organisms (and we use it frequently throughout the text), it's important to understand how these terms are used and their underlying biological significance.

Critical Thinking Questions

1. What are the two goals of classification? What happens when meeting both goals simultaneously becomes difficult or even impossible?

2. Remains of a fossil mammal have been found on your campus. If you adopt a cladistic approach, how would you determine (a) that it's a mammal rather than some other kind of vertebrate (discuss specific characters), (b) what kind of mammal it is (again, discuss specific characters), and (c) how it *might* be related to one or more living mammals (again, discuss specific characters)?

3. For the same fossil find (and your interpretation) in question 2, draw an interpretive figure using cladistic analysis (that is, draw a cladogram). Next, using more traditional evolutionary systematics, construct a phylogeny. Lastly, explain the differences between the cladogram and the phylogeny (be sure to emphasize the fundamental ways the two schemes differ).

4. a. Humans are fairly generalized mammals. What do we mean by this, and what specific features (characters) would you select to illustrate this statement?
   b. More precisely, humans are *placental* mammals. How do humans, and generally all other placental mammals, differ from the other two major groups of mammals?

Connections

Humans are both vertebrates and mammals and we've shared evolutionary history for millions of years.

Humans are primates and share many biological characteristics with other primates.

Due to our shared evolution, many human behaviors are also seen in other primates.

7

Survey of the Living Primates

Introduction

Chimpanzees aren't monkeys, and neither are gorillas or orangutans. They're apes, and even though most people think that monkeys and apes are basically the same, they aren't. Yet, how many times have you seen a greeting card or magazine ad with a picture of a chimpanzee and a caption that says something like, "Don't monkey around" or "No more monkey business"? Or maybe you've seen people at zoos teasing primates. Though these things may seem trivial, they really aren't, because they show just how little most people know about our closest relatives. This is extremely unfortunate, because by getting to know these relatives, we can better know ourselves. Even more importantly, we can try to preserve the many nonhuman primate species that are critically endangered today. Indeed, many will go extinct in the next 50 years or so if people don't act now to save them.

One way to understand any organism is to compare its anatomy and behavior with that of other, closely related species. This comparative approach helps explain how and why physiological and behavioral systems evolved as adaptive responses to various selective pressures. This statement applies to humans just as it does to any other species. So if we want to identify the components that have shaped the evolution of our species, a good starting point is to compare ourselves with our closest living relatives, the approximately 230 species of nonhuman primates (lemurs, lorises, tarsiers, monkeys, and apes).

This chapter describes the physical characteristics that define the order **Primates** (see next page for definitions of terms on this page), gives a brief overview of the major groups of living primates, and introduces some methods currently used to compare living primates genetically. (For a comparison of human and nonhuman skeletons, see Appendix A.) But before going any further, we again want to call attention to a few common misunderstandings about evolutionary processes.

Evolution is not a goal-directed process. Therefore, the fact that lemurs appeared earlier than **anthropoids** doesn't mean that lemurs "progressed" to become anthropoids. Living primates aren't in any way "superior" to their

◄ Female sifaka with infant.

evolutionary predecessors or to one another. Consequently, when we discuss major groupings of contemporary nonhuman primates, there's no implied superiority or inferiority of any of these groups. Each lineage or species has come to possess unique qualities that make it better suited to a particular habitat and lifestyle. You shouldn't make the mistake of thinking that contemporary primates (including humans) necessarily represent the final stage or apex of a lineage, because we all continue to evolve as lineages. Actually, the only species that represent final evolutionary stages of particular lineages are the ones that become extinct.

Primate Characteristics

As you learned in Chapter 6, all primates share many characteristics with other mammals. Some of these basic mammalian traits are body hair, a relatively long gestation period followed by live birth, mammary glands (thus the term *mammal*), different types of teeth (incisors, canines, premolars, and molars), the ability to maintain a constant internal body temperature through physiological means, or *endothermy* (see Chapter 6), increased brain size, and a considerable capacity for learning and behavioral flexibility. So, to differentiate primates as a distinct group from other mammals, we need to describe those characteristics that, taken together, set primates apart.

It isn't easy to identify single traits that define the primate order because, compared with most mammals, primates have remained quite *generalized*. This means that primates have retained several ancestral mammalian traits that some other mammals have lost over time. As we discussed in Chapter 6, many mammalian groups have become very specialized, or derived, at least with regard to certain traits. For example, through the course

of evolution, horses and cattle have undergone a reduction in the number of digits (fingers and toes) from the ancestral pattern of five to one and two, respectively. These species have also developed hard, protective coverings over their feet in the form of hooves (**Fig. 7-1a**). This limb structure is beneficial in prey species because their survival depends on speed and stability, but it restricts them to only one type of locomotion. Moreover, limb function is restricted to support and movement, and the ability to manipulate objects is completely lost.

Primates can't be defined by one or even a few traits they share in common because they *aren't* so specialized. Therefore, primatologists have drawn attention to a group of characteristics that, when taken together, more or less characterize the entire primate order. Still, these are a set of *general* tendencies that aren't all equally expressed in all primates. In addition, while some of these traits are unique to primates, many others are retained ancestral mammalian characteristics shared with other mammals. The following list is meant to give you a general anatomical and behavioral picture of the primates. In their limbs and locomotion, teeth, diet, senses, brain, and behavior, primates reflect a common evolutionary history with adaptations to similar environmental challenges, primarily as highly social, arboreal animals.

A. *Limbs and Locomotion*
  1. *A tendency toward an erect posture (especially in the upper body).* All primates show this tendency to some degree, and it's variously associated with sitting, leaping, standing, and, occasionally, bipedal walking.
  2. *A generalized limb structure, which allows most primates to practice numerous forms of locomotion.* Various aspects of hip and shoulder anatomy provide primates with a wide range of limb movement and function.

primates Members of the mammalian order Primates (pronounced "pry-may´-tees"), which includes lemurs, lorises, tarsiers, monkeys, apes, and humans.

anthropoids Members of the primate infraorder Anthropoidea (pronounced "an-thro-poid´-ee-uh"), which includes monkeys, apes, and humans.

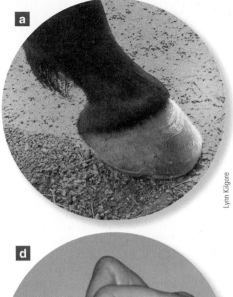

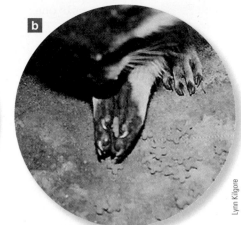

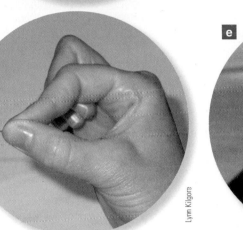

Lynn Kilgore

Lynn Kilgore

Lynn Kilgore

Lynn Kilgore

Lynn Kilgore

▲**Figure 7-1**
(a) A horse's front foot, homologous with a human hand, has undergone reduction from five digits to one. **(b)** While raccoons are capable of considerable manual dexterity and can readily pick up small objects with one hand, they have no opposable thumb. **(c)** Many monkeys are able to grasp objects with an opposable thumb, while others have very reduced thumbs. **(d)** Humans are capable of a "precision grip." **(e)** Chimpanzees, with their reduced thumbs, are capable of a precision grip but frequently use a modified form.

Thus, by maintaining a generalized locomotor anatomy, primates aren't restricted to one form of movement, like many other mammals are. Primates also use their limbs for many activities besides locomotion.

3. *Prehensile hands (and sometimes feet).* Many animals can manipulate objects, but not as skillfully as primates (**Fig. 7-1b**). All primates use their hands, and frequently their feet, to grasp and manipulate objects. This ability is variably expressed and is enhanced by several characteristics, including:
   a. *Retention of five digits on the hands and feet.* This trait varies somewhat throughout the order, with some species having reduced thumbs or second digits (first fingers).
   b. *An opposable thumb and, in most species, a divergent and partially opposable big toe.* Most primates are capable of moving the thumb so that it comes in contact with the second digit or with the palm of the hand (**Fig. 7-1c** through **e**).
   c. *Nails instead of claws.* This characteristic is seen in all primates except some New World monkeys (marmosets and tamarins). All lemurs and lorises also have a claw on one digit.
   d. *Tactile pads enriched with sensory nerve fibers at the ends of digits.* This characteristic enhances the sense of touch.

B. *Diet and Teeth*
   1. *Lack of dietary specialization.* This is typical of most primates, who tend to eat a wide assortment of food items. In general, primates are **omnivorous**.

omnivorous Having a diet consisting of many kinds of food including plants, meat, and insects.

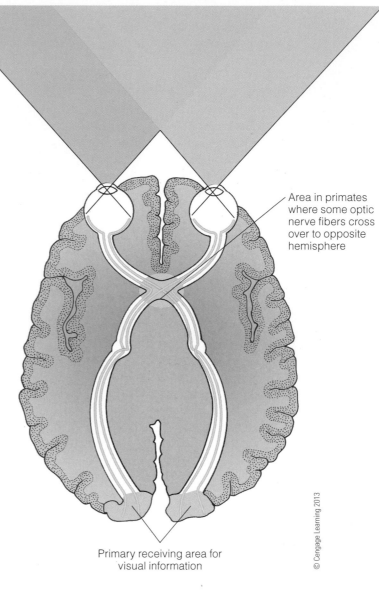

▶ **Figure 7-2**
Simplified diagram showing overlapping visual fields that permit binocular vision in primates with eyes positioned at the front of the face. (The green shaded area represents the area of overlap.) Stereoscopic (three-dimensional) vision is provided in part by binocular vision and in part by the transmission of visual stimuli from each eye to both hemispheres of the brain. (In nonprimate mammals, most, if not all, visual information crosses over to the hemisphere opposite the eye in which it was initially received.)

Area in primates where some optic nerve fibers cross over to opposite hemisphere

Primary receiving area for visual information

diurnal Active during the day.

nocturnal Active during the night.

stereoscopic vision The condition whereby visual images are, to varying degrees, superimposed. This provides for depth perception, or viewing the external environment in three dimensions. Stereoscopic vision is partly a function of structures in the brain.

binocular vision Vision characterized by overlapping visual fields provided by forward-facing eyes. Binocular vision is essential to depth perception.

hemispheres The two halves of the cerebrum that are connected by a dense mass of fibers. (The cerebrum is the large rounded outer portion of the brain.)

2. *A generalized dentition.* Primate teeth aren't specialized for processing only one type of food, a trait related to a general lack of dietary specialization.

C. *The senses and the brain.* Primates (**diurnal** ones in particular) rely heavily on vision and less on the sense of smell, especially when compared with other mammals. This emphasis is reflected in evolutionary changes in the skull, eyes, and brain.
  1. *Color vision.* This is a characteristic of all diurnal primates. **Nocturnal** primates don't have color vision.

2. *Depth perception.* Primates have **stereoscopic vision**, or the ability to perceive objects in three dimensions. This is made possible through a variety of mechanisms, including:
  a. *Eyes placed toward the front of the face (not to the sides).* This position provides for overlapping visual fields, or **binocular vision** (**Fig. 7-2**).
  b. *Visual information from each eye transmitted to visual centers in both **hemispheres** of the brain.* In nonprimate mammals, most optic nerve fibers cross to the opposite hemisphere through a struc-

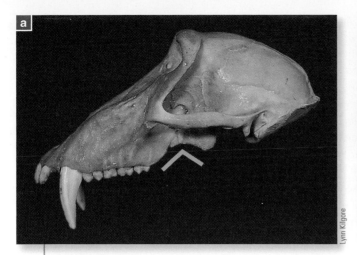

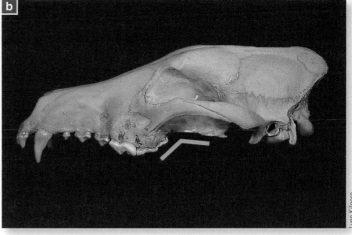

▲Figure 7-3

The skull of a male baboon **(a)** compared with a red wolf skull **(b)**. Forward-facing eyes are positioned above the snout in baboons; in wolves, the eyes are positioned more to the side of the face. Also, the baboon's large muzzle doesn't reflect a heavy reliance on the sense of smell as it does in the wolf. Rather, it supports the roots of the large canine teeth, which curve back through the bone for as much as 1½ inches.

ture at the base of the brain. In primates, about 40 percent of the fibers remain on the same side, so that both hemispheres receive much of the same information.

c. *Visual information organized into three-dimensional images by specialized structures in the brain itself.* The capacity for stereoscopic vision depends on each hemisphere of the brain receiving visual information from both eyes and from overlapping visual fields.

3. *Decreased reliance on the sense of smell.* This trend is expressed as an overall reduction in the size of olfactory structures in the brain. Corresponding reduction of the entire olfactory apparatus has also resulted in decreased size of the snout in most species. This is related to an increased dependence on vision. Some species, such as baboons, have large

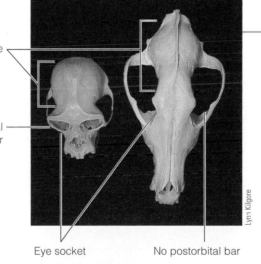

Braincase

Postorbital bar

Eye socket   No postorbital bar

◄Figure 7-4

The skull of a gibbon (left) compared with that of a red wolf (right). The absolute size of the gibbon braincase is slightly larger than the wolf's, even though the wolf (at about 80 to 100 pounds) is around six times the size of the gibbon (about 15 pounds).

muzzles, but this isn't related to **olfaction**, but rather to the need to accommodate large canine teeth (**Fig. 7-3**).

4. *Expansion and increased complexity of the brain.* This is a general trend among placental mammals, but it's especially true of primates (**Fig. 7-4**). In primates, this expansion is most evident in the visual and association areas of the **neocortex** (portions of the brain where information from different **sensory modalities** is combined).

olfaction The sense of smell.

neocortex The more recently evolved portion of the brain that is involved in higher mental functions and composed of areas that integrate incoming sensory information.

sensory modalities Different forms of sensation (e.g., touch, pain, pressure, heat, cold, vision, taste, hearing, and smell).

D. *Maturation, learning, and behavior*
   1. *A more efficient means of fetal nourishment, longer periods of gestation, reduced numbers of offspring (with single births the norm), delayed maturation, and extension of the entire life span.*
   2. *A greater dependence on flexible, learned behavior.* This trend is correlated with delayed maturation and subsequently longer periods of infant and adolescent dependency on at least one parent. Because of these trends, parental investment in each offspring is increased; although fewer offspring are born, they receive more intense parental care.
   3. *The tendency to live in social groups and the permanent association of adult males with the group.* Except for some nocturnal species, primates tend to associate with other individuals.
   4. *The tendency toward diurnal activity patterns.* This is seen in most primates. Lorises, tarsiers, one monkey species, and some lemurs are nocturnal; all the rest (the other monkeys, apes, and humans) are diurnal.

► **Figure 7-5**
Gray squirrels are well adapted to life in the trees, where they nest, sleep, play, and frequently eat; but they usually forage for food on the ground. Unlike primates, they don't have color vision or grasping hands and feet; and they have claws instead of nails.

arboreal Tree-living; adapted to life in the trees.

adaptive niche An organism's entire way of life: where it lives, what it eats, how it gets food, how it avoids predators, and so on.

Primate Adaptations

In this section, we consider how primate anatomical traits evolved as adaptations to environmental circumstances. It's important to remember that the phrase "environmental circumstances" refers to several interrelated variables, including climate, diet, habitat (woodland, grassland, forest, and so on), and predation.

Evolutionary Factors

Traditionally, the group of characteristics shared by primates has been explained as the result of an adaptation to **arboreal** living. While other mammals were adapting to various ground-dwelling lifestyles and marine environments, the primates found their **adaptive niche** in the trees. A number of other mammals were also adapting to arboreal living, but though many of them nested in the trees, they continued to forage for food on the ground (**Fig. 7-5**). Throughout the course of evolution, the primates increasingly found food (leaves, seeds, fruits, nuts, insects, and small mammals) in the trees themselves. Over time, this dietary shift enhanced a general trend toward *omnivory*, and this trend in turn led to the retention of the generalized dentition that's typical of most primates.

Increased reliance on vision, coupled with grasping hands and feet, are also adaptations to an arboreal lifestyle. In a complex, three-dimensional environment with uncertain footholds, acute color vision with depth perception is, for obvious reasons, extremely beneficial.

An alternative to this traditional *arboreal hypothesis* is based on the fact that animals such as squirrels and raccoons are also arboreal, yet they haven't evolved primate-like adaptations such as prehensile hands or forward-facing eyes. But visual predators, such as cats and owls, do have forward-facing eyes, and this fact may provide insight into an additional factor that could have shaped primate evolution.

Forward-facing eyes (which facilitate binocular vision), grasping hands and feet, and the presence of nails instead of claws may not have come about solely as adaptive advantages in a purely arboreal setting. They may also have been the hallmarks of an arboreal visual predator. So it's possible that early primates may first have adapted to shrubby forest undergrowth and the lowest tiers of the forest canopy, where they hunted insects and other small prey (Cartmill, 1972, 1992). In fact, many smaller primates occupy just such an econiche today.

In a third scenario, basic primate traits developed along with another major evolutionary occurrence, the appearance and diversification of flowering plants that began around 140 mya (Sussman, 1991). Flowering plants provide numerous resources for primates, including nectar, seeds, and fruits. Because visual predation isn't common among primates, forward-facing eyes, grasping hands and feet, omnivory, and color vision may have arisen in response to the demand for fine visual and tactile discrimination, necessary for feeding on small food items such as fruits, berries, and seeds among branches and stems (Dominy and Lucas, 2001).

These hypotheses aren't mutually exclusive. The complex of primate characteristics might well have originated in nonarboreal settings. These traits could also have been adaptive when evolving flowering plants opened up new econiches. But at some point, probably as a result of these and even other factors, primates did take to the trees, and that's where most of them still live today.

Geographical Distribution and Habitats

With just a couple of exceptions, nonhuman primates are found in tropical or semitropical areas of the New and Old Worlds. In the New World, these areas include southern Mexico, Central America, and parts of South America. Old World primates are found in Africa, India, Southeast Asia (including numerous islands), and Japan (**Fig. 7-6**).

Even though most nonhuman primates are arboreal and live in forest or woodland habitats, some Old World monkeys (for example, baboons) spend much of the day on the ground. The same is true for the African apes (gorillas, chimpanzees, and bonobos). Nevertheless, all nonhuman primates spend some time in the trees, especially when sleeping.

Diet and Teeth

Omnivory is one example of the overall lack of specialization in primates. Although all primates tend to favor some food items over others, most eat a combination of fruit, nuts, seeds, leaves, other plant materials, and insects. Many also get animal protein from birds, amphibians, and small mammals, including other primates. Others have become more specialized and mostly eat leaves. Such a wide array of choices is highly adaptive, even in fairly predictable environments.

Like nearly all other mammals, almost all primates have four kinds of teeth: incisors and canines for biting and cutting, and premolars and molars for chewing and grinding. Biologists use what's called a **dental formula** to describe the number of each type of tooth that typifies a species. A dental formula indicates the number of each tooth type in each quadrant of the mouth (**Fig. 7-7**). For example, all Old World *anthropoids* (monkeys, apes and humans) have two incisors, one canine, two premolars, and three molars on each side of the midline in both the upper and lower jaws, for a total of 32 teeth. This is represented by the following dental formula:

2.1.2.3 (upper)
2.1.2.3 (lower)

dental formula Numerical device that indicates the number of each type of tooth in each side of the upper and lower jaws.

Howler species
(Central and South
America)

Spider monkeys
and muriquis
(Central and South
America)

Prince Bernhard's titi
(Brazil, Amazon
rain forest)

Uakari
(Brazil, near Jurua River)

Squirrel monkeys
(South America)

White-faced
capuchins
(South America)

Muriqui
(southeastern Brazil)

Marmosets and
tamarins
(South America)

▲**Figure 7-6**
Geographical distribution of living nonhuman primates.
Much original habitat is now very fragmented.

Macaque species
(North Africa, India,
Southeast Asia,
China, and Japan

Jean De Rousseau

Gibbons and siamangs
(Southeast Asia,
islands, and China)

Lynn Kilgore

Baboon species
(throughout sub-Saharan
Africa)

Bonnie Pedersen / Arlene Kruse

Cercopithecus
species (throughout
sub-Saharan Africa)

Robert Jurmain

Tarsier species
(southeast
Asian islands)

© Steve Bloom Images / Alamy

Loris species
(Africa, India, and
Southeast Asia)

© Ian Bieller / Alamy

Mountain and lowland
gorillas (western and
central Africa)

Lynn Kilgore

Lemurs
(Madagascar)

Fred Jacobs

Langur species
(colobines) (India,
southern Asia, and
south China)

© Cyril Ruoso / Bios / Peter
Arnold / Photolibrary

Orangutans
(Borneo and Sumatra)

© Rolf Nussbaumer Photography / Alamy

Chimpanzees and
bonobos
(across central Africa)

Arlene Kruse / Bonnie Pedersen

Galago species
(throughout sub-Saharan
Africa)

© Federico Veronesi / Gallo
Images / Getty Images

Colobus species
(throughout sub-Saharan
Africa)

Robert Jurmain

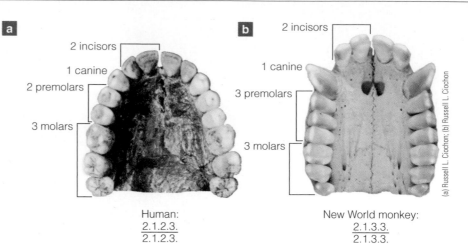

a

2 incisors
1 canine
2 premolars
3 molars

Human:
2.1.2.3.
2.1.2.3.

b

2 incisors
1 canine
3 premolars
3 molars

New World monkey:
2.1.3.3.
2.1.3.3.

(a) Russell L. Ciochon; (b) Russell L. Ciochon

▶ **Figure 7-7**
(a) The human maxilla illustrates a dental formula characteristic of all Old World monkeys, apes, and humans. **(b)** The New World monkey (*Cebus*) maxilla shows the dental formula that is typical of most New World monkeys. (Not to scale, the monkey maxilla is actually much smaller than the human maxilla.)

This formula differs from that of the New World monkeys in that there's one less premolar.

The overall lack of dietary specialization in primates is reflected in the lack of specialization in the size and shape of the teeth, because tooth shape and size are directly related to diet. For example, carnivores typically have premolars and molars with high, pointed **cusps** adapted for tearing meat; but herbivores, such as cattle and horses,

have premolars and molars with broad, flat surfaces suited to chewing tough grasses and other plant materials. Most primates have premolars and molars with low, rounded cusps, a pattern that enables them to process most types of foods. So, throughout their evolutionary history, the primates have developed a dentition adapted to a varied diet, and the capacity to exploit many foods has contributed to their overall success during the last 50 million years.

▶ **Figure 7-8**
Ring-tailed lemurs are one of several lemur species that use vertical clinging and leaping as one form of locomotion. (Tarsiers are also masters of vertical clinging and leaping.)

© Cyril Ruoso / JH Editorial / Minden Pictures

cusps The bumps on the chewing surface of premolars and molars.

quadrupedal Using all four limbs to support the body during locomotion; the basic mammalian (and primate) form of locomotion.

brachiation Arm swinging, a form of locomotion used by some primates. Brachiation involves hanging from a branch and moving by alternately swinging from one arm to the other.

Locomotion

Almost all primates are, at least to some degree, **quadrupedal**, whether they're entirely arboreal or spend some time on the ground. However, most primates use more than one form of locomotion, and they're able to do this because of their generalized anatomy.

Vertical clinging and leaping, another form of locomotion, is characteristic of some lemurs and tarsiers. As the term implies, vertical clingers and leapers support themselves vertically by grasping onto trunks of trees or other large plants while their knees and ankles are tightly flexed. By forcefully extending their long hind limbs, they can spring powerfully away either forward or backward (**Fig. 7-8**).

Brachiation,  or arm swinging, is a suspensory form of locomotion and the body moves by being alternatively suspended by one arm or the other.

▲ Figure 7-9
This spider monkey, a New World species, is using its prehensile tail to suspend itself from a tree branch.

▲ Figure 7-10
Chimpanzee knuckle walking. Note how the weight of the upper body is supported on the knuckles and not on the palm of the hand.

(You may have brachiated as a child on "monkey bars" in playgrounds.) Because of anatomical modifications at the shoulder joint, apes and humans are capable of true brachiation. However, only the small gibbons and siamangs of Southeast Asia use this form of locomotion almost exclusively.

Brachiation is seen in species characterized by arms longer than legs, a short, stable lower back, long curved fingers, and shortened thumbs. As these traits are seen in all the apes, it's believed that although none of the great apes (orangutans, gorillas, bonobos, and chimpanzees) habitually brachiates today, they probably inherited these characteristics from brachiating or climbing ancestors.

Some New World monkeys, such as spider monkeys and muriquis, are called *semibrachiators*, since they practice a combination of leaping and some arm swinging. Also, some New World monkeys enhance arm swing-

ing by using a *prehensile tail*, which in effect serves as an extra hand (**Fig. 7-9**). It's important to mention that no Old World monkeys have prehensile tails.

Lastly, all the apes, to varying degrees, have arms that are longer than legs, and some (gorillas, bonobos, and chimpanzees) practice a special form of quadrupedalism called knuckle walking. Because their arms are so long relative to their legs, they support the weight of their upper body on the back surfaces of their bent fingers (**Fig. 7-10**).

Primate Classification

The living primates are commonly categorized into their respective subgroups, as shown in **Figure 7-11**. This taxonomy is based on the system originally established by Linnaeus (see Chapter 2). The primate order, which includes approximately 230 species,

▼**Figure 7-11**
Primate taxonomic classification. This abbreviated taxonomy illustrates how primates are categorized from broader groupings (e.g., the order Primates) into increasingly specific ones (species). Only the more general categories are shown, except for the great apes and humans.

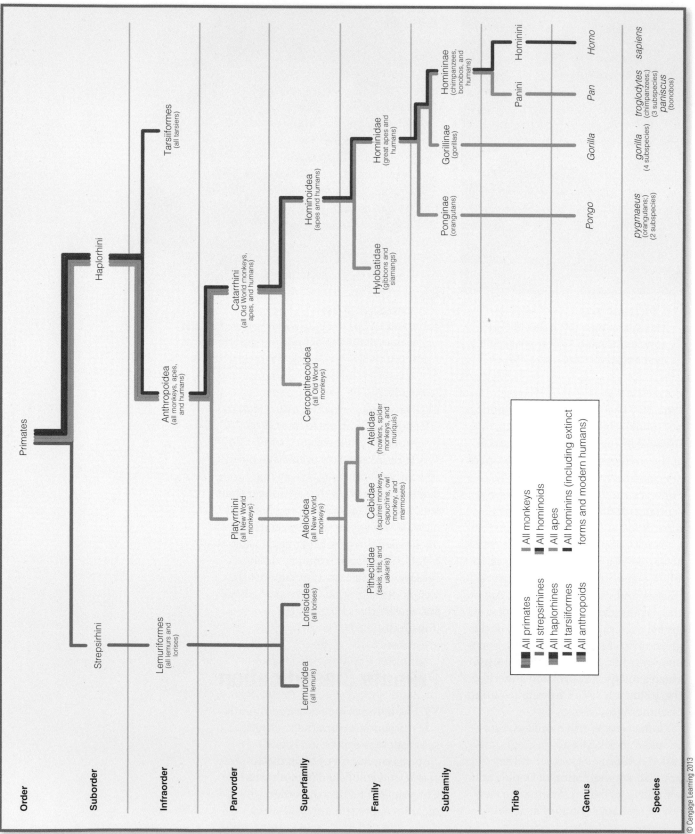

belongs to a larger group, the class Mammalia (see Chapter 6).

As you learned in Chapter 6, in any taxonomic system, animals are organized into increasingly specific categories. For example, the order Primates includes *all* primates. But at the next level down, the *suborder*, primates are divided into two smaller categories: **Strepsirhini** (lemurs and lorises) and **Haplorhini** (tarsiers, monkeys, apes, and humans). Therefore, the suborder distinction is more specific. At the suborder level, the lemurs and lorises are distinct as a group from all the other primates. This classification makes the biological and evolutionary statement that all the lemurs and lorises are more closely related to one another than they are to any of the other primates. Likewise, humans, apes, monkeys, and tarsiers are more closely related to one another than they are to the lorises and lemurs.

The taxonomy shown in Figure 7-11 is a modified version of a similar system that biologists and primatologists have used for decades. The traditional system was based on physical similarities between species and lineages. But that approach isn't foolproof. For instance, some New and Old World monkeys resemble each other anatomically, but evolutionarily they're quite distinct, having diverged from a common ancestor perhaps as long as 40 mya. By looking only at physical characteristics, it's possible to overlook the unknown effects of separate evolutionary histories. But thanks to the rapidly growing number of species whose genomes have been sequenced, geneticists can now make direct comparisons between the genes, and indeed the entire genetic makeup, of different species. This kind of analysis, called *comparative genomics*, provides a more accurate picture of evolutionary and biological relationships between species than was possible even as recently as the late 1990s. So once again, we see how changing technologies allow scientists to refine older hypotheses and develop new ones.

When a complete draft sequence of the chimpanzee genome was completed (The Chimpanzee Sequencing and Analysis Consortium, 2005), it was a major milestone in human comparative genomics. Comparisons of the genomes of different species are important because they reveal such differences in DNA as the number of nucleotide substitutions and/or deletions that have occurred since related species last shared a common ancestor.

For example, Wildman and colleagues (2003) compared nearly 100 human genes with their chimpanzee, gorilla, and orangutan counterparts. Their results supported some earlier studies indicating that humans are most closely related to chimpanzees and that the protein coding DNA sequences of the two species are 98.4 to 99.4 percent identical. This study also revealed that the chimpanzee and human lineages diverged between 7 and 6 mya. These results are consistent with the molecular findings of several other studies (Chen and Li, 2001; Clark et al., 2003; Steiper and Young, 2006). Other research has substantiated these figures but has also revealed more variation in non-protein coding DNA segments and portions that have been inserted, deleted, or duplicated. So when the *entire* genome is considered, reported DNA differences between chimpanzees and humans range from 2.7 percent (Cheng et al., 2005) to 6.4 percent (Demuth et al., 2006). These aren't substantial differences, but perhaps the most important discovery of all is that humans have much more non–protein coding DNA than do the other primates that have so far been studied. Now geneticists are beginning to understand some of the functions of non–protein coding DNA and they hope to explain why humans have so much of it and how it makes us different from our close relatives.

Strepsirhini (strep'-sir-in-ee) The primate suborder that includes lemurs and lorises.

Haplorhini (hap'-lo-rin-ee) The primate suborder that includes tarsiers, monkeys, apes, and humans.

A Survey of the Living Primates

In this section, we discuss the major primate subgroups. It's beyond the scope of this book to cover any species in great detail, so we present a brief description of each major grouping, taking a somewhat closer look at the apes.

Lemurs and Lorises

The suborder Strepsirhini includes the lemurs and lorises, the most non-derived or primitive living primates. Remember that by "primitive" we mean that lemurs and lorises are more similar anatomically to their earlier mammalian ancestors than are the other primates (tarsiers, monkeys, apes, and humans). For example, they retain certain ancestral characteristics, such as a greater reliance on *olfaction*. Their greater olfactory capabilities (compared to other primates) are reflected in the presence of a relatively long snout and a moist, fleshy pad, or **rhinarium**, at the end of the nose (**Fig. 7-12**).

Many other characteristics distinguish lemurs and lorises from the other primates, including eyes placed more to the side of the face, differences in reproductive physiology, and shorter gestation and maturation periods. Lemurs and lorises also have a unique, derived trait called a "dental comb" (**Fig. 7-13**) formed by forward-projecting lower incisors and canines. These modified teeth are used in grooming and feeding.

Lemurs Lemurs are found only on the island of Madagascar and adjacent islands off the east coast of Africa (**Fig. 7-14**). As the only nonhuman primates on Madagascar, lemurs diversified into numerous ecological niches without competition from monkeys

▶ **Figure 7-12**
As you can see, rhinaria come in different shapes and sizes, but they all enhance an animal's sense of smell.

▶ **Figure 7-13**
Lemur dental comb, formed by forward-projecting incisors and canines.

rhinarium (rine-air´-ee-um) (Plural: rhinaria) The moist, hairless pad at the end of the nose seen in most mammalian species. The rhinarium enhances an animal's ability to smell.

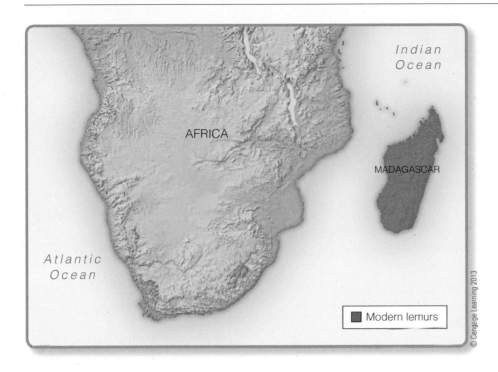

◄Figure 7-14
Geographical distribution of modern lemurs.

and apes. Thus, the approximately 60 surviving species of lemurs on Madagascar today represent an evolutionary pattern that vanished elsewhere.

Lemurs range in size from the small mouse lemur, with a body length (head and trunk) of only 5 inches, to the indri, with a body length of 2 to 3 feet (Nowak, 1999). Typically, the larger lemurs are diurnal and eat a wide variety of foods, such as leaves, fruits, buds, bark, and shoots, but the tiny mouse and dwarf lemurs are nocturnal and insectivorous.

There's a great deal of behavioral variation among lemurs. Some are mostly arboreal, and others, such as ring-tailed lemurs, are more terrestrial. Several species, such as ring-tailed lemurs (Fig. 7-8) and sifakas (**Fig. 7-15**) live in groups of 10 to 25 animals composed of males and females of all ages. Indris are among the few primates that live in "family" units composed of a mated pair and dependent offspring. In addition, several nocturnal species are mostly solitary.

Lorises Lorises (**Fig. 7-16**), which somewhat resemble lemurs, were able to survive in mainland areas by becoming nocturnal. In this way, they were

▼Figure 7-16
A slow loris in Malaysia. Note the large forward-facing eyes and rhinarium.

▼Figure 7-15
Sifakas.

▶ **Figure 7-17**
Galago or "bush baby."

(and are) able to avoid competition with more recently evolved primates (the diurnal monkeys).

There are at least eight loris species, all of which are found in tropical forest and woodland habitats of India, Sri Lanka, Southeast Asia, and Africa. Also included in the same general category are six to nine galago species, also called bush babies (Bearder, 1987; Nowak, 1999), which are widely distributed throughout

most of the forested and woodland savanna areas of sub-Saharan Africa (**Fig. 7-17**).

Locomotion in some lorises is a slow, cautious, climbing form of quadrupedalism. All galagos, however, are highly agile vertical clingers and leapers. Some lorises and galagos are almost entirely insectivorous, while others also eat fruits, leaves, and other plant products. Lorises and galagos frequently forage alone, but feeding ranges can overlap, and two or more females may feed and even nest together. Females also leave young infants behind in nests while they search for food, a behavior not seen in most primate species.

▼ **Figure 7-19**
Geographical distribution of tarsiers.

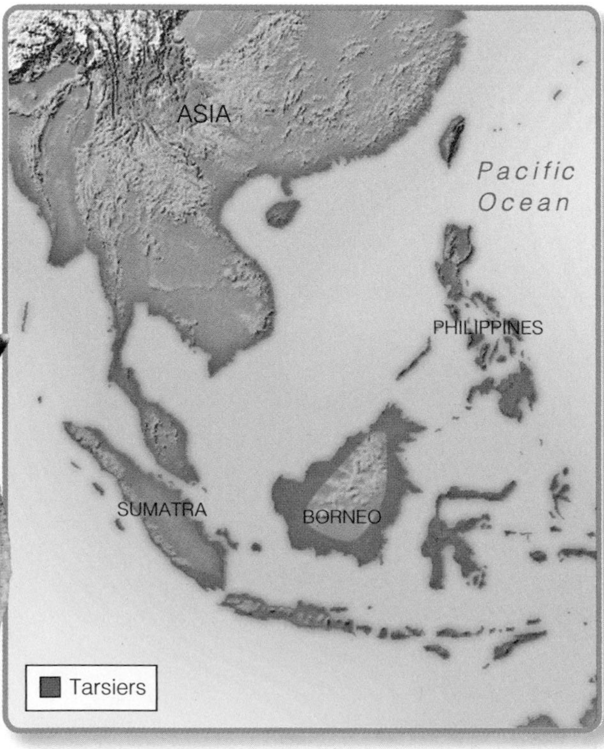

▼ **Figure 7-18**
Bornean tarsier. Tarsiers' eyes are almost as large as their brains.

ASIA

Pacific Ocean

PHILIPPINES

SUMATRA   BORNEO

■ Tarsiers

© Cengage Learning 2013

Tarsiers

There are five recognized tarsier species (Nowak, 1999), all of which are restricted to islands of Southeast Asia (Malaysia, Borneo, Sumatra, the Philippines), where they inhabit a wide range of habitats, from tropical forest to backyard gardens (**Figs. 7-18** and **7-19**). Tarsiers are nocturnal insectivores that leap from lower branches and shrubs onto small prey. They appear to form stable pair bonds, and the basic tarsier social unit is a mated pair and their young offspring (MacKinnon and MacKinnon, 1980).

Tarsiers are highly specialized (derived) animals that have several unique characteristics. In the past, primatologists believed that tarsiers were more closely related to lemurs and lorises than to other primates because they share several traits with them. However, they actually present a complex blend of characteristics not seen in any other primate. One of the most obvious is their enormous eyes, which dominate much of the face and are immobile within their sockets. To compensate for the inability to move their eyes, tarsiers, like owls, can rotate their heads 180°.

Anthropoids: Monkeys, Apes, and Humans

Although there is much variation among anthropoids, they share certain features that, when taken together, distinguish them as a group from lemurs and lorises. Here's a partial list of these anthropoid traits:

1. Larger average body size
2. Larger brain in absolute terms and relative to body weight
3. Reduced reliance on the sense of smell, as indicated by the absence of a rhinarium and reduction of olfactory-related brain structures
4. Increased reliance on vision, with forward-facing eyes placed more to the front of the face
5. Greater degree of color vision
6. Back of eye socket protected by a bony plate
7. Blood supply to the brain different from that of lemurs and lorises
8. Fusion of the two sides of the mandible at the midline to form one bone (in lemurs and lorises, they're two distinct bones joined by cartilage at the middle of the chin)
9. More generalized dentition, as seen in the absence of a dental comb
10. Differences in female internal reproductive anatomy
11. Longer gestation and maturation periods
12. Increased parental care
13. More mutual grooming

Approximately 85 percent of all primates are monkeys. Primatologists estimate that there are about 195 species, but it's impossible to give precise numbers because the taxonomic status of some monkeys remains in doubt, and previously unknown species are still being discovered. Monkeys are divided into two groups separated by geographical area (New World and Old World), as well as at least 40 million years of separate evolutionary history.

New World Monkeys The approximately 70 New World monkey species can be found in a wide range of environments throughout most forested areas in southern Mexico and Central and South America (**Fig. 7-20**). They

▼ **Figure 7-20**
Geographical distribution of New World monkeys.

▼ **Figure 7-21**
Some New World monkeys.

Female muriqui with infant

Squirrel monkeys

Prince Bernhard's titi monkey (discovered in 2002)

White-faced capuchins

Male uakari

exhibit considerable variation in size, diet, and ecological adaptations (**Fig. 7-21**). In size, they vary from the tiny marmosets and tamarins that weigh only about 12 ounces (**Fig. 7-22**) to the 20-pound howler monkeys (**Fig. 7-23**). New World monkeys are almost exclusively arboreal, and some never come to the ground. Like the Old World monkeys, all except one species (the owl monkey) are diurnal.

In addition to being the smallest of all monkeys, marmosets and tamarins have several other distinguishing features. They have claws instead of nails, and unlike other primates, they usually give birth to twins instead of one infant. They live in social groups usually composed of a mated pair, or a female and two adult males, and their offspring. This type of mating pattern is rare among mammals, and marmosets and tamarins are among the few primate species in which males are extensively involved in infant care.

New World monkeys rely on a combination of fruits and leaves supplemented to varying degrees with insects. Most are quadrupedal; but some, such as spider monkeys (Fig. 7-9), are semibrachiators. Howlers, muriquis, and spider monkeys also have prehensile tails that are used not only in locomotion but also for hanging from branches. Socially, most New World monkeys live in groups composed of both sexes and all age categories. Some (such as titis) form monogamous pairs and live with their subadult offspring.

Old World Monkeys Except for humans, Old World monkeys are the most widely distributed of all living primates. They're found throughout sub-Saharan Africa and southern Asia,

▲**Figure 7-22**
A pair of golden lion tamarins.

◀**Figure 7-23**
Male and female (with infant) howler monkeys. The adults are illustrating why they're called "howlers." The roaring sound they make is among the loudest of mammalian vocalizations.

ranging from tropical jungle habitats to semiarid desert and even to seasonally snow-covered areas in northern Japan (**Fig. 7-24**).

All Old World monkeys are placed in one taxonomic family, **Cercopithecidae**. In turn, this family is divided into two subfamilies: the **cercopithecines** and **colobines**. Most Old World monkeys are arboreal, but some (such as baboons) spend a great deal of time on the ground and return to the trees for the night. They have areas of hardened skin on the buttocks called **ischial callosities** that serve as sitting pads, making it possible to sit

Cercopithecidae
(serk-oh-pith´-eh-see-dee)

cercopithecines (serk-oh-pith´-eh-seens) The subfamily of Old World monkeys that includes baboons, macaques, and guenons.

colobines (kole´-uh-bines) Common name for members of the subfamily of Old World monkeys that includes the African colobus monkeys and Asian langurs.

ischial callosities Patches of tough, hard skin on the buttocks of Old World monkeys and chimpanzees.

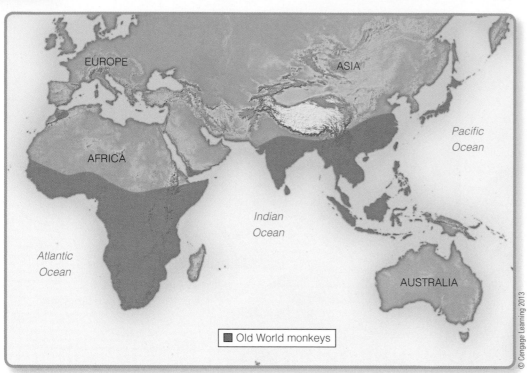

▲Figure 7-24
Geographical distribution of living Old World monkeys.

ans, small reptiles, and small mammals (the last seen in baboons).

The majority of cercopithecine species, such as the mostly arboreal guenons (**Fig. 7-25**) and the more terrestrial savanna and hamadryas baboons (**Fig. 7-26**), are found in Africa. The many macaque species (including the well-known rhesus monkeys), however, are widely distributed across southern Asia and India.

Colobine species have a narrower range of food preferences and mainly eat mature leaves, which is why they're also called "leaf-eating monkeys." The colobines are found mainly in Asia, but both red colobus and black-and-white colobus are exclusively African (**Fig. 7-27**).

Many Old World monkey species exhibit pronounced **sexual dimorphism**. This is especially true of the more terrestrial species (such as baboons) in which males may be almost twice the size of females (Fig. 7-26).

and sleep on tree branches for hours at a time.

The cercopithecines are more generalized than the colobines. They're more omnivorous, and as a group, they eat almost anything, including fruits, seeds, leaves, grasses, tubers, roots, nuts, insects, birds' eggs, amphibi-

▶Figure 7-25
Adult male sykes monkey, one of many guenon species.

sexual dimorphism Differences in physical characteristics between males and females of the same species. For example, humans are slightly sexually dimorphic for body size, with males being taller, on average, than females of the same population.

Females of several species (especially baboons and some macaques) have pronounced cyclical changes of the external genitalia. These changes, which include swelling and redness, are associated with **estrus**, a hormonally initiated period of sexual receptivity in female nonhuman mammals correlated with ovulation. They serve as visual cues to males that females are sexually receptive.

Old World monkeys live in a few different kinds of social groups. Colobines tend to live in small groups, with only one or two adult males. Savanna baboons and most macaque species are found in large social units comprising several adults of both sexes and offspring of all ages. Monogamous pairing isn't common in Old World monkeys, but it's seen in a few langurs and possibly one or two guenon species.

Hominoids: Apes and Humans

Apes and humans are classified together in the same superfamily, the **hominoids**. Apes are found in Asia and Africa. The small-bodied gibbons and siamangs live in Southeast Asia, and the two orangutan subspecies live on the islands of Borneo and Sumatra (**Fig. 7-28**). In Africa, until the mid- to late twentieth century, gorillas, chimpanzees, and bonobos occupied the forested areas of western, central, and eastern Africa, but their habitat is now extremely fragmented, and all are threatened or highly endangered. Apes and humans share the following characteristics that separate them from monkeys:

▲ **Figure 7-26**
Hamadryas baboons are found in Ethiopia. Notice how much larger the male (at right) is than the female. The male also has much longer hair around the head and shoulders, giving him a distinctive mane.

◄ **Figure 7-27**
Black-and-white colobus monkeys are mostly arboreal but do come down to the ground occasionally.

estrus Period of sexual receptivity in female mammals (except humans), correlated with ovulation. When used as an adjective, the word is spelled "estrous."

hominoids Members of the primate superfamily (Hominoidea) that includes apes and humans.

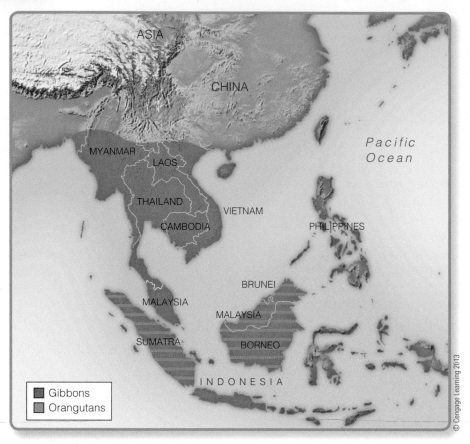

▲ **Figure 7-28**
Geographical distribution of living Asian apes.

Map legend:
- Gibbons
- Orangutans

Map labels: ASIA, CHINA, MYANMAR, LAOS, THAILAND, VIETNAM, CAMBODIA, PHILIPPINES, BRUNEI, MALAYSIA, MALAYSIA, SUMATRA, BORNEO, INDONESIA, *Pacific Ocean*

© Cengage Learning 2013

other primate, a fact reflected in their extremely long arms, long, permanently curved fingers, short thumbs, and powerful shoulder muscles. (Their arms are so long that when they're on the ground, they have to walk bipedally with their arms raised to the side.) Gibbons and siamangs mostly eat fruits, although they also consume a variety of leaves, flowers, and insects.

The basic social unit of gibbons and siamangs is an adult male and female with dependent offspring. Although they've been described as monogamous, in reality, members of a pair do sometimes mate with other individuals. As in marmosets and tamarins, male gibbons and siamangs are very much involved in rearing their young. Both males and females are highly **territorial** and protect their territories with elaborate whoops and siren-like "songs," lending them the name "the singing apes of Asia."

Orangutans Orangutans (*Pongo pygmaeus*; **Fig. 7-30**) are represented by two subspecies found today only in heavily forested areas on the Indonesian islands of Borneo and Sumatra. The name *orangutan* (which has no final g and should *never* be pronounced "o-rang-utang") means "wise man of the forest" in the language of the local people. But despite this somewhat affectionate-sounding label, orangutans are severely threatened with extinction in the wild due to poaching by humans and continuing habitat loss on both islands.

Orangutans are slow, cautious climbers whose locomotion can best be described as four-handed—referring to their use of all four limbs for grasping and support. Although they're almost completely arboreal, orangutans sometimes travel quadrupedally on the ground. Orangutans exhibit pronounced sexual dimorphism; males are very large and may weigh more than 200 pounds, while females weigh less than 100 pounds. In the wild, orangutans lead largely solitary lives, although adult females are usually

1. Generally larger body size (except for gibbons and siamangs)
2. No tail
3. Lower back is shorter and more stable
4. Arms longer than legs (only in apes)
5. Anatomical differences in the shoulder joint that facilitate suspensory feeding and locomotion
6. Generally more complex behavior
7. More complex brain and enhanced cognitive abilities
8. Increased period of infant development and dependency

Gibbons and Siamangs The eight gibbon species and closely related siamangs are the smallest of the apes, with a long, slender body weighing 13 pounds in gibbons (**Fig. 7-29**) and around 25 pounds in siamangs. Their most distinctive anatomical features are adaptations to feeding while hanging from tree branches, or brachiation. In fact, gibbons and siamangs are more dedicated to brachiation than any

territorial Pertaining to the protection of all or a part of the area occupied by an animal or group of animals. Territorial behaviors range from scent marking to outright attacks on intruders.

accompanied by one or two dependent offspring. They're primarily **frugivorous** but they may also eat bark, leaves, insects, and (rarely) meat.

Gorillas Gorillas (Gorilla gorilla) are the largest of all the living primates. Today, they are restricted to forested areas of western and eastern equatorial Africa (**Fig. 7-31**). Gorillas exhibit marked sexual dimorphism. Males may weigh as much as 400 pounds, while females weigh around 150 to 200 pounds. Adult gorillas, especially males, are primarily terrestrial, and like chimpanzees, they practice a type of quadrupedalism called knuckle walking.

Systematic studies of western lowland gorillas weren't begun until the mid-1980s, so even though they're the only gorillas you'll see in zoos, we don't know as much about them as we do about mountain gorillas. The social structure of western lowland gorillas is similar to that of mountain gorillas,

but groups are smaller and somewhat less cohesive.

Western lowland gorillas (**Fig. 7-32**), are found in several countries of west-central Africa. In 1998, Doran and McNeilage estimated their population size at perhaps 110,000, but Walsh and colleagues (2003) suggested that their numbers were far lower. Staggeringly, in August 2008, the Wildlife Conservation Society reported the discovery of an estimated 125,000 western lowland gorillas in the northern region of the Democratic Republic of the Congo (DRC—formerly Zaire)! This is extremely encouraging news, but it doesn't mean that gorillas are out of danger. To put

▲ **Figure 7-29**
Black-handed gibbon in Indonesia.

▲ **Figure 7-30**
Bornean orangutans.
(a) Female with infant. **(b)** Male.

frugivorous (fru-give´-or-us) Having a diet composed primarily of fruit.

◄Figure 7-31
Geographical distribution of living
African apes.

this figure into perspective, consider that a large football stadium can hold around 70,000 spectators. So, next time you see a stadium packed with fans, think about the fact that you're looking at a crowd that numbers around half of all the western lowland gorillas on earth.

Eastern lowland gorillas, which haven't really been studied, live near the eastern border of the DRC. At present, their numbers are unknown but suspected to be around 12,000. Because warfare is common in the region, researchers fear that many of these gorillas have been killed, but it's impossible to know how many.

Mountain gorillas (**Fig. 7-33**) have been extensively studied since the early 1970s. They're restricted to the mountainous areas of central Africa in Rwanda, the DRC, and Uganda, and

◄Figure 7-32
Western lowland gorillas.
(a) Male. (b) Female.

Chimpanzees
Bonobos
Gorillas

© Cengage Learning 2013

(a) © imagebroker/Alamy; (b) © Duncan Usher/Alamy

▲ **Figure 7-33**
Mountain gorillas. **(a)** A male silverback with his group in the background. **(b)** Female.

today they number only about 700 animals.

Mountain gorillas live in groups consisting of one, or sometimes two, large silverback males, a variable number of adult females, and their subadult offspring. (The term *silverback* refers to the saddle of white hair across the backs of fully adult males that appears around the age of 12 or 13.) A silverback male may tolerate the presence of one or more young adult "blackback" males (probably his sons) in his group. Typically, but not always, both females and males leave their **natal group** as young adults. Females join other groups; and males, who appear to be less likely to emigrate, may live alone for a while or may join up with other males before eventually forming their own group.

All gorillas are almost exclusively vegetarian. Mountain gorillas concentrate primarily on leaves, pith, and stalks, while western lowland gorillas eat more fruit. Unlike mountain gorillas (which avoid water), western lowland gorillas also frequently wade through swamps while foraging on aquatic plants (Doran and McNeilage, 1998).

Perhaps because of their large body size and enormous strength, gorillas have long been considered ferocious; in reality, they're usually shy and gentle. But this doesn't mean they're never aggressive. In fact, among males, competition for females can be extremely violent. As might be expected, males will attack and defend their group from any perceived danger, whether it's another male gorilla or a human hunter. Still, the reputation of gorillas as murderous beasts is the result of uninformed myth making and little else.

Chimpanzees Chimpanzees are probably the best known of all nonhuman primates, even though many people think they're monkeys (**Fig. 7-34**). Often misunderstood because of zoo exhibits, circus acts, and movies, the true nature of chimpanzees didn't become known until years of fieldwork with wild groups provided a more accurate picture. Today, chimpanzees

natal group The group in which an animal is born and raised. (*Natal* pertains to birth.)

© Morales / AGE / Photolibrary

▲ **Figure 7-34**
Male, female, and infant chimpanzees. Chimpanzees do not live in "nuclear families" as this photo might imply, and it's quite possible that the male at left is not the father of the infant.

small mammals such as young bushpigs and antelope. Their prey also includes monkeys, especially red colobus. When hunts are successful, the members of the hunting party share the meat.

Chimpanzees live in large communities ranging in size from 10 to as many as 100 individuals. A group of closely bonded males forms the core of chimpanzee communities in many locations, especially in East Africa (Wrangham and Smuts, 1980; Goodall, 1986; Wrangham et al., 1992). But for some West African groups, females appear to be more central to the community (Boesch, 1996; Boesch and Boesch-Acherman, 2000; Vigilant et al., 2001). Relationships among closely bonded males aren't always peaceful or stable, yet these males cooperatively defend their territory and are highly intolerant of unfamiliar chimpanzees, especially males.

Even though chimpanzees live in communities, it's rare for all members to be together at the same time. Rather, they tend to come and go, so that the individuals they encounter vary from day to day. Adult females usually forage either alone or with their offspring, a grouping that might include several animals, since females with infants sometimes accompany their own mothers and siblings. These associations have particularly been reported for the chimpanzees at Gombe National Park, Tanzania (Williams, 1999). But in most other areas, females leave their natal group to join another community. This behavioral pattern reduces the risk of mating with close male relatives, because males apparently never leave the group in which they were born.

Chimpanzee social behavior is complex, and individuals form lifelong attachments with friends and relatives. If they remain in their natal group, the bond between mothers and infants can remain strong until one of them dies. This may be a long time, because many wild chimpanzees live well into their 40s, and occasionally even longer.

are found throughout much of equatorial Africa (see Fig. 7-31). But within this large geographical area, their range is very patchy, and it's becoming even more so with continuous habitat destruction.

In many ways, chimpanzees are anatomically similar to gorillas. However, the ecological adaptations and behaviors of chimpanzees and gorillas differ, with chimpanzees spending more time in the trees. Chimpanzees are also frequently excitable, active, and noisy, while gorillas tend to be placid and quiet.

Chimpanzees are smaller and less sexually dimorphic than orangutans and gorillas. A male chimpanzee may weigh 150 pounds, but females can weigh at least 100 pounds. In addition to quadrupedal knuckle walking, chimpanzees may brachiate. When on the ground, they frequently walk bipedally for short distances, especially when carrying food or other objects.

Chimpanzees eat a huge variety of foods, including fruits, leaves, insects, birds' eggs, and nuts. Moreover, both males and females occasionally take part in group hunting efforts to kill

Bonobos Bonobos (*Pan paniscus*) are found only in an area south of the Zaire River in the DRC (see Figs. 7-31 and **7-35**), and they remain among the least studied of the great apes. Although ongoing field studies have produced much information (Susman, 1984; Kano, 1992), research has been hampered by civil war. There are currently no accurate counts of bonobos, but their numbers are believed to be between 29,000 and 50,000 (IUCN, 2011). The 50,000 estimate is probably optimistic at this point and bonobos are highly threatened by human hunting, warfare, and habitat loss.

Because bonobos bear a strong resemblance to chimpanzees, but are slightly smaller, they've been inappropriately called "pygmy chimpanzees." Actually, the differences in body size aren't great, although bonobos are less stocky. They also have longer legs relative to arms, a relatively smaller head, and a dark face from birth.

Bonobos are more arboreal than chimpanzees, and they're less excitable and aggressive. While aggression isn't unknown, it appears that physical violence both within and between groups is uncommon. Like chimpanzees, bonobos live in geographically based fluid communities, and they eat many of the same foods, including occasional meat derived from small mammals (Badrian and Malinky, 1984). But bonobo communities aren't centered around a group of males. Instead, male-female bonding is more important than in chimpanzees and most other nonhuman primates (Badrian and Badrian, 1984). This may be related to bonobo sexuality, which differs from that of other nonhuman primates in that copulation is frequent and occurs throughout a female's estrous cycle, so sex isn't linked solely to reproduction. In fact, bonobos are famous for their sexual behavior, copulating frequently and using sex to defuse potentially tense situations. Also, sexual activity between members of the same sex is common (Kano, 1992; de Waal and Lanting, 1997).

Humans Humans (*Homo sapiens*) are the only living representatives of the habitually bipedal primates (hominin tribe). Our primate heritage is evident in our overall anatomy, genetic makeup, and many behavioral aspects. Except for reduced canine size, human teeth are typical primate (especially ape) teeth. The human dependence on

◄**Figure 7-35**
Group of male, female, and subadult bonobos in the Democratic Republic of the Congo.

Lynn Kilgore

▲ Figure 7-36
Playground equipment frequently allows children to play in ways that reflect their arboreal heritage.

vision and decreased reliance on olfaction, as well as flexible limbs and grasping hands, are rooted in our primate, arboreal past (**Fig. 7-36**).

Humans in general are omnivorous, although all societies observe certain culturally based dietary restrictions. Even so, as a species with a rather generalized digestive system, we're physiologically adapted to digest an extremely wide assortment of foods. Perhaps to our detriment, we also share with our relatives a fondness for sweets that originates from the importance of high-energy fruits eaten by many nonhuman primates.

But humans are obviously unique among primates and indeed among all animals. No member of any other species has the ability to write or think about issues such as how it differs from other forms of life. This ability is rooted in the fact that during the last 800,000 years of human evolution, brain size has increased dramatically, and there have also been many other neurological changes.

Humans are also completely dependent on culture. Without cultural innovation, it would never have been possible for us to leave the tropics. As it is, humans inhabit every corner of the planet except for Antarctica, and we've established outposts there. Moreover, lest we forget, a fortunate few have even walked on the moon! None of the technologies (indeed, none of the other aspects of culture) that humans have developed over the last several thousand years would have been possible without the highly developed

cognitive abilities we alone possess. Nevertheless, the neurological basis for **intelligence** is rooted in our evolutionary past, and it's something that connects us to other primates. Indeed, research has demonstrated that several nonhuman primate species—most notably chimpanzees, bonobos, and gorillas—display a level of problem solving and insight that most people would have considered impossible just 30 years ago.

Humans are uniquely predisposed to use spoken language, and for the last 5,000 years or so, we've also used written language. This ability exists because during the course of human evolution, certain neurological and anatomical structures have been modified in ways not observed in any other species. But though nonhuman primates aren't anatomically capable of producing speech, research has shown that to varying degrees, the great apes are able to communicate by using symbols, which is a foundation for language that humans and the great apes (to a limited degree) have in common.

Aside from cognitive abilities, the one other trait that sets humans apart from other primates is our unique (among mammals) form of striding, *habitual* bipedal locomotion. This particular trait appeared early in the evolution of our lineage, and over time, we've become more efficient at it because of changes in the anatomy of our pelvis, leg, and foot. Still, although it's certainly true that human beings are unique intellectually, and in some ways anatomically, we're still primates. As a matter of fact, humans are basically exaggerated African apes.

Endangered Primates

In September 2000, scientists announced that a subspecies of red colobus, named Miss Waldron's red colobus, had officially been declared extinct. This announcement came after a six-year search for a monkey that hadn't been seen for 20 years

(Oates et al., 2000). Sadly, this monkey, indigenous to two West African countries, has the distinction of being the first nonhuman primate to be declared extinct in the twenty-first century. But it won't be the last. In fact, as of this writing, over half of all nonhuman primate species are in jeopardy, and some face almost certain extinction in the wild.

There are three basic reasons for the worldwide depletion of nonhuman primates: habitat destruction, human hunting, and live capture for export or local trade. Underlying these three causes is one major factor, unprecedented human population growth, particularly in developing countries, where most nonhuman primates live.

The developing nations of Africa, Asia, and Central and South America are home to over 90 percent of all nonhuman primate species. During the 1990s these countries, aided by Europe, China, and the United States, destroyed an average of 39 million acres of forest per year. The destruction declined between 2000 and 2010 to about 32 million acres a year, largely because of restrictions in Brazil (Food and Agriculture Organization of the United Nations, 2010; Tollefson, 2008). But whether these restrictions will hold remains to be seen.

Tropical forests are cleared for agriculture, pasture, lumber, and large-scale mining operations (with their necessary roads). Moreover, millions of people in many developing countries are critically short of fuel and, lacking electricity, their need for firewood is continuous. Lastly, the demand for tropical hardwoods (such as mahogany, teak, and rosewood) in the United States, Europe, and Japan continues unabated, creating an enormously profitable market for rain forest products.

The need for wood has resulted in conflict with conservationists, especially in central Africa. Mountain gorillas are one of the most endangered nonhuman primate species and tourism has been the only real hope of salvation for these magnificent animals. For this reason, several gorilla groups have been habituated to humans and are protected by park rangers. Nevertheless, poaching, civil war, and land clearing have continued to take a toll on these small populations. For example, between January and late July 2007, 10 mountain gorillas were shot in the Virunga Volcanoes Conservation Area shared by Uganda, Rwanda, and the DRC (**Fig. 7-37**). The gorillas weren't killed for meat or because they were raiding crops. They were shot because the presence and protection

◄**Figure 7-37**
Congolese villagers carrying the body of a silverback gorilla shot and killed in July 2007. His body was buried with other members of his group who were also killed.

WildlifeDirect.org

▶ **Figure 7-38**
(a) Red-eared guenons (with red tails) and Preuss's guenons for sale in a bushmeat market, Malabo, Equatorial Guinea.
(b) Body parts mostly from various monkey species, for sale in a West African market.

(a) John Oates; (b) © Jenny Pate / Robert Harding World Imagery / Getty Images

of mountain gorillas are obstacles to people who would destroy what remains of the forests. But gorillas are not the only primates to have been shot in the Virungas. In the past few years, more than 120 rangers have been killed while protecting wildlife.

Habitat loss used to be the single greatest threat to nonhuman primates. But in the past few years, human hunting has perhaps become an even more important factor (**Fig. 7-38**). During the 1990s, primatologists and conservationists became aware of a rapidly developing trade in *bushmeat*, meat from wild animals, especially in Africa. The current slaughter, which now accounts for the loss of tens of thousands of nonhuman primates and other animals annually, has been compared to the near extinction of the American bison in the nineteenth century.

Wherever nonhuman primates live, people have always hunted them for food. But in the past, subsistence hunting wasn't a serious threat to whole populations, and certainly not to entire species. But now, hunters armed with automatic rifles can, and do, wipe out an entire group of monkeys or gorillas in minutes. In fact, it's now possible to buy bushmeat in major cities throughout Europe and the United States. Illegal bushmeat is readily available to immigrants who want traditional foods; and to nonimmigrants who think it's trendy to eat meat from exotic, and frequently endangered, animals.

It's impossible to know how many animals are killed each year, but the estimates are staggering. The Society for Conservation Biology estimates that about 6,000 kg (13,228 pounds) of bushmeat are taken through just seven western cities (New York, London, Toronto, Paris, Montreal, Chicago, and Brussels) every month. No one knows how much of this meat is from primates, but this figure represents only a tiny fraction of all the animals being slaughtered because much smuggled meat is never detected. Moreover, the international trade is thought to account for only about 1 percent of the total (Marris, 2006). It's difficult to comprehend, but within a relatively short period of time, hunting wild animals for food, particularly in Africa, has shifted from being a subsistence activity to an international commercial enterprise.

Although the slaughter may be best known in Africa, it's by no means limited to that continent. Hunting and live capture of endangered primates continues unabated in China and Southeast Asia, where nonhuman primates are not only eaten but also funneled into the exotic pet trade. Just as importantly, primate body parts figure prominently in traditional medicines. With increasing human population size, the enormous demand for these products (and products from other, nonprimate species, such as tigers) has put many species in extreme jeopardy (**Table 7-1**).

Quite clearly, species that number only a few hundred or a few thousand animals, cannot survive this onslaught for more than a few years. In addition, hundreds of infants are orphaned and sold in markets as pets. Although a few of these traumatized orphans make it to sanctuaries, most die within days or weeks of capture (**Fig. 7-39**).

As a note of optimism, in November 2007, the DRC government and the Bonobo Conservation Initiative (in Washington, D.C.)

TABLE 7.1 African Primates in Danger of Extinction

Species/Subspecies Common Name	Location	Estimated Size of Remaining Population
Barbary macaque	North Africa	23,000
Tana River mangabey	Tana River, Kenya	800–1,100
Sanje mangabey	Uzungwa Mts., Tanzania	1,800–3,000
Drill	Cameroon, Bioko	?
Preuss' guenon	Cameroon, Bioko	?
White-throated guenon	Southwest Nigeria	?
Pennant's red colobus	Bioko	?
Preuss' red colobus	Cameroon	8,000
Bouvier's red colobus	Congo Republic	?
Tana River red colobus	Tana River, Kenya	200–300
Uhehe red colobus	Uzungwa Mts. Tanzania	10,000
Zanzibar red colobus	Zanzibar	1,500
Mountain gorilla	Virunga Volcanoes (Rwanda, Uganda, and Democratic Republic of the Congo) and Impenetrable Forest (Uganda)	550–650

▲ Figure 7-39
Orphaned bonobo infants being cared for at a bonobo sanctuary in The Democratic Republic of the Congo (DRC). It may not be possible to return them to the wild.

There are many conservation groups working to protect nonhuman primates. These include, among many others, Conservation International, the World Wildlife Fund, and the Jane Goodall Institute. It goes without saying that these and other organizations must succeed if the great apes are to survive in the wild even until the middle of this century.

If you are in your 20s or 30s, you will certainly live to hear of the extinction of some of our marvelous cousins. Many more will undoubtedly slip away unnoticed. Tragically, this will occur, in most cases, before we've even gotten to know them. Each species on earth is the current result of a unique set of evolutionary events that, over millions of years, has produced a finely adapted component of a diverse, interconnected ecosystem. When it becomes extinct, that adaptation and that part of biodiversity is lost forever. What a tragedy it will be if, through our own mismanagement and greed, we awaken to a world without chimpanzees, mountain gorillas, or the tiny, exquisite lion tamarin. When that day comes, we truly will have lost a part of ourselves, and we will certainly be the poorer for it.

created a bonobo reserve consisting of 30,500 km². This amounts to about 10 percent of the land in the DRC, and the government has stated that its goal is to set aside an additional 5 percent for wildlife protection (News in Brief, 2007). This is a huge step forward, but it remains to be seen if protection can be enforced.

Why It Matters

Most people don't know much about nonhuman primates, and of those who do, a majority don't realize how seriously endangered they are. What's worse, many who do know don't really care because their lives won't substantially change if, say, chimpanzees become extinct in the wild. (Although there could still be captive chimpanzees for a few more decades, this isn't seen as a viable long-term solution.)

The fact is, it *is* important that we know about nonhuman primates, not only for the anthropocentric reason that we can better understand ourselves (although this is true), but also because the living nonhuman primates are the current representatives of a lineage that goes back approximately 60 million years. They can provide a great deal of information as to how evolutionary processes have produced the diversity we see in our own lineage today. From comparative studies, we can identify the genetic causes for certain conditions (such as AIDS) that

humans are susceptible to but chimpanzees are able to resist. Although this information may not help us decide what kind of car to buy or what to have for dinner, it is permitting us to unravel the genetic and behavioral links that connect all primates, including ourselves, in a network of adaptation and evolution. Lastly, the nonhuman primates (and other species, too) are important in their own right, and it's up to us to make sure they survive into the next century. Indeed, this is going to be a truly formidable task.

Summary of Main Topics

- The mammalian order Primates includes humans and approximately 230 nonhuman species: apes, monkeys, tarsiers, and lemurs. Most nonhuman primates live in tropical and subtropical regions of Africa, India, Asia, Mexico, and Central and South America.
- The order Primates is divided into two suborders: Strepsirhini (lemurs and lorises) and Haplorhini (tarsiers, monkeys, apes, and humans).

- As a group, the primates are very generalized, meaning they've retained many anatomical characteristics that were present in early ancestral mammalian species. These traits include five digits on the hands and feet, different kinds of teeth, and a skeletal anatomy and limb structure that allow for different forms of locomotion (climbing, brachiation, quadrupedalism, and bipedalism).
- In general, primates have relatively larger, more complex brains than other mammals.

- Most primates are diurnal and live in social groups.
- Because of habitat loss and human hunting, the majority of nonhuman primates are endangered today, and some are on the verge of extinction. Without concerted efforts to preserve primate habitat and control hunting, many species, including mountain gorillas, bonobos, chimpanzees, and many monkeys, could well become extinct by 2050.

Critical Thinking Questions

1. How do you think continued advances in genetic research will influence how we look at our species' relationships with nonhuman primates in 10 years?

2. How does a classification scheme reflect biological and evolutionary relationships among different primate lineages?

3. What factors threaten the existence of nonhuman primates in the wild? How much do you care? What can you do to help save nonhuman primates from extinction?

Connections

Humans are primates and share many biological characteristics with other primates.

Due to our shared evolution, many human behaviors are also seen in other primates.

The first hominins appeared in Africa more than 6 mya.

8

Primate Behavior

Introduction

Do you think cats are cruel when they play with mice? Or if you've ever fallen off a horse when it suddenly jumped sideways for no apparent reason, did you think it threw you deliberately? If you answered yes to either of these questions, you're not alone. To most people, it does seem cruel for a cat to torment a mouse for no apparent reason; and more than one rider has blamed their horse for intentionally throwing them (it has been known to happen). But these views generally demonstrate how little most people really know about nonhuman animal **behavior** (see next page for definition of this term).

Behavior is extremely complex, especially in mammals and birds, because it's been shaped over evolutionary time by interactions between genetic and environmental factors. Most people don't give this much thought, and even those who do don't necessarily accept this basic premise. For example, many social scientists object to the notion of genetic influences on human behavior because of concerns that it implies that behaviors are fixed and can't be modified by experience (learning). This view could, in turn, be used to support racist and sexist ideologies.

Also, there's the prevailing notion of a fundamental division between humans and all other animals. In some cultures, this view is fostered by religion. Yet even when religion isn't a factor, most people see themselves as uniquely set apart from all other species. At the same time, and in obvious contradiction, people sometimes judge other species from a strictly human perspective and explain certain behaviors in terms of human motivations (for example, cats are cruel to play with mice). Of course, this isn't a valid thing to do for the simple reason that other animals aren't human. Cats sometimes play with mice because that's how, as kittens, they learned to hunt. Cruelty doesn't enter into it because the cat has no concept of cruelty and no idea of what it's like to be the mouse.

Likewise, a horse doesn't deliberately throw you off when it hears leaves rattling in a shrub. It jumps because its behavior has been shaped by thousands of generations of equine ancestors who leaped first and asked questions later. It's important

◄ Baboon infant playing with adult.

187

to understand that just as cats evolved as predators, horses evolved as prey animals, and their evolutionary history is littered with unfortunate animals that didn't jump at a sound in a shrub. In many cases, those ancestral horses learned, too late, that the sound wasn't caused by a breeze. This is a mistake that prey animals frequently don't survive, and those that don't leap first leave few if any descendants.

Obviously, this chapter isn't about cats and horses. It's about what we know and hypothesize about the individual and social behaviors of nonhuman primates. But we begin with the familiar examples of cats and horses because we want to point out that many basic behaviors have been shaped by the evolutionary history of particular species. So, if we want to discover the underlying principles of behavioral evolution, we first need to identify the interactions between a number of environmental and physiological variables.

The Evolution of Behavior

Scientists study behavior in free-ranging primates from an **ecological** and evolutionary perspective, focusing on the relationship between individual and social behaviors, the natural environment, and various physiological traits of the species in question. This approach is called **behavioral ecology**, and it's based on the underlying assumption that all of the interconnected biological components of ecological systems (animals, plants, and microorganisms) evolved together. Therefore, behaviors are adaptations to environmental circumstances that existed in the past as well as in the present.

Briefly, the cornerstone of this perspective is that *behaviors have evolved through the operation of natural selection*, and are therefore subject to natural selection in the same way physical traits are. (Remember that within

a specific environmental context, natural selection favors characteristics that provide a reproductive advantage to the individuals who possess them.) Therefore, behavior constitutes a phenotype, and individuals whose behavioral phenotypes increase reproductive fitness will pass on their genes at a faster rate than others. But this doesn't mean that primatologists think that genes code for specific behaviors, such as a gene for aggression, another for cooperation, and so on. Studying complex behaviors from an evolutionary viewpoint doesn't imply a one gene–one behavior relationship, nor does it suggest that behaviors that are influenced by genes can't be modified through learning.

In insects and other invertebrates, behavior is mostly under genetic control. In other words, most behavioral patterns in these species aren't learned; they're innate. But in many vertebrates, especially birds and mammals, the proportion of behavior that's due to learning is substantially increased, and the proportion under genetic control is reduced. This is especially true of primates; and, in humans, who are so much a product of culture, most behavior is learned. Still, we know that in mammals and birds, some behaviors are at least partly influenced by certain gene products such as hormones. You may be aware of studies showing that increased levels of testosterone increase aggression in many species. You may also know that abnormal levels of certain chemicals produced by brain cells cause conditions such as depression, schizophrenia, and bipolar disorder.

Brain cells are directed by the genes within them to produce these chemicals; therefore, in this way, genes can influence aspects of behavior. But *behavioral genetics*, or the study of how genes affect behavior, is a relatively new field, and we don't know the extent to which genes actually influence behavior in humans or other species. What we do know is that behavior must be viewed as the product of *complex*

---

behavior Anything organisms do that involves action in response to internal or external stimuli. The response of an individual, group, or species to its environment. Such responses may or may not be deliberate and they aren't necessarily the results of conscious decision making.

ecological Pertaining to the relationships between organisms and all aspects of their environment (temperature, predators, nonpredators, vegetation, availability of food and water, types of food, disease organisms, parasites, etc.).

behavioral ecology The study of the evolution of behavior, emphasizing the role of ecological factors as agents of natural selection. Behaviors and behavioral patterns have been favored because they increase the reproductive fitness of individuals (i.e., they are adaptive) in specific environmental contexts.

interactions between genetic and environmental factors. The limits and potentials for learning, and for behavioral flexibility, vary considerably among species. In some species, such as primates, the potentials are extremely broad; in others, such as insects, they aren't. Ultimately, those limits and potentials are set by genetic factors that have been subjected to natural selection throughout the evolutionary history of every species. That history, in turn, has been shaped by the ecological setting not only of living species *but also of their ancestors.*

One of the major goals of primatology is to discover how certain behaviors influence reproductive fitness and how ecological factors have shaped the evolution of those behaviors. Although the actual mechanics of behavioral evolution aren't yet fully understood, new technologies and methodologies are helping scientists answer many questions. For example, genetic analysis has recently been used to establish paternity in a few primate groups, and this has helped support hypotheses about some behaviors in males. But in general, an evolutionary approach to the study of behavior doesn't provide definitive answers to many research questions. Rather, it offers primatologists a valuable framework within which they

can analyze data and generate and test hypotheses concerning behavioral patterns. (Remember, the development and testing of new hypotheses is how scientific research is done.)

Because primates are among the most social of animals, social behavior is one of the major topics in primate research (**Fig. 8-1**). This is a broad subject that includes all aspects of behavior occurring in social groupings, even some you may not think of as social behaviors, such as feeding or mating. To understand the function of one behavioral element, it's necessary to determine how it's influenced by numerous interrelated factors. As an example, we'll consider some of the

▲ **Figure 8-1**
(a) These proboscis monkeys in Malaysia provide a good example of a small, nonhuman primate social group. **(b)** Imagine trying to recognize the red colobus monkeys as individuals. What tools and techniques would you use to identify them?

more important variables that influence **social structure**. Bear in mind that social structure itself influences individual behavior, so in many cases, the distinctions between social and individual behaviors are blurred.

Some Factors That Influence Social Structure

▲ **Figure 8-2**
This small mouse lemur has a much higher BMR and requires more energy per unit of body weight than a gorilla.

Body Size As a rule, larger animals require fewer calories per unit of weight than smaller animals because larger animals have less surface area relative to body mass than smaller animals. Since body heat is lost at the surface, larger animals can retain heat more efficiently, so they need less energy overall.

It may seem strange, but two 10-pound monkeys require more food than one 22-pound monkey (Fleagle, 1999).

Basal Metabolic Rate (BMR) The BMR concerns **metabolism**, the rate at which the body uses energy to maintain all bodily functions while in a resting state. It's closely correlated with body size, so in general, smaller animals have a higher BMR than larger ones (**Fig. 8-2**). Consequently, smaller primates, for instance galagos and marmosets, require an energy-rich diet high in protein (insects), fats (nuts and seeds), and carbohydrates (fruits and seeds). Some larger primates, which tend to have a lower BMR and reduced energy requirements relative to body size, can do well with less energy-rich foods, such as leaves.

Diet Because the nutritional requirements of animals are related to the previous two factors, all three have evolved together. Therefore, when primatologists study the relationships between diet and behavior, they consider the benefits in terms of energy (calories) derived from various food items against the costs (energy expended) of obtaining and digesting them. While small-bodied primates focus on high-energy foods, larger ones don't necessarily need to. For instance, gorillas eat leaves, pith from bamboo stems, and other types of vegetation, and they don't need to use much energy searching for food since they're frequently surrounded by it (**Fig. 8–3**).

Some monkeys, especially colobines (colobus and langur species), are primarily leaf eaters. Compared with many other monkeys, they're fairly large-bodied. They've also evolved elongated intestines and pouched stomachs that enable them, with the assistance of intestinal bacteria, to digest the tough fibers and cellulose in leaves. Moreover, in at least two langur species, there's a duplicated gene that produces an enzyme that further helps with digestion. This gene duplication isn't found in other primates that have been studied, so the duplication event

▲ **Figure 8-3**
This male mountain gorilla has only to reach out to find something to eat.

social structure The composition, size, and sex ratio of a group of animals. The social structure of a species is, in part, the result of natural selection in a specific habitat, and it guides individual interactions and social relationships.

metabolism The chemical processes within cells that break down nutrients and release energy for the body to use. (When nutrients are broken down into their component parts, such as amino acids, energy is released and made available for the cell to use.)

© Martin Harvey / Peter Arnold / Photolibrary

◄Figure 8-4
Gelada baboons live in one-male groups that combine to form troops that can number more than 300 animals.

probably occurred after colobines and cercopithecines last shared a common ancestor (Zhang et al., 2002). Having a second copy of the gene was advantageous to colobine ancestors, who were probably already eating some leaves, so natural selection favored it to the point that it was established in the lineage. (The discovery of this gene duplication is another example of how new technologies help explain behavior, in this case, dietary differences.)

Distribution of Resources Various kinds of foods are distributed in different ways. Leaves can be abundant and dense and will therefore support large groups of animals. Insects, on the other hand, may be widely scattered, and the animals that rely on them usually feed alone or with only one or two others.

Fruits, nuts, and berries occur in clumps in dispersed trees and shrubs. These are most efficiently exploited by smaller groups of animals, so large groups frequently break up into smaller subunits while feeding. Such subunits may consist of one-male–multifemale groups (some baboons) or **matrilines** (macaques). Species that feed on abundantly distributed resources may also live in one-male groups, and because food is plentiful, these one-male units

are able to join with others, to form large, stable communities (for example, howlers and some baboons) (**Fig. 8-4**). To the casual observer, these communities can appear to be multimale-multifemale groups.

Some species that depend on foods distributed in small clumps are protective of resources, especially if their feeding area is small enough to be defended. Some live in small groups composed of a mated pair (siamangs) or a female with one or two males (marmosets and tamarins). Lastly, foods such as fruits, nuts, and berries are only seasonally available, and primates that rely on them must eat a wide variety of items. This is another factor that tends to favor smaller feeding groups.

Predation Primates, depending on their size, are vulnerable to many types of predators, including snakes, birds of prey, leopards, wild dogs, and other primates. Their responses to predation depend on their body size, social structure, and the type of predator. Typically, where predation pressure is high and body size is small, large communities are advantageous. These may be multimale-multifemale groups or congregations of one-male groups.

matrilines Groups that consist of a female, her daughters, and their offspring. Matrilineal groups are common in macaques.

Dispersal Dispersal is another factor that influences social structure and relationships within groups. As is true of most mammals, members of one sex leave the group in which they were born about the time they become sexually mature. Male dispersal is the most common pattern (ring-tailed lemurs, vervets, and macaques, to name a few). But female dispersal is seen in some colobus species, hamadryas baboons, chimpanzees, and mountain gorillas. In species where the basic social structure is a mated pair, offspring of both sexes either leave or are driven away by their parents (gibbons and siamangs).

Dispersal may have more than one outcome. When females leave, they join another group. Males may do likewise but in some species (for example, gorillas), they may live alone for a time, or they may temporarily join an all-male "bachelor" group until they're able to establish a group of their own. But the common theme is that individuals who disperse usually find mates outside their natal group. This has led primatologists to conclude that the most valid explanations for dispersal are related to two major factors: reduced competition between males for mates and, more importantly, the decreased likelihood of close inbreeding.

Life Histories **Life history traits** are characteristics or developmental stages that typify members of a given species and therefore influence potential reproductive rates. Examples of life history traits include length of gestation, length of time between pregnancies (interbirth interval), period of infant dependency and age at weaning, age at sexual maturity, and life expectancy.

Life history traits have important consequences for many aspects of social life, and they can also be critical to species survival. Species that live only a few years mature rapidly, reproduce within a year or two after birth, and have short interbirth intervals. Thus, shorter life histories are advantageous to species that live in mar-

ginal or unpredictable habitats (Strier, 2003) because reproduction can occur at a relatively rapid rate. Conversely, longer-lived species, such as gorillas, are better suited to stable environmental conditions. The extended life spans of the great apes in particular, characterized by later sexual maturation and long interbirth intervals of 3 to 5 years, means that most females will raise only three or four offspring to maturity. Today, this slow rate of reproduction increases the threat of extinction for all the great apes, which are being hunted at a rate that far outpaces their replacement capacities.

Activity Patterns Most primates are diurnal, but galagos, lories, aye-ayes, tarsiers, and New World owl monkeys are nocturnal. Nocturnal primates tend to forage for food alone or in groups of two or three, and many hide to avoid predators.

Human Activities As you saw in Chapter 7, virtually all nonhuman primate populations are now impacted by human hunting and forest clearing. These activities severely disrupt and isolate groups, reduce numbers, reduce resource availability, and eventually can cause extinction.

Why Be Social?

Group living exposes animals to competition with other group members for resources, so why don't primates live alone? After all, competition can lead to injury or even death, and it's costly in terms of energy expenditure. One widely accepted answer to this question is that the costs of competition are offset by the benefits of predator defense. Multimale-multifemale groups are advantageous in areas where predation pressure is high, particularly in mixed woodlands and on open savannas. Leopards are the most significant predator of terrestrial primates (**Fig. 8–5**), and the chances of escaping a leopard

life history traits Characteristics and developmental stages that influence reproductive rates. Examples include longevity, age at sexual maturity, length of time between births, etc.

attack are greater for animals that live in groups where there are several pairs of eyes looking about. (There really is safety in numbers).

Savanna baboons have long been used as an example of these principles. They live in semiarid grassland and broken woodland habitats throughout sub-Saharan Africa. To avoid nocturnal predators, savanna baboons sleep in trees, but they spend much of the day on the ground foraging for food. If a predator appears, baboons flee back into the trees, but if they're some distance from safety, adult males (and sometimes females) may join forces to chase the intruder. The effectiveness of male baboons in this regard should not be underestimated, as they've been known to kill domestic dogs and even to attack leopards and lions.

There is probably no single answer to the question of why primates live in groups. More than likely, predator avoidance is a major factor but not the only one. Group living evolved as an adaptive response to a number of ecological variables, and it has served primates well for a very long time.

© Time Life Pictures / Getty Images

▲ **Figure 8-5**
When a baboon strays too far from its troop, as this one has done, it's more likely to fall prey to predators. Leopards are the most serious non-human threat to terrestrial primates.

Quick Review

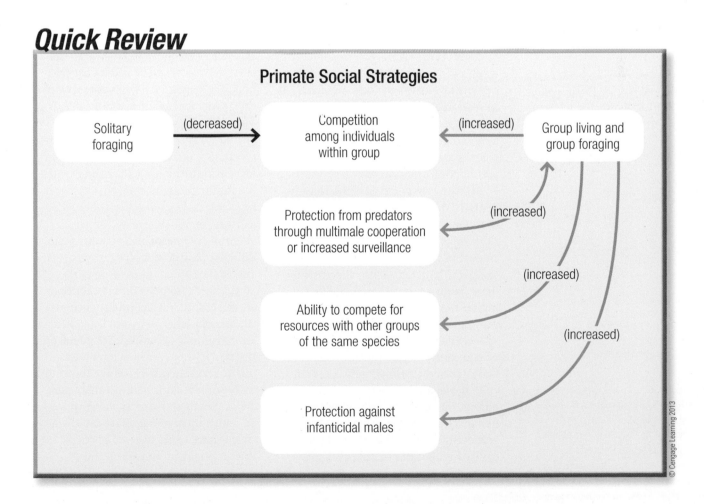

Primate Social Strategies

Solitary foraging → (decreased) → Competition among individuals within group ← (increased) — Group living and group foraging

Protection from predators through multimale cooperation or increased surveillance ← (increased)

Ability to compete for resources with other groups of the same species ← (increased)

Protection against infanticidal males ← (increased)

© Cengage Learning 2013

Primate Social Behavior

Because primates solve their major adaptive problems in a social context, we should expect them to behave in ways that reinforce the integrity of the group. The better known of these are described here. Remember, all these behaviors have evolved as adaptive responses during more than 50 million years of primate evolution.

Dominance

Many primate societies are organized into **dominance hierarchies**, which impose a certain degree of order by establishing parameters of individual behavior. Although aggression is frequently used to increase an animal's status, dominance hierarchies usually reduce the amount of actual physical violence. Not only are lower-ranking animals unlikely to attack or even threaten a higher-ranking one, but dominant animals are usually able to exert control simply by making a threatening gesture. Individual rank or status can be measured by access to resources, including food items and mating partners. Dominant animals (alpha males and females) are given priority by others, and they rarely give way in confrontations.

Many primatologists think that the primary benefit of dominance is the increased reproductive success of high-ranking animals. This is true in many cases, but there's good evidence that lower-ranking males also successfully mate. High-ranking females also have higher reproductive success because they have greater access to food than subordinate females. Therefore, they obtain more energy for the production and care of offspring (Fedigan, 1983).

Pusey et al. (1997) demonstrated that the offspring of high-ranking female chimpanzees at Gombe Stream National Park in Tanzania had significantly higher rates of infant survival. Moreover, their daughters matured faster, which meant they had shorter interbirth intervals and consequently produced more offspring.

An individual's position in the hierarchy isn't permanent. Instead, it changes throughout life. It's influenced by many factors, including sex, age, level of aggression, amount of time spent in the group, intelligence, perhaps motivation, and sometimes the mother's social position (particularly true of macaques).

In species organized into groups containing a number of females associated with one or several adult males, the males are generally dominant to females. Within such groups, males and females have separate hierarchies, although very high-ranking females can dominate the lowest-ranking males, particularly young ones. But there are exceptions to this pattern of male dominance. In many lemur species, females are the dominant sex. Moreover, in species that form bonded pairs (for example, indris and gibbons), males and females are codominant.

All primates *learn* their position in the hierarchy. From birth, an infant is carried by its mother, and it observes how she responds to every member of the group. Just as importantly, it sees how others react to her. Dominance and subordination are indicated by gestures and behaviors, some of which are universal throughout the primate order (including humans), and this gestural repertoire is part of every youngster's learning experience.

Young primates also acquire social rank through play with age peers, and as they spend more time with play groups, their social interactions widen. Competition and rough-and-tumble play allow them to learn the strengths and weaknesses of peers, and they carry this knowledge with them throughout their lives. Thus, through early contact with their mothers and subsequent exposure to peers, young primates learn to negotiate their way through the complex web of social interactions that makes up their daily lives.

dominance hierarchies Systems of social organization wherein individuals within a group are ranked relative to one another. Higher-ranking animals have greater access to preferred food items and mating partners than lower-ranking individuals. Dominance hierarchies are sometimes called "pecking orders."

Communication

Communication is universal among animals and includes scents and unintentional, **autonomic** responses, as well as behaviors that convey meaning. Such attributes as body posture provide information about an animal's emotional state. For example, a purposeful striding gait implies confidence. Moreover, autonomic responses to threatening or novel stimuli, such as raised body hair (most species) or enhanced body odor (gorillas), indicate excitement.

Many intentional behaviors also serve as communication. In primates, these include a wide variety of gestures, facial expressions, and vocalizations, some of which we humans share. Among many primates an intense stare indicates a mild threat; and indeed, we humans find prolonged eye contact with strangers very uncomfortable. (For this reason, people should avoid eye contact with captive primates.) Other threat gestures include a quick yawn to expose canine teeth (baboons, macaques) (**Fig. 8-6**); bobbing back and forth in a crouched position (patas monkeys); and branch shaking (many monkey species). High-ranking baboons *mount* the hindquarters of subordinates to express dominance (**Fig. 8-7**). Mounting may also serve to defuse potentially tense situations by indicating something like, "It's okay, I accept your apology."

© Martin B Withers / FLPA / Minden Pictures

▲ **Figure 8-6**
A "yawn" that exposes long canine teeth is a common threat gesture in many primate species. Here, an adult male baboon combines it with an "eyelid flash," closing the eyes to expose light-colored eyelids that enhance the visual effect of the threat.

Lynn Kilgore

◄ **Figure 8-7**
One young male savanna baboon mounts another as an expression of dominance.

Lynn Kilgore

▲ **Figure 8-8**
Adolescent savanna baboons holding hands.

Primates also use a variety of behaviors to indicate submission, reassurance, or amicable intentions. Most primates crouch to show submission and baboons also present or turn their hindquarters toward an animal they want to appease. Reassurance takes the form of touching, patting, hugging, and holding hands (**Fig. 8-8**). **Grooming** also serves in a number of situations to indicate submission or reassurance.

A wide variety of facial expressions indicating emotional state is seen in

communication Any act that conveys information, in the form of a message, to another individual. Frequently, the result of communication is a change in the behavior of the recipient. Communication may not be deliberate but may instead be the result of involuntary processes or a secondary consequence of an intentional action.

autonomic Pertaining to physiological responses not under voluntary control. An example in chimpanzees would be the erection of body hair during excitement. Blushing is a human example. Both convey information regarding emotional states, but neither is deliberate, and communication isn't intended.

grooming Picking through fur to remove dirt, parasites, and other materials that may be present. Social grooming is common among primates and reinforces social relationships.

| Relaxed | Relaxed with dropped lip | Horizontal pout face (distress) | Fear grin (fear/excitement) | Full play face |

© Cengage Learning 2013

▲ **Figure 8-9**
Chimpanzee facial expressions.

chimpanzees and, especially, in bonobos (**Fig. 8-9**). These include the well-known play face (also seen in several other primate and nonprimate species), associated with play behavior, and the fear grin to indicate fear and submission.

Not surprisingly, vocalizations play a major role in primate communication. Some, such as the bark of a baboon that has just spotted a leopard, are unintentional startled reactions. Others, such as the chimpanzee food grunt, are heard only in specific contexts; in this case in the presence of food. These vocalizations, whether deliberate or not, inform others of the possible presence of predators or food.

Primates (and other animals) also communicate through **displays**, which are more complicated, frequently elaborate combinations of behaviors. For example, the exaggerated courtship dances of many male birds, often enhanced by colorful plumage, are displays. Chest slapping and tearing vegetation are common gorilla threat displays.

All nonhuman animals use various body postures, vocalizations, and facial expressions to transmit information. But the array of communicative devices is much richer among nonhuman primates, even though they don't use language the way humans do. Communication is important, because it's what makes social living possible. Through submissive gestures, aggression is reduced and physical violence is less likely. Likewise, friendly intentions and relationships are reinforced through physical contact and grooming. Indeed, we humans can see ourselves in other primates most clearly in their use of nonverbal communication, particularly because some of their gestures and facial expressions carry the same meaning as ours do.

Aggressive Interactions

Within primate societies, there is an interplay between aggressive behaviors, which can lead to group disruption, and **affiliative behaviors**, which promote group cohesion. Conflict within a group frequently develops out of competition for resources, including mating partners or food. Instead of actual attacks or fighting, most **intragroup** aggression occurs in the form of various signals and displays, frequently within the context of a dominance hierarchy. The majority of tense situations are resolved through various submissive and appeasement behaviors.

But conflicts aren't always resolved peacefully; in fact, they can have serious and even fatal consequences. For example, high-ranking female macaques frequently intimidate, harass, and even attack lower-ranking females to keep them away from food. Dominant females consistently chase subordinates away from food and have even been observed taking food from their mouths. Eventually, these actions can cause weight loss and poor nutrition in low-ranking females. These, in turn, can reduce the reproductive success of these females because they're less able to rear offspring to maturity simply because they don't get enough to eat (Silk et al., 2003).

Competition between males for mates frequently results in injury and

displays Sequences of repetitious behaviors that serve to communicate emotional states. Nonhuman primate displays are most frequently associated with reproductive or agonistic behavior and examples include chest slapping in gorillas or, in male chimpanzees, dragging and waving branches while charging and threatening other animals.

affiliative behaviors Amicable associations between individuals. Affiliative behaviors, such as grooming, reinforce social bonds and promote group cohesion.

intragroup Within the group as opposed to intergroup (meaning between groups).

even death. In species that have a distinct breeding season, such as New World squirrel monkeys, conflict between males is most common during that time. In species not restricted to a mating season, such as baboons and chimpanzees, competition between males can be ongoing.

In recent years, some primatologists have focused on conflicts in which a number of individuals attack and sometimes kill one or two chimpanzees, who may or may not belong to the same group. Lethal aggression is relatively common between groups of chimpanzees, and it's also been reported for red colobus monkeys (Starin, 1994); spider monkeys, although no actual killings have been observed (Aureli et al., 2006; Campbell, 2006; and capuchin monkeys (Gros-Louis et al., 2003).

Between groups, aggression is often used to protect resources or **territories**. Primate groups are associated with a *home range* where they remain permanently. Although individuals may leave their home range and join another community, the group itself remains in a particular area. Within the home range is a portion called the **core area**, which contains the highest concentration of predictable resources, and this is where the group is most frequently found. Although parts of a group's home range may overlap with home ranges of other groups, core areas of adjacent groups don't overlap. The core area can also be said to be a group's territory, and it's the portion of the home range defended against intrusion. In some species, other areas of the home range may also be defended (**Fig. 8-10**)

Not all primates are territorial. In general, territoriality is typical of species whose ranges are small enough to be patrolled and protected (gibbons and vervets, for example). But male chimpanzees are highly intolerant of unfamiliar chimpanzees, especially other males, and they fiercely defend their resources. Therefore, chimpanzee intergroup interactions are almost always characterized by aggressive dis-

▲ **Figure 8-10**
A chimpanzee border patrol.

plays, chasing, and sometimes, very violent fighting (**Fig. 8-11**).

Beginning in 1974, Jane Goodall and her colleagues witnessed at least five unprovoked and extremely brutal attacks by groups of chimpanzees on other chimpanzees (Goodall, 1986). To

▲ **Figure 8-11**
Male chimpanzee display. Note how the hair on his arms and shoulders is raised to make him look larger. Erect hair is also an indication of excitement.

territories Portions of an individual's or group's home range that are actively defended against intrusion, especially by members of the same species.

core area The portion of a home range containing the highest concentration and most reliable supplies of food and water. The core area is defended.

explain these attacks, it's necessary to point out that by 1973, the original Gombe community had divided into two distinct groups, one located in the north and the other in the south of what had once been the original group's home range. In effect, the smaller offshoot group had denied the others access to part of their former home range.

By 1977, all seven males and one female of the splinter group were either known or suspected to have been killed. All observed incidents involved several animals, usually adult males, who brutally attacked lone individuals (**Fig. 8-12**). Whether the chimpanzees actually intended to kill their victims is difficult to know, because we don't know to what degree they have a concept of death.

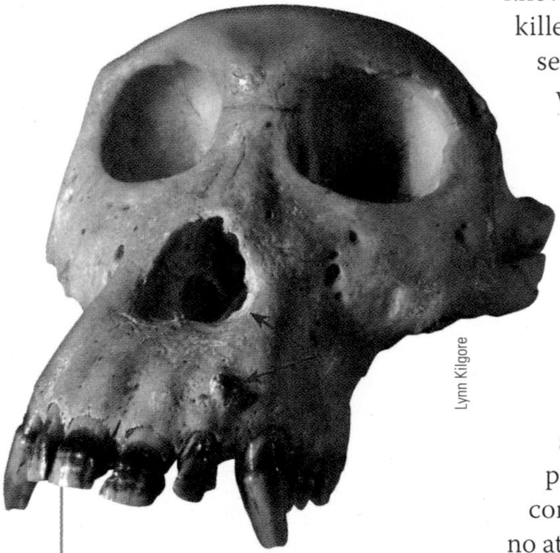

A similar situation was also reported for a chimpanzee group in the Mahale Mountains south of Gombe. Over a 17-year period, all the males of a small community disappeared. Although no attacks were actually observed, there was circumstantial evidence that most of these males met the same fate as the Gombe attack victims (Nishida et al., 1985, 1990).

Mitani et al. (2010) document a third such situation in a large chimpanzee community at Ngogo, Kibale National Park, Uganda. Between 1999 and 2009, members of this group were observed killing or fatally wounding 18 individuals from other groups, and all but one of the observed attacks were made by coalitions of males on patrol. The entire Ngogo community now regularly uses the area where they frequently conducted border patrols and where 13 of the attacks occurred. Meanwhile the former residents have not been seen. In effect, these chimpanzees have increased their territory by 2.5 square miles, or 22 percent. Given this fact, the researchers attribute the attacks on a neighboring group to territorial expansion, which increases the resource base of the attacking group and in turn may lead to greater reproductive success.

Even though chimpanzees engage in lethal attacks, the actual number of observed incidents is low. The major cause of death among the Mahale chimpanzees is actually disease (Nishida et al, 2003). This is probably true of most chimpanzee groups and perhaps early hominin populations as well. Though the precise motivation of chimpanzee intergroup aggression may never be fully explained, it appears that acquiring and protecting resources (including females) are involved (Nishida et al., 1985, 1990; Goodall, 1986; Manson and Wrangham, 1991; Nishida, 1991). Through careful examination of shared aspects of human and chimpanzee social life, we can develop hypotheses regarding how intergroup conflict may have arisen in our own lineage. Early hominins and chimpanzees may have inherited from a common ancestor the predispositions that lead to similar patterns of strife between populations. It's not possible to draw direct comparisons between chimpanzee conflict and modern human warfare because of human elaborations of culture: religion, use of symbols (such as flags), and language. But it's important to speculate on the fundamental issues that may have led to the development of similar patterns in both species.

Affiliation and Altruism

Even though conflict can be destructive, a certain amount of aggression helps protect resources and maintain order within groups. Fortunately, to minimize actual violence, promote group cohesion, and defuse potentially dangerous situations, there are many behaviors that reinforce bonds between individuals and enhance group stability. Common affiliative behaviors include reconciliation, consolation, and simple amicable interactions between friends and relatives. Most such behaviors involve various forms of physical contact such as touching,

▲ **Figure 8-12**
This male chimpanzee cranium from West Africa exhibits a healed bite wound beneath the nose (arrow), most likely inflicted by another chimpanzee. Also, the left margin of the nasal opening shows irregularities that may have been caused by an infection, perhaps related to the injury.

Lynn Kilgore

▲ **Figure 8-13**
Grooming primates.
(a) Drills
(b) Longtail macaques
(c) Japanese macaques
(d) Chimpanzees

hand-holding, hugging, and among chimpanzees, kissing. In fact, physical contact is one of the most important factors in primate development and it's crucial in promoting peaceful relationships and reinforcing bonds in many primate social groups.

There are also behaviors that indicate just how important bonds between individuals are; and some of these behaviors can perhaps be said to be examples of caregiving, or compassion. It's somewhat risky to use the term *compassion* because in humans, compassion is motivated by **empathy** for another person. We don't know for sure whether nonhuman primates can empathize with another's suffering or misfortune, but laboratory research has indicated that some of them probably do. The degree to which chimpanzees and other primates are capable of empathy is debated by primatologists. Some believe there is substantial evidence for it (deWaal, 2007, 1996), but others remain unconvinced (Silk, et al., 2005).

Certainly there are many examples, mostly from chimpanzee studies, of caregiving actions that resemble compassionate behavior in humans. Examples include protecting victims during attacks, helping younger siblings, and remaining near ill or dying relatives or friends. In a poignant example from Gombe, the young adult female Little Bee brought food to her mother at least twice while the latter lay dying of wounds inflicted by attacking males (Goodall, 1986). When chimpanzees have been observed sitting near a dying relative, they were occasionally seen shooing flies away or grooming the other individual, as if trying to help in some way.

Grooming is one of the most important affiliative behaviors in many primate species. Although grooming occurs in other animal species, social grooming is mostly a primate activity, and it plays an important role in day-to-day life (**Fig. 8–13**). Because grooming involves using the fingers to pick through the fur of another individual

empathy The ability to identify with the feelings and thoughts of another individual.

(or one's own) to remove insects, dirt, and other materials, it serves hygienic functions. But it's also an immensely pleasurable activity that members of some species, especially chimpanzees, engage in for long periods of time.

Grooming occurs in a variety of contexts. Mothers groom infants; males groom sexually receptive females; subordinate animals groom dominant ones, sometimes to gain favor; and friends groom friends. In general, grooming is comforting. It restores peaceful relationships after conflict, and provides reassurance during tense situations. In short, grooming reinforces social bonds and consequently helps strengthen and maintain a group's structure.

Conflict resolution through reconciliation is another important aspect of primate social behavior. Following a conflict, chimpanzee opponents frequently move, within minutes, to reconcile (de Waal, 1982). Reconciliation takes many forms, including hugging, kissing, and grooming. In addition, bonobos are unique in their use of sex to promote group cohesion, restore peace after conflicts, and relieve tension within the group (de Waal, 1987, 1989).

Social relationships are crucial to nonhuman primates, and bonds between individuals can last a lifetime. These relationships serve many functions. Individuals of many species form alliances in which members support each other against outsiders. Alliances, or coalitions, as they're also called, can be used to enhance the status of members. In fact, chimpanzees rely so heavily on coalitions and are so skillful politically that an entire book, appropriately titled *Chimpanzee Politics* (de Waal, 1982), is devoted to the topic.

Altruism is behavior that benefits another while involving some risk or sacrifice to the performer. Altruism, cooperation, and assistance are fairly common in many primate species, and altruistic acts sometimes contain elements of what might be interpret-ed as empathy. The most fundamental of altruistic behaviors, the protection of dependent offspring, is ubiquitous among mammals and birds, and in the majority of species, altruistic acts are confined to this context.

However, chimpanzees routinely come to the aid of relatives and friends; female langurs join forces to protect infants from infanticidal males; and male baboons protect infants and cooperate to chase predators. In fact, the primate literature abounds with examples of altruistic acts, whereby individuals place themselves at some risk to protect others from attacks by conspecifics or predators.

Adopting orphans is a form of altruism that has been reported for capuchins, macaques, baboons, gorillas, and especially chimpanzees. When chimpanzee youngsters are orphaned, they are almost always adopted, usually by older siblings who are attentive and highly protective. Adoption is crucial to the survival of orphans, who certainly wouldn't survive on their own. In fact, it's extremely rare for a chimpanzee orphan less than three years of age to survive, even if it is adopted.

There are now hundreds of documented examples of cooperation and altruism in nonhuman primates. Chimpanzees certainly have shown a tendency to perform altruistic acts and this fact has caused some primatologists to consider the possibility that the common ancestor of humans and chimpanzees had a propensity for cooperation and helping others, at least in certain circumstances (Warneken and Tomasello, 2006).

Evolutionary explanations of altruism are usually based on the premise that individuals are more likely to perform risky or self-sacrificing behaviors that benefit a relative. By helping a relative who otherwise might not survive to reproduce, the performer is helping promote the spread of genes they have in common. Another explanation, sometimes called "reciprocal altruism," emphasizes that performers help others

altruism Actions that benefit another individual but at some potential risk or cost to oneself.

◄**Figure 8-14**
Estrous swelling in a female
Celebes crested macaque.

in order to increase the chances that, at a future date, the recipient might return the favor.

Reproduction and Reproductive Behaviors

In most primate species, sexual behavior is tied to the female's reproductive cycle, with females being receptive to males only when they're in estrus. Estrus is characterized by behavioral changes that indicate that a female is receptive. In Old World monkeys and apes that live in multimale groups, estrus is also accompanied by swelling and changes in color of the skin around the genital area. These changes serve as visual cues of a female's readiness to mate (**Fig. 8–14**).

Permanent bonding between males and females isn't common among nonhuman primates. However, male and female savanna baboons sometimes form mating *consortships*. These temporary relationships last while the female is in estrus, and the two spend most of their time together, mating fre-

quently. Mating consortships are also sometimes seen in chimpanzees and are common in bonobos. In fact, male and female bonobos may spend several weeks primarily in each other's company. During this time, they mate often, even when the female isn't in estrus.

Such a male-female bond may result in increased reproductive success for both sexes. For the male, there is the increased likelihood that he will be the father of any infant the female conceives. At the same time, the female potentially gains protection from predators or other members of her group; and she may also gain some help in caring for offspring she may already have.

Female and Male Reproductive Strategies

Reproductive strategies, and especially how they differ between the sexes, have been a primary focus of primate research. The goal of these strategies is to produce and successfully rear to adulthood as many offspring as possible.

Primates are among the most **K-selected** of mammals. By this we mean that individuals produce only a

reproductive strategies
Behaviors or behavioral complexes that have been favored by natural selection to increase individual reproductive success. The behaviors need not be deliberate, and they often vary considerably between males and females.

K-selected Pertaining to K-selection, an adaptive strategy whereby individuals produce relatively few offspring, in whom they invest increased parental care. Although only a few infants are born, chances of survival are increased for each one because of parental investments in time and energy. Birds, elephants, and canids (wolves, coyotes, and dogs) are examples of K-selected nonprimate species.

few young, in whom they invest a tremendous amount of parental care. Contrast this pattern with **r-selected** species, where individuals produce large numbers of offspring but invest little or no energy in parental care. Good examples of r-selected species include insects, most fishes, and, among mammals, mice and rabbits.

Considering the degree of care required by young, dependent primate offspring, it's clear that enormous investment by at least one parent is necessary, and in a majority of species, the mother carries most of the burden, certainly before, but also after birth. Primates are completely helpless at birth. They develop slowly and, consequently, they're exposed to expanded learning opportunities within a *social* environment. This trend has been elaborated most dramatically in great apes and humans, especially the latter. So, what we see in ourselves and our close primate relatives (and presumably in our more recent ancestors as well) is a strategy in which at least one parent, usually the mother, makes an extraordinary investment to produce a few "high-quality," slowly maturing offspring.

Finding food and mates, avoiding predators, and caring for and protecting dependent young are difficult challenges for nonhuman primates. In most species, males and females use different strategies to meet these challenges.

Female primates spend almost all their adult lives either pregnant, lactating, and/or caring for offspring, and the resulting metabolic demands are enormous. A pregnant or lactating female, although perhaps only half the size of her male counterpart, may require about the same number of calories per day. Even if these demands are met, her physical resources may be drained. For example, analysis of chimpanzee skeletons from Gombe showed significant loss of bone and bone mineral in older females (Sumner et al., 1989).

Given these physiological costs, and the fact that her reproductive potential is limited by lengthy intervals between births, a female's best strategy is to maximize the amount of resources available to her and her offspring. Indeed, as we just discussed, females of many primate species are highly competitive with other females and aggressively protect resources. In other species, females distance themselves from others to avoid competition. Males, however, face a different set of challenges. Having little investment in the rearing of offspring and the continuous production of sperm, it's to the male's advantage to secure as many mates and produce as many offspring as possible.

Sexual Selection

Sexual selection is one outcome of different mating strategies. It was first described by Charles Darwin, and is a type of natural selection that operates on only one sex, usually males. The selective agent is male competition for mates and, in some species, mate choice by females. The long-term effect of sexual selection is to increase the frequency of those traits in males that lead to greater success in acquiring mates.

In the animal kingdom, numerous male attributes are the result of sexual selection. For example, female birds of many species are attracted to males with more vividly colored plumage. Selection has thus increased the frequency of alleles that influence brighter coloration in males, and in these species (peacocks are a good example) males are more colorful than females.

Sexual selection in primates is most common in species in which mating is **polygynous** and there is considerable male competition for females. In these species, sexual selection produces dimorphism with regard to a number of traits, most noticeably body size (**Fig. 8-15**). As you've seen, the males of many primate species are considerably larger than females, and they also have larger canine teeth. Conversely, in species that live in pairs (such as gibbons) or where male competition is reduced, sexual dimorphism in body size and

r-selected Pertaining to r-selection, a reproductive strategy that emphasizes relatively large numbers of offspring and reduced parental care compared to K-selected species. *K-selection* and *r-selection* are relative terms; e.g., mice are r-selected compared to primates but K-selected compared to insects.

sexual selection A type of natural selection that operates on only one sex within a species. It's the result of competition for mates, and it can lead to sexual dimorphism with regard to one or more traits.

polygynous Pertaining to polygyny. A mating system in which males, and in some cases females, have several mating partners.

canine teeth is either reduced or non-existent. For this reason, the presence or absence of sexual dimorphism in a species can be a reasonably good indicator of mating structure.

Infanticide as a Reproductive Strategy?

One way males may increase their chances of reproducing is to kill infants fathered by other males. This explanation was first offered in an early study of Hanuman langurs in India (Hrdy, 1977). Hanuman langurs (**Fig. 8–16**) typically live in groups composed of one adult male, several females, and their offspring. Other males without mates form "bachelor" groups that frequently forage within sight of one-male–multi-female units. These peripheral males occasionally attack and defeat a reproductive male and drive him from his group. Sometimes, following such a takeover, the new male kills some or all of the group's infants, fathered by the previous male.

At first glance, such behavior would seem to be counterproductive, especially for a species as a whole. However, individuals act to maximize their *own* reproductive success, no matter what effect their actions may have on the group or the species. By killing infants

▲**Figure 8-15**
Mandrills are one of many good examples of sexual dimorphism and sexual selection in primates. Fully adult males are about twice the size of females and are much more colorful.

fathered by other animals, male langurs may in fact increase their own chances of fathering offspring, albeit unknowingly. This is because, while a female is producing milk and nursing an infant, she doesn't come into estrus, and therefore she isn't sexually available. But when a female loses an infant, she resumes cycling and becomes sexually receptive. So, by killing nursing infants, a new male avoids waiting two to three years for them to be weaned before he can mate with their mothers. This could be advantageous for him because chances are good that he won't

◀**Figure 8-16**
Hanuman langurs.

▲**Figure 8-17**
An immigrant male chacma baboon chases a terrified female and her infant (clinging to her back). Resident males interceded to stop the chase.

even be in the group for 2 or 3 years. He also doesn't expend energy and put himself at risk defending infants who don't carry his genes.

Hanuman langurs aren't the only primates that practice infanticide. Infanticide has been observed or surmised in many species, including gorillas, chimpanzees (Struhsaker and Leyland, 1987), and humans. In the majority of reported nonhuman primate examples, infanticide coincides with the transfer of a new male into a group or, as in chimpanzees, an encounter with an unfamiliar female and infant. (It should also be noted that infanticide occurs in numerous nonprimate species, including rodents, cats, and horses.)

Numerous objections to this explanation of infanticide have been raised. Alternative explanations have included competition for resources (Rudran, 1973), aberrant behaviors related to human-induced overcrowding (Curtin and Dohlinow, 1978), and inadvertent killing during conflict between animals (Bartlett et al., 1993). Sussman and colleagues (1995), as well as others, have questioned the actual prevalence of infanticide, arguing that although it occurs, it's not particularly common. These authors have also suggested that if indeed male reproductive fitness is increased through the killing of infants, such increases are negligible. Yet others (Struhsaker and Leyland, 1987; Hrdy, 1995) maintain that the

incidence and patterning of infanticide by males are not only significant, but also consistent with the assumptions established by theories of behavioral evolution.

Henzi and Barrett (2003) reported that when chacma baboon males migrate into a new group, they "deliberately single out females with young infants and hunt them down" (**Fig. 8-17**). The importance of these findings is the conclusion that, at least in chacma baboons, newly arrived males consistently try to kill infants and their attacks are highly aggressive. However, reports such as these don't prove that infanticide increases a male's reproductive fitness. In order to do this, primatologists must demonstrate two crucial facts:

1. Infanticidal males *don't* kill their own offspring.
2. Once a male has killed an infant, he subsequently fathers another infant with the victim's mother.

The above statements are hypotheses that can be tested; and to do this, Borries et al. (1999) collected DNA samples from the feces of infanticidal males and their victims' remains in several groups of free-ranging Hanuman langurs. This was done to determine if these males killed their own offspring. Their results showed that in all 16 cases where infant and male DNA was available, the males were not related to the infants they either attacked or killed. Moreover, DNA analysis also showed that in four out of five cases in which a victim's mother subsequently gave birth, the new infant was fathered by the infanticidal male. The application of DNA technology to a long-unanswered question has provided strong evidence suggesting that infanticide may indeed give males an increased chance of fathering offspring. Moreover, this study provides another example of how hypotheses are further tested as new technologies are developed.

Mothers, Fathers, and Infants

The basic social unit among all primates is a female and her infants (**Fig. 8–18**). Except in those species in which monogamy or **polyandry** occurs, or in which the social group is a bonded pair, males usually don't directly participate in the rearing of offspring. The mother–infant bond begins at birth. Although the exact nature of the bonding process isn't fully understood, there appear to be predisposing innate

▶ **Figure 8-18**
Primate mothers with young
(a) Mongoose lemurs
(b) Chimpanzees **(c)** Sykes monkeys **(d)** Squirrel monkeys
(e) Japanese macaques

polyandry A mating system wherein a female continuously associates with more than one male (usually two or three) with whom she mates. Among nonhuman primates, polyandry is seen only in marmosets and tamarins. It also occurs in a few human societies.

◄**Figure 8-19**
(a) Male marmoset with youngster on his back. **(b)** Infant mountain gorilla with silverback male.

factors that strongly attract the female to her infant, so long as she herself has had a sufficiently normal experience with her own mother. This doesn't mean that primate mothers have innate knowledge of how to care for an infant. They don't. Monkeys and apes raised in captivity without contact with their own mothers not only don't know how to care for a newborn infant, they may reject or even injure it. Thus, learning is essential to establishing a mother's attraction to and proper care of her infant.

The importance of a normal relationship with the mother has been demonstrated by field and laboratory studies. From birth, infant primates are able to cling to their mother's fur, and they're in more or less constant physical contact with her for several months. During this critical period, infants develop a closeness with their mothers that doesn't always end with weaning. It may even be maintained throughout life. In some species, presumed fathers also participate in infant care (**Fig. 8–19**). Male siamangs are actively involved, and marmoset and tamarin infants are usually carried on the father's back and transferred to their mother only for nursing.

▲ Figure 8-20
(a) This little girl is learning basic computer skills by watching her older sister. **(b)** A chimpanzee learns the art of termiting through intense observation.

Primate Cultural Behavior

Cultural behavior is one important trait that makes primates, and especially chimpanzees and bonobos, attractive as models for behavior in early hominins. Although many cultural anthropologists and others prefer to apply the term *culture* specifically to human activities, most biological anthropologists consider it appropriate to apply the term to many nonhuman primate behaviors, too (McGrew, 1992, 1998; de Waal, 1999; Whiten et al., 1999).

Undeniably, most aspects of culture are uniquely human, and we should be cautious when we try to interpret nonhuman animal behavior. But, because humans are products of the same evolutionary forces that have produced other species, we can be expected to exhibit some of the same *behavioral patterns* seen in other primates. Because of increased brain size and learning capacities, humans express many characteristics to a greater degree, and culture is one of those characteristics.

Cultural behavior is *learned*. In other words, it's not genetically determined, although the capacity to learn is genetically influenced. Whereas humans deliberately teach their young, free-ranging nonhuman primates (with the exception of a few reports) don't appear to do so. But at the same time, like young nonhuman primates, human children also acquire a tremendous amount of knowledge through observation rather than instruction (**Fig. 8–20**). By watching their mothers and other members of their group, nonhuman primate infants learn about food items, appropriate behaviors, and how to use and modify objects to achieve certain ends. In turn, their own offspring will observe their activities. What emerges is a *cultural tradition* that may eventually come to typify an entire group or even a species.

The earliest reported example of cultural behavior concerned a study group of Japanese macaques on Koshima Island, Japan. In 1952, Japanese researchers began feeding the macaques sweet potatoes. The following year, a young female started washing her potatoes in a freshwater stream before eating them. Within 3 years,

© Thomas Breuer—WCS

▲ Figure 8-21
A female western lowland gorilla using a "wading stick" (in her right hand) for support.

several monkeys were washing their potatoes, though instead of using the stream, they were taking their potatoes to the ocean nearby. Maybe they liked the salt!

The researchers pointed out that dietary habits and food preferences are learned and that potato washing is an example of nonhuman culture. Because the practice arose as an innovative solution to a problem (removing dirt) and gradually spread through the troop until it became a tradition, it was seen as containing elements of human culture.

A study of orangutans listed 19 behaviors that showed sufficient regional variation to be classed as "very likely cultural variants" (van Schaik et al., 2003). Four of these were differences in how nests were used or built. Other behaviors that varied included the use of branches to swat insects and pressing leaves or hands to the mouth to amplify sounds.

Reports of tool use by gorillas aren't common, but recently Breuer et al. (2005) reported seeing two female lowland gorillas in the DRC using branches as tools. In one case, a gorilla used a branch to test the depth of a pool of water. Then, as she waded bipedally

through the pool, she used the branch again, this time as a walking stick (**Fig. 8-21**).

Chimpanzees exhibit more complex forms of tool use than any other nonhuman primate. This point is very important, because traditionally, tool use (along with language) was said to set humans apart from other animals. Chimpanzees crumple and chew handfuls of leaves, which they dip into tree hollows where water accumulates. Then they suck the water from the newly made "leaf sponges." Leaves are also used to wipe substances from fur. Twigs are used as toothpicks, stones as weapons, and objects, such as branches and stones, may be dragged or rolled to enhance displays.

"Termite fishing" is a common behavior among many chimpanzee groups. Chimpanzees routinely insert twigs and grass blades into termite mounds. The termites seize the twig and, unfortunately for them, they become a light snack once the chimpanzee pulls the twig out of the mound. Chimpanzees also modify some of their stems by stripping the leaves, or breaking them until they're the right length. In effect, this is making a tool, and chimpanzees have been seen making these tools even before the termite mound is in sight.

The modification of natural objects for use as tools has several implications for nonhuman primate intelligence. First, the chimpanzees are involved in an activity that prepares them for a future task at a somewhat distant location, and this implies planning and forethought. Second, attention to the shape and size of the raw material indicates that chimpanzees have a preconceived idea of what the finished product needs to be in order to be useful. To produce a tool, even a simple one, based on a concept is an extremely complex behavior that, as we now know, is not the exclusive domain of humans.

Primatologists have been aware of termite fishing and similar behaviors since the 1960s, but they were surprised by the discovery that chimpanzees also use tools to catch small prey. Preutz and Bertolani (2007) reported that savanna chimpanzees in Senegal, West Africa, sharpen small branches to use as thrusting spears for capturing galagos. This is the first report of a nonhuman primate hunting with what is basically a manufactured weapon.

On 22 occasions, 10 different animals jabbed sharpened sticks into cavities in branches and trunks to extract galagos from their sleeping nests. In much the same way they modify termiting sticks, these chimpanzees had stripped off side twigs and leaves. But they'd also chewed the ends to sharpen them, in effect producing small thrusting spears.

The spears weren't necessarily used to impale victims so much as to injure or immobilize them because galagos are extremely agile and hard to catch. Thus, after several thrusts the chimpanzee would reach into the opening to see if there was anything to be had. Observers only saw one galago being retrieved and eaten, and although it wasn't moving or vocalizing, it was unclear if it had actually been killed by the "spear" (Preutz and Bertolani, 2007).

In several West African study groups, chimpanzees use unmodified stones as hammers and anvils (**Fig. 8-22**) to crack nuts and hardshelled fruits (Boesch et al., 1994). Stone hammers and platforms are used only in West African groups and not in East Africa. Likewise, termite fishing is seen in Central and East Africa, but apparently it's not done in West African groups (McGrew, 1992). And using sharpened sticks to capture prey has been seen only in Senegal.

The fact that chimpanzees show regional variation in the types of tools they use is significant because these differences represent cultural variation from one area to another. Chimpanzees also show regional dietary preferences (Nishida et al., 1983; McGrew, 1992, 1998). For example, oil palm fruits and nuts are eaten at many locations, including Gombe. But even though oil palms also grow in the Mahale Mountains (only about 90 miles from Gombe), the chimpanzees there seem to ignore them. Such regional patterns in tool use and food preferences are very similar to the cultural differences that are typical of humans. Therefore, it's likely that this kind of variation existed in early hominins too.

So far, we've focused on tool use and culture in great apes, but they aren't the only nonhuman primates that consistently use tools and exhibit elements of cultural behavior. Primatologists have been studying tool use in capuchin or cebus monkeys for over 30 years. Capuchins are found in South America from Colombia and Venezuela, Brazil and Northern Argentina. They are the most encephalized of all monkeys and, while forest-dwelling capuchin species are arboreal, other species live in a more savanna-like habitat and these spend a fair amount of time on the ground. Many of the tool-using behaviors parallel those we've discussed for chimpanzees. Capuchins use leaves to extract water from cavities in trees (Phillips, 1998) and they use small, modified branches to probe into holes in logs for invertebrates (Westergaard and Fragaszy, 1987). But what they've really become known for is using stones to obtain food. They use stones to smash foods into smaller pieces and crack palm nuts; break open hollow tree branches and logs; and dig for tubers and insects. Capuchins are the only monkeys known to use stones as tools, and the only nonhuman primates

© Tetsuro Matsuzawa. Matsuzawa, et al. eds. *The Chimpanzees of Bossou and Nimba,* Springer 2011.

▲**Figure 8-22**
Chimpanzees in Bossou, Guinea, West Africa, use a pair of stones as hammer and anvil to crack oil palm nuts. Although the youngster isn't being taught to use stone tools, it's learning about them through observation.

▶**Figure 8-23**
This capuchin monkey is going to considerable effort, walking bipedally and carrying a heavy stone to a palm-nut cracking location.

▲**Figure 8-24**
This female capuchin must use most of her strength to smash a pine nut with a heavy stone, especially when carrying her infant on her back. Meanwhile, by watching her, the infant is learning the nut-smashing technique.

to dig with stones (Ottoni and Izar, 2008; Moura and Lee, 2004; Visalberghi, 1990).

The importance of palm nuts as a food source is revealed by the enormous effort expended in order to obtain them. Adult female and male capuchins weigh around 6 to 8 pounds respectively, yet they walk bipedally carrying stones that weigh as much as 2 pounds, (25 to 40 percent of their own body weight) (Visalberghi, et al., 2007; Fragaszy, et al., 2004). Because the stones are heavy, it's difficult for capuchins to sit while cracking nuts so they frequently stand bipedally, raise the hammer stone with both hands, and then pound the nut using their entire body (**Figs. 8-23** and **8-24**).

We've made it clear that even though chimpanzees and capuchins modify sticks to make tools, they haven't been observed modifying the stones they use. However, a male bonobo named Kanzi learned to strike two stones together to produce sharp-

edged flakes. In a study conducted by Sue Savage-Rumbaugh and archaeologist Nicholas Toth, Kanzi was allowed to watch as Toth produced stone flakes, which were then used to open a plastic food container (Savage-Rumbaugh and Lewin, 1994).

Bonobos don't commonly use objects as tools in the wild. But Kanzi readily appreciated the usefulness of the flakes to get food. What's more, he was able to master the basic technique of producing flakes without being taught, although at first his progress was slow. But then he realized that if he threw the stone onto a hard floor, it would shatter and he'd have lots of cutting tools. Although his solution wasn't the one that Savage-Rumbaugh and Toth had expected, it was even more significant because it provided an excellent example of bonobo insight and problem-solving ability. Kanzi did eventually learn to produce flakes by striking two stones together, and then he used these flakes to obtain food. These behaviors aren't just examples of tool manufacture and use, albeit in a captive situation; they're also very sophisticated goal-directed activities.

Culture has become the environment in which modern humans live. Quite clearly, the use of sticks in termite fishing and hammer stones to

◄ **Figure 8-25**
Group of vervets.

Lynn Kilgore

crack nuts is hardly comparable to modern human technology. However, modern human technology had its beginnings in these very types of behaviors. This doesn't mean that non-human primates are "on their way" to becoming human. Remember, evolution isn't goal directed and, even if it were, there's nothing to dictate that modern humans necessarily constitute an evolutionary goal. Such a conclusion is a purely **anthropocentric** view and has no validity in discussions of evolutionary processes.

Language

One of the most significant events in human evolution was the development of **language**. We've already described several behaviors and autonomic responses that convey information in primates. But although we emphasized the importance of communication to nonhuman primate social life, we also said that nonhuman primates don't use language the way humans do.

The view traditionally held by most linguists and behavioral psychologists was that nonhuman communication consists of mostly involuntary vocalizations and actions that convey information solely about the emotional state of the animal (anger, fear, etc.). Nonhuman animals haven't been considered capable of communicating about external events, objects, or other animals, either in close proximity or removed in space or time. For example, when a startled baboon barks, other group members know only that it may be startled. But they don't know what startled it, and they can only determine this by looking around to find the cause. In general, then, it's been assumed that in nonhuman animals, including primates, vocalizations, facial expressions, body postures, and so on don't refer to *specific* external phenomena.

For several years now, these views have been challenged (Steklis, 1985; King, 1994, 2004). For example, vervet monkeys (**Fig. 8–25**) use specific vocalizations to refer to particular categories of predators, such as snakes, birds of prey, and leopards (Struhsaker, 1967; Seyfarth, Cheney, and Marler, 1980a, 1980b). When researchers made tape recordings of various vervet alarm calls and played them back within hearing distance of wild vervets, they saw different responses to various calls. When they heard leopard-alarm calls, the

anthropocentric Viewing nonhuman organisms in terms of human experience and capabilities. Emphasizing the importance of humans over everything else.

language A standardized system of arbitrary vocal sounds, written symbols, and gestures used in communication.

monkeys climbed trees; they looked up when they heard eagle-alarm calls; and they responded to snake-alarm calls by looking at the ground around them.

These results show that vervets use distinct vocalizations to refer to specific components of the external environment. These calls aren't involuntary, and they don't refer solely to the emotional state (alarm) of the individual, although this information is conveyed. While these findings dispel certain long-held misconceptions about nonhuman communication (at least for some species), they also indicate certain limitations. Vervet communication is restricted to the present; as far as we know, no vervet can communicate about a predator it saw yesterday or one it might see tomorrow.

Humans use language, a set of written and/or spoken symbols that refer to concepts, other people, objects, and so on. This set of symbols is said to be *arbitrary* because the symbol itself has no inherent relationship with whatever it stands for. For example, the English word "flower," when written or spoken, doesn't look, sound, smell, or feel like the thing it represents. Humans can recombine their linguistic symbols in an infinite number of ways to create new meanings; and we can use language to refer to events, places, objects, and people far removed in both space and time. For these reasons, language is described as a form of communication, based on the human ability to think symbolically.

Language, as distinct from other forms of communication, has always been considered a uniquely human achievement, setting humans apart from the rest of the animal kingdom. But work with captive apes has somewhat revised this view. Although many researchers were skeptical about the capacity of nonhuman primates to use language, reports from psychologists, especially those who work with chimpanzees, leave little doubt that apes can learn to interpret visual signs and use them in communication. Other than humans, no mammal can speak.

However, the fact that apes can't speak has less to do with lack of intelligence than to differences in the anatomy of the vocal tract and language-related structures in the brain.

Beginning in the 1960s, after unsuccessful attempts to teach young chimpanzees to speak, researchers designed a study to evaluate language abilities in chimpanzees using *American Sign Language for the Deaf* (ASL). The research was a success and in 3 years a young female named Washoe was using at least 132 signs. Years later, an infant chimpanzee named Loulis was placed in Washoe's care. Psychologist Roger Fouts and colleagues wanted to know if Loulis would acquire signing skills from Washoe and other chimpanzees in the study group. Within just eight days, Loulis began to imitate the signs of others. Moreover, Washoe deliberately *taught* Loulis some signs.

There have been several other chimpanzee language experiments and work with orangutans, gorillas, and bonobos has shown that all the great apes have the capacity to use signs and symbols to communicate, not only with humans but also with each other. These abilities imply that, to some degree, the great apes are capable of symbolic thought.

Questions have been raised about this type of research. Do the apes really understand the signs they learn, or are they merely imitating their trainers? Do they learn that a symbol is a name for an object or simply that using it will produce that object? Partly in an effort to address some of these questions, psychologist Sue Savage-Rumbaugh demonstrated that chimpanzees can use symbols to categorize *classes* of objects. Using a symbol as a label is not the same thing as understanding the *representational value* of the symbol; but if the chimpanzees could classify things into groups, it would indicate that they can use symbols referentially. The chimps were taught that familiar food items (for which they used symbols) belonged to a broader category referred to by yet another sym-

◄**Figure 8-26**
The bonobo Kanzi, as a youngster, using lexigrams to communicate with human observers.

bol, "food." Then they were introduced to unfamiliar food items, for which they had no symbols, to see if they would put them in the food category. The fact that they both had excellent scores showed that they could categorize unfamiliar objects. This ability was a strong indication that the chimpanzees understood that the symbols represented objects and groups of objects (Savage-Rumbaugh and Lewin, 1994).

A major assumption, throughout the relatively brief history of ape language studies, has been that young chimpanzees must be *taught* to use symbols, in contrast to the ability of human children to learn language through exposure, without being taught. Therefore, it was significant when Savage-Rumbaugh and her colleagues reported that the young bonobo Kanzi, before his tool making days, was *spontaneously* acquiring and using symbols when he was just 2½ years old (Savage-Rumbaugh et al., 1986) (**Fig. 8-26**).

Although the great apes that have been involved in the language experiments have shown a remarkable degree of cognitive complexity, it nevertheless remains evident that they don't acquire and use language in the same way humans do. It also appears that not all signing apes understand the relationship between symbols and objects, people, or actions. Nonetheless, there's now abundant evidence that humans aren't the only species capable of some degree of symbolic thought and complex communication.

The Evolution of Language

From an evolutionary perspective, the ape language experiments may suggest clues to the origins of human language. It's quite possible that the last common ancestor we share with the living great apes had communication capabilities similar to those we see in these species. So, we need to identify the factors that enhanced the adaptive value of these abilities in our own lineage.

While increased brain size played a crucial role in human evolution, it was changes in preexisting neurological structures that permitted the development of language. Current evidence suggests that new structures and novel connections were not the basis for most of the neurological differences we see among species. Rather, changes to existing structures have been

Quick Review

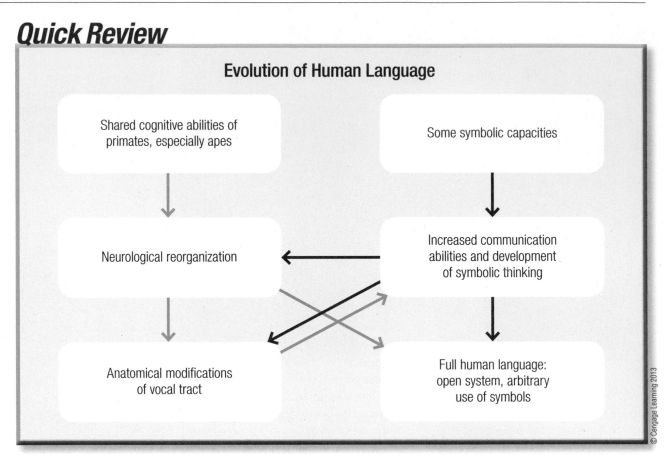

Evolution of Human Language

Shared cognitive abilities of primates, especially apes

Some symbolic capacities

Neurological reorganization

Increased communication abilities and development of symbolic thinking

Anatomical modifications of vocal tract

Full human language: open system, arbitrary use of symbols

© Cengage Learning 2013

far more important. It's also important to understand that the neurological changes that enhanced language development in humans would not have happened if early hominins hadn't already acquired the behavioral and neurological foundations that made them possible.

For reasons we don't yet fully understand, communication became increasingly important during the course of human evolution, and natural selection favored anatomical and neurological changes that enhanced our ancestors' ability to use spoken language.

Some researchers argue that language capabilities appeared late in human evolution with the wide dispersal of modern *Homo sapiens* some 100,000–30,000 years ago. Others favor a much earlier origin, possibly with the appearance of the genus *Homo* some 2 million years ago. Whichever scenario is correct, language came about as complex and efficient forms of communication gained selective value in our lineage.

The Primate Continuum

It's an unfortunate fact that humans generally view themselves as separate from the rest of the animal kingdom. This perspective is partly due to a prevailing lack of knowledge of the behavior and abilities of other species. Moreover, these notions are continuously reinforced through exposure to advertising, movies, and television (**Fig. 8–27**).

For decades, behavioral psychology taught that animal behavior represents nothing more than a series of conditioned responses to specific stimuli. (This perspective is very convenient for those who wish to exploit nonhuman animals, for whatever purposes, and remain guilt free.) Fortunately, this attitude has begun to change in recent years to reflect a growing awareness that humans, although in many ways unquestionably unique, are nevertheless part of a **biological continuum** and

biological continuum Refers to the fact that organisms are related through common ancestry and that behaviors and traits seen in one species are also seen in others to varying degrees. (When expressions of a phenomenon continuously grade into one another so that there are no discrete categories, they are said to exist on a continuum. Color is one such phenomenon.)

◄**Figure 8-27**
The unfortunate advertising display (a) and well-meaning but ill-informed poster (b) reinforce stereotypes and misconceptions many people have of our closest relatives.

behavioral continuum. We are connected, not only to our closest relatives, the other primates, but to all life on earth.

Where do humans fit in this continuum? The answer depends on the criteria used. Certainly, we're the most intelligent species if we define intelligence in terms of problem-solving abilities and abstract thought. However, if we look more closely, we recognize that the differences between ourselves and our primate relatives, especially chimpanzees and bonobos, are primarily quantitative and not qualitative.

Although the human brain is absolutely and relatively larger, neurological processes are functionally the same. The necessity of close bonding with at least one parent and the need for physical contact are essentially the same. Developmental stages and dependence on learning are similar. Indeed, even in the capacity for cruelty and aggression combined with compassion, tenderness, and altruism exhibited by chimpanzees, we see a close parallel to the dichotomy between "evil" and "good" so long recognized in ourselves. The main difference between how chimpanzees and humans express these qualities (and therefore the dichotomy) is one of degree. Humans are much more adept at cruelty and compassion, and we can reflect on our behavior in

ways that chimpanzees can't. Like the cat that plays with a mouse, chimpanzees don't seem to understand the suffering they inflict on others. But humans do. Likewise, while an adult chimpanzee may sit next to a dying relative, it doesn't seem to feel the intense grief a human normally does in the same situation.

To arrive at any understanding of what it is to be human, it's important to recognize that many of our behaviors are elaborate extensions of those of our hominin ancestors and close primate relatives. The fact that so many of us prefer to bask in the warmth of the "sun belt" with literally millions of others reflects our heritage as social animals adapted to life in the tropics. And the sweet tooth that afflicts so many of us is a result of our earlier primate ancestors' predilection for high-energy sugar contained in sweet, ripe fruit. Thus, it's important to recognize our primate heritage as we explore how humans came to be and how we continue to adapt.

Why It Matters

TV shows and popular articles about chimpanzee and other primate behavior are fun to watch and think about, but can we learn anything useful for our own species by observing primates in their natural settings? Many primatologists argue that it's important to observe other primates simply to learn as much as we can about other species, but there are ways in which knowledge about other primates' lives can be directly useful for humans.

One area that has attracted a great deal of attention is evidence of self-medication by chimpanzees, leading to the suggestion that we may be able to identify beneficial drugs for human diseases by observing chimpanzee dietary behaviors. While studying primate behavior in Tanzania, Harvard primatologist Richard Wrangham noted that occasionally chimpanzees would seek out a leaf that wasn't a normal part of the diet and swallow it whole and apparently undigested. Chemical analysis of the leaf revealed that it had high levels of a compound that had antibiotic properties, suggesting that the chimps were using

it for intestinal parasite control. Further observations revealed that chimpanzees occasionally use the same plants that are consumed by people in the area for intestinal parasites, skin infections, and ulcers. Perhaps most significant for human health, some of the other plants eaten by chimpanzees contain compounds that are potentially useful for controlling malaria, *Staphylococcus* infections, *E. coli*, and cancer. Perhaps our close relatives will show us as yet unknown medicinal properties of many plant species, but this will require ongoing careful observations of primate behavior.

Summary of Main Topics

- One of the major goals of primatology is to discover how certain behaviors influence reproductive fitness and how ecological factors have shaped the evolution of those behaviors.

- Behavioral ecology is the discipline that examines behavior from the perspective of complex ecological relationships and how they influence natural selection as it favors behaviors that increase reproductive fitness.

- Life history traits (developmental stages that characterize a species) are important to the reproductive success of individuals. These include length of gestation, number of offspring per birth, interbirth interval, age of sexual maturity, and longevity. Although these characters are strongly influenced by the genome of any species, they are also influenced by environmental and social

factors such as nutrition and social status. In turn, nutritional requirements are affected by body size, diet, and basal metabolic rate (BMR).

- Primates are among the most social of animals, but within social groups there is competition for resources, and conflict. Dominance hierarchies help reduce the amount of physical aggression. Also, there are numerous amicable behaviors, such as grooming, that maintain peaceful relationships between individuals.

- Affiliative behaviors such as grooming, hugging, and helping others (altruism) also promote group cohesion.

- Communication makes it possible to live in social groups. It occurs in many forms, including vocalizations and gestures. Some primate species are able to communicate about certain aspects of the exter-

nal environment, indicating some ability to think symbolically.

- Long-term language studies with the great apes have shown that these species have the ability to communicate using different kinds of symbols, including sign language. Some can also understand spoken language. This research has also revealed that some great apes understand that symbols represent objects and concepts.

- Several nonhuman primates exhibit aspects of culture, including tool use and regional variation in dietary preferences and tool use. For example, West African chimpanzees use stones to crack palm nuts but East African populations don't. Some savanna chimpanzees use sharpened sticks to hunt for galagos but this hasn't been seen in forest-dwelling groups. These variations represent cultural traditions that were perhaps present in early hominins. Capuchins that live in savanna-like habitats use stones to crack nuts and to dig for roots.

- Variation in cultural behavior and the transmission of these behaviors from one individual to another through observation and learning are hallmarks of human culture. Nonhuman primates exhibit certain aspects of culture, although none of these species have adopted culture as an adaptive strategy the way humans have.

- Biological and behavioral continuity within the primate order reveals how humans are connected to our closest relatives and allows us to explain some aspects of human behavior.

Critical Thinking Questions

1. Apply some of the topics presented in this chapter to some nonprimate species with which you are familiar. Can you develop some hypotheses to explain the behavior of some domestic species? You might want to speculate on how behavior in domestic animals may differ from that of their wild ancestors. (Chapter 2 might help you here.)

2. Speculate on how the behavioral ecology of nonhuman primates may be helpful in explaining some human behaviors.

3. How might infanticide be seen as a reproductive strategy for males? What would you say if you saw a newspaper article that applied this concept (not the act itself) to human males? Do you think some people would object? Why or why not?

4. Do you think that knowing about aggression between groups of chimpanzees is useful in understanding conflicts between human societies? Why or why not?

5. Why are the language capabilities of nonhuman primates important to our understanding of how our own species may have acquired language?

Connections

Due to our shared evolution, many human behaviors are also seen in other primates.

The first hominins appeared in Africa more than 6 mya.

Hominins dispersed out of Africa into Eurasia about 2 million years ago.

9

Primate and Hominin Origins

Today we humans dominate our planet as we use our brains and cultural inventions to invade every corner of the earth. Yet, 5 mya, our ancestors were little more than bipedal apes, confined to a few regions in Africa. What were these creatures like? How closely are they connected to us, and when and how did they begin their evolutionary journey?

In the last two chapters, we have seen how and why humans are classified as primates, both structurally and behaviorally, and how our evolutionary history connects humans with the other primates. However, we are a unique kind of primate, and our ancestors have been adapted to a particular kind of lifestyle for several million years. Some primitive hominoid may have begun this process more than 10 mya, but fossil evidence indicates a more definite hominin presence sometime after 7 mya. The hominin nature of these remains is revealed by more than the morphological structure of teeth and bones; in many cases, we know that these animals are **hominins** (see next page for definitions of terms on this page) also because of the way they behaved—emphasizing once again the **biocultural** nature of human evolution.

In this chapter, we turn first to the physical evidence of earlier primates and then to the hominin fossils themselves. The earliest fossils identifiable as hominins are all from Africa, and some of them may date back to more than six million years ago. It's fascinating to think about these early members of our family tree, with different species living side by side for millions of years. Most of these species became extinct. But why? What's more, were some of these apelike animals possibly our direct ancestors?

Hominins, of course, evolved from earlier primates (dating back to almost 50 mya). We'll briefly review this long and abundant prehominin fossil record to provide a better context for understanding the subsequent evolution of the human lineage.

◄ Artist's reconstruction of a female *Homo habilis* based on a cranium from East Lake Turkana.

In recent years, paleoanthropologists have made numerous exciting discoveries from several sites in Africa. However, because many finds have been made so recently, detailed evaluations are still in progress, and conclusions must remain tentative.

One thing is certain, however. The earliest members of the human family were confined to Africa. Only much later did their descendants disperse from the African continent to other areas of the Old World. (This "out of Africa" saga will be the topic of the next chapter.)

Early Primate Evolution

Long before bipedal hominins first evolved in Africa, more primitive primates had diverged from even more distant mammalian ancestors. The roots of the primate order go back to the early stages of the placental mammal radiation at least 65 mya. From this fact you can see that the earliest primates evolved from early and still primitive placental mammals.

We have seen (in Chapter 7) that strictly defining living primates using clear-cut derived features is not an easy task. The further back we go in the fossil record, the more primitive and, in many cases, the more generalized the fossil primates become. Such a situation makes classifying them all the more difficult.

The earliest primates date to the Paleocene (65–56 mya) and belong to a large and diverse group of primitive mammals called the plesiadapiforms. These very early primates have been controversial for several decades, with opinions varying whether they actually *are* primates or members of a closely related but different group of mammals. Quite complete fossils, recently discovered in Montana and Wyoming, have now more firmly placed these Paleocene animals as the earliest known primates.

Eocene Primates: Closer Connections to Living Primates

From the succeeding Eocene epoch (56–33 mya), a vast number of fossil primates have been discovered and now total more than 200 recognized species (see Chapter 6 for a geological chart). Unlike the available Paleocene forms, those from the Eocene display more clearly derived primate features. These fossils have been found at many sites in North America and Europe (which for most of the Eocene were still connected). In addition, more recent finds have shown that the radiation of Eocene primates extended to Asia and Africa. It's important to recall that the landmasses that connect continents, as well as the water boundaries that separate them, have an obvious impact on the geographical distribution of all land animals, including primates (see Chapter 6).

The most complete early primate fossil ever found was announced in 2009 and, in honor of the 200th anniversary of Darwin's birth, is called *Darwinius* (**Fig. 9–1**). It comes from the Eocene Messel site in Germany, dates to 47 mya (during the Eocene), and is extraordinarily well preserved (Franzen et al., 2009). At the time of its announcement, it created a public sensation, although the find has a complex and somewhat peculiar history.

Clearly, *Darwinius* was meant to make a big splash, and that it did; yet, virtually no other experts in early primate evolution have had an opportunity to see the original fossil, and thus the wide publicity it received wasn't accompanied by the normal assessments of other researchers. What so far has been tentatively concluded by a

▼**Figure 9-1**
Remarkably well-preserved remains of the Eocene primate *Darwinius*, dated to about 47 mya.

hominins Colloquial term for members of the tribe Hominini, which includes all bipedal hominoids back to the divergence with African great apes.

biocultural Pertaining to the concept that biology makes culture possible and that culture influences biology.

wide range of scholars shows that the claims made by the original researchers aren't substantiated and run counter to interpretations of other Eocene primate finds (Gibbons, 2009). There is much to learn about the adaptations of this small Eocene primate, but it seems unlikely that it provides direct evidence of a close connection to us and other anthropoids as claimed. Indeed, it may not be particularly closely related to any living primate.

Looking at this entire array of Eocene fossils, it's certain that they were (1) primates, (2) widely distributed, and (3) mostly extinct by the end of the Eocene. What is less certain is how any of them might be related to the living primates. Some of these forms were probably similar to and are potential ancestors of the lemurs and lorises.* Others are probably related to tarsiers. By far, however, most of the Eocene primates (including *Darwinius* and its close relatives) don't appear to have been ancestral to any later primate, and they became extinct before the end of the Eocene (around 33 mya).

_____

* In strict classification terms, especially from a cladistic point of view, lemurs and lorises should be referred to as strepsirhines (see Chapter 7).

Nevertheless, some fossil finds from late in the Eocene have derived features (such as a dental comb) that link them to modern lemurs and lorises.

New evidence of Eocene *anthropoid* origins has recently been discovered at a few sites in North Africa. The earliest of these African fossils go back to 50 mya, but the remains are very fragmentary. More conclusive evidence comes from Egypt and is well dated to 37 mya. At present, it looks likely that the earliest anthropoids first evolved in Africa.

Oligocene Primates: Anthropoid Connections

The Oligocene (33–23 mya) has yielded numerous additional fossil remains of several different early anthropoid species. Most of these are *Old World anthropoids*, all discovered at a single locality in Egypt, the Fayum (**Fig. 9-2**). In addition, there are a few known bits from North and South America that relate only to the ancestry of New World monkeys. By the early Oligocene, continental drift had separated the New World (that is, the Americas) from the Old World (Africa and Eurasia). Some of the earliest Fayum species, nevertheless, may potentially be close to the ancestry of both Old

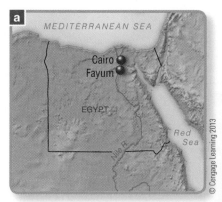

▲**Figure 9-2**
(a) Fayum site in Egypt **(b)** Excavations in progress at the Fayum, where dozens of fossil primates have been discovered.

© Cengage Learning 2013

© Russell L. Ciochon

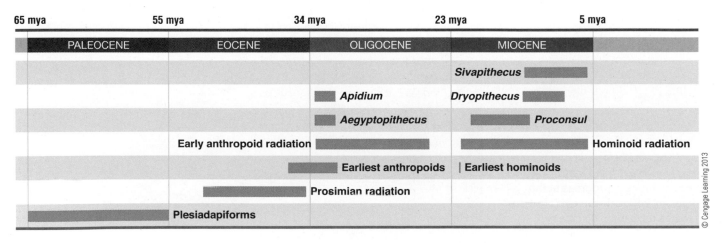

© Elwyn Simons

▲ Figure 9-3
Skull of *Aegyptopithecus*. This fossil primate from the Fayum has been suggested as a potential ancestor of both hominoids and Old World monkeys.

and New World anthropoids. It's been suggested that late in the Eocene or very early in the Oligocene, the first anthropoids (primitive "monkeys") arose in Africa and later reached South America by "rafting" over the water separation on drifting chunks of vegetation. What we call "monkey," then, may have a common Old World origin, but the ancestry of New and Old World monkeys was separate after about 35 mya. After this time, the closest evolutionary connections humans have are with other Old World anthropoids, that is, with Old World monkeys and apes.

The possible roots of anthropoid evolution are illustrated by different forms from the Fayum; one is the genus *Apidium*. Well known at the Fayum, *Apidium* is represented by several dozen jaws or partial dentitions as well as many **postcranial** remains. Owing to its primitive dental arrangement, some paleontologists have suggested that *Apidium* may lie near or even before the evolutionary divergence of Old and New World anthropoids. Because so much fossil material of teeth and limb bones of *Apidium*

has been found, some informed speculation regarding diet and locomotor behavior is possible. It's thought that this squirrel-sized primate ate mostly fruits and some seeds and was most likely an arboreal quadruped, adept at leaping and springing.

The other genus of importance from the Fayum is *Aegyptopithecus*. This genus is represented by several well-preserved crania and abundant jaws and teeth. The largest of the Fayum anthropoids, *Aegyptopithecus* is roughly the size of a modern howler monkey (13 to 18 pounds; Fleagle, 1983) and is thought to have been a short-limbed, slow-moving arboreal quadruped. *Aegyptopithecus* is important because, better than any other known form, it bridges the gap between the Eocene fossils and the succeeding Miocene hominoids (**Fig. 9-3**).

Nevertheless, *Aegyptopithecus* is a very primitive Old World anthropoid, with a small brain and long snout and not showing any derived features of either Old World monkeys or hominoids. Thus, it may be close to the ancestry of *both* major groups of living Old World anthropoids. Found in geological beds dating to 35–33 mya, *Aegyptopithecus* further suggests that the crucial evolutionary divergence of hominoids from other Old World anthropoids occurred *after* this time (**Fig. 9-4**).

▼ Figure 9-4
Major events in early primate evolution.

65 mya	55 mya	34 mya	23 mya	5 mya
PALEOCENE	EOCENE	OLIGOCENE	MIOCENE	
			Sivapithecus	
		Apidium	*Dryopithecus*	
		Aegyptopithecus	*Proconsul*	
	Early anthropoid radiation		Hominoid radiation	
		Earliest anthropoids	Earliest hominoids	
	Prosimian radiation			
	Plesiadapiforms			

© Cengage Learning 2013

Miocene Fossil Hominoids: Closer Connections to Apes and Humans

During the approximately 18 million years of the Miocene (23–5 mya), a great deal of evolutionary activity took place. In Africa, Asia, and Europe, a diverse and highly successful group of hominoids emerged (**Fig. 9-5**). Indeed, there were many more kinds of hominoids from the Miocene than there are today (now represented by just a few ape species and humans). In fact, the Miocene could be called "the golden age of hominoids." Many thousands of fossils have been found from dozens of sites scattered in East Africa, southern Africa, southwest Asia, into western and southern Europe, and extending into southern Asia and China.

During the Miocene, significant transformations relating to climate and repositioning of landmasses took place. By 23 mya, major continental locations approximated those of today (except that North and South America were separate). Nevertheless, the movements of South America and Australia farther away from Antarctica significantly altered ocean currents. Likewise, the continued collision between the South Asian Plate and southern Asia produced the Himalayan Plateau. Both of these geographical changes had significant impacts on the climate, and the early Miocene was considerably warmer than the preceding Oligocene. Moreover, by 19 mya, the Arabian Plate (which had been separate) "docked" with northeastern Africa. As a result, migrations of animals from Africa directly into southwest Asia (and in the other direction as well) became possible. Among the earliest transcontinental migrants (around 16 mya) were African hominoids that colonized both Europe and Asia at this time.

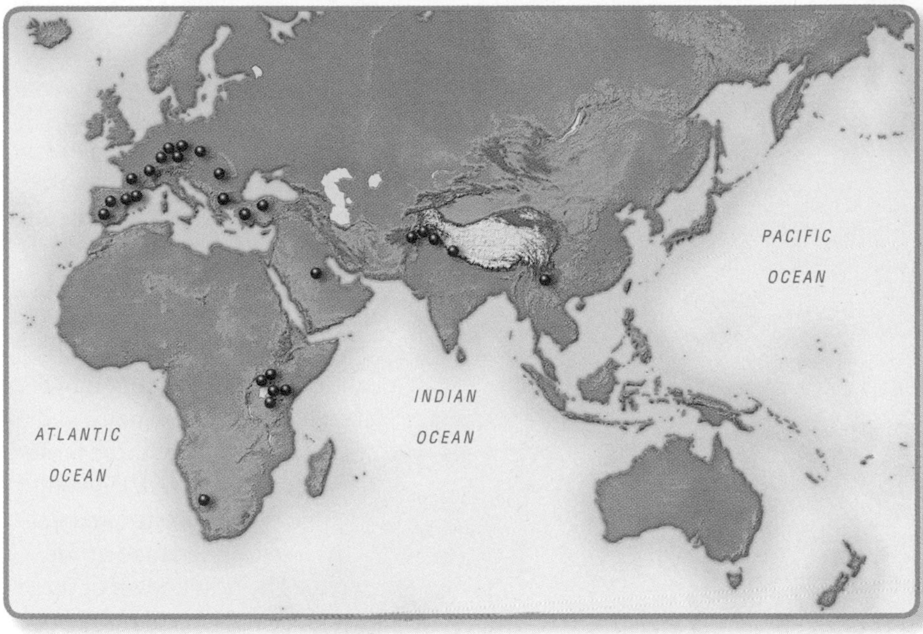

A problem arises in any attempt to simplify the complex evolutionary situation regarding Miocene hominoids. For example, for many years, paleontologists tended to think of these fossil forms as either "apelike" or "humanlike" and used modern examples as models. But as we have just noted, very few hominoids remain. Therefore, we should not hastily generalize from these few living forms to the much more diverse fossil forms; otherwise, we obscure the evolutionary uniqueness of these animals. In addition, we should not expect all fossil forms to be directly or even particularly closely related to living species. Indeed, we should expect the opposite; that is, most lines vanish without descendants.

Over the last three decades, the Miocene fossil hominoid assemblage has been interpreted and reinterpreted. As more fossils are found, the evolutionary picture becomes more complicated. What's more, most of the fossils haven't been completely studied, so conclusions remain tenuous. Given this uncertainty, it's probably best, for the present, to group Miocene hominoids geographically as follows:

1. *African forms (23–14 mya)* Known especially from western Kenya,

▲**Figure 9-5**
Miocene hominoid distribution, from fossils thus far discovered.

postcranial Referring to all or part of the skeleton not including the skull. The term originates from the fact that in quadrupeds, the body is in back of the head; the term literally means "behind the head."

these include quite generalized, and in many ways primitive, hominoids. The best-known genus is *Proconsul* (**Fig. 9-6**). In fact, *Proconsul* isn't much like an ape, and postcranially it more closely resembles a monkey. But there are some derived features of the teeth that link *Proconsul* to hominoids.

2. *European forms (16–11 mya)* Known from widely scattered localities in France, Spain, Italy, Greece, Austria, Germany, and Hungary, most of these forms are quite derived. However, this is a varied and not well-understood group. The best known of these are placed in the genus *Dryopithecus*; the Hungarian and Greek fossils are usually assigned to other genera. The Greek fossils, called *Ouranopithecus*, date to 10–9 mya. Evolutionary relationships are uncertain; some researchers have suggested a link with the African ape–hominin group, but most primatologists think these similarities result from homoplasy (Wood and Harrison, 2011; see Chapter 6).

3. *Asian forms (15–5 mya)* The largest and most varied group of Miocene fossil hominoids was geographically dispersed from Turkey through India/Pakistan and east to Lufeng, in southern China. The best-known genus is *Sivapithecus* (from Turkey and Pakistan), and fossil evidence indicates that most of these hominoids were *highly* derived (**Fig. 9-7**).

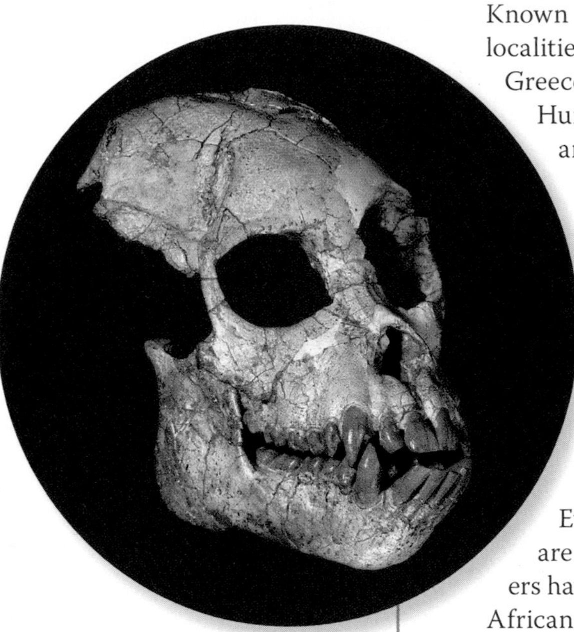

Four general points are certain concerning Miocene hominoid fossils: They are widespread geographically; they are numerous; they span essentially the entirety of the Miocene, with *known* remains dated between 23 and 6 mya; and at present, they are poorly understood. However, we can reasonably draw the following conclusions:

1. These are hominoids—more closely related to the ape-human lineage than to Old World monkeys.
2. They are mostly **large-bodied hominoids**, that is, more connected to the lineages of orangutans, gorillas, chimpanzees, and humans than to smaller-bodied apes (gibbons and siamangs).
3. Most of the Miocene species thus far discovered are so derived that

▲ **Figure 9-6**
Proconsul skull, an early Miocene hominoid.

▶ **Figure 9-7**
Skull of a juvenile *Lufengpithecus* from the late Miocene of China.

large-bodied hominoids Those hominoids including the great apes (orangutans, chimpanzees, gorillas) and hominins, as well as all ancestral forms back to the time of divergence from small-bodied hominoids (i.e., the gibbon lineage).

© David Pilbeam

▲**Figure 9-8**
Comparison of a modern chimpanzee (left), *Sivapithecus* (middle), and a modern orangutan (right). Notice that both *Sivapithecus* and the orangutan exhibit a dished face, broad cheekbones, and projecting upper jaw.

they are probably not ancestral to *any* living form.

4. One lineage that appears well established is *Sivapithecus* from Turkey and Pakistan. *Sivapithecus* shows some highly derived facial features similar to the modern orangutan, suggesting a fairly close evolutionary connection (**Fig. 9-8**).

5. Evidence of *definite* hominins from the Miocene hasn't yet been indisputably confirmed. However, exciting recent (and not fully studied) finds from Kenya, Ethiopia, and Chad (the latter dating as far back as 6–7 mya) suggest that hominins diverged sometime in the latter Miocene (see pp. 205–210 for further discussion). As we shall see shortly, the most fundamental feature of the early hominins is the adaptation to bipedal locomotion. In addition, recently discovered Miocene remains of the first fossils linked closely to gorillas (Suwa et al., 2007) provide further support for a late Miocene divergence (about 10–7 mya) of our closest ape cousins from the hominin line. The only fossil chimpanzee so far discovered has a much later date of around 500,000 years ago (ya), long after the time that hominins split from African apes (McBrearty and Jablonksi, 2005).

Understanding the Human Connection to Other Primates and Ways We Differ: Biocultural Evolution

One of the most distinctive behavioral features of humans is our extraordinary elaboration of and dependence on **culture**. Certainly other primates, and many other animals, for that matter, modify their environments. As we saw in Chapter 8, chimpanzees especially are now known for such behaviors as using termite sticks, and some chimps, as well as one capuchin species, even carry rocks to use for crushing nuts. Because of such observations, we're on shaky ground when it comes to drawing sharp lines between early hominin toolmaking behavior and that exhibited by other animals. It reminds us that most of our "connections" to other life-forms are best seen as part of a biological continuum.

Another point to remember is that human culture, at least as it's defined in contemporary contexts, involves much more than toolmaking capacity. For humans, culture integrates an entire adaptive strategy involving cognitive, political, social, and economic components. *Material culture*—or the tools

culture Nonbiological adaptations to the environment. This includes learned behaviors that can be communicated to others—especially from one generation to the next. Aspects of this capacity have been identified in our closest ape relatives.

humans use—is but a small portion of this cultural complex.

Still, when we examine the archaeological record of earlier hominins, what's available for study is almost exclusively limited to material culture, especially the bits and pieces of broken stone left over from tool manufacture. This is why it's extremely difficult to learn anything about the earliest stages of hominin cultural development before the regular manufacture of stone tools. As you'll see, this most crucial cultural development has been traced to approximately 2.6 mya (Semaw et al., 2003). Yet because of our contemporary primate models, we can assume that hominins were undoubtedly using other kinds of tools (made of perishable materials) and displaying a whole array of other cultural behaviors long before then. But with no "hard" evidence preserved in the archaeological record, our understanding of the early development of these nonmaterial cultural components remains elusive.

The fundamental basis for human cultural success relates directly to our cognitive abilities. Again, this isn't an absolute distinction, but a relative one. As you've already learned, great apes have some of the language capabilities exhibited by humans. Even so, modern humans display these abilities in a complexity several orders of magnitude beyond that of any other animal. What's more, only humans are so completely dependent on symbolic communication and its cultural by-products that we couldn't survive without them.

At this point, you may be wondering when the unique combination of cognitive, social, and material cultural adaptations became prominent in human evolution. In answering that question, we must be careful to recognize the complex nature of culture; we can't expect it to always contain the same elements across species (as when comparing ourselves with nonhuman primates) or through time (when trying to reconstruct ancient hominin behavior).

We know that the earliest hominins almost certainly didn't regularly manufacture stone tools (at least, none that have been found and identified as such). These earliest members of the hominin lineage, who lived prior to 5 mya, may have carried objects such as naturally sharp stones or stone flakes, parts of carcasses, and pieces of wood. At the very least, we would expect them to have displayed these behaviors to at least the same degree as living chimpanzees.

Also, as you'll see later in this chapter, by 6 mya—and perhaps as early as 7 mya—hominins had developed one crucial advantage: They were bipedal and so could more easily carry all kinds of objects from place to place. Ultimately, the efficient exploitation of widely distributed resources would probably have led to using "central" spots where the most important implements—especially stone objects—were cached, or collected (Potts, 1991).

What we know for sure is that over a period of several million years, during the formative stages of hominin emergence, many components interacted, but not all of them developed simultaneously. As cognitive abilities developed, more efficient means of communication and learning resulted. Largely because of consequent neurological reorganization, more elaborate tools and social relationships also emerged. These, in turn, selected for greater intelligence, which in turn selected for further neural elaboration. Quite clearly, these mutual dynamic interactions are at the very heart of what we call hominin *biocultural* evolution.

Discovering Human Evolution: The Science of Paleoanthropology

To adequately understand human biocultural evolution, we need a broad base of information. Paleoanthropologists must recover and interpret all the clues left by early hominins. Paleoanthropology is defined as the study of early humans. As such, it is a diverse **multidisciplinary** pursuit seeking to reconstruct every possible bit of information concerning the dating, anatomy, behavior, and ecology of our hominin ancestors. In the past few decades, the study of early hominins has marshaled the specialized skills of many different kinds of scientists. This growing and exciting adventure includes, but is not limited to, geologists, vertebrate paleontologists, archaeologists, physical anthropologists, and paleoecologists.

Geologists, usually working with other paleoanthropologists, do the initial survey to locate potential early hominin **sites**. Many sophisticated techniques can contribute to this search, including aerial and satellite photography. Vertebrate paleontologists are usually also involved in this early survey work, for they can help find geological beds containing **faunal** remains. (Where conditions are favorable for the preservation of bone from such species as ancient pigs or baboons, conditions may also be favorable for the preservation of hominin fossils.) Paleontologists can also (through comparison with known faunal sequences) give quick and dirty approximate ages of fossil sites in the field without having to wait for the expensive and time-consuming **chronometric** analyses.

Once identified, fossil beds likely to contain hominin finds become the focus for further extensive surveying. For some sites, generally those postdating 2.6 mya (the age of the oldest identified human artifacts), archaeologists take over in the search for hominin material traces. We don't necessarily have to find remains of early hominins themselves to know that they consistently occupied a particular area. Such material clues as **artifacts** inform us directly about early hominin activities. Modifying rocks according to a consistent plan or simply carrying them around from one place to another over fairly long distances (in a manner not easily explained by natural means, such as streams or glaciers) is characteristic of no other animal but hominins. So when we see such material evidence at a site, we know without a doubt that hominins were present.

Early Hominin Tools

As we've mentioned, the earliest definite tools date to about 2.6 mya, and these are made of stone. We've noted as well that other types of tools made of perishable materials were very likely used long before this time. Even relatively simple inventions, such as a digging stick or waterproof gourd, could have provided early hominins with crucial adaptive advantages. An unmodified stick could have allowed hominins to dig for roots, a vital resource in a variety of environments and one not generally available to competitors. A hollowed-out gourd could have been just as crucial (especially in more open environments), serving as an easily transportable water container (an ancient canteen, of sorts).

But such perishable materials leave no trace whatsoever in the archaeological record, so we're left with only our conjectures and nothing by which to test them. One thing is certain, however; being bipedal would have been a crucial adaptation allowing humans to carry sticks, gourds, bones, and chunks of stone over considerable distances.

Using stones to crack nuts or to smash bones to obtain marrow would have been likely adaptive behaviors practiced by hominins, but the battered rocks they would have left behind wouldn't be identifiable to us compared to other rocks scattered around ancient landscapes. Only rocks that have been altered according to a regular pattern are identifiable to us as *real* artifacts.

The first such stone tools are extremely simple, consisting of small sharp flakes removed from a rock nodule. These are, however, made to a

multidisciplinary Pertaining to research involving mutual contributions and cooperation of experts from various scientific fields (i.e., disciplines).

sites Locations of discoveries. In paleontology and archaeology, a site may refer to a region where a number of discoveries have been made.

faunal Referring to animal remains; in archaeology, specifically refers to the fossil (skeletonized) remains of animals.

chronometric (*chronos*, meaning "time," and *metric*, meaning "measure") Referring to a dating technique that gives an estimate in actual numbers of years.

artifacts Objects or materials made or modified for use by hominins. The earliest artifacts tend to be made of stone or occasionally bone.

Barry Lewis

▲ Figure 9-9
Oldowan tools, including flake tools as well as battered nodules probably used as hammerstones.

standard size and shape (and if you try this yourself, you'll quickly discover that it's far more difficult to do than it looks!). Early artifacts also include some battered rocks used as hammerstones (to knock flakes off another rock; see **Fig. 9-9**).

Such simple tools are found at several sites in Africa and are part of what has been called the **Oldowan industry**, named after Olduvai Gorge, in Tanzania. Owing to the pioneering research of Mary and Louis Leakey, this area has provided the most detailed information from anywhere in the world about early hominin tool use. Mary Leakey (**Fig. 9-10**), in particular, dedicated her career to excavating early hominin sites and analyzing ancient artifacts and the hominins who made them.

Beginning around 1.4 mya, some Oldowan tool types began to be replaced with larger, more complex stone tools (although many Oldowan tools continued to be produced as well). We'll discuss these later hominin cultural innovations in Chapter 10.

Connecting the Dots Through Time: Paleoanthropological Dating Methods

One of the essentials of paleoanthropology is placing sites and fossils into a time frame. In other words, we want to know how old they are. How, then, do we date sites—or, more precisely, how do we date the geological settings in which sites are found? The question is important, so let's examine some of the dating techniques used by paleontologists, geologists, and paleoanthropologists.

Scientists use two basic types of dating for this purpose: *relative dating* and *chronometric dating* (also known as *absolute dating*). Relative dating methods tell you that something is older or younger than something else, but not by how much. If, for example, a fossil cranium is found at a depth of 50 feet and another one at 70 feet at the same site, we usually assume that the cranium at 70 feet is older. We may not know the date (in years) of either one, but we would be able to infer a *relative* sequence. This method of dating is based on **stratigraphy** and is called *stratigraphic dating*. This was one of the first techniques used by scholars working with the vast expanses of geological time. Stratigraphic dating is based on the law of superposition, which states that a lower **stratum** (layer) is older than a higher one. Given the fact that much of the earth's crust has been laid down by layer after layer of sedimentary rock,

▶ Figure 9-10
Mary Leakey, one of the leading pioneers of paleoanthropology and the archaeologist who directed excavations at Olduvai Gorge for many years.

© John Reader / Photo Researchers, Inc.

Oldowan industry The earliest recognized stone tool culture, including very simple tools, mostly small flakes.

stratigraphy Study of the sequential layering of geological deposits.

stratum (*pl.,* strata) Geological layer.

stratigraphic relationships have provided a valuable tool in reconstructing the history of the earth and of life upon it.

Stratigraphic dating does, however, have a number of potential problems. Earth disturbances, such as volcanic activity, river action, and faulting, may shift the strata or materials in them, and the chronology may be difficult or impossible to reconstruct. What's more, given the widely different rates of accumulation, the elapsed time of any stratum cannot be determined with much accuracy.

Two other relative dating techniques, *biostratigraphy* and *paleomagnetism*, have also been used to date early hominin sites. Biostratigraphy is based on the fairly regular changes seen in the dentition and other anatomical structures in such groups as pigs, rodents, and baboons. Dating of sites is based on the presence of certain fossil species that also occur elsewhere in deposits whose dates have been determined. This technique has proved helpful in cross-correlating the ages of various sites in southern, central, and eastern Africa. Paleomagnetism is based on the shifting nature of the earth's geomagnetic pole. Although now oriented northward, the geomagnetic pole is known to have shifted several times in the past and at times was oriented to the south. By examining magnetically charged particles encased in rock, geologists can determine the orientation of these ancient "compasses." This technique doesn't provide exact dates but is used to double-check other techniques (**Fig. 9-11**).

In all these relative dating techniques, the age of geological layers or objects within them is impossible to calibrate. To determine age as precisely as possible, scientists have developed a variety of chronometric techniques, many based on radioactive decay. The principle is quite simple: Radioactive isotopes of certain elements are unstable, and they decay to form an isotopic variant of another element. Because the rate of decay follows a predictable

mathematical pattern, the radioactive material serves as an accurate geological clock. By measuring the amount of decay in a particular sample, scientists have devised techniques for dating the immense age of the earth (and of moon rocks) as well as material only a few hundred years old. Several such techniques have been employed for a number of years and are now quite well known.

The most important chronometric technique used to date early hominins involves potassium-40 (^{40}K), which has a half-life of 1.25 billion years and produces argon-40 (^{40}Ar). That is, half the ^{40}K isotope changes to ^{40}Ar in 1.25 billion years. In another 1.25 billion years, half the remaining ^{40}K would be converted (that is, only one-quarter of the original amount would still be present). Known as the K/Ar, or potassium-argon, method, this procedure has been extensively used in dating materials in the 5–1 mya range, especially in East Africa, where past volcanic activity makes this dating technique possible. Organic material, such as bone, cannot be measured, but the rock matrix that contains fossilized bones can be.

Strata that provide the best samples for K/Ar dating are those that have been heated to an extremely high temperature, such as that generated by volcanic activity. Heating drives off previously accumulated argon gas, thus "resetting" the clock to zero. As the material cools and solidifies, ^{40}K continues to break down to ^{40}Ar, but now the gas is physically trapped inside the cooling material. To date the geological material, it is reheated, and the escaping gas is then measured. Potassium-argon dating has been used to date very old events—such as the age of the earth—as well as those less than 2,000 years old. Another radiometric dating method, this one measuring the decay of uranium into lead (the U/Pb method, with a half-life of 4.47 billion years), has been used recently in South Africa to date hominin sites (De Ruiter et al., 2009; Dirks et al., 2010).

▲ **Figure 9-11**
A geologist carefully takes a sample of sediment containing magnetically charged particles for paleomagnetic dating. He must very precisely record the exact compass orientation so that it can be correlated with the sequence of magnetic orientations.

A well-known and commonly used chronometric technique involves carbon-14 (^{14}C), with a half-life of 5,730 years. This method is used to date organic material (such as wood, charcoal, and plant fibers) as recent as a few hundred years old and can be extended as far back as 75,000 years, although the probability of error rises rapidly after 40,000 years. The physical basis of this technique is also *radiometric*; that is, it's tied to the measurement of radioactive decay of an isotope (^{14}C) into another, more stable form. Radiocarbon dating has proved especially relevant for calibrating the latter stages of human evolution, including the Neandertals and the appearance of modern *Homo sapiens* (see Chapters 11 and 12).

Some inorganic artifacts can be directly dated through the use of **thermoluminescence (TL)**. This method, too, relies on the principle of radiometric decay. Stone used in tool manufacture invariably contains trace amounts of radioactive elements, such as uranium. When the stone is heated (perhaps deliberately as part of the toolmaking process), certain particles trapped within it are released. As they escape, they emit a dull glow known as thermoluminescence. After that, radioactive decay resumes within the fired stone, again building up electrons at a steady rate. To determine the age of an archaeological sample, the researcher must heat the sample to 500°C and measure its thermoluminescence; from that, the date can be calculated. Used especially by archaeologists to date ceramic pots from recent sites, TL can also be used to date burned flint tools from earlier hominin sites.

Like TL, two other techniques used to date sites from the latter phases of hominin evolution (where neither K/Ar nor radiocarbon dating is possible) are uranium series dating and electron spin resonance (ESR) dating. Uranium series dating relies on radioactive decay of short-lived uranium isotopes, and ESR is similar to TL because it's based on measuring trapped elec-

trons. However, whereas TL is used on heated materials such as clay or stone tools, ESR is used on the dental enamel of animals. All three of these dating methods have been used to provide key dating controls for hominin sites discussed in Chapters 11 and 12.

Many of the techniques just discussed are used together to provide *independent* checks for dating important early hominin sites. Each technique has a degree of error, and only by *cross-correlating* the results can paleoanthropologists feel confident about dating fossil and archaeological remains. This point is of the utmost importance, for a firm chronology forms the basis for making sound evolutionary interpretations (as discussed later in the chapter).

Understanding Our Direct Evolutionary Connections: What's a Hominin?

The earliest evidence of hominins dates to the end of the Miocene and mainly includes dental and cranial pieces. But dental remains alone don't describe the special features of hominins, and they certainly aren't distinctive of the later stages of human evolution. Modern humans, as well as our most immediate hominin ancestors, are distinguished from the great apes by more obvious features than tooth and jaw dimensions. For example, various scientists have pointed to such distinctive hominin characteristics as bipedal locomotion, large brain size, and toolmaking behavior as being significant (at some stage) in defining what makes a hominin a hominin.

It's important to recognize that not all these characteristics developed simultaneously or at the same pace. In fact, over the last several million years of hominin evolution, quite a different pattern has been evident, in which each of the components (dentition, locomo-

thermoluminescence (TL)
Technique for dating certain archaeological materials that were heated in the past (such as stone tools) and that release stored energy of radioactive decay as light upon reheating.

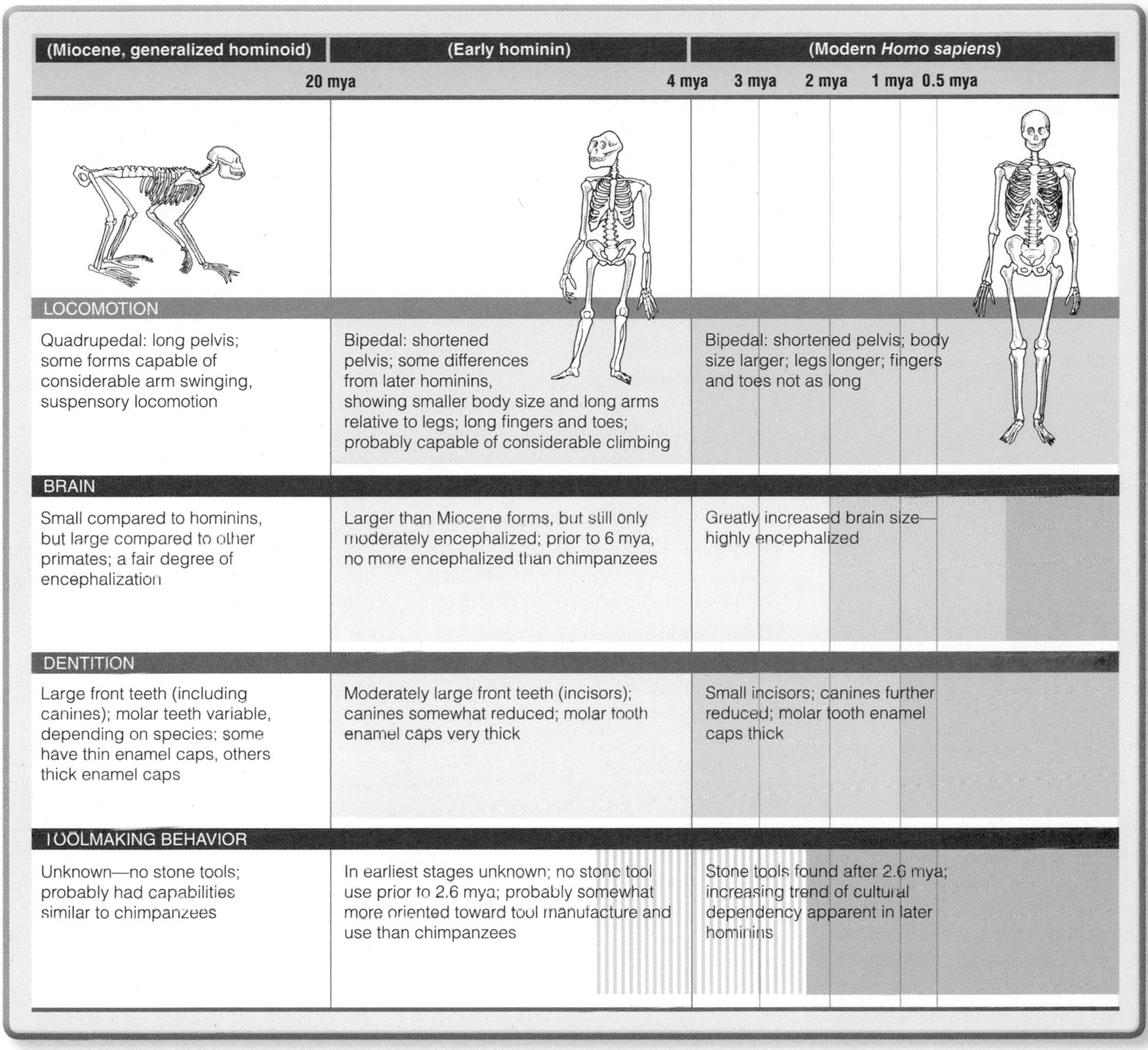

(Miocene, generalized hominoid)	(Early hominin)	(Modern *Homo sapiens*)
20 mya	4 mya 3 mya 2 mya 1 mya 0.5 mya	

LOCOMOTION

Quadrupedal: long pelvis; some forms capable of considerable arm swinging, suspensory locomotion	Bipedal: shortened pelvis; some differences from later hominins, showing smaller body size and long arms relative to legs; long fingers and toes; probably capable of considerable climbing	Bipedal: shortened pelvis; body size larger; legs longer; fingers and toes not as long

BRAIN

Small compared to hominins, but large compared to other primates; a fair degree of encephalization	Larger than Miocene forms, but still only moderately encephalized; prior to 6 mya, no more encephalized than chimpanzees	Greatly increased brain size— highly encephalized

DENTITION

Large front teeth (including canines); molar teeth variable, depending on species; some have thin enamel caps, others thick enamel caps	Moderately large front teeth (incisors); canines somewhat reduced; molar tooth enamel caps very thick	Small incisors; canines further reduced; molar tooth enamel caps thick

TOOLMAKING BEHAVIOR

Unknown—no stone tools; probably had capabilities similar to chimpanzees	In earliest stages unknown; no stone tool use prior to 2.6 mya; probably somewhat more oriented toward tool manufacture and use than chimpanzees	Stone tools found after 2.6 mya; increasing trend of cultural dependency apparent in later hominins

© Cengage Learning 2013

▲ **Figure 9-12**
Mosaic evolution of hominin characteristics: a postulated time line.

tion, brain size, and toolmaking) have developed at quite different rates. This pattern, in which physiological and behavioral systems evolve at different rates, is called **mosaic evolution**. As we first pointed out in Chapter 1 and will emphasize in this chapter, the single most important defining characteristic for the entire course of hominin evolution is **bipedal locomotion**. In the earliest stages of hominin emergence, skeletal evidence indicating bipedal locomotion is the only truly reliable indicator that these fossils were indeed hominins. But in later stages of hominin evolution, other features, especially those relating to brain development and behavior, become highly significant (**Fig. 9-12**).

What's in a Name?

Throughout this book, we refer to members of the human lineage as hominins (the technical name for members of the tribe Hominini). Most paleoanthropologists now prefer this terminology, because it more accurately reflects evolutionary relationships. As we mentioned briefly in Chapter 7, the more

mosaic evolution A pattern of evolution in which the rate of evolution in one functional system varies from that in other systems. For example, in hominin evolution, the dental system, locomotor system, and neurological system (especially the brain) all evolved at markedly different rates.

bipedal locomotion Walking on two feet. Walking on two legs is the single most distinctive feature of the hominins.

traditional classification of hominoids isn't as accurate and actually misrepresents key evolutionary relationships.

In the last several years, detailed molecular evidence clearly shows that the great apes (traditionally classified as pongids and including orangutans, gorillas, chimpanzees, and bonobos) don't make up a coherent evolutionary group sharing a single common ancestor. Indeed, the molecular/genetic data indicate that the African great apes (gorillas, chimpanzees, and bonobos) are significantly more closely related to humans than is the orangutan. What's more, at an even closer evolutionary level, we now know that chimpanzees and bonobos are yet more closely connected to humans than are gorillas. Hominoid classification has been significantly revised to show these more complete relationships, and two further taxonomic levels (subfamily and tribe) have been added (**Fig. 9-13**).

We should mention a couple of important ramifications of this new classification. First, it further emphasizes the *very* close evolutionary connection of humans with African apes and most especially that with chimpanzees and bonobos. Second, the term *hominid*, which has been used for decades to refer to our specific evolutionary lineage, has a quite different meaning in the revised classification; now it refers to *all* great apes and humans together.

Unfortunately, during the period of transition to the newer classification scheme, confusion is bound to result. For this reason, we won't use the term *hominid* in this book except where absolutely necessary (for example, in a formal classification; see Fig. 6-11). To avoid confusion, we'll simply refer to the grouping of great apes and humans as "large-bodied hominoids." And when you see the term *hominid* in earlier publications (including earlier editions of this text), simply regard it as synonymous with *hominin*, the term we use in this book.

▶ **Figure 9-13**
(a) Traditional classification of hominoids. **(b)** Revised classification of hominoids. Note that two additional levels of classification are added (subfamily and tribe) to show more precisely and more accurately the evolutionary relationships among the apes and humans. In this classification, "hominin" is synonymous with the use of "hominid" in part (a).

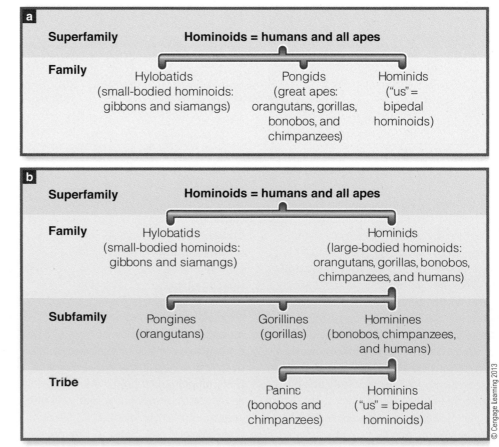

© Cengage Learning 2013

Walking the Walk: The Bipedal Adaptation

We discussed in Chapter 7 that all primates show adaptations for erect body posture and some species are occasionally bipedal. Of all living primates, however, efficient bipedalism as the primary form of locomotion is seen *only* in hominins. Functionally, the human mode of locomotion is most clearly shown in our striding gait, where weight is alternately placed on a single fully extended hind limb. This specialized form of locomotion has developed to a point where energy levels are used to near peak efficiency. This isn't true of nonhuman primates, who move bipedally with hips and knees bent in a much less efficient manner.

From a survey of our close primate relatives, it's apparent that while still in the trees, our ancestors were adapted to a fair amount of upper-body erectness. Lemurs, lorises, tarsiers, monkeys, and apes all spend considerable time sitting erect while feeding, grooming, or sleeping. Presumably, our early ancestors also displayed similar behavior. What caused them to come to the ground and embark on the unique way of life that would eventually lead to humans is still a mystery. Perhaps natural selection favored some Miocene hominoids coming occasionally to the ground to forage for food on the forest floor and forest fringe. In any case, once they were on the ground and away from the immediate safety offered by trees, bipedal locomotion could become a tremendous advantage.

First of all, bipedal locomotion freed the hands for carrying objects and for making and using tools. You need to realize, however, that early on the tools weren't made of stone; in fact, hominins were bipedal for at least 2 million years prior to the first archaeological evidence of stone tool use. Such early cultural developments had an even more positive effect on speeding the development of yet more efficient bipedalism—once again emphasizing the dual role of biocultural evolution. In addition, in a bipedal stance, animals have a wider view of the surrounding countryside, and in open (or semi-open) terrain, early spotting of predators (particularly large cats, such as lions, leopards, and saber-tooths) would be of critical importance. We know that modern ground-living primates, including savanna baboons and vervets, occasionally adopt this posture to "look around" when out in open country.

Moreover, bipedal walking is an efficient means of covering long distances, and when large game hunting came into play (several million years after the initial adaptation to ground living), further refinements increasing the efficiency of bipedalism may have been favored. It's hard to say exactly what initiated the process, but all these factors probably played a role in the adaptation of hominins to their special niche through a special form of locomotion.

The Mechanics of Walking on Two Legs

Our mode of locomotion is indeed extraordinary, involving, as it does, a unique kind of activity in which "the body, step by step, teeters on the edge of catastrophe" (Napier, 1967, p. 56). The problem is to maintain balance on the "stance" leg while the "swing" leg is off the ground. In fact, during normal walking, both feet are simultaneously on the ground only about 25 percent of the time, and as speed of locomotion increases, this percentage becomes even smaller.

Maintaining a stable center of balance calls for many drastic structural/anatomical alterations in the basic primate quadrupedal pattern. The most dramatic changes are seen in the pelvis. The pelvis is composed of three elements: two hip bones, or ossa coxae (*sing.*, os coxae), joined at the back to the sacrum (**Figs. 9-14** and **9-15**). In

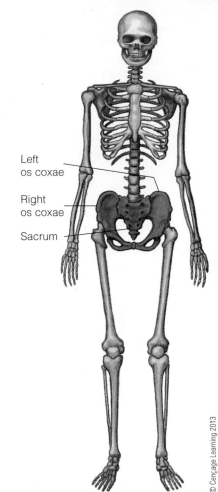

▲ **Figure 9-14**
The human pelvis: various elements shown on a modern skeleton.

Left os coxae

Right os coxae

Sacrum

© Cengage Learning 2013

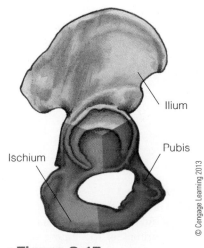

▲ **Figure 9-15**
The human os coxae, composed of three bones (right side shown).

Ilium

Pubis

Ischium

© Cengage Learning 2013

▼**Figure 9-16**

Ossa coxae. (a) *Homo sapiens*. (b) Early hominin (australopith) from South Africa. (c) Great ape. Note especially the length and breadth of the iliac blade (boxed) and the line of weight transmission (shown in red).

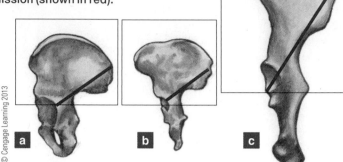

© Cengage Learning 2013

a quadruped, the ossa coxae are vertically elongated bones positioned along each side of the lower portion of the spine and oriented more or less parallel to it. In hominins, the pelvis is comparatively much shorter and broader and extends around to the side. This configuration helps to stabilize the line of weight transmission in a bipedal posture from the lower back to the hip joint (**Fig. 9-16**).

Moreover, the foot must act as a stable support instead of a grasping limb. When we walk, our foot is used like a prop, landing on the heel and pushing

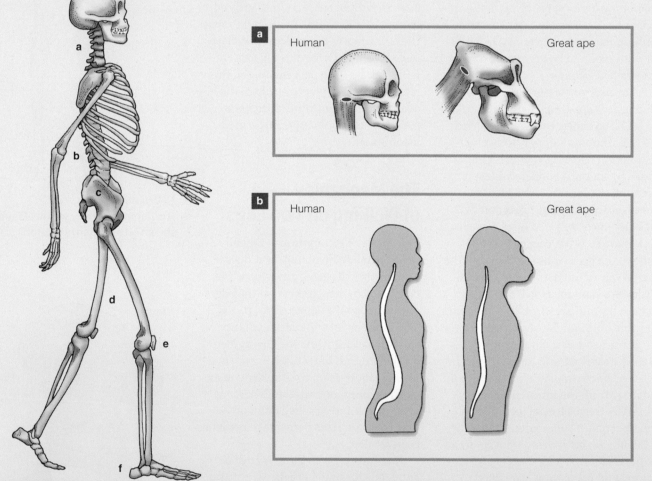

▲**Figure 9-17**

During hominin evolution, several major structural features throughout the body have been reorganized (from that seen in other primates), facilitating efficient bipedal locomotion. These are illustrated here, beginning with the head and progressing to the foot: (a) The foramen magnum (shown in blue) is repositioned farther underneath the skull, so that the head is more or less balanced on the spine (and thus requires less robust neck muscles to hold the head upright). (b) The spine has two distinctive curves—a backward (thoracic) one and a forward (lumbar) one—that keep the trunk (and weight) centered above the pelvis. (c) The pelvis is shaped more in the form of a basin to support internal organs; the ossa coxae (specifically, iliac blades) are also shorter and broader, thus

habitual bipedalism Bipedal locomotion as the form of locomotion shown by hominins most of the time.

off on the toes, particularly the big toe. In addition, our legs became elongated to increase the length of the stride. An efficient bipedal adaptation required further remodeling of the lower limb to allow full extension of the knee and to keep the legs close together during walking, in this way maintaining the center of support directly under the body (**Fig. 9-17**).

We say that hominin bipedalism is both habitual and obligate. By **habitual bipedalism**, we mean that hominins, unlike any other primate, move bipedally as their standard and most effi-

cient mode of locomotion. By **obligate bipedalism**, we mean that hominins are committed to bipedalism and cannot locomote efficiently in any other way. For example, the loss of grasping ability in the foot makes climbing much more difficult for humans. The central task, then, in trying to understand the earliest members of the hominin lineage is to identify anatomical features that indicate bipedalism and to interpret to what degree these individuals were committed to this form of locomotion (that is, was it habitual and obligate?).

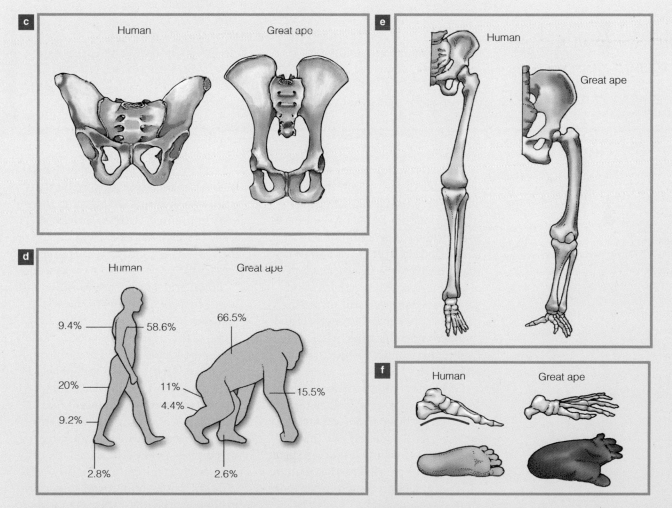

stabilizing weight transmission. **(d)** Lower limbs are elongated, as shown by the proportional lengths of various body segments (for example, in humans the thigh comprises 20 percent of body height, whereas in gorillas it comprises only 11 percent). **(e)** The femur is angled inward, keeping the legs more directly under the body; modified knee anatomy also permits full extension of this joint. **(f)** The big toe is enlarged and brought in line with the other toes; a distinctive longitudinal arch also forms, helping absorb shock and adding propulsive spring.

obligate bipedalism Bipedalism as the *only* form of hominin terrestrial locomotion. Major anatomical changes in the spine, pelvis, and lower limb are required for bipedal locomotion, so once hominins adapted this mode of locomotion, other forms of locomotion on the ground became impossible.

© Cengage Learning 2013

Quick Review

Key Pre-Australopith Discoveries

Date	Region	Hominin	Site	Evolutionary Significance
4.4 mya	East Africa	*Ardipithecus ramidus*	Aramis	Large collection of fossils, including partial skeletons; bipedal, but derived
5.8–5.2 mya		*Ardipithecus*	Middle Awash	Fragmentary, but possibly bipedal
~6.0 mya		*Orrorin tugenensis*	Tugen Hills	First hominin with post-cranial remains; possibly bipedal
~7.0–6.0 mya	Central Africa	*Sahelanthropus tchadensis*	Toros-Menalla	Oldest potential hominin; well-preserved cranium; very small-brained; bipedal?

© Cengage Learning 2013

What structural patterns are observable in early hominins, and what do they imply regarding locomotor function? By 4.4 mya, we have good evidence that hominins had adaptations in their pelvis and feet that allowed for fairly efficient bipedal locomotion while on the ground. They were, however, still surprisingly primitive in many other respects and spent considerable time in the trees (where they could also move about very efficiently).

Only after around 4 mya do we see all the major structural changes required for bipedalism. In particular, the pelvis, as clearly documented by several excellently preserved specimens, was remodeled further to more efficiently support weight in a bipedal stance (see Fig. 9-16b).

Other structural changes shown after 4 mya further confirm the pattern seen in the pelvis. For example, the vertebral column (as known from specimens in East and South Africa) shows the same curves as in modern hominins. The lower limbs are also elongated, and they seem to be proportionately about as long as in modern humans (although the arms are longer in these early hominins). Further, the carrying angle of weight support from the hip to the knee is very similar to that seen in ourselves.

Fossil evidence of early hominin foot structure has come from several sites in South and East Africa. Some of this evidence, especially well-preserved fossils (as well as footprints) from East Africa show a well-adapted form of bipedalism. However, some earlier (and recently analyzed) finds from East Africa as well as some from South Africa indicate that the large toe was divergent, like that seen in great apes. Such a configuration is an ancestral trait among hominoids, important in allowing the foot to grasp. In turn, this grasping ability (as in other primates) would have enabled early hominins to more effectively exploit arboreal habitats. Finally, because anatomical remodeling is always constrained by a set of complex functional compromises, a foot highly capable of grasping and climbing is less well adapted as a stable platform during bipedal locomotion.

From this evidence, some researchers have recently concluded that many forms of early hominins spent considerable time in the trees. What's more, the earliest hominins were likely habitual bipeds when they were on the ground, but they were not necessarily obligate bipeds. Only after about 4 mya did further adaptations lead to the fully committed form of bipedalism we see in all later hominins, including us.

Digging for Connections: Early Hominins from Africa

As you are now aware, a variety of early hominins lived in Africa, and we'll cover their comings and goings over a 5-million-year period, from at least 6 to 1 mya. It's also important to keep in mind that these hominins were geographically widely distributed, with fossil discoveries coming from central, East, and South Africa. Paleoanthropologists generally agree that among these early African fossils, there were at least 6 different genera, which in turn comprised upward of 13 different species. At no time, nor in any other place, were hominins ever as diverse as were these very ancient members of our family tree. As you'll see in a minute, some of the earliest fossils thought by many researchers to be hominins are primitive in some ways and unusually derived in others. In fact, some paleoanthropologists remain unconvinced that they are really hominins.

As you've already guessed, there are quite a few different fossils from many sites, and you'll find that their formal naming can be difficult to pronounce and not easy to remember. So we'll try to discuss these fossil groups in a way that's easy to understand. Our primary focus will be to organize them by

time and by major evolutionary trends. In so doing, we recognize three major groups:

- Pre-australopiths—the earliest and most primitive (possible) hominins (6.0+–4.4 mya)
- Australopiths—diverse forms, some more primitive, others highly derived (4.2–1.2 mya)
- Early *Homo*—the first members of our genus (2.0+–1.4 mya)

Pre-Australopiths (6.0+—4.4 mya)

The oldest and most surprising of these earliest hominins is represented by a cranium discovered at a central African site called Toros-Menalla in the modern nation of Chad (Brunet et al., 2002; **Fig. 9-18**). Provisional dating using faunal correlation (biostratigraphy) suggests a date of between 7 and 6 mya (Vignaud et al., 2002). Closer examination of the evidence used in obtaining this biostratigraphic date now has led many paleoanthropologists to suggest that the later date (6 mya) is more likely.

The morphology of the fossil is unusual, with a combination of characteristics unlike that found in other early hominins. The braincase is small, estimated at no larger than a modern chimpanzee's (preliminary estimate in the range of 320 to 380 cm³), but it is massively built, with huge browridges in front, a crest on top, and large muscle attachments in the rear. Yet, combined with these apelike features is a smallish vertical face containing front teeth very unlike an ape's. In fact, the lower face, being more tucked in under the brain vault (and not protruding, as in most other early hominins), is more of a *derived* feature more commonly expressed in much later hominins (especially members of genus *Homo*) (**Fig. 9-19**).

What's more, unlike the dentition seen in apes, the upper canine is

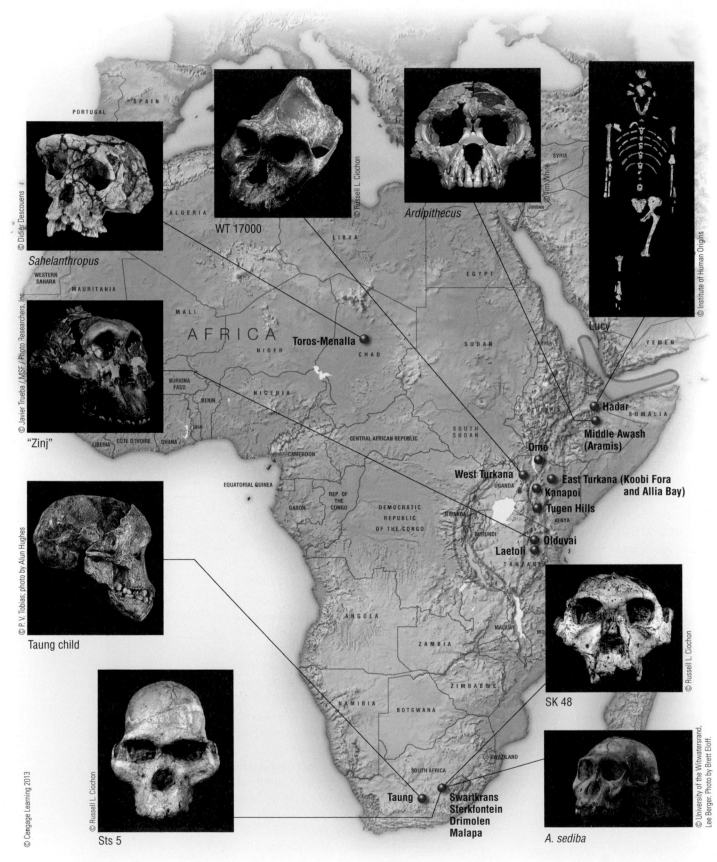

▲**Figure 9-18**
Early hominin fossil finds (pre-australopith and australopith localities). The Rift Valley in East Africa is shown in gold.

reduced and is worn down from the tip (rather than shearing along its side against the first lower premolar). The lack of such a shearing canine/ premolar arrangement (called a **honing complex**) (**Fig. 9-20**) is viewed by many researchers as an important derived characteristic of early hominins (White et al., 2009). Other experts are not entirely convinced and suggest it could just as easily have evolved in both hominins and other hominoids due to homoplasy (Wood and Harrison, 2011).

In recognition of this unique combination of characteristics, paleoanthropologists have placed the Toros-Menalla remains into a new genus and species of hominin, *Sahelanthropus tchadensis* (Sahel being the region of the southern Sahara in North Africa). These finds from Chad have forced an immediate and significant reassessment of early hominin evolution. Two cautionary comments, however, are in order. First, as we noted, the dating is only approximate, based, as it is, on biostratigraphic correlation with sites in Kenya (1,500 miles to the east). Second, and perhaps more serious, is the hominin status of the Chad fossil. Given the facial structure

and dentition, it's difficult to see how *Sahelanthropus* could be anything but a hominin. However, the position of its foramen magnum is intermediate between that of a quadrupedal ape and that of a bipedal hominin (**Fig. 9-21**); for this and other reasons, some researchers (Wolpoff et al., 2002) suggest that at this time, "ape" may be a better classification for *Sahelanthropus*. As we have previously said, the best-defining anatomical characteristics of hominins relate to bipedal locomotion. Unfortunately, no postcranial elements have been recovered from Chad—at least not yet. Consequently, we do not yet know the locomotor behavior of *Sahelanthropus*, and this raises even more fundamental questions: What if further finds show

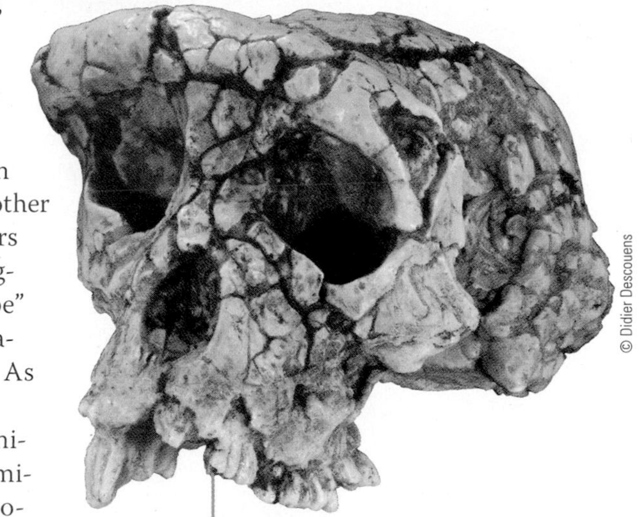

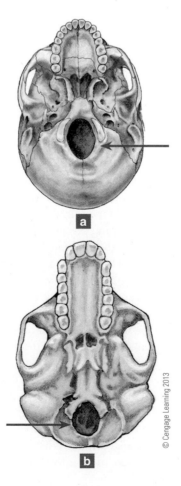

▲ **Figure 9-19**
A nearly complete cranium of *Sahelanthropus* from Chad, dating to approximately 6 mya or somewhat older.

© Didier Descouens

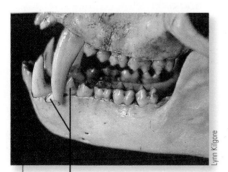

Sectorial lower 1st premolar

Lynn Kilgore

▲ **Figure 9-20**
Canine/lower 1st premolar honing complex, typical of most Old World anthropoids, but lacking in most hominins (shown here in a male patas monkey). Note how the large upper canine shears against the elongated surface of the lower first premolar.

◀ **Figure 9-21**
Position of the foramen magnum in (a) a human and (b) a chimpanzee. Note the more forward position in the human cranium.

a

b

© Cengage Learning 2013

honing complex The shearing of a large upper canine with the 1st lower premolar, with the wear leading to honing of the surfaces of both teeth. This anatomical pattern is typical of most Old World anthropoids, but is mostly absent in hominins.

this form not to be bipedal? Should we still consider it a hominin? What, then, are the defining characteristics of our lineage? For all these reasons, several paleoanthropologists have recently grown more skeptical regarding the hominin status of all the pre-australopith finds, and Bernard Wood (2010) prefers to call them "possible hominins."

Probably living at about the same time as *Sahelanthropus*, two other very early (possible) hominin genera have been found at sites in central Kenya in the Tugen Hills and from the Middle Awash area of northeastern Ethiopia. The earlier of these finds (dated by radiometric methods to around 6 mya) comes from the Tugen Hills and includes mostly dental remains, but also some quite complete lower limb bones. The fossils have been placed in a separate early hominin genus called *Orrorin*. The postcranial remains are especially important, because they seem to indicate bipedal locomotion (Pickford and Senut, 2001; Senut et al., 2001; Galik et al., 2004; Richmond and Jungers, 2008). As a result of these further analyses, *Orrorin* is the pre-australopith generally recognized as having the best evidence to establish it as a hominin (compared to less clear evidence for *Sahelanthropus* and *Ardipithecus*).

The last group of possible hominins dating to the late Miocene (that is, earlier than 5 mya) comes from the Middle Awash in the Afar Triangle of Ethiopia. Radiometric dating places the age of these fossils in the very late Miocene, 5.8–5.2 mya. The fossil remains themselves are very fragmentary. Some of the dental remains resemble some later fossils from the Middle Awash (discussed shortly), and Yohannes Haile-Selassie, the researcher who first found and described these earlier materials, has provisionally assigned them to the genus *Ardipithecus* (Haile-Selassie et al., 2004; see "Quick Review: Key Pre-Australopith Discoveries"). In addition, some postcranial elements have been preserved, most informatively a

toe bone, a phalanx from the middle of the foot (see Appendix A, Fig. A-8). From clues in this bone, Haile-Selassie concludes that this primate was a well-adapted biped (once again, the best-supporting evidence of hominin status).

From another million years or so later in the geological record in the Middle Awash region, a very large and significant assemblage of fossil hominins has been discovered at a site called **Aramis**. Radiometric dating firmly places these remains at about 4.4 mya. The site, represented by a 6-foot-thick bed of bones, has yielded more than 6,000 fossils. From this key site, excavations reveal both large and small vertebrates—birds and other reptiles and even very small mammals. Additionally, fossil wood and pollen samples have been recovered. All this information is important for understanding the environments in which these ancient hominins lived.

Hominin fossil remains from Aramis include several individuals, the most noteworthy being a partial skeleton. At least 36 other hominins are represented by isolated teeth, cranial bones, and a few limb bones. All the bones were extremely fragile and fragmentary and required many years of incredibly painstaking effort to clean and reconstruct. Indeed, it took 15 years before the partial skeleton was in adequate condition to be intensively studied. But the wait was well worth it, and in 2009, Tim White and colleagues published their truly remarkable finds. By far, the most informative fossil is the partial skeleton. Even though it was found crushed and fragmented into hundreds of small pieces, years of work and computer imaging have now allowed researchers to interpret this 4.4-million-year-old individual. The skeleton, nicknamed "Ardi," has more than 50 percent of the skeleton represented; however, because it was found in such poor condition, any reconstruction must be seen as provisional and open to varying interpretations. Ardi has been sexed as female and contains several key portions,

Aramis (air-ah-miss)

including a skull, a pelvis, and almost complete hands and feet (White et al., 2009; **Fig. 9-22**).

Brain size, estimated between 300 and 350 cm³, is quite small, being no larger than a chimpanzee's. However, it is much like that seen in *Sahelanthropus*, and overall, the skulls of the two hominins also appear to be similar. The fact that remains of the postcranial skeleton are preserved is potentially crucial, because key body elements, such as the pelvis and the foot, are only very rarely discovered. This is the *earliest* hominin for which we have so many different parts of the body represented, and it permits researchers to hypothesize more confidently about body size and proportions and, perhaps most crucially of all, the mode of locomotion.

Height is estimated at close to 4 feet, with a body weight of around 110 pounds. Compared to other early hominins, such a body size would be similar to that of a male and well above average for a female. The pelvis and foot are preserved well enough to allow good-quality computer reconstructions. According to Tim White and colleagues, both areas of the body show key anatomical changes indicating that *Ardipithecus* was a competent biped. For example, the ilium is short and broad (see Figs. 9-14 and 9-15), and the foot has been modified to act as a prop for propulsion during walking.

However, Ardi also contains some big surprises. Although the shape of the ilium seems to show bipedal abilities, other parts of the pelvis show more ancestral ("primitive") hominoid characteristics. In fact, the paleoanthropologists who analyzed the skeleton concluded that Ardi likely walked quite adequately, but might well have had difficulty running (Lovejoy et al., 2009a, 2009b). The foot is also an odd mix of features, showing a big toe that is highly divergent and capable of considerable grasping. Some researchers are not convinced that Ardi was bipedal, and considering all her other primi-

◄**Figure 9-22**
A mostly complete (but fragmented) skeleton of *Ardipithecus*. Dating to about 4.4 mya, this is the earliest hominin skeleton yet found containing so many different portions of the body.

© David L. Brill / Atlanta

tive characteristics, some have questioned whether *Ardipithecus* was really a hominin at all (Sarmiento, 2010). The extreme degree of reconstruction that was required (for the skull and pelvis especially) adds further uncertainty to understanding this crucial discovery. One thing that everyone agrees on is that Ardi was an able climber who likely was well adapted to walking on all fours along the tops of branches. It seems clear that she spent a lot of time in the trees.

Accepting for the moment that *Ardipithecus* was a hominin, it was a very primitive one, displaying an array of characteristics quite distinct from all later members of our lineage. The new evidence that Ardi provides has not convinced all paleoanthropologists that *Ardipithecus* or any of the other very early pre-australopiths are hominins; indeed, Ardi's very odd anatomy has caused doubts to increase. One thing is for sure: It would take a considerable adaptive shift in the next 200,000 years to produce the more derived hominins we'll discuss in a moment. All of these considerations have not only intrigued professional anthropologists, they have also captured the imagination of the general public. When did the earliest member of our lineage first appear? The search still goes on, and professional reputations are made and lost in this quest.

Another intriguing aspect of all these late Miocene/early Pliocene locales (that is, Toros-Menalla, Tugen Hills, early Middle Awash sites, and Aramis) relates to the ancient environments associated with these potentially earliest hominins. Rather than the more open grassland savanna habitats so characteristic of most later hominin sites, the environment at all these early locales is more heavily forested. Perhaps we are seeing at Aramis and these other ancient sites the very beginnings of hominin divergence, not long after the division from the African apes.

Australopiths (4.2–1.2 mya)

The best-known, most widely distributed, and most diverse of the early African hominins are colloquially called **australopiths**. In fact, this diverse and very successful group of hominins is made up of two closely related genera, *Australopithecus* and *Paranthropus*. These homi-

nins have an established time range of over 3 million years, stretching back as early as 4.2 mya and not apparently becoming extinct until close to 1 mya—making them the longest-enduring hominins yet documented. In addition, these hominins have been found in all the major geographical areas of Africa that have, to date, produced early hominin finds, namely, South Africa, central Africa (Chad), and East Africa. From all these areas combined, there appears to have been considerable complexity in terms of evolutionary diversity, with numerous species now recognized by most paleoanthropologists.

There are two major subgroups of australopiths, an earlier one that is more anatomically primitive and a later one that is much more derived. These earlier australopiths, dated 4.2–3.0 mya, show several more primitive (ancestral) hominin characteristics than the later australopith group, whose members are more derived, some extremely so. These more derived hominins lived after 2.5 mya and are composed of two different genera, together represented by at least five different species (see Appendix B for a complete listing and more information about early hominin fossil finds).

Given the 3-million-year time range as well as quite varied ecological niches, there are numerous intriguing adaptive differences among these varied australopith species. We'll discuss the major adaptations of the various species in a moment. But first let's emphasize the major features that all australopiths share.

1. They are all clearly bipedal (although not necessarily identical to *Homo* in this regard).
2. They all have relatively small brains (at least compared to *Homo*).
3. They all have large teeth, particularly the back teeth, with thick to very thick enamel on the molars.

australopiths A colloquial name referring to a diverse group of Plio-Pleistocene African hominins. Australopiths are the most abundant and widely distributed of all early hominins and are also the most completely studied.

In short, then, all these australopith species are relatively small-brained, big-toothed bipeds.

The earliest australopiths, dating to 4.2–3.0 mya, come from East Africa from a couple of sites in northern Kenya. Among the fossil finds of these earliest australopiths so far discovered, a few postcranial pieces clearly indicate that locomotion was bipedal.

Because these particular fossils have initially been interpreted as more primitive than all the later members of the genus *Australopithecus*, paleo-anthropologists have provisionally assigned them to a separate species. This important fossil species is now called *Australopithecus anamensis*, and some researchers suggest that it is a potential ancestor for many later australopiths as well as perhaps early members of the genus *Homo* (White et al., 2006).

Australopithecus afarensis

Slightly later and much more complete remains of *Australopithecus* have come primarily from the sites of Hadar (in Ethiopia) and Laetoli (in Tanzania). Much of this material has been known for three decades, and the fossils have been very well studied; indeed, in certain instances, they are quite famous. For example, the Lucy skeleton was discovered at Hadar in 1974, and the Laetoli footprints were first found in 1978. These hominins are classified as members of the species *Australopithecus afarensis*.

Literally thousands of footprints have been found at Laetoli, representing more than 20 different kinds of animals (Pliocene elephants, horses, pigs, giraffes, antelopes, hyenas, and an abundance of hares). Several hominin footprints have also been found, including a trail more than 75 feet long made by at least two—and perhaps three—individuals (Leakey and Hay, 1979; **Fig. 9-23**). Such discoveries of well-preserved hominin footprints are extremely important in furthering our understanding of human evolution. For the first time, we can make *definite* statements regarding the locomotor pattern and stature of early hominins.

Studies of these impression patterns clearly show that the mode of locomotion of these hominins was bipedal (Day and Wickens, 1980). Some researchers, however, have concluded that *A. afarensis* was not bipedal in quite the same way that modern humans are. From detailed comparisons with modern humans, estimates of stride length, cadence, and speed of walking have been ascertained, indicating that the Laetoli

◄ **Figure 9-23**
Hominin footprint from Laetoli, Tanzania. Note the deep impression of the heel and the large toe (arrow) in line (adducted) with the other toes.

▶ **Figure 9-24**
(a) "Lucy," a partial hominin skeleton, discovered at Hadar in 1974. This individual is assigned to *Australopithecus afarensis*. **(b)** Artist's reconstruction of a female *A. afarensis* derived from study of the Lucy skeleton.

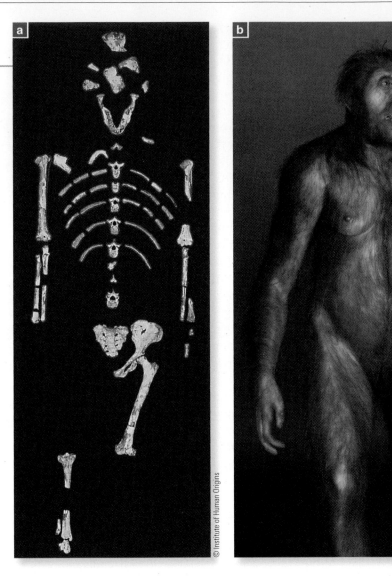

© Institute of Human Origins

© 2010 Photo E. Daynès – Reconstruction Atelier Daynès Paris

hominins moved in a slow-moving ("strolling") fashion with a rather short stride.

One extraordinary discovery at Hadar is the Lucy skeleton (**Fig. 9-24**), found eroding out of a hillside by Don Johanson. This fossil is scientifically designated as Afar Locality (AL) 288-1, but is usually just called Lucy (after the Beatles song "Lucy in the Sky with Diamonds"). Representing almost 40 percent of a skeleton, this is one of the most complete individuals from anywhere in the world for the entire period before about 100,000 years ago.

Because the Laetoli area was covered periodically by ashfalls from nearby volcanic eruptions, accurate dating is possible and has provided dates of 3.7–3.5 mya. Dating from the Hadar region isn't as straightforward, but more complete dating calibration using a variety of techniques has determined a range of 3.9–3.0 mya for the hominin discoveries from this area.

Several hundred *A. afarensis* specimens, representing a minimum of 60 individuals (and perhaps as many as 100), have been removed from Laetoli and Hadar. At present, these materials represent the largest *well-studied* collection of early hominins and are among the most significant of the hominins discussed in this chapter.

Without question, *A. afarensis* is more primitive than any of the other later australopith fossils from South or East Africa (discussed shortly). By "primitive" we mean that *A. afarensis*

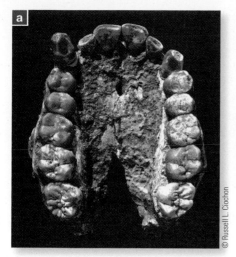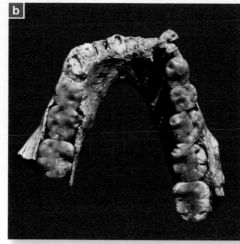

© Russell L. Ciochon

© Carol Ward

◀**Figure 9-25**
Jaws of *Australopithecus afarensis*. **(a)** Maxilla, AL 200-1a, from Hadar, Ethiopia. (Note the parallel tooth rows and large canines.) **(b)** Mandible, LH 4, from Laetoli, Tanzania. This fossil is the type specimen for the species *Australopithecus afarensis*.

is less evolved in any particular direction than are later-occurring hominin species. That is, *A. afarensis* shares more primitive features with late Miocene apes and with living great apes than do later hominins, who display more derived characteristics.

For example, the teeth of *A. afarensis* are quite primitive. The canines are often large, pointed teeth. Moreover, the lower first premolar provides a shearing surface for the upper canine (although it is not a full honing complex as seen in many monkeys and apes). Lastly, the tooth rows are parallel, even converging somewhat toward the back of the mouth (**Fig. 9-25**).

The cranial portions that are preserved also display several primitive hominoid characteristics, including a crest in the back as well as several primitive features of the cranial base. Cranial capacity estimates for *A. afarensis* show a mixed pattern when compared with later hominins. A provisional estimate for the one partially complete cranium—apparently a large individual—gives a figure of 500 cm^3, but another, even more fragmentary cranium is apparently quite a bit smaller and has been estimated at about 375 cm^3 (Holloway, 1983). Thus, for some individuals (males?), *A. afarensis* is well within the range of other australopith species, but others (females?) may have a significantly smaller cranial capacity. However, a detailed depiction of cra-

nial size for *A. afarensis* is not possible at this time; this part of the skeleton is unfortunately too poorly represented. One thing is clear: *A. afarensis* had a small brain, probably averaging for the whole species not much over 420 cm^3.

On the other hand, a large assortment of postcranial pieces representing almost all portions of the body of *A. afarensis* has been found. Initial impressions suggest that relative to lower limbs, the upper limbs are longer than in modern humans (also a primitive Miocene ape condition). (This statement does not mean that the arms of *A. afarensis* were longer than the legs.) In addition, the wrist, hand, and foot bones show several differences from modern humans (Susman et al., 1985). From such excellent postcranial evidence, stature can be confidently estimated: *A. afarensis* was a short hominin. From her partial skeleton, Lucy is estimated to be only 3 to 4 feet tall. However, Lucy—as demonstrated by her pelvis—was probably a female, and there is evidence of larger individuals as well. The most economical hypothesis explaining this variation is that *A. afarensis* was quite sexually dimorphic: The larger individuals are male, and the smaller ones, such as Lucy, are female. Estimates of male stature can be approximated from the larger footprints at Laetoli, inferring a height of not quite 5 feet. If we accept this interpretation, *A. afarensis* was a very sexually dimorphic form indeed.

In fact, for overall body size, this species may have been as dimorphic as *any* living primate (that is, as much as gorillas, orangutans, or baboons).

Significant further discoveries of *A. afarensis* have come from Ethiopia in the last few years, including two further partial skeletons. The first of these is a mostly complete skeleton of an *A. afarensis* infant discovered at the Dikika locale in northeastern Ethiopia, very near the Hadar sites mentioned earlier (**Fig. 9-26**). What's more, the infant comes from the same geological horizon as Hadar, with very similar dating: of 3.3–3.2 mya (Alemseged et al., 2006).

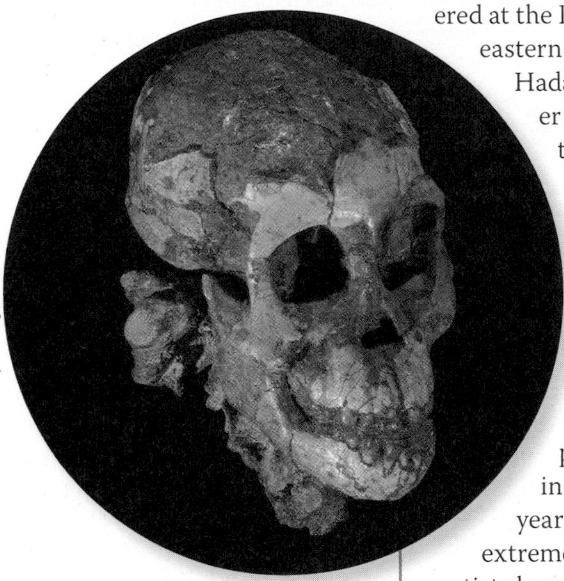

This find of a 3-year-old infant is remarkable because it's the first example of a very well-preserved immature hominin prior to about 100,000 years ago. From the infant's extremely well-preserved teeth, scientists hypothesize that she was female. A comprehensive study of her developmental biology has already begun, and many more revelations are surely in store as the Dikika infant is more completely cleaned and studied. For now, and accounting for her immature age, the skeletal pattern appears to be quite similar to what we'd expect in an *A. afarensis* adult. The limb proportions, anatomy of the hands and feet, and shape of the scapula (shoulder blade) reveal a similar "mixed" pattern of locomotion. The foot and lower limb indicate that this infant would have been a terrestrial biped; yet, the shoulder and (curved) fingers suggest that she was also capable of climbing about quite ably in the trees.

The second recently discovered *A. afarensis* partial skeleton comes from the Woranso-Mille research area in the central Afar, only about 30 miles north of Hadar (Haile-Selassie et al., 2010). The dating places the find at close to 3.6 mya (almost 400,000 years earlier than Lucy). Moreover, the individual was considerably larger than Lucy and likely was male. Analysis of bones preserved in this new find reinforces what was previously known about *A. afarensis* as well as adding some further insights. The large degree of sexual dimorphism and well-adapted bipedal locomotion agree with prior evidence. A portion of a shoulder joint (with a scapula; see Appendix A) confirms that suspensory locomotion was not a mode of arboreal locomotion; nevertheless, arboreal habitats could still have been effectively exploited.

What makes *A. afarensis* a hominin? The answer is revealed by its manner of locomotion. From the abundant limb bones recovered from Hadar and other locales, as well as those beautiful footprints from Laetoli, we know unequivocally that *A. afarensis* walked bipedally when on the ground. (At present, we do not have nearly such good evidence concerning locomotion for *any* of the earlier hominin finds.) Whether Lucy and her contemporaries still spent considerable time in the trees, and just how efficiently they walked, have become topics of some controversy. Most researchers, however, agree that *A. afarensis* was an efficient habitual biped while on the ground. These hominins were also clearly *obligate* bipeds, which would have hampered their climbing abilities but would not necessarily have precluded arboreal behavior altogether.

Australopithecus afarensis is a crucial hominin group. Because it comes after the earliest, poorly known group of pre-australopith hominins, but prior to all later australopiths as well as *Homo*, it is an evolutionary bridge, connecting together much of what we assume are the major patterns of early hominin evolution. The fact that there are many well-preserved fossils and that they have been so well studied also adds to the paleoanthropological significance of *A. afarensis*. The consensus among most experts over the last several years has been that *A. afarensis* is a potentially strong candidate as the ancestor of *all* later hominins.

© Zeresenay Alemseged

▲ **Figure 9-26**
Complete skull with attached vertebral column of the infant skeleton from Dikika, Ethiopia (dated to about 3.3 mya).

Some ongoing analysis has recently challenged this hypothesis (Rak et al., 2007) but, at least for the moment, this new interpretation has not been widely accepted. Still, it reminds us that science is an intellectual pursuit that constantly reevaluates older views and seeks to provide more systematic explanations about the world around us. When it comes to understanding human evolution, we should always be aware that things might change. So stay tuned.

Later More Derived Australopiths (3.0–1.2 mya)

Following 3.0 mya, hominins became more diverse in Africa. As they adapted to varied niches, australopiths became considerably more derived. In other words, they show physical changes making them quite distinct from their immediate ancestors.

In fact, there were at least three separate lineages of hominins living (in some cases side by side) between 2.0 and 1.2 mya. One of these is a later form of *Australopithecus*; another is represented by the highly derived three species that belong to the genus *Paranthropus*; and the last consists of early members of the genus *Homo*. Here we'll discuss *Paranthropus* and *Australopithecus*. *Homo* will be discussed in the next section.

The most derived australopiths are the various members of *Paranthropus*. Though all australopiths are big-toothed, *Paranthropus* has the biggest teeth of all, especially as seen in its huge premolars and molars. Along with their massive back teeth, these hominins show a variety of other specializations related to powerful chewing (**Fig. 9-27**). For example, they all have large, deep lower jaws and large attachments for muscles associated with chewing. In fact, these chewing muscles are so prominent that major anatomical alterations evolved in the architecture of their face and skull vault. In particular, the *Paranthropus* face is flatter than that of any other australopith; the broad cheekbones (to which the masseter muscle attaches) flare out; and a ridge develops on top of the skull (this is called a **sagittal crest**, and it's where the temporal muscle attaches).

All these morphological features suggest that *Paranthropus* was adapted for a diet emphasizing rough vegetable foods. However, this does not mean that these very big-toothed hominins did not also eat a variety of other foods, perhaps including some meat. In fact, sophisticated recent chemical analyses of *Paranthropus* teeth suggest that their diet may have been quite varied (Sponheimer et al., 2006).

The first member of the *Paranthropus* evolutionary group (clade) comes from a site in northern Kenya on the west side of Lake Turkana. This key find is that of a nearly complete skull, called the "Black Skull" (owing to chemical staining during fossilization), and it dates to approximately 2.5 mya (**Fig. 9-28**). This skull, with a cranial capacity of only 410 cm^3, is among the smallest for any hominin known, and it has other primitive traits reminiscent of *A. afarensis*.

But here's what makes the Black Skull so fascinating: Mixed into this array of distinctively primitive traits are a host of derived ones that link it to other, later *Paranthropus* species (including a broad face, a very large palate, and a large area for the back teeth). This mosaic of features seems to place this individual between earlier *A. afarensis* on the one hand and the later *Paranthropus* species on the other. Because of its unique position in hominin evolution, the Black Skull (and the population it represents) has been placed in a new species, *Paranthropus aethiopicus*.

Around 2 mya, different varieties of even more derived members of the *Paranthropus* lineage were on the scene in East Africa. Well documented by

sagittal crest A ridge of bone that runs down the middle of the cranium like a short Mohawk. This serves as the attachment for the large temporal muscles, indicating strong chewing.

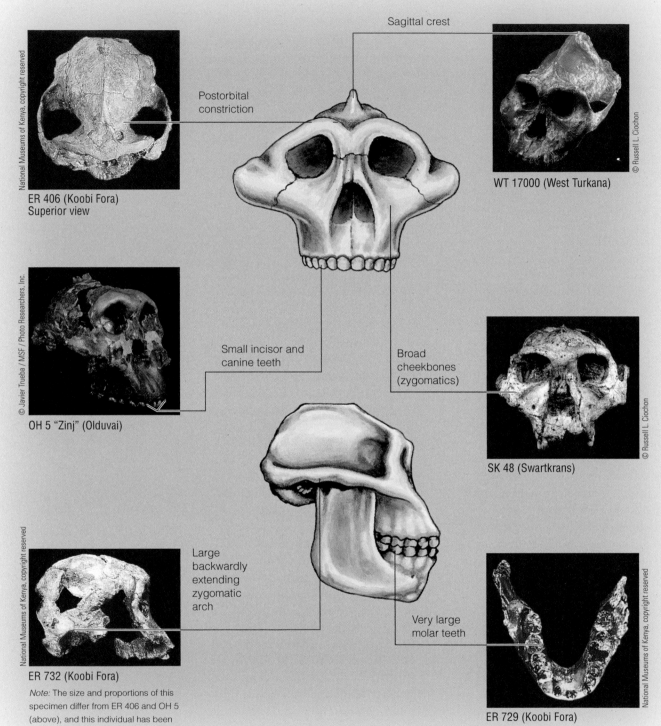

ER 406 (Koobi Fora)
Superior view

WT 17000 (West Turkana)

OH 5 "Zinj" (Olduvai)

SK 48 (Swartkrans)

ER 732 (Koobi Fora)

Note: The size and proportions of this specimen differ from ER 406 and OH 5 (above), and this individual has been suggested as a female *Paranthropus*.

ER 729 (Koobi Fora)

Sagittal crest

Postorbital constriction

Small incisor and canine teeth

Broad cheekbones (zygomatics)

Large backwardly extending zygomatic arch

Very large molar teeth

▲**Figure 9-27**
Morphology and variation in *Paranthropus*. (Note both typical features and range of variation as shown in different specimens.)

finds dated after 2 mya from Olduvai and East Turkana, *Paranthropus* continues to have relatively small cranial capacities (ranging from 510 to 530 cm³) and very large, broad faces with massive back teeth and lower jaws. The larger (probably male) individuals also show that characteristic raised ridge (sagittal crest) along the midline of the cranium. Females are not as large or as robust as the males, indicating a fair degree of sexual dimorphism. In any case, the East African *Paranthropus* individuals are all extremely robust in terms of their teeth and jaws—although in overall body size they are much like other australopiths. Because these somewhat later East African *Paranthropus** fossils are so robust, they are usually placed in their own separate species, *Paranthropus boisei*.

Paranthropus fossils have also been found at several sites in South Africa. As we discussed earlier, the geological context in South Africa usually does not allow as precise chronometric dating as is possible in East Africa. Based on these less precise dating methods, *Paranthropus* in South Africa existed about 2.0–1.2 mya.

Paranthropus in South Africa is very similar to its close cousin in East Africa, but it's not quite as dentally robust. As a result, paleoanthropologists prefer to regard South African *Paranthropus* as a distinct species—one called *Paranthropus robustus*.

What became of *Paranthropus*? After 1 mya, these hominins seem to vanish without descendants. Nevertheless, we should be careful not to think of them as "failures." After all, they lasted for 1.5 million years, during which time they expanded over a considerable area of sub-Saharan Africa. Moreover, although their extreme dental/chewing adaptations may seem peculiar to us, it was a fascinating "evolutionary experiment" in hominin evo-

lution. And it was an innovation that worked for a long time. Still, these big-toothed cousins of ours did eventually die out. It remains to us, the descendants of another hominin lineage, to find their fossils, study them, and ponder what these creatures were like.

No sites dating after 3 mya in East Africa have yielded fossil finds of the genus *Australopithecus*. As you know, their close *Paranthropus* kin were doing quite well during this time. Whether *Australopithecus* actually did become extinct in East Africa following 3 mya or whether we just haven't yet found their fossils is impossible to say.

South Africa, however, is another story. A very well-known *Australopithecus* species has been found at four sites in southernmost Africa, in a couple of cases in limestone caves very close to where *Paranthropus* fossils have also been found.

In fact, the very first early hominin discovery from Africa (indeed, from *anywhere*) came from the Taung site, discovered back in 1924. The discovery of the beautifully preserved child's skull from Taung is a fascinating tale (**Fig. 9-29**). When first published in 1925 by a young anatomist named Raymond Dart, most experts were unimpressed. They thought Africa to be an unlikely place for the origins of hominins. These skeptics, who had been long focused on European and Asian hominin finds, were initially unprepared to acknowledge Africa's central place in human evolution. Only years later, following many more African discoveries from other sites, did professional opinion shift. With this admittedly slow scientific awareness came the eventual consensus that Taung (which Dart classified as *Australopithecus africanus*) was indeed an ancient member of the hominin family tree.

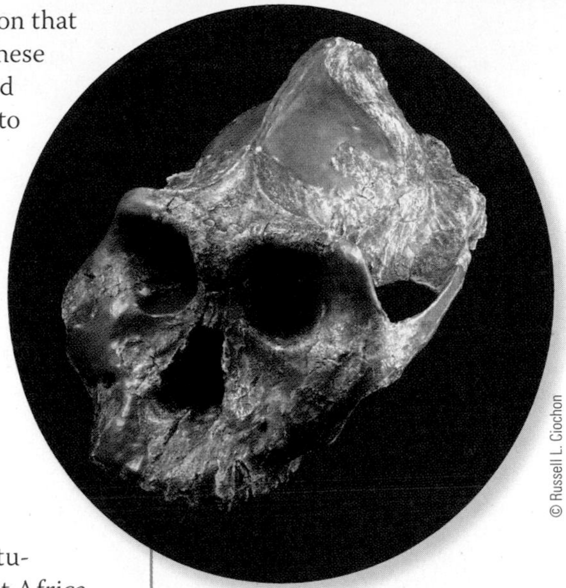

▲ Figure 9-28
The "Black Skull," discovered at West Lake Turkana. This specimen is usually assigned to *Paranthropus aethiopicus*. It's called the Black Skull due to its dark color from the fossilization (mineralization) process.

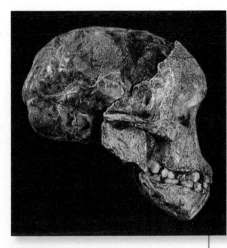

▲ Figure 9-29
The Taung child's skull, discovered in 1924. There is a fossilized endocast of the brain in back, with the face and lower jaw in front.

*Note that these later East African *Paranthropus* finds are at least 500,000 years later than the earlier species (*P. aethiopicus*, exemplified by the Black Skull).

▲ Figure 9-30
Australopithecus africanus adult cranium from Sterkfontein.

Like other australopiths, the "Taung baby" and other *A. africanus* individuals (**Fig. 9-30**) were small-brained, with an adult cranial capacity of about 440 cm³. They were also big-toothed, although not as extremely so as in *Paranthropus*. Moreover, from very well-preserved postcranial remains from Sterkfontein, we know that they also were well-adapted bipeds.

The ongoing excavation of a remarkably complete skeleton at Sterkfontein should tell us about *A. africanus'* locomotion, body size and proportions, and much more (**Fig. 9-31**).

The precise dating of *A. africanus*, as with most other South African hominins, has been disputed. Over the last several years, it's been assumed that this species existed as far back as 3.3 mya. However, the most recent analysis suggests that *A. africanus* lived approximately between 3 and 2 mya (Walker et al., 2006; Wood, 2010; **Fig. 9-32**).

New Connections: A Transitional Australopith?

As we'll see in the next section, almost all the evidence for the earliest appearance of our genus, *Homo*, has come from East Africa. So it's no surprise that most researchers have assumed that *Homo* probably first evolved in this region of Africa.

However, new and remarkably well-preserved fossil discoveries from South Africa may challenge this view. In 2008, paleoanthropologists discovered two partial skeletons at the Malapa Cave, located just a few miles from Sterkfontein and Swartkrans. Actually, the first find was made by the lead researcher's 9-year-old son, Matthew. His father (Lee Berger, from the University of Witwatersrand) and colleagues have been further investigating inside the cave, where several skeletons may be buried, and they announced and described these finds in 2010 (Berger et al., 2010).

▶ Figure 9-31
Paleoanthropologist Ronald Clarke carefully excavates a 2-million-year-old skeleton from the limestone matrix at Sterkfontein Cave. Clearly seen are the cranium (with articulated mandible) and the upper arm bone.

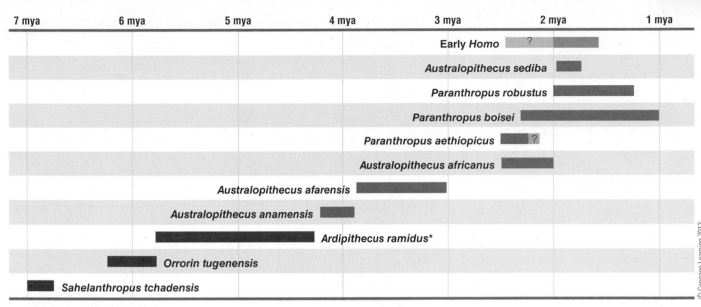

	7 mya	6 mya	5 mya	4 mya	3 mya	2 mya	1 mya

Early *Homo*

Australopithecus sediba

Paranthropus robustus

Paranthropus boisei

Paranthropus aethiopicus

Australopithecus africanus

Australopithecus afarensis

Australopithecus anamensis

*Ardipithecus ramidus**

Orrorin tugenensis

Sahelanthropus tchadensis

© Cengage Learning 2013

*The earlier *Ardipithecus* specimens (5.8–5.2 mya) are placed in a separate species.

▲ **Figure 9-32**
Time line of early African hominins. Note that most dates are approximations. Question marks indicate those estimates that are most tentative.

Using paleomagnetic dating as well as more precise radiometric techniques than have been used before in South Africa (Dirks et al., 2010; Pickering et al. 2011), the fossils are dated to just a little less than 2 mya and show a fascinating mix of australopith characteristics along with a few features more suggestive of *Homo*. Because of this unique anatomical combination, these fossils have been assigned to a new species, *Australopithecus sediba* (sediba means "wellspring" or "fountain" in the local language). Australopith-like characteristics seen in *A. sediba* include a small brain (estimated at 420 cm^3), long arms with curved fingers, and several primitive traits in the feet. In these respects *A. sediba* most resembles its potential immediate South African predecessor, *A. africanus* (see **Figs. 9-33** and **9-34**).

On the other hand, some other aspects of *A. sediba* more resemble *Homo*. Among these characteristics are short fingers and possible indications of brain reorganization.

All this is very new and quite complex. Indeed, initial paleoanthropological interpretations are highly varied (Balter, 2010; Gibbons, 2011). It will take some time for experts to figure it out. Remember, too, that there are more fossils still in the cave. The initial consensus among paleoanthropologists is that *A. sediba* is quite

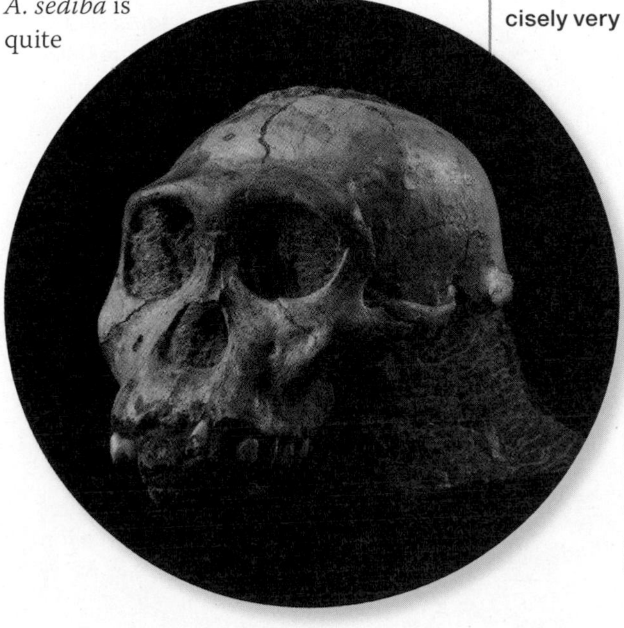

▼ **Figure 9-33**
A. sediba skull, found at Malapa Cave, South Africa, dated precisely very close to 2 mya.

© University of the Witwatersrand, Lee Berger. Photo by Brett Eloff.

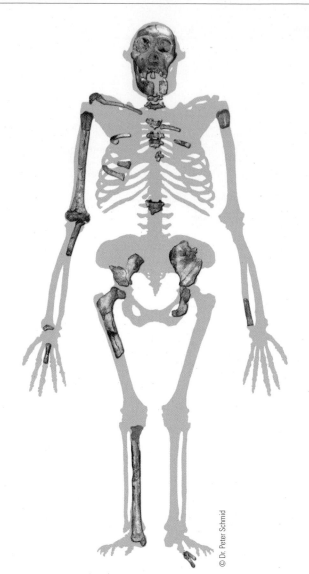

© Dr. Peter Schmid

▲Figure 9-34
One of the two partial *A. sediba* skeletons so far discovered at Malapa Cave, showing those elements that were preserved.

different from other australopiths. and shows a surprising and unique mix of primitive and derived characteristics. How it fits in with the origins of *Homo* remains to be determined. Certainly, more detailed studies of the *A. sediba* fossils, including further comparisons with other early hominins will help further our understanding. For the moment, most paleoanthropologists still think the best evidence for the origins of our genus comes from East Africa.

Plio-Pleistocene Pertaining to the Pliocene and first half of the Pleistocene, a time range of 5–1 mya. For this time period, numerous fossil hominins have been found in Africa.

Closer Connections: Early *Homo* (2.0+–1.4 mya)

In addition to the australopith remains, there's another largely contemporaneous hominin that is quite distinctive and thought to be more closely related to us. In fact, as best documented by fossil discoveries from Olduvai and East Turkana, these materials have been assigned to the genus *Homo*—and thus are different from all species assigned to either *Australopithecus* or *Paranthropus*.

The earliest appearance of genus *Homo* in East Africa may date back well before 2 mya (and thus considerably before *A. sediba*). A discovery in the 1990s from the Hadar area of Ethiopia suggested to many paleoanthropologists that early *Homo* was present in East Africa by 2.3 mya; however, we should be cautious, because the find is quite incomplete (including only one upper jaw).

Better-preserved evidence of a **Plio-Pleistocene** hominin with a significantly larger brain than seen in australopiths was first suggested by Louis Leakey in the early 1960s, on the basis of fragmentary remains found at Olduvai Gorge. Leakey and his colleagues gave a new species designation to these fossil remains, naming them *Homo habilis*. There may, in fact, have been more than one species of *Homo* living in Africa during the Plio-Pleistocene. So, more generally, we'll refer to them all as "early *Homo*." The species *Homo habilis* refers particularly to those early *Homo* fossils from Olduvai and the Turkana Basin.

The *Homo habilis* material at Olduvai dates to about 1.8 mya, but due to the fragmentary nature of the fossil remains, evolutionary interpretations have been difficult. The most immediately obvious feature distinguishing the *H. habilis* material from

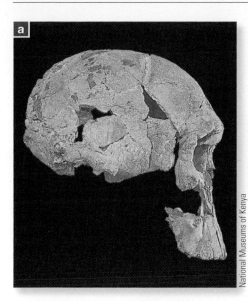

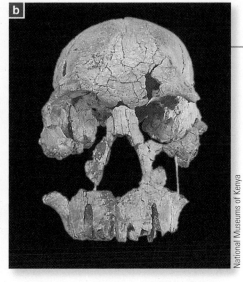

National Museums of Kenya

National Museums of Kenya

◄ **Figure 9-35**
A nearly complete early *Homo* cranium from East Lake Turkana (ER 1470), one of the most important single fossil hominin discoveries from East Africa. **(a)** Lateral view. **(b)** Frontal view.

the australopiths is cranial size. For all the measurable early *Homo* skulls, the estimated average cranial capacity is 631 cm³, compared to 520 cm³ for all measurable *Paranthropus* specimens and 442 cm³ for *Australopithecus* crania (McHenry, 1988), including *A. sediba*. Early *Homo*, therefore, shows an increase in cranial size of about 20 percent over the larger of the australopiths and an even greater increase over some of the smaller-brained forms. In their initial description of *H. habilis*, Leakey and his associates also pointed to differences from australopiths in cranial shape and in tooth proportions (with early members of genus *Homo* showing larger front teeth relative to back teeth and narrower premolars).

The naming of this fossil material as *Homo habilis* ("handy man") was meaningful from two perspectives. First of all, Leakey argued that members of this group were the early Olduvai toolmakers. Second, and most significantly, by calling this group *Homo*, Leakey was arguing for at least *two separate branches* of hominin evolution in the Plio-Pleistocene. Clearly, only one could be on the main branch eventually leading to *Homo sapiens*. By labeling this new group *Homo* rather than *Australopithecus*, Leakey was guessing that he had found our ancestors.

Much better-preserved fossils from East Turkana have shed further light on early *Homo* in the Plio-Pleistocene.* The most important of this additional material is a nearly complete cranium (**Fig. 9-35**). With a cranial capacity of 775 cm³, this individual is well outside the known range for australopiths and actually overlaps the lower boundary for later species of *Homo* (that is, *H. erectus*, discussed in the next chapter). In addition, the shape of the skull vault is in many respects unlike that of australopiths. However, the face is still quite robust (Walker, 1976), and the fragments of tooth crowns that are preserved indicate that the back teeth in this individual were quite large.† The East Turkana early *Homo* material is generally contemporaneous with the Olduvai remains. The oldest date back to about 1.8 mya, but recently discovered specimen dates to 1.44 mya, making it by far the latest

_____

* Some early *Homo* fossils from East Turkana are classified by a minority of paleoanthropologists as a different species (*Homo rudolfensis*; see Appendix B). These researchers often identify both *H. habilis* and *H. rudolfensis* at Turkana but only *H. habilis* at Olduvai.

† In fact, some researchers have suggested that all these "early *Homo*" fossils are better classified as *Australopithecus* (Wood and Collard, 1999a).

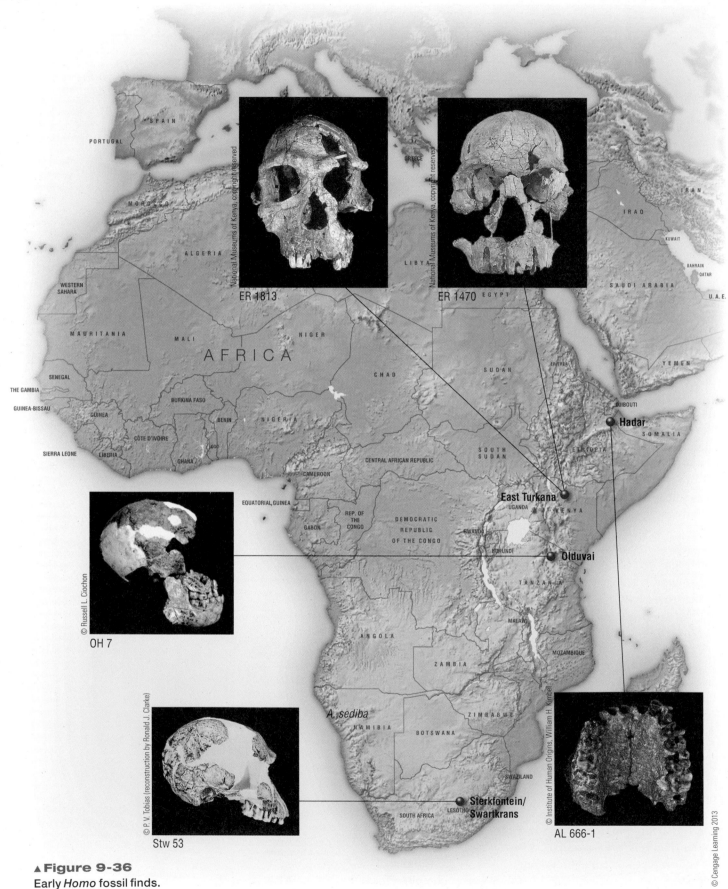

ER 1813

ER 1470

OH 7

Stw 53

A. sediba

East Turkana

Olduvai

Hadar

Sterkfontein/
Swartkrans

AL 666-1

▲**Figure 9-36**
Early *Homo* fossil finds.

surviving early *Homo* fossil yet found (Spoor et al., 2007). In fact, this discovery indicates that a species of early *Homo* coexisted in East Africa for several hundred thousand years with *H. erectus*, with both species living in the exact same area on the eastern side of Lake Turkana. This new evidence raises numerous fascinating questions regarding how two closely related species existed for so long in the same region.

As in East Africa, early members of the genus *Homo* have also been found in South Africa, and these fossils are considered more distinctive of *Homo* than is the *transitional* australopith, *A. sediba.* At both Sterkfontein and Swartkrans, fragmentary remains have been recognized as most likely belonging to *Homo* (**Fig. 9-36**).

On the basis of evidence from Olduvai, East Turkana, and Hadar, we can reasonably postulate that at least one species (and possibly two) of early *Homo* was present in East Africa perhaps a little prior to 2.0 mya, developing in parallel with an australopith species. These hominin lines lived contemporaneously for a minimum of 1 million years, after which time the australopiths apparently disappeared forever. One lineage of early *Homo* likely evolved into *H. erectus* about 1.8 mya. Any other species of early *Homo* became extinct sometime after 1.4 mya.

Interpretations: What Does It All Mean?

By this time, you may think that anthropologists are obsessed with finding small scraps buried in the ground and then assigning them confusing numbers and taxonomic labels impossible to remember. But it's important to realize that the collection of all the basic fossil data is the foundation of human evolutionary research. Without fossils, our specu-lations would be largely hollow—and most certainly not scientifically testable. Several large, ongoing paleoanthropological projects are now collecting additional data in an attempt to answer some of the more perplexing questions about our evolutionary history.

The numbering of specimens, which may at times seem somewhat confusing, is an effort to keep the designations neutral and to make reference to each individual fossil as clear as possible. The formal naming of finds as *Australopithecus*, *Paranthropus*, or *Homo habilis* should come much later, because it involves a lengthy series of complex interpretations. Assigning generic and specific names to fossil finds is more than just a convenience; when we attach a particular label, such as *A. afarensis*, to a particular fossil, we should be fully aware of the biological implications of such an interpretation.

From the time that fossil sites are first located until the eventual interpretation of hominin evolutionary patterns, several steps take place. Ideally, they should follow a logical order, for if interpretations are made too hastily, they confuse important issues for many years. Here's a reasonable sequence:

1. Selecting and surveying sites
2. Excavating sites and recovering fossil hominins
3. Designating individual finds with specimen numbers for clear reference
4. Cleaning, preparing, studying, and describing fossils
5. Comparing with other fossil material—in a chronological framework if possible
6. Comparing fossil variation with known ranges of variation in closely related groups of living primates and analyzing ancestral and derived characteristics
7. Assigning taxonomic names to fossil material

But the task of interpretation still isn't complete, for what we really want to know in the long run is what

▶ **Figure 9-37**
A tentative early hominin phylogeny. Note the numerous question marks, indicating continuing uncertainty regarding evolutionary relationships.

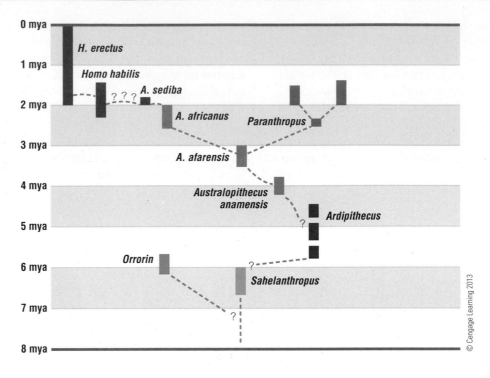

happened to the populations represented by the fossil remains. In looking at the fossil hominin record, we're actually looking for our ancestors. In the process of eventually determining those populations that are our most likely antecedents, we may conclude that some hominins are on evolutionary side branches. If this conclusion is accurate, those hominins necessarily must have become extinct. It's both interesting and relevant to us as hominins to try to find out what influenced some earlier members of our family tree to continue evolving while others died out.

Although a clear evolutionary picture is not yet possible for organizing all the early hominins discussed in this chapter, there are some general patterns that for now make good sense (**Fig. 9-37**). New finds may of course require serious alterations to this scheme. Science can be exciting but can also be frustrating to many in the general public looking for simple answers to complex questions. For well-informed students of human evolution, it's most important to grasp the basic principles of paleoanthropology and *how* interpretations are made and

why they sometimes must be revised. This way you'll be prepared for whatever shows up tomorrow.

Seeing the Big Picture: Adaptive Patterns of Early African Hominins

As you are by now aware, there are several different African hominin genera and certainly lots of species. This, in itself, is interesting. Speciation was occurring quite frequently among the various lineages of early hominins—more frequently, in fact, than among later hominins. What explains this pattern?

Evidence has been accumulating at a furious pace in the last decade, but it's still far from complete. What's clear is that we'll never have anything approaching a complete record of early hominin evolution, so some significant gaps will remain. After all, we're able to discover hominins only in those special environmental contexts where fossilization was likely. All the other potential habitats they might have exploited are now invisible to us.

Still, patterns are emerging from the fascinating data we do have. First, it appears that early hominin species (pre-australopiths, *Australopithecus*, *Paranthropus*, and early *Homo*) all had restricted ranges. It's therefore likely that each hominin species exploited a relatively small area and could easily have become separated from other populations of its own species. So genetic drift (and to some extent natural selection) could have led to rapid genetic divergence and eventual speciation.

Second, most of these species appear to be at least partially tied to arboreal habitats, although there's disagreement on this point regarding early *Homo* (see Wood and Collard, 1999b; Foley 2002). Also, *Paranthropus* was probably somewhat less arboreal than *Ardipithecus* or *Australopithecus*. These very large-toothed hominins apparently concentrated on a diet of coarse, fibrous plant foods, such as roots. Exploiting such resources may have routinely taken these hominins farther away from the trees than their dentally more gracile—and perhaps more omnivorous—cousins.

Third, except for some early *Homo* individuals, there's very little in the way of an evolutionary trend of increased body size or of markedly greater encephalization. Beginning with *Sahelanthropus*, brain size was no more than that in chimpanzees—although when controlling for body size, this earliest of all known hominins may have had a proportionately larger brain than any living ape. Close to 5 million years later (that is, the time of the last surviving australopith species), relative brain size increased by no more than 10 to 15 percent. Perhaps tied to this relative stasis in brain capacity, there's no absolute association of any of these hominins with patterned stone tool manufacture.

Although conclusions are becoming increasingly controversial, for the moment, early *Homo* appears to be a

Why It Matters

This chapter argues that becoming bipedal contributed to the success of our ancestors and perhaps to our own success as well. But so many people have back problems, and certainly the narrow pelvis of women complicates childbirth. So why hasn't evolution done a better job of making us into well-adapted bipeds?

First, it's important to remember that the evolutionary process is a series of trade-offs rather than a course to perfection, so it's not surprising that some of the anatomical changes allowing bipedalism seem less than optimal. In fact, the "imperfections" are pretty good evidence against intelligent design. What sort of designer would have a birth canal so narrow and twisted that the baby has to undergo a series of rotations in order to pass its head and shoulders through the canal (see Chapter 13)? In fact, complications of birth are a major cause of death in women throughout the world today, especially in the less industrialized nations.

W. M. Krogman wrote a thought-provoking article in 1951 entitled "The Scars of Human Evolution," in which he discussed the ubiquitous back problems that most of us have as a result of being bipedal. After all, the limb structure we have inherited initially evolved over millions of years in quadrupeds and has since been "jerry-rigged" to function in an animal walking around on just two legs.

The difficulties have probably gotten worse since Krogman wrote the article, given that one of the reasons we have back problems is all the sitting (often with bad posture) that we do—like sitting in front of the computer or being hunched over a textbook. Anthropologist Robert Anderson, who also happens to be a chiropractor, argues that if we are taught proper walking techniques as children and are more careful of the way we sit, walk, lift, and carry, then we can prevent many of the back problems (especially lower back pain) so often encountered as people enter midlife. In this way, by considering how bipedalism evolved, we may be able to adopt walking and sitting habits that keep our spines more healthy throughout our lives.

partial exception. This group shows both increased encephalization and numerous occurrences of likely association with stone tools (though at many of the sites, australopith fossils were *also* found).

Lastly, all of these early African hominins show an accelerated developmental pattern (similar to that seen in African apes), one quite different from the *delayed* developmental pattern characteristic of *Homo sapiens* (and our immediate precursors). This apelike development is also seen in some early *Homo* individuals (Wood and Collard, 1999a). Rates of develop-

ment can be accurately reconstructed by examining dental growth markers (Bromage and Dean, 1985), and these data may provide a crucial window into understanding this early stage of hominin evolution.

These African hominin predecessors were rather small, able bipeds, but still closely tied to arboreal and/or climbing niches. They had fairly small brains and, compared to later *Homo*, matured rapidly. It would take a major evolutionary jump to push one of their descendants in a more human direction. For the next chapter in this more human saga, read on.

Summary of Main Topics

- The earliest very primitive primates evolved in the Paleocene around 65 mya.
- Many primate fossil forms, more similar to living primates, evolved in the Eocene (56–33 mya). Most of these species went extinct, although some show connections to modern lemurs/lorises or to tarsiers.
- The first anthropoids likely appear in the late Eocene, but are much better documented from the Fayum Oligocene site (about 33 mya).
- Large-bodied hominoids are widespread and diverse in the Old World throughout the entire Miocene (23–5 mya).

- Paleoanthropology is the multidisciplinary science that studies early human evolution.
- Accurately dating early hominins is essential and there are two major types of dating techniques: relative and chronometric.
- The first hominins appear 7–6 mya, and for the next 5 my are all restricted to Africa.
- Many species of these early African hominins have been identified and can be summarized within three major subgroups:
  - Pre-australopiths (6.0+–4.4 mya) Including three genera of very early, and still primitive (possi-

ble) hominins: *Sahelanthropus*, *Orrorin*, and *Ardipithecus*
  - Australopiths (4.2–1.2 mya) Early, more primitive australopith species (4.2–3.0 mya), including *Australopithecus anamensis* and *Australopithecus afarensis*

  Later, more derived australopith species (2.5–1.2 mya), including two genera: *Paranthropus* and a later species of *Australopithecus*
  - Early *Homo* (2.4–1.4 mya) The first members of our genus, who around 2 mya likely diverged into more than one species

What's Important

Key Early Hominin Fossil Discoveries from Africa

Dates	Hominins	Sites/Regions	The Big Picture
1.8–1.4 mya	Early *Homo*	Olduvai; E. Turkana (E. Africa)	Bigger-brained; possible ancestor of later *Homo*
1.9 mya	*Australopithecus sediba*	Malapa (S. Africa)	Possibly a transitional species between *Australopithecus* and *Homo,* but this interpretation is controversial
2.5–2.0 mya	Later *Australopithecus* (*A. africanus*)	Taung; Sterkfontein (S. Africa)	Quite derived; likely evolutionary dead end
2.0–1.0 mya	Later *Paranthropus*	Several sites (E. and S. Africa)	Highly derived; very likely evolutionary dead end
2.4 mya	*Paranthropus aethiopicus*	W. Turkana (E. Africa)	Earliest robust australopith; likely ancestor of later *Paranthropus*
3.6–3.0 mya	*Australopithecus afarensis*	Laetoli; Hadar (E. Africa)	Many fossils; very well studied; earliest well-documented biped; possible ancestor of all later hominins
4.4 mya	*Ardipithecus ramidus*	Aramis (E. Africa)	Many fossils; comprehensive studies completed in 2010, but interpretations are controversial. Some characteristics indicate a hominin pattern, including bipedal locomotion, but other traits show a very unusual and highly derived adaptation.
7.0–6.0 mya	*Sahelanthropus*	Toros-Menalla (central Africa)	The earliest hominin; bipedal?

© Cengage Learning 2013

Critical Thinking Questions

1. Assume you have been asked to compare the paleoanthropological evidence (including hominin fossils) from two sites in East Africa. What sorts of dating techniques might you use and why would you choose one vs. another? Be sure to discuss and compare at least one relative dating and one chronometric dating technique.

2. In what ways are the remains of *Sahelanthropus* and *Ardipithecus* primitive? Why do many paleoanthropologists classify these forms as hominins? How sure are we?

3. Assume that you are in the laboratory analyzing the Lucy *A. afarensis* skeleton. You also have complete skeletons from a chimpanzee and a modern human. (a) Which parts of the Lucy skeleton are more similar to the chimpanzee? Which are more similar to the human? (b) Which parts of the Lucy skeleton are most informative?

4. What is a phylogeny? Construct one for early hominins (7.0–1.0 mya). Make sure you can describe what conclusions your scheme makes. Also, try to defend it.

Paleoanthropology:
On the Trail of Our Early Ancestors and the Environments in Which They Lived

© Russell L. Ciochon

◀ Researchers from the University of Iowa and the Bandung Institue of Technology working in Java (Indonesia) on geological beds to gather data on ancient environments.

As we discussed in Chapter 9, paleoanthropology is a multidisciplinary science, drawing on the skills of many experts. Because sites are often found in remote, largely inaccessible locales, their discovery has traditionally been arduous and time-consuming. In fact, sites of the appropriate age and with any likelihood of containing fossils are generally found in very restricted areas of the world (especially in Africa).

After a potentially productive region has been identified, many long hours of ground surveying are required to find the fossils themselves. In most cases, and with any good fortune at all, numerous remains of nonhominin animals (such as elephant, pig, and antelope) will be found. However, the discovery of hominin fossils themselves is always a problematic undertaking. Thus, a truly successful paleoanthropological project (i.e., one that attracts public attention and funding) requires not just good science, but a considerable degree of luck as well.

Fossils are most often found scattered on the ground surface as they erode out from sediments (through the combined action of wind, rain, and gravity). When fossils are located, their precise position is recorded.

The fossils frequently are found heavily encrusted in hard rock (called matrix) and thus require many years of enormous effort in their cleaning and reconstruction (i.e., putting the fragments back together).

. . . a truly successful paleoanthropological project requires not just good science, but a considerable degree of luck as well.

◀ Top: When large areas of geological exposures are surveyed, geological and paleontological localities are mapped.

◀ Upper middle: Areas where exposures occur and weathering exposes fossils are carefully inspected to identify significant finds (even fragments) of non-hominin as well as hominin remains.

◀ Lower middle: If (and with considerable good fortune) hominin remains are found, they are collected very carefully. Here, Yoel Rak of Tel Aviv University and the Institute of Human Origins flags the precise location of each fragment of an *Australopithecus afarensis* cranium from Hadar, Ethiopia.

◀ Bottom: Even the most careful searching and hand sifting cannot locate all the fossil fragments. As shown at a hominin site at Olduvai Gorge, Tanzania, to retrieve the small fragments, the surrounding soil is screened through a fine mesh and then sifted again by hand.

▲ In many cases, fossils are found completely embedded in surrounding matrix, and much patience and skill are required to remove the fossil fragments from the rock. This specimen comes from Sterkfontein in South Africa, where fossils are typically embedded in limestone matrix called breccia.

261

The first hominins appeared in Africa more than 6 mya.

Hominins dispersed out of Africa into Eurasia about 2 million years ago.

Premodern humans, including Neandertals, were the immediate predecessors of modern humans.

10

The First Dispersal of the Genus *Homo*: *Homo erectus* and Contemporaries

It's estimated that more than 1 million people now cross national borders every day. Some travel for business, some for pleasure, and others may be seeking refuge from persecution in their own countries. Regardless, it seems that modern humans have wanderlust—a desire to see distant places. Our most distant hominin ancestors were essentially homebodies, staying in fairly restricted areas, exploiting the local resources, and trying to stay out of harm's way. In this respect, they were much like other primate species.

One thing is certain: All these early hominins were restricted to Africa. When did hominins first leave Africa? What were they like, and why did they leave their ancient homeland? Did they differ physically from their australopith and early *Homo* forebears, and did they have new behavioral and cultural capabilities that helped them successfully exploit new environments?

It would be a romantic misconception to think of these first hominin transcontinental emigrants as "brave pioneers, boldly going where no one had gone before." They weren't deliberately striking out to go someplace in particular. It's not as though they had a map! Still, for what they did, deliberate or not, we owe them a lot.

Sometime close to 2 mya, something decisive occurred in human evolution. As the title of this chapter suggests, for the first time, hominins expanded widely out of Africa into other areas of the Old World. Because all the early fossils have been found *only* in Africa, it seems that hominins were restricted to that continent for perhaps as long as 5 million years. The later, more widely dispersed hominins were quite different both anatomically and behaviorally from their African ancestors. They were much larger, more committed to a completely terrestrial habitat, used more elaborate stone tools, and probably ate meat.

There is some variation among the different geographical groups of these highly successful hominins, and anthropologists still debate how to classify them. In particular, new discoveries from Europe are forcing a major reevaluation of exactly which were the first to leave Africa (**Fig. 10-1**).

◄ Dmanisi cranium.

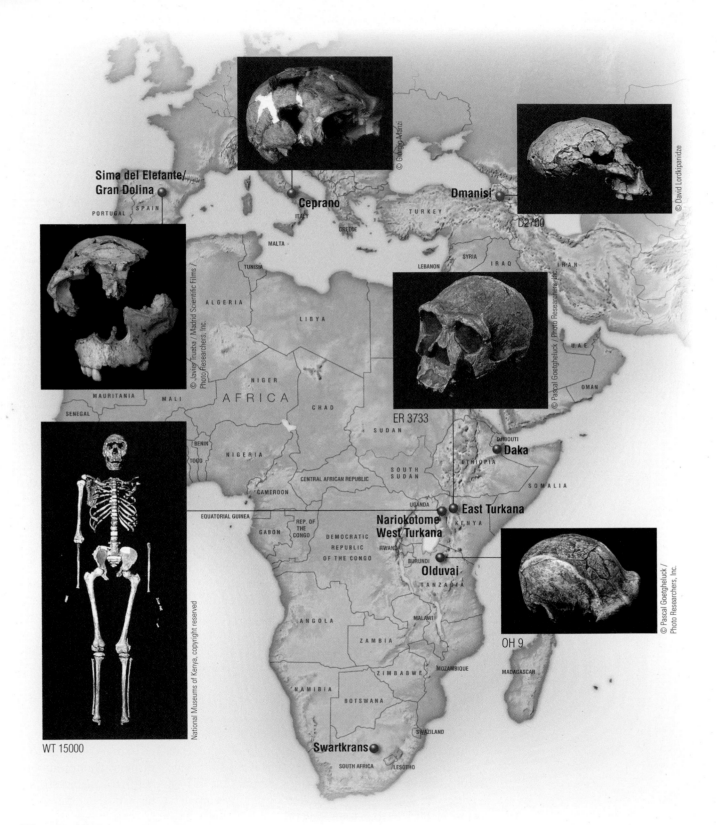

▲ **Figure 10-1**
Major *Homo erectus* sites and localities
of other contemporaneous hominins.

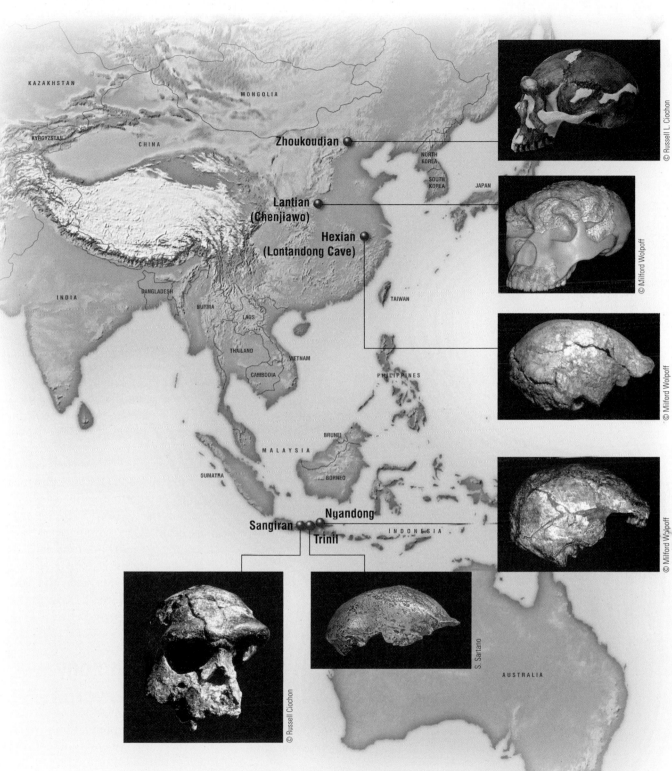

Zhoukoudian

Lantian
(Chenjiawo)

Hexian
(Lontandong Cave)

Ngandong

Sangiran

Trinil

© Russell L. Ciochon

© Milford Wolpoff

© Milford Wolpoff

© Milford Wolpoff

© Russell Ciochon

S. Sartano

© Cengage Learning 2013

Nevertheless, after 2 mya, there's less diversity among these hominins than is apparent in their pre-australopith and australopith predecessors. Consequently, there is universal agreement that the hominins found outside of Africa are all members of genus *Homo*. Thus, taxonomic debates focus solely on how many species are represented. The species for which we have the most evidence is called *Homo erectus*. Furthermore, this is the one group that most paleoanthropologists have recognized for decades and still agree on. Thus, in this chapter we'll focus our discussion on *Homo erectus*. We will, however, also discuss alternative interpretations that "split" the fossil sample into more species.

A New Kind of Hominin

The discovery of fossils now referred to as *Homo erectus* began in the nineteenth century. Later in this chapter, we'll discuss the historical background of these earliest discoveries in Java and the somewhat later discoveries in China. For these fossils, as well as several from Europe and North Africa, a variety of taxonomic names were suggested.

It's important to realize that such taxonomic *splitting* was quite common in the early years of paleoanthropology. More systematic biological thinking came to the fore only after World War II, with the incorporation of the Modern Synthesis into paleontology. Most of the fossils that were given these varied names are now placed in the species *Homo erectus*—or at least they've all been lumped into one genus (*Homo*).

In the last few decades, discoveries from East Africa of firmly dated fossils have established the clear presence of *Homo erectus* by 1.7 mya. Some researchers see several anatomical differences between these African representatives of an *erectus*-like hominin

and their Asian cousins (hominins that almost everybody refers to as *Homo erectus*). Thus, they place the African fossils into a separate species, one they call *Homo ergaster* (Andrews, 1984; Wood, 1991).

Though there are some anatomical differences between the African specimens and those from Asia, they are all clearly *closely* related and quite possibly represent geographical varieties of a single species. We'll thus refer to them collectively as *Homo erectus*.

Most analyses show that *H. erectus* represents a quite different kind of hominin than their more ancient African predecessors. Increase in body size and robustness, changes in limb proportions, and greater encephalization all indicate that these hominins were more like modern humans in their adaptive pattern than their African ancestors were. It's clear from most of the fossils usually classified as *Homo erectus* that a major adaptive shift had taken place—one setting hominin evolution in a distinctly more human direction.

We mentioned that there is considerable variation among different regional populations defined as *Homo erectus*. New discoveries show even more dramatic variation, suggesting that some of these hominins may not fit closely with this general adaptive pattern (more on this presently). For the moment, however, let's review what most of these fossils look like.

The Morphology of *Homo erectus*

Homo erectus populations lived in very different environments over much of the Old World. They all, however, shared several common physical traits.

Body Size

Anthropologists estimate that some *H. erectus* adults weighed well over

100 pounds, with an average adult height of about 5 feet 6 inches (McHenry, 1992; Ruff and Walker, 1993; Walker and Leakey, 1993). Another point to keep in mind is that *H. erectus* was quite sexually dimorphic—at least as indicated by the East African specimens. Some adult males may have weighed considerably more than 100 pounds.

Increased height and weight in *H. erectus* are also associated with a dramatic increase in robusticity. In fact, a heavily built body was to dominate hominin evolution not just during *H. erectus* times, but through the long transitional era of premodern forms as well. Only with the appearance of anatomically modern *H. sapiens* did a more gracile skeletal structure emerge, one that still characterizes most modern populations.

Brain Size

Although *Homo erectus* differs in several respects from both early *Homo* and *Homo sapiens*, the most obvious feature is cranial size—which is closely related to brain size. Early *Homo* had cranial capacities ranging from as small as 500 cm^3 to as large as 800 cm^3. *H. erectus*, on the other hand, shows considerable brain enlargement, with a cranial capacity of about 700* to 1,250 cm^3 (and a mean of approximately 900 cm^3).

As we've discussed, brain size is closely linked to overall body size. So it's important to note that along with an increase in brain size, *H. erectus* was also considerably larger than earlier members of the genus *Homo*. In fact, when we compare *H. erectus* with the larger-bodied early *Homo* individuals, *relative* brain size is about the same (Walker, 1991). What's more, when we compare the relative brain size of

*Even smaller cranial capacities are seen in recently discovered fossils from the Caucasus region of southeastern Europe at a site called Dmanisi. We'll discuss these fossils in a moment.

H. erectus with that of *H. sapiens*, we see that *H. erectus* was considerably less encephalized than later members of the genus *Homo*.

Cranial Shape

Homo erectus crania display a highly distinctive shape, partly because of increased brain size, but probably more correlated with increased body size. The ramifications of this heavily built cranium are reflected in thick cranial bone (in most specimens), large browridges (supraorbital tori) above the eyes, and a projecting **nuchal torus** at the back of the skull (**Fig. 10-2**).

The braincase is long and low, receding from the large browridges with little forehead development. Also, the cranium is wider at the base compared with earlier *and* later species of genus *Homo*. The maximum cranial breadth is below the ear opening, giving the cranium a pentagonal shape (when viewed from behind). In contrast, the skulls of early *Homo* and *H. sapiens* have more vertical sides, and the maximum width is *above* the ear openings.

Most specimens also have a sagittal keel running along the midline of the skull. Very different from a sagittal crest, the keel is a small ridge that runs front to back along the sagittal suture. The sagittal keel, browridges, and nuchal torus don't seem to have served an obvious function, but most likely reflect bone buttressing in a very robust skull.

The First *Homo erectus: Homo erectus* from Africa

Where did *Homo erectus* first appear? The answer seems fairly simple: Most likely, this species initially evolved in Africa. Two important pieces of evidence help confirm this hypothesis. First, *all* of the earlier

nuchal torus (nuke´-ul) (*nucha*, meaning "neck") A projection of bone in the back of the cranium where neck muscles attach. These muscles hold up the head.

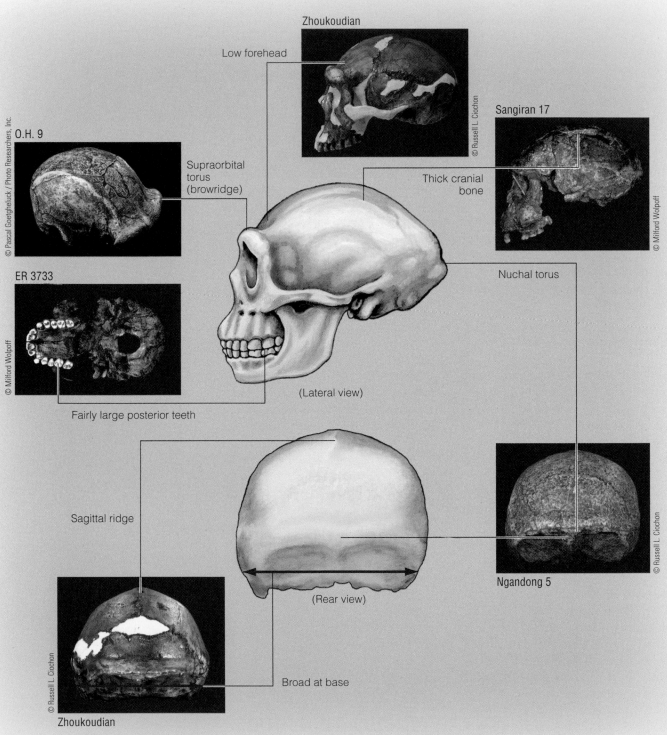

▲ **Figure 10-2**
Morphology and variation in *Homo erectus*.

hominins prior to the appearance of *H. erectus* come from Africa. What's more, by 1.7 mya, there are well-dated fossils of this species at East Turkana, in Kenya, and not long after that at other sites in East Africa.

But there's a small wrinkle in this neat view. We now know that at about 1.8 mya, similar populations were already living far away in southeastern Europe, and by 1.6 mya, in Indonesia. So, adding these pieces to our puzzle, it seems likely that *H. erectus* first arose in East Africa and then very quickly migrated to other continents; nevertheless, as we'll see shortly, the dating of sites from Africa and elsewhere does not yet clearly confirm this hypothesis. Let's first review the African *H. erectus* specimens dated at 1.7–1 mya, and then we'll discuss those populations that emigrated to Europe and Asia.

The earliest of the East African *H. erectus* fossils come from East Turkana, from the same area where earlier australopith and early *Homo* fossils have been found (see Chapter 9). Indeed, it seems likely that in East Africa around 2.0–1.8 mya, some form of early *Homo* evolved into *H. erectus*.

The most significant *H. erectus* fossil from East Turkana is a nearly complete skull (ER 3733, **Fig. 10-3**). Recently redated at 1.7 mya, this fossil is about the same age (or even just a little younger) than some other fossils outside of Africa; nevertheless, for now, it certainly is the oldest known member of this species from Africa (Lepre and Kent, 2010). The cranial capacity is estimated at 848 cm³, in the lower range for *H. erectus* (700 to 1,250 cm³), which isn't surprising considering its early date. A second very significant new find from East Turkana is notable because it has the smallest cranium of any *H. erectus* specimen from anywhere in Africa. Dated to around 1.5 mya, the skull has a cranial capacity of only 691 cm³. As we'll see shortly, there are a couple of crania from southeastern Europe that are even smaller. The small skull from East Turkana also shows more gracile features (such as

smaller browridges) than do other East African *H. erectus* individuals, but it preserves the overall *H. erectus* vault shape. It's been proposed that perhaps this new find is a female and that the variation indicates a very high degree of sexual dimorphism in this species (Spoor et al., 2007).

Another remarkable discovery was made in 1984 by Kamoya Kimeu, a member of Richard Leakey's team known widely as an outstanding fossil hunter. Kimeu discovered a small piece of skull on the west side of Lake Turkana at a site known as **Nariokotome**. Excavations produced the most complete *H. erectus* skeleton ever found (**Fig. 10-4**). Known properly as WT 15000, the almost complete skeleton includes facial bones, a pelvis, and most of the limb bones, ribs, and vertebrae, and is chronometrically dated to about 1.6 mya.

Such well-preserved postcranial elements make for a very unusual and highly useful discovery, because these elements are scarce at other *H. erectus* sites. The skeleton is that of an adolescent about 8 years of age with an estimated height of about 5 feet 3 inches (Walker and Leakey, 1993; Dean and Smith, 2009). Some estimates have hypothesized that the adult height of this individual could have been about 6 feet. However, this conclusion is contentious, because it assumes that the growth pattern of this species was similar to that of modern humans. But more recent and more detailed analyses find the developmental pattern in this and other *H. erectus* individuals to actually be more like that of an ape (Dean and Smith, 2009).

Nevertheless, the postcranial bones look very similar, though not quite identical, to those of modern humans. The cranial capacity of WT 15000 is estimated at 880 cm³; brain growth was nearly complete, and the adult cranial capacity would have been approximately 909 cm³ (Begun and Walker, 1993).

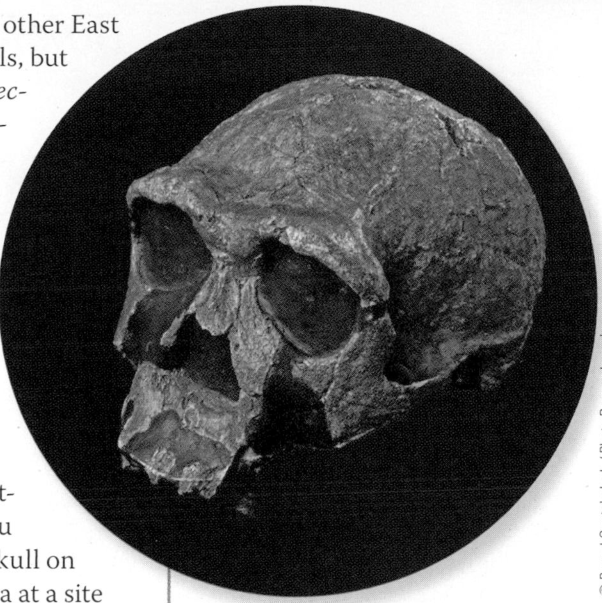

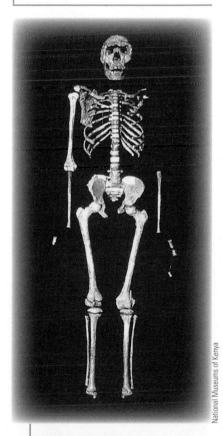

© Pascal Goetgheluck / Photo Researchers, Inc.

▲ **Figure 10-3**
Nearly complete skull of *Homo erectus* from East Lake Turkana, Kenya, dated to approximately 1.7 mya.

National Museums of Kenya

▲ **Figure 10-4**
WT 15000 from Nariokotome, Kenya: The "Nariokotome boy" is the most complete *H. erectus* specimen yet found.

Nariokotome (nar´-ee-oh-koh´-tow-may)

Quick Review

Key *Homo erectus* Discoveries from Africa

Date	Site	Evolutionary Significance
1.4 mya	Olduvai	Large individual, very robust (male?) *H. erectus*
1.6 mya	Nariokotome, W. Turkana	Nearly complete skeleton; young male
1.7 mya	E. Turkana	Oldest well-dated *H. erectus* in Africa; great amount of variation seen among individuals, possibly due to sexual dimorphism

© Cengage Learning 2013

Other important *H. erectus* finds have come from Olduvai Gorge, in Tanzania, and they include a very robust skull discovered there by Louis Leakey in 1960. The skull is dated at 1.4 mya and has a well-preserved cranial vault with just a small part of the upper face. Estimated at 1,067 cm³, the cranial capacity is the largest of all the African *H. erectus* specimens. The browridge is huge, the largest known for any hominin, but the walls of the braincase are thin. This latter characteristic is seen in most East African *H. erectus* specimens; in this respect, they differ from Asian *H. erectus*, in which cranial bones are thick.

Three other sites from Ethiopia have yielded *H. erectus* fossils, the most noteworthy coming from the Gona area and the Daka locale, both in the Awash River region of eastern Africa (Gilbert and Asfaw, 2008). As you've seen, numerous remains of earlier hominins have come from this area (see Chapter 9 and Appendix B).

A recently discovered nearly complete female *H. erectus* pelvis comes from the Gona area in Ethiopia and is dated to approximately 1.3 mya (Simpson et al., 2008). This find is particularly interesting because *H. erectus* postcranial remains are so rare, and this is the first *H. erectus* female pelvis yet found. This new pelvis is very different from that of the Nariokotome pelvis and may reflect considerable sexual dimorphism in skeletal anatomy linked to reproduction as well as body size. This fossil also reveals some tantalizing glimpses of likely *H. erectus* development. The pelvis has a very wide birth canal, indicating that quite large-brained infants could have developed *in utero* (before birth); in fact, it's possible that a newborn *H. erectus* could have had a brain that was almost as large as what's typical for modern human babies.

This evidence has led Scott Simpson and his colleagues to suggest that *H. erectus* prenatal brain growth was more like that of later humans and quite different from that found in apes or in australopiths such as Lucy. However, it's also evident that *H. erectus* brain growth after birth was more rapid than in modern humans.

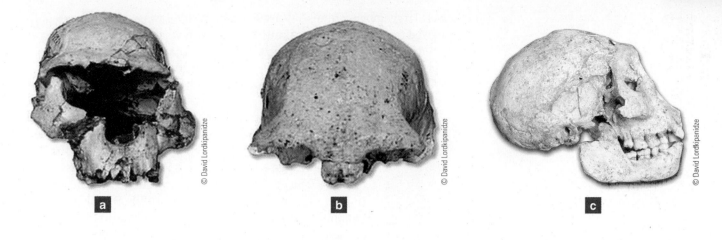

a

b

c

© David Lordkipanidze

© David Lordkipanidze

▲ **Figure 10-5**
Dmanisi crania discovered in 1999 and 2001 and dated to 1.8–1.7 mya. **(a)** Specimen 2282. **(b)** Specimen 2280. **(c)** Specimen 2700.

Another recent discovery from the Middle Awash of Ethiopia of a mostly complete cranium from Daka is also important because this individual (dated at approximately 1 mya) is more like Asian *H. erectus* than are most of the earlier East African remains we've discussed (Asfaw et al., 2002). Consequently, the suggestion by several researchers that East African fossils are a different species from (Asian) *H. erectus* isn't supported by the morphology of the Daka cranium.

Who Were the Earliest African Emigrants?

The fossils from East Africa imply that a new adaptive pattern in human evolution appeared in Africa not long after 2 mya. Until recently, *H. erectus* sites outside Africa all have shown dates later than the earliest finds of this species in Africa, leading paleoanthropologists to assume that the hominins who migrated to Asia and Europe descended from earlier African ancestors. Also, these travelers look like *Homo*, with longer limbs and bigger brains. Because *H. erectus* originated in East Africa, they were close to land links to Eurasia (through the Middle East) and thus were probably the first to leave the continent. We can't be sure why these hominins left— were they following animal migrations,

or was it simply population growth and expansion?

What we do know is that we're seeing a greater range of physical variation in the specimens outside of Africa and that the emigration out of Africa happened earlier than we had previously thought. Current evidence shows *H. erectus* in East Africa about 1.7 mya, while similar hominins were living in the Caucasus region of southeastern Europe *even a little earlier*, about 1.8 mya.* Eventually, hominins made it all the way to the island of Java, Indonesia, by 1.6 mya! It took *H. erectus* less than 200,000 years to travel from East Africa to Southeast Asia. Let's look at this fascinating evidence.

The site of **Dmanisi**, in the Republic of Georgia, has produced several individuals, giving us a unique look at these first possible travelers. The age of this crucial site has recently been radiometrically redated to 1.81 mya (Garcia et al., 2010). The Dmanisi crania are similar to those of *H. erectus* (for example, the long, low braincase, wide base, and sagittal keeling; see especially **Fig. 10-5b**, and compare with Fig. 10-2). However, other characteristics of the Dmanisi individuals are different from other hominins outside Africa. In particular, the most complete fossil (specimen 2700; see **Fig. 10-5c**) has a less robust and thinner browridge, a projecting lower face, and

---

* Note that these dates are based solely on what has been discovered so far.

Dmanisi (dim´-an-eese´-ee)

a relatively large upper canine. At least when viewed from the front, this skull is more reminiscent of the smaller early *Homo* specimens from East Africa than it is of *H. erectus*. Also, specimen 2700's cranial capacity is very small—estimated at only 600 cm³, well within the range of early *Homo*. In fact, all four Dmanisi crania so far described have relatively small cranial capacities—the other three estimated at 630 cm³, 650 cm³, and 780 cm³.

Probably the most remarkable find from Dmanisi is the most recently discovered skull. This nearly complete cranium is of an older adult male; and surprisingly for such an ancient find, he died with only one tooth remaining in his jaws (Lordkipanidze et al., 2006). Because his jawbones show advanced bone loss (which occurs after tooth loss), it seems that he lived for several years without being able to efficiently chew his food (**Fig. 10-6**). As a result, it probably would have been difficult for him to maintain an adequate diet.

Researchers have also recovered some stone tools at Dmanisi. The tools are similar to the Oldowan industry from Africa, as would be expected for a site dated earlier than the beginning of the **Acheulian** industry; this later and very important tool industry is first found associated with African *H. erectus* after 1.6 mya.

The newest evidence from Dmanisi includes several postcranial bones coming from at least four individuals (Lordkipanidze et al., 2007). This new evidence is especially important because it allows us to make comparisons with what is known of *H. erectus* from other areas. The Dmanisi fossils have an unusual combination of traits. They weren't especially tall, having an estimated height ranging from about 4 feet 9 inches to 5 feet 5 inches. Certainly, based on this evidence, they seem much smaller than the full *H. erectus* specimens from East Africa or Asia. Yet, although very short in stature, they still show body proportions (such as leg length) like that of *H. erectus* (and *H. sapiens*) and quite different from that seen in earlier hominins.

Based on the evidence from Dmanisi, we can assume that *Homo erectus* was the first hominin to leave Africa. Although the Dmanisi specimens are small in both stature and cranial capacity, they have specific characteristics that identify them as *H. erectus* (for example, a sagittal keel and low braincase). So, for now, the Dmanisi hominins are thought to be *H. erectus*, although an early and quite different variety from that found almost anywhere else.

Though new and thus tentative, the recent evidence raises important and exciting possibilities. The Dmanisi findings suggest that the first hominins to leave Africa were quite possibly a small-bodied very early form of *H. erectus*, possessing smaller brains than later *H. erectus* and carrying with them a typical African Oldowan stone tool culture.

Also, the Dmanisi hominins had none of the adaptations hypothesized to be essential to hominin migration—that is, being tall and having relatively large brains. Another explanation may be that there were *two* migrations out of Africa at this time: one consisting of the small-brained, short-statured Dmanisi hominins and an almost immediate second migration that founded the well-recognized *H. erectus* populations of Java and China. All this evidence is so new, however, that it's too soon even to predict what further revisions may be required.

▲ Figure 10-6
Most recently discovered cranium from Dmanisi, almost totally lacking in teeth (with both upper and lower jaws showing advanced bone resorption).

© David Lordkipanidze

Acheulian (ash´-oo-lay-en) Pertaining to a stone tool industry from the Early and Middle Pleistocene; characterized by a large proportion of bifacial tools (flaked on both sides). Acheulian tool kits are common in Africa, Southwest Asia, and western Europe, but they're thought to be less common elsewhere. Also spelled Acheulean.

Homo erectus from Indonesia

After the publication of *On the Origin of Species*, debates about evolution were prevalent throughout Europe. While many theorists simply stayed home and debated the merits of natural selection and the likely course of human evolution, one young Dutch anatomist decided to go find evidence of it. Eugene Dubois (1858–1940) enlisted in the Dutch East Indian Army and was shipped to the island of Sumatra, Indonesia, to look for what he called "the missing link."

In October 1891, after moving his search to the neighboring island of Java, Dubois' field crew unearthed a skullcap along the Solo River near the town of Trinil—a fossil that was to become internationally famous as the first recognized human ancestor (**Fig. 10-7**). The following year, a human femur was recovered about 15 yards upstream in what Dubois claimed was the same level as the skullcap, and he assumed that the skullcap (with a cranial capacity of slightly over 900 cm³) and the femur belonged to the same individual.

Counting the initial find plus later discoveries, so far, all the *H. erectus* fossil remains have come from six sites located in eastern Java. The dating of these fossils has been hampered by the complex nature of Javanese geology, but it's generally accepted that most of the fossils belong to the Early to Middle **Pleistocene** and are between 1.6 and 1 million years old. What's more, there was also a very late surviving *H. erectus* group in Java that apparently managed to survive there until less than 100,000 years ago.

These fossils from the Ngandong site are by far the most recent group of *H. erectus* fossils from Java or anywhere else. At Ngandong, an excavation along an ancient river terrace produced 11 mostly complete hominin skulls. Some estimates of the age of the Ngandong *H. erectus* fossils suggest-ed an age of only 50,000–25,000 years ago (ya). These dates are quite controversial, and further evidence is better establishing a *very* late survival of *H. erectus* in Java (approximately 70,000–40,000 ya) (Yokoyama et al., 2008). So these individuals would be contemporary with *H. sapiens*—which, by this time, had expanded widely throughout the Old World and into Australia around 60,000–40,000 ya. Recent work on the old excavation site of Ngandong (first excavated in the early 1930s) has led to a rediscovery of the fossil bed where the 14 individuals had been found (Ciochon et al., 2009). New dating techniques and fossil identification will be undertaken to better understand site formation and taphonomy. As we'll see in Chapter 12, even later—and very unusual—hominins have been found not far away, apparently evolving while isolated on another Indonesian island.

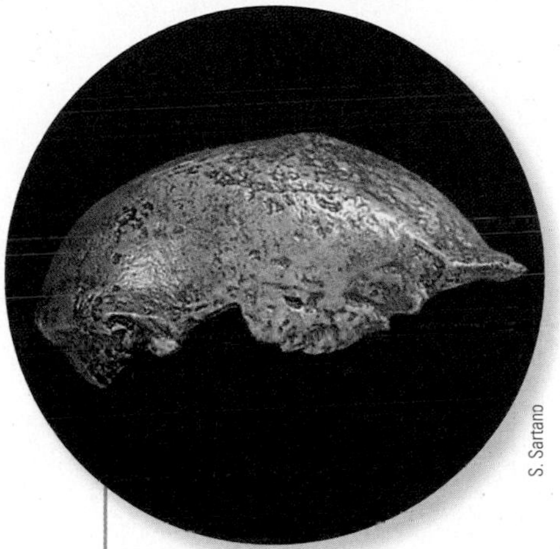

Homo erectus from China

The story of the first discoveries of Chinese *H. erectus* is another saga filled with excitement, hard work, luck, and misfortune. Europeans had known for a long time that "dragon bones," used by the Chinese as medicine and aphrodisiacs, were actually ancient mammal bones. Scientists eventually located one of the sources of these bones near Beijing at a site called **Zhoukoudian**. Serious excavations were begun there in the 1920s, and in 1929, a fossil skull was discovered. The skull turned out to be a juvenile's, and although it was thick, low, and relatively small, there was no doubt that it belonged to an early hominin.

Zhoukoudian *Homo erectus*

The fossil remains of *H. erectus* discovered in the 1920s and 1930s, as well

S. Sartano

▲ **Figure 10-7**
The famous Trinil skullcap discovered by Eugene Dubois near the Solo River in Java. Discovered in 1891, this was the first fossil human found outside of Europe or Africa.

Pleistocene The epoch of the Cenozoic from 1.8 mya until 10,000 ya. Frequently referred to as the Ice Age, this epoch is associated with continental glaciations in northern latitudes.

Zhoukoudian (Zhoh´-koh-dee´-en)

▼ Figure 10-8
Zhoukoudian cave.

© Russell L. Ciochon

as some more recent excavations at Zhoukoudian (**Fig. 10-8**), are by far the largest collection of *H. erectus* material found anywhere. This excellent sample includes 14 skullcaps (**Fig. 10-9**), other cranial pieces, and more than 100 isolated teeth, but only a scattering of postcranial elements (Jia and Huang, 1990). Various interpretations to account for this unusual pattern of preservation have been offered, ranging from ritualistic treatment or cannibalism to the more mundane suggestion that the *H. erectus* remains are simply the leftovers of the meals of giant hyenas. The hominin remains were studied, and casts were made immediately, which proved invaluable, because the original specimens were lost during the American evacuation of China at the start of World War II.

The hominin remains belong to upward of 40 adults and children and together provide a good overall picture of Chinese *H. erectus*. Like the materials from Java, they have typical *H. erectus* features, including a large browridge and nuchal torus. Also, the skull has thick bones, a sagittal keel, and a protruding face and is broadest near the bottom. This site, along with others in China, has been difficult to date accurately. Although Zhoukoudian was previously dated to about 500,000 ya, a new radiometric dating technique that measures isotopes of aluminum and beryllium shows that Zhoukoudian is actually considerably older, with a dating estimate of approximately 780,000 ya (Ciochon and Bettis, 2009; Shen et al., 2009).

Cultural Remains from Zhoukoudian

More than 100,000 artifacts have been recovered from this vast site, which was occupied intermittently for many thousands of years. The earliest tools are generally crude and shapeless, but they become more refined over time. Common tools at the site are choppers and chopping tools, but retouched flakes were fashioned into scrapers, points, burins, and awls (**Fig. 10-10**).

The way of life at Zhoukoudian has traditionally been described as that of hunter-gatherers who killed deer, horses, and other animals. Fragments of charred ostrich eggshells and abundant deposits of hackberry seeds unearthed in the cave suggest that these hominins supplemented their diet of meat by gathering herbs, wild fruits, tubers, and eggs. Layers of what has long been thought to be ash in the cave (over 18 feet deep at one point) have been interpreted as indicating the use of fire by *H. erectus*.

More recently, several researchers have challenged this picture of Zhoukoudian life. Lewis Binford and colleagues (Binford and Ho, 1985; Binford and Stone, 1986a, 1986b) reject the description of *H. erectus* as hunters and argue that the evidence clearly points more accurately to scavenging. Using advanced archaeological anal-

▶ Figure 10-9
Composite cranium of Zhoukoudian *Homo erectus*, reconstructed by Ian Tattersall and Gary Sawyer, of the American Museum of Natural History in New York.

© Russell L. Ciochon

Graver, or burin

Flint awl

Flint point

Quartzite chopper

◄ **Figure 10-10**
Chinese tools from Middle Pleistocene sites. (Adapted from Wu and Olsen, 1985.)

yses, Noel Boaz and colleagues have even questioned whether the *H. erectus* remains at Zhoukoudian represent evidence of hominin habitation of the cave. By comparing the types of bones, as well as the damage to the bones, with that seen in contemporary carnivore dens, Boaz and Ciochon (2001) have suggested that much of the material in the cave likely accumulated through the activities of extinct giant hyenas. In fact, they hypothesize that most of the *H. erectus* remains, too, are the leftovers of hyena meals. Boaz and his colleagues do recognize that the tools in the cave, and possibly the cut marks on some of the animal bones, provide evidence of hominin activities at Zhoukoudian.

Probably the most intriguing archaeological aspect of the presumed hominin behavior at Zhoukoudian has been the long-held assumption that *H. erectus* deliberately used fire inside the cave. Controlling fire was one of the major cultural breakthroughs of all prehistory. By providing warmth, a means of cooking, light to further modify tools, and protection, controlled fire would have been a giant technological innovation. Though some potential early African sites have yielded evidence that to some have suggested hominin control of fire, it's long been assumed that the first *definite* evidence of hominin fire use comes from Zhoukoudian. Now even this assumption has been challenged.

In the course of further excavations at Zhoukoudian during the 1990s, researchers carefully collected and analyzed soil samples for distinctive chemical signatures that would show whether fire had been present in the cave (Weiner et al., 1998). They determined that burnt bone was only rarely found in association with tools. And in most cases, the burning appeared to have taken place *after* fossilization—that is, the bones weren't cooked. In fact, it turns out that the "ash" layers aren't actually ash, but naturally accumulated organic sediment. This last conclusion was derived from chemical testing that showed absolutely no sign of wood having been burnt inside the cave. Finally, the "hearths" that have figured so prominently in archaeological reconstructions of presumed fire control at this site are apparently not hearths at all. They are simply round depressions formed in the past by water.

Another provisional interpretation of the cave's geology suggests that the cave wasn't open to the outside as a habitation site would be, but was accessed only through a vertical shaft. This theory has led archaeologist Alison Brooks to remark, "It wouldn't have been a shelter, it would have been a trap" (quoted in Wuethrich, 1998). These serious doubts about control of fire, coupled with the suggestive evidence of bone accumulation by carnivores, have led anthropologists Boaz and Ciochon to conclude that "Zhoukoudian cave was neither hearth nor home" (Boaz and Ciochon, 2001).

Other Chinese Sites

More work has been done at Zhoukoudian than at any other Chinese site. Even so, there are other paleoanthropological sites worth mentioning. Three of the more important regions outside of Zhoukoudian are Lantian County (including two sites, often simply referred to as Lantian), Yunxian County, and several discoveries in Hexian County (usually referred to as the Hexian finds).

Dated to 1.15 mya, Lantian is older than Zhoukoudian (Zhu et al., 2003). From the Lantian sites, the cranial remains of two adult *H. erectus* females have been found in association with fire-treated pebbles and flakes as well as ash (Woo, 1966; **Fig. 10-11a**). One of the specimens, an almost complete mandible containing several teeth, is quite similar to those from Zhoukoudian.

Two badly distorted crania were discovered in Yunxian County, Hubei Province, in 1989 and 1990 (Li and Etler, 1992). A combination of ESR and paleomagnetism dating methods (see Chapter 9) gives us an average dating estimate of 800,000–580,000 ya. If the dates are correct, this would place Yunxian at a similar age to Zhoukoudian in the Chinese sequence. Due to extensive distortion of the crania from ground pressure, it was very difficult to compare these crania with other *H. erectus* fossils; recently, however, French paleoanthropologist Amélie Vialet has restored the crania using sophisticated imaging techniques (Vialet et al., 2005). And from a recent analysis of the fauna and paleoenvironment at Yunxian, the *H. erectus* inhabitants are thought to have had limited hunting capabilities, since they appear to have been restricted to the most vulnerable prey, namely, the young and old animals.

In 1980 and 1981, the remains of several individuals, all bearing some resemblance to similar fossils from Zhoukoudian, were recovered from Hexian County, in southern China (Wu and Poirier, 1995; see **Fig. 10-11b**). A close relationship has been postulated between the *H. erectus* specimens from the Hexian finds and from Zhoukoudian (Wu and Dong, 1985). Dating of the Hexian remains is unclear, but they appear to be later than Zhoukoudian, perhaps by several hundred thousand years.

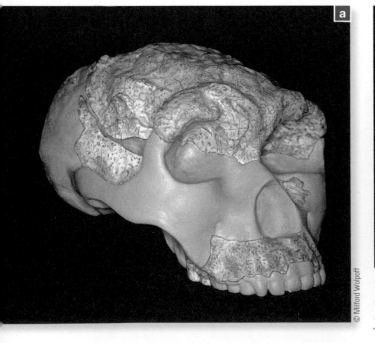

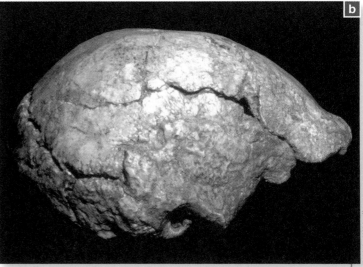

◀ **Figure 10-11**
(a) Reconstructed cranium of *Homo erectus* from Lantian, China, dated to approximately 1.15 mya. **(b)** Hexian cranium.

© Milford Wolpoff

Quick Review

Key *Homo Erectus* Discoveries from Asia

Date	Site	Evolutionary Significance
70,000–40,000 ya	Ngandong (Java)	Very late survival of *H. erectus* in Java
780,000 ya	Zhoukoudian (China)	Large sample; most famous *H. erectus* site; shows some *H. erectus* populations well adapted to temperate (cold) environments
1.6 mya	Sangiran (Java)	First discovery of *H. erectus* from anywhere; shows dispersal out of Africa into southeast Asia by 1.6 mya

© Cengage Learning 2013

The Asian crania from Java and China share many similar features, which could be explained by *H. erectus* migration from Java to China perhaps around 1 mya. Asia has a much longer *H. erectus* habitation than Africa (1.8 mya–40,000 or 70,000 ya versus 1.7–1 mya), and it's important to understand the variation seen in this geographically dispersed species.

Asian and African *Homo erectus*: A Comparison

The *Homo erectus* remains from East Africa show several differences from the Javanese and Chinese fossils. Some African cranial specimens—particularly ER 3733, presumably a female, and WT 15000, presumably a male—aren't as strongly buttressed at the browridge and nuchal torus, and their cranial bones aren't as thick. Indeed, some researchers are so impressed by these differences, as well as others in the postcranial skeleton, that they're arguing for a *separate* species status for the African material, to distinguish it from the Asian samples. Bernard Wood, the leading proponent of this view, has suggested that the name *Homo ergaster* be used for the African remains and that *H. erectus* be reserved solely for the Asian material (Wood, 1991). In addition, the very early dates now postulated for the dispersal of *H. erectus* into Asia (Java) would argue that the Asian and African populations were separate (distinct) for more than 1 million years.

As a result of the discovery of the Daka cranium in Ethiopia and continued comparison of these specimens, this species division has not been fully accepted; the current consensus (and the one we prefer) is to continue referring to all these hominins as *Homo erectus* (Kramer, 1993; Conroy, 1997;

Rightmire, 1998; Asfaw et al., 2002). So, as with some earlier hominins, our interpretation of *H. erectus* requires us to recognize a considerable degree of variation within this species.

Later *Homo erectus* from Europe

We've talked about *H. erectus* in Africa, the Caucasus region, and Asia, but there are European specimens as well, found in Spain and Italy. Though not as old as the Dmanisi material, fossils from the Atapuerca region in northern Spain are significantly extending the antiquity of hominins in western Europe. There are several caves in the Atapuerca region, two of which (Sima del Elefante and Gran Dolina) have yielded hominin fossils contemporaneous with *H. erectus*.

The earliest find from Atapuerca (from Sima del Elefante) has been recently discovered and dates to 1.2 mya, making it clearly the oldest hominin yet found in western Europe (Carbonell et al., 2008). So far, just one specimen has been found here, a partial jaw with a few teeth. Very provisional analysis suggests that it most closely resembles the Dmanisi fossils. There are also tools and animal bones

from the site. As at the Dmanisi site, the implements are simple flake tools similar to that of the Oldowan. Some of the animal bones also bear the scars of hominin activity, with cut marks indicating butchering.

Gran Dolina is a later site, and based on specialized techniques discussed in Chapter 9, it's dated to approximately 850,000–780,000 ya (Parés and Pérez-González, 1995; Falguères et al., 1999). Because all the remains so far identified from both these caves at Atapuerca are fragmentary, assigning these fossils to particular species poses something of a problem. Spanish paleoanthropologists who have studied the Atapuerca fossils have decided to place these hominins into another (separate) species, one they call *Homo antecessor* (Bermúdez de Castro et al., 1997; Arsuaga et al., 1999). However, it remains to be seen whether this newly proposed species will prove to be distinct from other species of *Homo*.

Finally, the southern European discovery of a well-preserved cranium from the Ceprano site in central Italy may be the best evidence yet of *H. erectus* in Europe (Ascenzi et al., 1996). Provisional dating suggested a date between 900,000 and 800,000 ya (**Fig. 10-12**), but more recent paleomagnetic studies have indicated a date of 450,000 ya (Muttoni et al., 2009). Philip Rightmire (1998) has concluded that cranial morphology places this specimen quite close to *H. erectus*. Italian researchers have proposed a different interpretation that classifies the Ceprano hominin as a species separate from *H. erectus*. For the moment, the exact relationship of the Ceprano find to *H. erectus* remains to be fully determined.

After about 400,000 ya, the European fossil hominin record becomes increasingly abundant. More fossils mean more variation, so it's not surprising that interpretations regarding the proper taxonomic assessment of many of these remains have been debated, in some cases for decades. In recent years, several of these some-

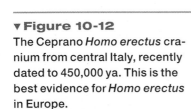
▼ Figure 10-12
The Ceprano *Homo erectus* cranium from central Italy, recently dated to 450,000 ya. This is the best evidence for *Homo erectus* in Europe.

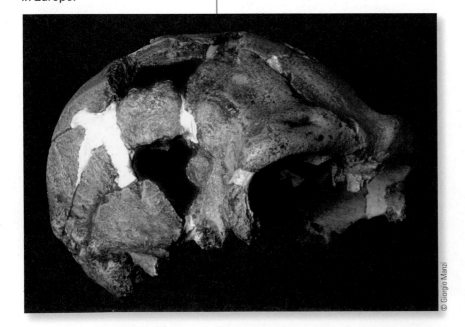

Quick Review

Key *Homo Erectus* and Contemporaneous Discoveries from Europe

Date	Site	Evolutionary Significance
900,000–450,000 ya	Ceprano (Italy)	Well-preserved cranium; best evidence of full *H. erectus* morphology from any site in Europe
1.2 mya	Sima del Elefante (Atapuerca, Spain)	Oldest evidence of hominins in western Europe, possibly not *H. erectus*
1.75 mya	Dmanisi (Republic of Georgia)	Oldest well-dated hominins outside of Africa; not like full *H. erectus* morphology, but are small-bodied and small-brained

© Cengage Learning 2013

what later "premodern" specimens have been regarded either as early representatives of *H. sapiens* or as a separate species, one immediately preceding *H. sapiens*. These enigmatic premodern humans are discussed in Chapter 11. A time line for the *H. erectus* discoveries discussed in this chapter, as well as other finds of more uncertain status, is shown in **Figure 10-13**.

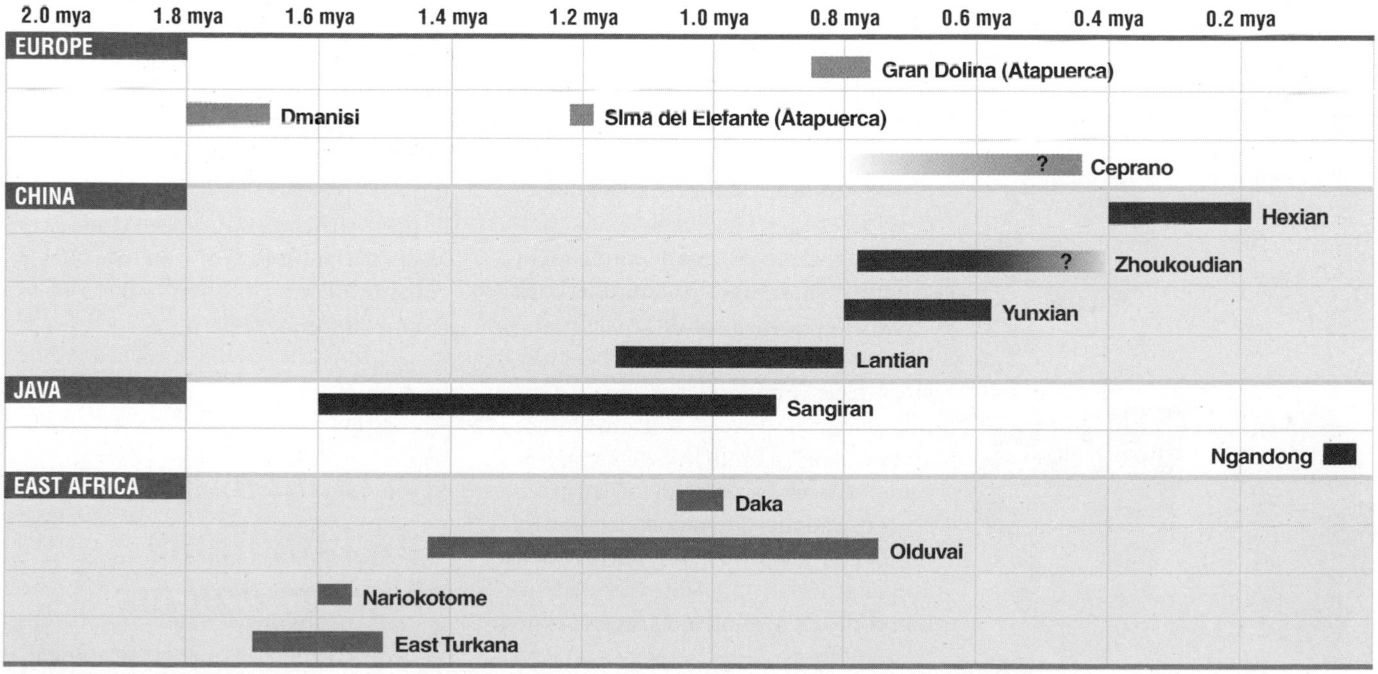

▲ Figure 10-13

Time line for *Homo erectus* discoveries and other contemporary hominins. (*Note:* Most dates are only imprecise estimates. However, the dates from East African sites are chronometrically determined and are thus much more secure. The early dates from Java are also radiometric and are gaining wide acceptance.)

▲ **Figure 10-14**
Acheulian biface ("hand axe"), a basic tool of the Acheulian tradition.

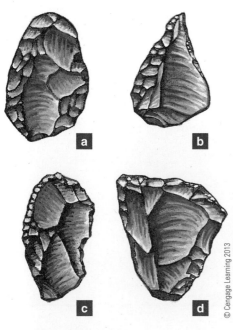

▲ **Figure 10-15**
Small tools of the Acheulian industry. **(a)** Side scraper. **(b)** Point. **(c)** End scraper. **(d)** Burin.

Technological Trends During *Homo erectus* Times

The temporal span of *H. erectus* includes two different stone tool industries, one of which was probably first developed by *H. erectus*. Earlier finds indicate that *H. erectus* started out using Oldowan tools, which the *H. erectus* emigrants took with them to Dmanisi, Java, and Spain. The newer industry was invented (about 1.6 mya) *after* these early African emigrants left their original homeland for other parts of the Old World. This new tool kit is called the Acheulian. The important change in this kit was a core worked on both sides, called a *biface* (known widely as a hand axe or cleaver; **Fig. 10-14**). The biface had a flatter shape than seen in the rounder earlier Oldowan cores (which were worked to make quick and easy flakes and were soon discarded). Beginning with the Acheulian culture, we find the first evidence that raw materials were being transported more consistently and for longer distances. When Acheulian tool users found a suitable piece of stone, they often would take it with them as they traveled from one place to another. This behavior suggests foresight: They likely knew that they might need to use a stone tool in the future and that this chunk of rock could later prove useful. This is a major change from the Oldowan, where all stone tools are found very close to their raw-material sources. With the biface as a kind of "Acheulian Swiss army knife," these tools served to cut, scrape, pound, and dig. This most useful tool has been found in Africa, parts of Asia, and later in Europe. Note that Acheulian tool kits also include several types of small tools (**Fig. 10-15**).

For many years, scientists thought that a cultural "divide" separated the Old World, with Acheulian technology found *only* in Africa, the Middle East, and parts of Europe (elsewhere, the Acheulian was presumed to be absent). But more recently reported excavations from many sites in southern China have forced reevaluation of this hypothesis (Hou et al., 2000). The archaeological assemblages from southern China are securely dated at about 800,000 ya and contain numerous bifaces, very similar to contemporaneous Acheulian bifaces from Africa (see Fig. 10-14). New evidence from India dates the Acheulian in southern Asia to at least 1 mya (Pappu et al., 2011). It now appears likely that cultural traditions relating to stone tool technology were largely equivalent over the *full* geographical range of *H. erectus* and its contemporaries.

Evidence of butchering is widespread at *H. erectus* sites, and in the past, such evidence has been cited in arguments for consistent hunting (researchers formerly interpreted any association of bones and tools as evidence of hunting). But many studies now suggest that cut marks on bones from the *H. erectus* time period often overlay carnivore tooth marks. This means that hominins weren't necessarily hunting large animals but were scavenging meat from animals killed by carnivores. It's also crucial to mention that they obtained a large amount of their daily calories from gathering wild plants, tubers, and fruits. Like hunter-gatherers of modern times, *H. erectus* individuals were most likely consuming most of their daily calories from plant materials.

Seeing the Connections: Interpretations of *Homo erectus*

Several aspects of the geographical, physical, and behavioral patterns shown by *Homo erectus* seem clear. But new discoveries and more in-depth analyses are helping us to reevaluate our prior ideas. The fascinating fossil hominins discovered at Dmanisi are perhaps the most challenging piece of this puzzle.

Past theories suggest that *H. erectus* was able to emigrate from Africa owing to more advanced tools and a more modern anatomy (longer legs, larger brains) compared to earlier African predecessors. Yet, the Dmanisi cranial remains show that these very early Europeans still had small brains; and *H. erectus* in Dmanisi, Java, and Spain was still using Oldowan-style tools.

So it seems that some key parts of earlier hypotheses are not fully accurate. At least some of the earliest emigrants from Africa didn't yet show the entire suite of *H. erectus* physical and behavioral traits. How different the Dmanisi hominins are from the full *H. erectus* pattern remains to be seen, and the discovery of more complete postcranial remains will be most illuminating.

Going a step further, the four crania from Dmanisi are extremely variable; one of them, in fact, does look more like *H. erectus*. It would be tempting to conclude that more than one type of hominin is represented here, but they're all found in the same geological context. The archaeologists who excavated the site conclude that all the fossils are closely associated with each other. The simplest hypothesis is that they're all members of the *same* species. This degree of apparent intraspecific variation is biologically noteworthy, and it's influencing how paleoanthropologists interpret all of these fossil samples.

This growing awareness of the broad intraspecific variation among some hominins brings us to our second consideration: Is *Homo ergaster* in Africa a separate species from *Homo erectus*, as strictly defined in Asia? Although this interpretation was popular in the last decade, it's now losing support. The finds from Dmanisi raise fundamental issues of interpretation. Among these four crania from one locality (see Fig. 10-5), we see more variation than between the African and Asian forms, which many researchers have interpreted as different species. Also, the new discovery from Daka (Ethiopia) of a young African specimen with Asian traits further weakens the separate-species interpretation of *H. ergaster*.

The separate-species status of the early European fossils from Spain (Sima del Elefante and Gran Dolina) is also not yet clearly established. We still don't have much good fossil evidence from these two sites; but dates going back to 1.2 mya for the earlier site are well confirmed. Recall also that no other western European hominin fossils are known until at least 500,000 years later, and it remains to be seen if any of these European hominins dating prior to 500,000 ya are ancestors of any later hominin species. Nevertheless, it's quite apparent that later in the Pleistocene, well-established hominin populations were widely dispersed in both Africa and Europe. These later premodern humans are the topic of the next chapter.

When looking back at the evolution of *H. erectus*, we realize how significant this early human was. *H. erectus* had greater limb length and thus more efficient bipedalism; was the first species with a cranial capacity approaching the range of *H. sapiens*; became a more efficient scavenger and exploited a wider range of nutrients, including meat; and ranged across the Old World, from Spain to Indonesia. In short, it was *H. erectus* that transformed hominin evolution to human evolution. As Richard Foley states, "The appearance and expansion of *H. erectus* represented a major change in adaptive strategy that influenced the subsequent process and pattern of human evolution" (1991, p. 425).

Why It Matters

Question: In this chapter, we've suggested that increased meat consumption *may* have been an important behavioral adaptation that led to increased brain and body size in *Homo erectus* and, ultimately, to geographical expansion. Does that mean that modern humans have to eat meat in order to maintain healthy brains and bodies?

Answer: One of the most significant characteristics of humans is that we are a generalized species with flexible adaptations, including diet. But for natural selection to favor increased brain size in the human lineage, as reflected in *Homo erectus*, diet had to change to maintain the energetically expensive brain. In other words, to allow for evolutionary increases in brain size, our ancestors would have had to spend all day gathering and eating the same sorts of plant foods consumed by their ancestors (the australopiths) or they would have had to find foods with greater nutrients per unit of weight. And the food category with the greatest amount of energy and other nutrients per weight is animal protein. Additionally, the pattern of amino acids that humans need for good health matches the pattern found in animal protein, providing more evidence that meat was an important component of ancestral diets. Although animal food sources, including insects, have been consumed by humans for thousands of generations, the types of animal products consumed by most people today are much higher in fat than those consumed in the past. This fat content, as well as the monetary and environmental costs attached to meat, has led many people today to minimize the amount of meat in their diet or to eliminate it entirely. It's probably fine for humans to be entirely vegetarian, as long as combinations of plant foods are used in such a way as to approximate the amino acid content of animal protein. But it's particularly important that infants and children obtain appropriate nutrients to maintain healthy brain growth in the first four to five years of life. *Homo erectus* may have been the first of our ancestors to rely on appreciable amounts of animal protein, but as descendants, we are "stuck with" not only a large brain but also the pattern of nutrients required to maintain it.

Summary of Main Topics

- *Homo erectus* remains have been found in Africa, Europe, and Asia dating from about 1.8 mya to at least 100,000 ya—and probably even later—and thus this species spanned a period of more than 1.5 million years.
- *H. erectus* likely first appeared in East Africa and later migrated to other areas. This widespread and highly successful hominin displays a new and more modern pattern of human evolution.
- *H. erectus* differs from early *Homo*, with a larger brain, taller stature, robust build, and changes in facial structure and cranial buttressing.
- *H. erectus* and contemporaries introduced more sophisticated tools (as part of the Acheulian industry) and probably ate novel foods processed in new ways. By using these new tools—and at later sites possibly fire as well—they were also able to move into different environments and successfully adapt to new conditions.

The most important fossil discoveries discussed in this chapter are summarized in "What's Important."

What's Important

Key Fossil Discoveries of *Homo erectus*

Dates	Region	Site	The Big Picture
1.6 mya–25,000 ya	**Asia** Indonesia	Java (Sangiran and other sites)	Shows *H. erectus* early on (by 16 mya) in tropical areas of Southeast Asia. *H. erectus* persisted here for more than 1 million years
780,000–(?)400,000 ya	China	Zhoukoudian	Largest, most famous sample of *H. erectus*, shows adaptation to colder environments; conclusions regarding behavior at this site have been exaggerated and are now questioned
?800,000–450,000 ya	**Europe** (Italy)	Ceprano	Likely best evidence of full-blown *H. erectus* morphology in Europe
1.8–1.7 mya	Republic of Georgia	Dmanisi	Very early dispersal to southeastern Europe (by 1.8 mya) of small-bodied, small-brained *H. erectus* populations; may represent an earlier dispersal from Africa than one that led to wider occupation of Eurasia
1.6 mya	**Africa** (Kenya)	Nariokotome	Beautifully preserved nearly complete skeleton, best post-cranial evidence of *H. erectus* from anywhere
1.7 mya		East Turkana	Earliest *H. erectus* from Africa; some individuals more robust, others smaller and more gracile; such variation has been suggested to represent sexual dimorphism

© Cengage Learning 2013

Critical Thinking Questions

1. Why is the nearly complete skeleton from Nariokotome so important? What kinds of evidence does it provide?

2. Assume that you're in the laboratory and have the Nariokotome skeleton, as well as a skeleton of a modern human. First, given a choice, what age and sex would you choose for the comparative human skeleton, and why? Second, what similarities and differences do the two skeletons show?

3. What fundamental questions of interpretation do the fossil hominins from Dmanisi raise? Does this evidence completely overturn the earlier views (hypotheses) concerning *H. erectus* dispersal from Africa? Explain why or why not.

4. How has the interpretation of *H. erectus* behavior at Zhoukoudian been revised in recent years? What kinds of new evidence from this site have been used in this reevaluation, and what does that tell you about modern archaeological techniques and approaches?

Connections

Hominins dispersed out of Africa into Eurasia about 2 million years ago.

Premodern humans, including Neandertals, were the immediate predecessors of modern humans.

Modern humans first evolved in Africa and later spread to other areas of the world.

11

Premodern Humans

What do you think of when you hear the term *Neandertal*? Most people think of imbecilic, hunched-over brutes. Yet, Neandertals were quite advanced; they had brains at least as large as ours, and they showed many sophisticated cultural capabilities. What's more, they definitely weren't hunched over, but fully erect (as hominins had been for millions of years). In fact, Neandertals and their immediate predecessors could easily be called human.

That brings us to possibly the most basic of all questions: What does it mean to be human? The meaning of this term is highly varied, encompassing religious, philosophical, and biological considerations. As you know, physical anthropologists primarily concentrate on the biological aspects of the human organism. All living people today are members of one species, sharing a common anatomical pattern and similar behavioral potentials. We call hominins like us "modern *Homo sapiens*," and in the next chapter, we'll discuss the origin of forms that were essentially identical to people living today.

When in our evolutionary past can we say that our predecessors were obviously human? Certainly, the further back we go in time, the less hominins look like modern *Homo sapiens*. This is, of course, exactly what we'd expect in an evolutionary sequence.

We saw in Chapter 10 that *Homo erectus* took crucial steps in the human direction and defined a new adaptive level in human evolution. In this chapter, we'll discuss the hominins who continued this journey. Both physically and behaviorally, they're much like modern *Homo sapiens*, though they still show several significant differences. So while most paleoanthropologists are comfortable referring to these hominins as "human," we need to qualify this recognition a bit to set them apart from fully modern people. Thus, in this text, we'll refer to these fascinating immediate predecessors as "premodern humans."

◄ Excavation at El Sidrón cave in Spain.

When, Where, and What

Most of the hominins discussed in this chapter lived during the **Middle Pleistocene**, a period beginning 780,000 ya and ending 125,000 ya. In addition, some of the later premodern humans, especially the Neandertals, lived well into the **Late Pleistocene** (125,000–10,000 ya).

The Pleistocene

The Pleistocene has been called the Ice Age because, as had occurred before in geological history, it was marked by periodic advances and retreats of massive continental **glaciations**. During glacial periods, when temperatures dropped dramatically, ice accumulated as a result of more snow falling each year than melted, causing the advance of massive glaciers. As the climate fluctuated, at times it became much warmer. During these **interglacials**, the ice that had built up during the glacial periods melted, and the glaciers retreated back toward the earth's polar regions. The Pleistocene was characterized by numerous advances and

retreats of ice, with at least 15 major and 50 minor glacial advances documented in Europe alone (Delson et al., 1988).

These glaciations, which enveloped huge swaths of Europe, Asia, and North America as well as Antarctica, were mostly confined to northern latitudes. Hominins living at this time—all still restricted to the Old World—were severely affected as the climate, flora, and animal life shifted during these Pleistocene oscillations. The most dramatic of these effects were in Europe and northern Asia—less so in southern Asia and in Africa.

Still, the climate also fluctuated in the south. In Africa, the main effects were changing rainfall patterns. During glacial periods, the climate in Africa became more arid, while during interglacials, rainfall increased. The changing availability of food resources certainly affected hominins in Africa; but probably even more importantly, migration routes also swung back and forth. For example, during glacial periods (**Fig. 11-1**), the Sahara Desert expanded, blocking migration in and out of sub-Saharan Africa (Lahr and Foley, 1998).

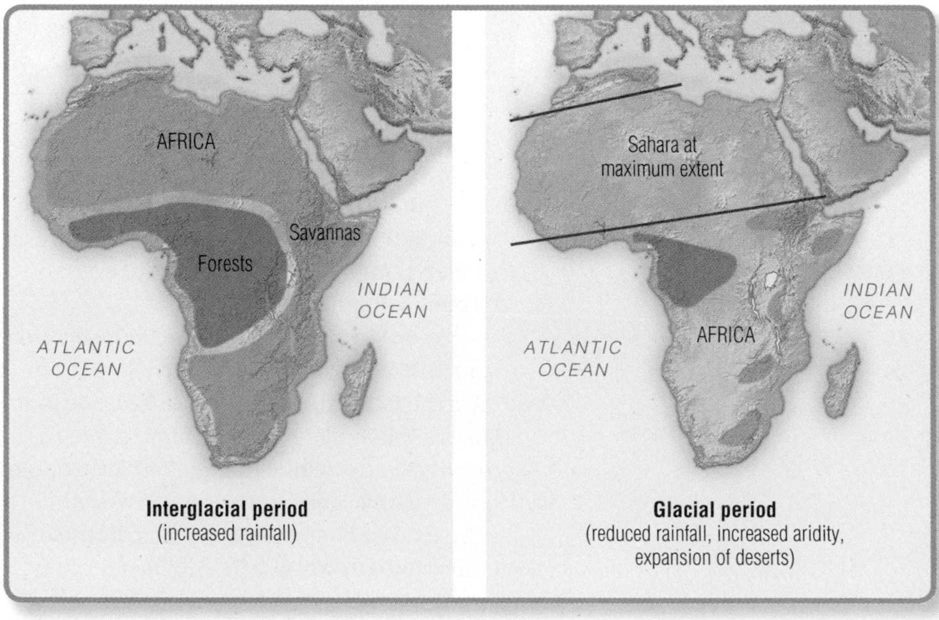

Middle Pleistocene The portion of the Pleistocene epoch beginning 780,000 ya and ending 125,000 ya.

Late Pleistocene The portion of the Pleistocene epoch beginning 125,000 ya and ending approximately 10,000 ya.

glaciations Climatic intervals when continental ice sheets cover much of the northern continents. Glaciations are associated with colder temperatures in northern latitudes and more arid conditions in southern latitudes, most notably in Africa.

interglacials Climatic intervals when continental ice sheets are retreating, eventually becoming much reduced in size. Interglacials in northern latitudes are associated with warmer temperatures, while in southern latitudes the climate becomes wetter.

▲ **Figure 11-1**
Changing Pleistocene environments in Africa.

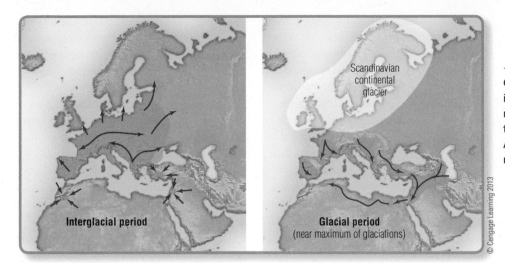

◀**Figure 11-2**
Changing Pleistocene environments in Eurasia. Orange areas show regions of likely hominin occupation. White areas are major glaciers. Arrows indicate likely migration routes.

In Eurasia, glacial advances also greatly affected migration routes. As the ice sheets expanded, sea levels dropped, more northern regions became uninhabitable, and some key passages between areas became blocked by glaciers. For example, during glacial peaks, much of western Europe would have been cut off from the rest of Eurasia (**Fig. 11-2**).

During the warmer—and, in the south, wetter—interglacials, the ice sheets shrank, sea levels rose, and certain migration routes reopened (for example, from central Europe into western Europe). Clearly, to understand Middle Pleistocene hominins, it's crucial to view them within their shifting Pleistocene world.

Dispersal of Middle Pleistocene Hominins

Like their *Homo erectus* predecessors, later hominins were widely distributed in the Old World, and discoveries of their presence have come from three continents—Africa, Asia, and Europe. For the first time, Europe became more permanently and densely occupied, as evidence of Middle Pleistocene hominins has been discovered widely from England, France, Spain, Germany, Italy, Hungary, and Greece. Africa, as well, probably continued as a central area of hominin occupation, and finds have come from North, East, and South

Africa. Finally, Asia has yielded several important finds, especially from China. We should point out, though, that these Middle Pleistocene premodern humans didn't vastly extend the geographical range of *Homo erectus*, but rather largely replaced the earlier hominins in previously exploited habitats. One exception appears to be the more successful occupation of Europe, a region where earlier hominins have only sporadically been found.

Middle Pleistocene Hominins: Terminology

The premodern humans of the Middle Pleistocene (that is, after 780,000 ya) generally succeeded *H. erectus*. Still, in some areas—especially in Southeast Asia—there apparently was a long period of coexistence, lasting 300,000 years or longer; you'll recall the very late dates for the Javanese Ngandong *H. erectus* (see Chapter 10).

The earliest premodern humans exhibit several *H. erectus* characteristics: The face is large, the brows are projected, the forehead is low, and in some cases the cranial vault is still thick. Even so, some of their other features show that they were more derived toward the modern condition than were their *H. erectus* predecessors. Compared with *H. erectus*, these premodern humans possessed an increased brain size, a more rounded braincase (that is, maximum breadth is higher up on the sides), a more vertical nose, and a less angled back of the skull (occipital). We should note that the time span encompassed by Middle Pleistocene premodern humans is at least 500,000 years, so it's no surprise that over time we can observe certain trends. Later Middle Pleistocene hominins, for example, show even more brain expansion and an even less angled occipital than do earlier forms.

We know that premodern humans were a diverse group dispersed over three continents. Deciding how to classify them has been disputed for decades, and anthropologists still have disagreements. However, a growing consensus has recently emerged. Beginning perhaps as early as 850,000 ya and extending to about 200,000 ya, the fossils from Africa and Europe are placed within *Homo heidelbergensis*, named after a fossil found in Germany in 1907. What's more, some Asian specimens possibly represent a regional variant of *H. heidelbergensis*.

Until recently, many researchers regarded these fossils as early, but more primitive, members of *Homo sapiens*. In recognition of this somewhat transitional status, the fossils were called "archaic *Homo sapiens*," with all later humans also belonging to the species *Homo sapiens*. However, most paleoanthropologists now find this terminology unsatisfactory. For example, Phillip Rightmire concludes that "simply lumping diverse ancient groups with living populations obscures their differences" (1998, p. 226). In our own discussion, we recognize *H. heidelbergensis* as a transitional species between *H. erectus* and later hominins (that is, primarily *H. sapiens*). Keep in mind, however, that this species was probably an ancestor of both modern

humans and Neandertals. It's debatable whether *H. heidelbergensis* actually represents a fully separate species in the *biological* sense, that is, following the biological species concept (see Chapter 6). Still, it's useful to give this group of premodern humans a separate name to make this important stage of human evolution more easily identifiable. (We'll return to this issue later in the chapter when we discuss the theoretical implications in more detail.)

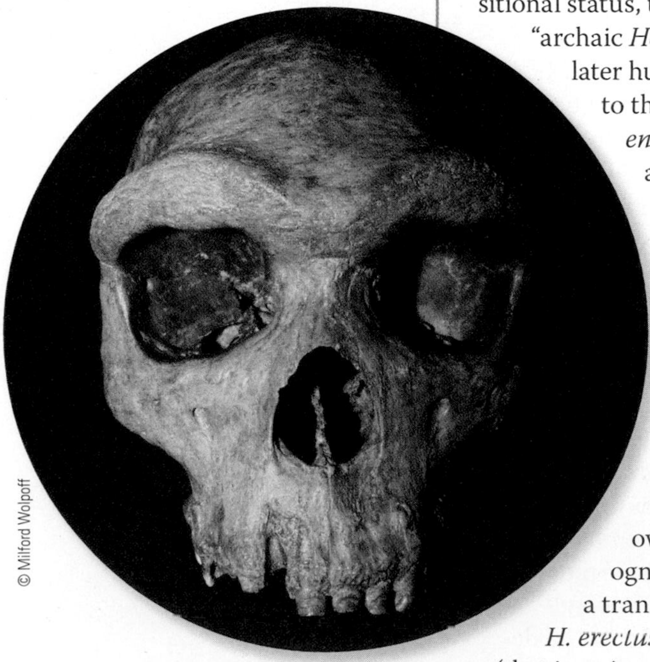

Premodern Humans of the Middle Pleistocene

Africa

In Africa, premodern fossils have been found at several sites. One of the best known is Kabwe (Broken Hill). At this site in Zambia, fieldworkers discovered a complete cranium (**Fig. 11-3**), together with other cranial and postcranial elements belonging to several individuals. In this and other African premodern specimens, we can see a mixture of primitive and more derived traits. The skull's massive browridge (one of the largest of any hominin), low vault, and prominent occipital torus recall those of *H. erectus*. On the other hand, the occipital region is less angulated, the cranial vault bones are thinner, and the cranial base is essentially modern. Dating estimates of Kabwe and most of the other premodern fossils from Africa have ranged throughout the Middle and Late Pleistocene, but recent estimates have given dates for most of the sites in the range of 600,000 to 125,000 ya.

Bodo is another significant African premodern fossil (**Fig. 11-4**). A nearly complete cranium, Bodo has been dated to relatively early in the Middle Pleistocene (estimated at 600,000 ya), making it one of the oldest specimens of *H. heidelbergensis* from the African continent. The Bodo cranium is par-

▼**Figure 11-3**
The Kabwe (Broken Hill) *Homo heidelbergensis* skull from Zambia. Note the very robust browridges.

© Milford Wolpoff

ticularly interesting because it shows a distinctive pattern of cut marks, similar to modifications seen on butchered animal bones. Researchers have thus hypothesized that the Bodo individual was defleshed by other hominins, but for what purpose is not clear. The defleshing may have been related to cannibalism, though it also may have been for some other purpose, such as ritual. In any case, this is the earliest evidence of deliberate bone processing of hominins *by* hominins (White, 1986).

A number of other crania from South and East Africa also show a combination of retained ancestral with more derived (modern) characteristics, and they're all mentioned in the literature as being similar to Kabwe. The most important of these African finds come from the sites of Florisbad and Elandsfontein (in South Africa) and Laetoli (in Tanzania).

The general similarities in all these African premodern fossils indicate a close relationship between them, almost certainly representing a single species (most commonly referred to as *H. heidelbergensis*). These African premodern humans also are quite similar to those found in Europe.

Europe

More fossil hominins of Middle Pleistocene age have been found in Europe than in any other region. Maybe it's because more archaeologists have been searching longer in Europe than anywhere else. In any case, during the Middle Pleistocene, Europe was more widely and consistently occupied than it was earlier in human evolution.

The time range of European premodern humans extends the full length of the Middle Pleistocene and beyond. At the earlier end, the Gran Dolina finds from northern Spain (discussed in Chapter 10) are definitely not *Homo erectus*. The Gran Dolina remains may, as proposed by Spanish researchers, be members of a new hominin species. However, Rightmire (1998) has suggested that the Gran Dolina hominins may simply represent the earliest well-dated occurrence of *H. heidelbergensis*, possibly dating as early as 850,000 ya.

More recent and more completely studied *H. heidelbergensis* fossils have been found throughout much of Europe. Examples of these finds come from Steinheim (Germany), Petralona (Greece), Swanscombe (England), Arago (France), and another cave site at Atapuerca (Spain), known as Sima de los Huesos. Like their African counterparts, these European premoderns have retained certain *H. erectus* traits, but they're mixed with more derived ones—for example, increased cranial capacity, less angled occiput, parietal expansion, and reduced tooth size (**Figs. 11-5** and **11-6**).

The hominins from the Atapuerca site of Sima de los Huesos are especially interesting. These finds come from another cave in the same area as the Gran Dolina discoveries, but are slightly younger, likely dating to between 500,000 and 400,000 ya. Using a different dating method, a date as early as 600,000 ya has been proposed (Bischoff et al., 2007), but most researchers prefer the more conservative later dating (Green et al., 2010; Wood, 2010). A total of at least 28 individuals has been recovered from Sima de los Huesos, which literally means "pit of bones." In fact, with more than 4,000 fossil fragments recovered, Sima de los Huesos

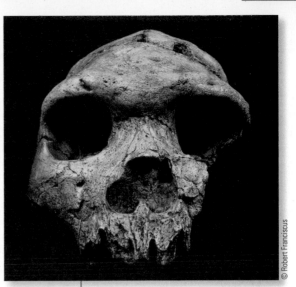

▲**Figure 11-4**
Bodo cranium, the earliest evidence of *Homo heidelbergensis* in Africa.

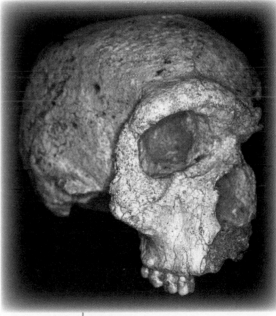

▲**Figure 11-5**
Steinheim cranium, a representative of *Homo heidelbergensis* from Germany.

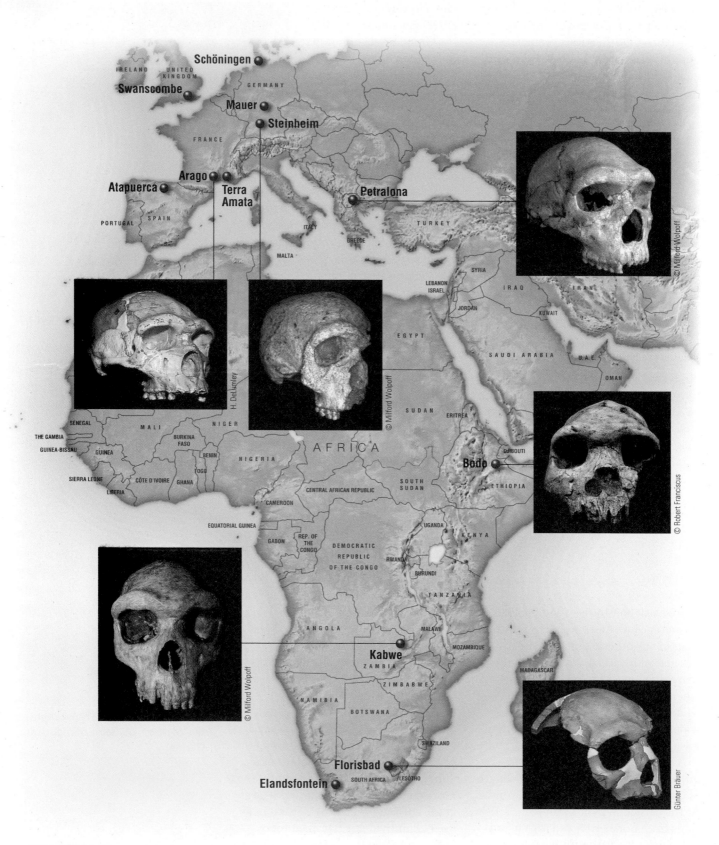

▲Figure 11-6
Fossil discoveries and archaeological localities of
Middle Pleistocene premodern hominins.

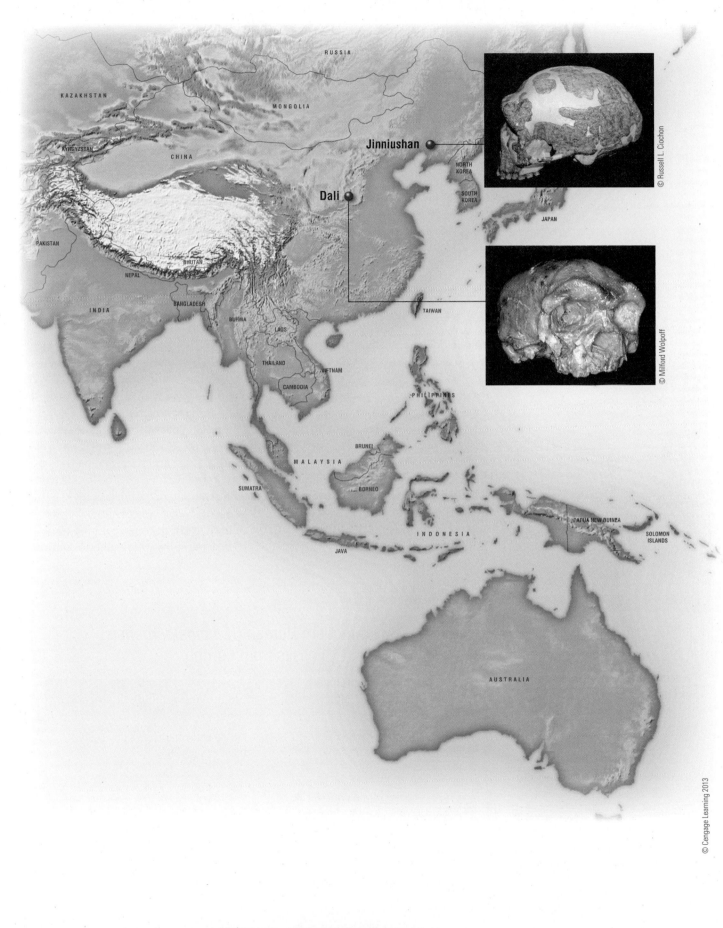

© Russell L. Ciochon

© Milford Wolpoff

© Cengage Learning 2013

Quick Review

Key Premodern Human (*H. heidelbergensis*) Fossils from Africa

Date	Site	Evolutionary Significance
130,000+ ya	Kabwe (Broken Hill, (Zambia)	Nearly complete skull; mosaic of features (browridge very robust, but braincase expanded)
600,000 ya	Bodo (Ethiopia)	Earliest example of African *H. heidelbergensis;* likely evidence of butchering

© Cengage Learning 2013

contains more than 80 percent of all Middle Pleistocene hominin remains in the world (Bermúdez de Castro et al., 2004). Excavations continue at this remarkable site, where bones have somehow accumulated within a deep chamber inside a cave. From initial descriptions, paleoanthropologists interpret the hominin morphology as showing several indications of an early Neandertal-like pattern, with arching browridges, projecting midface, and other Neandertal features (Rightmire, 1998).

Asia

Like their contemporaries in Europe and Africa, Asian premodern specimens discovered in China also display both earlier and later characteristics. Chinese paleoanthropologists suggest that the more ancestral traits, such as a sagittal ridge and flattened nasal bones, are shared with *H. erectus* fossils from Zhoukoudian. They also point out that some of these features can be found in modern *H. sapiens* in China today, indicating substantial genetic continu-

Quick Review

Key Premodern Human (*H. heidelbergensis*) Fossils from Europe

Date	Site	Evolutionary Significance
300,000?– 259,000? ya	Swanscombe (England)	Partial skull, but shows considerable brain expansion
?600,000– 400,000 ya	Sima de los Huesos (Atapuerca, northern Spain)	Large sample; very early evidence of Neandertal ancestry (>400,000 ya); earliest evidence of deliberate body disposal of the dead anywhere

© Cengage Learning 2013

Quick Review

Key Premodern Human (*H. heidelbergensis*) Fossils from Asia

Date	Site	Evolutionary Significance
230,000–180,000 ya	Dali (China)	Nearly complete skull; best evidence of *H. heidelbergensis* in Asia
200,000 ya	Jinniushan (China)	Partial skeleton with cranium showing relatively large brain size; some Chinese scholars suggest it as possible ancestor of early Chinese *H. sapiens*

© Cengage Learning 2013

ity. That is, some Chinese researchers have argued that, anatomically, modern Chinese didn't evolve from *H. sapiens* in either Europe or Africa; instead, they evolved locally in China from a separate *H. erectus* lineage. Whether such regional evolution occurred or whether anatomically modern migrants from Africa displaced local populations is the subject of a major ongoing debate in paleoanthropology. This important controversy will be a central focus of the next chapter.

Dali, the most complete skull of the later Middle or early Late Pleistocene fossils in China, displays *H. erectus* and *H. sapiens* traits, with a cranial capacity of 1,120 cm³ (**Fig. 11-7**). Like Dali, several other Chinese specimens combine both earlier and later traits. In addition, a partial skeleton from Jinniushan, in northeast China, has been given a provisional date of 200,000 ya (Tiemel et al., 1994). The cranial capacity is fairly large (approximately 1,260 cm³), and the walls of the braincase are thin. These are both modern features, and they're somewhat unexpected in an individual this ancient—if the dating estimate is indeed correct. Just how to classify these Chinese Middle Pleistocene hominins has been a subject of debate and controversy. More recently, though, a leading paleoanthropologist has concluded that they're regional variants of *H. heidelbergensis* (Rightmire, 2004).

A Review of Middle Pleistocene Evolution

Premodern human fossils from Africa and Europe resemble each other more than they do the hominins from Asia. The mix of some ancestral characteristics—retained from *Homo erectus* ancestors—with more derived features gives the African and European fossils a distinctive look; thus, Middle Pleistocene hominins from these two continents are usually referred to as *H. heidelbergensis*.

The situation in Asia isn't so tidy. To some researchers, the remains, especially those from Jinniushan, seem more modern than do contemporary fossils from either Europe or Africa. This observation explains why Chinese paleoanthropologists and some American colleagues conclude that the

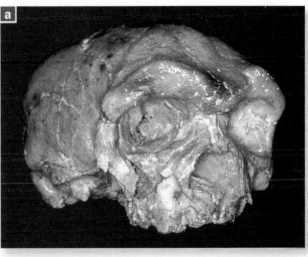
a

© Milford Wolpoff

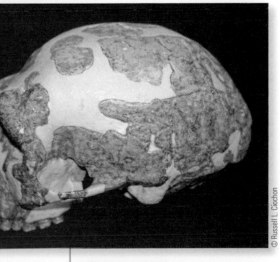
b

© Russell L. Ciochon

▲ **Figure 11-7**
(a) Dali skull and **(b)** Jinniushan skull, both from China. These two crania are considered by some to be Asian representatives of *Homo heidelbergensis*.

Jinniushan remains are early members of *H. sapiens*. Other researchers (for example, Rightmire, 1998, 2004) suggest that they represent a regional branch of *H. heidelbergensis*.

The Pleistocene world forced many small populations into geographical isolation. Most of these regional populations no doubt died out. Some, however, did evolve, and their descendants are likely a major part of the later hominin fossil record. In Africa, *H. heidelbergensis* is hypothesized to have evolved into modern *H. sapiens*. In Europe, *H. heidelbergensis* evolved into Neandertals. Meanwhile, the Chinese premodern populations may all have met with extinction. Right now, though, there's no consensus on the status or the likely fate of these enigmatic Asian Middle Pleistocene hominins (**Fig. 11-8**).

Middle Pleistocene Culture

The Acheulian technology of *H. erectus* carried over into the Middle Pleistocene with relatively little change until near the end of the period, when it became slightly more sophisticated. Bone, a high-quality tool material, remained practically unused during this time. Stone flake tools similar to those of the earlier era persisted, possibly in greater variety. Some of the later premodern humans in Africa and Europe invented a method—the Levallois technique (**Fig. 11-9**)—for controlling flake size and shape, resulting in a "turtleback" profile. The Levallois technique required several complex and coordinated steps, suggesting increased cognitive abilities in later premodern populations.

Premodern human populations continued to live in both caves and open-air sites, but they may have increased their use of caves. Did these hominins control fire? Klein (1999), in interpreting archaeological evidence from France, Germany, and Hungary, suggests that they did. What's more, Chinese archaeologists insist that many Middle Pleistocene sites in China contain evidence of human-controlled fire. Still, not everyone is convinced.

We know that Middle Pleistocene hominins built temporary structures, because researchers have found concentrations of bones, stones, and artifacts at several sites. We also have evidence that they exploited many different food sources—fruits, vegeta-

▼ **Figure 11-8**
Time line of Middle Pleistocene hominins. Note that most dates are approximations. Question marks indicate those estimates that are most tentative.

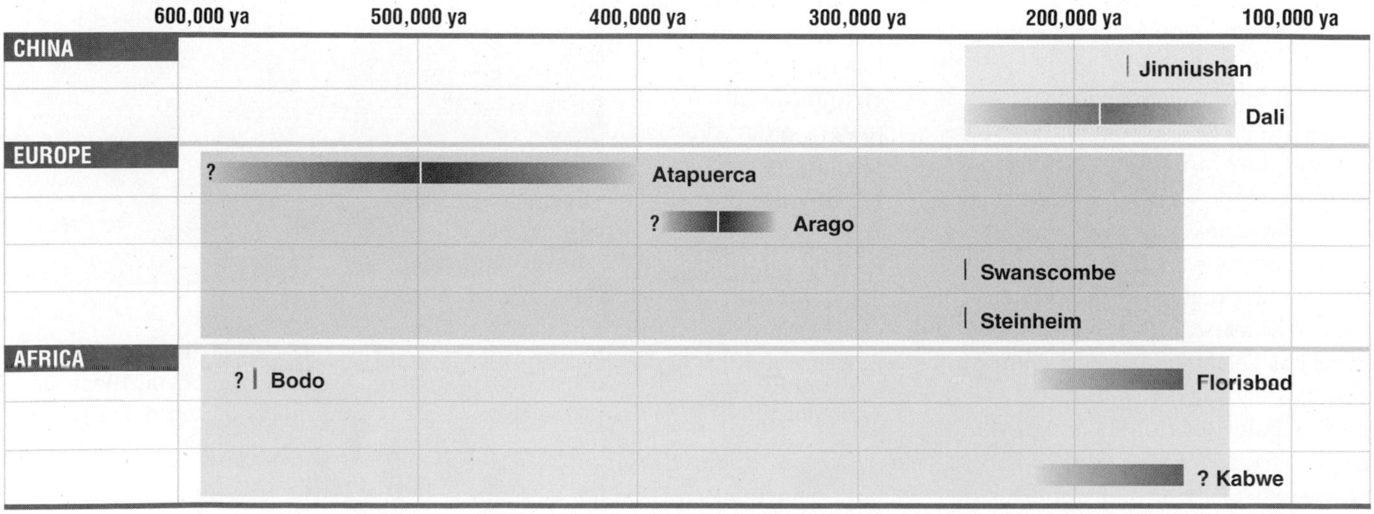

© Cengage Learning 2013

bles, seeds, nuts, and bird eggs, each in its own season. Importantly, they also exploited marine life, a new innovation in human biocultural evolution.

The hunting capabilities of premodern humans, as for earlier hominins, are still greatly disputed. Most researchers have found little evidence supporting widely practiced advanced hunting. Some more recent finds, however, are beginning to change this view—especially the discovery in 1995 of remarkable wood spears from the Schöningen site, in Germany (Thieme, 1997). These large, extremely well-preserved weapons (provisionally dated to about 400,000–300,000 ya) were most likely used as throwing spears, presumably to hunt large animals. Also interesting in this context, the bones of numerous horses were recovered at Schöningen.

As documented by the fossil remains as well as artifactual evidence from archaeological sites, the long period of transitional hominins in Europe continued well into the Late Pleistocene (after 125,000 ya). But with the appearance and expansion of the Neandertals, the evolution of premodern humans took a unique turn.

Neandertals: Premodern Humans of the Late Pleistocene

Since their discovery more than a century ago, the Neandertals have haunted the minds and foiled the best-laid theories of paleoanthropologists. They fit into the general scheme of human evolution, and yet they're misfits. Classified variously either as *H. sapiens* or as belonging to a separate species, they are like us and yet different. It's not easy to put them in their place. Many anthropologists classify Neandertals within *H. sapiens*, but as a distinctive subspecies, *Homo sapi-*

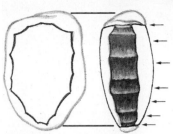

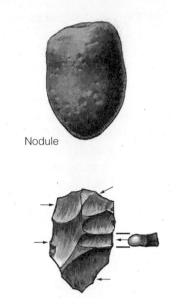

Nodule

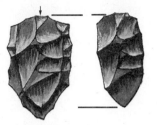

Flakes are radially removed from top surface.

The nodule is chipped on the perimeter.

A final blow struck at one end removes a large flake. The flake on the right is the goal of the whole process and is the completed tool.

© Cengage Learning 2013

▲ **Figure 11-9**
The Levallois technique.

*ens neanderthalensis,** with modern *H. sapiens* designated as *Homo sapiens sapiens*. However, not all experts agree with this interpretation. The most recent genetic evidence of interbreeding between Neandertals and early modern humans (Green et al., 2010) suggests that complete speciation was never attained. This argues against a clear designation of Neandertals as a species separate from *H. sapiens*. We'll discuss this important evidence in more detail in a moment.

Neandertal fossil remains have been found at dates approaching 130,000 ya, but in the following discussion of Neandertals, we'll focus on those populations that lived especially during the last major glaciation, which began about 75,000 ya and ended about 10,000 ya (**Fig. 11-10**). We should also note that the evolutionary roots of Neandertals apparently reach quite far back in western Europe, as evidenced

---

**Thal*, meaning "valley," is the old spelling; due to rules of taxonomic naming, this spelling is retained in the formal species designation *Homo neanderthalensis* (although the *h* was *never* pronounced). The modern spelling, *tal*, is used today in Germany; we follow contemporary usage in the text with the spelling of the colloquial *Neandertal*.

by the 400,000+-year-old remains from Sima de los Huesos, Atapuerca, in northern Spain. The majority of fossils have been found in Europe, where they've been most studied. Our description of Neandertals is based primarily on those specimens, usually called classic Neandertals, from western Europe. Not all Neandertals—including others from eastern Europe and western Asia and those from the interglacial period just before the last glacial one—exactly fit our description of the classic morphology. They tend to be less robust, possibly because the climate in which they lived was not as cold as in western Europe during the last glaciation.

One striking feature of Neandertals is brain size, which was actually larger than that of *H. sapiens* today. The average for contemporary *H. sapiens* is between 1,300 and 1,400 cm³, while for Neandertals it was 1,520 cm³. The larger size may be associated with the metabolic efficiency of a larger brain in cold weather. The Inuit (Eskimo), also living in very cold areas, have a larger average brain size than most other modern human populations. We should also point out that the larger brain size in both premodern and contemporary human populations adapted to cold climates is partially correlated with larger body size, which has also evolved among these groups (see Chapter 5).

The classic Neandertal cranium is large, long, low, and bulging at the sides. Viewed from the side, the occipital bone is somewhat bun-shaped, but the marked occipital angle typical of many *H. erectus* crania is absent. The forehead rises more vertically than that of *H. erectus*, and the browridges arch over the orbits instead of forming a straight bar (see **Fig. 11-11**).

Compared with anatomically modern humans, the Neandertal face stands out. It projects almost as if it were pulled forward. Postcranially, Neandertals were very robust, barrel-chested, and powerfully muscled. This robust skeletal structure, in fact, dominates hominin evolution

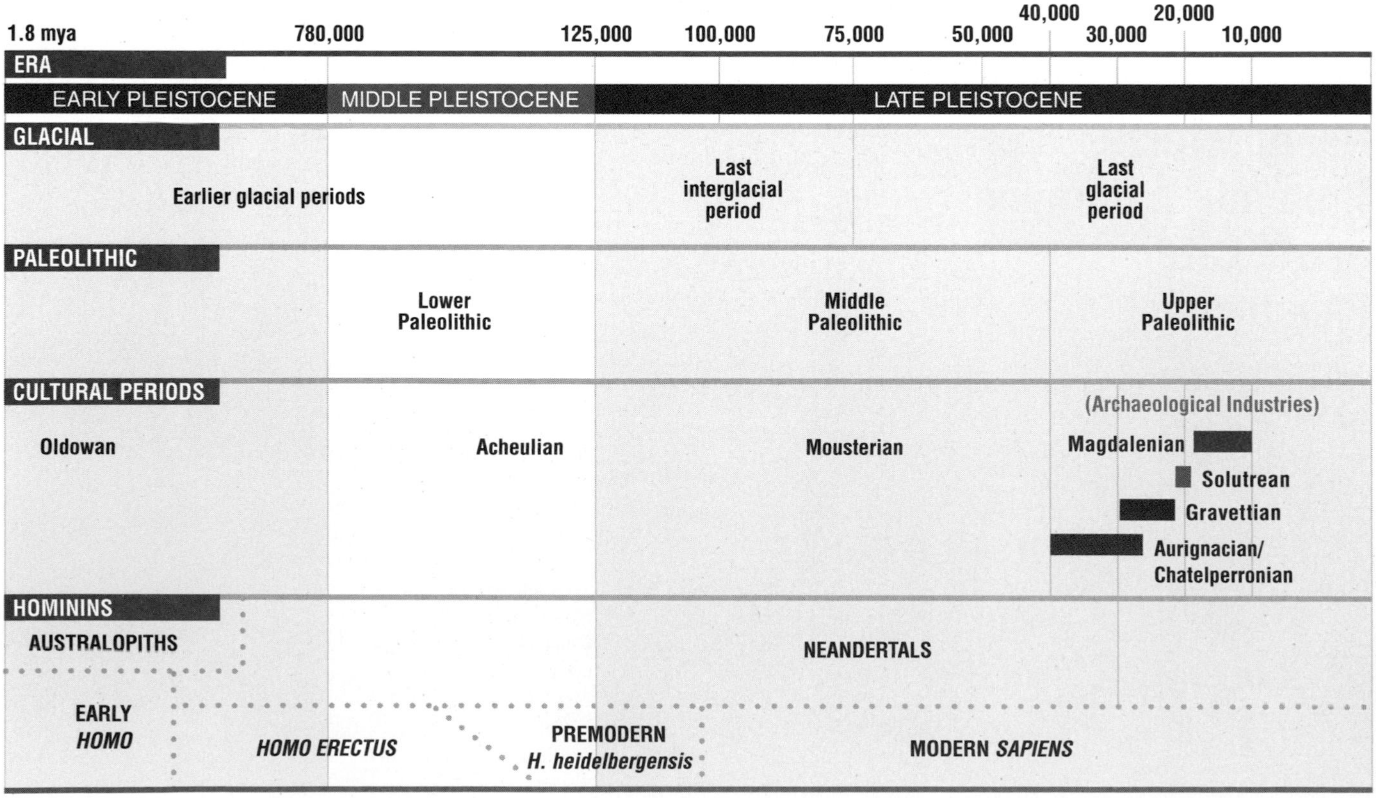

▼**Figure 11-10**
Correlation of Pleistocene subdivisions with archaeological industries and hominins. Note that the geological divisions are separate and different from the archaeological stages (e.g., Late Pleistocene is not synonymous with Upper Paleolithic).

© Cengage Learning 2013

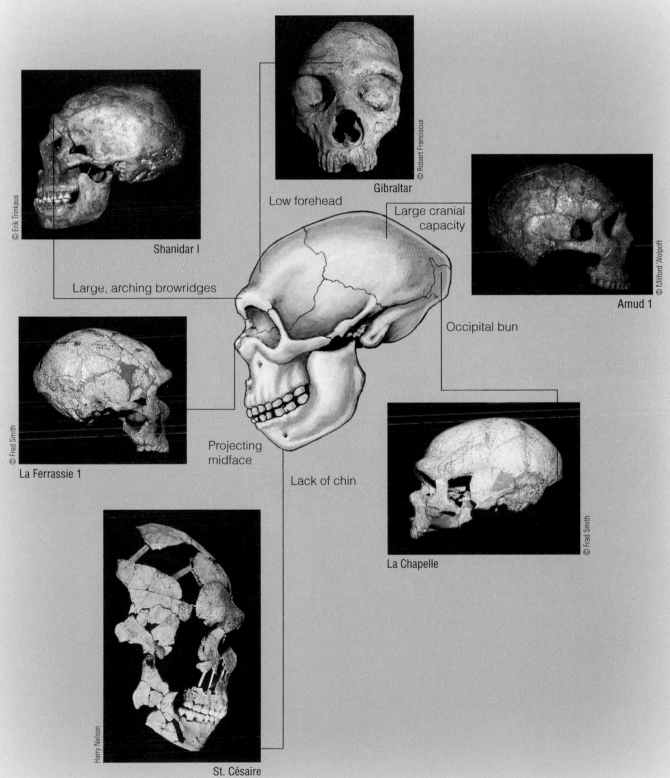

▲ **Figure 11-11**

Morphology and variation in Neandertal crania.

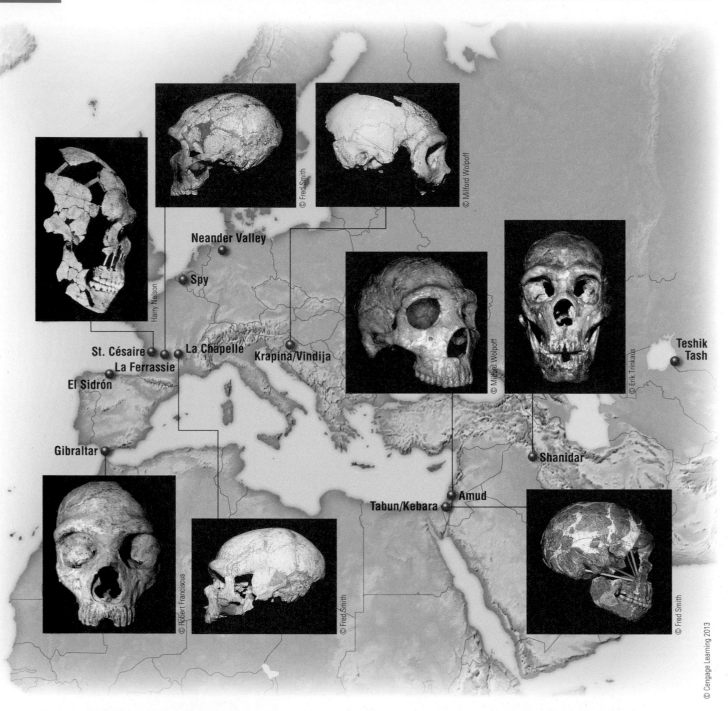

Neander Valley

Spy

St. Césaire   La Chapelle   Krapina/Vindija
La Ferrassie
El Sidrón

Gibraltar   Shanidar

                              Amud
              Tabun/Kebara

Teshik Tash

▲ **Figure 11-12**
Fossil discoveries of Neandertals.

from *H. erectus* through all premodern forms. Still, the Neandertals appear particularly robust, with shorter limbs than seen in most modern *H. sapiens* populations. Both the facial anatomy and the robust postcranial structure of Neandertals have been interpreted by Erik Trinkaus, of Washington University in St. Louis, as adaptations to rigorous living in a cold climate.

For about 100,000 years, Neandertals lived in Europe and western Asia (see **Fig. 11-12**), and their coming and going have raised more questions and controversies than for any other hominin group. As we've noted, Neandertal forebears were transitional forms dating to the later Middle Pleistocene. However, it's not until the Late Pleistocene that Neandertals become fully recognizable.

Western Europe

One of the most important Neandertal discoveries was made in 1908 at La Chapelle-aux-Saints, in southwestern France. A nearly complete skeleton was found buried in a shallow grave in a **flexed** position (**Fig. 11-13**). Several fragments of nonhuman long bones had been placed over the head, and over them, a bison leg. Around the body were flint tools and broken animal bones.

The skeleton was turned over for study to a well-known French paleontologist, Marcellin Boule, who subsequently depicted the La Chapelle Neandertal as a brutish, bent-kneed, not fully erect biped. Because of this exaggerated interpretation, some scholars, and certainly the general public, concluded that all Neandertals were highly primitive creatures.

Why did Boule draw these conclusions from the La Chapelle skeleton? Today, we think he misjudged the Neandertal posture because this adult male skeleton had arthritis of the spine. Also, and probably more importantly, Boule and his contemporaries found it difficult to accept an individual who appeared in any way to depart from the modern pattern as a human ancestor.

The skull of this male, who was possibly at least 40 years of age when he died, is very large, with a cranial capacity of 1,620 cm³. Typical of western European classic forms of Neandertal, the vault is low and long; the browridges are immense, with the typical Neandertal arched shape; the forehead is low and retreating; and the face is long and projecting. The back of the skull is protuberant and bun-shaped (see Figs. 13-12 and **11-14**).

The La Chapelle skeleton actually isn't a typical Neandertal, but an unusually robust male who "evidently represents an extreme in the Neandertal range of variation" (Brace et al., 1979, p. 117). Unfortunately, this skeleton, which Boule claimed didn't even walk completely erect, was widely accepted as "Mr. Neandertal." But

◄**Figure 11-13**
Artist's reconstruction of an adult male Neandertal based on skeletal remains from La Chapelle, France.

few other Neandertal individuals possess such an exaggerated expression of Neandertal traits as the "Old Man of La Chapelle-aux-Saints."

Dramatic new evidence of Neandertal behavior comes from the El Sidrón site in northern Spain. Dated to about 49,000 ya, fragmented remains of 12 individuals show bone changes indicating they were smashed, butchered, and likely cannibalized—presumably by other Neandertals (Lalueza-Fox et al., 2011).

Because the remains of all 12 individuals were found together in a cave where their remains had accidentally fallen, they all probably died (were killed) at about the same time. Lying there undisturbed for almost 50,000 years, these individuals reveal several secrets about Neandertals. First, they are hypothesized to all have belonged

▲**Figure 11-14**
La Chapelle-aux-Saints. Note the occipital bun, projecting face, and low vault.

flexed The position of the body in a bent orientation, with arms and legs drawn up to the chest.

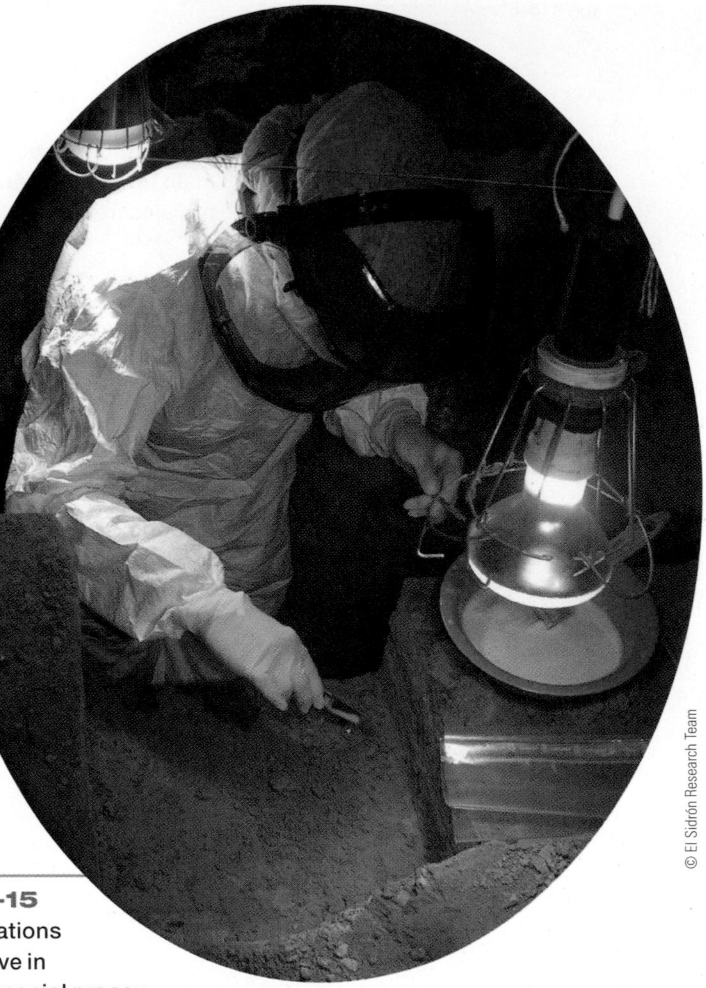

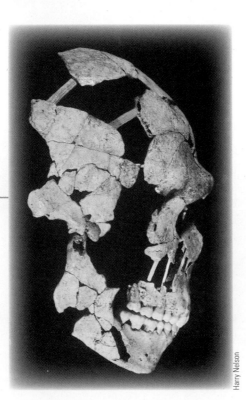

► **Figure 11-15**
"Clean" excavations
at El Sidrón cave in
Spain, where special precautions are used to prevent contamination and allow more
controlled later DNA analyses.
From this site recent evidence
from mtDNA analyses suggests
that males likely practiced a
patrilocal mating pattern.

► **Figure 11-16**
St. Césaire, among the "last"
Neandertals.

Upper Paleolithic A cultural
period usually associated with modern
humans, but also found with some
Neandertals, and distinguished by
technological innovation in various stone
tool industries. Best known from western Europe, similar industries are also
known from central and eastern Europe
and Africa.

to the same social group, representing a band of hunter-gatherers. Their
ages and sex support this interpretation: three adult males, three adult
females, five children/adolescents, and
one infant.

What's more, genetic evidence
shows that the adult males were all
closely related, but the females weren't.
It seems that Neandertals practiced
a patrilocal form of mating, in which
related males stay together and mate
with females from other groups (see
Fig. 11-15).

Some of the most recent of the western European Neandertals come from
St. Césaire, in southwestern France,
and are dated at about 35,000 ya
(**Fig. 11-16**). At St. Césaire, Neandertal
remains were recovered from an
archaeological level that also included discarded chipped blades, hand
axes, and other stone tools of an **Upper
Paleolithic** tool industry associated
with Neandertals.

Central Europe

There are quite a few other European classic Neandertals, including significant finds from central Europe
(see Fig. 10-12). At Krapina, Croatia,
researchers have recovered an abundance of bones—1,000 fragments representing up to 70 individuals—and
1,000 stone tools or flakes (Trinkaus
and Shipman, 1992). Krapina is an old
site, possibly the earliest showing the
full suite of classic Neandertal morphology (**Fig. 11-17**), dating back to the
beginning of the Late Pleistocene (estimated at 130,000–110,000 ya). Krapina is also important as an intentional
burial site—one of the oldest on record.

About 30 miles from Krapina,
Neandertal fossils have also been discovered at Vindija. This site is an
excellent source of faunal, cultural,
and hominin materials stratified in
sequence throughout much of the Late
Pleistocene. Neandertal fossils from
Vindija consist of some 35 specimens
dated to between 42,000 and 32,000 ya,

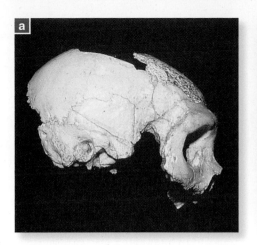

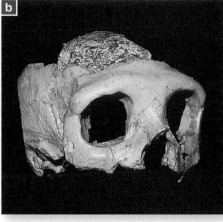

© Fred Smith

◄**Figure 11-17**
Krapina cranium. **(a)** Lateral
view showing characteristic
Neandertal traits. **(b)** Three-
quarters view.

making them some of the most recent Neandertals ever discovered (Higham et al., 2006). Given these dates, it seems that the most recent Neandertal remains yet recovered come from Vindija.

As we've seen, the Neandertals from St. Césaire are only slightly older than those from Vindija, making these two sites important for several reasons. Anatomically modern humans were living in both western and central Europe by about 35,000 ya or a bit earlier. So it's possible that Neandertals and modern *H. sapiens* were living quite close to each other for several thousand years (**Fig. 11-18**). How did these two groups interact? Evidence from a number of French sites indicates that Neandertals may have borrowed technological methods and tools (such as blades) from the anatomically modern populations and thereby modified their own tools, creating a new industry, the **Chatelperronian**. It's also possible, of course, that early modern *H. sapiens* borrowed cultural innovations from the Neandertals (who, as we'll soon see, were in many ways also quite sophisticated). What's more, we now know they very likely were *interbreeding* with each other!

	140,000 ya	120,000 ya	100,000 ya	80,000 ya	60,000 ya	40,000 ya	20,000 ya
SOUTHWEST ASIA			Tabun C				
					? Shanidar		
					Kebara		
						Amud	
EUROPE			Krapina				
			Moula-Guercy				
				La Ferrassie			
						La Chapelle	
						El Sidrón	
							Vindija
							St. Césaire

Last interglacial   Last glacial

© Cengage Learning 2013

▲**Figure 11-18**
Time line for Neandertal fossil discoveries.

Chatelperronian Pertaining to
an Upper Paleolithic industry found in
France and Spain, containing blade
tools and associated with Neandertals.

Western Asia

Israel Many important Neandertal discoveries have also been made in southwest Asia. Neandertal specimens from Israel are less robustly built than the classic Neandertals of Europe, though again, the overall pattern is clearly Neandertal. One of the best known of these discoveries is from Tabun (**Fig. 11-19**). Tabun, excavated in the early 1930s, yielded a female skeleton, dated by thermoluminescence (TL) at about 120,000–110,000 ya. (TL dating is discussed in Chapter 9.) If this dating is accurate, Neandertals at Tabun were generally contemporary with early modern *H. sapiens* found in nearby caves.

A more recent Neandertal burial of a large male comes from Kebara, a neighboring cave at Mt. Carmel. A partial skeleton, dated to 60,000 ya, contains the most complete Neandertal thorax and pelvis yet found. Also recovered at Kebara is a hyoid—a small bone located in the throat, and the first ever found from a Neandertal; this bone is especially important because of its usefulness in reconstructing language capabilities.*

Iraq A most remarkable site is Shanidar Cave, in the Zagros Mountains of northeastern Iraq, where fieldworkers found partial skeletons of nine individuals, four of them deliberately buried. One of the more interesting skeletons recovered from Shanidar is that of a male (Shanidar 1) who lived to be approximately 30 to 45 years old, a considerable age for a prehistoric human (**Fig. 11-20**). He is estimated to have stood 5 feet 7 inches tall, with a cranial capacity of 1,600 cm³. The skeletal remains of Shanidar 1 also exhibit several other fascinating features.

> There had been a crushing blow to the left side of the head, fracturing the eye socket, displacing the left eye, and probably causing blindness on that side. He also sustained a massive blow to the right side of the body that so badly damaged the right arm that it became withered and useless; the bones of the shoulder blade, collar bone, and upper arm are much smaller and thinner than those on the left. The right lower arm and hand are missing, probably not because of poor preservation . . . but because they either atrophied and dropped off or because they were amputated. (Trinkaus and Shipman, 1992, p. 340)

Besides these injuries, the man had further trauma to both legs, and he probably limped. It's hard to imagine how he could have performed day-to-day activities without assistance. This is why Erik Trinkaus, who has studied the Shanidar remains, suggests that to survive, Shanidar 1 must have been helped by others: "A one-armed, partially blind, crippled man could have made no pretense of hunting or gathering his own food. That he survived for years after his trauma was a testament to Neandertal compassion and humanity" (Trinkaus and Shipman, 1992, p. 341).

*The Kebara hyoid is identical to that of modern humans, suggesting that Neandertals did not differ from modern *H. sapiens* in this key element.

▼ **Figure 11-19**
Excavation of the Tabun Cave, Mt. Carmel, Israel.

Harry Nelson

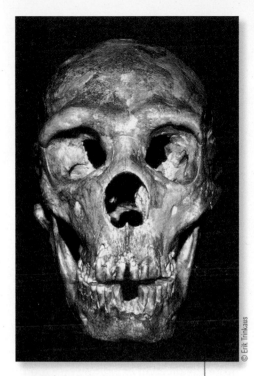

▲ **Figure 11-20**
Shanidar 1. Does he represent
Neandertal compassion for the
disabled?

Central Asia

Neandertals extended their range even
farther to the east, far into central Asia.
A discovery made in the 1930s at the
site of Teshik-Tash, in Uzbekistan, of a
Neandertal child associated with tools
of the Mousterian industry suggested
that this species had dispersed a long
way into Asia. However, owing to poor
archaeological control during excavation and the young age of the individual, the find was not considered by all
paleoanthropologists as clearly that
of a Neandertal. New finds and molecular evaluation have provided crucial
evidence that Neandertals did in fact
extend their geographical range far
into central Asia and perhaps even farther east.

DNA analysis of the Teshik-Tash
remains shows that they are clearly
Neandertal. What's more, other fragments from southern Siberia also show
a distinctively Neandertal genetic pattern (Krause et al., 2007a). As we'll see

shortly, researchers have recently been
able to identify and analyze DNA from
several Neandertal specimens. It's been
shown that Neandertals and modern
humans differ in both their mitochondrial DNA (mtDNA) and nuclear
DNA, and these results are extremely significant in determining the evolutionary status of the Neandertal
lineage. Moreover, in the case of the
fragmentary remains from southern Siberia (dating to 44,000–37,000
ya), it was the DNA findings that provided the key evidence in determining whether the hominin is even a
Neandertal. In a sense, this is analogous to doing forensic analysis on our
ancient hominin predecessors.

Surprising Connections: Another Contemporary Hominin?

In 2000 and
2008 researchers found more fragmentary hominin remains in another cave
(Denisova Cave) in the Altai Mountains of southern Siberia. Only a finger
bone and one tooth were found, and
these are dated to 50,000–30,000 ya.
From such incomplete skeletal remains,
accurate anatomical species identification is impossible. In prior years,
this seemingly meager find would
have been stashed away in a cabinet in
a museum or a university laboratory
and mostly forgotten. But in the twenty-first century, we have new ways to
study bits and pieces of ancient hominins. So the finger bone was sent to the
Max-Planck Institute for Evolutionary Biology in Germany to see if DNA
analysis could determine to which species it belongs.

Initially, mitochondrial DNA analysis was performed and provided a big
surprise: The mtDNA from the hominin at Denisnova Cave did not match
that of either a modern *H. sapiens* or a
Neandertal! What's more, the degree
of genetic distance suggested to the
researchers that the hominin line of
this "new" hominin diverged from the
modern *H. sapiens*/Neandertal line
almost 1 million years ago (Krause et
al., 2010). These results suggest that
these hominins were a completely new

species, different from modern humans or Neandertals.

Lying in a cool and dry stable environment inside the cave, the Denisnova remains stood a good chance of preserving even more complete ancient DNA. So, the Max Planck team, along with many colleagues from around the world, decided to attempt to sequence the nuclear genome derived from DNA in the finger bone (in which DNA preservation was exceptionally good). Within less than two years they successfully sequenced the *entire* genome from this one small bone, in other words, more than three billion base pairs, a truly amazing scientific accomplishment (Reich et al., 2010). These far more complete data confirmed the earlier findings, most notably that the "Denisovans" were a separate branch of hominins living side-by-side in central Asia with two other lineages of hominins (Neandertals and modern humans). The complete genome also provided another big surprise regarding how these ancient Denisovans are genetically connected to some living human populations (see "Molecular Connections" below).

Culture of Neandertals

Anthropologists almost always associate Neandertals, who lived in the cultural period known as the Middle Paleolithic, with the **Mousterian** industry—although they don't always associate the Mousterian industry with just Neandertals (since it sometimes is also found with modern humans). Early in the last glacial period, Mousterian culture extended across Europe and North Africa into the former Soviet Union, Israel, Iran, and as far east as central Asia and possibly even China. Also, in sub-Saharan Africa, the contemporaneous Middle Stone Age industry is broadly similar to the Mousterian.

Technology

Neandertals extended and diversified traditional methods of making tools, and there's some indication that they developed specialized tools for skinning and preparing meat, hunting, woodworking, and hafting (**Fig. 11-21**).

Even so, in strong contrast to the following cultural period, the Upper Paleolithic, there's almost no evidence that they used bone tools. Still, Neandertals advanced their technology well beyond that of earlier hominins. It's possible that their technological advances helped provide part of the basis for the remarkable changes of the Upper Paleolithic, which we'll discuss in the next chapter. What's more, Neandertals also were quite advanced in exploiting new food resources, as well as fashioning personal adornments.

Subsistence

We know, from the abundant remains of animal bones at their sites, that Neandertals were successful hunters. But though it's clear that Neandertals could hunt large mammals, they may not have been as efficient at this task as Upper Paleolithic modern humans. For example, it wasn't until the beginning of the Upper Paleolithic that the spear-thrower, or atlatl, came into use (see Chapter 12). Soon after that, in Upper Paleolithic groups, the bow and arrow greatly increased efficiency (and safety) in hunting large mammals by putting distance between the hunters and the hunted. Because Neandertals had no long-distance weaponry and were mostly limited to thrusting spears, they may have been more prone to serious injury—a hypothesis supported by paleoanthropologists Thomas Berger and Erik Trinkaus. Berger and Trinkaus (1995) analyzed the pattern of trauma, particularly fractures, in Neandertals and compared it with that seen in

Mousterian Pertaining to the stone tool industry associated with Neandertals and some modern *H. sapiens* groups; also called Middle Paleolithic. This industry is characterized by a larger proportion of flake tools than is found in Acheulian tool kits.

◄**Figure 11-21**
Examples of the Mousterian tool kit, including (from left to right) a Levallois point, a perforator, and a side scraper.

contemporary human samples. Interestingly, the pattern in Neandertals, especially the relatively high proportion of head and neck injuries, was most similar to that seen in contemporary rodeo performers. Berger and Trinkaus concluded that "the similarity to the rodeo distribution suggests frequent close encounters with large ungulates unkindly disposed

to the humans involved" (Berger and Trinkaus, 1995, p. 841).

Recent archaeological discoveries have shown that Neandertals also expanded their range of available foods to include marine resources—a subsistence strategy previously thought to have been developed later by modern humans during the Upper Paleolithic. From the island of Gibraltar, new

Quick Review

Key Neandertal Fossil Discoveries

Date	Site	Evolutionary Significance
42,000–28,000 ya	Vindija (Croatia)	Large sample (best evidence of Neandertals in eastern Europe); latest well-dated Neandertal site
50,000 ya	La Chapelle (France)	Most famous Neandertal site; historically provided early, but distorted, interpretation of Neandertals
70,000–60,000 ya	Shanidar (Iraq)	Several well-preserved skeletons; good example of Neandertals from southwestern Asia; one individual with multiple injuries
110,000 ya; date uncertain	Tabun (Israel)	Well-preserved and very well-studied fossils showing early evidence of Neandertals in southwestern Asia

evidence has shown that some Neandertals gathered shellfish and hunted seals and dolphins, displaying no difference in their hunting behavior from modern humans of the same region (Stringer et al., 2008).

Speech and Symbolic Behavior

There are a variety of hypotheses concerning the speech capacities of Neandertals, and many of these views are contradictory. Although some researchers argue that Neandertals were incapable of human speech, the prevailing consensus has been that they *were* capable of articulate speech and possibly capable of producing the same range of sounds as modern humans.

Recent genetic evidence likely will help us determine when fully human language first emerged (Enard et al., 2002; Fisher and Scharff, 2009). In humans today, mutations in a particular gene (locus) are known to produce serious language impairments. From an evolutionary perspective, what is perhaps most significant is the greater variability seen in the alleles at this locus in modern humans as compared to other primates. One explanation for this increased variation is intensified selection acting on human populations, and as we'll see shortly, DNA evidence from Neandertal fossils shows that these hominins had already made this transformation.

Many researchers are convinced that Upper Paleolithic *H. sapiens* had some significant behavioral advantages over Neandertals and other premodern humans. Was it some kind of new and expanded ability to symbolize, communicate, organize social activities, elaborate technology, obtain a wider range of food resources, or care for the sick or injured? Or was it some other factor? Compared with modern *H. sapiens*, were the Neandertals limited by neurological differences that may have contributed to their demise?

The direct anatomical evidence derived from Neandertal fossils isn't much help in answering these questions. Ralph Holloway (1985) has maintained that Neandertal brains—at least as far as the fossil evidence suggests (from endocasts—both natural and artificial)—aren't significantly different from those of modern *H. sapiens*. What's more, the positioning of the Neandertal vocal tract (determined by the shape of the hyoid bone), as well as other morphological features, doesn't appear to have seriously limited them.

Most of the reservations about advanced cognitive abilities in Neandertals have been based on archaeological data. However, as more archaeological data have been collected and better dating controls applied to a large number of sites bridging the Mousterian–Upper Paleolithic transition, many of the proposed behavioral differences between Neandertals and early modern humans have blurred. For example, it is now known that, like early *H. sapiens*, Neandertals sometimes used pigment (probably as body ornamentation) and wore jewelry. The most significant recent finds come from two sites in Spain dating to 50,000–37,000 ya, and both have a Mousterian stone tool industry. Since these sites were occupied *before* modern *H. sapiens* reached this part of Europe, the most likely conclusion is that the objects found were made by Neandertals (Zilhão et al., 2010). The finds include perforated shells, ostensibly drilled to be used as jewelry, as well as natural pigments that were deliberately brought to the site and applied to the shells and some animal bones (see **Fig. 11-22**).

Neandertals and modern humans coexisted in some parts of Europe for up to 15,000 years, so Neandertals didn't disappear suddenly. Nevertheless, shortly after 30,000 ya, they disappear from the fossil and archaeological record. At some point, as a recognizable human group, Neandertals became an evolutionary dead end. Right now, we can't say exactly what caused their disappearance and ultimate replacement by anatomically modern Upper Paleolithic peoples. Indeed, Neandertals didn't really disappear altogether, since a few of their genes still can be found today in many human groups.

Burials

Anthropologists have known for some time that Neandertals deliberately buried their dead. Undeniably, the spectacular discoveries at La Chapelle, Shanidar, and elsewhere were the direct results of ancient burial, which permits preservation that's much more complete. Such deliberate burial treatment goes back at least 90,000 years at Tabun. From a much older site, some form of consistent "disposal" of the dead—not necessarily below-ground burial—is evidenced. As previously discussed, at the site of Sima de los Huesos in Spain, archaeologists found thousands of fossilized bone fragments in a cave at the end of a deep vertical shaft. From the nature of the site and the accumulation of hominin remains, Spanish researchers are convinced that the site demonstrates some form of human activity involving deliberate disposal of the dead (Arsuaga et al., 1997).

The recent dating of Sima de los Huesos to more than 400,000 ya suggests that Neandertal precursors were already handling their dead in special ways during the Middle Pleistocene. Such behavior was previously thought to have emerged only much later, in the Late Pleistocene. As far as current data indicate, this practice is seen in western European contexts well before it appears in Africa or eastern Asia. For example, in the premodern sites at Kabwe and Florisbad (discussed earlier), deliberate disposal of the dead is not documented. Nor is it seen in African early modern sites—for example, the Klasies River Mouth, dated at 120,000–100,000 ya (see Chapter 12).

Yet, in later contexts (after 35,000 ya), where modern *H. sapiens* remains are found in clear burial contexts, their treatment is considerably more complex than in Neandertal burials. In these later (Upper Paleolithic) sites, grave goods, including bone and stone tools as well as animal bones, are found more consistently and in greater concentrations. Because many Neandertal sites were excavated in the nineteenth or early twentieth century, before more rigorous archaeological methods were developed, many of these supposed burials are now in question. Still, the evidence seems quite clear that deliberate burial was practiced not only at La Chapelle, La Ferrassie (eight graves), Tabun, Amud, Kebara, Shanidar, and Teshik-Tash, but also at several other localities, especially in France. In many cases, the body's position was deliberately modified, with it placed in the grave in a flexed posture. This flexed position has been found in 16 of the 20 best-documented Neandertal burial contexts (Klein, 1999).

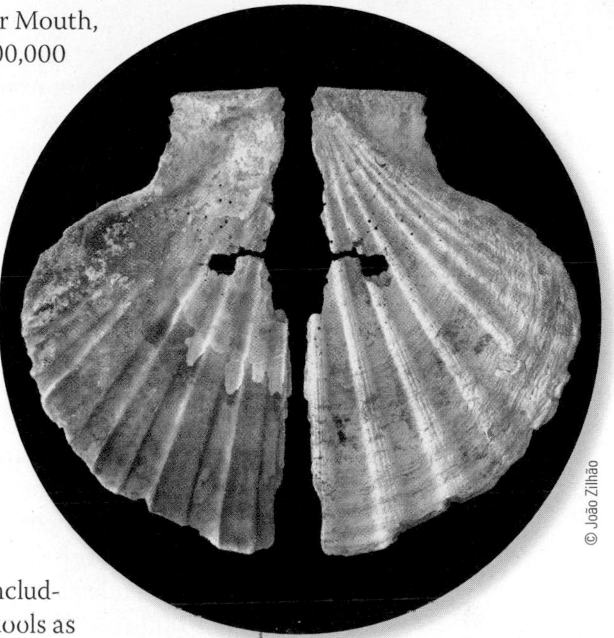

▲ **Figure 11-22**
Upper portion of a bivalve shell that has been perforated and stained with pigment, from the Antón rock-shelter site in Spain (dated around 44,000–37,000 ya). The reddish inner surface (left) is natural, but the yellow colorant on the outer whitish surface (right) was the result of an added pigment.

Molecular Connections: The Genetic Evidence

With the revolutionary advances in molecular biology (discussed in Chapter 3), fascinating new avenues of research have become possible in the study of earlier hominins. It's becoming fairly commonplace to extract, amplify, and sequence ancient DNA from contexts spanning the last 10,000 years or so. For example, researchers have analyzed DNA from the 5,000-year-old "Iceman" found in the Italian Alps as well as the entire nuclear genome from a 4,000-year-old Inuit (Eskimo) from Greenland (Rasmussen et al., 2010).

It's much harder to find usable DNA in even more ancient remains, because the organic components, often including the DNA, have been destroyed during the mineralization process. Still, in the past few years, exciting results have been announced about DNA found in more than a dozen different Neandertal fossils dated between 50,000 and 32,000 ya. These fossils come from sites in France (including La Chapelle), Germany (from the original Neander Valley locality), Belgium, Italy, Spain, Croatia, and Russia (Krings et al., 1997, 2000; Ovchinnikov et al., 2000; Schmitz et al., 2002; Serre et al., 2004; Green et al., 2006). As we previously mentioned, recently ascertained ancient DNA evidence strongly suggests that other fossils from central Asia (Uzbekistan and two caves in southern Siberia) dated at 48,000–30,000 ya are also Neandertals (Krause et al., 2007b) or even an entirely different species (Krause et al., 2010; Reich et al., 2010).

The technique most often used in studying most Neandertal fossils involves extracting mitochondrial DNA (mtDNA), amplifying it through polymerase chain reaction (PCR; see Chapter 3), and sequencing nucleotides in parts of the molecule. Initial results from the Neandertal specimens show that these individuals are genetically more different from contemporary *Homo sapiens* populations than modern human populations are from each other—in fact, about three times as much.

Major advances in molecular biology have allowed much more of the Neandertal genetic pattern to be determined, with the ability to now sequence the entire mtDNA sequence in several individuals (Briggs et al., 2009) as well as big chunks of the *nuclear* DNA (which, as you may recall, contains more than 99 percent of the human genome). In fact, the most exciting breakthrough yet in ancient DNA studies was achieved in 2010 with the completion of the *entire* nuclear genome of European Neandertals (Green et al., 2010). Just a couple of years ago, this sort of achievement would have seemed like science fiction.

This new information has already allowed for crucial (as well as quite surprising) revisions in our understanding of Neandertal and early modern human evolution. First of all, Neandertal DNA is remarkably similar to modern human DNA, with 99.84 percent of it being identical. However, to detect those few (but possibly informative) genes that do differ, the team sequenced the entire genome of five modern individuals (two from Africa and one each from China, France, and New Guinea). To the surprise of almost everyone, the researchers found that many people today still have Neandertal genes! What's more, these Neandertal genes are found only in non-Africans, strongly suggesting that interbreeding occurred between Neandertals and modern *H. sapiens* after the latter had emigrated out of Africa. In fact, the three modern non-African individuals used for comparison in this study all had the same amount of Neandertal DNA. What makes this finding even more startling is the modern non-African humans evaluated come from widely scattered regions (western Europe, China, and the far South Pacific). Further evidence, including complete genomes from another seven modern people from even more dispersed populations have further confirmed these findings (Reich et al., 2010).

The best (and simplest) hypothesis for this genetic pattern is that shortly after modern *H. sapiens* migrants left Africa, a few of them interbred with Neandertals *before* these people and their descendants dispersed to other areas of the world. The best guess is that this intermixing between the two groups occurred in the Middle East, likely sometime between 80,000 and 50,000 ya. DNA data from more individuals, both within and outside of Africa, will help substantiate this hypothesis. For the moment, the degree of interbreeding appears to be small but still significant—about 1 to 4 percent of the total genome for living non-Africans.

Another quite astonishing molecular finding also came in 2010 during the analysis of the Denisovan DNA from Siberia (see above). These ancient hominins from central Asia quite possibly represent a different branch of recent human evolution (Reich et al., 2010). They are also more closely related to just *some* populations of modern humans, sharing about 4–5% of genes with contemporary people from Melanesia (a region of islands in the south Pacific, including New Guinea, located north and east of Australia). We will focus much more on the ancestral connections of modern humans in the next chapter. As you'll see, all of us derive mostly from fairly recent African ancestors. But, when these African migrants came into contact with premodern humans living in Eurasia, some interbreeding occurred with at least two of these premodern groups. We can tell this by distinctive genetic "signatures" that can still be found in living people.

What's more, we've already had tantalizing clues of how we differ from Neandertals in terms of specific genes. As the data are further analyzed and expanded, we will surely learn more about the evolutionary development of human anatomy *and* human behavior. In so doing, we'll be able to answer far more precisely that age-old question, What does it mean to be human?

Seeing Close Human Connections: Understanding Premodern Humans

As you can see, the Middle Pleistocene hominins are a very diverse group, broadly dispersed through time and space. There is considerable variation among them, and it's not easy to get a clear evolutionary picture. We know that regional populations were small and frequently isolated, and many of them probably died out and left no descendants. So it's a mistake to see an "ancestor" in every fossil find.

Still, as a group, these Middle Pleistocene premoderns do reveal some general trends. In many ways, for example, it seems that they were *transitional* between the hominins that came before them (*H. erectus*) and the ones that followed them (modern *H. sapiens*). It's not a stretch to say that all the Middle Pleistocene premoderns derived from *H. erectus* forebears and that some of them, in turn, were probably ancestors of the earliest fully modern humans.

Paleoanthropologists are certainly concerned with such broad generalities as these, but they also want to focus on meaningful anatomical, environmental, and behavioral details as well as the underlying processes. So they consider the regional variability displayed by particular fossil samples as significant—but just *how* significant is debatable. In addition, increasingly sophisticated theoretical and technological approaches are being used to better understand the processes that shaped the evolution of later *Homo* at both macroevolutionary and microevolutionary levels.

Scientists, like all humans, assign names or labels to phenomena, a point we addressed in discussing classification in Chapter 6. Paleoanthropologists are certainly no exception. Yet, working from a common evolutionary foundation, paleoanthropologists still come to different conclusions about the most appropriate way to interpret the Middle/Late Pleistocene hominins. Consequently, a variety of species names have been proposed in recent years.

Paleoanthropologists who advocate an extreme lumping approach recognize only one species for all the premodern humans discussed in this chapter. These premoderns are classified as *Homo sapiens* and are thus lumped together with modern humans, although they're partly distinguished by such terminology as "archaic *H. sapiens*." As we've noted, this degree of lumping is no longer supported by most researchers. Alternatively, a second, less extreme view postulates modest species diversity and labels the earlier premoderns as *H. heidelbergensis* (**Fig. 11-23a**).

At the other end of the spectrum, more enthusiastic paleontological splitters have identified at least two (or more) species distinct from *H. sapiens*. The most important of these, *H. heidelbergensis* and *H. neanderthalensis*, have been discussed earlier. This more complex evolutionary interpretation is shown in **Figure 11-23b**.

We addressed similar differences of interpretation in Chapters 9 and 10, and we know that disparities such as these can be frustrating to students who are new to paleoanthropology. The proliferation of new names is confusing, and it might seem that experts in the field are endlessly arguing about what to call the fossils.

Fortunately, it's not quite that bad. There's actually more agreement than you might think. No one doubts that all these hominins are closely related to each other as well as to modern humans. And everyone agrees that only some of the fossil samples represent populations that left descendants. Where paleoanthropologists disagree is when they start discussing which hominins are the most likely to be closely related to later hominins. The grouping of hominins into evolutionary clusters (clades) and assigning of

different names to them is a reflection of differing interpretations—and, more fundamentally, of somewhat differing philosophies.

But we shouldn't emphasize these naming and classification debates too much. Most paleoanthropologists recognize that a great deal of these disagreements result from simple, practical considerations. Even the most enthusiastic splitters acknowledge that the fossil "species" are not true species as defined by the biological species concept (see Chapter 6). As prominent paleoanthropologist Robert Foley puts it, "It is unlikely they are all biological species. . . . These are probably a mixture of real biological species and evolving lineages of subspecies. In other words, they could potentially have interbred, but owing to allopatry [that is, geographical separation] were unlikely to have had the opportunity" (Foley, 2002, p. 33).

Even so, Foley, along with an increasing number of other professionals, distinguishes these different fossil samples with species names to highlight their distinct position in hominin evolution. That is, these hominin groups are more loosely defined as a type of paleospecies (see Chapter 6) rather than as fully biological species. Giving distinct hominin samples a separate (species) name makes them more easily identifiable to other researchers and makes various cladistic hypotheses more explicit—and equally important, more directly testable.

The hominins that best illustrate these issues are the Neandertals. Fortunately, they're also the best known, represented by dozens of well-preserved individuals and also a complete genome. With all this evidence, researchers can systematically test and evaluate many of the differing hypotheses.

Are Neandertals very closely related to modern *H. sapiens*? Certainly. Are they physically and behaviorally somewhat distinct from both ancient and fully modern humans? Yes. Does this mean that Neandertals are a fully

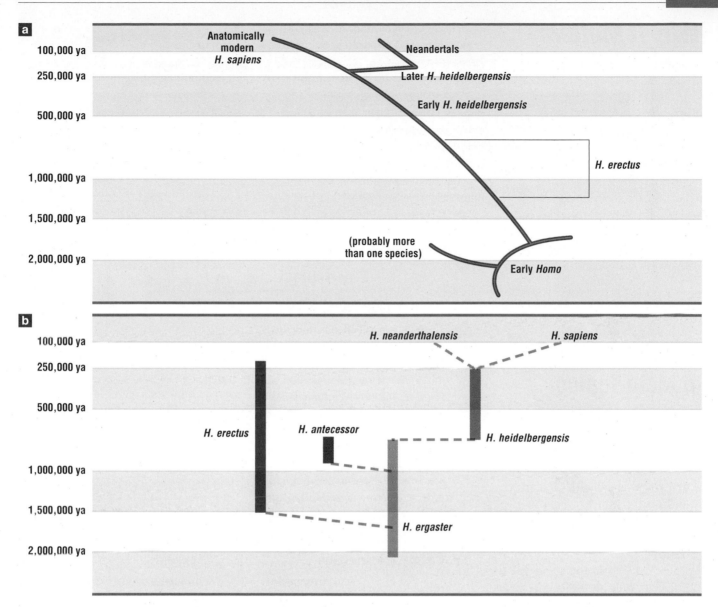

▲ **Figure 11-23**
(a) Phylogeny of genus *Homo*. Only very modest species diversity is implied. (b) Phylogeny of genus *Homo* showing considerable species diversity (after Foley, 2002)

separate biological species from modern humans and therefore theoretically incapable of fertilely interbreeding with modern people? Almost certainly not. Finally, then, should Neandertals really be placed in a separate species from *H. sapiens*? For most purposes, it doesn't matter, since the distinction at some point is arbitrary. Speciation is, after all, a *dynamic* process. Fossil groups such as the Neandertals represent just one point in this process (see Chapter 6).

We can view Neandertals as a distinctive side branch of later hominin evolution. It is not unreasonable to say that Neandertals were likely an incipient species. The much less well-known "Denisovans" from Siberia also likely represent another partially distinct incipient species, separate from both Neandertals and early modern humans. Given enough time and enough isolation, Neandertals and Denisovans likely would have separated completely from their modern human contemporaries. The new DNA evidence suggests that they were partly on their way, but had not reached full speciation from *Homo sapiens*. Their fate, in a sense, was decided for them as more successful competitors expanded into their habitats. These highly successful hominins were fully modern humans, and in the next chapter we'll focus on their story.

Why It Matters

Question: Why should knowing the full genome of Neandertals help us learn something important about ourselves?

Answer: Neandertals are our closest not fully human cousin to ever walk the earth, but they disappeared more than 25,000 years ago. What we have left of them are some very nice fossils, of course. And now, we also have begun to sequence their DNA (which is still found in many Neandertal fossils). Moreover, advanced genetic sequencing has recently allowed us to know the entire Neandertal genomic pattern. Science fiction buffs might easily conjure Jurassic Park and imagine recreating a living Neandertal This is not quite as crazy as it may sound.

But far more important (and more realistic) is what Neandertal DNA can tell us about ourselves. What exactly is it that makes us human, with our full use of language, artistic expression, human emotions, and so forth? Much of what makes the human animal such an unusual hominin is coded in perhaps just a few dozen genes that have been altered by evolution in just the last few hundred thousand years.

By looking at the precise sequences in Neandertal DNA, we have a good chance of seeing which specific genes have been modified. We can then try to find out how these genes function and begin to explain the biological bases of human intelligence and even perhaps the nature of consciousness.

Summary of Main Topics

- Premodern humans from the Middle Pleistocene show similarities both with their predecessors (*H. erectus*) and with their successors (*H. sapiens*). They've also been found in many areas of the Old World—in Africa, Asia, and Europe.
- Most paleoanthropologists call the majority of Middle Pleistocene fossils *H. heidelbergensis*. Similarities between the African and European Middle Pleistocene hominin samples suggest that they all can be reasonably seen as part of this same species, but contemporaneous Asian fossils don't fit as neatly into this model.
- Some of the later *H. heidelbergensis* populations in Europe likely evolved into Neandertals, and abundant Neandertal fossil and archaeological evidence has been collected from the Late Pleistocene time span of Neandertal existence, about 130,000–30,000 ya.
- Neandertals are more geographically restricted than earlier premoderns and are found in Europe, southwest Asia, and central Asia.
- Neandertals have been considered quite distinct from modern *H. sapiens*, but recent genetic evidence confirms that some interbreeding took place between these hominins (likely 80,000–50,000 years ago).

In "What's Important," you'll find a useful summary of the most significant premodern human fossils discussed in this chapter.

What's Important

Key Fossil Discoveries of Premodern Humans

Dates	Region	Site	Hominin	The Big Picture
50,000 ya	Western Europe	*La Chapelle* (France)	Neandertal	Most famous Neandertal discovery; led to false interpretation of primitive, bent-over creature
110,000 ya	Southwestern Asia	*Tabun* (Israel)	Neandertal	Best evidence of early Neandertal morphology in S. W. Asia
130,000 ya	South Africa	*Kabwe* (Broken Hill, Zambia)	*H. heidelbergensis*	Transitional-looking fossil; perhaps a close ancestor of early *H. sapiens* in Africa
?600,000– 400,000 ya	Western Europe	*Sima de los Huesos* (Atapuerca, northern Spain)	*H. heidelbergensis* (early Neandertal)	Very early evidence of Neandertal ancestry.
600,000 ya	East Africa	*Bodo* (Ethiopia)	*H. heidelbergensis*	Earliest evidence of *H. heidelbergensis* in Africa—and possibly ancestral to later *H. sapiens*

Critical Thinking Questions

1. Why are the Middle Pleistocene hominins called premodern humans? In what ways are they human?

2. What is the general popular conception of Neandertals? Do you agree with this view? (Cite both anatomical and archaeological evidence to support your conclusion.)

3. What evidence suggests that Neandertals deliberately buried their dead? Do you think the fact that they buried their dead is important? Why? How would you interpret this behavior (remembering that Neandertals were not identical to us)?

4. How are species defined, both for living animals and for extinct ones? Use the Neandertals to illustrate the problems encountered in distinguishing species among extinct hominins. Contrast specifically the interpretation of Neandertals as a distinct species with the interpretation of Neandertals as a subspecies of *H. sapiens*.

Connections

Premodern humans, including Neandertals, were the immediate predecessors of modern humans.

Modern humans first evolved in Africa and later spread to other areas of the world.

Modern human variation is best understood by looking at patterns of DNA in different populations.

12

The Origin and Dispersal of Modern Humans

T oday, our species numbers more than 7 billion individuals, spread all over the globe, but there are no other living hominins but us. Our last hominin cousin disappeared several thousand years ago. Perhaps about 80,000 ya, modern peoples in the Middle East encountered beings that walked on two legs, hunted large animals, made fire, lived in caves, and fashioned complex tools. These beings were the Neandertals, and imagine what it would have been like to be among a band of modern people following game into what is now Israel and coming across these other *humans*, so like yourself in some ways, yet so different in others. It's almost certain that such encounters took place, perhaps many times. How strange would it have been to look into the face of a being sharing so much with you, yet being a total stranger both culturally and, to some degree, biologically? What would you think seeing a Neandertal for the first time? What do you imagine a Neandertal would think seeing you?

Sometime, probably close to 200,000 ya, the first modern *Homo sapiens* populations appeared in Africa. Within 150,000 years or so, their descendants had spread across most of the Old World, even expanding as far as Australia (and somewhat later to the Americas).

Who were they, and why were these early modern people so successful? What was the fate of the other hominins, such as the Neandertals, who were already long established in areas outside Africa? Did they evolve as well, leaving descendants among some living human populations? Or were they completely swept aside and replaced by African emigrants?

In this chapter, we'll discuss the origin and dispersal of modern *H. sapiens*. All contemporary populations are placed within this species (and the same subspecies as well). Most paleoanthropologists agree that several fossil forms, dating back as far as 100,000 ya, should also be included in the same *fully* modern group as us. In addition, some recently discovered fossils from Africa also are clearly *H. sapiens*, but they show some (minor) differences from living people and could thus be described as *near-modern*. Still, we can think of these early African humans as well as their somewhat later relatives as "us."

◄ Archaeological excavations at the Blombos Cave site in South Africa.

These first modern humans, who evolved by 195,000 ya, are probably descendants of some of the premodern humans we discussed in Chapter 11. In particular, African populations of *H. heidelbergensis* are the most likely ancestors of the earliest modern *H. sapiens*. The evolutionary events that took place as modern humans made the transition from more ancient premodern forms and then dispersed throughout most of the Old World were relatively rapid, and they raise several basic questions:

1. When (approximately) did modern humans first appear?
2. Where did the transition take place? Did it occur in just one region or in several?
3. What was the pace of evolutionary change? How quickly did the transition occur?
4. How did the dispersal of modern humans to other areas of the Old World (outside their area of origin) take place?

These questions concerning the origins and early dispersal of modern *Homo sapiens* continue to fuel much controversy among paleoanthropologists. And it's no wonder, for at least some early *H. sapiens* populations are the direct ancestors of all contemporary humans. They were much like us skeletally, genetically, and (most likely) behaviorally. In fact, it's the various hypotheses regarding the behaviors and abilities of our most immediate predecessors that have most fired the imaginations of scientists and laypeople alike. In every major respect, these are the first hominins that we can confidently refer to as *fully* human.

In this chapter, we'll also discuss archaeological evidence coming from the Upper Paleolithic cultures. This evidence will give us a better understanding of the technological and social developments during the period when modern humans arose and quickly came to dominate the planet.

The evolutionary story of *Homo sapiens* is really the biological autobiography of all of us. It's a story that still has many unanswered questions; but some general theories can help us organize the diverse information that's now available.

Approaches to Understanding Modern Human Origins

In attempting to organize and explain modern human origins, paleoanthropologists have proposed a few major theories that can be summarized into two contrasting views: the *regional continuity model* and various versions of *replacement* models. These two views are quite distinct, and in some ways they're completely opposed to each other. Since so much of our contemporary view of modern human origins is influenced by the debates linked to these differing theories, let's start by briefly reviewing them. Then we'll turn to the fossil evidence itself to see what it can contribute to answering the four questions we've posed.

The Regional Continuity Model: Multiregional Evolution

The regional continuity model is most closely associated with paleoanthropologist Milford Wolpoff, of the University of Michigan, and his associates (Wolpoff et al., 1994, 2001). They suggest that local populations—not all, of course—in Europe, Asia, and Africa continued their indigenous evolutionary development from premodern Middle Pleistocene forms to anatomically modern humans. But if that's true, then we have to ask how so many different local populations around the globe happened to evolve with such similar morphology. In other words, how could anatomically modern humans arise separately in different continents and end up so much alike, both physically and genetically? The multiregional model answers this question by (1) denying that the earliest modern *H. sapiens* populations originated *exclusively* in Africa and (2) asserting that significant levels of gene flow (migration) between various geographically dispersed premodern populations were extremely likely throughout the Pleistocene.

Through gene flow and natural selection, according to the multiregional hypothesis, local populations would *not* have evolved totally independently from one another, and such mixing would have "prevented speciation between the regional lineages and thus maintained human beings as a *single*, although obviously *polytypic* [see Chapter 5], species throughout the Pleistocene" (Smith et al., 1989). Thus, under a multiregional model, there are no taxonomic distinctions between modern and premodern hominins. That is, all hominins following *H. erectus* are classified as a single species: *H. sapiens*.

In light of emerging evidence over the last few years, advocates of the multiregional model generally aren't dogmatic about the degree of regional continuity. They recognize that a strong influence of modern humans evolving *first* in Africa has left an imprint on populations throughout the world that is still detectable today. Nevertheless, the most recent data suggest that multiregional models no longer tell us much useful about the origins of modern humans; nor do they seem to provide much information regarding the dispersal of modern *H. sapiens*.

Replacement Models

Replacement models all emphasize that modern humans first evolved in Africa and only later dispersed to other parts of the world, where they replaced those hominins already living in these other regions. In recent years, two versions of such replacement models have been proposed, the first emphasizing *complete* replacement. The complete replacement model proposes that anatomically modern populations arose in Africa within the last 200,000 years and then migrated from Africa, completely replacing populations in Europe and Asia (Stringer and Andrews, 1988). It's important to note that this model doesn't account for a transition from premodern forms to modern *H. sapiens* anywhere in the world except Africa. A critical deduction of the original Stringer and Andrews theory argued that anatomically modern humans appeared as the result of a biological speciation event. So in this view, migrating African modern *H. sapiens* could not have interbred with local non-African populations, because the African modern humans were a *biologically* different species. Taxonomically, all of the premodern populations outside Africa would, in this view, be classified as belonging to different species of *Homo*. For example, the Neandertals would be classified as *H. neanderthalensis*. This speciation explanation fits nicely with, and in fact helps explain, *complete* replacement; but Stringer has more recently stated that he isn't insistent on this issue. He does suggest that even though there may have been potential for interbreeding, apparently very little actually took place.

Interpretations of the latter phases of human evolution have recently been greatly extended by newly available genetic techniques, and they've recently been applied to the question of modern human origins. Using numerous contemporary human populations as a data source, geneticists have precisely determined and compared a wide variety of DNA sequences. The theoretical basis of this approach assumes that at least some of the genetic patterning seen today can act as a kind of window into the past. In particular, the genetic patterns observed today between geographically widely dispersed humans are thought to partly reflect migrations occurring in the Late Pleistocene. This hypothesis can be further tested as contemporary population genetic patterning is better documented.

As these new data have accumulated, consistent relationships are emerging, especially in showing that indigenous African populations have far greater diversity than do populations from elsewhere in the world. The consistency of the results is highly significant, because it strongly supports an African origin for modern humans and some mode of replacement elsewhere. What's more, as we will discuss in Chapter 5, new, even more complete data on contemporary population patterning for large portions of nuclear DNA further confirm these conclusions.

Certainly, most molecular data come from contemporary species, since DNA is not *usually* preserved in long-dead individuals. Even so, exceptions do occur, and these cases open another genetic window—one that can directly illuminate the past. As discussed in Chapter 11, mtDNA has been recovered from more than a dozen Neandertal fossils.

In addition, researchers have recently sequenced the mtDNA of nine ancient fully modern *H. sapiens* skeletons from sites in Italy, France, the Czech Republic, and Russia (Caramelli et al., 2003, 2006; Kulikov et al., 2004; Serre et al., 2004). MtDNA data, however, are somewhat limited because mtDNA is a fairly small segment of DNA, and it is transmitted between generations as a single unit; genetically it acts like a single gene. Indeed, in just the last few years, comparisons of Neandertal and early modern mtDNA led to some significant misinterpretations. Clearly, data from the vastly larger nuclear genome are far more informative.

As we discussed in Chapter 11, a giant leap forward occurred in 2010 when sequencing of the entire Neandertal nuclear genome was completed. Researchers immediately compared the Neandertal genome with that of people living today and discovered that some populations still retain some Neandertal genes (Green et al., 2010). Without doubt, we can now conclude that some interbreeding took place between Neandertals and modern humans, arguing against *complete* replacement and supporting some form of *partial* replacement.

Partial Replacement Models For a number of years, several paleoanthropologists, such as Günter Bräuer, of the University of Hamburg, suggested that very little interbreeding occurred—a view supported more recently by John Relethford (2001) in what he described as "mostly out of Africa." The new findings from DNA analysis confirm that the degree of interbreeding was modest, ranging from 1 to 4 percent in modern populations outside Africa, while also revealing that contemporary Africans have no trace of Neandertal genes, suggesting the interbreeding occurred *after* modern humans migrated out of Africa. This would seem obvious when you consider that (as far as we know) Neandertals never lived anywhere in Africa. For our African ancestors to even have the opportunity to mate with a Neandertal, they would first have to leave their African homeland. Another fascinating discovery is that among the modern people so far sampled (five individuals), the three non-Africans all have some Neandertal DNA. The tentative conclusion from these preliminary findings suggests that the interbreeding occurred soon after modern humans emigrated out of Africa. The most likely scenario suggests that the intermixing occurred around 80,000–50,000 ya, quite possibly in the Middle East.

These results are very new and are partly based on very limited samples of living people. Technological innovations in DNA sequencing are occurring at an amazing pace, making it faster and cheaper. But it is still a challenge to sequence all the 3 billion+ nucleotides each of us has in our nuclear genome.

When we have full genomes from more individuals living in many more geographical areas, the patterns of modern human dispersal should become clearer. Did the modern human-Neandertal interbreeding occur primarily in one area, or did it happen in several regions? Moreover, did some modern human populations several thousand years ago interbreed with their Neandertal cousins more than others did? Even more interesting, were there still other premodern human groups still around when modern humans emigrated from Africa—and did they interbreed, too?

From his study of fossil remains, Fred Smith, of Illinois State University, has proposed an "assimilation" model that hypothesizes that more interbreeding did take place, at least in some regions (Smith, 2002). To test these hypotheses and answer all the fascinating questions, we will also need more whole-genome DNA from ancient remains, particularly from early modern human skeletons. This, won't be an easy task; remember, it took four years of intensive effort to decode and reassemble the Neandertal genome. Then, too, we need to be aware that DNA thousands of years old can be obtained from hominin remains that are found in environments that have been persistently cold (or at least cool). In tropical areas, DNA degrades rapidly; so it seems a long shot that any usable DNA can be obtained from hominins that lived in many extremely large and significant regions (for example, Africa and Southeast Asia).

The Earliest Discoveries of Modern Humans

Africa

In Africa, several early (around 200,000–100,000 ya) fossils have been interpreted as fully anatomically modern forms (**Fig. 12-2** on p. 320). The earliest of these specimens comes from Omo Kibish, in southernmost Ethiopia. Using radiometric techniques, redating of a fragmentary skull (Omo 1) demonstrates that, coming from 195,000 ya, this is the earliest modern human yet found in Africa— or, for that matter, anywhere (McDougall et al., 2005). An interesting aspect of fossils from this site concerns the variation shown between the two individuals. Omo 1 (**Fig. 12-1**) is essentially modern in most respects (note the presence of a chin; see **Fig. 12-3**, where a variety of modern human cranial characteristics are shown). But another ostensibly contemporary cranium

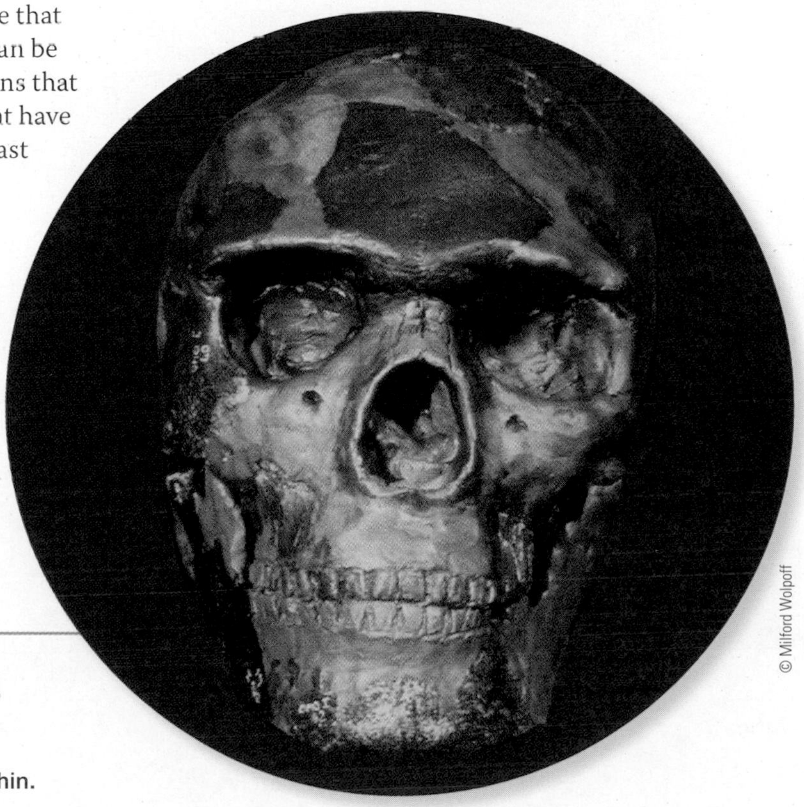

▼ **Figure 12-1**
Reconstructed skull of Omo 1, an early modern human from Ethiopia, dated to 195,000 ya. Note the clear presence of a chin.

© Milford Wolpoff

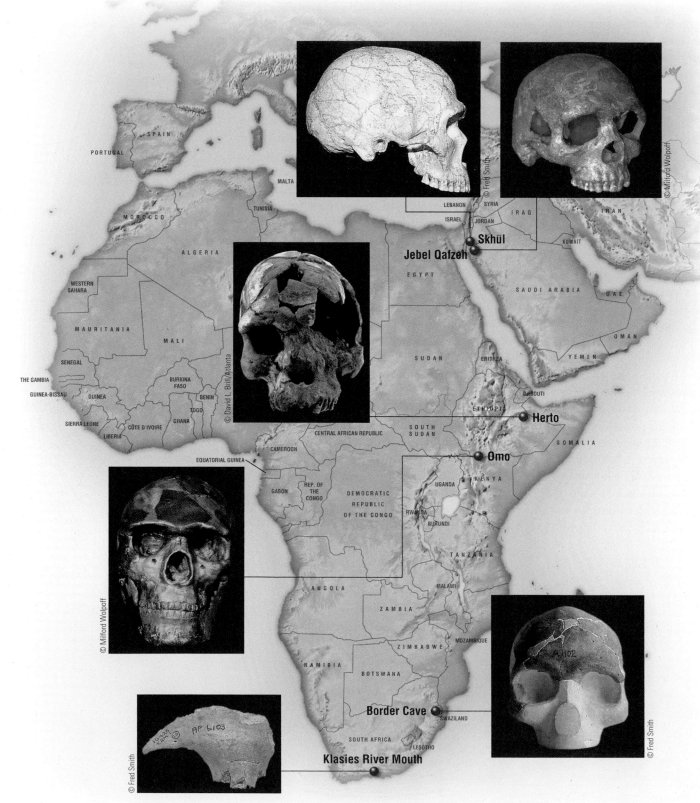

▲ **Figure 12-2**
Modern humans from Africa
and the Near East.

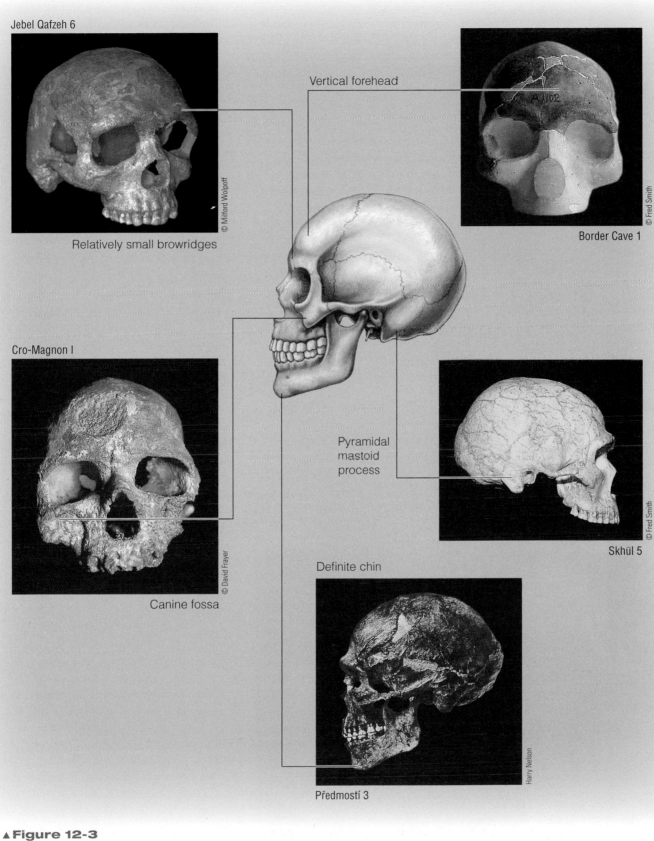

Jebel Qafzeh 6

Relatively small browridges

© Milford Wolpoff

Vertical forehead

Border Cave 1

© Fred Smith

Cro-Magnon I

© David Frayer

Canine fossa

Pyramidal mastoid process

Skhūl 5

© Fred Smith

Definite chin

Předmostí 3

Harry Nelson

▲ **Figure 12-3**
Morphology and variation in early specimens
of modern *Homo sapiens*.

© Cengage Learning 2013

(Omo 2) is much more robust and less modern in morphology.

Somewhat later modern human fossils come from the Klasies River Mouth on the south coast of Africa and Border Cave, just slightly to the north. Using relatively new techniques, paleoanthropologists have dated both sites to about 120,000–80,000 ya. The original geological context at Border Cave is uncertain, and the fossils may be younger than those at Klasies River Mouth. Although recent reevaluation of the Omo site has provided much more dependable dating, there are still questions remaining about some of the other early African modern fossils. Nevertheless, it now seems very likely that early modern humans appeared in East Africa by shortly after 200,000 ya and had migrated to southern Africa by approximately 100,000 ya. More recently discovered fossils are helping confirm this view.

Herto   The announcement in 2003 of well-preserved *and* well-dated *H. sapiens* fossils from Ethiopia has gone a long way toward filling gaps in the African fossil record. As a result, these fossils are helping to resolve key issues regarding modern human origins. Tim White, of the University of California, Berkeley, and his colleagues have been working for three decades in the Middle Awash area of Ethiopia. They've discovered a remarkable array of early fossil hominins (*Ardipithecus* and *Australopithecus*) as well as somewhat later forms (*H. erectus*). From this same area in the Middle Awash, highly significant new discoveries came to light in 1997. For simplicity, these new hominins are referred to as the Herto remains.

These Herto fossils include a mostly complete adult cranium, an incomplete adult cranium, a fairly complete (but heavily reconstructed) child's cranium, and a few other cranial fragments. Following lengthy reconstruction and detailed comparative studies, White and colleagues were prepared to announce their findings in 2003.

What they said caused quite a sensation among paleoanthropologists, and it was reported in the popular press as well. First, well-controlled radiometric dating (^{40}Ar/^{39}Ar) securely places the remains at between 160,000 and 154,000 ya, making these the best-dated hominin fossils from this time period from anywhere in the world. Note that this date is clearly *older* than for any other equally modern *H. sapiens* from anywhere else in the world. Moreover, the preservation and morphology of the remains leave little doubt about their relationship to modern humans. The mostly complete adult cranium (**Fig. 12-4**) is very large, with an extremely long cranial vault. The cranial capacity is 1,450 cm^3, well within the range of contemporary *H. sapiens* populations. The skull is also in some respects heavily built, with a large, arching browridge in front and a large, projecting occipital protuberance in back. The face does not project, in stark contrast to Eurasian Neandertals.

The overall impression is that this individual is clearly *Homo sapiens*— as are the other fossils from the site. Following comprehensive statistical studies, Tim White and colleagues concluded that, though not identi-

▲ **Figure 12-4**
Herto cranium from Ethiopia, dated 160,000–154,000 ya. This is the best-preserved early modern *H. sapiens* cranium yet found.

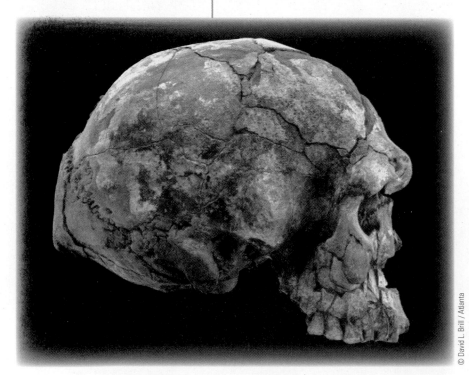

© David L. Brill / Atlanta

cal to modern people, the Herto fossils are near-modern. That is, these fossils "sample a population that is on the verge of anatomical modernity but not yet fully modern" (White et al., 2003, p. 745). To distinguish these individuals from fully modern humans (*H. sapiens sapiens*), the researchers have placed them in a newly defined subspecies: *Homo sapiens idaltu*. The word *idaltu*, from the Afar language, means "elder."

What, then, can we conclude? First, we can say that these new finds strongly support an African origin of modern humans. The Herto fossils are the right age, and they come from the right place. Besides that, they look much like what we might have predicted. Considering all these facts, they're the most conclusive fossil evidence yet indicating an African origin of modern humans. What's more, this fossil evidence is compatible with a great deal of strong genetic data indicating some form of replacement model for human origins.

The Near East

In Israel, researchers found early modern *H. sapiens* fossils, including the remains of at least 10 individuals, in the Skhūl Cave at Mt. Carmel (**Figs. 12-5** and **12-6a**). Also from Israel, the Qafzeh Cave has yielded the remains of at least 20 individuals (**Fig. 12-6b**). Although their overall configuration is definitely modern, some specimens show certain premodern features. Skhūl has been dated to between 130,000 and 100,000 ya (Grün et al., 2005), while Qafzeh has been dated to around 120,000–92,000 ya (Grün and Stringer, 1991). The time line for these fossil discoveries is shown in **Figure 12-7**.

Such early dates for modern specimens pose some problems for those advocating the influence of local evolution, as proposed by the multiregional model. How early do the premodern populations—that is, Neandertals—appear in the Near East? A recent chronometric calibration for the

Quick Review

Key Early Modern *Homo sapiens* Discoveries from Africa and the Near East

Date	Site	Hominin	Evolutionary Significance
110,000 ya	Qafzeh (Israel)	*H. sapiens sapiens*	Large sample (at least 20 individuals); definitely modern, but some individuals fairly robust; early date (>100,000 ya)
115,000 ya	Skhūl (Israel)	*H. sapiens sapiens*	Minimum of 10 individuals; like Qafzeh modern morphology, but slightly earlier date (and earliest modern humans known outside of Africa)
160,000–154,000 ya	Herto (Ethiopia)	*H. sapiens idaltu*	Very well-preserved cranium; dated > 150,000 ya, the best-preserved early modern human found anywhere
195,000 ya	Omo (Ethiopia)	*H. sapiens*	Dated almost 200,000 ya and the oldest modern human found anywhere; two crania found, one more modern looking than the other

▶ **Figure 12-5**
Mt. Carmel, studded with caves, was home to *H. sapiens sapiens* at Skhūl (and to Neandertals at Tabun and Kebara).

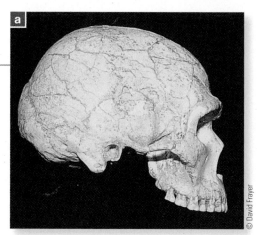 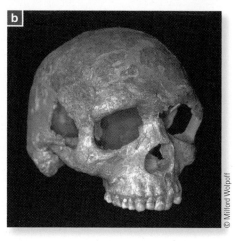

▶ **Figure 12-6**
(a) Skhūl 5. **(b)** Qafzeh 6. These specimens from Israel are thought to be representatives of early modern *Homo sapiens*. The vault height, forehead, and lack of prognathism are modern traits.

Tabun Cave suggests a date as early as 120,000 ya. This dating for these sites, all located *very* close to each other, suggests that there's considerable chronological overlap in the occupation of the Near East by Neandertals and modern humans. This chronological overlap in such a small area is the reason anthropologists have suggested this region as a likely place where Neandertals and modern humans might well have interbred.

Asia

There are seven early anatomically modern human localities in China, the most significant of which are Upper Cave at Zhoukoudian, Tianyuan Cave (very near Zhoukoudian), and Ordos, in Mongolia (**Fig. 12-8**). The fossils from these Chinese sites are all fully modern, and all are considered to be from the Late Pleistocene, with dates probably less than 40,000 ya. Upper Cave at Zhoukoudian has been dated to 27,000 ya, and the fossils consist of three skulls found with cultural remains in a cave site that humans clearly regularly inhabited. Considerable antiquity has also been proposed for the Mongolian Ordos skull, but this dating is not very secure and has therefore been questioned (Trinkaus, 2005).

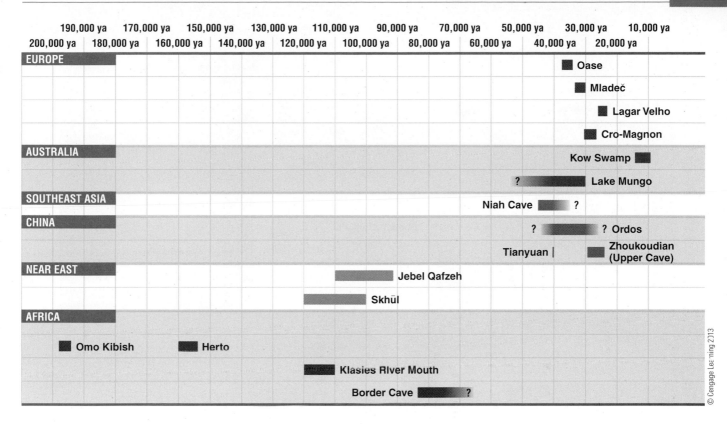

▲ Figure 12-7
Time line of modern *Homo sapiens* discoveries. Note that most dates are approximations. Question marks indicate those estimates that are most tentative.

In addition, some researchers (Tiemel et al., 1994) have suggested that the Jinniushan skeleton discussed in Chapter 11 hints at modern features in China as early as 200,000 ya. If this date—as early as that proposed for direct antecedents of modern *H. sapiens* in Africa—should prove accurate, it would cast doubt on replacement models. This position, however, is a minority view and is not supported by more recent and more detailed analyses.

Just about four miles down the road from the famous Zhoukoudian Cave is another cave called Tianyuan, the source of an important find in 2003. Consisting of a fragmentary skull, a few teeth, and several postcranial bones, this fossil is accurately dated by radiocarbon at close to 40,000 ya (Shang et al., 2007). The skeleton shows mostly modern features, but has a few archaic characteristics as well. The Chinese and American team that has analyzed the remains from Tianyuan proposes that they indicate an African origin of modern humans, but there is also evidence of at least

some interbreeding in China with resident archaic (that is, premodern) populations. More complete analysis and (with some luck) further finds at this new site will help provide a better picture of early modern *H. sapiens* in China. For the moment, this is the best-dated early modern *H. sapiens* from China and one of the two earliest from anywhere in Asia.

The other early fossil is a partial skull from Niah Cave, on the north coast of the Indonesian island of Borneo (see Fig. 12-8). This is actually not a new find and was, in fact, first excavated more than 50 years ago. However, until recent more extensive analysis, it had been relegated to the paleoanthropological back shelf due to uncertainties regarding its archaeological context and dating. Now all this has changed with a better understanding of the geology of the site and new dates strongly supporting an age of more than 35,000 ya and most likely as old as 45,000–40,000 ya, making it perhaps older than Tianyuan (Barker et al., 2007). Like its Chinese counterparts,

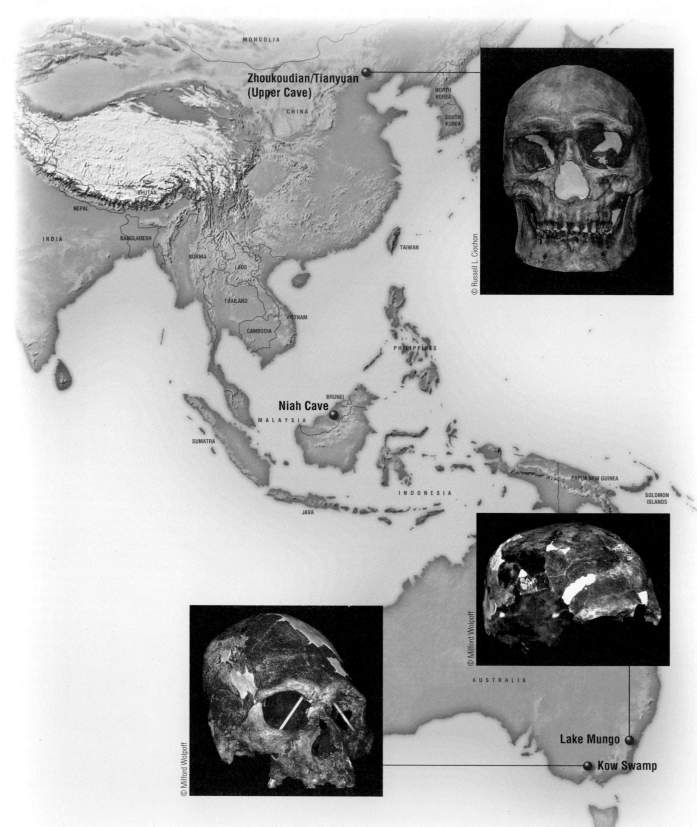

▲ **Figure 12-8**
Anatomically modern *Homo sapiens*
in Asia and Australia.

the Niah skull is modern in morphology. It's hypothesized that some population contemporaneous with Niah or somewhat earlier inhabitants of Indonesia was perhaps the first group to colonize Australia.

Australia

During glacial times, the Indonesian islands were joined to the Asian mainland, but Australia wasn't. It's likely that by 50,000 ya, modern humans inhabited Sahul—the area including New Guinea and Australia. Bamboo rafts may have been used to cross the ocean between islands, though this would certainly have been dangerous and difficult. It's not known just where the ancestral Australians came from, but as noted, Indonesia has been suggested.

Human occupation of Australia appears to have occurred quite early, with some archaeological sites dating to 55,000 ya. There's some controversy about the dating of the earliest Australian human remains, which are all modern *H. sapiens*. The earliest finds so far discovered have come from Lake Mungo, in southeastern Australia (see Fig. 12-8). In agreement with archaeological context and radiocarbon dates, the hominins from this site have been dated at approximately 30,000–25,000 ya.

Fossils from a site called Kow Swamp suggest that the people who lived there between about 14,000 and 9,000 ya were different from the more gracile early Australian forms from Lake Mungo (see Fig. 12-8). The Kow Swamp fossils display certain archaic cranial traits—such as receding foreheads, heavy supraorbital tori, and thick bones—that are difficult to explain, since these features contrast with the postcranial anatomy, which matches that of living indigenous Australians. Regardless of the different morphology of these later Australians, new genetic evidence indicates that all native Australians are descendants of a *single* migration dating back to about 50,000 ya (Hudjashou et al., 2007).

Central Europe

Central Europe has been a source of many fossil finds, including the earliest anatomically modern *H. sapiens* yet discovered anywhere in Europe. Dated to 35,000 ya, these early *H. sapiens* fossils come from recent discoveries at the Oase Cave in Romania (**Fig. 12-9**). Here, cranial remains of three individuals were recovered, including a complete mandible and a partial skull. While quite robust, these individuals are similar to later modern specimens, as seen in the clear presence of both a chin and a canine fossa (see Fig. 12-3; Trinkaus et al., 2003).

Another early modern human site in central Europe is Mladeč, in the Czech Republic (**Fig. 12-10**). Several individuals have been excavated here and are dated to approximately 31,000 ya. Although there's some variation among the crania, including some with big browridges, Fred Smith (1984) is confident that they're all best classified as modern *H. sapiens* (**Fig. 12-11a**). It's clear that by 28,000 ya, modern

▼ Figure 12-9
Excavators at work within the spectacular cave at Oase, in Romania. The floor is littered with the remains of fossil animals, including the earliest dated cranial remains of *Homo sapiens* in Europe.

© Mircea Gherase

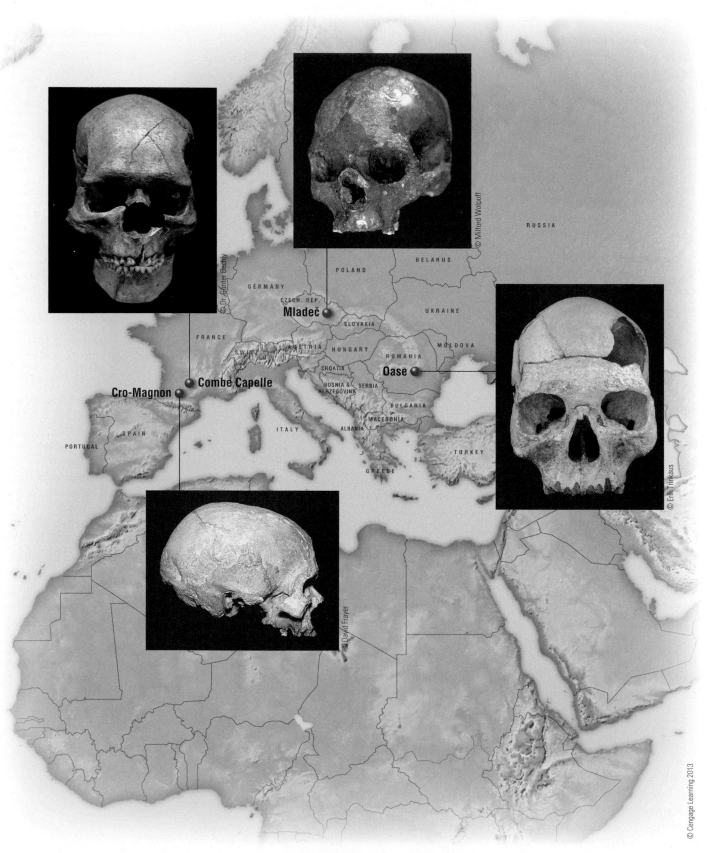

▲ **Figure 12-10**
Anatomically modern humans in Europe.

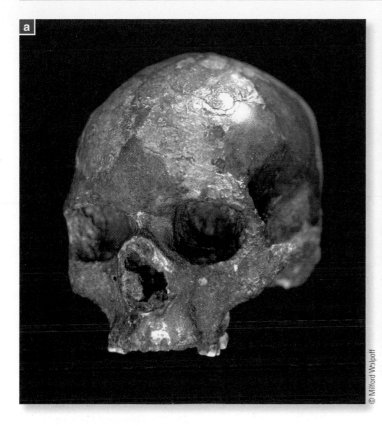

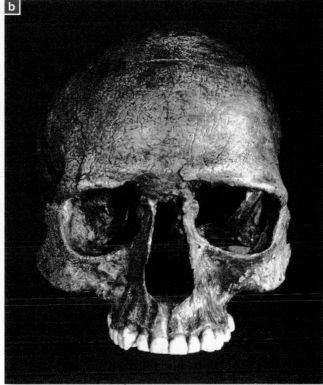

▲ **Figure 12-11**
The Mladeč **(a)** and Dolní Věstonice **(b)** crania, both from the Czech Republic, represent good examples of early modern *Homo sapiens* in central Europe. Along with Oase, in Romania, the evidence for early modern *Homo sapiens* appears first in central Europe before the later finds in western Europe.

humans were widely dispersed in central and western Europe (Trinkaus, 2005). Also from the Czech Republic and dated at about 26,000 ya, Dolní Věstonice provides another example of a central European early modern human (see **Fig. 12-11b**).

Western Europe

For several reasons, western Europe and its fossils have received more attention than other regions. Over the last 150 years, many of the scholars doing this research happened to live in western Europe, and the southern region of France turned out to be a fossil treasure trove.

As a result of this scholarly interest, a great deal of data accumulated beginning back in the nineteenth century, with little reliable comparative information available from elsewhere in the world. Consequently, theories of human evolution were based almost exclusively on the western European material. It's only been in more recent years, with growing evidence from

other areas of the world and with the application of new dating techniques, that recent human evolutionary dynamics are being seriously considered from a worldwide perspective.

Western Europe has yielded many anatomically modern human fossils, but by far the best-known sample of western European *H. sapiens* is from the **Cro-Magnon** site, a rock-shelter in southern France. At this site, the remains of eight individuals were discovered in 1868.

The Cro-Magnon materials are associated with an **Aurignacian** tool assemblage, an Upper Paleolithic industry. Dated at about 28,000 ya, these individuals represent the earliest of France's anatomically modern humans. The so-called Old Man (Cro-Magnon 1) became the original model for what was once termed the Cro-Magnon, or Upper Paleolithic, "race" of Europe (**Fig. 12-12**). Actually, of course, there's no such valid biological category, and Cro-Magnon 1 is not typical of Upper Paleolithic western Europeans—and not even all that

Cro-Magnon (crow-man´-yon)

Aurignacian Pertaining to an Upper Paleolithic stone tool industry in Europe beginning at about 40,000 ya.

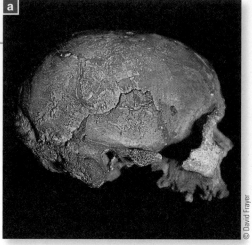

► **Figure 12-12**
Cro-Magnon 1 (France). In this specimen, modern traits are quite clear. **(a)** Lateral view. **(b)** Frontal view.

© David Frayer

similar to the other two male skulls found at the site.

Most of the genetic evidence, as well as the newest fossil evidence from Africa, argues against continuous local evolution producing modern groups directly from any Eurasian premodern population (in Europe, these would be Neandertals). Still, for some researchers, the issue isn't completely settled.

With all the latest evidence, there's no longer much debate that a *large* genetic contribution from migrating early modern Africans influenced other groups throughout the Old World. What's being debated is just how much admixture might have occurred between these migrating Africans and the resident premodern groups. For those paleoanthropologists (for exam-

Quick Review

Key Early Modern *Homo sapiens* Discoveries from Europe and Asia

Date	Site	Hominin	Evolutionary Significance
24,500 ya	Abrigo do Lagar Velho (Portugal)	*H. sapiens sapiens*	Child's skeleton; some suggestion of possible hybrid between Neandertal and modern human—but is controversial
30,000 ya	Cro-Magnon (France)	*H. sapiens sapiens*	Most famous early modern human find in world; earliest evidence of modern humans in France
40,000 ya	Tianyuan Cave (China)	*H. sapiens sapiens*	Partial skull and a few postcranial bones; oldest modern human find from China
45,000–40,000 ya	Niah Cave (Borneo, Indonesia)	*H. sapiens sapiens*	Partial skull recently redated more accurately; oldest modern human find from Asia

© Cengage Learning 2013

ple, Trinkaus, 2005) who hypothesize that significant admixture (assimilation) occurred in western Europe as well as elsewhere, a recently discovered child's skeleton from Portugal provides some of the best skeletal evidence of possible interbreeding between Neandertals and anatomically modern *H. sapiens.* This important discovery from the Abrigo do Lagar Velho site was excavated in late 1998 and is dated to 24,500 ya—that's at least 5,000 years more recent than the last clearly identifiable Neandertal fossil. Associated with an Upper Paleolithic industry and buried with red ocher and pierced shell is a fairly complete skeleton of a 4-year-old child (Duarte et al., 1999). In studying the remains, Cidália Duarte, Erik Trinkaus, and colleagues found a highly mixed set of anatomical features. From this evidence they concluded that the young child was the result of interbreeding between Neandertals and modern humans, and thus supports a partial replacement model of human origins. It's still debatable from this fossil evidence whether interbreeding with Neandertals took place in Portugal this late in time. Nevertheless, the genetic evidence is unequivocal: Neandertals and modern humans *did* interbreed at some point.

Something New and Different: The "Little People"

As we've seen, by 25,000 years ago, modern humans had dispersed to all major areas of the Old World, and they would soon journey to the New World as well. But at about the same time, remnant populations of earlier hominins still survived in a few remote and isolated corners. We mentioned in Chapter 10 that populations of *Homo erectus* in Java managed to survive on this island long after their cousins had disappeared from other areas

(for example, China and East Africa). What's more, even though they persisted well into the Late Pleistocene, physically these Javanese hominins were still similar to other *H. erectus* individuals.

Even more surprising, it seems that other populations possibly branched off from some of these early inhabitants of Indonesia and either intentionally or accidentally found their way to other, smaller islands to the east. There, under even more extreme isolation pressures, they evolved in an astonishing direction. In late 2004, the world awoke to the startling announcement that an extremely small-bodied, small-brained hominin had been discovered in Liang Bua Cave, on the island of Flores, east of Java (see **Fig. 12-13**). Dubbed the "Little Lady of Flores" or simply "Flo," the remains consist of an incomplete skeleton of an adult female (LB1) as well as additional pieces from approximately 13 other individuals, which the press has collectively nicknamed "hobbits." The female skeleton is remarkable in several ways (**Fig. 12-14**), though in some ways similar to the Dmanisi hominins. First, she was barely 3 feet tall—as short as the smallest australopith—and her brain, estimated at a mere 417 cm^3 (Falk et al., 2005), was no larger than that of a chimpanzee (Brown et al., 2004). Possibly most startling of all, these extraordinary hominins were still living on Flores just 13,000 ya (Morwood et al., 2004, 2005; Wong, 2009b)!

Where did they come from? As we said, their predecessors were perhaps *H. erectus* populations like those found on Java. How they got to Flores—some 400 miles away, partly over open ocean—is a mystery. There are several connecting islands, and to get from one to another these hominins may have drifted across on rafts; but there's no way to be sure of this. What's more, these little hominins were apparently living on Flores for a very long time; recently discovered stone tools have been radiometrically dated to at least 1 mya (Brumm et al., 2010). Such

▶ **Figure 12-13**
Location of the Flores site in Indonesia.

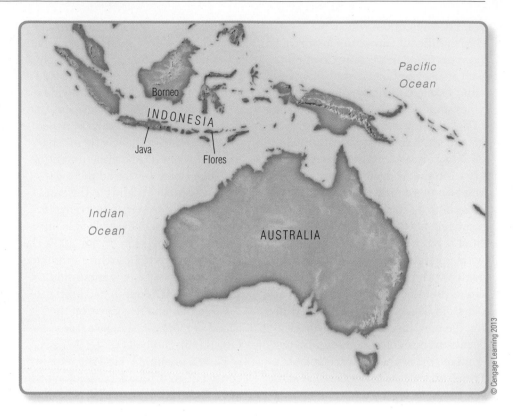

© Cengage Learning 2013

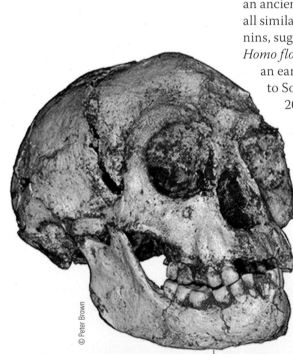

© Peter Brown

▲ **Figure 12-14**
Cranium of adult female *Homo floresiensis* from Flores, Indonesia, dated 18,000 ya.

an ancient date, as well as the overall similarities to the Dmanisi hominins, suggest to some researchers that *Homo floresiensis* may derive from an early migration of early *Homo* to Southeast Asia (Jungers et al., 2009; Wong, 2009b). In other words, this highly unusual hominin might have evolved from ancestors that left Africa even before *H. erectus* did.

How did they get to be so physically different from all other known hominins? Here we're a little more certain of the answer. Isolated island populations can quite rapidly diverge from their relatives elsewhere. Among such isolated animals, natural selection frequently favors reduced body size. For example, remains of dwarfed elephants have been found on islands in the Mediterranean as well as on some channel islands off the coast of southern California. And perhaps most interesting of all, dwarf elephants *also*

evolved on Flores; they were found in the same geological beds with the little hominins. The evolutionary mechanism (called "insular dwarfing") thought to explain such extreme body size reduction in both the elephants and the hominins is an adaptation to reduced resources, with natural selection favoring smaller body size (Schauber and Falk, 2008).

Other than short stature, what did the Flores hominins look like? In their cranial shape, thickness of cranial bone, and dentition, they most resemble *H. erectus*, and specifically those from Dmanisi. Still, they have some derived features that also set them apart from all other hominins. For that reason, many researchers have placed them in a separate species, *Homo floresiensis*.

Immediately following the first publication of the Flores remains, intense controversy arose regarding their interpretation (Jacob et al., 2006; Martin et al., 2006). Some researchers have argued that the small-brained hominin (LB1) is actually a pathological modern *H. sapiens* afflicted with a severe disorder (microcephaly and others have been proposed). The researchers who did most of the initial work reject this conclusion and provide some further details to support their original inter-pretation (for example, Dean Falk and colleagues' further analysis of microce-phalic endocasts; Falk et al., 2009).

The conclusion that among this already small-bodied island popula-tion the one individual found with a preserved cranium happened to be afflicted with a severe (and rare) growth defect is highly unlikely. Yet, it must also be recognized that long-term, extreme isolation of hominins on Flores leading to a new species show-ing dramatic dwarfing and even more dramatic brain size reduction is quite unusual.

So where does this leave us? Because a particular interpretation is unlike-ly, it's not necessarily incorrect. We do know, for example, that such "insu-lar dwarfing" has occurred in other mammals. For the moment, the most comprehensive analyses indicate that a recently discovered hominin spe-cies (*H. floresiensis*) did, in fact, evolve on Flores (Nevell et al., 2007; Tocheri et al., 2007; Falk et al., 2008; Schauber and Falk, 2008; Jungers et al., 2009). The more detailed studies of hand and foot anatomy suggest that in sev-eral respects the morphology is like that of *H. erectus* (Nevell et al., 2007; Tocheri et al., 2007) or even early *Homo* (Jungers et al., 2009). In any case, the morphology of the Flores hominins is different in several key respects from

that of *H. sapiens*, even those who show pathological conditions. There is some possibility that DNA can be retrieved from the Flores bones and sequenced. Although considered a long shot due to poor bone preservation, analysis of this DNA would certainly help solve the mystery.

Technology and Art in the Upper Paleolithic

Europe

The cultural period known as the Upper Paleolithic began in west-ern Europe approximately 40,000 ya (**Fig. 12-15**). Upper Paleolithic cultures are usually divided into five different industries, based on stone tool tech-nologies: Chatelperronian, Aurigna-cian, Gravettian, Solutrean, and Mag-dalenian. Major environmental shifts were also apparent during this period. During the last glacial period, about 30,000 ya, a warming trend lasting several thousand years partially melt-ed the glacial ice. The result was that much of Eurasia was covered by tun-dra and steppe, a vast area of treeless country dotted with lakes and marsh-es. In many areas in the north, per-mafrost prevented the growth of trees but permitted the growth, in the short summers, of flowering plants, moss-es, and other kinds of vegetation. This

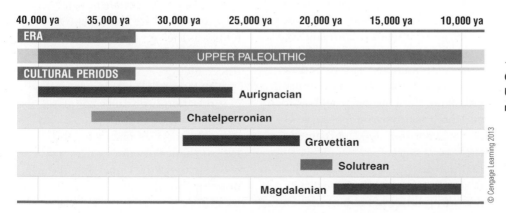

◄**Figure 12-15**
Cultural periods of the European Upper Paleolithic and their approxi-mate beginning dates.

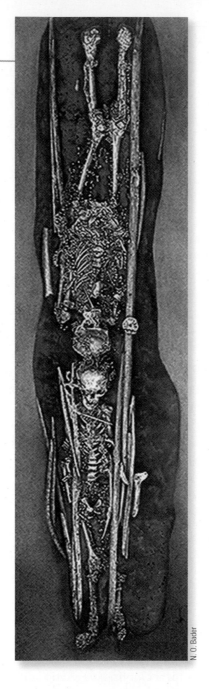

N. O. Bader

▶ **Figure 12-16**
Skeletons of two teenagers, a male and a female, from Sungir, Russia. Dated 24,000 ya, this is the richest find of any Upper Paleolithic grave.

humans exploited fish and fowl systematically for the first time. It was a time of relative abundance, and ultimately Upper Paleolithic people spread out over Eurasia, living in caves and open-air camps and building large shelters. We should recall that many of the cultural innovations seen in the Upper Paleolithic had begun with Neandertals (see Chapter 11). Nevertheless, when looking at the entire Upper Paleolithic, there are notable differences. For example, far more elaborate burials are found, most spectacularly at the 24,000-year-old Sungir site near Moscow (**Fig. 12-16**), where grave goods included a bed of red ocher, thousands of ivory beads, long spears made of straightened mammoth tusks, ivory engravings, and jewelry (Formicola and Buzhilova, 2004). During this period, either western Europe or perhaps portions of Africa achieved the highest population density in human history up to that time.

Humans and other animals in most of Eurasia had to cope with shifts in climate conditions, some of them quite rapid. For example, at 20,000 ya, another climatic "pulse" caused the weather to become noticeably colder in Europe and Asia as the continental glaciations reached their maximum extent for this entire glacial period, which is called the Würm in Eurasia.

As a variety of organisms attempted to adapt to these changing conditions, *Homo sapiens* had a major advantage: the elaboration of increasingly sophisticated technology and probably other components of culture as well. In fact, one of the greatest challenges facing numerous Late Pleistocene mammals was the ever more dangerously equipped humans—a trend that continues today.

The Upper Paleolithic was an age of innovation that can be compared to the past few hundred years in our recent history of amazing technological change. Anatomically modern humans of the Upper Paleolithic not only invented new and specialized tools (**Fig. 12-17**), but, as we've seen,

vegetation served as an enormous pasture for herbivorous animals, large and small, and carnivorous animals fed off the herbivores. It was a hunter's paradise, with millions of animals dispersed across expanses of tundra and grassland, from Spain through Europe and into the Russian steppes.

Large herds of reindeer roamed the tundra and steppes, along with mammoths, bison, horses, and a host of smaller animals that served as a bountiful source of food. In addition,

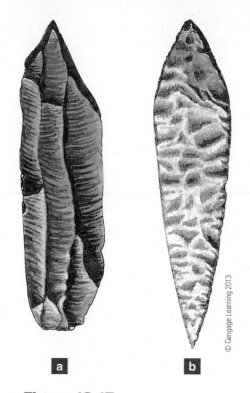

▲ Figure 12-17

(a) A burin, a very common Upper Paleolithic tool. (b) A Solutrean blade. This is the best-known work of the Solutrean tradition. Solutrean stonework is considered the most highly developed of any Upper Paleolithic industry.

also experimented with and greatly increased the use of new materials, such as bone, ivory, and antler.

Solutrean tools are good examples of Upper Paleolithic skill and likely aesthetic appreciation as well (see Fig. 12-17b). In this lithic (stone) tradition, skill in modifying rock (called "knapping") developed to the finest degree ever known. Using specialized flaking techniques, the artist/technicians made beautiful parallel-flaked lance heads, expertly flaked on both surfaces. The lance points are so delicate that they can be considered works of art that quite possibly never served, nor were they intended to serve, a utilitarian purpose.

The last stage of the Upper Paleolithic, known as the **Magdalenian**, saw even more advances in technology. The spear-thrower, or atlatl, was a wooden or bone hooked rod that extended the hunter's arm, enhancing the force and distance of a spear throw (**Fig. 12-18**). For catching salmon and other fish, the barbed harpoon is a good example of skillful craftsmanship. There's also evidence that bows and arrows may have been used for the first time during this period. The introduction of much more efficient manufacturing methods, such as the punch blade technique (**Fig. 12-19**), provided an abundance of standardized stone blades. These could be fashioned into **burins** (see Fig. 12-17a) for working wood, bone, and antler; borers for drilling holes in skins, bones, and shells; and knives with serrated or notched edges for scraping wooden shafts into a variety of tools.

By producing many more specialized tools, Upper Paleolithic peoples probably had more resources available to them; moreover, these more effective tools may also have had an impact on the biology of these populations. Emphasizing a biocultural interpretation, C. Loring Brace, of the University of Michigan, has suggested that with more effective tools as well as the use of fire allowing for more efficient food

◄ Figure 12-18
Spear-thrower (atlatl). Note the carving.

Magdalenian Pertaining to the final phase of the Upper Paleolithic stone tool industry in Europe.

burins Small, chisel-like tools with a pointed end; thought to have been used to engrave bone, antler, ivory, or wood.

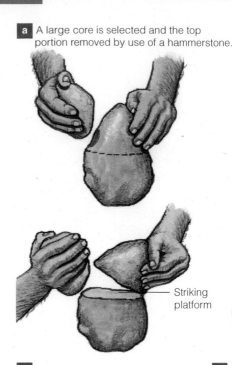

a A large core is selected and the top portion removed by use of a hammerstone.

Striking platform

b The objective is to create a flat surface called a striking platform.

c Next, the core is struck by use of a hammer and punch (made of bone or antler) to remove the long narrow flakes (called blades).

d Or the blades can be removed by pressure flaking.

e The result is the production of highly consistent sharp blades, which can be used, as is, as knives; or they can be further modified (retouched) to make a variety of other tools (such as burins, scrapers, and awls).

© Cengage Learning 2013

▲ **Figure 12-19**
The punch blade technique.

processing, anatomically modern *H. sapiens* wouldn't have required the large teeth and facial skeletons seen in earlier populations.

In addition to their reputation as hunters, western Europeans of the Upper Paleolithic are even better known for their symbolic representation (what we today recognize as art). There's an extremely wide geographical distribution of symbolic images, best known from many parts of Europe but now also well documented from Siberia, North Africa, South Africa, and Australia. Given a 25,000-year time depth of what we call Paleolithic art, along with its nearly worldwide distribution, we can indeed observe marked variability in expression.

Besides cave art, there are many examples of small sculptures excavated from sites in western, central, and eastern Europe. Perhaps the most famous of these are the female figurines, popularly known as "Venuses," found at such sites as Brassempouy, in France, and

Grimaldi, in Italy. Some of these figures were realistically carved, and the faces appear to be modeled after actual women. Other figurines may seem grotesque, with sexual characteristics exaggerated, perhaps to promote fertility or serve some other ritual purpose.

Beyond these quite well-known figurines, there are numerous other examples of what's frequently called portable art, including elaborate engravings on tools and tool handles (see Fig. 12-18). Such symbolism can be found in many parts of Europe and was already well established early in the Aurignacian, by 33,000 ya. Innovations in symbolic representations also benefited from, and probably further stimulated, technological advances. New methods of mixing pigments and applying them were important in rendering painted or drawn images. Bone and ivory carving and engraving were made easier with the use of special stone tools (see Fig. 11-17). At two sites in the Czech Republic, Dolní Věstonice and

Předmostí (both dated at approximately 27,000–26,000 ya), small animal figures were fashioned from fired clay. This is the first documented use of ceramic technology anywhere; in fact, it precedes later pottery invention by more than 15,000 years.

But it wasn't until the final phases of the Upper Paleolithic, particularly during the Magdalenian, that European prehistoric art reached its climax. Cave art is now known from more than 150 separate sites, the vast majority from southwestern France and northern Spain. Apparently, in other areas the rendering of such images did not take place in deep caves. People in central Europe, China, Africa, and elsewhere certainly may have painted or carved representations on rock faces in the open, but these images long since would have disappeared. So we're fortunate that the people of at least one of the many sophisticated cultures of the Upper Paleolithic chose to journey belowground to create their artwork, preserving it not just for their immediate descendants, but for us as well. The most spectacular and most famous of the cave art sites are Lascaux and Grotte Chauvet (in France) and Altamira (in Spain).

In Lascaux Cave, for example, immense wild bulls dominate what's called the Great Hall of Bulls; and horses, deer, and other animals drawn with remarkable skill adorn the walls in black, red, and yellow. Equally impressive, at Altamira the walls and ceiling of an immense cave are filled with superb portrayals of bison in red and black. The artist even took advantage of bulges in the walls to create a sense of relief in the paintings. The cave is a treasure of beautiful art whose meaning has never been satisfactorily explained. It could have been religious or magical, a form of visual communication, or simply art for the sake of beauty.

Inside the cave called Grotte Chauvet, preserved unseen for thousands of years, are a multitude of images, including dots, stenciled human handprints, and, most dramatically, hundreds of animal representations. Radiocarbon dating has placed the paintings during the Aurignacian, likely more than 35,000 ya, making Grotte Chauvet considerably earlier than the Magdalenian sites of Lascaux and Altamira (Balter, 2006).

Africa

Early accomplishments in rock art, possibly as early as in Europe, are seen in southern Africa (Namibia) at the Apollo 11 rock-shelter site, where painted slabs have been identified as dating to between 28,000 and 26,000 ya (Freundlich et al., 1980; Vogelsang, 1998). At Blombos Cave, farther to the south, remarkable bone tools, beads, and decorated ocher fragments are all dated to 73,000 ya (Henshilwood et al., 2004; Jacobs et al., 2006). The most recent and highly notable discovery from South Africa comes from another cave located at Pinnacle Point, not far from Blombos. At Pinnacle Point, ocher has been found (perhaps used for personal adornment) as well as clear evidence of systematic exploitation of shellfish and use of very small stone blades (microliths). What is both important and surprising is that the site is dated to approximately 165,000 ya, providing the earliest evidence from anywhere of these behaviors thought by many as characteristic of modern humans (Marean et al., 2007). The microliths also show evidence that the stone had been carefully heated, making it easier to modify into such small tools (Brown et al., 2009; Marean, 2010). Other recent finds from Sibudu, another cave site in South Africa dated to around 70,000 ya, show what archaeologist Lyn Wadley and colleagues think are traces of adhesives used to haft stone tools to handles (Wadley et al., 2009) as well as indirect evidence indicating possible use of snares and traps to catch small animals (Wadley, 2009). In both cases,

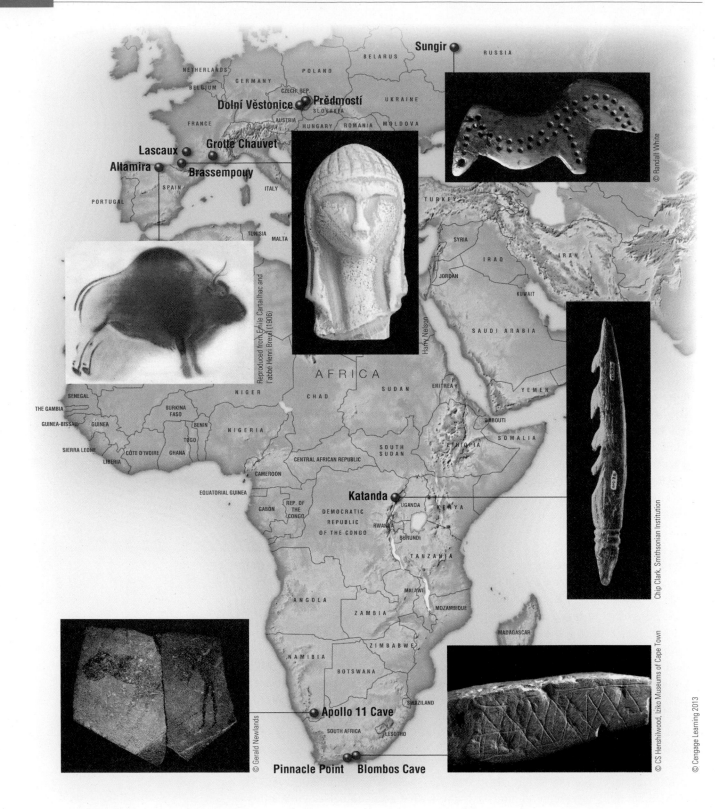

▲**Figure 12-20**

Symbolic artifacts from the Middle Stone Age of Africa and the Upper Paleolithic in Europe. It is notable that evidence of symbolism is found in Blombos Cave (77,000 ya) and Katanda (80,000 ya), both in Africa, about 45,000 years before any comparable evidence is known from Europe.

Lyn Wadley concludes such traces of behavior show evidence of what she terms "complex cognition."

In central Africa, there was also considerable use of bone and antler, some of it possibly quite early. Excavations in the Katanda area of the eastern portion of the Democratic Republic of the Congo (**Fig. 12-20**) have shown remarkable development of bone craftwork. Dating of the site is quite early. Initial results using ESR and TL dating indicate an age as early as 80,000 ya (Feathers and Migliorini, 2001). Preliminary reports have demonstrated that these technological achievements rival those of the more renowned European Upper Paleolithic (Yellen et al., 1995).

Summary of Upper Paleolithic Culture

In looking back at the Upper Paleolithic, we can see it as the culmination of 2 million years of cultural development. Change proceeded incredibly slowly for most of the Pleistocene; but as cultural traditions and materials accumulated, and the brain—and, we assume, intelligence—expanded and reorganized, the rate of change quickened.

Cultural evolution continued with the appearance of early premodern humans and moved a bit faster with later premodern humans. Neandertals in Eurasia and their contemporaries elsewhere added deliberate burials,

body ornamentation, technological innovations, and much more.

Building on existing cultures, Late Pleistocene populations attained sophisticated cultural and material heights in a seemingly short (by previous standards) burst of exciting activity. In Europe and southern and central Africa, particularly, there seem to have been dramatic cultural innovations, among them big game hunting with new weapons, such as harpoons, spear-throwers, and eventually bows and arrows. Other innovations included needles, "tailored" clothing, hafting of tools, and burials with elaborate grave goods—a practice that may indicate some sort of status hierarchy.

This dynamic age was doomed, or so it seems, by the climate changes of about 10,000 ya. As the temperature slowly rose and the glaciers retreated, animal and plant species were seriously affected, and these changes, in turn, affected humans. As traditional prey animals were depleted or disappeared altogether, humans had to seek other means of obtaining food.

Grinding hard seeds or roots became important, and as humans grew more familiar with propagating plants, they began to domesticate both plants and animals. Human dependence on domestication became critical, and with it came permanent settlements, new technology, and more complex social organization. This continuing story of human biocultural evolution will be the topic of the remainder of this text.

Why It Matters

Question: Do you think we are all originally Africans?

Answer: The answer to this question is easy: Yes, without a doubt. As you know, all the early hominins evolved first in Africa and migrated to other parts of the world only subsequent to several million years of evolutionary history confined solely to Africa. So it's clear that we are all descendants of African ancestors. How recently were all of our ancestors strictly African? Accumulating evidence is strongly suggesting that we all share an African heritage dating back to no more than 200,000 ya and perhaps as recently as 40,000–30,000 ya.

Most of humanity's genetic patterning arose in the evolutionary crucible of the African continent. These highly successful African hominins then dispersed widely to other areas and did so on several occasions. There were at least two major emigrations out of Africa and perhaps as many as four. The features we see as most distinctive of our species, such as bipedal locomotion, large brain size, and culture, all began in Africa. The most recent evidence provided by fossils, highly detailed genetic data, and archaeological finds further points to our most distinctive fully "human" characteristics also originating in Africa. Artistic expression, body ornamentation, full use of language, complex social organization, and elaborate tools also perhaps all first developed in the savannas, near the forest edge, or along stream channels in Africa. Only later, as African migrants spread to other areas, do we find these human characteristics outside of Africa.

Our origins are clearly African. Our bodies and brains were shaped as they evolved largely in Africa. All humans share most of their genes with each other, more so than do other primates. This, too, suggests a recent origin of humanity from a restricted ancestral population—one that almost certainly was African. So in every meaningful evolutionary and biocultural aspect, we are all Africans. The practical implications are clear as they apply to human social relations. The next time you seriously consider the meaning of race, think about your African roots.

Summary of Main Topics

- Two main hypotheses have been used to explain the origin and dispersal of modern humans:
  - The regional continuity model suggests that different groups of modern people evolved from local populations of premodern humans.
  - Various replacement models, especially those emphasizing partial replacement, suggest that modern humans originated in Africa and migrated to other parts of the world. However, when they came into contact with premodern human groups, they did not completely replace them, but interbred with them to some extent.

- New DNA evidence from ancient Neandertals as well as from modern people demonstrate that some modest interbreeding did take place, probably between 80,000 and 50,000 ya. These findings clearly support a partial replacement model.
- Archaeological finds and some fossil evidence (although the latter is not as well established) also support the view that intermixing occurred between modern *H. sapiens* and Neandertals.
- The earliest finds of modern *H. sapiens* come from East Africa (Ethiopia), with the oldest dating to about 200,000 ya. The second find from Herto is very well dated (160,000 ya) and is the best evidence of an early modern human from anywhere at this time.
- Modern humans are found in South Africa beginning around 100,000 ya, and the first anatomical modern *H. sapiens* are found in the Middle East dating to perhaps more than 100,000 ya.
- The Upper Paleolithic is a cultural period showing many innovations in technology, development of more sophisticated (cave) art, and, in many cases, very elaborate burials rich in grave goods. Similar cultural developments occurred in both Eurasia and Africa.

In "What's Important," you'll find a useful summary of the most significant fossil discoveries discussed in this chapter.

What's Important

Key Fossil Discoveries of Early Modern Humans and *Homo floresiensis*

Dates	Region	Site	Hominin	The Big Picture
95,000–13,000 ya	Southeast Asia	Flores (Indonesia)	*H. floresiensis*	Late survival of very small-bodied and small-brained hominin on island of Flores; designated as different species (*H. floresiensis*) from modern humans
30,000 ya	Europe	Cro-Magnon (France)	*H. sapiens sapiens*	Famous site historically; good example of early modern humans from France
35,000 ya	Europe	Oase Cave (Romania)	*H. sapiens sapiens*	Earliest well-dated modern human from Europe
110,000 ya	Southwest Asia	Qafzeh (Israel)	*H. sapiens sapiens*	Early site; shows considerable variation
115,000 ya	Southwest Asia	Skhūl (Israel)	*H. sapiens sapiens*	Earliest well-dated modern human outside of Africa; perhaps contemporaneous with neighboring Tabun Neandertal site
160,000–154,000 ya	Africa	Herto (Ethiopia)	*H. sapiens idaltu*	Best-preserved and best-dated early modern human from anywhere; placed in separate subspecies from living *H. sapiens*

© Cengage Learning 2013

Critical Thinking Questions

1. What anatomical characteristics define *modern* as compared with *premodern* humans? Assume that you're analyzing an incomplete skeleton that may be early modern *H. sapiens*. Which portions of the skeleton would be most informative, and why?

2. What recent evidence supports a partial replacement model for an African origin and later dispersal of modern humans? Do you find this evidence convincing? Why or why not? Can you propose an alternative that has better data to support it?

3. Why are the fossils recently discovered from Herto so important? How does this evidence influence your conclusions in question 2?

4. What archaeological evidence shows that modern human behavior during the Upper Paleolithic was significantly different from that of earlier hominins? Do you think that early modern *H. sapiens* populations were behaviorally superior to the Neandertals? Be careful to define what you mean by "superior."

5. Why do you think some Upper Paleolithic people painted in caves? Why don't we find such evidence of cave painting from a wider geographical area?

Connections

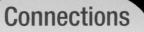

Modern human variation is best understood by looking at patterns of DNA in different populations.

Human development and adaptation is best understood from an evolutionary perspective.

Humans have recently become disconnected from other life and are rapidly altering the planet.

13

The Anthropological Perspective on the Human Life Course

Introduction

You've now read 12 chapters that have emphasized human biological evolution and adaptation. You have followed along as we've talked about genetics, evolutionary factors, nonhuman primates, fossil hominins, and how humans vary from one another. But you have also learned that we are remarkably genetically uniform when compared to most other primate species. One of the keys to our evolutionary success, as discussed in previous chapters, is that modern human beings are a highly generalized and behaviorally flexible species. This means that we can live in a great variety of climates, eat a wide variety of foods, and respond to most environmental challenges in myriad ways. As the environments of our ancestors changed, those who were able to survive and reproduce in the new environments passed along advantageous characteristics to their offspring so that today humans continue to survive and reproduce under a great variety of conditions, including high altitudes, extreme temperatures, high levels of environmental pollution, dense urban populations, and with diets and lifestyles that differ radically from those of our ancestors only a few generations ago. In fact, the human environment has changed more radically in the last few decades than it has at any point in the entire course of human evolutionary history. What are the consequences of these tremendous changes, some of which you have seen in your own lifetimes? In this chapter and the next, we'll explore ways in which the legacies of human evolution continue to have profound impacts on our biology and behavior throughout our lives and on the planet we inhabit even in the face of ever-increasing rates of cultural and technological change.

◄ Two extremes of the human life course: fetal development and old age.

Evolved Biology and Contemporary Lifestyles — Is There a Mismatch?

A frequently expressed concern today is that our evolved biology may not be well matched with our contemporary lives, resulting in poorer health and shorter lives than those of even our recent ancestors. This is referred to variously as a mismatch or discordance. Reflecting the "connections" theme of this book we will propose that our modern lives are in some ways *dis*connected from our evolved biology, with occasional harmful consequences. There are some who argue that if we could only return to the ways of living of our ancestors ("stone-age lives"), we would all become healthier. Certainly there are aspects of ancestral ways of life that would probably result in improved health if adopted (specifically, exercise and dietary changes), but with more than 7 billion people living on earth, "returning" to lifestyles like those of our ancestors is highly unlikely (**Fig. 13-1**).

For most of human history, individuals were born and grew up in environments not very different from those of their parents and grandparents. They faced few challenges in their lives that

▲ **Figure 13-1**
The lives of our ancestors differ in many ways from the lives of people today in nations like the United States and Japan.

required significant cultural or biological adaptations. With the origin of food production approximately 10,000 years ago, however, the pace of cultural change began to speed up. And though biological evolution didn't cease 10,000 years ago, since that time there has been a veritable explosion of culture and technology, whereas biological change has been relatively slow (Pritchard, 2010). With so many changes occurring within single lifetimes, many people are stressed to their limits to adapt physically, emotionally, and materially. How far can our flexible and generalized biology take us in this rapidly changing world? These are some of the questions we will explore in this chapter as we consider ways in which culture interacts with biology throughout the life course and in our everyday lives, and ways in which this interaction sometimes provides challenges to our health and lifestyles.

Biocultural Evolution and the Life Course

A good place to explore the interaction of biology and culture and potential mismatches is the human life course. If we consider how a human develops from an embryo into an adult and examine the forces that operate on that process, we will have a better perspective of how both biology and culture influence our own lives and how our evolutionary history creates opportunities and sets limitations.

Of course, cultural factors interact with genetically based biological characteristics to widely varying degrees; these variable interactions influence how characteristics are expressed in individuals. Some genetically based characteristics will be exhibited no matter what the cultural context of a person's life happens to be. If a woman inherits two alleles for albinism, for example, she will be deficient in the production of the pigment melanin, resulting in lightly colored skin, hair,

and eyes. This phenotype will emerge regardless of the woman's cultural environment. Likewise, the sex-linked allele for hemophilia will be exhibited by all males who inherit it, no matter where they live.

Other characteristics, such as intelligence, body shape, and growth, reflect the interaction of environment and genes. We know, for example, that each of us is born with a genetic makeup that influences the maximum stature we can achieve in adulthood. But to reach that maximum stature, we must be properly nourished during growth (including during fetal development), and we must avoid many childhood diseases and other factors that inhibit growth. What factors determine whether we are well fed and receive good medical care? In the United States, socioeconomic status is probably the primary factor that determines nutrition and health. Socioeconomic status is thus an example of a cultural factor that affects growth. But in another culture, diet and health status might be influenced by whether the individual is male or female. In some cultures, males receive the best care in infancy and childhood and are thus often larger and healthier as adults than are females (**Fig. 13-2**). If there's a cultural value on slimness in women, young girls may try to restrict their food intake in ways that affect their growth; but if the culture values plumpness, the effect on diet in adolescence will likely be different. These are all examples of how cultural values affect growth and development. The ability of our bodies to develop in

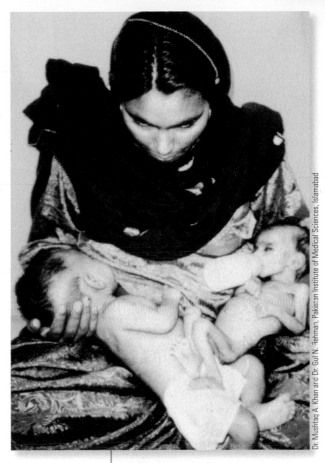

Dr. Mushtaq A. Khan and Dr. Gul N. Rehman, Pakistan Institute of Medical Sciences, Islamabad

▲ **Figure 13-2**
This is a mother with her twin children. The one on the left is a boy and is breast-fed. The girl, on the right, is bottle-fed. This illustrates both differential treatment of boys and girls in many societies and the potential negative effects of bottle feeding for people with few resources.

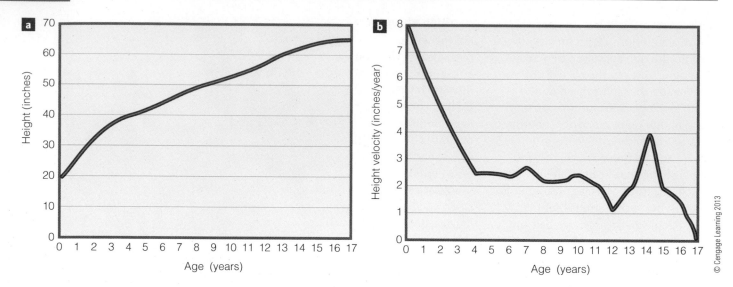

© Cengage Learning 2013

▲ **Figure 13-3**
Distance and velocity curves of growth in height for a healthy American girl. **(a)** The distance curve shows the height attained in a given year. **(b)** The velocity curve plots the amount gained in a given year.

Human Growth and Development Today and in the Past

In humans, growth begins at conception and continues until the late teens or early 20s. Typically, well-nourished humans grow fairly rapidly during the first two trimesters (six months) of fetal development, but growth slows during the third trimester. After birth, growth rates increase and remain fairly rapid for about four years, at which time they decrease again to relatively slow, steady levels that are maintained until puberty. At puberty, there's another very pronounced increase in growth. During this so-called **adolescent growth spurt**, Western teenagers typically grow around 4 inches per year. Following the adolescent growth spurt, the rate of growth declines again and remains slower until adult stature is achieved by the late teens (**Fig. 13-3**).

Growth curves for boys and girls are significantly different, with the adolescent growth spurt occurring approximately two years earlier in girls than in boys. At birth, there's a slight *sexual dimorphism* in many body mea-

different ways under varying circumstances is a product of our evolutionary history.

sures (for example, height, weight, head circumference, and body fat), but the major divergence in these characteristics doesn't occur until puberty.

The head is a relatively large part of the body at birth. The continued growth of the brain after birth occurs at a rate far greater than that of any other part of the body, with the exception of the eyeball. At birth, the human brain is about 25 percent of its adult size. By 6 months of age, the brain has doubled in size, reaching 50 percent of adult size. It reaches 75 percent of adult size at age 2½ years, 90 percent by age 5, and 95 percent by age 10. There's only a very small spurt in brain growth at adolescence, making the brain an exception to the growth curves characteristic of most other parts of the body. As we'll see later in this chapter, this pattern of brain growth, including the relatively small amount of growth before birth, is unusual among primates and other mammals. By contrast, the typical picture for most mammalian species is that at least 50 percent of adult brain size has been attained prior to birth. For humans, however, the narrow pelvis necessary for walking bipedally provides limits on the size of the neonatal head that can be delivered through it (Rosenberg and Trevathan, 2001). That limitation, in addition to the value of having most brain growth occur in the more stimulating environment outside the womb,

adolescent growth spurt The period during adolescence when well-nourished teens typically increase in stature at greater rates than at other times in the life cycle.

has resulted in human infants being born with far less of their total adult brain size than most other mammals.

Nutritional Requirements for Growth

Nutrition has an impact on human growth at every stage of the life cycle, and few aspects of the human environment have changed as much in the last 10,000 years as diet. It is therefore not surprising that there have also been changes in growth rates and outcomes. During pregnancy, for example, a woman's diet can have a profound effect on the development of her fetus and the eventual health of the child. Moreover, the effects are transgenerational, because a woman's own supply of eggs is developed while she herself is *in utero*. Thus, if a woman is malnourished during pregnancy, the eggs that develop in her female fetus may be damaged in a way that will impact the health of her future grandchildren.

What's more, nutritional stress during pregancy commonly results in low-birth-weight babies that are at great risk for developing hypertension, cardiovascular disease, and diabetes later in life (Barker, 2004; Gluckman and Hanson, 2005). Low-birth-weight babies are particularly at risk if they are born into a world of abundant food resources (especially cheap fast food), and they gain weight rapidly in childhood (Kuzawa, 2005, 2008). These findings have clear implications for public health efforts to provide adequate nutritional support to pregnant women and infants throughout the world.

Nutrients needed for growth, development, and body maintenance include proteins, carbohydrates, lipids (fats), vitamins, and minerals. The specific amount that we need of each of these nutrients coevolved with the types of foods that were available to human ancestors throughout our evolutionary history. For example, the specific pattern of amino acids required in human nutrition (the **essential amino acids**) reflects an ancestral diet high in animal protein. Unfortunately for modern humans, these coevolved nutritional requirements are often incompatible with the foods that are available and typically consumed today. To understand this mismatch of our nutritional needs and contemporary diets, we need to examine the impact of agriculture on human evolutionary history.

The preagricultural diet, basically encompassing the entirety of our evolutionary history prior to 10,000 years ago, was typically high in animal protein, but was low in fats, particularly saturated fats. That diet was also high in complex carbohydrates (including fiber), low in salt, and high in calcium. We don't need to be reminded that the contemporary diet that typifies many industrialized societies has the opposite configuration of the one just described. It's high in saturated fats and salt and low in complex carbohydrates, fiber, and calcium (**Fig. 13-4**). Although humans are notable for the great flexibility in their diets (Leonard, 2002), there is very good evidence that many of today's diseases in industrialized countries are related to the lack of fit between our diet today and the one with which we evolved (Gluckman et al., 2009).

Along with agriculture and animal domestication came a number of "new" food types that are important and common today but were rare or nonexistent in ancestral diets. Two examples include dairy products and cereal grains. In a previous chapter we discussed the difficulty that some people have digesting dairy products because they lack the enzyme necessary for breaking down the milk sugar lactose. Others have difficulty digesting the gluten found in some cereal grains, most commonly wheat and its close relatives. Intolerance for both lactose and gluten is more common in populations that have only recently adopted milk products and cereal grains into their diets (Wiley, 2008). The introduction of cattle and grains into early

essential amino acids The 9 (of 22) amino acids that must be obtained from the food we eat because they are not synthesized in the body in sufficient amounts.

▼**Figure 13-4**

The photos show diets that were likely consumed by our ancestors (left) and those that are commonly consumed in nations such as the United States today (right). The graphs compare the composition of the two diets for selected nutri- ents. Human nutritional requirements co-evolved with the foods consumed during the long period of human evolution- ary history before agriculture, resulting in a mismatch between what we need to eat today and the composition of contemporary diets.

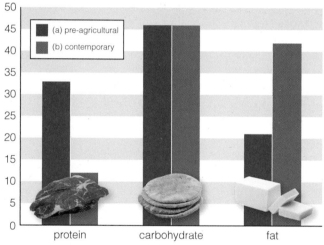

Percent of calories from protein, carbohydrates, and fats of preagricultural (a) and contemporary (b) diets.

Amount of sodium (mg) in preagricultural (a) and contemporary (b) diets.

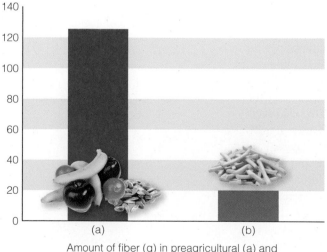

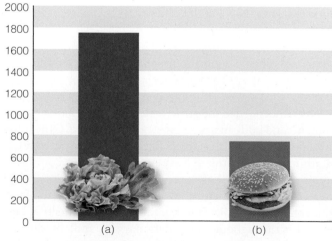

Amount of fiber (g) in preagricultural (a) and contemporary (b) diets.

Amount of calcium (mg) in preagricultural (a) and contemporary (b) diets.

agricultural populations may have increased food availability for many people, but for some people, specific foods that were not part of their ancestral diets are mismatched with their bodies in ways that lead to diarrhea and gastrointestinal upset. Unfortunately, food aid programs originating in parts of the world where milk and grains are staples sometimes have negative impacts on the malnourished populations they target.

Although we might reasonably expect that nutrition and health would have improved with the development of agriculture, human health actually declined in most parts of the world beginning about 10,000 years ago. Some have referred to the changing patterns of disease that occurred with agriculture as an "epidemiological transition," marked by the rise of infectious and nutritional deficiency diseases. In many places, skeletal signs of malnutrition (for example, iron-deficiency anemia; **Fig. 13-5**) appear for the first time with domesticated crops such as corn (Cohen and Armelagos, 1984; Larsen, 2002). Life expectancy also appears to have dropped. Clark Larsen refers to the adoption of agriculture as an "environmental catastrophe" (Larsen,

2006), and Jared Diamond has called it the worst mistake humans ever made (Diamond, 1987). But whether for better or worse, we're stuck with agriculture as a way of acquiring food because the planet couldn't possibly support the billions that live on it today without agriculture.

Many of our biological and behavioral characteristics evolved because in the past they contributed to adaptation, but today these same characteristics may be maladaptive. An example is our ability to store fat. This capability was an advantage in the past, when food availability often alternated between abundance and scarcity. Those who could store fat during times of abundance could draw on those stores during times of scarcity and remain healthy, resist disease, and, for women, maintain the ability to reproduce. Today, people with adequate economic resources spend much of their lives with a relative abundance of foods. Considering the number of disorders associated with obesity, the formerly positive ability to store extra fat has now turned into a liability. Our "feast or famine" biology is now incompatible with the constant feast many of us indulge in today.

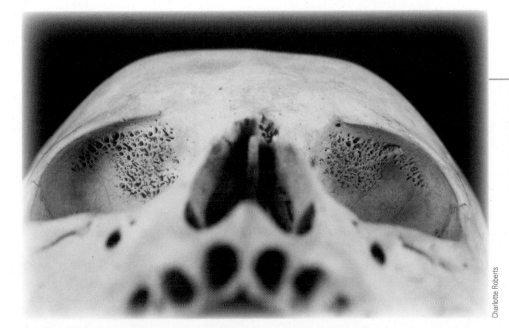

Charlotte Roberts

◄ Figure 13-5
Bone changes to the eye orbits that likely indicate anemia caused by vitamin deficiency or perhaps iron deficiency. Other conditions can also cause these bone changes.

Perhaps no disorder is as clearly linked with dietary and lifestyle behaviors as the form of diabetes mellitus that typically has its onset in later life, referred to variously as type 2 diabetes or NIDDM (non-insulin-dependent diabetes mellitus). A few years ago, type 2 diabetes was something that happened to older people living primarily in the developed world. Sadly, this is no longer true. The World Diabetes Foundation estimates that 80 percent of the new cases of type 2 diabetes that appear between now and 2025 will be in developing nations, and the World Health Organization (WHO) predicts that more than 70 percent of *all* diabetes cases in the world will be in developing nations in 2025. Furthermore, type 2 diabetes is occurring in children as young as 4 (Pavkov et al., 2006), and the mean age of diagnosis in the United States dropped from 52 to 46 between 1988 and 2000 (Koopman et al., 2005). In fact, we would guess that almost everyone reading this book has a friend or family member who has diabetes. What's happened to make this former "disease of old age" and "disease of civilization" reach what some have described as epidemic proportions?

Although there appears to be a genetic link (type 2 diabetes tends to run in families), most fingers point to lifestyle factors. Two lifestyle factors that have been implicated in this epidemic are poor diet and inadequate exercise. Noting that our current diets and activity levels are very different from those of our ancestors, proponents of *evolutionary medicine* suggest that diabetes is the price we pay for consuming excessive sugars and other refined carbohydrates while spending our days in front of the TV set or computer monitor. The reason that the incidence of diabetes is increasing in developing nations is that these bad habits are spreading to those nations. In fact, we may soon see what can be called an "epidemiological collision" in countries such as Zimbabwe,

Ecuador, and Haiti, where malnutrition and infectious diseases are rampant but obesity is on the rise, so that people are dying not only from diseases of poverty but also from those more characteristic of wealthier populations (Trevathan, 2010).

It's clear that both deficiencies and excesses of nutrients can cause health problems and interfere with childhood growth and adult health. Certainly, many people in all parts of the world, both industrialized and developing, suffer from inadequate supplies of food of any quality. We read daily of thousands dying from starvation due to drought, warfare, or political instability. The blame must be placed not only on the narrowed food base that resulted from the emergence of agriculture, but also on the increase in human population that occurred when people began to settle in permanent villages and have more children. Today, the crush of billions of humans almost completely dependent on cereal grains means that millions face undernutrition, malnutrition, and even starvation. Even with these huge populations, however, food scarcity may not be as big a problem as food inequality. In other words, there may be enough food produced for all people on earth, but economic and political forces keep it from reaching those who need it most. Of increasing concern are the effects of globalization (including liberalization of trade and agricultural policies) on food security, especially in developing nations, and what has become known as the "Global South." In particular, the adoption of Western diets and lifestyles has contributed to declining health in much of the world (Young, 2004).

Thirty years ago, the primary focus of international health and nutrition organizations, including the World Health Organization, was undernutrition and infectious diseases (Prentice, 2006). Today, more and more attention is focused on overnutrition and the diseases and disorders associ-

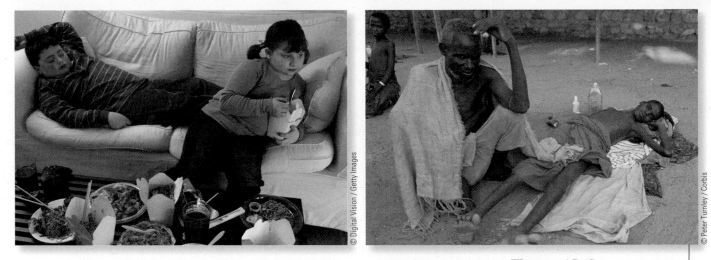

ated with obesity. By 2006, the number of people in the world who were overweight exceeded the number who were malnourished and underweight (Popkin, 2007). In many countries, including the United States, more than half of the population is overweight or obese (Mexico has the highest rate at almost 70%, with the United States not far behind). (To see obesity trends in the United States, visit the website http://www.cdc.gov/obesity/data/trends.html.). Clearly, diets for many people are mismatched with the nutrients required for healthy bodies.

In summary, our nutritional adaptations were shaped in environments that included times of scarcity alternating with times of abundance. The variety of foods consumed was so great that nutritional deficiency diseases were rare. Small amounts of animal foods were probably an important part of the diet in many parts of the world. In northern latitudes, after about 1 mya, meat was an important part of the diet. But because meat from wild animals is low in saturated fats, the negative effects of high meat intake that we see today were rare. Our diet today is often *dis*connected from the adaptations that evolved in the millions of years preceding the development of agriculture. The consequences of that mismatch include both starvation and obesity (**Fig. 13-6**).

Other Factors Influencing Growth and Development: Genes and Environment

Genetic factors set the underlying limitations and potentialities for growth and development, but the life experiences and environment of the organism determine how the body grows within those parameters. In fact, there is increasing evidence that environmental factors can change the ways in which genes are expressed without having an effect on the genes themselves. and that people with identical genotypes (i.e., identical twins) could have very different phenotypes. In other words, identical twins aren't really identical, and they become even more different as they age (Frago et al., 2005; Gluckman et al., 2009). Phenotypic differences emerge in identical twins because of the "software" that provides instructions to the unfolding genotype. These instructions are known as the **epigenome**, and they are responsible for turning some genes on and some genes off. All of the cells in our body have the same genes (except the sex cells), but they do different things because of the epigenome. In different individuals, the epigenome may turn off some genes or turn on others, resulting in different phenotypes. This is one of the main ways in which the environment interacts with genes and helps explain why

epigenome The instructions that determine how genes are expressed in a cell.

one member of a pair of identical twins may suffer from a genetically based cancer while the other is disease-free. Lifestyle factors are particularly important influences on the epigenome, especially diet and smoking.

The ongoing "nature–nurture debate" has pitted genetic factors against environmental factors in determining how an individual grows, develops, and behaves. The field of **epigenetics** helps to resolve this conflict by revealing that structural changes to DNA and associated proteins (without accompanying changes in the nucleotide sequence) can underlie gene expression. The changes are transmitted through mitosis, so that when they are established during development, they persist with further cell division. In this way, environmental factors (such as smoke or air pollution) can bring about changes during development that affect a person in adulthood, partially explaining differences in disease risk. Although these changes in gene expression are not usually passed on to offspring, there is increasing evidence of epigenetic inheritance that transcends generations (Whitelaw and Whitelaw, 2006). Certainly, research in epigenetics calls into question the whole idea of genetic determinism for many traits. Of interest to social scientists is the suggestion that social factors may have an effect on the epigenetic programming of behavior throughout the life course (Szyf et al., 2008).

Hormones

One of the primary ways in which genes have an effect on growth and development is through their effects on hormones. Hormones are substances produced in one cell that have an effect on another cell , and examples include estrogen, testosterone, cortisol, and insulin. Most hormones are produced by **endocrine glands**, such as the pituitary, thyroid, and adrenal glands, in addition to the ovaries and testes. Hormones are transported in the blood-

stream, and almost all have an effect on growth. The hypothalamus (located at the base of the forebrain) can be considered the relay station, control center, or central clearinghouse for most hormonal action. This control center receives messages from the brain and other glands and sends out messages that stimulate hormonal action. Most of the hormonal messages transmitted from the hypothalamus result in the inhibition or release of other hormones.

Two hormones that are especially important in growth are growth hormone and insulin. Growth hormone, secreted by the anterior pituitary, promotes growth and has an effect on just about every cell in the body. Tumors and other disorders can cause excessive or insufficient amounts of growth hormone secretion, which in turn can result in gigantism or dwarfism. One group of people who have notably short stature are African Efe pygmies (**Fig. 13-7**). Research suggests that altered levels of growth hormone and its controlling factors interact with nutritional factors and infectious diseases to produce the relatively short adult stature of these people (Shea and Bailey, 1996), providing another example of the interaction of biological and cultural forces.

Another hormone that influences growth and development is cortisol, which is elevated during stress. Up to a point, cortisol elevation is adaptive, but if the response is prolonged or severe, there appear to be negative effects on health and behavior (Flinn, 1999; Flinn and England, 2003). Under conditions of chronic emotional and psychosocial stress, cortisol levels may remain high and suppress normal immune function. This means that a child living in a stressful situation is more vulnerable to infectious diseases and may experience periods of slowed growth if the stress is prolonged. A reasonable argument could be made that people today of all ages and in all parts of the world experience significantly higher levels

epigenetics Changes in phenotype that are not related to changes in underlying DNA and that may result from the interaction between the genotype and the environment.

endocrine glands glands responsible for the secretion of hormones into the bloodstream.

◀**Figure 13-7**
Charles Knowles of the Wildlife Conservation Network stands beside three Mbuti (Efe) staff members of the Okapi Conservation Project.

of stress than our ancestors did. suggesting that effects on growth may also be different. This is not to suggest that our ancestors didn't experience stress (few things are more stressful than a lion chasing you and your children), but the sources and duration of stressors were probably very different from those we experience today.

The levels of reproductive hormones in women from health-rich nations appear to be elevated over what is reported for women in traditional societies and what was probably the ancestral profile (Vitzthum, 2009; **Fig. 13-8**). Furthermore, women who use contraception and have few or no children and breastfeed for only a few months have repeated menstrual cycles and the associated high levels of estrogen for the majority of their reproductive lives. This is a very

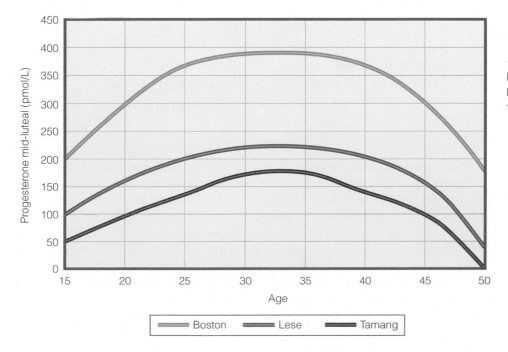

◀**Figure 13-8**
Hormonal variation in three populations. Re-drawn from Ellison, 1994.

different hormonal profile from ancestral women, who spent most of their adult years pregnant or nursing infants, yielding very few menstrual cycles. This disconnection between today's hormonal profiles and those of our ancestors may result in a higher incidence of reproductive cancers, especially when coupled with high-fat diets and low levels of exercise (Trevathan, 2010).

The Human Life Cycle

As noted in earlier chapters, primatologists and other physical anthropologists view primate and human growth and development from an evolutionary perspective, with an interest in how natural selection has operated on the life cycle from conception to death, a perspective known as life history theory. Why, for example, do humans have longer periods of infancy and childhood compared with other primates? What accounts for differences seen in the life cycles of such closely related species as humans and chimpanzees? Life history research seeks to answer such questions (see Mace, 2000, for a review).

Life history theory allows us to predict the timing of reproduction under favorable circumstances. It begins with the premise that there's only a certain amount of energy available to an organism for growth, maintenance of life, and reproduction. Energy invested in one of these processes isn't available to another. Thus, the entire life course represents a series of trade-offs among various life history traits, such as length of gestation, age at weaning, time spent in growth to adulthood, adult body size, and length of life span. For example, life history theory provides the basis for understanding how fast an organism will grow and to what size, how many offspring can be produced, how long gestation will last, and how long an individual will live. Crucial to understanding life history theory is its link to the evolu-

tionary process: It's the action of natural selection that shapes life history traits, determining which ones will succeed or fail in a given environment. Although it isn't clear if life history theory works in contemporary human populations (Strassman and Gillespie, 2002), it serves as a useful guide for examining the various life cycle phases from evolutionary and ecological perspectives.

Most life cycle stages are well marked by biological transitions such as those that occur at birth and puberty. Biological markers associated with life cycle changes are similar among higher primates, but for humans, there's an added complexity: They occur in cultural contexts that define and characterize them. Puberty, for example, has very different meanings in different cultures. A girl's first menstruation (**menarche**) is often marked with ritual and celebration, and a change in social status typically occurs with this biological transition. Likewise, **menopause** is often associated with a rise in status for women in non-Western societies, whereas it's commonly seen as a negative transition for women in many Western societies. As we shall see, collective and individual attitudes toward these life cycle transitions have an effect on growth, development, and health.

Pregnancy, Birth, and Infancy

The biological aspects of conception and gestation can be discussed in a fairly straightforward way, drawing information from what is known about reproductive biology at the present time: A sperm fertilizes an egg; the resulting zygote travels through a uterine (fallopian) tube to become implanted in the uterine lining; and the embryo develops until it's mature enough to survive outside the womb, at which time birth occurs. But this is clearly not all there is to human pregnancy and birth. Female biology may

menarche The first menstruation in girls, usually occurring in the early to mid-teens.

menopause The end of menstruation in women, usually occurring around age 50.

be similar the world over, but cultural rules and practices are the primary determinants of who will get pregnant, as well as when, where, how, and by whom.

Once a pregnancy has begun, there's much variation in how a woman should behave, what she should eat, where she should and should not go, and how she should interact with other people. Almost every culture known imposes dietary restrictions on pregnant women. Many of these appear to serve an important biological function, particularly that of keeping the woman from ingesting toxins that would be dangerous for the fetus. (Alcohol is a good example of a potential toxin whose consumption in pregnancy is discouraged in the United States.) The food aversions to coffee, alcohol, and other bitter substances that many women experience during pregnancy may be evolved adaptations to protect the embryo from toxins. The nausea of early pregnancy may also function to limit the intake of foods potentially harmful to the embryo at a critical stage of development (Profet, 1988; Williams and Nesse 1991; but see Pike, 2000).

As noted above, there is increasing evidence that what happens during prenatal development has lifelong consequences, many of which are irreversible. Scholars of fetal origins research propose that conditions during pregnancy affect such factors as disease susceptibility and metabolism (Kuzawa, 2008); some go even further to suggest that prenatal factors can affect intelligence and temperament as well (Paul, 2010). The old adage of "eating for two" during pregnancy can be expanded to "living for two" with evidence that stress, emotions, and pollution in addition to food and drink have an effect on a developing fetus. Given the effects on metabolism, it may be that pregnancy is the best place to focus efforts to curb rising obesity rates worldwide.

Birth is an event that's celebrated with ritual in almost every culture

studied. In fact, the relatively little fanfare associated with childbirth in the United States is unusual by world standards. Because risk of death for both mother and child is so great at birth, it's not surprising that it's surrounded with ritual significance. Perhaps, because of the high risk of death, we tend to think that birth is far more difficult for humans than it is for other mammals. But since almost all primate infants have large heads relative to body size, birth is challenging to many primates (**Fig. 13-9**)

An undeveloped brain seems necessary for birth to occur through a narrow pelvis, but it may also be advantageous for other reasons. For a species as dependent on learning as we are for survival, it may be adaptive for most of our brain growth to take place in the presence of environmental stimuli rather than in the relatively unstimulating environment of the uterus. This

▼**Figure 13-9**
The relationship between the average diameter of the birth canal of adult females and the average head size of newborn infants of the same species (after Jolly, 1985).

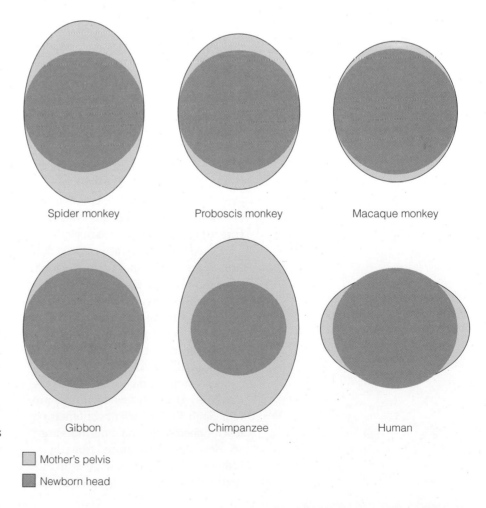

Spider monkey   Proboscis monkey   Macaque monkey

Gibbon   Chimpanzee   Human

☐ Mother's pelvis
☐ Newborn head

may be particularly true for a species dependent on language. The language centers of the brain develop in the first three years of life, when the brain is undergoing its rapid expansion; these three years are considered a critical period for the development of language in the human child.

Infancy, as we noted, is the period of nursing, and it typically lasts two to three years in humans. When we consider how unusual it is for a mother to nurse her child for even a year in the United States or Canada, this figure may surprise us. But considering that three or four years of nursing is the norm for the great apes and for women in some foraging societies, most anthropologists conclude that three to four years was the norm for most humans in the evolutionary past (Eaton et al., 1988; Dettwyler, 1995). On the other hand, mother's milk alone may not be sufficient to support the rapidly growing infant brain, so supplementation may have been important early in our evolutionary history, just as it is today (Kennedy, 2005). High-quality foods for infant supplementation may have been limited before the origin of agriculture and the domestication of milk-producing animals, however. In fact, if the mother died during childbirth in preagricultural populations, it's very likely that the child died also unless there was another woman available who could nurse the child. Jane Goodall has noted that this is also true for chimpanzees: Infants who are orphaned before they are weaned don't usually survive. Even those orphaned after weaning are still emotionally dependent on their mothers and exhibit clinical signs of depression for a few months or years after the mother's death, assuming they survive the trauma (Goodall, 1986).

Human milk, like that of other primates, is extremely low in fats and protein. Such a low-nutrient content is typical for species in which mothers are seldom or never separated from their infants and nurse in short, frequent bouts. Not coincidentally, prolonged, frequent nursing suppresses ovulation in marginally nourished women (Konner and Worthman, 1980), especially when coupled with high activity levels and few calorie reserves (Ellison, 2001). Under these circumstances, breast-feeding can help maintain a four-year birth interval, during which infants have no nutritional competition from siblings. Thus, nursing served as a natural (but not foolproof) birth control mechanism in the evolutionary past, as it does in some populations today.

The fact that infants born today can survive and grow without breast milk is further evidence of our species' flexibility and how cultural mechanisms have enabled us to transcend some of the biological limitations placed on our ancestors and on other mammalian species. But breast milk also provides important antibodies that contribute to infant survival and that are not available in formula and other milk substitutes. Throughout the world, breast-fed infants have far greater survival rates than those who aren't breast-fed or who are weaned too early. The only exception is in societies where scientifically developed milk substitutes are readily available and appropriately used, and even then, infants don't get several important antibodies and other immune factors. The importance of adequate nutrients during this period of rapid brain growth can't be overestimated. Thus, it's not surprising that there are many cultural practices designed to ensure successful nursing. Furthermore, there is increasing evidence that breast-feeding may be protective against later-life obesity, types 1 and 2 diabetes, and hypertension (Pollard, 2008). Like prenatal care, increasing rates of successful breast-feeding around the world is a worthy public health goal.

Childhood

Humans have unusually long childhoods, reflecting the importance of learning for our species (Bogin, 2006). Childhood is that time between weaning and puberty when the brain is completing its growth and the acquisition of technical and social skills is taking place. For most other mammals, once weaning has occurred, getting food is left to individual effort. Humans may be unique in the practice of providing food for juveniles (Lancaster and Lancaster, 1983). In the course of human evolution, it's possible that provisioning children between weaning and puberty may have doubled or even tripled the number of offspring that survived to adulthood (**Table 13-1**). This long period of extended child care by older children and adults (especially fathers) probably enhanced the time for learning technological and social skills, also contributing to greater survival and reproductive success. Thus, the costs of extensive parental care were outweighed in human evolutionary history by the benefits of greater reproductive success.

The major causes of childhood death worldwide today are infectious diseases exacerbated by poor nutrition (Caulfield et al., 2004; Pellitier et al., 1995). Noting how important it is to have sufficient caloric intake in infancy while the brain is developing, Christopher Eppig and his colleagues have suggested that infectious diseases and parasitic infections drain nutrients and energy necessary for brain development in ways that threaten cognitive development and may help explain variation in IQ scores seen across nations (Eppig, et al., 2010). It's notable that the leading causes of childhood death in the United States and Western Europe aren't typically related to malnutrition; for children under 5 years of age, accidents are the leading cause of death, followed by preterm births.

Adolescence

For most animals, infancy ends with weaning as adulthood begins. For many social species such as most primates, cetaceans, and carnivores, there's an additional life cycle stage called the juvenile stage (childhood in humans) when the young are weaned but not reproductively mature and are still dependent on adults for food. For humans there is yet another stage, adolescence, a period of extremely rapid growth (the "adolescent growth spurt") that is not seen in other primates (Bogin, 1999; 2010). A number of biological events mark the transition to adolescence for both males and females. These include increase in body size, change in body shape, and the increased development and enlargement of testes and penises in boys and breasts in girls. Hormonal changes are the driving forces behind all these physical alterations, especially increased testosterone production in boys and increased estrogen production in girls. As already noted, menarche is a clear sign of puberty in girls and is usually the marker of this transition in cultures where the event is ritually celebrated.

A number of factors affect the onset of puberty in humans, including genetics, gestational experience, nutrition, disease, activity levels, and stress. In humans and other primates, females

TABLE 13.1 Providing for Juveniles

	Percent of Those Who Survive	
	Weaning	**Adolescence**
Lion	28	15
Baboon	45	33
Macaque	42	13
Chimpanzee	48	38
Provisioned macaques	82	58
Human Populations		
!Kung*	80	58
Yanomamo†	73	50
Paleoindian‡	86	50

* A hunting and gathering population of southern Africa.
† A horticultural population of South America.
‡ A preagricultural people of the Americas.
Source: Adapted from Lancaster and Lancaster, 1983.

reach sexual maturity before males do. An illustration of the "mismatch" effect of diet and other lifestyle factors on puberty is seen in the trend toward a lower age of menarche that has been noted in human populations in the last hundred years (**Fig. 13-10**) and the tendency for girls who are very active and thin to mature later than those who are heavier and less active. Socioeconomic factors are also implicated in this trend: In less industrialized nations, girls from higher social classes tend to mature earlier than girls from lower social classes. In general, physical development has accelerated in the past several decades along with worldwide improvements in public health and nutrition. Although we have emphasized the gradual decline in the age of maturity observed in the last century, there's a great range of variation within every population. An important lesson from life history theory is that maturation is sensitive to local environmental situations, including diet, health care, and parental care practices.

Until the advent of settled living, it's likely that females became pregnant as soon as they were biologically able to do so, that is, as soon as they had finished growing. This would have been advantageous under conditions when individual life expectancy would have been low. Paleodemographic studies indicate a mortality rate of at least 50 percent in subadults in preindustrial populations; and of the half that survived to adulthood, most did not survive to age 50. Considering the reality of short life spans combined with the long period of infant dependency, producing offspring as early as possible may have contributed to the reproductive success of females, particularly early hominin females. By giving birth as soon as she reached sexual maturity, an early hominin female enhanced her chances of rearing at least one offspring to the point it could survive without her.

Adulthood

Pregnancy and child care occupy much of a woman's adult life in most cultures, as they likely did throughout hominin evolution. For most women, the years from menarche to menopause are marked by monthly menstruation except when they are pregnant or nursing. A normal menstrual cycle has two phases: the follicular phase, during which the egg is preparing for ovulation, marked by high estrogen produc-

▶ **Figure 13-10**

The secular trend in age of menarche in Western nations.

From James W. Wood, Dynamics of Human Reproduction (New York: Aldine de Gruyter, 1994); original redrawn from P. B. Eveleth and J. M. Tanner, Worldwide Variation in Human Growth (New York: Cambridge University Press, 1976).

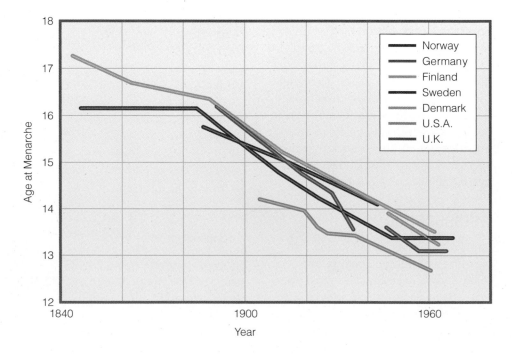

tion; and the luteal phase, during which the uterus is preparing for implantation, marked by high progesterone production. If the egg is not fertilized, progesterone production drops off and menstruation, the shedding of the uterine lining, occurs. A woman who never becomes pregnant may have as many as 400 cycles between menarche and menopause. Because reliable contraceptives were unavailable in the past, this high number of menstrual cycles is probably a relatively recent phenomenon. It's been suggested, in fact, that highly frequent menstrual cycling may be implicated in several cancers of the female reproductive organs, especially of the breast, uterus, and ovaries (Eaton et al., 1994; Strassman, 1999; Greaves, 2008). During the course of human evolution, females may have had as few as 60 menstrual cycles in their entire lives unless they were sterile or not sexually active.

Furthermore, research conducted by several biological anthropologists presents evidence that the levels of hormones produced during the menstrual cycle may be higher in women from industrialized economies than for women living lives more similar to those of our ancestors (Vitzthum, 2009). Thus, the hormonal milieu of contemporary women may be different from the conditions under which we evolved, with negative consequences for reproductive health. This is another example of the *dis*connections or mismatches between our evolved biology and the lives many of us live today.

For women, menopause, or the end of menstruation, is a sign of entry into a new phase of the life cycle. Estrogen and progesterone production begins to decline toward the end of the reproductive years until ovulation (and thus menstruation) ceases altogether. This occurs at approximately age 50 in all parts of the world. As an example of the continuing effects of natural selection, there is evidence that women with a later age at menopause have more surviving offspring (Stearns et al., 2010). If this pattern continues,

the authors suggest, the average age of menopause may increase by a year in the next 10 generations or 200 years.

Throughout human evolution, the majority of females (and males) did not survive to age 50; thus, few women lived much past menopause. But today, this event occurs when women have as much as one-third of their active and healthy lives ahead of them. As already noted, such a long postreproductive period isn't found in other primates. Female chimpanzees and monkeys experience decreased fertility in their later years, but most continue to have monthly cycles until their deaths. Occasional reports of menopause in apes and monkeys have been noted, but it's far from a routine and expected event.

Why do human females have such a long period during which they can no longer reproduce? One theory relates to parenting. Because it takes about 12 to 15 years before a child becomes independent, it's been argued that females are biologically "programmed" to live 12 to 15 years beyond the birth of their last child . This hypothesis assumes that the maximum human life span for preagricultural humans was about 65 years, a figure that corresponds to what is known for contemporary hunter-gatherers and for prehistoric populations.

Another theory about a long postreproductive life is known as the "grandmother hypothesis." This proposal argues that natural selection may have favored this long period in women's lives because by ceasing to bear and raise their own children, postmenopausal women would be freed to provide high-quality care for their grandchildren (**Fig. 13-11**). In other words, an older woman would be more likely to increase her reproductive fitness by enhancing the survival of her grandchildren (who share one-quarter of her genes) than by having her own, possibly low-quality infants (Hawkes et al., 1997; Lahdenperä et al., 2004; but see Peccei, 2001). This is an example of

▲ **Figure 13-11**
Hadza woman and grandchild.

the trade-offs considered by life history theory.

A third theory regarding menopause suggests that it wasn't itself favored by natural selection; rather it's an artifact of the extension of the human life span that's occurred in the last several centuries. To put it another way, the long postreproductive years and associated menopause in women have been "uncovered" by an extended life expectancy because many causes of death are now reduced (Sievert, 2006).

Aging and Longevity

Postreproductive years are physiologically defined for women, but "old age" is a very ambiguous concept. In the United States, we tend to associate old age with physical ailments and decreased activity. Thus, a person who's vigorous and active at age 70 might not be regarded as "old," whereas another who's frail and debilitated at age 55 may be considered old.

One reason we're concerned with this definition is that old age is generally regarded negatively and is typically unwelcome in the United States, a culture noted for its emphasis on youth. This attitude is quite different from that of many other societies, where old age brings with it wealth, higher status, and new freedoms, particularly for women. This is because high status is often correlated with knowledge, experience, and wisdom, which are themselves associated with greater age in most societies. Such has been the case throughout most of history, but today,

in technologically developed countries, information is changing so rapidly that the old may no longer control the most relevant knowledge.

By and large, people are living longer today than they did in the past because, in part, they aren't dying from infectious disease. Currently, the top five killers in the United States, for example, are heart disease, cancer, stroke, chronic obstructive lung disease, and accidents. Together these account for almost 70 percent of deaths (CDC National Vital Statistics Report, 2009). All these conditions are considered "diseases of civilization" in that most can be accounted for by conditions in the modern environment that weren't present in the past, another example of the mismatch. Examples include cigarette smoke, air and water pollution, alcohol, automobiles, high-fat diets, and environmental carcinogens. It should be noted, however, that the high incidence of these diseases is also a result of people living to older ages because of factors such as improved hygiene, regular medical care, and new medical technologies.

Relative to most other animals, humans have a long life span (**Table 13-2**). The maximum life span potential, estimated to be about 120 years, has probably not changed in the last several thousand years, although life expectancy at birth (the average length of life) has increased significantly in the last 100 years, probably owing to increased standards of living and the decreased influence of infectious disease, which typically takes its toll on the young (Crews and Harper, 1998).

To some extent, aging is something we do throughout our entire lives. But we usually think of aging as **senescence**, the process of physiological decline in all systems of the body that occurs toward the end of the life course. Actually, throughout adulthood, there's a gradual decline in our cells' ability to synthesize proteins, in immune system function, in muscle mass (with a corresponding increase in fat mass) and strength, and in bone mineral density (Lamberts et al. 1997). This decline is associated with an increase in risk for the chronic degenerative diseases that are usually listed as the primary causes of death in industrialized nations.

Most causes of death that have their effects after the reproductive years won't necessarily be subjected to the forces of natural selection. In evolutionary terms, reproductive success isn't measured by how long we live; rather, as we've emphasized throughout this book, it's measured by how many offspring we produce. So organisms need to survive only long enough to produce offspring and rear them to maturity. Most wild animals die young of infection, starvation, predation, injury, and cold. Obviously, there are exceptions to this statement, especially in larger-bodied animals. Elephants, for example, may live over 50 years, and we know of several chimpanzees at Gombe that have survived into their 40s and even 50s.

One explanation for why we age and are affected by chronic degenerative diseases such as atherosclerosis, cancer, and hypertension is that genes that enhance reproductive success in earlier years (and thus were favored by natural selection) may have detrimental effects in later years. These are referred to as **pleiotropic genes**, meaning that they have multiple effects at different times in the life span or under different conditions (Williams, 1957). For example, genes that enhance the function of the immune system in the early years may also damage tissue so that cancer susceptibility increases in later life (Nesse and Williams, 1994).

Pleiotropy may help us understand evolutionary reasons for aging, but what are the causes of senescence in the individual? Much attention has been focused recently on free radicals, highly reactive molecules that can damage cells. Protection against these by-products of normal metabolism is provided by antioxidants such as vitamins A, C, and E and by a number of enzymes (Kirkwood, 1997).

TABLE 13.2	Maximum Life Spans for Selected Species

Organism	Approximate Maximum Life Span (in years)
Bristlecone pine	5,000
Tortoise	170
Rockfish	140
Human	120
Blue whale	80
Indian elephant	70
Gorilla	39
Domestic dog	34
Rabbit	13
Rat	5

Source: Stini, 1991.

Ultimately, damage to DNA can occur, which in turn contributes to the senescence of cells, the immune system, and other functional systems of the body. Additionally, there is evidence that programmed cell death is also a part of the normal process of development that can obviously contribute to senescence.

The mitochondrial theory of aging proposes that the free radicals produced by the normal action of the cell's mitochondria as by-products of daily living (for example, eating, breathing, walking) contribute to declining efficiency of energy production and accumulating mutations in mitochondrial DNA (mtDNA). When the mitochondria of an organ fail, there's a greater chance that the organ itself will fail. In this view, as mitochondria lose their ability to function, the body ages as well (Loeb et al., 2005; Kujoth et al., 2007). Two of the most promising strategies for enhancing health in later life are calorie reduction and aerobic exercise, both of which appear to improve mitochondrial function in later life (Lanza and Nair, 2010).

Another hypothesis for senescence is known as the "telomere hypothesis."

pleiotropic genes Genes that have more than one effect; genes that have different effects at different times in the life cycle.

▲ **Figure 13-12**

Telomeres are repeated sequences of DNA at the ends of chromosomes and the sequences appear to be the same in all animals. They stabilize and protect the ends of chromosomes, and as they shorten with each cell division the chromosomes eventually become unstable.

In this view, the DNA sequence at the end of a chromosome, known as the telomere, is shortened each time a cell divides (**Fig. 13-12**). Cells that have divided many times throughout the life course have short telomeres, eventually reaching the point at which they can no longer divide and are unable to maintain healthy tissues and organs. Changes in telomere length have also been implicated in cancers and other diseases associated with aging (Oeseburg et al., 2010). Furthermore, shorter telomeres are associated with excess body fat, suggesting that obesity may hasten the aging process (Lee et al., 2011).

In the laboratory, the enzyme telomerase can lengthen telomeres, allowing the cell to continue to divide. For this reason, the gene for telomerase has been called the "immortalizing gene." But this may not be a good thing, since the only cells that can divide indefinitely are cancer cells. Although this research isn't likely to lead to a lengthening of the life span, it may contribute to a better understanding of cellular functions and cancer.

Far more important than genes in the aging process, however, are lifestyle factors, such as smoking, physical activity, diet, and medical care. Life expectancy at birth varies considerably from country to country and among socioeconomic classes within a country. Throughout the world, women have higher life expectancies than men. A Japanese girl born in 2009, for example, can expect to live to age 86, a boy to age 80. Girls and boys born in that same year in the United States have life expectancies of 81 and 76, respectively. Unfortunately, gains in life expectancy in the United States appear to be slowing relative to other industrialized nations, primarily due to smoking, obesity, and sedentary habits (Seppa, 2011). In 2006, the latest year for which data were available, the United States ranked 36th in life expectancy among nations of the world (UN Life Expectancy 2005–2010).

In contrast to children in industrialized nations, girls and boys in Malawi have life expectancies of only 51 and 44, respectively (data from World Health Organization, WHO Global Health Indicators, 2011). Many African nations have seen life expectancy drop below 40 due to deaths from AIDS. For example, before the AIDS epidemic, Botswanans had a life expectancy of almost 65 years; at the height of the AIDS epidemic, life expectancy in Botswana was slightly more than 40 (**Fig. 13-13**). In 1990, Zimbabweans could expect to live to 61, but by 2000 that figure had dropped to 45.

One consequence of improved health and longer life expectancy in conjunction with declining birth rates is an aging population, leading in some parts of the world to a shift toward older median ages and greater numbers of people older than 65 than younger than 20. In demographic terms, these two groups represent dependent categories, and there's increasing concern about the decline in the number of working-aged adults available to support the younger and older segments of a population. In other words, the dependency ratio is increasing, with significant consequences for local and global economies. This phenomenon is of increasing concern in the United States and Western Europe, where it is estimated that more than a third of the population will be older than age 65 and fewer than half will be in the workforce.

Effects of Technology on the Brain

Aspects of the human cultural environment that are changing especially rapidly are computer technology and the ways in which people gather information. In the past, information was based on environmental cues derived from sights, sounds, smells, and tactile sensations. Although these sensory sources of information are still very important, people are increasing-

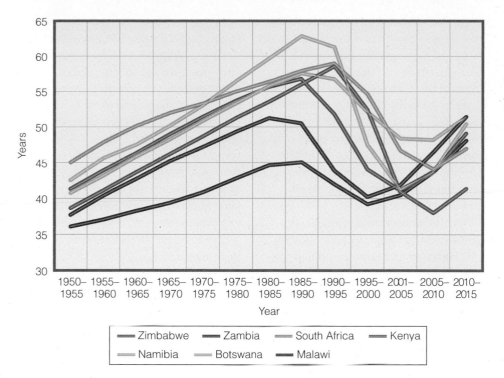

◄ **Figure 13-13**
Changes in life expectancy due to AIDS in seven African nations (from United Nations, 1998).

ly turning to the Internet for information and social contact. What effect will this change have on our brains? As we have argued throughout this text, our brains coevolved with technology and language development and it is reasonable to think that evolutionary processes continue for the brain, but like so much of what has occurred in the last hundred or so years, the pace of technological change is becoming faster and faster. One concern is that as our brains adapt to new technological innovations there may be decreases in the development of social skills (Small, 2008).

Brain plasticity is well known, as demonstrated by the brains of musicians (showing more gray matter in the areas of the brain responsible for finger movement) and athletes (more neurons for hand-eye coordination), so it is reasonable to assume that spending hours on the Internet searching for information and playing computer games will result in brain modifications that are different from those seen in our grandparents and great grandparents. This is not the same as evolution, of course, but it does suggest that the distinctive human brain is being modified

by technology in new and unforeseen ways. The speed of change also raises concerns about generational differences and what has become known as the "digital divide." Other concerns include addiction to Internet browsing, decreased attention span, and effect on young children (**Fig. 13-14**). In fact, the American Academy of Pediatrics issued a warning against too much screen time (computers and television) for children under 2 for fear of negative consequences for the rapidly developing brain in those years (AAP, 2001). On the other hand, there is evidence that becoming proficient in Internet skills may have a positive effect on the aging brain (Small et al., 2009).

Are We Still Evolving?

In many ways, it seems that culture has enabled us to transcend most of the limitations our biology imposes on us. But that biology was shaped during millions of years of evolution in environments very different from those in which most of us live today. There is, to a great extent, a lack of fit or a "mismatch" between our biology and our

© iStockphoto.com / Ana Abejon

▲ **Figure 13-14**
Exposure to computers at a very young age and for many hours per day may have effects on the developing brain.

twenty-first-century cultural environments, resulting in health challenges at all ages. Our expectations that scientists can easily and quickly discover a "magic bullet" to enable us to resist any disease that arises have been painfully dashed as death tolls from AIDS reach catastrophic levels in many parts of the world. Obesity and related disorders are beginning to have a greater impact on human lives than undernutrition and infectious diseases.

Socioeconomic and political concerns also have powerful effects on our species today. Whether you die of starvation or succumb to disorders associated with overconsumption depends a great deal on where you live, what your socioeconomic status is, and how much power and control you have over your life—factors not related to biology. These factors also affect whether you'll be killed in a war or spend most of your life in a safe, comfortable community. Your chances of being exposed to one of the "new" pathogens such as HIV, SARS, or tuberculosis have a lot to do with your lifestyle and other cultural factors. But your chances of dying from the disease or failing to reproduce because of it still have a lot to do with your biology. The millions of children dying annually from respiratory infections and diarrhea are primarily those in the developing world, with limit-

ed access to adequate medical care—clearly a cultural factor. But in those same areas, lacking that same medical care, are millions of other children who aren't getting the infections or aren't dying from them. Presumably, among the factors affecting this difference is resistance afforded by genes. It is clear that human gene frequencies are still changing from one generation to the next in response to selective agents such as disease; thus, our species is still evolving.

We can't predict whether we will become a different species or become extinct as a species (remember, that is the fate of almost every species that has ever existed). Will our brains get larger, or will our hands evolve solely to push buttons? Or will we change genetically so that we no longer have to eat food? This is the stuff of science fiction, not anthropology. But as long as new pathogens appear or new environments are introduced by technology, there's little doubt that just like every other species on earth, the human species will either continue to evolve or become extinct.

Has our evolutionary history prepared us for the twenty-first century? We have discussed a number of the *dis*-connections between our evolved biologies and contemporary lives, but we have also emphasized that one of the

Why It Matters

For children who grow up in poverty with limited access to good food, isn't it better that they are small as adults so that they don't require as much food?

This argument was presented several years ago as the "small but healthy hypothesis" (Seckler, 1982), which stated that small adult stature under circumstances of low resource availability was adaptive in that small adults would need fewer resources and would fare better under chronically stressful conditions. In fact, a

great deal of public policy was based on this "small but healthy" hypothesis, but the broader anthropological and evolutionary perspectives reveal that small body size also means small organs, less ability to perform work, and lower reproductive success (Martorell, 1989), all of which mean "not healthy" from evolutionary and life span perspectives. And even if a baby whose mother was malnourished during pregnancy is well nourished from birth on (as often happens in adoptions), the child's growth, health, and, for females, future pregnancies appear to be

compromised, perhaps even for several generations (Kuzawa, 2005). This awareness has clear implications for public health efforts that attempt to provide adequate nutritional support to pregnant women throughout the world. One of the best predictors of lifelong health is infant birth weight (Barker, 2004), so if public health programs could focus only on one goal, improving this statistic would have far-reaching impacts. Over and over again, we find that the nutritional requirements of our ancestors still have profound effects on us today.

most significant legacies from our evolutionary history is our biological and behavioral flexibility provided in part by the all-important phenomenon of culture. Culture has enabled us to transcend many limits imposed by our biology. Today, people who never would have been able to do so in the past are surviving and having children. This in itself means that we are adapting and evolving. How many of you would be reading this text if you had been born under the health and economic conditions prevalent 500 years ago?

Summary of Main Topics

- Our evolved biology, resulting from millions of years of evolution, may not be well matched with the diets and lifestyles we have today, perhaps contributing to myriad health challenges we now face.
- Nutrition has an impact on human growth at every stage of the life cycle and few aspects of the human environment have changed as much in the last 10,000 years as diet.
- Prenatal nutrition and infant birth weight have profound effects on lifelong health.
- In some ways, human health may have declined with the onset of agriculture and animal domestication approximately 10,000 years ago.

- One result of the mismatch between contemporary diets and evolved biology may be a rise in the worldwide incidence of type 2 diabetes and obesity.
- Studies in epigenetics have revealed that structural changes to DNA and associated proteins caused by developmental and environmental factors can underlie gene expression, helping to resolve the age-old conflict between nature and nurture.
- Women in health-rich nations today have reproductive hormonal profiles that may differ greatly from those under which our ancestors evolved, suggesting a link to various reproductive disorders and diseases.

- Humans have an unusually long period of childhood during which time much learning takes place.
- Unlike most mammals, human women live several years beyond the termination of their reproductive years, suggesting a value in the contributions of grandmothers.
- A new set of questions about the effects of technology on the developing and mature human brain has arisen with rapidly increasing developments in computers and other forms of information technology.
- Although it appears that culture has enabled us to transcend biological evolutionary processes, there is little doubt that our species continues to evolve.

Critical Thinking Questions

1. What is meant by the analogy "Water is to fish as culture is to humans"? Do you think that humans could survive without culture?
2. Several times in this chapter the authors talk about a "mismatch" between our evolved biology and our contemporary lifestyles and they suggest that this mismatch has negative consequences for health. Do you agree that many of our health problems result from this mismatch or do you think our health is generally much better than that of our ancestors?
3. Consider the following statement: "In the United States, socioeconomic status is the primary determinant of nutrition and health." Do you agree or disagree with this statement? Why or why not?
4. How many hours a day do you spend with your computer or cell phone? Do you think that these forms of technology may have negative effects on your health? Why or why not?
5. What evidence is there that humans are still evolving?

Connections

Human development and adaptation is best understood from an evolutionary perspective.

Humans have recently become disconnected from other life and are rapidly altering the planet.

Legacies of Human Evolutionary History: Effects on the Individual

While reading this book, you have accompanied us through geological time to the present state of *Homo sapiens:* connecting us with earlier life through 225 million years of mammalian evolution, 65 million years of primate evolution, 6 million years of hominin evolution, and 2 million years of evolution of the genus *Homo.* So, what do you think now? Are we just another mammal—or just another primate? In most ways, of course, we *are* like other mammals and primates. But as we have emphasized throughout the text, modern human beings are the result of *biocultural evolution.* In other words, modern human biology and behavior have been shaped by the biological and cultural forces that operated on our ancestors. In fact, it would be fruitless to attempt an understanding of modern human biology and diversity without considering that humans have evolved in the context of culture. It would be like trying to understand the biology of fish without considering that they live in water.

In the last few chapters, we saw how the choices we make as cultural animals have profound effects on our health and on the health of other people. Although culture and technology have allowed us to adapt beyond our biology, they have also impacted other species and, indeed, the planet. The human species now has the ability to preserve or destroy a significant portion of the earth's life-forms— the results of billions of years of evolution. Here we will briefly discuss some of the challenges that have emerged as a result of our own actions. Though many people refuse to believe that humans are responsible for global climate change, the overwhelming consensus among climate scientists is that we are, and the truth is that the results of such rapid climate change are going to be more than "inconvenient."

Although physical anthropology textbooks don't usually dwell on the topics included here, we feel that it's important to consider them, however brief and simplified our treatment must be. We are living during a critical period in the earth's history. Indeed, the future of much of life as we know it will be decided in the next few decades, and these decisions will be irrevocable. It's crucial that we, as individuals, cities, and nations, make wise decisions, and to do this we must be

◄ A polar bear jumping between ice floes.

well informed. We also think that it's important to consider these problems from an anthropological perspective. This is something not usually done in the media and certainly not by politicians and heads of state. But if we are truly to comprehend the impact that human activities have had on the planet, then surely we must consider our biological and cultural evolution. And we must also emphasize our place in nature and focus on how, from the time we began to domesticate plants and animals, we've altered the face of our planet, at the same time shaping the destiny of thousands of species, including our own.

Human Impact on the Planet and Other Life-Forms

By most standards, *Homo sapiens* is a successful species. There are currently 7 billion humans living on this planet. Even so, we and all other multicellular organisms contribute only a small fraction of all the cells on the planet—most of which are bacteria. So if we see life ultimately as a competition among reproducing organisms, bacteria are the winners, hands down.

Nevertheless, no matter what criterion for success is used, there's no question that humans have had an inordinate impact on the earth and all other forms of life. In the past, our ancestors had to respond primarily to challenges in the natural world; today the greatest challenges for our species (and all others) are the vastly altered environments of our own making. By our actions, which have caused such widespread devastation of ecosystems all over the world, from every continent, from the deep seas to the upper atmosphere, we have disconnected our species from its long evolutionary legacy. But we are still dependent on the ecosystems of which we remain a part. Can we sur-

vive as a species if we continue to challenge Mother Nature? Perhaps, but things will certainly be different and, undoubtedly, the planet will be able to support far fewer humans.

Increasing population size is perhaps the single most important reason that our impact has been so great. As human population pressure increases, more and more land is converted to crops, pasture, and construction, providing more opportunities for still more humans and fewer (or no) habitats for most other species.

Scientists estimate that around 10,000 years ago, only about 5 million people inhabited the earth (not even half as many as live in Los Angeles County or New York City today). By the year 1650, there were perhaps 500 million, and by 1800, around 1 billion (**Fig. 14-1**). Today we add 1 billion people to the world's population approximately every 11 to 13 years. That comes out to 90 to 95 million every year and roughly a quarter of a million every day—or more than 10,000 an hour.

The rate of growth is not equally distributed among all nations. The most recent United Nations report on world population notes that 95 percent of population growth is occurring in the developing world. Likewise, resources are not distributed equally among all nations. Only a small percentage of the world's population, located in a few industrialized nations, controls and consumes most of the world's resources. A 2009 study estimated that 48 percent of the world's population exists on less than $2 per day (Population Reference Bureau, 2009).

Humans and the Impact of Culture

For most of human history, technology remained simple, and the rate of culture change was slow. From the archaeological record, it appears that around 15,000 ya, influenced in part by cli-

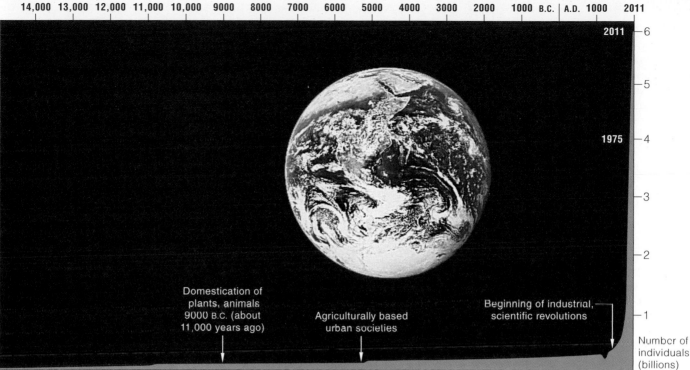

14,000 13,000 12,000 11,000 10,000 9000 8000 7000 6000 5000 4000 3000 2000 1000 B.C. | A.D. 1000 2011

2011 — 6

— 5

1975 — 4

— 3

— 2

Domestication of plants, animals 9000 B.C. (about 11,000 years ago)

Agriculturally based urban societies

Beginning of industrial, scientific revolutions — 1

Number of individuals (billions)

© Cengage Learning 2013 ; Photo of earth: Earth Data Analysis Center

▲ Figure 14-1

Growth curve (orange) depicting the exponential growth of the human population. The vertical axis shows the world population in billions. It wasn't until 1804 that the world's human population reached 1 billion, but we now add 1 billion people every 12 years. Population increase occurs as a function of some percentage (in developing countries, the annual rate is over 3 percent). With advances in food production and medical technologies, humans are undergoing a population explosion, as this figure illustrates.

mate change (not induced by human activity) and the extinction of many large-bodied prey species, some human groups began to abandon their nomadic lifestyles and settle down. Moreover, by about 10,000 ya (and probably earlier), some peoples had learned that by keeping domestic animals and growing crops, they had more abundant and reliable food supplies. The domestication of plants and animals is seen as one of the most significant events in human history, one that was eventually to have far-reaching consequences for the entire planet. Human impact on local environments increased dramatically as soon as people began to live in permanent settlements.

Unfortunately, humans began to exploit, and increasingly depend on, nonrenewable resources. Forests can be viewed as renewable resources, provided they're given the opportunity for regrowth. But in many areas, forest clearing was virtually complete and was inevitably followed by soil erosion, frequent overgrazing, and overcultivation, which in turn led to further

soil erosion (**Fig. 14-2**). In those areas, trees became a nonrenewable resource, perhaps the first resource to have this distinction.

Destruction of natural resources in the past has also had severe consequences for people living today. In 1990, a typhoon and subsequent flooding killed over 100,000 people in Bangladesh, and the flooding was at least partly due to previous deforestation in parts of the Himalayas of northern India. There is also evidence that deforestation has contributed to continued erosion and flooding in China. And millions of people in Pakistan were affected by flooding in 2010 and 2011 that resulted in part from deforestation and dam building along tributaries of the Indus River. The flooding affected one-fifth of the country and set back years of infrastructure development (**Fig. 14-3**).

Global Climate Change

Consider for a moment the fact that much of the energy used for human

▶**Figure 14-2**
Stumps of recently felled forest trees are still visible in this newly cleared field in the Amazon.

© iStockphoto.com / Joseph Luoman

▼**Figure 14-3**
Pakistani villagers move to higher ground as the Indus River floods in 2010. The floods were partially due to years of deforestation and dam building.

© AP Images / Mohammad Sajjad

activities is derived from the burning of fossil fuels, such as oil and coal. The burning of fossil fuels releases carbon dioxide into the atmosphere, and this, in turn, traps heat. Increased production of carbon dioxide and other *greenhouse gases*, such as methane and chlorofluorocarbons (CFCs), is of great concern to many in the scientific community, who anticipate dramatic climate change in the form of global warming. Deforestation, particularly in the tropics, also contributes greatly to global warming, since we're reducing the number of trees available to absorb carbon dioxide.

Certainly, there have been dramatic climatic fluctuations throughout earth's history that had nothing to do with human activity. Many of these fluctuations were sudden and had devastating consequences. But even if the current warming were part of a natural cycle, scientists are concerned that human-produced greenhouse gases could tip the balance toward a catastrophic global climate change. In fact, ice core data show that today there is significantly more carbon dioxide in the earth's atmosphere than at any other time in the last 800,000 years.

Global warming is the result of the interactions of thousands of factors, and the consequences of these interactions aren't possible to predict with complete accuracy. Nevertheless, the strong consensus among most scientists is that we can expect dramatic fluctuations in weather patterns along with alterations in precipitation levels. The results of changing temperatures and rainfall include loss of agricultural lands due to desertification in some regions and flooding in others; rising sea levels inundating vast coastal areas throughout the world; increased human hunger; extinction of numerous plant and animal species; and altered patterns of infectious disease. Regarding the latter, health officials are particularly concerned about the spread of mosquito-borne diseases, such as malaria, dengue fever, and yellow fever, as warmer temperatures increase the geographical range of mosquitoes.

Another consequence of human-caused global climate change is increasing acidification of the oceans due to absorption of greater amounts of CO_2. The global dangers to ecosystems from ocean acidification are potentially as great as global warming, so much so, in fact, that some marine biologists have termed it "the other CO_2 problem" (Doney et al., 2009). Since the beginning of industrialization, ocean acidity has already increased by 30 percent. If current CO_2 emission rates continue, it could double in the next one hundred, reaching levels not seen in the oceans for the past 20 million years (Turley et al., 2007).

The most immediate risk of acidification is to tropical coral reefs. Coral reefs constitute the most diverse marine ecosystems on earth, containing up to 25 percent of all ocean-dwelling species. In addition to a tragic loss of biodiversity, there are direct economic effects of the destruction of coral reefs because more than 100 million people depend on them for food (Harrould-Kolieb and Savitz, 2009). As bad as this sounds, the longer-term effects of ocean acidification could be far more catastrophic, affecting thou-

sands of other species. Unless major action is taken soon to reduce CO^2 emissions, ocean ecosystems will be severely affected worldwide by 2050; these changes could prove irreversible, or at least will take generations to rebound. If you think this won't impact you and all of humanity, just consider that today 20–25 percent of the animal protein consumed by humans comes from marine sources (Guinotte and Fabry, 2009) (see **Fig. 14-4**).

There has been international recognition of the enormity of the problems associated with global climate change, and unprecedented international cooperation has begun. All this is happening because virtually every world government understands the gravity of the impending crisis. This is true despite what many radio or TV commentators and even some members of Congress want you to believe.

In December 2009, a U.N.-sponsored International Convention on Climate Change took place in Copenhagen, Denmark, and was attended by nearly 200 countries. Leading up to this meeting, worldwide expectations ran high that earlier agreements (reached in 1997 at a prior international convention in Kyoto, Japan) would be expanded and strengthened with broader and more rigorous binding agreements to cut carbon emissions.

The world looked especially to the United States for leadership and, even more, for signs of real commitment. Yet nothing substantive occurred in Copenhagen. Most world leaders indicated that they were fully prepared to commit to major cuts in carbon emissions. But widespread lack of trust in American willingness to make real political commitments (that is, serious

▼ **Figure 14-4**
Coral reefs are the most biologically diverse habitats in the oceans, and also the most threatened.

© iStockphoto.com / John Anderson

legislation passed by Congress) as well as weak support from China led to no formal and certainly no binding agreements. Instead, only a broad statement of goals was made, with no mechanisms to ensure that even these would be met.

Deep disappointment from every corner of the planet greeted the lack of progress in Copenhagen. Where we go from here is not clear, but one thing is certain: The climate will continue to change. It will likely be at least 4–5 years before another truly global effort can be made. What will come of that? And will it be in time?

Impact On Biodiversity

According to biologist Stephen Palumbi (2001), humans are the "world's greatest evolutionary force." What Palumbi means is that we humans, like no other species before us, have a profound effect on the evolutionary histories of almost all forms of life, including the potential to alter global ecology and destroy ourselves and much life on earth. Even massive geological events and mass extinctions did not wreak the havoc that may result from modern human technology.

The geological record indicates that in the last 570 million years, there have been at least 15 mass extinction events, two of which altered all of the earth's ecosystems (Ward, 1994). The first of these occurred some 250 mya and resulted from climate change that followed the joining of all the earth's landmasses into one supercontinent. The second event happened around 65 mya and eradicated tens of thousands of species, including most dinosaurs (recalling from Chapter 6 that birds are their living descendants).

A third major extinction event, perhaps of the same magnitude, is occurring now, and according to some scientists, it may have begun in the late Pleistocene or early **Holocene** (Ward, 1994). Unlike all other mass extinctions, this one hasn't been caused by

continental drift or collisions with asteroids. Today it's due to the activities of a single species, *Homo sapiens*.

The overall effects of human activities, particularly in the last 250 years, have made such a profound effect on the earth that many scientists are now recognizing these sudden and dramatic changes as marking a new geological era, called the "Anthropocene" (Vince, 2011). Like earlier major shifts in the earth's geology and biodiversity, the Anthropocene is comparable to the two planetary events mentioned above. These, however, were caused by gigantic asteroid collisions or super volcanoes; the Anthropocene ("the age of humans") is the result of human behavior.

For at least the past 15,000 years, human activities such as hunting and clearing land for cultivation have taken their toll on nonhuman species, but today species are disappearing at an unprecedented rate. Hunting, which occurs for reasons other than acquiring food, is a major factor (particularly true for tigers and rhinoceroses used in traditional medicines). Competition with introduced nonnative species, such as pigs, goats, and rats, has also contributed enormously to the problem (**Fig. 14-5**). And in many cases, the most important cause of extinction is habitat reduction. (Although in some regions, habitat loss has become less important than hunting.)

Habitat loss is a direct result of the burgeoning human population and the resulting need for building materials, grazing and agricultural land, and ever-expanding living areas for people (**Fig. 14-6**). We're all aware of the risk to such visible species as elephants, pandas, rhinoceroses, tigers, and mountain gorillas, to name a few. These risks are real, and within your lifetime, some of these species will certainly become extinct, at least in the wild. But the greatest threats to biodiversity are to the countless unknown species that live in the world's rain forests and in the oceans (most particularly, coral reefs). By the year 2022, half

Holocene The most recent epoch of the Cenozoic. Following the Pleistocene, it's estimated to have begun 10,000 years ago.

◀**Figure 14-5**
Feral goats, introduced into the Galápagos Islands, threaten the habitat of the giant Galápagos tortoise.

the world's remaining rain forests will be gone if destruction continues at its current rate. This will result in a loss of between 10 and 22 percent of all rain forest species, or 5 to 10 percent of all plant and animal species on earth (Wilson, 1992).

Should we care about the loss of biodiversity? If so, why? In truth, many people don't seem very concerned. What's more, in explaining why we should care, we usually point out the benefits (known and unknown) that

humans may derive from wild species of plants and animals. An example of such a benefit is the chemical taxol (derived from the Pacific yew tree), which may be an effective treatment for ovarian and breast cancer.

The United Nations recently organized a large international conference to address pressing issues concerning biodiversity. The conference (an extension of the Convention on Biological Diversity) took place October

▼**Figure 14-6**
(a) Agricultural fields in China's Yunnan Province and **(b)** aerial view of Sao Paulo, Brazil; with a population of about 19 million people, it is one of the 10 largest cities in the world. The fields and city occupy land that was formerly home to hundreds of plants and animals that no longer live there.

2010 in Nagoya, Japan, and was attended by representatives from 193 countries. Unlike the lack of agreement that characterized the conference on global climate change, the results from the biodiversity meeting were quite encouraging. Conference members agreed to increase cooperation and to share financial benefits that come from the development of new drugs from wild plants and animals. What's more, they produced an impressive list of significant international goals to be reached by 2020, including to reduce to half or bring close to zero the rate of loss of all natural habitats; to reduce pollution to levels that are not detrimental to ecosystems and biodiversity; to conserve at least 17 percent of terrestrial areas and 10 percent of coastal and marine areas in protected zones; to prevent the extinction of known threatened species; and to restore at least 15 percent of degraded ecosystems.

Acceleration of Evolutionary Processes

Another major impact of human activities is the acceleration of the evolutionary process for hundreds of bacteria and viruses. Many of these changes have occurred over a single human generation (that is, during the lifetime of many people living today), not the millions of years usually associated with evolution. As noted earlier, our use of antibiotics has dramatically altered the course of evolution of several bacterial diseases to the point that many bacteria have become resistant to antibiotics. Human-invented antibiotics have now become the most significant selective factors causing many bacteria to evolve into more virulent forms. It's even likely that human technology and lifestyles are responsible for the deadly nature of some of the so-called new diseases that have arisen in recent decades, such as HIV/AIDS, dengue hemorrhagic fever, Legionnaires' disease, Lyme disease, and resistant strains of tuberculosis, *Staphylococcus*, and *E. coli*. We could reach a point where we have no antibiotics capable of fighting dangerous bacteria that live and constantly mutate in our midst. For example, each one of us has billions of beneficial bacteria in our digestive tracts. We couldn't live without these bacteria, but some can and occasionally do mutate into varieties that cause serious illness and even death. Without antibiotics, these and many other bacteria in our environment would have the ability to drastically increase mortality due to infectious disease.

A similar phenomenon has occurred with the overuse and misuse of insecticides and pesticides on agricultural crops (Palumbi, 2001). As mentioned previously, DDT is perhaps the best-known insecticide to have altered the course of a species' evolution. When this insecticide was first developed, it was hailed as the best way to reduce malaria, eliminating the mosquitoes that transmit the disease. DDT was highly effective when it was first applied to mosquito-ridden areas; but soon, mosquitoes had evolved resistance to the powerful agent, rendering it almost useless in the fight against malaria. Moreover, the use of DDT proved disastrous to many bird species, including the bald eagle (**Fig 14-7**). In the 1970s, its use was curtailed, even banned in some countries, but the failure of other efforts to treat malaria has led to a recent call to begin using DDT again.

From these examples, it's clear that the human-caused accelerated process of evolution is something that can result in great harm to our species and the planet. Certainly, none of the scientists developing antibiotics, insecticides, pesticides, and other biological tools intend to cause harm. But unless they understand the evolutionary process, they may not be able to foresee the

▼**Figure 14-7**
DDT almost caused the extinction of the American bald eagle, the bird featured on the Great Seal of the United States.

U.S. Government

long-term consequences of their work. As the great geneticist Theodosius Dobzhansky (1973) said, "Nothing in biology makes sense except in the light of evolution." Indeed, we can't afford even a single generation of scientists who lack knowledge about the process of evolution. If human actions can cause an organism to evolve from a relatively benign state to a dangerously virulent one, then there is no reason why we can't turn that process around. In other words, it is theoretically possible to direct the course of evolution of a dangerous virus such as HIV to a more benign, less harmful state (Ewald, 1999). But using evolution to solve health problems requires that medical researchers have a very sophisticated understanding of the evolutionary process, and unfortunately, evolutionary theory isn't usually offered as part of medical training.

Looking for Solutions

The problems facing our planet reflect an adaptive strategy gone awry. Indeed, it would seem that we no longer enjoy a harmonious relationship with culture or with the planet. Instead, culture has become an unintentional transformer of the environment in which we live. All we need to do is examine the very air we breathe to realize that we have overstepped our limits (**Fig. 14-8**).

Can the problems we've created be solved? Perhaps, but any objective assessment of the future offers little optimism. Climate change, air pollution, depletion of the ozone layer, and loss of biodiversity are catastrophic problems in a world of 7 billion people. How well does the world *now* cope with feeding, housing, and educating its inhabitants? What quality of life

▼ **Figure 14-8**
Today, air pollution is a worldwide problem. **(a)** Two Vietnamese girls using scarves as protective masks. **(b)** Sunrise over Delhi, India. **(c)** Toronto, Canada, in the gloom. **(d)** Sunset over Beijing, China. **(e)** A smoggy day in Los Angeles.

do the majority of the world's people enjoy right now? What kind of world have we wrought for the other organisms that share our planet as many are steadily isolated into fragments of what were once large habitats? If these concerns aren't overwhelming enough now, what kind of world will we see in the year 2050, when the world's population could reach 10 billion? Among other consequences of this population growth, the world's food production may need to double in order to adequately feed everyone (something we don't do now). Since our window of opportunity shrinks every year, industrialized nations must immediately help developing countries adopt fuel-efficient technologies that allow them to raise their standard of living without increasing their output of greenhouse gases. Furthermore, family planning must be adopted to slow population growth. In most societies, however, behavioral change is very difficult, and sacrifice on the part of the developing world alone wouldn't adequately stem the tide. It's entirely too easy for someone from North America to ask that the people of Bangladesh control their rate of reproduction (it runs two to three times that of the United States). But consider this: The average American uses an estimated 400 times the resources consumed by a resident of Bangladesh. The United States *alone* produces 25 to 30 percent of all carbon dioxide emissions that end up in the earth's atmosphere. In 2007, China caught up with the United States in this regard, but over 1.3 billion people live in China, compared with 312 million in the United States. In his book *The Future of Life* (2002), E.O. Wilson discusses the issue in terms of "ecological footprints," or the average amount of land and sea required for each person to support his or her lifestyle. This includes all resources consumed for energy, housing, transportation, food, water, and waste disposal. In nonindustrialized nations, the ecological footprint per capita is about 2.5 acres, but in the United States it's 24 acres! Wilson goes on to point out that four additional planet earths would be needed for every person on the planet to reach the current levels of consumption in the United States. Clearly, much of the responsibility for the world's problems rests squarely on the shoulders of the industrialized West.

Is There Any Good News?

Although world population growth continues, it appears that the rate of growth has slowed somewhat. It's common knowledge among economists that as income and education increase, family size decreases, and as infant and child mortality rates decrease, families have fewer children. In fact, one of the best strategies for reducing family size and thus world population is to educate girls and women. Educated woman are more likely to be in the labor force and are better able to provide food for their families, seek health care for themselves and their children, delay marriage, and practice family planning.

With decreases in family size and improvements in education and employment opportunities for both men and women throughout the world, we are also likely to see improvements in environmental conservation and habitat preservation. The small Central American country of Costa Rica has recognized the economic importance of its abundant and beautiful natural resources. By developing ecotourism as a means of generating income, Costa Rica has been able, for the present, to preserve much of its forests and wildlife. In fact, ecotourism has become its primary industry, and Costa Rica's poverty levels are the lowest in Central America. Habitat destruction and poverty often go hand in hand. Although successes like those accomplished in Costa Rica can't be replicated everywhere, this small nation has been a model for making environmental concerns integral to social and economic development.

Annually since 2005, leaders from both developing and developed countries have come together to discuss new ways of reducing global poverty, especially in sub-Saharan Africa. Additionally, some of the wealthiest people in the world (including Bill and Melinda Gates, George Soros, Warren Buffet, Richard Branson, and Ted Turner) have begun to invest their personal fortunes to help reduce poverty and poor health to try to achieve global peace and prosperity. Lastly, the degree of international cooperation shown at the 2010 conference on biodiversity is a hopeful development that could be a foundation for slowing species extinctions and maintaining natural habitats.

What should be obvious is that only by working together can nations and individuals hope to bring about solutions to the world's problems. As we argued earlier in the book, despite occasional evidence to the contrary, cooperation may have been more important in human evolution than

conflict. The question now is whether or not we have the collective will to see that our admirable goals are met. Many people believe that it's our only hope.

Studies of human evolution have much to contribute to our understanding of how we, as a single species, came to exert such control over the destiny of our planet. It's a truly phenomenal story of how a small apelike creature walking on two feet across the African savanna challenged nature by learning to make stone tools. From these humble beginnings came large-brained humans who, instead of stone tools, have telecommunications satellites, computers, and nuclear arsenals at their fingertips. The human story is indeed unique and wonderful. Our two feet have carried us not only across the plains of Africa, but onto the polar caps, the ocean floor, and even on the surface of the moon! Surely, if we can accomplish so much in so short a time, we can act responsibly to preserve our home and the wondrous creatures that share it with us.

Summary of Main Topics

- Humans are the product of millions of years of biocultural evolution, but in just the last few hundred years have exerted huge influences on other life-forms and the planet itself, unlike that by any other organism in the history of life.
- A major contributor to the scope of recent human disruptions of the earth's ecosystems is population growth.
- Probably the most immediate and crucial challenge we face is to rapidly slow our harmful influence on global climate change, including that from warming of the atmosphere and acidification of the ocean.

Critical Thinking Questions

1. What effects have recent population growth caused in the city or area in which you live? What do you think will happen in your local area, to the country, and to the planet if population growth continues?

2. Why does a large majority of scientists support the conclusion that CO_2 emissions are the primary cause of global climate change? If you think this conclusion is not correct, can you point to a body of scientific evidence that supports your view?

3. What do you personally think individuals, large corporations, and world leaders should do to address the world's ecological problems?

Appendix A

Atlas of Primate Skeletal Anatomy

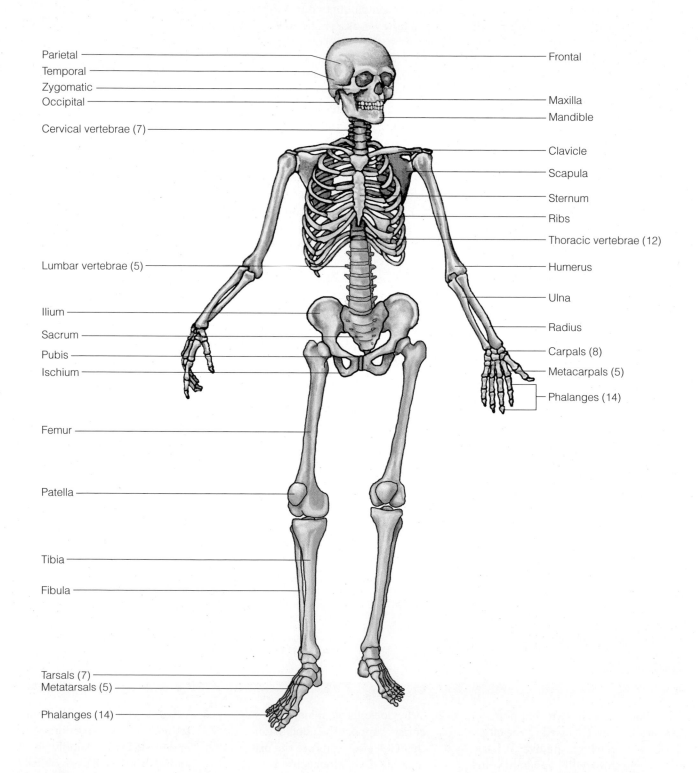

Parietal
Temporal
Zygomatic
Occipital
Cervical vertebrae (7)
Lumbar vertebrae (5)
Ilium
Sacrum
Pubis
Ischium
Femur
Patella
Tibia
Fibula
Tarsals (7)
Metatarsals (5)
Phalanges (14)

Frontal
Maxilla
Mandible
Clavicle
Scapula
Sternum
Ribs
Thoracic vertebrae (12)
Humerus
Ulna
Radius
Carpals (8)
Metacarpals (5)
Phalanges (14)

▲ Figure A–1
Human skeleton (*Homo sapiens*)—
bipedal hominin.

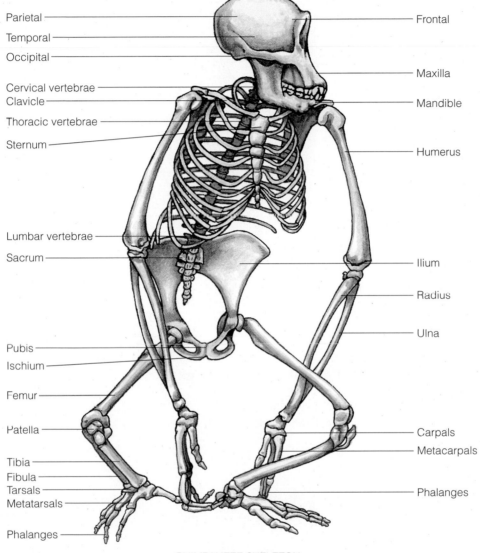

Parietal — Frontal
Temporal —
Occipital —
Maxilla
Cervical vertebrae —
Clavicle —
Mandible
Thoracic vertebrae —
Sternum —
Humerus
Lumbar vertebrae —
Sacrum —
Ilium
Radius
Ulna
Pubis —
Ischium —
Femur —
Patella —
Carpals
Metacarpals
Tibia —
Fibula —
Tarsals —
Metatarsals —
Phalanges
Phalanges —

CHIMPANZEE SKELETON

▲ **Figure A-2**
Chimpanzee skeleton (*Pan troglodytes*)—
knuckle-walking ape.

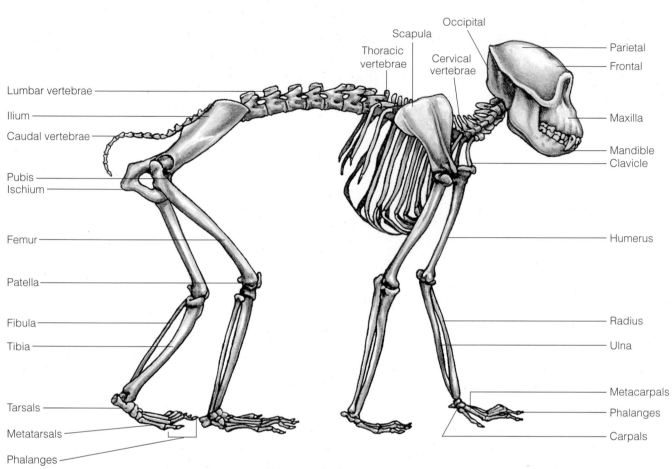

MONKEY SKELETON

▲ **Figure A-3**
Monkey skeleton (rhesus macaque;
Macaca mulatta)—a typical
quadrupedal primate.

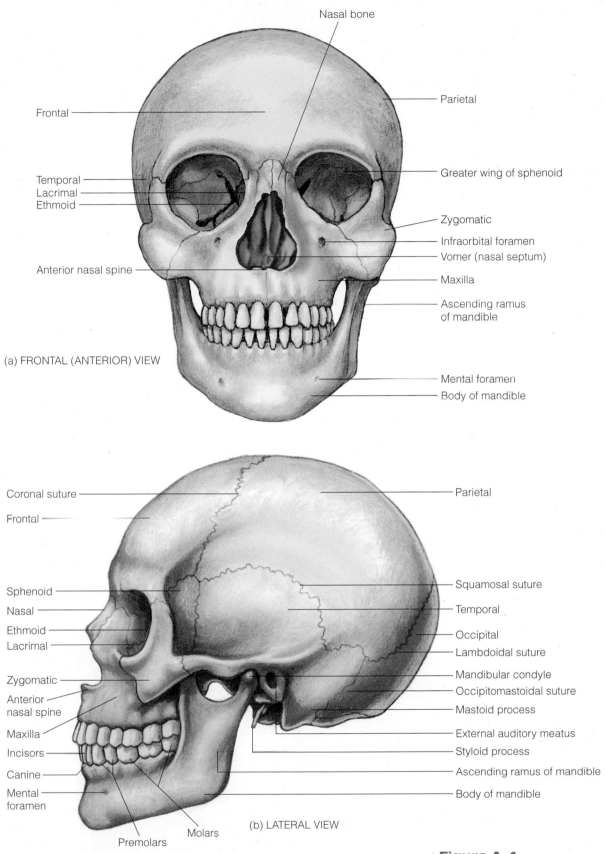

Nasal bone

Frontal

Parietal

Temporal
Lacrimal
Ethmoid

Greater wing of sphenoid

Zygomatic

Infraorbital foramen

Vomer (nasal septum)

Anterior nasal spine

Maxilla

Ascending ramus
of mandible

(a) FRONTAL (ANTERIOR) VIEW

Mental foramen

Body of mandible

Coronal suture

Parietal

Frontal

Sphenoid

Squamosal suture

Nasal

Temporal

Ethmoid

Occipital

Lacrimal

Lambdoidal suture

Zygomatic

Mandibular condyle

Anterior
nasal spine

Occipitomastoidal suture

Mastoid process

Maxilla

External auditory meatus

Incisors

Styloid process

Canine

Ascending ramus of mandible

Mental
foramen

Body of mandible

Premolars

Molars

(b) LATERAL VIEW

▲ **Figure A-4**
Human cranium.

(continued on next page)

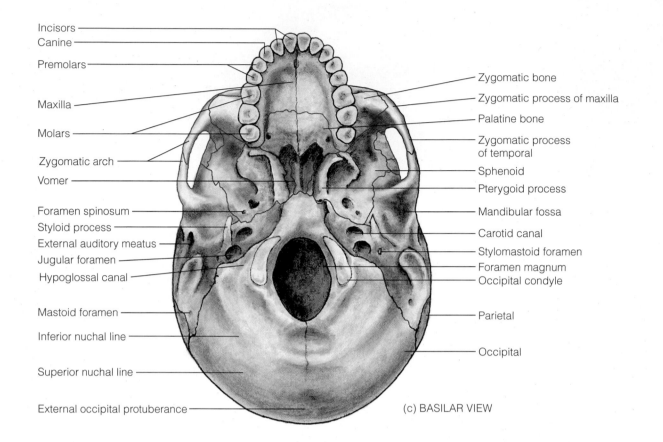

Incisors
Canine
Premolars
Maxilla
Molars
Zygomatic arch
Vomer
Foramen spinosum
Styloid process
External auditory meatus
Jugular foramen
Hypoglossal canal
Mastoid foramen
Inferior nuchal line
Superior nuchal line
External occipital protuberance

Zygomatic bone
Zygomatic process of maxilla
Palatine bone
Zygomatic process of temporal
Sphenoid
Pterygoid process
Mandibular fossa
Carotid canal
Stylomastoid foramen
Foramen magnum
Occipital condyle
Parietal
Occipital

(c) BASILAR VIEW

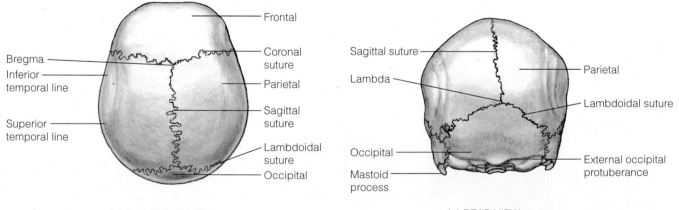

Bregma
Inferior temporal line
Superior temporal line

Frontal
Coronal suture
Parietal
Sagittal suture
Lambdoidal suture
Occipital

(d) SUPERIOR VIEW

Sagittal suture
Lambda
Occipital
Mastoid process

Parietal
Lambdoidal suture
External occipital protuberance

(e) REAR VIEW

▲ **Figure A-4**
Human cranium.

(continued)

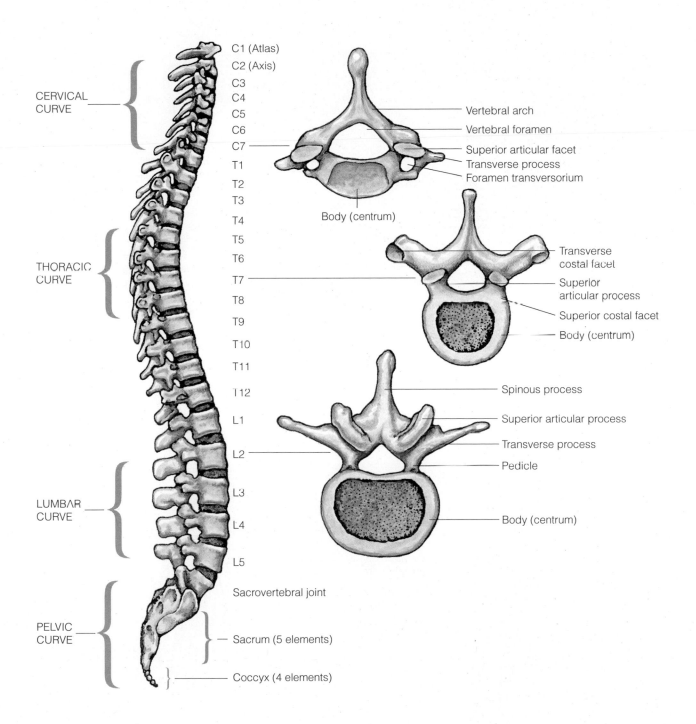

CERVICAL
CURVE

C1 (Atlas)
C2 (Axis)
C3
C4
C5
C6
C7

T1
T2
T3
T4
T5
T6
T7
T8
T9
T10
T11
T12

L1

L2

THORACIC
CURVE

LUMBAR
CURVE

L3

L4

L5

PELVIC
CURVE

Sacrovertebral joint

Sacrum (5 elements)

Coccyx (4 elements)

Vertebral arch
Vertebral foramen
Superior articular facet
Transverse process
Foramen transversorium

Body (centrum)

Transverse
costal facet

Superior
articular process

Superior costal facet

Body (centrum)

Spinous process

Superior articular process

Transverse process

Pedicle

Body (centrum)

▲ **Figure A-5**
**Human vertebral column (lateral
view) and representative cervical,
thoracic, and lumbar vertebrae
(superior views).**

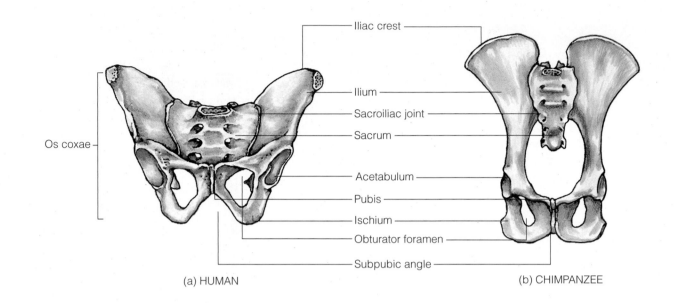

(a) HUMAN

(b) CHIMPANZEE

▲**Figure A-6**
Pelvic girdles.

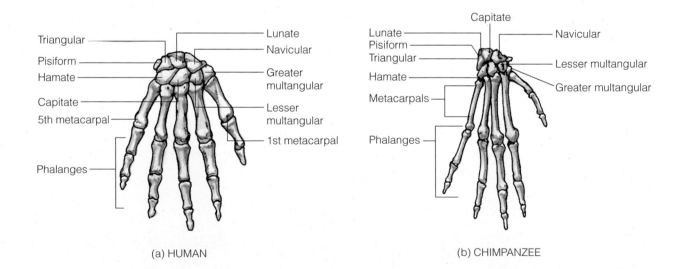

(a) HUMAN

(b) CHIMPANZEE

▲**Figure A-7**
Hand anatomy.

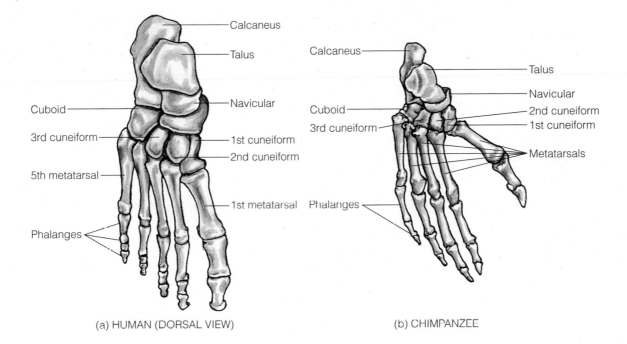

Calcaneus

Talus

Navicular

Cuboid

3rd cuneiform

5th metatarsal

1st cuneiform

2nd cuneiform

1st metatarsal

Phalanges

(a) HUMAN (DORSAL VIEW)

Calcaneus

Talus

Navicular

Cuboid

3rd cuneiform

2nd cuneiform

1st cuneiform

Metatarsals

Phalanges

(b) CHIMPANZEE

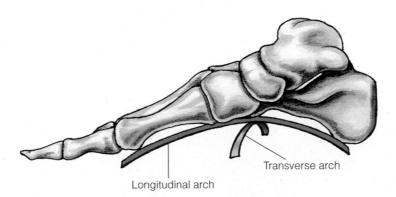

Transverse arch

Longitudinal arch

(c) HUMAN (MEDIAL VIEW)

▲ **Figure A-8**
Foot (pedal) anatomy.

Appendix B

Summary of Early Hominin Fossil Finds from Africa

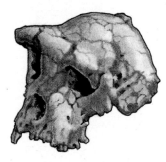

Sahelanthropus

Taxonomic designation:
Sahelanthropus tchadensis

Year of first discovery: 2001

Dating: ~7–6 mya

Fossil material: Nearly complete cranium, 2 jaw fragments, 3 isolated teeth

Orrorin

Taxonomic designation:
Orrorin tugenensis

Year of first discovery: 2000

Dating: ~6 mya

Fossil material: 2 jaw fragments, 6 isolated teeth, postcranial remains (femoral pieces, partial humerus, hand phalanx). No reasonably complete cranial remains yet discovered.

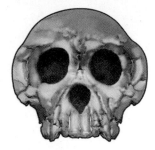

Ardipithecus

Taxonomic designation:
Ardipithecus ramidus; earlier species designated as *Ardipithecus kadabba*

Year of first discovery: 1992

Dating: Earlier sites, 5.8–5.6 mya; Aramis, 4.4 mya

Fossil material: Earlier materials: Jaw fragment, isolated teeth, 5 postcranial remains. Later sample (Aramis): partial skeleton, 110 other specimens representing at least 36 individuals

Location of finds: Toros-Menalla, Chad, central Africa

Location of finds: Lukeino Formation, Tugen Hills, Baringo District, Kenya, East Africa

Location of finds: Middle Awash region, including Aramis (as well as earlier localities), Ethiopia, East Africa

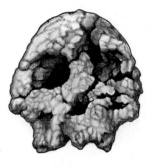

Australopithecus anamensis

Taxonomic designation:
Australopithecus anamensis

Year of first discovery: 1965 (but not recognized as separate species at that time); more remains found in 1994 and 1995

Dating: 4.2–3.9 mya

Fossil material: Total of 22 specimens, including cranial fragments, jaw fragments, and postcranial pieces (humerus, tibia, radius). No reasonably complete cranial remains yet discovered.

Australopithecus afarensis

Taxonomic designation:
Australopithecus afarensis

Year of first discovery: 1973

Dating: 3.6–3.0 mya

Fossil material: Large sample, with up to 65 individuals represented: 1 partial cranium, numerous cranial pieces and jaws, many teeth, numerous postcranial remains, including partial skeleton. Fossil finds from Laetoli also include dozens of fossilized footprints.

Kenyanthropus

Taxonomic designation:
Kenyanthropus platyops

Year of first discovery: 1999

Dating: 3.5 mya

Fossil material: Partial cranium, temporal fragment, partial maxilla, 2 partial mandibles

Location of finds: Kanapoi, Allia Bay, Kenya, East Africa

Location of finds: Laetoli (Tanzania), Hadar/Dikika (Ethiopia), also likely found at East Turkana (Kenya) and Omo (Ethiopia), East Africa

Location of finds: Lomekwi, West Lake Turkana, Kenya, East Africa

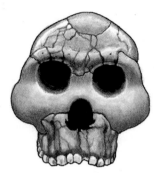

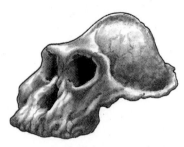

Paranthropus boisei

Taxonomic designation:
Paranthropus boisei (also called *Australopithecus boisei*)

Year of first discovery: 1959

Dating: 2.2–1.0 mya

Fossil material: 2 nearly complete crania, several partial crania, many jaw fragments, dozens of teeth. Postcrania less represented, but parts of several long bones recovered.

Australopithecus garhi

Taxonomic designation:
Australopithecus garhi

Year of first discovery: 1997

Dating: 2.5 mya

Fossil material: Partial cranium, numerous limb bones

Paranthropus aethiopicus

Taxonomic designation:
Paranthropus aethiopicus (also called *Australopithecus aethiopicus*)

Year of first discovery: 1985

Dating: 2.4 mya

Fossil material: Nearly complete cranium

Location of finds: Bouri, Middle Awash, Ethiopia, East Africa

Location of finds: West Lake Turkana, Kenya

Location of finds: Olduvai Gorge and Peninj (Tanzania), East Lake Turkana (Koobi Fora), Chesowanja (Kenya), Omo (Ethiopia)

Paranthropus robustus

Taxonomic designation:
Paranthropus robustus
(also called *Australopithecus robustus*)

Year of first discovery: 1938

Dating: ~2–1 mya

Fossil material: 1 complete cranium, several partial crania, many jaw fragments, hundreds of teeth, numerous postcranial elements

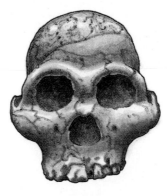

Australopithecus africanus

Taxonomic designation:
Australopithecus africanus

Year of first discovery: 1924

Dating: ~3.0?–2.0 mya

Fossil material: 1 mostly complete cranium, several partial crania, dozens of jaws/partial jaws, hundreds of teeth, 4 partial skeletons representing significant parts of the postcranium

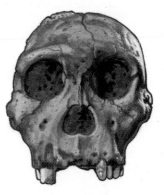

Australopithecus sediba

Taxonomic designation:
Australopithecus sediba
(also called *Homo sediba*)

Year of first discovery: 2008

Dating: 1.95-1.78 mya

Fossil material: 2 partial skeletons (Note: further fossils remains still in cave but not yet published)

Location of finds: Kromdraai, Swartkrans, Drimolen, Cooper's Cave, possibly Gondolin (all from South Africa)

Location of finds: Taung, Sterkfontein, Makapansgat, Gladysvale (all from South Africa)

Location of finds: Malapa Cave (South Africa)

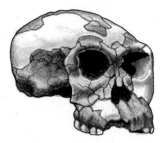

Early *Homo*

Taxonomic designation:
Homo habilis

Year of first discovery:
1959/1960

Dating: ?2.4–1.8 mya

Fossil material: 2 partial crania, other cranial pieces, jaw fragments, several limb bones, partial hand, partial foot, partial skeleton

Location of finds: Olduvai Gorge (Tanzania), Lake Baringo (Kenya), Omo (Ethiopia), Sterkfontein (?) (South Africa)

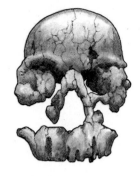

Early *Homo*

Taxonomic designation:
Homo rudolfensis

Year of first discovery: 1972

Dating: 1.8–1.4 mya

Fossil material: 4 partial crania, 1 mostly complete mandible, other jaw pieces, numerous teeth, a few postcranial elements (none directly associated with crania)

Location of finds: East Lake Turkana (Koobi Fora), Kenya, East Africa

Abbreviations Used for Fossil Hominin Specimens

For those hominin sites where a number of specimens have been recovered, standard abbreviations are used to designate the site as well as the specimen number (and occasionally museum accession information as well).

Abbreviation	Explanation	Example
AL	Afar locality	AL-288-1
LH	Laetoli hominin	LH 4
OH	Olduvai hominin	OH 5
KNM-ER (or simply ER)	Kenya National Museums, East Rudolf*	ER 1470
KNM-WT (or simply WT)	Kenya National Museums, West Turkana	WT 17000
Sts	Sterkfontein, main site	Sts 5
Stw	Sterkfontein, west extension	Stw 53
SK	Swartkrans	SK 48

* East Rudolf is the former name for Lake Turkana; the abbreviation was first used before the lake's name was changed. All these fossils (as well as others from sites throughout Kenya) are housed in Nairobi at the National Museums of Kenya.

Appendix C

Population Genetics

As noted in Chapter 5, the basic approach in population genetics makes use of a mathematical model called the Hardy-Weinberg equilibrium equation. The Hardy-Weinberg theory of genetic equilibrium postulates a set of conditions in a population where *no* evolution occurs. In other words, none of the forces of evolution are acting, and all genes have an equal chance of recombining in each generation (that is, there is random mating of individuals). More precisely, the hypothetical conditions that such a population would be *assumed* to meet are as follows:

1. The population is infinitely large. This condition eliminates the possibility of random genetic drift or changes in allele frequencies due to chance.
2. There is no mutation. Thus, no new alleles are being added by molecular changes in gametes.
3. There is no gene flow. There is no exchange of genes with other populations that can alter allele frequencies.
4. Natural selection is not operating. Specific alleles confer no advantage over others that might influence reproductive success.
5. Mating is random. There are no factors that influence who mates with whom. Thus, any female is assumed to have an equal chance of mating with any male.

If all these conditions are satisfied, allele frequencies will not change from one generation to the next (that is, no evolution will take place), and a permanent equilibrium will be maintained as long as these conditions prevail. An evolutionary "barometer" is thus provided that may be used as a standard against which actual circumstances are compared. Similar to the way a typical barometer is standardized under known temperature and altitude conditions, the Hardy-Weinberg equilibrium is standardized under known evolutionary conditions.

Note that the idealized conditions that define the Hardy-Weinberg equilibrium are just that: an idealized, *hypothetical* state. In the real world, no actual population would fully meet any of these conditions. But do not be confused by this distinction. By explicitly defining the genetic distribution that would be *expected* if *no* evolutionary change were occurring (that is, in equilibrium), we can compare the *observed* genetic distribution obtained from actual human populations. The evolutionary barometer is thus evaluated through comparison of these observed allele and genotype frequencies with those expected in the predefined equilibrium situation.

If the observed frequencies differ from those of the expected model, then we can say that evolution is taking place at the locus in question. The alternative, of course, is that the observed and expected frequencies do not differ sufficiently to state unambiguously that evolution is occurring at a locus in a population. Indeed, this is frequently the result that is obtained, and in such cases, population geneticists are unable to delineate evolutionary changes at the particular locus under study. Put another way, geneticists are unable to reject what statisticians call the *null hypothesis* (where "null" means nothing, a statistical condition of randomness).

The simplest situation applicable to a microevolutionary study is a genetic trait that follows a simple Mendelian pattern and has only two alleles (*A*, *a*). As you recall from earlier discussions, there are then only three possible genotypes: *AA*, *Aa*, *aa*. Proportions of these genotypes (*AA:Aa:aa*) are a function of the *allele frequencies* themselves (percentage of *A* and percentage of *a*). To provide uniformity for all genetic loci, a standard notation is employed to refer to these frequencies:

Frequency of dominant allele (*A*) = *p*
Frequency of recessive allele (*a*) = *q*

Since in this case there are only two alleles, their combined total frequency must represent all possibilities. In other words, the sum of their separate frequencies must be 1.

p	+	q	=	1
(frequency of *A* alleles)		(frequency of *a* alleles)		(100% of alleles at that locus)

To ascertain the expected proportions of genotypes, we compute the chances of the alleles combining with one another into all possible combinations. Remember, they all have an equal chance of combining, and no new alleles are being added.

These probabilities are a direct function of the frequency of the two alleles. The chances of all possible combinations occurring randomly can be simply shown as

$$\begin{array}{r} p + q \\ \underline{p + q} \\ pq + q^2 \\ \underline{p^2 + \ pq} \\ p^2 + 2pq + q^2 \end{array}$$

Mathematically, this is known as a binomial expansion and can also be shown as

$$(p + q)(p + q) = p^2 + 2pq + q^2$$

What we have just calculated is simply:

Allele Combination	Genotype Produced	Expected Proportion in Population
Chances of *A* combining with *A*	*AA*	$p \times p = p^2$
Chances of *A* combining with *a*;	*Aa*	$p \times q$
a combining with *A*	*aA*	$p \times q$ = 2*pq*
Chances of *a* combining with *a*	*aa*	$q \times q = q^2$

Thus, p^2 is the frequency of the *AA* genotype, 2*pq* is the frequency of the *Aa* genotype, and q^2 is the frequency of the *aa* genotype, where *p* is the frequency of the dominant allele and *q* is the frequency of the recessive allele in a population.

Calculating Allele Frequencies: An Example

How geneticists use the Hardy-Weinberg formula is best demonstrated through an example. Let us assume that a population contains 200 individuals, and use the MN blood group locus as the gene to be measured. This gene produces a blood group antigen—similar to ABO—located on red blood cells. Because the *M* and *N* alleles are codominant, we can ascertain everyone's phenotype by taking blood samples and observing reactions with specially prepared antisera. From the phenotypes, we can then directly calculate the *observed* allele frequencies. So let us proceed.

   All 200 individuals are tested, and the results are shown in Table C-1. Although the match between observed and expected frequencies is not perfect, it is close enough statistically to satisfy equilibrium conditions. Since our population is not a large one, sampling may easily account for the small observed deviations. Our population is therefore probably in equilibrium (that is, at this locus, it is not evolving). At the minimum, what we can say scientifically is that we cannot reject the *null hypothesis*.

TABLE C-1 Calculating Allele Frequencies in a Hypothetical Population

Observed Data

Genotype	Number of Individuals	Percentage	Number of Alleles M	Number of Alleles N			
MM	80	40%	160	0			
MN	80	40%	80	80			
NN	40	20%	0	80			
Totals	200	100%	240	+ 160	=	400	
		Proportion:	0.6	+ 0.4	=	1	

*Each individual has two alleles. Thus, a person who is *MM* contributes two *M* alleles to the total gene pool. A person who is *MN* contributes one *M* and one *N*. Two hundred individuals, then, have 400 alleles for the *MN* locus.

Observed Allele Frequencies

$M = 0.6(p)$
$N = 0.4(q)$ ($p + q$ should equal 1, and they do)

Expected Frequencies

What are the predicted genotypic proportions if genetic equilibrium (no evolution) applies to our population? We simply apply the Hardy-Weinberg formula: $p^2 + 2pq + q^2$.

p^2	=	(.6)(.6) =	.36
$2pq$	=	2(.6)(.4) = 2(.24) =	.48
q^2	=	(.4)(.4) =	.16
Total			1.00

There are only three possible genotypes (*MM:MN:NN*), so the total of the relative proportions should equal 1; as you can see, they do.

Comparing Frequencies

How do the expected frequencies compare with the observed frequencies in our population?

	Expected Frequency	Expected Number of Individuals	Observed Frequency	Actual Number of Individuals with Each Genotype
MM	.36	72	.40	80
MN	.48	96	.40	80
NN	.16	32	.20	40

Appendix D

Sexing and Aging the Skeleton

The field of physical anthropology that is directly concerned with the analysis of skeletal remains is called *osteology.* Using an osteological perspective allows researchers to study skeletons of both human and nonhuman primates to understand the ways in which hominins are similar to, and distinct from, other primates. Moreover, paleoanthropologists also use many of the same techniques to analyze the remains of fossil hominins (which mostly consist of teeth and bones). In more recent contexts, encompassing the last few thousand years, skeletal remains of *Homo sapiens* have been investigated by osteologists to learn about the size, nutritional status, and diseases present in prior human populations.

Two very important questions that osteologists ask when analyzing a skeleton are the sex and age of the individual. Such basic demographic variables as sex and age are crucial in any comprehensive osteological analysis, especially of human remains.

Sexing the Skeleton

During infancy and childhood, male and female skeletons do not differ much. Consequently, osteologists usually cannot determine the sex of a skeleton of someone who died before 13 to 15 years of age. However, during development, *sexual dimorphism* is increasingly manifested in the skeleton, making sex determination feasible in adult remains, provided enough of the skeleton is present. We should mention that molecular techniques are sometimes able to detect the presence of the Y chromosome from bone or dental tissue (thus determining that a skeleton is that of a male). Though not yet used widely, molecularly based sexing is becoming more common in osteological analyses.

The differences between male and female skeletons are most clearly expressed in the pelvis (*pl.*, pelves), and this variation is due to the requirements of childbirth in females. In particular, during hominin evolution, the dual influences of bipedal locomotion and relatively large-brained newborns placed adaptive constraints on pelvic anatomy. As a result, in females the pelvis is generally broader and more splayed out than in males. The most useful criteria for sex determination are listed in **Table D-1** and illustrated in **Figure D-1**. Although these criteria, taken together, are good indicators of sex, you should be aware that none, taken in isolation, is accurate in all cases. Moreover, this is not a complete listing of all traits used in sexing skeletons, although it does include those most commonly used.

There are also sex differences in cranial dimensions, most especially relating to facial proportions. However, these differences are not as consistent as those in the pelvis. Therefore, it is important to recognize patterns of cranial variation as they are expressed in different populations. The cranial features most commonly used for sex determination are listed in **Table D-2** (see also **Fig. D-2**). These differences reflect the fact that in males, the skeleton is larger than in females. The bones are denser, and areas of muscle attachment are frequently more robust. However, such

TABLE **D-1**	Differences Between the Male and Female Pelvis	

Pelvic Characteristic	Female	Male
General	Muscle attachments less robust; overall appearance sometimes less massive	Muscle attachments more robust; overall appearance sometimes more massive
Subpubic angle	Wider (more than 90°)	Narrower (less than 90°)
Greater sciatic notch	Wider—more open (more than 68°)	Narrower—more closed (less than 68°)
Ischiopubic ramus (medial view)	Thinner	Thicker
Ventral arc (elevated ridge on ventral surface of pubis)	Frequently present	Absent
Sacrum	Wider and straighter	Narrower and more curved

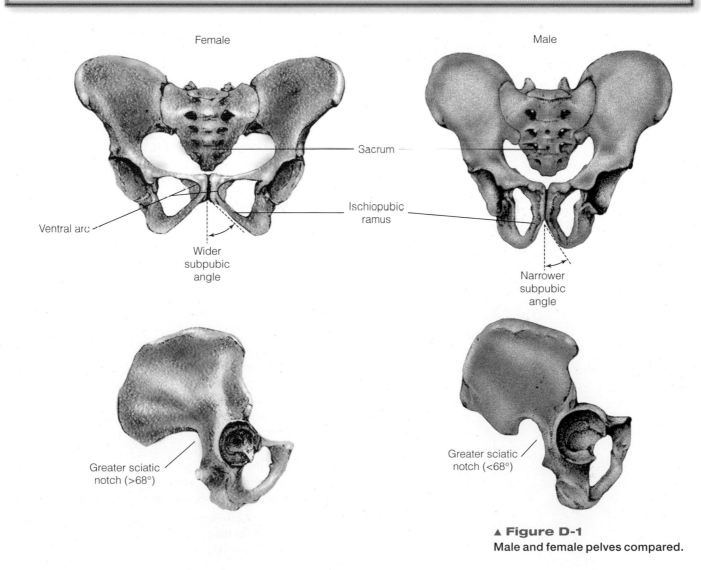

▲ **Figure D-1**
Male and female pelves compared.

TABLE D-2	Differences Between the Male and Female Cranium	
Cranial Feature	**Female**	**Male**
Points of muscle attachment (e.g., mastoid process)	Less pronounced	Larger, more pronounced
Supraorbital torus (browridge)	Less pronounced or absent	More pronounced
Supraorbital rim (upper margin of eye orbit)	Sharper	More rounded
Palate	More shallow	Deeper

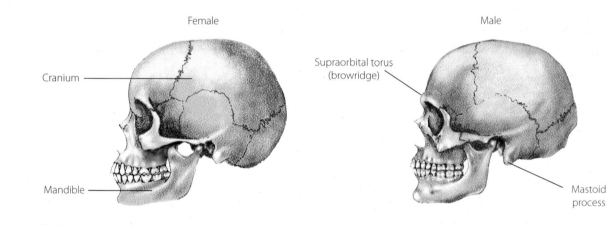

▲ Figure D-2
Male and female cranium and mandible.

differences are not consistently expressed across various populations, and knowledge of relevant population variation is thus important in drawing reasonable determinations of sex.

Determining Age

During growth, the skeleton and dentition undergo developmental changes that occur within known age ranges. Thus, estimating age in individuals who were younger than 20 when they died is based primarily on the presence of deciduous (baby) and permanent teeth, the appearance of ossification centers of bones, and the fusion of the ends of long bones to bone shafts.

Dental Eruption

Age estimation based on dental eruption is useful in individuals up to approximately 15 years of age. The third molar (wisdom tooth) erupts after this time, but the age of eruption of this tooth (if it forms at all) is highly variable. Thus, the third molar is not a very reliable indicator of age except that its presence indicates that the individual was at least a young adult (**Fig. D-3**).

Bone Growth

The size of the long bones, the development of secondary ossification centers (epiphyses), and the degree of fusion of epiphyses (ends of the bones) to diaphyses (bone shafts) are just as important as dental eruption. Post-cranial bones are preceded by a cartilage model that is gradually replaced by bone, both in the diaphyses and the secondary centers (epiphyses). In children and adolescents, bones continue to grow until the epiphyses fuse to the diaphyses. Because this fusion occurs within different age ranges in different bones, the age of an individual can be estimated by determining which epiphyses have fused and which have not (**Fig. D-4**). The characteristic undulating appearance of the unfused surfaces helps differentiate immature elements from the broken end of a mature bone.

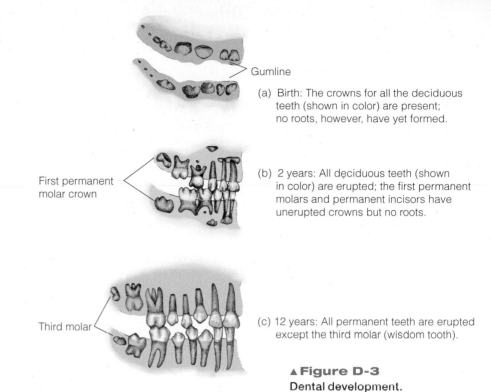

Gumline

(a) Birth: The crowns for all the deciduous teeth (shown in color) are present; no roots, however, have yet formed.

First permanent molar crown

(b) 2 years: All deciduous teeth (shown in color) are erupted; the first permanent molars and permanent incisors have unerupted crowns but no roots.

Third molar

(c) 12 years: All permanent teeth are erupted except the third molar (wisdom tooth).

▲**Figure D-3**
Dental development.

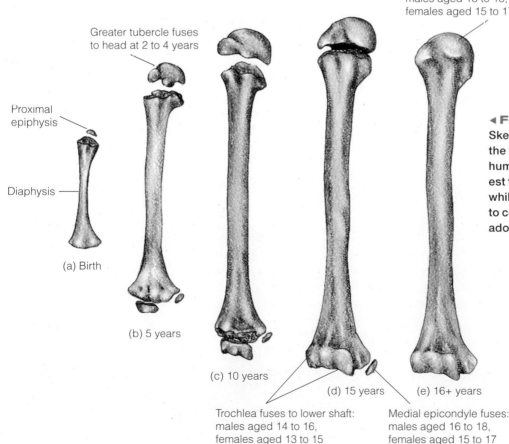

Greater tubercle fuses to head at 2 to 4 years

Head fuses to shaft: males aged 16 to 18, females aged 15 to 17

Proximal epiphysis

Diaphysis

(a) Birth

(b) 5 years

(c) 10 years

(d) 15 years

(e) 16+ years

Trochlea fuses to lower shaft: males aged 14 to 16, females aged 13 to 15

Medial epicondyle fuses: males aged 16 to 18, females aged 15 to 17

◄**Figure D-4**
Skeletal age: epiphyseal union in the humerus. Some regions of the humerus exhibit some of the earliest fusion centers in the body, while others are among the latest to complete fusion (not until late adolescence).

Other Skeletal Changes

Once a person has reached physiological maturity (by the early 20s), determinations of age become more difficult and less precise. Several techniques are used, and these are based on the occurrence of progressive, regular changes in the face of the pubic symphysis (the most common technique), in the sternal ends of the ribs, and in the auricular surface of the ilium (where the ilium articulates with the sacrum). Other indicators are closure of the cranial sutures and cellular changes that are determined by microscopic examination of cross sections of long bones. Degenerative changes, such as arthritis, osteoporosis, and wear of dental enamel, can also aid in the determination of relative age (older versus younger), but they provide imprecise estimates. In fact, it is very difficult to age the skeletons of adults accurately. For example, the presence of severe tooth wear would imply that the individual was not young, but enamel attrition varies between populations and depends on many factors, including diet. Moreover, the appearance of many degenerative changes is influenced by disease, trauma, and the biological make-up of individuals. Thus, at present, osteologists must be content to use broad age ranges when estimating age at death in mature skeletons.

Pubic Symphyseal Face   The face of the pubic symphysis in young individuals is characterized by a billowing surface (with ridges and furrows) such as that seen on the surface of an epiphysis (**Fig. D-5**). The symphyseal face undergoes regular age-related changes from the age of about 18 onward.

The first aging technique based on alterations of the pubic symphysis was developed by T. W. Todd (1920, 1921), utilizing dissection room cadavers. McKern and Stewart (1957) developed a technique by analyzing a sample of American males killed in the Korean War. Both of the samples from which these systems were derived, however, had limitations. The dissection room sample used by Todd contained some individuals of uncertain age, and the Korean War sample was predominantly made up of young white males, with few being older than 35.

More recently, a system has been developed by Judy Suchey and colleagues (Katz and Suchey, 1986) based on very well-documented autopsy samples of males and females. These samples have proven more representative of the general population than the earlier samples. Because this technique is derived from data collected from a large sample of people of known age at death, it is currently the most accurate method available for estimating age in adult human skeletal remains.

▼ **Figure D-5**
Skeletal age: remodeling of the pubic symphysis. This area of the pelvis shows systematic changes progressively throughout adult life. Two of these stages are shown in **(b)** and **(c)**.

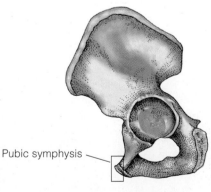

(a) Position of the pubic symphysis.

(b) Age 21. The face of the symphysis shows the typical "billowed" appearance of a young joint; no rim present.

(c) Age mid-50s. The face is mostly flat, with a distinct rim formed around most of the periphery.

Glossary

acclimatization Physiological responses to changes in the environment that occur during an individual's lifetime. Such responses may be temporary or permanent, depending on the duration of the environmental change and when in the individual's life it occurs. The capacity for acclimatization may typify an entire population or species, and because it's under genetic influence, it's subject to evolutionary factors such as natural selection and genetic drift.

Acheulian (ash´-oo-lay-en) Pertaining to a stone tool industry from the Early and Middle Pleistocene; characterized by a large proportion of bifacial tools (flaked on both sides). Acheulian tool kits are common in Africa, Southwest Asia, and western Europe, but they're thought to be less common elsewhere. Also spelled Acheulean.

adaptation An anatomical, physiological, or behavioral response of organisms or popula tions to the environment. Adaptations result from evolutionary change (specifically, as a result of natural selection).

adaptive niche An organism's entire way of life: where it lives, what it eats, how it gets food, how it avoids predators, and so on.

adaptive radiation The relatively rapid expansion and diversification of life-forms into new ecological niches.

adolescent growth spurt The period during adolescence when well-nourished teens typically increase in stature at greater rates than at other times in the life cycle.

affiliative behaviors Amicable associations between individuals. Affiliative behaviors, such as grooming, reinforce social bonds and promote group cohesion.

allele frequency In a population, the percentage of all the alleles at a locus accounted for by one specific allele.

alleles Alternate forms of a gene. Alleles occur at the same locus on both members of a pair of chromosomes, and they influence the same trait. But because they're slightly different from one another, their action may result in different expressions of that trait. The term *allele* is sometimes used synonymously with *gene*.

altruism Actions that benefits another individual but at some potential risk or cost to oneself.

amino acids Small molecules that are the components of proteins.

analogies Similarities between organisms based strictly on common function, with no assumed common evolutionary descent.

ancestral Referring to characters inherited by a group of organisms from a remote ancestor and thus not diagnostic of groups (lineages) that diverged after the character first appeared; also called primitive.

anthropocentric Viewing nonhuman organisms in terms of human experience and capabilities. Emphasizing the importance of humans over everything else.

anthropoids Members of the primate infraorder Anthropoidea (pronounced "an-thropoid´-ee-uh"), which includes monkeys, apes, and humans.

anthropology The field of inquiry that studies human culture and evolutionary aspects of human biology; includes cultural anthropology, archaeology, linguistics, and physical, or biological, anthropology.

antigens Large molecules found on the surface of cells. Several different loci govern various antigens on red and white blood cells. (Foreign antigens provoke an immune response.)

applied anthropology The practical application of anthropological and archaeological theories and techniques. For example, many biological anthropologists work in the public health sector.

arboreal Tree-living; adapted to life in the trees.

artifacts Objects or materials made or modified for use by hominins. The earliest artifacts are usually tools made of stone or, occasionally, bone.

Aurignacian Pertaining to an Upper Paleolithic stone tool industry in Europe beginning at about 40,000 ya.

australopiths A colloquial name referring to a diverse group of Plio-Pleistocene African hominins. Australopiths are the most abundant and widely distributed of all early hominins and are also the most completely studied.

autonomic Pertaining to physiological responses not under voluntary control. An example in chimpanzees would be the erection of body hair during excitement. Blushing is a human example. Both convey information regarding emotional states, but neither is deliberate, and communication isn't intended.

autosomes All chromosomes except the sex chromosomes.

behavior Anything organisms do that involves action in response to internal or external stimuli; the response of an individual, group, or species to its environment. Such responses may or may not be deliberate, and they aren't necessarily the result of conscious decision making (which is absent in single-celled organisms, insects, and many other species).

behavioral ecology The study of the evolution of behavior, emphasizing the role of ecological factors as agents of natural selection. Behaviors and behavioral patterns have been favored because they increase the reproductive fitness of individuals (i.e., they are adaptive) in specific environmental contexts.

binocular vision Vision characterized by overlapping visual fields provided by forward-facing eyes. Binocular vision is essential to depth perception.

binomial nomenclature (*binomial*, meaning "two names") In taxonomy, the convention established by Carolus Linnaeus whereby genus and species names are used to refer to species. For example, *Homo sapiens* refers to human beings.

bioarchaeology The study of skeletal remains from archaeological sites.

biocultural Pertaining to the concept that biology makes culture possible and that culture influences biology.

biocultural evolution The mutual, interactive evolution of human biology and culture; the concept that biology makes culture possible and that developing culture further influences the direction of biological evolution; a basic concept in understanding the unique components of human evolution.

biological continuity A biological continuum. When expressions of a phenomenon continuously grade into one another so that there are no discrete categories, they exist on a continuum. Color is one such phenomenon, and life-forms are another.

biological continuum Refers to the fact that organisms are related through common ancestry and that behaviors and traits seen in one species are also seen in others to varying degrees. (When expressions of a phenomenon continuously grade into one another so that there are no discrete categories, they are said to exist on a continuum. Color is one such phenomenon.)

biological determinism The concept that phenomena, including various aspects of behavior (e.g., intelligence, values, morals) are governed by biological (genetic) factors; the inaccurate association of various behavioral attributes with certain biological traits, such as skin color.

biological species concept A depiction of species as groups of individuals capable of fertile interbreeding but reproductively isolated from other such groups.

bipedal locomotion Walking on two feet. Walking on two legs is the single most distinctive feature of the hominins.

bipedally On two feet; walking habitually on two legs.

brachiation Arm swinging, a form of locomotion used by some primates. Brachiation involves hanging from a branch and moving by alternately swinging from one arm to the other.

breeding isolates Populations that are clearly isolated geographically and/or socially from other breeding groups.

burins Small, chisel-like tools with a pointed end; thought to have been used to engrave bone, antler, ivory, or wood.

catastrophism The view that the earth's geological landscape is the result of violent cataclysmic events. Cuvier promoted this view, especially in opposition to Lamarck.

cercopithecines (serk-oh-pith´-eh-seens) The subfamily of Old World monkeys that includes baboons, macaques, and guenons.

Chatelperronian Pertaining to an Upper Paleolithic industry found in France and Spain, containing blade tools and associated with Neandertals.

Chordata The phylum of the animal kingdom that includes vertebrates.

Christian fundamentalists Adherents to a movement in American Protestantism that began in the early twentieth century. This group holds that the teachings of the Bible are infallible and that the scriptures are to be taken literally.

chromosomes Discrete structures composed of DNA and proteins found only in the nucleus of cells. Chromosomes are visible under magnification only during certain phases of cell division.

chronometric (*chronos*, meaning "time," and *metric*, meaning "measure") Referring to a dating technique that gives an estimate in actual numbers of years.

clade A group of organisms sharing a common ancestor. The group includes the common ancestor and all descendants.

cladistics An approach to classification that attempts to make rigorous evolutionary interpretations based solely on analysis of certain types of homologous characters (those considered to be derived characters).

cladogram A chart showing evolutionary relationships as determined by cladistic analysis. It's based solely on interpretation of shared derived characters. It contains no time component and does not imply ancestor-descendant relationships.

classification In biology, the ordering of organisms into categories, such as orders, families, and genera, to show evolutionary relationships.

clones Organisms that are genetically identical to another organism.

codominance The expression of two alleles in heterozygotes. In this situation, neither allele is dominant or recessive, so they both influence the phenotype.

codons Triplets of messenger RNA bases that code for specific amino acids during protein synthesis.

colobines (kole´-uh-bines) Common name for members of the subfamily of Old World monkeys that includes the African colobus monkeys and Asian langurs.

communication Any act that conveys information, in the form of a message, to another individual. Frequently, the result of communication is a change in the behavior of the recipient. Communication may not be deliberate but may instead be the result of involuntary processes or a secondary consequence of an intentional action.

complementary In genetics, referring to the fact that DNA bases form pairs (called base pairs) in a precise manner. For example, adenine can bond only to thymine. These two bases are said to be complementary because one requires the other to form a complete DNA base pair.

continental drift The movement of continents on sliding plates of the earth's surface. As a result, the positions of large landmasses have shifted drastically during the earth's history.

continuum A set of relationships in which all components fall along a single integrated spectrum (for example, color). All life reflects a single biological continuum.

core area The portion of a home range containing the highest concentration and most reliable supplies of food and water. The core area is defended.

culture Behavioral aspects of human adaptation, including technology, traditions, language, religion, marriage patterns, and social roles. Culture is a set of learned behaviors transmitted from one generation to the next by nonbiological (i.e., nongenetic) means.

cusps The bumps on the chewing surface of premolars and molars.

cytoplasm The semifluid substance contained within the cell membrane. The nucleus and numerous other kinds of structures involved with cell function are found within the cytoplasm.

data (*sing.*, datum) Facts from which conclusions can be drawn; scientific information.

dental formula Numerical device that indicates the number of each type of tooth in each side of the upper and lower jaws.

derived (modified) Referring to characters that are modified from the ancestral condition and thus diagnostic of particular evolutionary lineages.

displays Sequences of repetitious behaviors that serve to communicate emotional states. Nonhuman primate displays are most frequently associated with reproductive or agonistic behavior and examples include chest slapping in gorillas or, in male chimpanzees, dragging and waving branches while charging and threatening other animals.

diurnal Active during the day.

DNA (deoxyribonucleic acid) The double-stranded molecule that contains the genetic code. DNA is a main component of chromosomes.

dominance hierarchies Systems of social organization wherein individuals within a group are ranked relative to one another. Higher-ranking animals have greater access to preferred food items and mating partners than lower-ranking individuals. Dominance hierarchies are sometimes called "pecking orders."

dominant In genetics, describing a trait governed by an allele that's expressed in the presence of another allele (that is, in heterozygotes). Dominant alleles prevent the expression of recessive alleles in heterozygotes. (This is the definition of *complete* dominance.)

ecological Pertaining to the relationships between organisms and all aspects of their environment (temperature, predators, nonpredators, vegetation, availability of food and water, types of food, disease organisms, parasites, etc.).

ecological niche The position of a species within its physical and biological environments. A species' ecological niche is defined by such components as diet, terrain, vegetation, type of predators, relationships with other species, and activity patterns, and each niche is unique to a given species. Together, ecological niches make up an ecosystem.

empathy The ability to identify with the feelings and thoughts of another individual.

empirical Relying on experiment or observation; from the Latin *empiricus*, meaning "experienced."

endemic Continuously present in a population.

endocrine glands glands responsible for the secretion of hormones into the bloodstream.

endothermic (*endo*, meaning "within" or "internal") Able to maintain internal body temperature by producing energy through metabolic processes within cells; characteristic of mammals, birds, and perhaps some dinosaurs.

enzymes Specialized proteins that initiate and direct chemical reactions in the body.

epigenetics Changes in phenotype that are not related to changes in underlying DNA and that may result from the interaction between the genotype and the environment.

epigenome The instructions that determine how genes are expressed in a cell.

epochs Categories of the geological time scale; subdivisions of periods. In the Cenozoic era, epochs include the Paleocene, Eocene, Oligocene, Miocene, and Pliocene (from the Tertiary Period) and the Pleistocene and Holocene (from the Quaternary Period).

essential amino acids The 9 (of 22) amino acids that must be obtained from the food we eat because they are not synthesized in the body in sufficient amounts.

estrus Period of sexual receptivity in nonhuman female mammals correlated with ovulation. When used as an adjective, it is spelled "estrous."

ethnocentric Viewing other cultures from the inherently biased perspective of one's own culture. Ethnocentrism often results in other cultures being seen as inferior to one's own.

ethnographies Detailed descriptive studies of human societies. In cultural anthropology, an ethnography is traditionally the study of a non-Western society.

eugenics The philosophy of "race improvement" through the forced sterilization of members of some groups and increased reproduction among others; an overly simplified, often racist view that's now discredited.

evaporative cooling A physiological mechanism that helps prevent the body from overheating. It occurs when perspiration is produced from sweat glands and then evaporates from the surface of the skin.

evolution A change in the genetic structure of a population. The term is also frequently used to refer to the appearance of a new species.

evolutionary systematics A traditional approach to classification (and evolutionary interpretation) in which presumed ancestors and descendants are traced in time by analysis of homologous characters.

exons Segments of genes that are transcribed and are involved in protein synthesis. (The prefix *ex* denotes that these segments are expressed.)

faunal Referring to animal remains; in archaeology, specifically refers to the fossil (skeletonized) remains of animals.

fertility The ability to conceive and produce healthy offspring.

fitness Pertaining to natural selection, a measure of the relative reproductive success of individuals. Fitness can be measured by an individual's genetic contribution to the next generation compared with that of other individuals. The terms genetic fitness, reproductive fitness, and *differential reproductive success* are also used.

flexed The position of the body in a bent orientation, with arms and legs drawn up to the chest.

forensic anthropology An applied anthropological approach dealing with legal matters. Forensic anthropologists work with coroners and others in identifying and analyzing human remains.

fossils Traces or remnants of organisms found in geological beds on the earth's surface.

founder effect A type of genetic drift in which allele frequencies are altered in small populations that are taken from, or are remnants of, larger populations.

frugivorous (fru-give´-or-us) Having a diet composed primarily of fruit.

gametes Reproductive cells (eggs and sperm in animals) developed from precursor cells in ovaries and testes.

gene A sequence of DNA bases that specifies the order of amino acids in an entire protein, a portion of a protein, or any functional product (for example., RNA). A gene may be made up of hundreds or thousands of DNA bases organized into coding and noncoding segments.

gene flow Exchange of genes between populations.

gene pool The total complement of genes shared by the reproductive members of a population.

genetic Having to do with the study of gene structure and action and the patterns of inheritance of traits from parent to offspring. Genetic mechanisms are the foundation for evolutionary change.

genetic drift Evolutionary changes, or changes in allele frequencies, that are produced by random factors in small populations. Genetic drift is a result of small population size.

genome The entire genetic makeup of an individual or species.

genotype The genetic makeup of an individual. Genotype can refer to an organism's entire genetic makeup or to the alleles at a particular locus.

genus (*pl.*, genera) A group of closely related species.

geological time scale The organization of earth history into eras, periods, and epochs; commonly used by geologists and paleoanthropologists.

glaciations Climatic intervals when continental ice sheets cover much of the northern continents. Glaciations are associated with colder temperatures in northern latitudes and more arid conditions in southern latitudes, most notably in Africa.

grooming Picking through fur to remove dirt, parasites, and other materials that may be present. Social grooming is common among primates and reinforces social relationships.

habitual bipedalism Bipedal locomotion as the form of locomotion shown by hominins most of the time.

Haplorhini (hap'-lo-rin-ee) The primate suborder that includes tarsiers, monkeys, apes, and humans.

Hardy-Weinberg equilibrium The mathematical relationship expressing—under conditions in which no evolution is occurring—the predicted distribution of alleles in populations; the central theorem of population genetics.

hemispheres The two halves of the cerebrum that are connected by a dense mass of fibers. (The cerebrum is the large rounded outer portion of the brain.)

hemoglobin A protein molecule that occurs in red blood cells and binds to oxygen molecules.

heterodont Having different kinds of teeth; characteristic of mammals, whose teeth consist of incisors, canines, premolars, and molars.

heterozygous Having different alleles at the same locus on members of a pair of chromosomes.

Holocene The most recent epoch of the Cenozoic. Following the Pleistocene, it's estimated to have begun 10,000 years ago.

homeobox genes An evolutionarily ancient group of regulatory genes. One type (called *Hox* genes) directs segmentation of the body during embryonic development.

homeostasis A condition of balance, or stability, within a biological system, maintained by the interaction of physiological mechanisms that compensate for changes (both external and internal).

hominins Colloquial term for members of the evolutionary group that includes modern humans and now-extinct bipedal relatives.

hominoids Members of the primate superfamily (Hominoidea) that includes apes and humans.

homologies Similarities between organisms based on descent from a common ancestor.

homoplasy (*homo*, meaning "same," and *plasy*, meaning "growth") The separate evolutionary development of similar characteristics in different groups of organisms.

homozygous Having the same allele at the same locus on both members of a pair of chromosomes.

honing complex The shearing of a large upper canine with the 1st lower premolar, with the wear leading to honing of the surfaces of both teeth. This anatomical pattern is typical of most Old World anthropoids, but is mostly absent in hominins.

hormones Substances (usually proteins) that are produced by specialized cells and that travel to other parts of the body, where they influence chemical reactions and regulate various cellular functions.

Human Genome Project An international effort aimed at sequencing and mapping the entire human genome, completed in 2003.

hybrids Offspring of parents who differ from each other with regard to certain traits or certain aspects of genetic makeup; heterozygotes.

hypotheses (*sing.*, hypothesis) A provisional explanation of a phenomenon. Hypotheses require verification or falsification through testing.

intelligence Mental capacity; ability to learn, reason, or comprehend and interpret information, facts, relationships, and meanings; the capacity to solve problems, whether through the application of previously acquired knowledge or through insight.

interglacials Climatic intervals when continental ice sheets are retreating, eventually becoming much reduced in size. Interglacials in northern latitudes are associated with warmer temperatures, while in southern latitudes the climate becomes wetter.

interspecific Between species; refers to variation beyond that seen within the same species to include additional aspects seen between two different species.

intragroup Within the group as opposed to intergroup (meaning between groups).

intraspecific Within species; refers to variation seen within the same species.

introns Segments of genes that are initially transcribed and then deleted. Because they aren't expressed, they aren't involved in protein synthesis. However, a DNA sequence that is deleted during the manufacture of one protein may not be deleted in another. Therefore, the terms "introns" and "noncoding DNA" aren't synonymous.

ischial callosities Patches of tough, hard skin on the buttocks of Old World monkeys and chimpanzees.

K-selected Pertaining to K-selection, an adaptive strategy whereby individuals produce relatively few offspring, in whom they invest increased parental care. Although only a few infants are born, chances of survival are increased for each one because of parental investments in time and energy. Birds, elephants, and canids (wolves, coyotes, and dogs) are examples of K-selected nonprimate species.

lactase persistence In adults, the continued production of lactase, the enzyme that breaks down lactose (milk sugar). This allows adults in some human populations to digest fresh milk products. The discontinued production of lactase in adults leads to lactose intolerance and the inability to digest fresh milk.

language A standardized system of arbitrary vocal sounds, written symbols, and gestures used in communication.

large-bodied hominoids Those hominoids including the great apes (orangutans, chimpanzees, gorillas) and hominins, as well as all ancestral forms back to the time of divergence from small-bodied hominoids (i.e., the gibbon lineage).

Late Pleistocene The portion of the Pleistocene epoch beginning 125,000 ya and ending approximately 10,000 ya.

life history traits Characteristics and developmental stages that influence reproductive rates. Examples include longevity, age at sexual maturity, length of time between births, etc.

locus (*pl.*, loci) (lo-kus, lo-sigh) The position on a chromosome where a given gene occurs. The term is frequently used interchangeably with *gene*.

macroevolution Changes produced only after many generations, such as the appearance of a new species.

Magdalenian Pertaining to the final phase of the Upper Paleolithic stone tool industry in Europe.

matrilines Groups that consist of a female, her daughters, and their offspring. Matrilineal groups are common in macaques.

meiosis Cell division in specialized cells in ovaries and testes. Meiosis involves two divisions and results in four daughter cells, each containing only half the original number of chromosomes. These cells can develop into gametes.

menarche The first menstruation in girls, usually occurring in the early to midteens.

Mendelian traits Characteristics that are influenced by alleles at only one genetic locus. Examples include many blood types, such as ABO. Many genetic disorders, including sickle-cell anemia and Tay-Sachs disease, are also Mendelian traits.

menopause The end of menstruation in women, usually occurring around age 50.

messenger RNA (mRNA) A form of RNA that's assembled on a sequence of DNA bases. It carries the DNA code to the ribosome during protein synthesis.

metabolism The chemical processes within cells that break down nutrients and release energy for the body to use. (When nutrients are broken down into their component parts, such as amino acids, energy is released and made available for the cell to use.)

microevolution Small changes occurring within species, such as changes in allele frequencies.

Middle Pleistocene The portion of the Pleistocene epoch beginning 780,000 ya and ending 125,000 ya.

mineralization The process in which parts of animals (or some plants) become transformed into stone-like structures. Mineralization usually occurs very slowly as water carrying minerals, such as silica or iron, seeps into the tiny spaces within a bone. In some cases, the original minerals within the bone or tooth can be completely replaced, molecule by molecule, with other minerals.

mitochondria (*sing.*, mitochondrion) Structures contained within the cytoplasm of eukaryotic cells that convert energy, derived from nutrients, to a form that can be used by the cell.

mitochondrial DNA (mtDNA) DNA found in the mitochondria. Mitochondrial DNA is inherited only from the mother.

mitosis Simple cell division; the process by which somatic cells divide to produce two identical daughter cells.

molecules Structures made up of two or more atoms. Molecules can combine with other molecules to form more complex structures.

mosaic evolution A pattern of evolution in which the rate of evolution in one functional system varies from that in other systems. For example, in hominin evolution, the dental system, locomotor system, and neurological system (especially the brain) all evolved at markedly different rates.

Mousterian Pertaining to the stone tool industry associated with Neandertals and some modern *H. sapiens* groups; also called Middle Paleolithic. This industry is characterized by a larger proportion of flake tools than is found in Acheulian tool kits.

multidisciplinary Pertaining to research involving mutual contributions and cooperation of experts from various scientific fields (i.e., disciplines).

mutation A change in DNA. The term can refer to changes in DNA bases (specifically called point mutations) as well as to changes in chromosome number and/or structure.

natal group The group in which an animal is born and raised. (*Natal* pertains to birth.)

natural selection The most critical mechanism of evolutionary change, first described by Charles Darwin; refers to genetic change or changes in the frequencies of certain traits in populations due to differential reproductive success between individuals.

neocortex The more recently evolved portion of the brain that is involved in higher mental functions and composed of areas that integrate incoming sensory information.

neural tube In early embryonic development, the anatomical structure that develops to form the brain and spinal cord.

nocturnal Active during the night.

noncoding DNA DNA that does not direct the production of proteins. However, such DNA segments may produce other important molecules, so the term *noncoding* DNA is not really accurate.

nuchal torus (nuke´-ul) (*nucha*, meaning "neck") A projection of bone in the back of the cranium where neck muscles attach. These muscles hold up the head.

nucleotides Basic units of the DNA molecule, composed of a sugar, a phosphate, and one of four DNA bases.

nucleus A structure (organelle) found in all eukaryotic cells. The nucleus contains DNA that, during cell division, is organized into chromosomes.

obligate bipedalism Bipedalism as the *only* form of hominin terrestrial locomotion. Major anatomical changes in the spine, pelvis, and lower limb are required for bipedal locomotion, so once hominins adapted this mode of locomotion, other forms of locomotion on the ground became impossible.

Oldowan industry The earliest recognized stone tool culture, including very simple tools, mostly small flakes.

olfaction The sense of smell.

omnivorous Having a diet consisting of many kinds of food including plants, meat, and insects.

osteology The study of skeletal material. Human osteology focuses on the interpretation of the skeletal remains from archaeological sites, skeletal anatomy, bone physiology, and growth and development. Some of the same techniques are used in paleoanthropology to study early hominins.

paleoanthropology The interdisciplinary approach to the study of earlier hominins—their chronology, physical structure, archaeological remains, habitats, and so on.

paleopathology The branch of osteology that studies the evidence of disease and injury in human skeletal (or, occasionally, mummified) remains from archaeological sites.

paleospecies Species defined from fossil evidence, often covering a long time span.

pandemic An epidemic that spreads through many populations and may affect people worldwide. Examples include HIV/ AIDS and the "Spanish flu" pandemic of 1918-1919.

phenotypes The observable or detectable physical characteristics of an organism; the detectable expressions of genotypes, frequently influenced by environmental factors.

phylogenetic tree A chart showing evolutionary relationships as determined by evolutionary systematics. It contains a time component and implies ancestor–descendant relationships.

pigment In this context, a molecule that influences the color of skin, hair, and eyes.

placental A type (subclass) of mammal. During the Cenozoic, placentals became the most widespread and numerous mammals and today are represented by upward of 20 orders, including the primates.

pleiotropic genes Genes that have more than one effect; genes that have different effects at different times in the life cycle.

Pleistocene The epoch of the Cenozoic from 1.8 mya until 10,000 ya. Frequently referred to as the Ice Age, this epoch is associated with continental glaciations in northern latitudes.

Plio-Pleistocene Pertaining to the Pliocene and first half of the Pleistocene, a time range of 5–1 mya. For this time period, numerous fossil hominins have been found in Africa.

polyandry A mating system wherein a female continuously associates with more than one male (usually two or three) with whom she mates. Among nonhuman primates, polyandry is seen only in marmosets and tamarins. It also occurs in a few human societies.

polygenic Referring to traits that are influenced by genes at two or more loci. Examples include stature, skin color, eye color, and hair color. Many (but not all) polygenic traits are influenced by environmental factors such as nutrition and exposure to sunlight.

polygynous Pertaining to polygyny. A mating system in which males, and in some cases females, have several mating partners.

polymerase chain reaction (PCR) A method of producing thousands of copies of a DNA sample.

polymorphisms Loci with more than one allele. Polymorphisms can be expressed in the phenotype as the result of gene action (as in ABO), or they can exist solely at the DNA level within noncoding regions.

polytypic Referring to species composed of populations that differ in the expression of one or more traits.

population Within a species, a community of individuals where mates are usually found.

population genetics The study of the frequency of alleles, genotypes, and phenotypes in populations from a microevolutionary perspective.

postcranial Referring to all or part of the skeleton not including the skull. The term originates from the fact that in quadrupeds, the body is in back of the head; the term literally means "behind the head."

primates Members of the mammalian order Primates (pronounced "pry-may´-tees"), which includes lemurs, lorises, tarsiers, monkeys, apes, and humans.

primatology The study of the biology and behavior of nonhuman primates (lemurs, lorises, tarsiers, monkeys, and apes).

principle of independent assortment The distribution of one pair of alleles into gametes does not influence the distribution of another pair. The genes controlling different traits are inherited independently of one another.

principle of segregation Genes (alleles) occur in pairs because chromosomes occur in pairs. During gamete formation, the members of each pair of alleles separate, so that each gamete contains one member of each pair.

protein synthesis The manufacture of proteins; the assembly of chains of amino acids into functional protein molecules. Protein synthesis is directed by DNA.

proteins Three-dimensional molecules that serve a wide variety of functions through their ability to bind to other molecules.

quadrupedal Using all four limbs to support the body during locomotion; the basic mammalian (and primate) form of locomotion.

quantitatively Pertaining to measurements of quantity and including such properties as size, number, and capacity. When data are quantified, they're expressed numerically and can be tested statistically.

r-selected Pertaining to r-selection, a reproductive strategy that emphasizes relatively large numbers of offspring and reduced parental care compared to K-selected species. *K-selection* and *r-selection* are relative terms; e.g., mice are

r-selected compared to primates but K-selected compared to insects.

random assortment The chance distribution of chromosomes to daughter cells during meiosis. Along with recombination, random assortment is an important source of genetic variation (but not new alleles).

recessive Describing a trait that isn't expressed in heterozygotes; also refers to the allele that governs the trait. For a recessive allele to be expressed, an individual must have two copies of it (that is, the individual must be homozygous).

recombination The exchange of genetic material between paired chromosomes during meiosis; also called *crossing over*.

regulatory genes Genes that influence the activity of other genes. Regulatory genes direct embryonic development and are involved in physiological processes throughout life. They are extremely important to the evolutionary process.

relativistic Viewing entities as they relate to something else. Cultural relativism is the view that cultures have merits within their own historical and environmental contexts.

replicate To duplicate. The DNA molecule is able to make copies of itself.

reproductive strategies Behaviors or behavioral complexes that have been favored by natural selection to increase individual reproductive success. The behaviors need not be deliberate, and they often vary considerably between males and females.

reproductive success The number of offspring an individual produces and rears to reproductive age; an individual's genetic contribution to the next generation.

reproductively isolated Pertaining to groups of organisms that, mainly because of genetic differences, are prevented from mating and producing offspring with members of other such groups. For example, dogs cannot mate and produce offspring with cats.

rhinarium (rine-air´-ee-um) (Plural: rhinaria) The moist, hairless pad at the end of the nose seen in most mammalian species. The rhinarium enhances an animal's ability to smell.

ribosomes Structures composed of a form of RNA called ribosomal RNA (rRNA) and protein. Ribosomes are found in a cell's cytoplasm and are essential to the manufacture of proteins.

RNA (ribonucleic acid) A single-stranded molecule similar in structure to DNA. Three forms of RNA are essential to protein synthesis: messenger RNA (mRNA), transfer RNA (tRNA), and ribosomal RNA (rRNA).

sagittal crest A ridge of bone that runs down the middle of the cranium like a short Mohawk. This serves as the attachment for the large temporal muscles, indicating strong chewing.

savanna (also spelled savannah) A large flat grassland with scattered trees and shrubs. Savannas are found in many regions of the world with dry and warm-to-hot climates.

science A body of knowledge gained through observation and experimentation; from the Latin *scientia*, meaning "knowledge."

scientific method An approach to research whereby a problem is identified, a hypothesis (provisional explanation) is stated, and that hypothesis is tested by collecting and analyzing data.

scientific testing The precise repetition of an experiment or expansion of observed data to provide verification; the procedure by which hypotheses and theories are verified, modified, or discarded.

selective breeding A practice whereby animal or plant breeders choose which individual animals or plants will be allowed to mate based on the traits (such as body size) they hope to produce in the offspring. Animals or plants that don't have the desirable traits aren't allowed to breed.

selective pressures Forces in the environment that influence reproductive success in individuals.

senescence Decline in physiological functioning usually associated with aging.

sensory modalities Different forms of sensation (e.g., touch, pain, pressure, heat, cold, vision, taste, hearing, and smell).

sex chromosomes In mammals, the X and Y chromosomes.

sexual dimorphism Differences in physical characteristics between males and females of the same species. For example, humans are slightly sexually dimorphic for body size, with males being taller, on average, than females of the same population. Sexual dimorphism is very pronounced in many species, such as gorillas.

sexual selection A type of natural selection that operates on only one sex within a species. It's the result of competition for mates, and it can lead to sexual dimorphism with regard to one or more traits.

shared derived Relating to specific character traits shared in common between two life-forms and considered the most useful type of characteristic for making evolutionary interpretations.

sickle-cell anemia A severe inherited hemoglobin disorder in which red blood cells collapse when deprived of oxygen. It results from inheriting two copies of a mutant allele. This allele is caused by a single base substitution in the DNA.

sickle-cell trait Heterozygous condition in which a person has one Hb^A allele and one Hb^S allele. Thus they have some normal hemoglobin.

sites Locations of discoveries. In paleontology and archaeology, a site may refer to a region where a number of discoveries have been made.

slash-and-burn agriculture A traditional land-clearing practice involving the cutting and burning of trees and vegetation. In many areas, fields are abandoned after a few years and clearing occurs elsewhere.

social structure The composition, size, and sex ratio of a group of animals. The social structure of a species is, in part, the result of natural selection in a specific habitat, and it guides individual interactions and social relationships.

somatic cells Basically, all the cells in the body except those involved with reproduction.

speciation The process by which a new species evolves from an earlier species. Speciation is the most basic process in macroevolution.

species A group of organisms that can interbreed to produce fertile offspring. Members of one species are reproductively isolated from members of all other species (i.e., they cannot mate with them to produce fertile offspring).

spina bifida A condition in which the arch of one or more vertebrae fails to fuse and form a protective barrier around the spinal cord. This can lead to spinal cord damage and paralysis.

stereoscopic vision The condition whereby visual images are, to varying degrees, superimposed. This provides for depth perception, or viewing the external environment in three dimensions. Stereoscopic vision is partly a function of structures in the brain.

stratigraphy Study of the sequential layering of geological deposits.

stratum (*pl.*, strata) Geological layer.

Strepsirhini (strep'-sir-in-ee) The primate suborder that includes lemurs and lorises.

stress In a physiological context, any factor that acts to disrupt homeostasis; more precisely, the body's response to any factor that threatens its ability to maintain homeostasis.

taphonomy The study of how bones and other materials come to be buried in the earth and preserved as fossils.

taxonomy The branch of science concerned with the rules of classifying organisms on the basis of evolutionary relationships.

territorial Pertaining to the protection of all or a part of the area occupied by an animal or group of animals. Territorial behaviors range from scent marking to outright attacks on intruders.

territories Portions of an individual's or group's home range that are actively defended against intrusion, especially by members of the same species.

theory A broad statement of scientific relationships or underlying principles that has been substantially verified through the testing of hypotheses.

thermoluminescence (TL) Technique for dating certain archaeological materials that were heated in the past (such as stone tools) and that release stored energy of radioactive decay as light upon reheating.

transfer RNA (tRNA) The form of RNA that binds to specific amino acids and transports them to the ribosome during protein synthesis.

uniformitarianism The theory that the earth's features are the result of long-term processes that continue to operate in the present just as they did in the past. Elaborated on by Lyell, this theory opposed catastrophism and contributed strongly to the concept of immense geological time.

Upper Paleolithic A cultural period usually associated with modern humans, but also found with some Neandertals, and distinguished by technological innovation in various stone tool industries. Best known from western Europe, similar industries are also known from central and eastern Europe and Africa.

variation In genetics, inherited differences among individuals; the basis of all evolutionary change.

vasoconstriction Narrowing of blood vessels to reduce blood flow to the skin. Vasoconstriction is an involuntary response to cold and reduces heat loss at the skin's surface.

vasodilation Expansion of blood vessels, permitting increased blood flow to the skin. Vasodilation permits warming of the skin and facilitates radiation of warmth as a means of cooling. Vasodilation is an involuntary response to warm temperatures, various drugs, and even emotional states (blushing).

vectors Agents that transmit disease from one carrier to another. Mosquitoes are vectors for malaria, just as fleas are vectors for bubonic plague.

vertebrates Animals with segmented, bony spinal columns; includes fishes, amphibians, reptiles (including birds), and mammals.

worldview General cultural orientation or perspective shared by members of a society.

zoonotic (zoh-oh-no´-tic) Pertaining to a zoonosis (*pl.*, zoonoses), a disease that's transmitted to humans through contact with nonhuman animals.

zygote A cell formed by the union of an egg cell and a sperm cell. It contains the full complement of chromosomes (in humans, 46) and has the potential to develop into an entire organism.

Bibliography

Alemseged, Z., F. Spoor, W. H. Kimbel, et al.
2006   A juvenile early hominin skeleton from Dikika, Ethiopia. *Nature* 443:296–301.

American Academy of Pediatrics
2001   Children, adolescents, and television. *Pediatrics* 107:423–426.

Andrews, P.
1984   An alternative interpretation of the characters used to define *Homo erectus. Cour Forschungist Senckenb* 69:167–175.

Ardrey, R.
1961   *African Genesis.* New York: Macmillan.

Arsuaga, Juan Luis, C. Lorenzo, A. Gracia, et al.
1999   The human cranial remains from Gran Dolina Lower Pleistocene site (Sierra de Atapuerca, Spain). *Journal of Human Evolution* 37:431–457.

Arsuaga, J. L., I. Martinez, A. Gracia, et al.
1997   Sima de los Huesos (Sierra de Atapuerca, Spain): The site. *Journal of Human Evolution* 33:109–127.

Ascenzi, A., I. Bidditu, P. F. Cassoli, et al.
1996   A calvarium of late *Homo erectus* from Ceprano, Italy. *Journal of Human Evolution* 31:409–423.

Asfaw, B., W. H. Gilbert, Y. Beyene, et al.
2002   Remains of *Homo erectus* from Bouri, Middle Awash, Ethiopia. *Nature* 416:317–320.

Aureli, F., C. M. Schaffner, et al.
2006   Raiding parties of male spider monkeys: Insights into human warfare? *American Journal of Physical Anthropology* 131(4).486–497.

Badrian, A., and N. Badrian
1984   Social organization of *Pan paniscus* in the Lomako Forest, Zaire. In: *The Pygmy Chimpanzee,* Randall L. Susman (ed.), pp. 325–346. New York: Plenum Press.

Badrian, N., and R. K. Malenky
1984   Feeding ecology of *Pan paniscus* in the Lomako Forest, Zaire. In: *The Pygmy Chimpanzee,* Randall L. Susman (ed.), pp. 275–299. New York: Plenum Press.

Balter, M.
2006   Radiocarbon dating's final frontier. *Science* 313:1560–1563.

———
2010   Candidate human ancestor from South Africa sparks praise and debate. *Science* 328:154–155.

Barker, D. J. P.
2004   The developmental origins of adult disease. *Journal of the American College of Nutrition* 23:588S–595S.

Barker, G.,H. Barton, M.Bird, et al.
2007   The human revolution in lowland tropical Southeast Asia: The antiquity and behavior of anatomically modern humans at Niah Cave (Sarawak, Borneo). *Journal of Human Evolution* 52:243–261.

Bearder, S. K.
1987   Lorises, bushbabies & tarsiers: Diverse societies in solitary foragers. In: *Primate Societies,* B. B. Smuts, D. L. Cheney, and R. M. Seyfath (eds.), pp. 11–24. Chicago: University of Chicago Press.

Begun, D., and A. Walker
1993   The Endocast. In: *The Nariokotome* Homo erectus *Skeleton,* A. Walker and R. E. Leakey (eds.), pp. 326–358. Cambridge, MA: Harvard University Press.

Beja-Pereira, A., G. Luikart, P. R. England, et al.
2003   Gene-culture coevolution between cattle milk protein genes and human lactase genes. *Nature Genetics* 35:311–313.

Bell, M., and M. J. C. Walker
1992   *Late Quaternary Environmental Change.* New York: John Wiley and Sons.

Belluscio, A.
2009   Argentina's forests dwindle. *Nature News* doi:10.1038/news.2009.984.

Berger, L. R., D. J. de Ruiter, S. E. Churchill, et al.
2010   *Australopithecus sediba:* A new species of *Homo*-like australopith from South Africa. *Science* 328:195–204.

Berger, T., and E. Trinkaus
1995   Patterns of trauma among the Neandertals. *Journal of Archaeological Science,* 22:841–852.

Bermejo, M., J. Rodriguez, et al.
2006   Ebola outbreak killed 5000 gorillas. *Science* 314:1564.

Bermúdez de Castro, J. M., J. Arsuaga, E. Carbonell, et al.
1997   A hominid from the Lower Pleistocene of Atapuerca, Spain. Possible ancestor to Neandertals and modern humans. *Science* 276:1392–1395.

Bermúdez de Castro, J. M., M. Martinon-Torres, E. Carbonell, et al.
2004   The Atapuerca sites and their contribution to the knowledge of human evolution in Europe. *Evolutionary Anthropology* 13:25–41.

Biasutti, R.
1959   Razze e Popoli della Terra. *Turin: Unione-Tipografico-Editrice.*

Binford, L. R., and C. K. Ho
1985   Taphonomy at a distance: Zhoukoudian, 'the cave home of Beijing Man'? *Current Anthropology* 26:413–442.

Binford, L. R., and N. M. Stone
1986a   The Chinese Paleolithic: An outsider's view. *AnthroQuest* 1986:14–20.

———
1986b   Zhoukoudian: A closer look. *Current Anthropology* 27(5):453–475.

Bininda-Emonds, R. P. Olaf, Marcel Cordillo, et al.
2007   The delayed rise of present-day mammals. *Nature* 446:507–512

Bischoff, J. L., R. W. Williams, R. J. Rosebauer, et al.
2007   High-resolution U-series dates from the Sima de los Huesos hominids yields 600+∨/-66 kyrs: Implications for the evolution of the early Neanderthal lineage. *Journal of Archaeological Science* 34:763–770.

Boaz, N. T., and R. L. Ciochon
2001   The scavenging of *Homo erectus pekinensis. Natural History* 110:46–51.

Boesch, C.
1996   Social grouping Tai chimpanzees. In: *Great Ape Societies,* W. C. McGrew, L. Marchant, and T. Nishida (eds.), pp.101–113. Cambridge, UK: Cambridge University Press.

Boesch, C., and H. Boesch-Achermann
2000   *The Chimpanzees of the Tai Forest.* Oxford, UK: Oxford University Press.

Bogin, B.
1988   *Patterns of Human Growth.* Cambridge: Cambridge University Press.

————
2006   Modern human life history: the evolution of human childhood and fertility. In: *The Evolution of Human Life History*, K. Hawkes and R. R. Paine (eds.). Santa Fe, NM: SAR Press.

————
2010   Evolution of Human Growth. In: *Human Evolutionary Biology*, Michael Muehlenbein (ed.), pp. 379–395. Cambridge, UK: Cambridge University Press.

Borries, C., K. Launhardt, C. Epplen, et al.
1999   DNA analyses support the hypothesis that infanticide is adaptive in langur monkeys. *Proceedings of the Royal Society of London* 266:901–904.

Bower, B.
2006   Evolution's mystery woman. *Science News* 170:330–332.

Brace, C. L., H. Nelson, and N. Korn
1979   *Atlas of Human Evolution*, 2nd ed. New York: Holt, Rinehart & Winston.

Breuer, T., M. Ndoundou-Hockemba, and V. Fishlock
2005   First observations of tool use in wild gorillas. *PloS Biology* 3(11):e380. doi:10.1371/journal.pbio.0030380.

Briggs, A., J. M. Good, R. E. Green, et al.
2009   Targeted retrieval and analysis of five Neandertal mtDNA genomes. *Science* 325:318–320.

Bromage, T. G., and C. Dean
1985   Re-evaluation of the age at death of immature fossil hominids. *Nature* 317:525–527.

Brown, K. S., C. W. Marean, A. I. R. Herries, et al.
2009   Fire as an engineering tool of early modern humans. *Science* 325:859–862.

Brown, P., T. Sutiikna, M. K. Morwood, et al.
2004   A new small-bodied hominin from the Late Pleistocene of Flores, Indonesia. *Nature* 431:1055–1061.

Brunet, M., F. Guy, D. Pilbeam, et al.
2002   A new hominid from the Upper Miocene of Chad, Central Africa. *Nature* 418:145–151.

Campbell, C. J.
2006   Lethal intragroup aggression by adult male spider monkeys (*Ateles geoffroyi*). *American Journal of Physical Anthropology* 68:1197–1201.

Caramelli, D., C. Lalueza-Fox, S. Condemi, et al.
2006   A highly divergent mtDNA sequence in a Neandertal individual from Italy. *Current Biology* 16:R630–R632.

Caramelli, D., C. Lalueza-Fox, C. Vernesi, et al.
2003   Evidence for genetic discontinuity between Neandertals and 24,000-year-old anatomically modern humans. *Proceedings of the National Academy of Sciences USA* 100:6593–6597.

Carbonell, E., J. M. Bermuda de Castro, J. M. Pares, et al.
2008   The first hominin of Europe. *Nature* 452:465–469.

Cartmill, M.
1972   Arboreal adaptations and the origin of the order Primates. In: *The Functional and Evolutionary Biology of Primates*, R. H. Tuttle (ed.), pp. 97–122. Chicago: Aldine-Atherton.

————
1992   New views on primate origins. *Evolutionary Anthropology* 1:105–111.

Caulfield, L. E., M. de Onis, M. Blössner, and R. E. Black
2004   Undernutrition as an underlying cause of child deaths associated with diarrhea, pneumonia, malaria, and measles. *American Journal of Clinical Nutrition* 80:193–198.

Centers for Disease Control
2009   www.cdc.gov/flu/about/disease

Chen, F-C., and W-H. Li
2001   Genomic divergences between humans and other hominoids and the effective population size of the common ancestor of humans and chimpanzees. *American Journal of Human Genetics* 68:444–456.

Chen, F. C., E. J. Vallender, H. Wang, C. S. Tzeng, and W. H. Li
2001   Genomic divergence between human and chimpanzee estimated from large-scale alignments of genomic sequences. *Journal of Heredity* 92:481–489.

Cheng, Z., M. Ventura, X. She, P. Khaitovich, T. Graves, et al.
2005   A genome-wide comparison of recent chimpanzee and human segmental duplications. *Nature* 437:88–93.

Chimpanzee Sequencing and Analysis Consortium.
2005   Initial sequence of the chimpanzee genome and comparison with the human genome. *Nature* 437:69–87.

Chisholm, J. S.
1993   Death, hope, and sex: Life-history theory and the development of reproductive strategies. *Current Anthropology* 34(1):1–24.

Ciochon, R. L., and E. Arthur Bettis
2009   Asian *Homo erectus* converges in time. *Nature* 458:153–154.

Ciochon, R. L., and R. S. Corruccini (eds.)
1983   *New Interpretations of Ape and Human Ancestry.* New York: Plenum Press.

Ciochon, R. L., F. Huffman, et al.
2009   Rediscovery of the *Homo erectus* bed at Ngandong: Site formation of a Late Pleistocene hominin site in Asia. *American Journal of Physical Anthropology* (Supplement 48):110.

Clark, A. G., S. Glanowski, et al.
2003   Inferring nonneutral evolution from human-chimp-mouse orthologous gene trios. *Science* 302(5652):1960–1963.

Cohen, M. L, G. Armelagos, eds.
1984   *Paleopathology at the Origins of Agriculture.* New York: Academic Press.

Colwell, R. R.
1996   Global climate and infectious disease: The cholera paradigm. *Science* 274:2025–2031.

Crews, D. E., and G. J. Harper
1998   Ageing as part of the developmental process. In: *The Cambridge Encyclopedia of Human Growth and Development*, S. J. Ulijaszek et al. (eds.), pp. 425–427. Cambridge, UK: Cambridge University Press.

Cummings, M.
2000   *Human Heredity. Principles and Issues*, 5th ed. St. Paul, MN: Wadsworth/West.

Currat, M., G. Trabuchet, D. Rees, et al.
2002   Molecular analysis of the beta-globin gene cluster in the Niokholo Mandenka population reveals a recent origin of the beta S Senegal mutation. *American Journal of Human Genetics* 70:207–223.

Daeschler, E. B., N. H. Shubin, and F. A. Jenkins, Jr.
2006   A Darwinian tetrapod-like fish and the evolution of the tetrapod body plan. *Nature* 440:757–763.

Darwin, C.
1859   *On the Origin of Species.* A Facsimile of the First Edition. Cambridge, MA: Harvard University Press (1964).

————
1871   *The Descent of Man and Selection in Relation to Sex.* Princeton, NJ: Princeton University Press (1981).

Darwin, F.
1950   *The Life and Letters of Charles Darwin.* New York: Henry Schuman.

Day, M. H., and E. H. Wickens
1980   Laetoli Pliocene hominid footprints and bipedalism. *Nature* 286:385–387.

Dean, M., M. Carring, C. Winkler, et al.
1996   Genetic restriction of HIV-1 infection and progression to AIDS by a deletion allele of the CKR5 structural gene. *Science* 273:1856–1862.

Dean, M. C., and B. H. Smith
2009   Growth and development of the Nariokotome youth, KNM-ER-15000. In: *The First Humans. Origin and Evolution of the Genus* Homo, F. E. Grine, J. J. Fleagle, and R. E. Leakey (eds.), pp. 101–120. New York: Springer.

Defleur, A., T. White, et al.
1999   Neanderthal cannibalism at Moula-Guercy, Ardèche, France. *Science* 286:128–131.

de Lumley, H., and M. de Lumley
1973   Pre-Neanderthal human remains from Arago Cave in southeastern France. *Yearbook of Physical Anthropology* 16:162–168.

de Ruiter, D. J., R. Pickering, C. M. Steininger, et al.
2009   New *Australopithecus robustus* fossils and associated U-Pb dates from Cooper's Cave (Gauteng, South Africa). *Journal of Human Evolution* 56:497–513.

de Waal, F.
1982   *Chimpanzee Politics*. London: Jonathan Cape.

1987   Tension regulation and nonreproductive functions of sex in captive bonobos *(Pan paniscus). National Geographic Research* 3:318–335.

1989   *Peacemaking Among Primates*. Cambridge, MA: Harvard University Press.

1996   *Good Natured: The Origins of Right and Wrong in Humans and Other Animals*. Cambridge, MA.: Harvard University Press.

2007   With a little help from a friend. *PloS Biology* 5(7):1406–1408.

de Waal, F., and F. Lanting.
1997   *Bonobo: The Forgotten Ape*. Berkeley, CA: University of California Press.

Demuth, J. P., T. D. Bie, J. E. Stajich, N. Cristianini, and M. W. Hahn
2006   The evolution of mammalian gene families. *PloS ONE* 1(1):e85. doi:10.1371/journal.pone.0000085.

Desmond, A., and J. Moore
1991   *Darwin*. New York: Warner Books.

Dettwyler, K. A.
1994   *Dancing Skeletons*. Prospect Heights, IL: Waveland Press.

1995   A Time to wean: The hominid blueprint for the natural age of weaning in modern human populations. In: *Breastfeeding: Biocultural Perspectives*, P.Stuart-Macadam and K. A. Dettwyler (eds.), pp. 39–73. New York: Aldine de Gruyter.

Diamond, J.
1987   The worst mistake in the history of the human race. *Discover* May:64–66.

Dirks, P. H. G. M., J. M. Kibii, B. F. Kuhn, et al.
2010   Geological setting and age of *Australopithecus sediba* from southern Africa. *Science* 328:205–208.

Dobzhansky, T.
1973   Nothing in biology makes sense except in the light of evolution. *American Biology Teacher* 35:125–129.

Dominy, N. J., and P. W. Lucas
2001   Ecological importance of trichromatic vision to primates. *Nature* 410:363–366.

Doney, S. C., V. J. Fabry, R. A. Feely, and J. A. Kleypas
2009   Ocean acidification: The other CO2 problem. *Annual Review of Marine Science*, online journal, doi: 10.1146/annurev.marine .010908.163834

Doran, D. M., and A. McNeilage
1998   Gorilla ecology and behavior. *Evolutionary Anthropology* 6:120–131.

Dressler, W. W., K. S. Oths, and C. G. Gravlee
2005   Race and ethnicity in public health research: Models to explain Health disparities. *Annual Review of Anthropology* 34:231–252.

Duarte, C., J. Mauricio, P. B. Pettitt, et al.
1999   The early Upper Paleolithic human skeleton from the Abrigo do Lagar Velho (Portugal) and modern human emergence in Iberia. *Proceedings of the National Academy of Sciences USA* 96:7604–7609.

Durham, W.
1981   Paper presented to the Annual Meeting of the American Anthropological Association, Washington, DC., December 1980. Reported in *Science* 211:40.

Eaton, S. B., M. C. Pike, R. V. Short, et al.
1994   Women's reproductive cancers in evolutionary context. *Quarterly Review of Biology* 69(3):353–367.

Eaton, S. B., M. Shostak, and M. Konner
1988   *The Paleolithic Prescription*. New York: Harper and Row.

Ehrlich, P. R., and A. H. Ehrlich
1990   *The Population Explosion*. New York: Simon & Schuster.

Ellison, P. T.
1994   Salivary steroids and natural variation in human ovarian function. *Annals of the New York Academy of Science* 709:287–298.

2001   *On Fertile Ground: A Natural History of Human Reproduction*. Cambridge, MA: Harvard University Press

Enard, W., M. Przeworski, S. E. Fisher, et al.
2002   Molecular evolution of FOXP2, a gene involved in speech and language. *Nature* 418:869–872.

Eppig, C., C. L. Fincher, and R. Thornhill
2010   Parasite prevalence and the worldwide distribution of cognitive ability. *Proceedings of the Royal Society of London*. B. 277:3801–3808.

Erickson, C.
1998   Applied archaeology and rural development: Archaeology's potential contribution to the future. In: *Crossing Currents: Continuity and Change in Latin America*, M. Whiteford and S. Whiteford (eds.), pp. 34–45. Upper Saddle River, NJ: Prentice-Hall.

Eswaran, V., H. Harpending, and A. R. Rogers
2005   Genomics refutes an exclusively African origin of humans. *Journal of Human Evolution* 49:1–18.

Evans, D., C. Pottier, R. Fletcher, et al.
2007   A comprehensive archaeological map of the world's largest pre-industrial settlement complex at Angkor, Cambodia. *Proceedings of the National Academy of Sciences USA* 104:14277–14282.

Ewald, P. W.
1994   *Evolution of Infectious Disease*. New York: Oxford University Press.

1999   Evolutionary control of HIV and other sexually transmitted viruses. In: *Evolutionary Medicine*, W. R. Trevathan, E. O. Smith, and J. J. McKenna, (eds.), New York: Oxford University Press.

Falguères, C., J. J. Bahain, Y. Yokoyama, et al.
1999   Earliest humans in Europe: The age of TD6 Gran Dolina, Atapuerca, Spain. *Journal of Human Evolution* 37:345–352.

Falk, D., C. Hildebolt, K. Smith, et al.
2005   The brain of LB1, *Homo floresiensis. Science* 308:242–245.

Falk, D., C. Hildebolt, K. Smith, et al.
2008   LB1 did not have Laron Syndrome. *American Journal of Physical Anthropology, Supplement* 43:95 (abstract).

Falk, D., C. Hildebolt, K. Smith, et al.
2009   LM1's virtual endocast, microcephaly, and hominin brain evolution. *Journal of Human Evolution* 57:597–607.

Feathers, J. K., and E. Migliorini
2001   Luminescence dating at Katanda—A reassessment. *Quaternary Science Reviews* 20:961–966.

Fedigan, L. M.
1983   Dominance and reproductive success in primates. *Yearbook of Physical Anthropology* 26:91–129.

Fisher, S. E., and C. Scharff
2009   FOXP2 as a molecular window into speech and language. *Trends in Genetics* 25:166–177.

Fleagle, J.
1983   Locomotor adaptations of Oligocene and Miocene hominoids and their phyletic implications. In: *New Interpretations of Ape and Human Ancestry*, R. L. Ciochon and R. S. Corruccini (eds.), pp. 301–324. New York: Plenum Press.

_____
1999   *Primate Adaptation and Evolution*, 2nd ed. New York: Academic Press.

Flinn, M. V.
1999   Family environment, stress, and health during childhood. In: *Hormones, Health, and Behavior*, C. Panter-Brick and C. M. Worthman (eds.), pp. 105–138. Cambridge, UK: Cambridge University Press.

Flinn, M. V., and B. G. England
2003   Childhood stress: Endocrine and immune responses to psychosocial events. In: *Social and Cultural Lives of Immune Systems*, James MacLynn Wilce (ed.), pp. 107–147. London: Routledge Press.

Foley, R. A.
1991   How many species of hominid should there be? *Journal of Human Evolution* 30:413–427.

_____
2002   Adaptive radiations and dispersals in hominin evolutionary ecology. *Evolutionary Anthropology* 11(Supplement 1):32–37.

Foley, R. A., and M. M. Lahr
1997   Mode 3 technologies and the evolution of modern humans. *Cambridge Archaeological Journal* 7:3–36.

Formicola, V., and A. P. Buzhilova
2004   Double child burial from Sunghir (Russia): Pathology and inferences for Upper Paleolithic funerary practices. *American Journal of Physical Anthropology* 124:189–198.

Fraga, M. F., E. Ballestar, M. F. Paz, et al.
2005   Epigenetic differences arise during the lifetime of monozygotic twins. *Proceedings of the National Academy of Sciences* 102:10604–10609.

Fragaszy, D., P. Izar, et al.
2004   Wild capuchin monkeys (*Cebus libidinosus*) use anvils and stone pounding tools. *American Journal of Primatology* 64: 359–366.

Franzen, J. L., P. D. Gingerich, J. Habensetzer, et al.
2009   Complete primate skeleton from the Middle Eocence of Messel in Germany: Morphology and paleobiology. *PLoS One* 4:1–27.

Freundlich, J. C., H. Schwabedissen, and E. Wendt
1980   Köln radiocarbon measurements II. *Radiocarbon* 22:68–81.

Frisancho, A. R.
1993   *Human Adaptation and Accommodation*. Ann Arbor: University of Michigan Press.

Galik, K., B. Senut, M. Pickford, et al.
2004   External and internal morphology of the bar, 1002'00 *Orrorin tugenensis* femur. *Science* 305:1450–1453.

Gao, F., E. Bailes, D. L. Robertson, et al.
1999   Origin of HIV-1 in the chimpanzee *Pan troglodytes troglodytes*. *Nature* 397:436–441.

Garcia, T., G. Féraud, C. Falguères, et al.
2010   Earliest human remains in Eurasia: New ^{40}Ar/^{39}Ar dating of the Dmanisi hominid-bearing levels, Georgia. *Quaternary Geochronology* 5:443–451.

Garner, K. J., and O. A. Ryder
1996   Mitochondrial DNA diversity in gorillas. *Molecular Phylogenetics and Evolution* 6(1): 39–48.

Gibbons, A.
2008   The birth of childhood. *Science* 322:1040–1043.

_____
2009   Celebrity fossil primate: Missing link or weak link? *Science* 324:1124-1125.

_____
2011   Skeletons present an exquisite paleo-puzzle. Newsfocus, *Science* 333:1370–1372.

Giles, J., and J. Knight
2003   Dolly's death leaves researchers woolly on clone ageing issue. *Nature* 421:776.

Gill, J. L., J. W. Williams, S. T. Jackson, K. B., et al.
2009   Pleistocene Megafaunal Collapse, Novel Plant Communities, and Enhanced Fire Regimes in North America. *Science* 326:1100–1103.

Gluckman, P., A. Beedle, and M. Hanson
2009   *Principles of Evolutionary Medicine*. Oxford, UK: Oxford University Press.

Gluckman, P. D., and M. Hanson
2005   *The Fetal Matrix: Evolution, Development, and Disease*. New York: Cambridge University Press.

Goodall, J.
1986   *The Chimpanzees of Gombe*. Cambridge, MA: Harvard University Press.

Gossett, T. F.
1963   *Race, the History of an Idea in America*. Dallas: Southern Methodist University Press.

Gould, S.
1981   *The Mismeasures of Man*. New York: W. W. Norton.

_____
1985   Darwin at sea—and the virtues of port. In: *The Flamingo's Smile. Reflections in Natural History*, S. J. Gould (ed.), pp. 347–359. New York: W.W. Norton.

_____
1987   *Time's Arrow, Time's Cycle*. Cambridge, MA: Harvard University Press.

Grant, P. R.
1986   *Ecology and Evolution of Darwin's Finches*. Princeton, NJ: Princeton University Press.

Greaves, M.
2008   Cancer: evolutionary origins of vulnerability. In *Evolution in Health and Disease*, Second Edition. S. C. Stearns and J. C. Koella (eds), pp. 277–287. Oxford: Oxford University Press.

Green, R. E., J. Krause, E. Ptak, A. W. Briggs, et al.
2006   Analysis of one million base pairs of Neanderthal DNA. *Nature* 444:330–336.

Green, R. E., J. Krause, A. W. Briggs, et al.
2010   A draft sequence of the Neandertal genome. *Science* 328:710–722.

Greene, J. C.
1981   *Science, Ideology, and World View*. Berkeley: University of California Press.

Greenwood, B., and T. Mutabingwa
2002   Malaria in 2000. *Nature* 415:670–672.

Gros-Louis, J., H. Perry, et al.
2003   Violent coalitionary attacks and intraspecific killing in wild white-faced capuchin monkeys (*Cebus capucinus*). *Primates* 44:341–346.

Grün, R., and C. B. Stringer
1991   ESR dating and the evolution of modern humans. *Archaeometry* 33:153–199.

Grün, R., C. B. Stringer, F. McDermott, et al.
2005   U-series and ESR analysis of bones and teeth relating to the human burials from Skhūl. *Journal of Human Evolution* 49:316–334.

Guinotte, J., and V. J. Fabry
2009   The threat of acidification to ocean ecosystems. *The Journal of Marine Education* Vol. 25, Number 1.

Haile-Selassie, Y., B. M. Latimer, M. Alene, et al.
2010   An early *Australopithecus afarensis* postcranium from Woranso-Mille, Ethiopia. *Proceedings of the National Academy of Sciences* 107:12121–12126.

Haile-Selassie, Y., G. Suwa, and T. D. White
2004   Late Miocene teeth from Middle Awash, Ethiopia, and early hominid dental evolution. *Science*, 303:1503–1505.

Hanna, J. M.
1999   Climate, altitude, and blood pressure. *Human Biology* 71:553–582.

Harlow, H. F.
1959   Love in infant monkeys. *Scientific American* 200:68–74.

Harlow, H. F., and M. K. Harlow
1961   A study of animal affection. *Natural History* 70:48–55.

Harrould-Kolieb, E., and J. Savitz
2009   Can we save our oceans from CO2? Oceana: Protecting the World's Oceans, Second Edition. Online publication, June 2009, na.oceana.org/sites/default/files/o/.../Acid.../Acidification_Report.pdf.

Hawkes, K., J. F. O'Connell, and N. G. Blurton Jones
1997   Hadza women's time allocation, offspring provisioning, and the evolution of long postmenopausal life spans. *Current Anthropology* 38:551–577.

Henshilwood, C. S., F. d'Errico, M. Vanhaeren, et al.
2004   Middle Stone Age shell beads from South Africa. *Science* 304:404.

Henzi, P., and L. Barrett
2003   Evolutionary ecology, sexual conflict, and behavioral differentiation among baboon populations. *Evolutionary Anthropology* 12:217–230.

Higham, T., C. B. Ramsey, I. Karavanic, et al.
2006   Revised direct radiocarbon dating of the Vindija G_1 Upper Paleolithic Neandertals. *Proceedings of the National Academy of Sciences* 103:553–557.

Holloway, R. L.
1983   Cerebral brain endocast pattern of *Australopithecus afarensis* hominid. *Nature* 303:420–422.

———
1985   The poor brain of *Homo sapiens neanderthalensis*. In: *Ancestors, The Hard Evidence*, E. Delson (ed.), pp. 319–324. New York: Alan R. Liss.

Hrdy, S. B.
1977   *The Langurs of Abu*. Cambridge, MA: Harvard University Press.

Hudjashou, G., T. Kivisid, P. A. Underhill, et al.
2007   Revealing the prehistoric settlement of Australia by Y chromosome and mtDNA analysis. *Proceedings of the National Academy of Sciences* 104:8726–8730.

Intergovernmental Panel on Climate Change.
2007   *Contribution of Working Group I to the Fourth Assessment Report of the Intergovernmental Panel on Climate Change*. Solomon, S, D. Qin, M. Manning, et al (eds.). New York: Cambridge University Press.

International Human Genome Sequencing Consortium
2001   Initial sequencing and analysis of the human genome. *Nature* 409:860–921.

International SNP Map Working Group
2001   A map of human genome sequence variation containing 1.42 million single nucleotide polymorphisms. *Nature* 409:928–933.

IUCN (International Union for Conservation of Nature and Natural Resources)
2009   Red list of threatened species. www.iucnredlist.org

Jablonski, N. G.
1992   Sun, skin colour, and spina bifida: An exploration of the relationship between ultraviolet light and neural tube defects. *Proceedings of the Australian Society of Human Biology* 5:455–462.

Jablonski, N. G., and G. Chaplin
2000   The evolution of skin coloration. *Journal of Human Evolution* 39:57–106.

———
2002   Skin Deep. *Scientific American* 287:74–81.

Jacob, T., E. Indriati, R. P. Soejono, et al.
2006   Pygmoid Australomelanesian *Homo sapiens* skeletal remains from Liang Bua, Flores: Population affinities and pathological abnormalities. *Proceedings of the National Academy of Sciences* 103:13421–13426.

Jacobs, Z. G.A.T. Duller, A.G. Wintle, and C.S. Heshilwood
2006   Extending the chronology of deposits at Blombos Cave, South Africa, back to 140 ka using optical dating of single and multiple grains of quartz. *Journal of Human Evolution* 51:255–273.

Jakobsson, M., S. W. Scholz, P. Scheet, et al.
2008   Genotype, haplotype and copy-number variation in worldwide human populations. *Nature* 451:998–1003.

Jia, L., and W. Huang
1990   *The Story of Peking Man*. New York: Oxford University Press.

Johnson, C.
2009   Megafaunal Decline and Fall. *Science* 326:1072–1073.

Jolly, A.
1985   *The Evolution of Primate Behavior*, 2nd ed. New York: Macmillan.

Jungers, W. L., W. E. H. Harcourt-Smith, R. E. Wunderlich, et al.
2009   The Foot of *Homo floresiensis*. *Nature*, 459:81–84.

Kano, T.
1992   *The Last Ape. Pygmy Chimpanzee Behavior and Ecology*. Stanford, CA: Stanford University Press.

Katz, D., and J. M. Suchey
1986   Age determination of the male os pubis. *American Journal of Physical Anthropology* 69:427–435.

Kennedy, G. E.
2005   From the ape's dilemma to the weanling's dilemma: early weaning and its evolutionary context. *Journal of Human Evolution* 48:123–145.

Keynes, R.
2002   *Darwin, His Daughter and Human Evolution*. New York: Riverhead Books.

King, B. J.
1994   *The Information Continuum*. Santa Fe, NM: School of American Research.

———
2004   *Dynamic Dance: Nonvocal Communication in the African Great Apes*. Cambridge, MA: Harvard University Press.

Kirkwood, T. B. L.
1997   The origins of human ageing. *Philosophical Transactions of the Royal Society of London B*. 352:1765–1772.

Klein, R. G.
1999   *The Human Career. Human Biological and Cultural Origins*, 2nd ed. Chicago: University of Chicago Press.

Konner, M., and C. Worthman
1980   Nursing frequency, gonadal function, and birth spacing among !Kung hunter-gatherers. *Science* 207:788–791.

Koopman, R. J., A. G. Mainous, V. A. Diaz, et al.
2005   Changes in age at diagnosis of type 2 diabetes mellitus in the United States, 1988 to 2000. *Annals of Family Medicine* 3:60–69.

Kramer, A.
1993 Human taxonomic diversity in the Pleistocene: Does *Homo erectus* represent multiple hominid species? *American Journal of Physical Anthropology* 91:161–171.

Krause, J., Q. Fu, J. M. Good, et al.
2010 The complete mitochondrial DNA genome of an unknown hominin from southern Siberia. *Nature* 464:894–896.

Krause, J., C. Lalueza-Fox, et al.
2007b The derived FOXP2 variant of modern humans was shared with Neandertals. *Current Biology* 17:1908–1912.

Krause, J., L. Orlando, D. Serre, et al.
2007a Neanderthals in central Asia and Siberia. *Nature* 449:902–904.

Krings, M., C. Capelli, et al.
2000 A view of Neandertal genetic diversity. *Nature Genetics* 26(2): 144–146.

Krings, M., A. Stone, R. W. Schmitz, et al.
1997 Neandertal DNA sequences and the origin of modern humans. *Cell* 90:19–30.

Kujoth, G. C., P. C. Bradshaw, S. Haroon, and T. A. Prolla.
2007 The role of mitochondrial DNA mutations in mammalian aging. *PLoS Genetics* 3:e24.

Kulikov, E. E., A. B. Poltaraus, and I. A. Lebedeva
2004 DNA analysis of Sunghir remains: Problems and perspectives. Poster presentation, European Paleopathology Association Meetings, Durham, UK, August 2004.

Kuzawa, C. W.
1998 Adipose tissue in human infancy and childhood: An evolutionary perspective. *American Journal of Physical Anthropology* 10:177–209.

———
2005 The fetal origins of developmental plasticity: Are maternal cues reliable predictors of future nutritional environments? *American Journal of Human Biology* 17:5–21.

———
2008 The developmental origins of adult health: Intergenerational inertia in adaptation and disease. In *Evolutionary Medicine and Health: New Perspectives*, W. R. Trevathan, E. O. Smith, and J. J. McKenna (eds.), pp. 325–349. New York: Oxford University Press.

Lack, D.
1966 *Population Studies of Birds*. Oxford: Clarendon.

Lahdenperä, M., V. Lummaa, S. Helle, M. Tremblay, and A. F. Russell
2004 Fitness benefits of prolonged post-reproductive lifespan in women. *Nature* 428:178–181.

Lahr, M. M., and R. Foley
1998 Towards a theory of human origins: Geography, demography, and diversity in recent human evolution. *Yearbook of Physical Anthropology* 41:137–176.

Lalueza-Fox, C., H. Römpler, D. Caramelli, et al.
2007 A melanocortin receptor allele suggests varying pigmentation among Neanderthals. *Science Express* Oct. 25, 2007.

Lalueza-Foxa, C., A. Rosas, A. Estalrrich, et al.
2011 Genetic evidence for patrilocal mating behavior among Neandertal groups. *Proceedings of the National Academy of Sciences* 108:250–253.

Lamason, R. L., M-A. P. K. Mohideen, J. R. Mest, et al.
2005 SLC24A5, a putative cation exchanger, affects pigmentation in zebrafish and humans. *Science* 310:1782–1786.

Lamberts, S. W. J., A. W. van den Beld, and A. J. van der Lely
1997 The endocrinology of aging. *Science* 278:419–424.

Lancaster, J. B., and C. S. Lancaster
1983 Prenatal investment: The hominid adaptation. In: *How Humans Adapt: A Biocultural Odyssey*, D. J. Ortner (ed.). Washington, DC: Smithsonian Institution Press.

Lanza, I. R., and K. S. Nair
2010 Mitochondrial function as a determinant of life span. *European Journal of Physiology* 459:277–289.

Larsen, C. S.
2002 *Skeletons in Our Closet: Revealing Our Past through Bioarchaeology*. Princeton, NJ: Princeton University Press.

———
2006 The agricultural revolution as environmental catastrophe: Implications for health and lifestyle in the Holocene. *Quaternary International* 150:12–20.

Leakey, M. D., and R. L. Hay
1979 Pliocene footprints in Laetolil beds at Laetoli, Northern Tanzania. *Nature* 278:317–323.

Lee, M., H. Martin, M. A. Firpo, and E. W. Demerath
2011 Inverse association between adiposity and telomere length: The Fels longitudinal study. *American Journal of Human Biology* 23:100–106.

Lentz, D. L., and B. Hockaday
2009 Timbers and temples, ancient Maya agroforestry and the end of time. *Journal of Archaeological Science* 36:1342–1353.

Lepre, C. J., and D. V. Kent
2010 New magnetostratigraphy for the Olduvai Subchron in the Koobi Fora Formation, northwest Kenya, with implications for early *Homo*. *Earth and Planetary Science Letters* 290:362–374.

Lerner, I. M., and W. J. Libby
1976 *Heredity, Evolution, and Society*. San Francisco: W. H. Freeman.

Leroy, E. M., B. Kumulungui, et al.
2005 Fruit bats as reservoirs of Ebola virus. *Nature* 438:575–576.

Leroy, E. M., P. Rouquet, et al.
2004 Multiple Ebola virus transmission events and rapid decline of central African wildlife. *Science* 303(5656): 387–390.

Lewin, R.
1986 Damage to tropical forests, or why were there so many kinds of animals? *Science* 234:149–150.

Li, J. Z., D. M. Assher, H. Tang, et al.
2008 Worldwide human relationships inferred from genome-wide patterns of variation. *Science* 319:1100–1104.

Li, T., and D. A. Etler
1992 New Middle Pleistocene hominid crania from Yunxian in China. *Nature* 357:404–407.

Lin, D. R., and J. H. White
2004 Pleiotropic actions of vitamin D. *BioEssays* 26(1):21–28.

Lin, J. Y., and D. E. Fisher
2007 Melanocyte biology and skin pigmentation. *Nature* 445:843–850.

Loeb, L. A., D. C. Wallace, and G. M. Martin.
2005 The mitochondrial theory of aging and its relationship to reactive oxygen species damage and somatic mtDNA mutations. *Proceedings of the National Academy of Sciences (PNAS)* 102:18769–18770.

Lohmueller, K. E., A. R. Indap, S. Schmidt, et al.
2008 Proportionally more deleterious genetic variation in European than in African populations. *Nature* 451:994–997.

Lordkipandize, D., T. Jashashuil, A. Vekua, et al.
2007 Postcranial evidence from early *Homo* from Dmanisi, Georgia. *Nature* 449:305–310.

Lordkipandize, D., A. Vekua, R. Ferring, et al.
2005 The earliest toothless hominin skull. *Nature* 434:717–718.

Lordkipandize D., A. Vekua, R. Ferring, P. Rightmire, et al.
2006 A fourth hominid skull from Dmanisi, Georgia. *The Anatomical Record: Part A* 288:1146–1157.

Lovejoy, C. O., B. Latimer, G. Suwa, et al.
2009a Combining prehension and propulsion: The foot of *Ardipithecus ramidus*. *Science* 72e1–72e8.

Lovejoy, C. O., G. Suwa, S. W. Simpson, et al.
2009b The great divides: *Ardipithecus ramidus* reveals the postcrania of our last common ancestors with African great apes. *Science* 326:100–106.

Mace, R.
2000 Evolutionary ecology of human life history: A review. *Animal Behaviour* 59:1–10.

MacKinnon, J., and K. MacKinnon
1980 The behavior of wild spectral tarsiers. *International Journal of Primatology* 1:361–379.

Malhi, Y., J. T.Roberts, R. A. Betts, et al.
2008 Climate change, deforestation, and the fate of the Amazon. *Science* 319:169–172.

Manson, J. H., and R. Wrangham
1991 Intergroup aggression in chimpanzees and humans. *Current Anthropology* 32:369–390.

Marean, C. M.
2010 When the sea saved humanity. *Scientific American* 303 (August):54–61.

Marean, C. W., M. Bar-Matthews, J. Bernatchez, et al.
2007 Early human use of marine resources and pigment in South Africa during the Middle Pleistocene. *Nature* 449:905–908.

Marris, E.
2006 Bushmeat surveyed in Western cities. Illegally hunted animals turn up in markets from New York to London. *News@Nature.com*, doi:10 1038/news060626 10

Martin, R. D., A. M. Maclaranon, J. C. Phillips, and W. B. Dobyns
2006 Flores hominid: New species or microcephalic dwarf? *The Anatomical Record: Part A* 288:1123–1145.

Martorell, R.
1989 Body size, adaptation, and function. *Human Organization* 48(1):15–20.

Mayr, E.
1970 *Population, Species, and Evolution*. Cambridge, MA: Harvard University Press.

———
1981 *The Growth of Biological Thought*. Cambridge: Harvard University Press.

McBrearty, S., and N. G. Jablonski
2005 First fossil chimpanzee. *Nature* 437:105–108.

McDougall, I., F. H. Brown, and J. G. Fleagle
2005 Stratigraphic placement and age of modern humans from Kibish, Ethiopia. *Nature*, 433:733–736.

McGrew, W. C.
1992 *Chimpanzee Material Culture. Implications for Human Evolution*. New York: Cambridge University Press.

———
1998 Culture in nonhuman primates? *Annual Review of Anthropology* 27:301–328.

McHenry, H.
1988 New estimates of body weight in early hominids and their significance to encephalization and megadontia in 'robust' australopithecines. In: *Evolutionary History of the Robust Australopithecines* (Foundations of Human Behavior), pp. 133–148, F. E. Grine (ed.), Somerset, NJ: Aldine Transaction.

———
1992 Body size and proportions in early hominids. *American Journal of Physical Anthropology* 87:407–431.

McKern, T. W., and T. D. Stewart
1957 *Skeletal Age Changes in Young American Males*. Natick, MA: Quartermaster Research and Development Command, Technical Report EP-45.

McKusick, V. A. (with S. E. Antonarakis, et al.)
1998 *Mendelian Inheritance in Man*, 12th ed. Baltimore, MD: Johns Hopkins University Press.

Miller, G. H., J. W. Magee, B. J. Johnson, et al.
1999 Pleistocene extinction of *Genyornis newtoni*: Human impact on Australian megafauna. *Science* 283:205–208.

Miniño, A. M., E. Arias, K. D. Kochanek, et al.
2002 Deaths: Final Data for 2000 National Vital Statistics Reports 50(15):2. Division of Vital Statistics.

Molnar, S.
1983 *Human Variation. Races, Types, and Ethnic Groups*, 2nd ed. Englewood Cliffs, NJ: Prentice-Hall.

Moore, L. G., S. Niermeyer, and S. Zamudio
1998 Human adaptation to high altitude: Regional and life-cycle perspectives. *American Journal of Physical Anthropology, Suppl.* 27:25–64.

Moore, L. G., and J. G. Regensteiner
1983 Adaptation to high altitude. *Annual Reviews of Anthropology* 12:285–304.

Moore, L.G., M. Shriver, L. Bemis, and E. Vargas
2006 An evolutionary model for identifying genetic adaptation to high altitude. *Advances in Experimental Medicine and Biology* 588:101–118.

Moore, L. G., S. Zamudio, J. Zhuang, et al.
2001 Oxygen transport in Tibetan women during pregnancy at 3,658 m. *American Journal of Physical Anthropology* 114:42–53.

Morris, D.
1967 *The Naked Ape*. New York: Dell.

Morwood, M. J., P. Brown, T. Jatmiko, et al.
2005 Further evidence for small-bodied hominins from the Late Pleistocene of Flores, Indonesia. *Nature* 437:1012–1017.

Morwood, M. J., R. P. Suejono, R. G. Roberts, et al.
2004 Archaeology and age of a new hominin from Flores in eastern Indonesia. *Nature* 431:1087–1091.

Moura, A. C. A., and P. C. Lee
2004 Capuchin tool use in Caatinga dry forest. *Science* 306(5703):1909.

Mourant, A. E., A. C. Kopec, and K. Domaniewska-Sobczak.
1976 *The Distribution of the Human Blood Groups and Other Polymorphisms*, 2d ed. London: Oxford University Press.

Muchmore, E. A., S. Diaz, and A. Varki
1998 A structural difference between the cell surfaces of humans and the great apes. *American Journal of Physical Anthropology* 107:187–198.

Muttoni, G., G. Scardia, D. Kent, et al.
2009 Pleistocene magnetochronology of early hominin sites at Ceprano and Fontana Ranuccio, Italy. *Earth and Planetary Science Letters* 286:255–268.

Napier, J.
1967 The antiquity of human walking. *Scientific American* 216:56–66.

Napier, J. R., and P. H. Napier
1985 *The Natural History of the Primates*. London: British Museum of Natural History.

National Snow and Ice Data Center.
2007 http://nsdic.org/

———
2009 Arctic sea ice extent remains low; 2009 sees third lowest mark. Press release. http://nsidc.org/news/press/20091005_minimumpr.html

Nesse, R. M., and G. C. Williams
1994 *Why We Get Sick. The New Science of Darwinian Medicine*. New York: Vintage Books.

Nevell, L., A. Gordon, and B. Wood
2007 *Homo floresiensis* and *Homo sapiens* size-adjusted cranial shape variations. *American Journal of Physical Anthropology, Supplement* 14:177–178 (abstract).

News in Brief
2007 Congolese government creates bonobo reserve. *Nature* 450:470 doi:10.1038450470f.

Nishida, T., M. Hiraiwa-Hasegawa, T. Hasegawa, and Y. Takahata
1985   Group extinction and female transfer in wild chimpanzees in the Mahale National Park, Tanzania. *Zeitschrift Tierpsychologie* 67:284–301.

Nishida, T., H. Takasaki, and Y. Takahata
1990   Demography and reproductive profiles. In: *The Chimpanzees of the Mahale Mountains*, T. Nishida (ed.), pp. 63–97. Tokyo: University of Tokyo Press.

Nishida, T., R. W. Wrangham, J. Goodall, and S. Uehara
1983   Local differences in plant-feeding habits of chimpanzees between the Mahale Mountains and Gombe National Park, Tanzania. *Journal of Human Evolution* 12:467–480.

Noonan, J. P., G. Coop, S. Kudaravalli, D. Smith, et al.
2006   Sequencing and analysis of Neanderthal genomic DNA. *Science* 314:1113–1118.

Nowak, R. M.
1999   *Walker's Primates of the World*. Baltimore, MD: Johns Hopkins University Press.

Oates, J. F., M. Abedi-Lartey, W. S. McGraw, et al.
2000   Extinction of a West African red colobus monkey. *Conservation Biology* 14:1526–1532.

Oates, J. F., R. A. Bergl, J. Sunderland-Groves, and A. Dunn
2007   *Gorilla gorilla* ssp. *Diehli*. In IUCN 2007. *2007 IUCN Red List of Threatened Species*.

Oeseburg, H., R. A. de Boer, W. H. van Gilst, and P. van der Harst
2010   Telomere biology in health aging and disease. *European Journal of Physiology* 459:259–268.

Ottoni, E. B., and P. Izar
2008   Capuchin monkey tool use: Overview and implications. *Evolutionary Anthropology* 17:171–178.

Ovchinnikov, I. V., A. Gotherstrom, G. P. Romanova, et al.
2000   Molecular analysis of Neanderthal DNA from the northern Caucasus. *Nature* 404:490–493.

Padian, K., and L. M. Chiappe
1998   The origin of birds and their flight. *Scientific American*, 278:38–47.

Page, S. E., F. Siegert, J. O. Rieley, H-D. V. Boehm, A. Jaya, and S. Limin
2002   The amount of carbon released from peat and forest fires in Indonesia during 1997. *Nature* 420:61–65.

Pagel, M., C. Venditti, and A. Meade
2006   Large punctuational contribution of speciation to evolutionary divergence at the molecular level. *Science* 314:119–121.

Palmer, S. K., L. G. Moore, D. Young, et al.
1999   Altered blood pressure course during normal pregnancy and increased preeclampsia at high altitude (3100 meters) in Colorado. *American Journal of Obstetrics and Gynecology* 189:1161–1168.

Palumbi, S. R.
2001   *The Evolution Explosion: How Humans Cause Rapid Evolutionary Change*. New York: W.W. Norton.

Pappu, S., Y. Gunnell, K. Akhilesh, et al.
2011   Early Pleistocene presence of Acheulian hominins in South India. *Science* 331:1596–1599.

Parés, J. M., and A. Pérez-González
1995   Paleomagnetic age for hominid fossils at Atapuerca archaeological site, Spain. *Science* 269:830–832.

Pavkov, M. E., P. H. Bennett, et al.
2006   Effect of young-onset type 2 diabetes mellitus on incidence of end-stage renal disease and mortality in young and middle-aged Pima Indians. *Journal of the American Medical Association* 296(4):421–426.

Pavkov, M. E., R. L. Hanson, et al.
2006   Secular trends in the prevalence and incidence rate of type 2 diabetes. *Diabetes* 55:A224-A224.

Peccei, J. S.
2001   Menopause: Adaptation or epiphenomenon? *Evolutionary Anthropology* 10:43–57.

Pelletier, D. L., E. A. Frongillo, D. G. Schroeder, and J. P. Habicht
1995   The effects of malnutrition on child mortality in developing countries. *Bulletin of the World Health Organization* 73:443–448.

Pennisi, E.
2007   No sex please, we're Neandertals. *Science* 316:967

Peres, C. A.
1990   Effects of hunting on western Amazonian primate communities. *Biological Conservation* 54:47–59.

Phillips, K. A.
1998   Tool use in wild capuchin monkeys. *American Journal of Primatology* 46:259–261.

Pickering, R., P. H. G. M. Dirks, Z. Jinnah, et al.
2011   *Australopithecus sediba* at 1.977 Ma and implications for the origins of the genus *Homo*. *Science* 333:1421–1423.

Pickford, M., and B. Senut
2001   The geological and faunal context of late Miocene hominid remains from Lukeino, Kenya. *Comptes Rendus de l'Académie des Sciences, Ser. 11A, Earth and Planetary Science* 332:145–152.

Pike, I. L.
2000   The nutritional consequences of pregnancy sickness: A critique of a hypothesis. *Human Nature* 11 (3), 207–232.

Pinner, R. W., S. M. Teutsch, L. Simonson, et al.
1996   Trends in infectious diseases mortality in the United States. *Journal of the American Medical Association* 275:189–193.

Pollard, T. M.
2008   *Western Diseases: An Evolutionary Perspective*. Cambridge, UK: Cambridge University Press.

Popkin, B. M.
2007   The World Is Fat. *Scientific American*, 297(3), 88–95.

Population Reference Bureau
2009   2009 World Population Data Sheet. http://www.prb.org/Publications/Datasheets/2009/2009wpds .aspx

Potts, R.
1991   Why the Oldowan? Plio-Pleistocene toolmaking and the transport of resources. *Journal of Anthropological Research* 47:153–176.

————
1993   Archeological interpretations of early hominid behavior and ecology. In: *The Origin and Evolution of Humans and Humanness*, D. T. Rasmussen (ed.), pp. 49–74. Boston: Jones and Bartlett.

Pritchard, J. K.
2010   How we are evolving. *Scientific American*, October, pp. 41–47.

Proctor, R.
1988   From anthropologie to rassenkunde. In: *Bones, Bodies, Behavior. History of Anthropology* (Vol. 5), W. Stocking, Jr. (ed.), pp. 138–179. Madison, WI: University of Wisconsin Press.

Profet, M.
1988   The evolution of pregnancy sickness as a protection to the embryo against Pleistocene teratogens. *Evolutionary Theory* 8:177–190.

Pruetz, J. D., and P. Bertolani
2007   Savanna chimpanzees, *Pan troglodytes verus*, hunt with tools. *Current Biology* 17:412–417

Pusey, A., J. Williams, and J. Goodall
1997   The influence of dominance rank on the reproductive success of female chimpanzees. *Science* 277:828–831.

Rak, Y., A. Ginzburg, and E. Geffen
2007   Gorilla-like anatomy on *Australopithecus afarensis* mandibles suggests *Au. afarensis* link to robust australopiths. *Proceedings of the National Academy of Sciences* 104:6568–6572.

Rasmussen, M., Y. Li, S. Lindgreen, et al.
2010   Ancient human genome sequence of an extinct Palaeo-Eskimo. *Nature* 463:757–762.

Reich, D., R. E. Green, and M. Kircher
2010   Genetic history of an archaic hominin group from Denisova Cave in Siberia. *Nature* 468:1053–1060.

Reinberg, S.
2009   Swine flu has infected 1 in 6 Americans:CDC. *U.S. News and World Reports*. www.usnews.com/health [posted December 10, 2009]

Relethford, J. H.
2001   *Genetics and the Search for Modern Human Origins*. New York: Wiley-Liss.

Reno, P. L., R. S. Meindl, et al.
2003   Sexual dimorphism in *Australopithecus afarensis* was similar to that of modern humans. *Proceedings of the National Academy of Sciences of the United States of America* 100(16):9404–9409.

Rhesus Macaque Genome Sequencing and Analysis Consortium.
2007   Evolutionary and biomedical insights from the rhesus macaque genome. *Science* 316:222–234.

Richards, G. D.
2006   Genetic, physiologic, and ecogeographic factors contributing to variation in *Homo sapiens: Homo floresiensis* reconsidered. *Journal of Evolutionary Biology* 19:1744–1767.

Richmond, B. G., and W. L. Jungers
2008   *Orrorin tugenensis* femoral morphology and the evolution of hominin bipedalism. *Science* 319:1662–1665.

Riddle, R. D., and C. J. Tabin
1999   How limbs develop. *Scientific American* 280:74–79.

Ridley, M.
1993   *Evolution*. Boston: Blackwell Scientific Publications.

Rightmire, G. P.
1998   Human evolution in the Middle Pleistocene: The role of *Homo heidelbergensis*. *Evolutionary Anthropology* 6:218–227.

———
2004   Affinities of the Middle Pleistocene cranium from Dali and Jinniushan. *American Journal of Physical Anthropology, Supplement* 38:167 (abstract).

Roberts, D. F.
1973   *Climate and Human Variability*. An Addison-Wesley Module in Anthropology, No. 34. Reading, MA: Addison-Wesley.

Rosenberg, K., and W. Trevathan
2001   The evolution of human birth. *Scientific American* 285:72–77.

Rouquet, P., J. Froment, et al.
2005   Wild animal mortality monitoring and human Ebola outbreaks, Gabon and Republic of Congo. *Emerging Infectious Diseases* 11(2):283–290.

Rudran, R.
1973   Adult male replacement in one-male troops of purple-faced langurs (*Presbytis senex senex*) and its effect on population structure. *Folia Primatologica* 19:166–192.

Ruff, C. B., and A. Walker
1993   The body size and shape of KNM-WT 15000. In: *The Nariokotome* Homo erectus *Skeleton*, A. Walker and R. E. Leakey (eds.), pp. 234–265. Cambridge, MA: Harvard University Press.

Ruvolo, M., D. Pan, et al.
1994   Gene trees and hominoid phylogeny. *Proceedings of the National Academy of Sciences of the United States of America* 91(19):8900–8904.

Samson, M., F. Libert, B. J. Doranz, et al.
1996   Resistance to HIV-1 infection in Caucasian individuals bearing mutant alleles of the CCR-5 chemokine receptor gene. *Nature* 382:722–725.

Sarmiento, E. E.
2010   Comment on the paleobiology and classification of *Ardipithecus ramidus*. *Science* 328:1105-b.

Savage-Rumbaugh, S., and R. Lewin
1994   *Kanzi: The Ape at the Brink of the Human Mind*. New York: Wiley.

Savage-Rumbaugh, S., K. McDonald, R. A. Sevic, W. D. Hopkins, and E. Rupert
1986   Spontaneous symbol acquisition and communicative use by pygmy chimpanzees *(Pan paniscus)*. *Journal of Experimental Psychology: General* 115:211–235.

Schauber, A.D., and D. Falk
2008   Proportional dwarfism in foxes, mice, and humans: implications for relative brain size in *Homo floresiensis*. *American Journal of Phsyical Anthropology, Supplement* 43:185 (abstract).

Schmitz, R. W., D. Serre, G. Bonani, et al.
2002   The Neandertal type site revisited: Interdisciplinary investigations of skeletal remains from the Neander Valley, Germany. *Proceedings of the National Academy of Sciences* 99:13342–13347.

Scriver, C. R.
2001   *The Metabolic and Molecular Bases of Inherited Disease*. New York: McGraw-Hill.

Seckler, D.
1982   Small but healthy? A basic hypothesis in the theory, measurement and policy of malnutrition. In *Newer Concepts in Nutrition and Their Implications for Policy*, P. V. Sukhatme (ed.), pp. 127–137. Pune, India: Maharashtra Association for the Cultivation of Science Research Institute.

Semaw, S., M. J. Rogers, J. Quade, et al.
2003   2.6-million-year-old stone tools and associated bones from OGS-6 and OGS-7, Gona, Afar, Ethiopia. *Journal of Human Evolution* 45:169–177.

Senut, B., M. Pickford, D. Grommercy, et al.
2001   First hominid from the Miocene (Lukeino Formation, Kenya). *Comptes Rendus de l'Académie des Sciences, Ser. 11A, Earth and Planetary Science* 332:137–144.

Seppa, N.
2011   U.S. falters in life expectancy gains. *Science News*. February 26, p. 10.

Serre, D., A. Langaney, M. Chech, et al.
2004   No evidence of Neandertal mtDNA contribution to early modern humans. *PloS Biology* 2:313–317.

Seyfarth, R. M.
1987   Vocal communication and its relation to language. In: *Primate Societies*, B. Smuts, D. L. Cheney, R. M. Seyfarth, et al. (eds.), pp. 440–451. Chicago: University of Chicago Press.

Seyfarth, R. M., D. L. Cheney, and P. Marler
1980a   Monkey responses to three different alarm calls. *Science* 210:801–803.

———
1980b   Vervet monkey alarm calls. *Animal Behavior* 28:1070–1094.

Shang, H., H. Tong, S. Zhang, et al.
2007   An early modern human from Tianyuan Cave, Zhoukoudian, China. *Proceedings of the National Academy of Sciences* 104:6573–6578.

Shea, B. T., and R. C. Baily
1996   Allometry and adaptation of body proportions and stature in African pygmies. *American Journal of Physical Anthropology* 100:311–340.

Shea, J. J.
1998   Neandertal and early modern human behavioral variability— A regional-scale approach to lithic evidence for hunting in the Levantine Mousterian. *Current Anthropology* 39: S45–S78.

Shen, G., X. Gao, B. Gao, and D. E. Granger
2009   Age of Zhoukoudian *Homo erectus* with 26Ar/10Be burial dating. *Nature* 458:198–200.

Shubin, N. H., E. B. Daeschler, and F. A. Jenkins, Jr.
2006   The pectoral fin of *Tiktaalik roseae* and the origin of the tetrapod limb. *Nature* 440:764–771.

Shubin, N., C. Tabin, and S. Carroll
1997   Fossil genes, and the evolution of animal limbs. *Nature* 388:639–648.

Sievert, L. L.
2006 *Menopause: A Biocultural Perspective.* New Brunswick, NJ: Rutgers University Press.

Silk, J. B., S. C. Alberts, and J. Altmann
2003 Social bonds of female baboons enhance infant survival. *Science* 302:1231–1234.

Silk, J. B., S. F. Brosman, J. Vonk, et al.
2005 Chimpanzees are indifferent to the welfare of unrelated group members. *Nature* 437:1357–1359.

Simmons, J. G.
1989 *Changing the Face of the Earth.* Oxford: Basil Blackwell.

Simons, E. L.
1972 *Primate Evolution.* New York: Macmillan.

Simpson, S. W., J. Quade, N. E. Levin, et al.
2008 A female *Homo erectus* pelvis from Gona, Ethiopia. *Science* 322:1089–1092

Small, G. W., T. D. Moody, P. Siddarth, and S. Y. Bookheimer
2009 Your Brain on Google: Patterns of Cerebral Activation during Internet Searching. *American Journal of Geriatric Psychiatry* 17:116–126.

Small, G., and G. Vogan
2008 *iBRAIN: Surviving the Technological Alteration of the Modern Mind.* New York: HarperCollins.

Smith, F. H.
1984 Fossil hominids from the Upper Pleistocene of central Europe and the origin of modern Europeans. In: *The Origins of Modern Humans,* F. H. Smith and F. Spencer (eds.), pp. 187–209. New York: Alan R. Liss.

——— 2002 Migrations, radiations and continuity: patterns in the evolution of Late Pleistocene humans. In: *The Primate Fossil Record,* W. Hartwig (ed.), pp. 437–456. New York: Cambridge University Press.

Smith, F. H., A. B. Falsetti, and S. M. Donnelly
1989 Modern human origins. *Yearbook of Physical Anthropology* 32:35–68.

Smith, F. H., E. Trinkaus, P. B. Pettitt, et al.
1999 Direct radiocarbon dates for Vindija G1 and Velika Pécina Late Pleistocene hominid remains. *Proceedings of the National Academy of Sciences* 96:12281–12286.

Snyder, M., and M. Gerstein
2003 Genomics. Defining genes in the genomics era. *Science* 300:258–260.

Sponheimer, M., B. H. Passey, D. J. de Ruiter, et al.
2006 Isotopic evidence for dietary variability in the early hominin *Paranthropus robustus. Science* 314:980–982.

Spoor, F., M. G. Leakey, P. N. Gathago, et al.
2007 Implications of new early *Homo* fossils from Ileret, East of Lake Turkana, Kenya. *Nature* 448:688–691.

Starin, E. D.
1994 Philopatry and affiliation among red colobus. *Behaviour* 130:253–270.

Steiper, M. E., and N. M. Young
2006 Primate molecular divergence dates. *Molecular Phylogenetics and Evolution* 41(2): 384–394.

Steklis, H. D.
1985 Primate communication, comparative neurology, and the origin of language reexamined. *Journal of Human Evolution,* 14:157–173.

Stearns, S. C., S. G. Byars, D. R. Govindaraju, et al.
2010 Measuring selection in contemporary human populations. *Nature Reviews: Genetics* 11:611–622.

Stini, W. A.
1991 Body composition and longevity: is there a longevous morphotype? *Medical Anthropology* 13:215–229.

Strassmann, B. I.
1999 Menstrual cycling and breast cancer: An evolutionary perspective. *Journal of Women's Health* 8(2), 193–202.

Strassmann, B. I., and B. Gillespie
2002 Life-history theory, fertility, and reproductive success in humans. *Proceedings of the Royal Society of London B* 269:553–562.

Straus, L. G.
1995 The Upper Paleolithic of Europe: An overview. *Evolutionary Anthropology* 4:4–16.

Strier, K. B.
2003 *Primate Behavioral Ecology,* 2nd ed. Boston: Allyn and Bacon.

Stringer, C. B., and P. Andrews
1988 Genetic and fossil evidence for the origin of modern humans. *Science* 239:1263–1268.

Stringer, C. B., J. C. Finlayson, R. N. E. Barton, et al.
2008 Neanderthal exploitation of marine mammals in Gibralter. *Proceedings of the National Academy of Sciences* 105:14319–14324.

Struhsaker, T. T.
1967 Auditory communication among vervet monkeys (*Cercopithecus aethiops*). In: *Social Communication Among Primates,* S. A. Altmann (ed.). Chicago: University of Chicago Press.

Sumner, D. R., M. E. Morbeck, and J. Lobick
1989 Age-related bone loss in female Gombe chimpanzees. *American Journal of Physical Anthropology* 72:259.

Susman, R. L. (ed.)
1984 *The Pygmy Chimpanzee: Evolutionary Biology and Behavior.* New York: Plenum Press.

Susman, R. L., J. T. Stern, and W. L. Jungers
1985 Locomotor adaptations in the Hadar hominids. In: *Ancestors: The Hard Evidence,* E. Delson (ed.), pp. 184–192. New York: Alan R. Liss.

Sussman, R. W.
1991 Primate origins and the evolution of angiosperms. *American Journal of Primatology* 23:209–223.

Suwa, G., R. T. Kono, S. Katch, B. Asfaw, and Y. Beyene
2007 A new species of great ape from the late Miocene epoch in Ethiopia. *Nature* 448:921–924.

Swisher, C. C., W. J. Rink, S. C. Anton, et al.
1996 Latest *Homo erectus* of Java: Potential contemporaneity with *Homo sapiens* in Southwest Java. *Science* 274:1870–1874.

Szyf, M., P. McGowan, and M. J. Meaney
2008 The Social Environment and the Epigenome. *Environmental and Molecular Mutagenesis* 49:46–60.

Tattersall, I., E. Delson, and J. Van Couvering
1988 *Encyclopedia of Human Evolution and Prehistory.* New York: Garland Publishing.

Tavera-Mendoza, L. E., and J. H. White
2007 Cell defenses and the sunshine vitamin. *Scientific American* 297:62–72.

Teresi, D.
2002 *Lost Discoveries. The Ancient Roots of Modern Science—from the Babylonians to the Maya.* New York: Simon and Schuster.

Thieme, H.
1997 Lower Palaeolithic hunting spears from Germany. *Nature* 385:807–810.

Tiemel, C., Y. Quan, and W. En
1994 Antiquity of *Homo sapiens* in China. *Nature* 368:55–56.

Tishkoff, S. A., F. A. Reed, et al.
2007 Convergent adaptation of human lactase persistence in Africa and Europe. *Nature Genetics* 39(1): 31–40.

Tocheri, M. W., C. M. Orr, S. G. Larson, et al.
2007 The primitive wrist of *Homo floresiensis* and its implications for hominin evolution. *Science* 1743–1745.

Todd, T. W.
1920 Age changes in the pubic bone. I. The male white pubis. *American Journal of Physical Anthropology* 3:285–339.

1921   Age changes in the pubic bone. III. The pubis of the white female. *American Journal of Physical Anthropology* 4:26–39.

Tollefson, J.
2008   Brazil goes to war against logging. *Nature* 452:134–135.

Trevathan, W.
2010   *Ancient Bodies, Modern Lives: How Evolution Has Shaped Women's Health*. New York: Oxford University Press.

Trinkaus, E.
2005   Early modern humans. *Annual Reviews of Anthropology* 34:207–230.

Trinkaus, E., S. Milota, R. Rodrigo, et al.
2003   Early modern human cranial remains from Pestera cu Oase, Romania. *Journal of Human Evolution* 45:245–253.

Trinkaus, E., and P. Shipman
1992   *The Neandertals*. New York, NY: Alfred A. Knopf.

Turley, C. M., J. M. Roberts, and J. M. Guinotte
2007   Corals in deepwater: Will the unseen hand of ocean acidification destroy cold-water ecosystems? *Coral Reefs* 26:445–448.

United Nations Population Division
1998   *World Population Prospects: The 1998 Revision*.

van Schaik, C. P., M. Ancrenaz, G. Bogen, et al.
2003   Orangutan cultures and the evolution of material culture. *Science* 299:102–105.

Varki, A.
2000   A chimpanzee genome project is a biomedical imperative. *Genome Research* 8:1065–1070.

Venter, J. C., M. D. Adams, E. W. Myers, et al.
2001   The sequence of the human genome. *Science* 291:1304–1351.

Vialet, A., L. Tianyuan, D. Grimaud-Herve, et al.
2005   Proposition de reconstitution du deuxième crâne d'*Homo erectus* de Yunxian (Chine). *Comptes rendus. Palévol* 4:265–274.

Vigilant, L., M. Hofreiter, H. Siedel, and C. Boesch
2001   Paternity and relatedness in wild chimpanzee communities. *Proceedings of the National Academy of Sciences* 98:12890–12895.

Vignaud, P., P. Duringer, H. MacKaye, et al.
2002   Geology and palaeontology of the Upper Miocene Toros-Menalla hominid locality, Chad. *Nature* 418:152–155.

Villa, P.
1983   *Terra Amata and the Middle Pleistocene Archaeological Record of Southern France*. University of California Publications in Anthropology, Vol. 13. Berkeley: University of California Press.

Vince, G.
2011   An epoch debate. News Focus, *Science* 334:33–37.

Visalberghi, E.
1990   Tool use in Cebus. *Folia Primatologica* 54:146–154.

Visalberghi, E. D. F., E. Ottoni, et al.
2007   Characteristics of hammer stones and anvils used by wild bearded capuchin monkeys (*Cebus libidinosus*) to crack open palm nuts. *American Journal of Physical Anthropology* 132:426–444.

Vitzthum, V.
2009   The ecology and evolutionary endocrinology of reproduction in the human female. Yearbook of Physical Anthropology 52:95–136.

Vogelsang, R.
1998   *The Middle Stone Age Fundstellen in Süd-west Namibia*. Köln: Heinrich Barth Institut.

Wadley, L.
2009   Were snares and traps used in the Middle Stone Age and does it matter? A review and a case study from Sibudu, South Africa. *Journal of Human Evolution* 58(2):179–92.

Wadley, L., T. Hodgskiss, and M. Grant
2009   Implications for complex cognition from the hafting of tools with compound adhesives in the Middle Stone Age, South

Africa. *Proceedings of the National Academy of Sciences* 106:9590–9594.

Wakayama, S., H. Ohta, T. Hikichi, et al.
2008   Production of healthy cloned mice from bodies frozen at –20 C for 16 years. *Proceedings of the National Academy of Sciences* 105:17318–17322

Walker, A.
1976   Remains attributable to *Australopithecus* from East Rudolf. In: *Earliest Man and Environments in the Lake Rudolf Basin*, Y. Coppens (ed.), pp. 484–489. Chicago: University of Chicago Press.

_____
1991   The origin of the genus *Homo*. In: *Evolution of Life*, S. Osawa and T. Honjo (eds.), pp. 379–389. Tokyo: Springer-Verlag.

_____
1993   The origin of the genus *Homo*. In: *The Origin and Evolution of Humans and Humanness*, D. T. Rasmussen (ed.), pp. 29–47. Boston: Jones and Bartlett.

Walker, A., and R. E. Leakey
1993   *The Nariokotome* Homo erectus *Skeleton*. Cambridge, MA: Harvard University Press.

Walker, J., R. A. Cliff, and A. G. Latham
2006   U-Pb isoptoic age of the Stw 573 hominid from Sterkfontein, South Africa. *Science* 314:1592–1594.

Walker, P. L., R. R. Bathurst, R. Richman, et al.
2009   The causes of porotic hyperostosis and cribra orbitalia: A reappraisal of iron-deficiency anemia hypothesis. *American Journal of Physical Anthropology* 139:109–125.

Walsh, P. D., K. A. Abernathy, M. Bermejo, et al.
2003   Catastrophic ape decline in western equatorial Africa. *Nature* 422:611–614.

Ward, P.
1994   *The End of Evolution*. New York: Bantam.

Warneken, F., and M. Tomasello
2006   Altruistic helping in human infants and young chimpanzees. *Science* 311:1301–1303.

Warren, W. C., L. W. Hillier, J. A. Marshall, et al.
2008   Genome analysis of the platypus reveals unique signatures of evolution. *Nature* 453.175–183.

Waterston, R. H., K. Lindblad-Toh, E. Birney, et al. (Mouse Genome Sequencing Consortium)
2002   Initial sequencing and comparative analysis of the mouse genome. *Nature* 421:520–562.

Watson, J. D., and F. H. C. Crick
1953a   Genetical implications of the structure of the deoxyribonucleic acid. *Nature* 171:964–967.

_____
1953b   A structure for deoxyribonucleic acid. *Nature* 171:737–738.

Weiner, S., Q. Xu, P. Goldberg, et al.
1998   Evidence for the use of fire at Zhoukoudian, China. *Science* 281:251–253.

Weiss, K.
2003   Come to me my melancholic baby! *Evolutionary Anthropology* 12:3–6.

Weiss, R. A., and R. W. Wrangham
1999   From Pan to pandemic. *Nature* 397:385–386.

Weiss, U.
2002   Nature insight: Malaria. *Nature* 415:669.

Westergaard, G. C., and D. M. Fragaszy
1987   The manufacture and use of tools by capuchin monkeys (*Cebus apella*). *Journal of Comparative Psychology* 101:159–168.

White, T. D.
1986   Cut marks on the Bodo cranium: A case of prehistoric defleshing. *American Journal of Physical Anthropology* 69:503–509.

White, T. D., Berhane Asfaw, Yonas Beyene, et al.
2009   *Ardipithecus ramidus* and the paleobiology of early hominids. *Science* 326:75–86.

White, T. D., B. Asfaw, D. DeGusta, et al.
2003   Pleistocene *Homo sapiens* from Middle Awash Ethiopia. *Nature* 423:742–747.

White, T. D., B. Asfaw, D. DeGusta, et al.
1995   Corrigendum (White, et al., 1994). *Nature* 375:88.

White, T. D., G. WoldeGabriel, B. Asfaw, et al.
2006   Asa Issie, Aramis and the origin of *Australopithecus*. *Nature* 440:883–889.

Whitelaw, N. C., and E. Whitelaw
2006   How lifetimes shape epigenotype within and across generations. *Human Molecular Genetics* 15:R131–R137.

Whiten, A., J. Goodall, W. C. McGrew, et al.
1999   Cultures in chimpanzees. *Nature* 399:682–685.

WHO
2009   http://www.who.int/whosis/whostat/EN_WHS08_Table1_Mort.pdf. Accessed 10/12/09.

Wildman, D. E., M. Uddin, G. Liu, et al.
2003   Implications of natural selection in shaping 99.4% nonsynonymous DNA identity between humans and chimpanzees: Enlarging genus *Homo*. *Proceedings of the National Academy of Sciences* 100:7181–7188.

Wiley, A. S.
2008   Cow's milk consumption and health: An evolutionary perspective. In *Evolutionary Medicine and Health: New Perspectives*. Wenda Trevathan, E. O. Smith, James J. McKenna (eds.), pp. 116–133. New York: Oxford University Press.

Williams, G. C.
1957   Pleiotopy, natural selection, and the evolution of senescence. *Evolution* 11:398–411.

Williams, G. C., and R. M. Nesse
1991   The dawn of Darwinian medicine. *The Quarterly Review of Biology* 66:1–22.

Williams, J. M.
1999   *Female Strategies and the Reasons for Territoriality in Chimpanzees. Lessons from Three Decades of Research at Gombe.* Unpublished Ph.D. thesis. University of Minnesota.

Wilmut, I., A. E. Schnieke, J. McWhir, et al.
1997   Viable offspring derived from fetal and adult mammalian cells. *Nature* 385:810–813.

Wilson, E. O.
1992   *The Diversity of Life*. Cambridge, MA: The Belknap Press of Harvard University Press.

————   2002   *The Future of Life*. New York: Alfred A. Knopf.

Wilson, R. S.
1979   Twin growth: initial deficit, recovery, and trends in concordance from birth to nine years. *Annals of Human Biology* 6:205–220.

Wolpoff, M. H.
1999   *Paleoanthropology*, 2nd ed. New York: McGraw-Hill.

Wolpoff, M. H., J. Hawks, D. Frayer, and K. Hunley
2001   Modern human ancestry at the peripheries: A test of the replacement theory. *Science* 291:293–297.

Wolpoff, M. H., B. Senut, M. Pickford, and J. Hawks
2002   Paleoanthropology (communication arising): *Sahelanthropus* or 'Sahelpithecus'? *Nature* 419:581–582.

Wolpoff, M. H., A. G. Thorne, F. H. Smith, et al.
1994   Multiregional evolutions: A world-wide source for modern human populations. In: *Origins of Anatomically Modern Humans*, M. H. Nitecki and D. V. Nitecki (eds.), pp. 175–199. New York: Plenum Press.

Wong, K.
2009a   Twilight of the Neandertals. *Scientific American* 301(August):32–37.

2009b   "Rethinking the Hobbits of Indonesia." *Scientific American* 301 (November):66–73.

Woo, J.
1966   The skull of Lantian Man. *Current Anthropololgy* 5:83–86.

Wood, B.
1991   *Koobi Fora Research Project IV: Hominid Cranial Remains from Koobi Fora*. Oxford: Clarendon Press.

————   1992   Origin and evolution of the genus *Homo*. *Nature* 355:783–790.

Wood, B., and M. Collard
1999a   The human genus. *Science* 284:65–71.

————   1999b   The changing face of genus *Homo*. *Evolutionary Anthropology* 8:195–207.

————   2010   Reconstructing human evolution: Achievements, challenges, and opportunities. *Proceedings of the National Academy of Sciences* 107(Suppl. 2):8902–8909.

Wood, B., and T. Harrison
2011   The evolutionary context of the first hominins. *Nature* 470:347–352.

World Health Organization
2011   WHO Global Health Indicators, 2011.

Wrangham, R. W., and D. Peterson
1996   *Demonic Males: Apes and the Origins of Human Violence*. New York: Houghton Mifflin.

Wrangham, R. W., and B. B. Smuts
1980   Sex differences in the behavioural ecology of chimpanzees in Gombe National Park, Tanzania. *J. Reprod. Fert., Supplement* 28:13–31.

Wu, Rukang, and Xingren Dong
1985   *Homo erectus* in China. In: *Palaeoanthropology and Palaeolithic Archaeology in the People's Republic of China*, R. Wu and J. W. Olsen (eds.), pp. 79–89. New York: Academic Press.

Wu, R., and J. W. Olsen (eds.)
1985   *Palaeoanthropology and Palaeolithic Archaeology in the People's Republic of China*. Orlando, FL: Academic Press.

Wu, X., and F. E. Poirier
1995   *Human Evolution in China*. Oxford: Oxford University Press.

Wuethrich, B.
1998   Geological analysis damps ancient Chinese fires. *Science* 28:165–166.

Yamei, H., R. Potts, Y. Baoyin, et al.
2000   Mid-Pleistocene Acheulean-like stone technology of the Bose Basin, South China. *Science* 287:1622–1626.

Yellen, J. E., A. S. Brooks, E. Cornelissen, et al.
1995   A Middle Stone Age worked bone industry from Katanda, Upper Semliki Valley, Zaire. *Science* 268:553–556.

Yokoyama, Y., C. Falguères, F. Sémah, et al.
2008   Gamma-ray spectrometric dating of late *Homo erectus* skulls from Ngandong and Sambungmacan, Central Java, Indonesia. *Journal of Human Evolution* 55:274–277.

Young, D.
1992   *The Discovery of Evolution*. Cambridge, UK: Natural History Museum Publications, Cambridge University Press.

Young, E. M.
2004   Globalization and food security: novel questions in a novel context? *Progress in Development Studies* 4:1–21.

Zhang, F., S. L. Kearns, P. J. Orr, et al.
2010   Fossilized melanosomes and the colour of Cretaceous dinosaurs and birds. *Nature* 463:1075–1078.

Zhu, R. X., Z. S. An, R. Potts, et al.
2003   Magnetostratigraphic dating of early humans in China. *Earth Science Reviews* 61:341–359.

Index

World Political Map